Foundations of American Political Thought

American political thought was shaped by a unique combination of theoretical influences: republicanism, liberalism, and covenant theology. This reader shows how these influences came together. Organized chronologically from the Puritans' arrival in the New World to the Civil War, each chapter includes carefully selected primary sources and substantial commentary to explain the historical context and significance of the excerpts. A coherent interpretative framework is offered by focusing the analysis on the different assumptions about the "people" – the republican understanding of the people as a corporate whole and the liberal understanding of the people as a multitude of individuals – that were intertwined during the founding. The book features, for the first time, two chapters on non-American authors, who capture the main tenets of republicanism and liberalism and were widely quoted in the era, as well as excerpts from lesser-known sources, including Puritan covenants, the first state constitutions, and Native American speeches.

ALIN FUMURESCU is Associate Professor in the Department of Political Science at the University of Houston, Texas.

ANNA MARISA SCHÖN is a PhD candidate in Political Science at the University of Houston, Texas.

Foundations of American Political Thought

Readings and Commentary

Alin Fumurescu
University of Houston

Anna Marisa Schön
University of Houston

 **CAMBRIDGE**
UNIVERSITY PRESS

Shaftesbury Road, Cambridge CB2 8EA, United Kingdom

One Liberty Plaza, 20th Floor, New York, NY 10006, USA

477 Williamstown Road, Port Melbourne, VIC 3207, Australia

314–321, 3rd Floor, Plot 3, Splendor Forum, Jasola District Centre, New Delhi – 110025, India

103 Penang Road, #05–06/07, Visioncrest Commercial, Singapore 238467

Cambridge University Press is part of Cambridge University Press & Assessment, a department of the University of Cambridge.

We share the University's mission to contribute to society through the pursuit of education, learning and research at the highest international levels of excellence.

www.cambridge.org
Information on this title: www.cambridge.org/9781108733557

DOI: 10.1017/9781108774154

First published 2021
First paperback edition 2023

A catalogue record for this publication is available from the British Library

Library of Congress Cataloging-in-Publication data
Names: Fumurescu, Alin, 1967– author. | Schön, Anna Marisa, author.
Title: Foundations of American political thought : readings and commentary / Alin Fumurescu, University of Houston, Anna Marisa, University of Houston.
Description: Cambridge, United Kingdom ; New York, NY: Cambridge University Press, 2021. | Includes bibliographical references and index.
Identifiers: LCCN 2021002311 (print) | LCCN 2021002312 (ebook) | ISBN 9781108489188 (hardback) | ISBN 9781108733557 (paperback) | ISBN 9781108774154 (ebook)
Subjects: LCSH: Political science – United States – History – Sources. | Political science – Philosophy – Sources. | United States – Politics and government – Sources.
Classification: LCC E183 .F86 2021 (print) | LCC E183 (ebook) | DDC 320.973–dc23
LC record available at https://lccn.loc.gov/2021002311
LC ebook record available at https://lccn.loc.gov/2021002312

ISBN   978-1-108-48918-8   Hardback
ISBN   978-1-108-73355-7   Paperback

Contents

Preface

Alexis de Tocqueville opened the first chapter of his second volume of *Democracy in America* with a provocative statement: "I think there is no country in the civilized world where they are less occupied with philosophy than the United States."[1] If this feature is indeed part of the American exceptionalism, it is not one that most Americans are likely to brag about, even if some might find it amusingly accurate. Yet it may explain why scholars and teachers of American political thought have so much trouble offering a coherent framework of interpretation, and why disagreements about the subject matter are so pervasive. From the very beginning, the yet-to-be Americans paid little or no attention to the theoretical consistency of their arguments, focusing more on the practical results. In Tocqueville's words, the philosophical method of the Americans is "to seek the reason for things by themselves and in themselves alone, to strive for a result without letting themselves be chained to the means."[2] True, sometimes they invoked thinkers from the distant or more recent past, from Aristotle and Polybius to Locke, Blackstone, or Montesquieu, in order to support their arguments. But, more often than not, this amounted to little more than name-dropping, with no solid evidence that they carefully read these authors or properly understood their basic assumptions.[3] As we shall see throughout this volume, more than once, the very same texts were used to justify either rebellion against or loyalty to a certain form of government, either slavery or abolitionism, either majority or minority rights, either equality or freedom.

To give just one example for now: Decades after penning the Declaration of Independence, in a letter to James Madison dated August 30, 1823, Thomas Jefferson made no claim to originality for the famous document. "All of its authority rests on the harmonizing sentiments of the day, whether expressed in conversations, in letters, printed essays, or in the elementary books of public right, as Aristotle, Cicero, Locke, Sidney, &c." It is quite clear that for Jefferson, as for many of his contemporaries, "the sentiments of the day" could accommodate, without any theoretical angst, the fundamental differences between, say, Aristotle and Locke. Examples of such accommodations are legion and cannot but frustrate anyone who tries to arrange the American political thinkers according to neatly defined and theoretically consistent labels.

---

[1] A. de Tocqueville [1838], *Democracy in America*, translated by A. Goldhammer (New York: The Library of America, 2004).

[2] Tocqueville, *Democracy in America*, Vol. II, chapter 1.

[3] See, for example, B. Baylin, *The Ideological Origins of the American Revolution*, enlarged ed. (Cambridge, MA: The Belknap Press of Harvard University Press, 1992).

Gone are the decades when the American founding was interpreted as a purely **classical liberal** one, as Louis Hartz, for example, argued.[4] After J. G. A. Pocock published his seminal book, *The Machiavellian Moment*, in 1975, the picture was complicated by a mounting body of evidence which stressed the **republican** influence (sometimes labeled as **conservative**) throughout the period.[5] Since then, the influence of religious beliefs (sometimes labeled as **biblical thought**) on American political thought has also been well documented.[6] Other theoretical influences have been added to the mixture, from the **Scottish Enlightenment** to the **civil disobedience** promoted by thinkers like Thoreau, and the voices of **Native Americans**, **women**, and **African Americans** – to name just a few. Alan Gibson identifies no less than <u>six approaches</u> or organizing frameworks for understanding the founding: progressive, Lockean or liberal, republican, Scottish Enlightenment, a multiple-tradition approach, and the study of the dispossessed groups.[7]

For the sake of offering students a wide and comprehensive view of American political thought, both at an undergraduate and at a graduate level, most professors choose the **multiple-traditions approach**, but this cannot fully ease the feeling of frustration on both sides of the podium in dealing with these "cacophonous strains."[8] Simply calling them a "synthesis"[9] or an "amalgam"[10] mainly between **liberalism** and **republicanism** does not help much. We hope that, by offering a coherent interpretative framework, this volume will help to alleviate some, if not all, of these feelings of frustration, while also providing a fresh perspective on American exceptionalism.

Putting together such a handbook requires a high degree of dexterity in keeping the proper balance between so many different requirements – from the selection of the primary sources to the length of the explanatory considerations, and from the time frame to the amount of (inherently) subjective interpretation. Hard choices had to be made. Like acrobats spinning plates in the air, sometimes we had to let some of them drop, in order to preserve the most important ones. Surely, the result may not be satisfactory to everyone, but this is also a lesson to be learned: In books, as in life, one should struggle for the ideal while remaining fully aware that one cannot reach it.

Compared to other attempts of this kind, our project is at once more modest and more ambitious. It is more modest, in several respects. First, it does not attempt to cover the entire field of American political thought, from the colonial era up until Trump's presidency. We have chosen to focus strictly on the *Foundations* of American political thought, with the conviction that a proper understanding of the

---

[4] L. Hartz, *The Liberal Tradition in America* (New York: Harcourt, Brace and World, 1955).

[5] J. G. A. Pocock, *The Machiavellian Moment: Florentine Political Thought and the Atlantic Republican Tradition* (Princeton: Princeton University Press, 1975).

[6] See, for example, B. A. Shain, *The Myth of American Individualism: The Protestant Origins of American Political Thought* (Princeton: Princeton University Press, 1996); M. A. Noll, *America's God: From Jonathan Edwards to Abraham Lincoln* (Oxford and New York: Oxford University Press, 2002).

[7] A. Gibson, *Interpreting the Founding: Guide to the Enduring Debates over the Origins and Foundations of the American Republic* (Lawrence: University Press of Kansas, 2006).

[8] P. Abbott, *Political Thought in America: Conversations and Debates*, 4th ed. (Long Grove, IL: Waveland Press, 2010), p. 5.

[9] Noll, *America's God*.

[10] M. P. Zuckert, "Natural Rights and Imperial Constitutionalism: The American Revolution and the Development of the American Amalgam" in E. Frankel Paul, F. D. Miller Jr., and J. Paul (eds.), *Natural Rights Liberalism from Locke to Nozick* (Cambridge: Cambridge University Press, 2005).

roots can help in understanding the ramifications to follow, from the late nineteenth all the way up to the twenty-first century. Many if not all of today's political battles can be explained by rediscovering their roots. Second, it is more modest in that we did not try to offer the reader thousands of pages of selections from the primary sources. Even a thousand-page anthology cannot cover all the primary sources of the period and, realistically, it is impossible for any student or professor, no matter how committed, to seriously engage with such a vast amount of literature in the span of a single semester or even a full academic year. Nevertheless, for the reader willing to go the extra mile, we have included suggestions for additional primary sources.

Yet, in other respects, it is a more ambitious undertaking than other endeavors meant to serve a similar purpose. Defining the time frame of the founding was a challenge in itself. The scholarly jury is still out on when the American founding began and when it ended. For some, it started in 1611, with the *Virginia Articles, Laws, and Orders*; for others, in 1619, when the first slaves (or indentured servants)[11] were brought into the New World; for yet others, in the 1730s, with Benjamin Colman's sermon, *Government the Pillar of Earth*, or as late as in the 1760s, with Abraham Williams's *An Election Sermon* (1762). It also may have ended (or even begun) in 1787, in 1805, or in 1860.[12] We have decided to expand these limits. As the end of the founding period we have chosen the American Civil War, for only after more than 600,000 deaths was the formula "the United States *are*" formally replaced by the now usual "the United States *is*." And while we agree that the American beginnings are to be found with the first colonists coming to the shores of the New World, we are also persuaded that the full story starts even earlier, in the Old World. Hence, unlike any other textbooks of this kind, we are dedicating two full chapters to selections from European authors who helped to define the main tenets of **republicanism** and **liberalism** as well as some who have blurred the lines between the two, which we are labeling **liberal-conservatives** and **conservative-liberals**, respectively. It is hard to understand the significant differences in the basic assumptions about the state, people, representation, and the like, absent a recourse to some of the representative figures often invoked, properly or not, by the founders themselves. After all, there cannot be a *New* World absent an *Old* one, against which to define one's exceptionalism.

---

[11] The distinction between slaves and indentured servants, together with its racial connotations, would consolidate only decades later.

[12] See, for example, B. Frohnen (ed.), *The American Republic: Primary Sources* (Indianapolis: Liberty Fund, 2002); C. S. Hyneman and D. S. Lutz, *American Political Writing during the Founding Era, 1760–1805* (Indianapolis: Liberty Press, 1983); E. Sandoz (ed.), *Political Sermons of the American Founding Era, 1730–1805* (Indianapolis: Liberty Press, 1998); P. B. Knupfer, *The Union As It Is: Constitutional Unionism and Sectional Compromise, 1787–1861* (Chapel Hill: University of North Carolina Press, 1991).

Acknowledgements

Most books have more authors than appear on the front cover – and this one is no exception. Putting together such a volume would not have been possible absent the professionalism (and patience) of the Cambridge University Press's editorial team. Special thanks are due to our publisher, Robert Dreesen, whose unshakeable enthusiasm for this project from its very inception proved contagious. We would also like to thank the anonymous reviewers for useful suggestions from the initial proposal all the way to the final version.

While it might be true that man does not live by bread only, some bread definitely helps. The University of Houston provided not just a friendly and intellectually stimulating atmosphere, but also a grant that helped with the completion of the manuscript. For the past five years, various cohorts of undergraduate students sitting in the Foundations of American Political Thought classes at the University of Houston unknowingly made a substantial contribution to the final selection of primary sources. Year after year they signaled, as only undergraduate students know how to persuasively do, which authors and which texts are most useful in understanding the theoretical foundations of the American founding. They deserve our gratitude.

Last but not least, we would like to thank our loved ones for putting up with some unusual working hours, while reminding us, in peculiar ways, that despite its shortcomings, the United States of America remains an experiment to be cherished and worth understanding in order to preserve and improve it.

Alin Fumurescu and Anna Marisa Schön

1 Introduction

The People's Two Bodies

If you think contemporary American politics is messier than ever, think again. Even a cursory look at its founding period reveals a far from rosy picture. There was slavery, there was discrimination, intolerance against any perceived "otherness," and religious persecution. People were killing each other over different ideas of freedom and of justice. What's more, we have to keep in mind that back then the stakes were higher than today, for every decision came with significant long-term consequences, setting precedents difficult to ignore. The future was filled with big promises, but also fraught with worrisome dangers. How to sort them out? As the saying goes, the road to hell is paved with good intentions. When one takes a closer look at the founding period, one easily feels trapped in a maze of endless theoretical arguments and disagreements – some of them (and not just a few) ending in bloodbaths. So here is the first lesson from the past: ideas can do a lot of good, but also plenty of evil. In short, ideas matter. If nowadays one fights over symbols – statues, monuments, street names, and so forth – it is because those theoretical puzzles have remained unsolved.

According to an old Greek myth, when trapped in the labyrinth that hid the Minotaur, Theseus was able to find his way out thanks to the famous Ariadne's thread. Taking inspiration from this strategy, what, in this intellectual maze of the founding, could be the thread that helps us orient ourselves? Where should we start?

We propose to begin with the one thing that remains a constant fixture: the enduring belief in an American exceptionalism. If nowadays such a claim is relatively easy to make, consider the handful of people that arrived on the shores of what would come to be known as New England in the 1620s. They were thousands of miles from home, in the middle of a wilderness they were utterly unfamiliar with, doubtlessly hungry and scared. Nevertheless, they dared to make the bold claim that they would become a beacon of light for the rest of the world! The fact that their confidence was fed by their religious beliefs is secondary. Following in their footsteps, generation after generation of Americans of various confessions (if any) shared the same unshakeable belief: What was happening in the New World was of concern not just to its inhabitants, but to all of humanity.

Even before reaching the shores of the new settlement, John Winthrop demanded exemplary conduct from his companions: "For wee must consider that we shall be [. . .] as a city upon a hill. *The eies of all people are upon us*" (Chapter 4). "The cause of America is in a great measure *the cause of all mankind*," wrote Thomas Paine, in *Common Sense*, even before the Revolutionary War was in full force (Chapter 5). Such claims appeared to be confirmed when the first state constitutions were widely republished and discussed in Europe, as the first written constitutions made under the authority of sovereign peoples, no matter how ambiguous the concept of "the people" remained (Chapter 6). During the Philadelphia Convention Gouverneur Morris "flattered himself he came here in some degree as a Representative of the whole human race; for *the whole human race* will be affected by the proceedings of this Convention" (Chapter 7). In his Inaugural Address, John Adams told his audience that it "is very certain, that to a benevolent human mind there can be *no spectacle presented by any nation* more pleasing, more noble, majestic, or august, than an assembly like [this]" (Chapter 8). Thomas Skidmore tried to solve, once and for all, "the effect, *in all ages and countries*, of the possession of great and undue wealth" (Chapter 9). And in his Special Session Message, on July 4, 1861, Abraham Lincoln told Congress that the Civil War "presents *to the whole family of man* the question whether a constitutional republic, or democracy – a government of the people by the same people – can or cannot maintain its territorial integrity against its own domestic foes" (Chapter 10). The examples could go on and on.

Hence, it might be useful to start with this very question: If indeed there is such a thing as an American exceptionalism, what is it? What are its main features? What makes the American people not just *different* from, say, the French or the Chinese people, but also *exemplary*? After all, the French or the Chinese are also proud of their unicity. Being proud of one's nation, language, ethnicity, religion, or even continent appears to be a universal feature. Is there then something more, something distinctly American, in this claim? What can be exceptional about a country founded, like all the other ones, on a series of accidents, oftentimes involving injustice and violence? Furthermore, whenever we are talking about the American exceptionalism, what are we actually talking about? The United States of America as a country? The American nation? Or the American people? Which people? Many questions and many possible answers.

1.1 A Political People

Generally speaking, **modern nations** are different from the **peoples** composing them.[1] The Swiss **nation**, for example, is composed of French, German, and Italian **people**. The Jewish **people** live in the nation of Israel, but also among many other **nations**. *The modern nation is a political (and cultural) construct*, despite the claims that it is based upon an (imagined) community of ethnicity, language, religion, traditions, and the like. The reality simply does not endorse such claims. Most nations are composed of different ethnicities, languages, religions, and traditions, and are held together by a political system that applies to all the people encompassed by the respective nation, despite all the differences mentioned above. Of course, so is the American nation.

---

[1] The understanding of the nation in antiquity and medieval times differed drastically from the modern one, but this is of no interest to us here.

The difference is that, unlike other cases, ***the American nation coincides with the American people***. In the United States, multiple ethnicities live together, multiple religions are practiced, multiple languages are spoken (unlike in many other nations, the Constitution does not impose an official language), but there are not *multiple peoples* – just the American *people*. Here, from the very beginning, "a people" was defined, like a modern nation, not by any other commonality, but by an elective government. As we shall see in more detail in Chapter 4, the Puritans that arrived on the shores of the New World created not just new theological-political communities, but, as Donald Lutz has persuasively argued, new *peoples*.[2] They were all British subjects, most of them *formally* members of the same Church of England, they spoke the same language and shared the same traditions, but they considered themselves different *peoples* because they had consented to subject themselves to the leaders of their choice.

Or think about the famous beginning of the Declaration of Independence (Chapter 5): "When in the Course of human events, it becomes necessary for *one people to dissolve the political bands which have connected them with another* … " The assumption, conscious or not, is that people are connected solely by "political bands" and nothing else. "[O]ur *British brethren* […] have been deaf to the voice of justice and of *consanguinity*. We must, therefore, acquiesce in the necessity, which denounces our Separation, and hold them, as we hold the rest of mankind, Enemies in War, in Peace Friends." Thus, a **political nation** and a **political people** were born at the same time. As we shall see in Chapter 10 this understanding would create a huge set of problems leading to the American Civil War. Once again, ideas do matter.

Abraham Lincoln understood this very well. During the famous Lincoln–Douglas debates, he elaborates on this point – and deserves a lengthier quotation:

> We are now a mighty *nation* […] We run our memory back over the pages of history for about eighty-two years […] We find a race of men living in that day whom we claim as our fathers and grandfathers; they were iron men, they fought for the principle that they were contending for; […] We have besides these men – descended *by blood* from our ancestors – among us perhaps half *our people* who are *not* descendants at all of these men, they are men who have come from Europe – German, Irish, French and Scandinavian – men that have come from Europe themselves, or whose ancestors have come hither and settled here, *finding themselves our equals in all things. If they look back through this history to trace their connection with those days by blood, they find they have none*, they cannot carry themselves back into that glorious epoch and make themselves feel that they are part of us, but when they look through that old Declaration of Independence they find that those old men say that "We hold these truths to be self-evident, that all men are created equal," and then they feel that […] *they have a right to claim it as though they were blood of the blood, and flesh of the flesh of the men who wrote that Declaration*, and so they are. That is the electric cord in that Declaration that links the hearts of patriotic and liberty-loving men together, that will link those patriotic hearts as long as the love of freedom exists in the minds of men throughout the world.[3]

[2] D. S. Lutz, *The Origins of American Constitutionalism* (Baton Rouge: Louisiana State University Press, 1988).

[3] Quoted in R. P. Basler (ed.), *The Collected Works of Abraham Lincoln*, Vol. II (New Brunswick, NJ: Rutgers University Press, 1953), pp. 499–500 (emphasis added).

Because of this American overlapping of "nation" and "people," the contemporary focus on nation and nationalism risks obscuring what we believe is a more important concept, namely "the people." After all, the American nation is no longer a questionable concept. The role of the people in American democracy, however, remains heavily disputed. The Constitution starts with the words *"We the People,"* yet leaves the definition of the people open to interpretation.

1.2 The Foundational Double Helix: The People as One and Many

It might not be an accident that the English language allows one to say both "the American people *is* a hard-working people" and "the American people *are* hard-working people."[4] In the first case, one conceives the people as a corporate entity; in the second, as a multitude of individuals.[5] For both the British and the American colonists, the people were primarily conceived as a *political* people, hence assimilated with the "nation." As Sir Roger L'Estrange put it in 1683 as a widely accepted truth, *"The people are the nation; and the nation is the people."*[6] Therefore, unlike in continental Europe, in Great Britain and in the United States, there are no references to "national minorities," but instead to "ethnic minorities."

There was, however, from the very beginning, a crucial difference between the two: while for the British the idea of a political people was just that – an idea – for the American colonists it was a living reality. Furthermore, in seventeenth-century Great Britain, the understanding of the people was sharply divided between that of the Tories, for whom the multitude was but an unruly mob, and that of the Whigs, for whom the *legal* equality of the individuals was a fundamental assumption. For people like L'Estrange, this latter approach was opening the gates of anarchy. After positing what he saw as a self-evident truth, "the people are the nation; and the nation is the people," he continued with what, for him, was the crux of the matter: *"But do we speak of the multitude or of the community?"* For the fervent royalist the answer was clear: "If of the community, why do ye not rather call it *the government*? If of the multitude; they have no right of acting, judging, or interposing … "[7] By contrast, the American strength was to be the ability to accommodate both visions of the people, without creating an insurmountable gap between the two.

The **paradigm of the people's two bodies** may be nothing more than a fiction, but it is a useful one – like all other fictions upon which any government rests. They are the bread and butter of politics. Edmund Morgan's observation is not to be ignored:

---

[4] In contrast, for example, in French (*le peuple*), Italian (*il popolo*), German (*das Volk*), or Romanian (*poporul*), the only possible usage of "the people" is in the singular, like a corporate entity.

[5] For a full treatment of this subject, see A. Fumurescu, *Compromise and the American Founding: The Quest for the People's Two Bodies* (Cambridge: Cambridge University Press, 2019).

[6] R. L'Estrange [February 10, 1683], *Observator in Dialogue*, quoted in S. C. A. Pincus, *England's Glorious Revolution, 1688–1689: A Brief History with Documents* (New York: Palgrave Macmillan, 2006), p. 143 (emphasis added).

[7] L'Estrange, *Observator*, p. 143 (emphasis added).

> Governments require make-believe. [...] Make believe that the people *have* a voice or make believe that the representatives of the people *are* the people. Make believe that governors are the servants of the people. Make believe that all men are equal or make believe that they are not. [...] Because fictions are necessary, because we cannot live without them, we often take pains to prevent their collapse by moving the facts to fit the fiction.[8]

The idea of the people being conceived *at once* as a multitude prone to errors *and* as a sovereign corporate entity that cannot err is not an American invention, and it enjoys a long pedigree. Even if the label of the people's two bodies is recent, the idea behind it is not. It predates the transfer of sovereignty from kings to people, and hence the transfer of the idea of the king's two bodies to the people's two bodies that came to characterize the revolutionary eighteenth century.[9] Throughout the Middle Ages, "the people" were conceived simultaneously as a whole and as a multitude, as One and as Many. That the body politic was to be distinguished – as later on the political body of the king would be as well – from the physicality of its members, was a certitude for the famous commentator Baldus de Ubaldis, who wrote in the fourteenth century: "Therefore separate individuals do not make up the people, and thus properly speaking the people is not men, but a collection of men into a body which is mystical and taken as abstract, and the significance of which has been discovered by the intellect."[10] The difference between the people as One or as Many was insurmountable. For the medieval understanding, this "mystical body of the commonwealth" (*corpus mysticum republicae*) could not err. By contrast, the people as a multitude was not to be trusted, and the rule of the majority was viewed as a dangerous procedure. As Jean Bodin, a famous French jurist and political philosopher, put it in the sixteenth century, "in popular assemblies votes are counted, not weighed, and the number of fools, sinners, and dolts is a thousand times that of honest men."[11]

By contrast, in the New World the understanding of "the people" took a peculiar twist. As we shall see in detail in Chapter 4, thanks to the Puritan **bi-dimensional covenant**, the idea of equal individuals consenting to form a new political body and to subject themselves to a new form of government was far from a mere philosophical idea. It was a living reality, hence the later attractiveness of the **social contract theory** for American political thinking. At the same time, however, once this new body of people was formed, the details of setting up a specific form of government and its daily function was entrusted to an **elected aristocracy of merit**, moving many scholars to claim that the Puritans were, in effect, more medieval than modern.

---

[8] E. S. Morgan, *Inventing the People: The Rise of Popular Sovereignty in England and America* (New York and London: W. W. Norton & Co., 1988), pp. 13–14 (emphasis in the original).

[9] According to Queen Elizabeth's lawyers, "the King has in him two Bodies, viz., a Body natural and a Body politic. [...] [H]is Body politic is a Body that cannot be seen or handled, consisting of Policy and Government, and constituted for the Direction of the People, and the Management of the public weal, and this Body is utterly void of Infancy, and old Age." For a full development of this topic, see E. H. Kantorowicz, *The King's Two Bodies* (Princeton: Princeton University Press, 1957).

[10] Quoted in J. Canning, *The Political Thought of Baldus de Ubaldis* (Cambridge: Cambridge University Press, 1987), p. 187.

[11] J. Bodin [1606], *Six Books of the Commonwealth*, Vol. VI.4, abridged and translated by M. J. Tooley (Oxford: Basil Blackwell, 1955), p.193.

In reality, they simply assumed that people enjoyed *equal constituent power, but different political skills*. This dual understanding of the people, both horizontal (egalitarian) and vertical (hierarchical), proved to be, politically speaking, a long-lasting legacy.

What sets the American case apart is that they had the opportunity to actually implement both understandings of "the people" without really favoring one at the expense of the other. Some scholars have noticed that "democratic tides" come and go throughout American history. The approach that we propose here overcomes this binary thinking, divided between "democrats" and "anti-democrats," or "liberals" and "republicans." As in the story of the blind men and the elephant, all interpretations are partially right, and the main problem remains the inability to seize the paradigm of the people's two bodies underlying these labels. By contrast, the interpretation suggested here invites the reader to see the whole elephant.

This paradigm does not merely recognize the existence of these different understandings. Instead, it reveals why they were accepted by most of the founders, *at the same time*, in a display of dialectic thinking that is hard to conceive today when talking about "the people." As hard as it is to accept today, the idea of an "aristocracy of merit" dominated the American psyche and rhetoric for more than a century before it was replaced by competing concepts, such as "democracy." Yet, at the same time, equally indisputable was the right of ordinary citizens to approve the general form of government, and to elect or remove their representatives from office. Thus, the paradigm of the people's two bodies was, for a long period of time, a suitable way for dealing with a political reality that could not (and still cannot) be confined in the peculiarly contemporaneous "either/or" model of the people: either ruled by wills or by reason, either One or Many.

By now, we are better equipped to understand the basic tenets of **republicanism** and **liberalism**, but also the largely disregarded distinction between the **political** (or **governmental**) **contract** and the much more popular **social contract**, so often invoked in the wrong context.

1.3 Republicanism and Liberalism

Words change their meanings and their connotations over time. For the ancient Greeks, for example, "**democracy**" (a word that they coined from *demos* = "people" and *kratos* = "power") meant **direct democracy**. The Athenians took the principle of equality so seriously that most of their elections were by lot! (Imagine electing the President of the United States or the members of the Supreme Court by pulling their names from a huge hat!) For them, what we today call "democracy", i.e. **representative democracy**, would not have qualified as a democracy at all, but at best as a **mixed regime** (Chapter 2). They didn't even have a word for "representation" – it was a concept alien to them. Despite the fact that in the Western world representative democracy came to be accepted as "democracy," the word carried primarily negative connotations for centuries. With very few exceptions (see, for example, John Wise in Chapter 4 or Thomas Paine in Chapter 5), up until the beginning of the 1800s, the words "democracy" and "democratic" were used with pejorative connotations in the American rhetorical battles. Back then, being labeled as a "democrat" by your political opponents carried the same negative connotations as being labeled as an "anarchist" or a "radical" today. In contrast, the original meaning of "**aristocracy**" carried positive connotations, as long as it was associated with "merit." (See especially Chapters 6 and 7.) It was not a hereditary title but, as the Greek word indicates, the rule of the best ones, the most virtuous (*aristoi* = "the best ones"; *kratos* = "power"). Hence, the expression "**aristocracy of merit**," so often used by the founders, would, in fact, have been redundant if not for the later meaning of the word.

The same applies to "republicanism" and "liberalism." Whenever we use these words throughout this volume, one has to remember that, today, neither word carries the same connotations as it did in the past – at least not for the general public, hence the often used qualifiers, "**classical republicanism**" and "**classical liberalism**," respectively, in order to avoid confusion. The former has nothing to do with today's Republican Party (Chapter 10), the latter nothing to do with the contemporary appellative "liberal" in American politics. More will be said in the introduction to the next two chapters, especially dedicated to these topics. For now, it suffices to sketch the two different *Weltanschauungen* (*Weltanschauung* = a comprehensive world view) and their relationship with the two different apprehensions of the people and of political representation.

Nowadays, we tend to think about "republic" and "republicanism" as opposed to monarchy and its supporters, but this is a relatively new development in the history of the concept. According to the classical understanding, a monarchy can very well also be a republic, for the word, of Latin origin, comes from *respublica* (literally, "the *public things*," and, by extension, "the *public or common good*"). Thus, any political regime that cares for the common good as opposed to the good of the ruling class is, properly speaking, a republic. (See, for example, Aristotle's division of political regimes in Chapter 2.) The emphasis is on the good of the *whole* community, not just a part of it, even if the major one. Hence, as a general rule, republicanism tends to embrace the vision of a **corporate people** – and an **organic vision of the state**. In republican parlance, one would say the American people "*is*," not the American people "*are*." The people is One, not Many. Yet an organic, corporate vision of the people also implies a certain hierarchy and a differentiation of roles. Think about the political body as a human body (the word "corporate" has a Latin etymology, from *corpus* = "body"). As a human body has a certain "hierarchy" among its members, each performing a unique role, so does in classical republican-ism the body politic.

The entire **medieval *Weltanschauung*** was permeated by this hierarchical, cor-poratist, and organic vision of the people, in which every single individual was supposed to play a *unique role*, hence the emphasis on **virtue**, for virtue cannot be represented by someone else. The same rationale informed both the Church and the state, and one of the consequences was the apprehension of **representation** as **descending**. For centuries, the basic assumption was that one cannot represent someone or something that is superior to oneself. The whole of the Church was above the pope, even though the pope was above each individual believer, for even the head is not above the whole body, but part of it. In a similar way, the whole of the people was considered superior to the king (or any generic "ruler" or "representative"), even if the king was above each individual subject.

Think about it this way: The president of your university (from Latin *universitas* = "a corporate whole") represents the university, but the university as a whole is superior to the president. The university elects him or her and can also dismiss him or her in case he or she fails to fulfill the obligations of a president in a satisfactory manner. This was precisely the medieval understanding of the people. The community (*universitas*) as a whole had the power to elect the rulers, and to depose them, if necessary. This was the **political or governmental contract** (or compact) between the people *as a whole* and its ruler. In Britain, Charles I, during the **Civil War**, and James II, during the **Glorious Revolution**, were accused of breaking precisely this contract with the British people. Remember that this was a *political people*, hence it was the **legislative**, i.e. the Parliament, who was entitled to speak in the name of the British people.

Nevertheless, this republican *Weltanschauung* came with a major deficiency: Since the political body was supposed to be ruled by reason, the one(s) entitled to speak for and in the name of the *whole* and of the *common good* remained open to questioning and contestation. The solution of early modernity was straightforward: If **reason** is debatable and hard to define, **will** is not. One could always argue (and disagree) about "why" one should vote for X instead of Y, i.e. about the **reason** to cast one's vote one way or another, so why not ignore the reason for the vote and focus exclusively on the **will** to vote for X instead of Y? Unlike reason, impossible to quantify, the wills can be easily counted, hence the general acceptance of the **rule of the majority**. This is precisely what Hobbes argued for.

To consider **Thomas Hobbes** (Chapter 3) the father of classical liberalism is open to contestation, because he appears to many a totalitarian thinker. He claimed that the sovereign, be it one, a few, or many, can do no wrong, since he/she (or they) are the one(s) determining what is right and what is wrong. Yet Hobbes is also the first to boldly claim that the authority of the sovereign comes from the voluntary transfer of rights from each individual into the hands of the majority, and also the first one to theorize a new, **ascending** understanding of **representation**.[12] He openly opposed the republican theory of **descending representation**, where the people qua *universitas* are above the ruler(s), arguing that the people are only a *societas*, held together by their elected sovereign(s). Thus, "there is little ground for the opinion of them, that say of sovereign kings, though they be *singulis majores*, of greater power than every one of their subjects, yet they be *universis minores*, of less power than them all together."[13] Such an argument, he claimed, is plainly absurd. For Hobbes, a people, any people, is but a voluntary, political construct that lasts only as long as its elected "head" survives. This is the **instrumental vision of the state**, according to which the

---

[12] For a detailed discussion of the two *Weltanschauungen*, see A. Fumurescu, *Compromise: A Political and Philosophical History* (Cambridge: Cambridge University Press, 2013).

[13] T. Hobbes, *Leviathan, or The Matter, Form, and Power of a Common-Wealth Ecclesiastical and Civil* (London: Andrew Crooke, 1651), part 2, chapter 18.

individuals agree to create the state as an instrument meant to protect their **private interest**. Absent the head, this *artificial* body would disintegrate and the individuals composing it would then return to the original state – the **state of nature**. As we shall see in Chapter 3, **John Locke** would adapt and qualify Hobbes's theory, while leaving intact the main theoretical frame. Both of them think of individuals in the abstract, stripped of their personal, unique qualities that make, say, Mary different from both John and Susan. Their theories are meant to apply universally, regardless of the geographical or historical context.

But since both republicanism and liberalism come with strengths and shortcomings, it goes almost without saying that not every political thinker fits nicely into one of the two camps. Several attempts have been made to combine the two *Weltanschauungen*, thus reducing the shortcomings of each. In the beginning of this volume, we offer two examples of thinkers that, while mainly conservative, also acknowledge an important set of liberal values – **William Blackstone** and **Edmund Burke**. For this reason, we have labeled these authors **liberal-conservatives** (Chapter 2). We are also offering selections from two other authors, who, while mainly liberal, share some conservative concerns – Charles-Louis de Secondat, Baron de La Brède et de Montesquieu (for short, **Montesquieu**) and **David Hume**, an exponent of the Scottish Enlightenment. We have labeled them **conservative-liberals** (Chapter 3). All four of them were heavily invoked and quoted during the American founding – and with cause. As Americans, we like to have our cake and eat it too. We like to have the best of both worlds, and even if it is not possible, we keep trying to find solutions to this conundrum.

1.4 The History of the Founding

As previously mentioned, the Puritans that arrived on the shores of the New World might not have been full-fledged political philosophers (even though their degree of literacy and knowledge of the classics was staggering when compared to the rest of Europe). Yet they turned out to be great at actually implementing the **paradigm of the people's two bodies** (Chapter 4) before it was ever specifically thought about. Their own bi-dimensional founding covenant allowed them to accept not only the **liberal** apprehension of free and equal individuals consenting to create a new people by electing rulers that could eventually be removed (*equal constitutional power*), but also the **republican** vision of an organic people, structured according to a hierarchy of merit (*the visible saints*), in which each individual plays a unique role (his or her *calling*). Thus, they also accepted both the **ascending** and the **descending** understandings of political representation.

As shown in Chapter 5, this foundational double helix proved its efficiency during the debates between the **Patriots** and the **Loyalists**. While the colonists maintained that the people for each colony were *created and maintained* by their elective colonial legislatures (the **social contract** argument), they also ended up claiming that the people of each colony ought to be apprehended as a corporate whole connected with Great Britain not via the British Parliament, as the liberal

Weltanschauung had it, but solely via the **political contract** between each colony and the king. From here, it was but a small step to accuse the king of breach of contract (as their British brethren had done already twice, with Charles I and James II), and declare their independence.

This corporatist understanding is evident in the framing of the first Constitution of the United States (or **united States**, as it was capitalized in the Declaration of Independence), the **Articles of Confederation**. As in the largely forgotten **Articles of the Confederation of the United Colonies** instituted by the Puritans more than a century before, the theoretical equality of all the colonies, regardless of their size and population, was accepted as a matter of fact (Chapter 6). At the same time, most of the first state constitutions granted a significant amount of power to the state legislatures, considered by many the true expression of the will of majority.

But, as Tocqueville noted, while Americans might love general ideas, they are also pragmatic; whenever the practice contradicts the theory, they are willing to adapt the theory, rather than forcing the practice to fit the abstract theory.[14] Once the Articles of Confederation and the supremacy of the legislative power proved deficient, the founders started looking for solutions (Chapter 7). After long theoretical debates, the second Constitution of the United States formalized the paradigm of the people's two bodies for the first time. The fact that the Constitution starts with the famous words "We the People," without clarifying the definition of "the people," allowed the founders to combine in an entire set of institutions both understandings of the people.

Nevertheless, the struggle for the United States (only *now* capitalized as such) was far from over. As we shall see in Chapter 8, the fears of factionalism proved to be well founded. Multiple lines of fracture threatened the newly created Union. There were **political** divisions, mostly based upon the different apprehensions of "the people," that led to the emergence of the *first party systems*. Once again, the question of whether there is one American people or many American peoples, and how this people or these peoples were to be understood, created major divisions. Additionally, there were **philosophical disagreements** about how much control the government ought to have over the lives of individuals, as well as **gender, ethnic, and racial inequalities** that needed to be addressed (Chapter 9.) The selections from these two chapters are meant to give the reader a taste of how these issues were theoretically addressed during the first half of the nineteenth century. As we shall see, regardless of what type of minority we are concerned with, the choice between integration and segregation is not an easy one, for each comes with advantages and shortcomings. The first option presupposes an abstract equality which gives the upper hand to the **liberal** principle of majority rule. The second one, while acknowledging the unicity of both individuals and groups, as does the **republican** *Weltanschauung*, is also more willing to accommodate a certain hierarchical ordering of them. No matter what path one chooses, the end result will, most likely, be unsatisfactory.

Last but not least, Chapter 10 offers samples from the theoretical battles that led up to the bloodiest event in American history: **the American Civil War**. It was, in

---

[14] Tocqueville, *Democracy in America*, Vol. II, part 1, chapter 4.

Abraham Lincoln's interpretation, "essentially a people's contest." Somewhat ironically, like the Patriots before them, the Southerners endorsed the argument of a corporatist understanding of the people from each state. For them, the American people was built "bottom-up" from the Virginian people, the Georgian people, and so forth. That is why, when offered the command of the Northern troops by Lincoln, General Robert E. Lee declined, arguing that he was an American *because* he was a Virginian, and thus his first allegiance ought to be to his native state.[15] If the Declaration of Independence maintained that "When in the Course of human events, it becomes necessary for *one people to dissolve the political bands which have connected them with another* ... ", so be it. On the contrary, for the Northerners, as for the Loyalists before them, the Virginian or, say, the Georgian peoples were but parts of the all-encompassing American people, who made their particular existence possible.

After the Civil War, when the official formula "the United States *are*" was replaced with "the United States *is*," the issue of how many peoples live in the US was finally put to rest, yet the saga of the American people was far from over. It is still unfolding. We are all part of it.

1.5 Old Lessons for a New World

By now, the differences between the seventeenth or eighteenth century's New World and that of the twenty-first century are far greater than those between the Old and the New Worlds of the seventeenth or eighteenth century. History moves faster than ever, the past is written and rewritten, new scientific and technological developments happen every day, and the whole of humankind, let alone the Americans, are more connected than ever. One may change existing institutions, create new institutions, reform the public administration, the laws, or the electoral system; one may even amend the Constitution. Yet the basic concepts and ideas underlying and motivating any political action and any policy tend to be extremely resilient. As long as human nature stays the same, it makes little difference if one travels by horse, by ship, or by plane; if one sends the mail by Pony Express or instantly, via the Internet. The problems of the founders are still our problems.

People will always try to balance equality with freedom, common good with individual rights, **positive** (the right and the ability *to do* something) with **negative liberty** (the right *not to* be prevented from doing something), and so forth. People will always want to be recognized as both equal to everyone else and unique. In short, people will always continue to argue. Aristotle might have been right when he claimed that the human being is a *zoon politikon*, a political animal, because we are creatures of meaning. Contrary to common belief, we are not in effect arguing over money, freedom, rights, healthcare, foreign or domestic policies, etc. We are arguing over the *meanings* of money, of freedom, of rights, of foreign or domestic

---

[15] Contrary to popular opinion, Robert E. Lee opposed both secession and slavery. He was among the few Southerners to free his slaves before Lincoln's Emancipation Declaration.

policies, and so forth. And that's precisely why political thought is so important, to clarify what we are *actually* talking about.

Probably the most important lesson to be learned from the foundations of American political thought is that the greatest moments of the founding happened when the two apprehensions of the people discussed above, together with liberty and equality, or virtue and self-interest, were properly balanced, i.e. when the republican and the liberal *Weltanschauungen* were apprehended as **two sides of the same coin**. By the same token, the worst moments of the founding happened whenever the two visions found themselves at odds, with each side sticking to its guns (sometimes literally). Considering today's polarization of political life, it is a lesson worth remembering. Freedom *and* equality. Uniqueness *and* sameness. One does not have to choose between the people's two bodies. It is worth trying to have the cake and eat it too.

As the saying goes, "Those who cannot remember the past are condemned to repeat it."

2 Republicanism

The People "Is"

Ideas are not just resilient, but also versatile – they can be expressed in different words in different times and different contexts. Aristotle, born in the fourth century BCE in the city of Stagira, Greece, lived in a different world than Polybius, also Greek, who was born "only" a couple of centuries later.[1] At the time when Aristotle wrote, the Romans were only an insignificant political and military player in the Mediterranean world. By the time Polybius wrote, the republic of Rome controlled most of the known world, including Greece, and was still expanding. And yet the two authors share the same basic assumptions about the people, politics, and the best regime.

Fast-forwarding almost two millennia, to a different kind of empire – the British one – during the eighteenth century, we encounter another set of republican thinkers. **William Blackstone** was a Tory, i.e. a member of the so-called "Court party," while **Edmund Burke** was a member of the Whig Party, i.e. the "Country party." Yet, despite their practical political differences, they shared many theoretical assumptions, and they both exercised a significant influence on the American founding. Edmund Burke famously stated that Blackstone's *Commentaries* were as widely purchased in America as in Great Britain.[2] As a matter of fact, both authors were highly popular in America, both before and after the Revolutionary War,[3] even though some of the founders (like Thomas Jefferson) had mixed feelings about them.

The reason for the popularity of these authors in America may be found in the fact that, writing a century after the emergence of **classical liberalism** (Chapter 3), they both tried to accommodate some of the new liberal ideas in their theoretical framework, which, however, remained largely **republican** and **conservative**. Such dualism was highly attractive to the Americans, who, as we have seen in the introduction and shall see in more detail in the following chapters, were trying from the beginning to *practically* reconcile *theoretically* opposed visions: republicanism and liberalism,

---

[1] In order to better realize what two centuries can do in terms of change, think how different your world is compared with the one in which people lived at the beginning of the 1800s or at the beginning of the 1600s.

[2] E. Burke, "On Moving His Resolutions for Conciliation with the Colonies" (March 22, 1775) in *The Works of Edmund Burke, with a Memoir*, Vol. I (New York, Harper & Brothers, 1855), pp. 222, 230.

[3] The American edition of Blackstone's *Commentaries on the Laws of England* (four volumes) was published in Philadelphia in 1771–1772. The first edition of 1,400 copies quickly sold out and a second edition soon appeared. As for Burke, his works enjoyed sixteen editions before the Civil War. By comparison, John Locke's work was first published in America in 1773, without any further reprints for the next 164 years.

conservatism and progress, community and individual, public and private good, order and freedom, etc.

As explained before, by focusing on the *respublica*, the common good, **classical republicanism** embraces a **holistic, corporatist, and organic** vision of both the people and the state. The "**body politick**," as it was called, was literally envisioned as a human body. Like the human body, the assumption was that it grows naturally; it has different organs and members, each performing a unique role for the sake of the whole body. The feet have their role, as do the eyes, the heart, the brain, and so forth. Sure, some members are more important than others, but the health of each individual is important for the health of the whole body. Yet, by the same token, if the whole body gets sick, every part of the body suffers as well. It means that the *eudaimonia* (the Greek word for a happy and blessed life) of the individual, no matter how "insignificant" the role, depends on the *eudaimonia* of the community – and vice versa.

But the parallels with the human body do not stop there. Like humans, in order to grow and stay healthy, political bodies have to **adapt** to particular circumstances and to the environment: what might be beneficial for a child growing up in, say, a tribe in the Amazonian jungle may very well be detrimental for one growing up in an affluent, gated community in the suburbs of Philadelphia. And what might be beneficial for an adult may be detrimental for a teenager. Different strategies and different approaches for their education are required. In a similar vein, different types of constitutions may be suitable for different political bodies at certain moments in time. According to this theory, depending on the size of the territory, the differences in wealth and virtue among the inhabitants, their customs, and so forth, a healthy political body can be better ruled by one, by few, or by many. One size, i.e. one type of constitution, does not fit all.

Furthermore, the metaphor of an organic political body implies that, no matter how hard one tries to live a healthy life, **corruption** is unavoidable. No matter how healthy the lives they live, or how virtuous they are, humans get old, lose their strength, and eventually die. The same rationale applies to political bodies. Kingdoms, empires, or popular states have risen and fallen throughout history, no matter how successful or "healthy" they appeared to be – sometimes for centuries. If the process is "unavoidable," how can one slow it down? One republican answer, embraced by many from **Aristotle** to **James Madison**, and from **Polybius** to **John Adams**, is to combine the strengths of different types of constitutions – the rule of one, the rule of few, and the rule of many – and, in so doing, to incorporate different interests to check upon each other and rein in each other's possible excesses. *The best constitutions*, so the argument goes, *are **mixed** ones*: In Rome there were the consuls (the monarchical element), the Senate (the few, the aristocratic component), and the tribunes, elected by the people (the many, i.e. the democratic ingredient). In Great Britain, we have the king or the queen, the House of Lords and the House of Commons. In the US, we ended up having the president, the Senate, and the House of Representatives. Once again, contexts vary, labels vary, and particular details vary as well, but the main idea behind all these institutions stayed the same.

Yet, no matter how well the constitution is crafted, as circumstances change, the constitution must adapt as well. The question is, how fast? Edmund Burke's answer was that changes should be made gradually and with caution, for at least a couple of reasons: first, because once people get used to a certain type of government and certain institutions, a sudden change will create more problems than it will solve. Second, because a gradual change will allow those making the changes to gauge the unintended consequences in the long run, and to adapt the strategy accordingly. Not surprisingly, Burke is seen by many as the father of **modern conservatism**. The story, though, begins much earlier, in ancient Greece.

Aristotle (384–322 BCE) is considered to be one of the greatest philosophers of all times and the "father" of many sciences, from biology to rhetoric, and from physics to ethics and logic. Compared to **Plato** (*c.*423–*c.*347 BCE), the master under whom he studied for some twenty years, Aristotle was more pragmatic when it came to politics and spent more time studying how different constitutions work in the *real* world, instead of arguing how a constitution should look *ideally*. Two key concepts characterize his approach. The first is **mesotes** – the right measure, *in between* excess and deficiency, but far from mediocrity. Most virtues, he claimed, exist in *mesotes*. Courage, for example, is "in *mesotes*" between cowardice and foolishness. The second concept is **telos**, or the final aim. In order to discover the true nature of anything, one must discover its *telos* – what it is for – because nature does nothing in vain, or without purpose. According to Aristotle, man's *telos* is to be a political animal, a *zoon politikon*, in *mesotes* between gods and beasts. Human beings are not meant to live by themselves; only gods and beasts are self-sufficient. Hence, education can move humans in one direction or the other.

Aristotle defines three types of rule – the rule of one, of the few, and of the many – which, according to their *telos*, can be subdivided into good and corrupted regimes. **Monarchy** is the rule of one for the common good. When it is corrupted, it becomes a **tyranny**. **Aristocracy** is the rule of the best few (the *aristoi*) for the sake of the whole people. When it is corrupted, becoming the rule of the few wealthy ones, it is called an **oligarchy**. For Aristotle, **democracy** is still a corrupt regime, although a less dangerous one, because it is the rule of the many (the poor ones) for the benefit of the majority, in disregard of the (wealthy) minority. Its non-corrupted version is the *politeia*, or the **constitutional regime**, which is a <u>mixture</u> between oligarchy and democracy, in *mesotes* between the rule of the few and the rule of the many. According to Aristotle, the main cause for a regime change is a misinterpretation of equality. For Aristotle, true equality is <u>equity</u>, which means giving equal things to equals, and unequal things to unequals. People will be dissatisfied, and will attempt to change the regime, whenever they feel either that they are discriminated against or, on the contrary, that they are treated equally when they feel they are deserving of more.

Polybius (*c.*208–*c.*125 BCE) expanded Aristotle's theory and applied it to particular historical contexts, most notably to explain the success of the Romans, who came to control the entire Mediterranean world in the span of a mere few decades. Polybius is considered by many to be the successor of the historian **Thucydides** (*c.*460–*c.*400 BCE) in terms of objectivity and critical reasoning, and the forefather of historical research in the modern scientific sense. He was among the first to champion the necessity of factual integrity in historical writing. He also claimed that the profession of a historian required political experience (which aids in differentiating between fact and fiction) and familiarity with the geography surrounding one's subject matter to supply an accurate version of the events. Polybius himself exemplified these principles, as he was well traveled and had both political and military experience. Born in Megalopolis, Arcadia, he spent a good part of his life in Rome and thus he acquired first-hand knowledge of the workings of politics, both at a small scale (the *polis*) and at a large one (the empire).

Like Aristotle, Polybius identified six forms of government, three good and three corrupted forms; however, he placed **democracy** among the three good ones. Its corrupted counterpart was *mob rule*, or **anarchy**. In order for a **monarchy** to function properly, it ought to be accepted voluntarily, by an appeal to reason, rather than being imposed by fear or force. Similarly, **aristocracy** should be the rule of the most just and wise men, selected for their merit. Finally, a **democracy** cannot work absent reverence for the gods, succor of parents, respect of elders, and obedience to the laws. Nevertheless, corruption is to be expected, "for just as rust is the natural dissolvent of iron, wood-worms and grubs to timber [. . .] so in each constitution there is naturally engendered a particular vice inseparable from it." The solution would be to combine all three forms, because, "each power being checked by the others, no one part should turn the scale or decisively out-balance the others; but that, by being accurately adjusted and in exact equilibrium, the whole might remain long steady like a ship sailing close to the wind." It was the beginning of the **checks and balances theory**.

Yet, argued Polybius, no matter how well balanced the institutions were, or how well crafted the laws, something more was needed for the stability of the regime, especially one with a democratic component, namely customs based upon religious beliefs – "it is the very thing that keeps the Roman commonwealth together." He went on to explain why:

> If it were possible to form a state wholly of philosophers, such a custom would perhaps be unnecessary. [. . .] Wherefore, to my mind, the ancients were not acting without purpose or at random, when they brought in among the vulgar those opinions about the gods, and the belief in the punishments in Hades: much rather do I think that men nowadays are acting rashly and foolishly in rejecting them.

Some two millennia later, Alexis de Tocqueville found the explanation for the success of the American democratic revolution in the use of religion for nurturing democratic instincts. Respect for the laws comes from *mores*. Unlike many European supporters of the Enlightenment, he famously declared: "I doubt that man can ever tolerate both religious independence and total political liberty, and I am inclined to think that if he has no faith, he must serve, and if he is free, he must believe."[4]

Two millennia after Polybius, Sir **William Blackstone** (1723–1780) lived in a different kind of empire – the British – but also praised its government for combining the monarchical, aristocratic, and democratic principles into a well-

---

[4] Tocqueville, *Democracy in America*, Vol. I, part 1, chapter 5.

functioning whole. Born into a middle-class family, he rose to fame for being the first to survey and organize the ever-growing system of English customary law. His works, most notably his *Commentaries on the Laws of England*, became the basis for legal education in both England and North America, while also bringing him a fortune in royalties (the equivalent of some two million pounds in today's terms) during his lifetime.

Blackstone admitted wholeheartedly that laws are meant to protect rights and to punish transgressors, yet he carefully distinguished between private and public rights, or private and public wrongs, while also pairing rights with duties. The **political contract** between the people, on the one hand, and its rulers, i.e. the magistrates, implies that there are reciprocal rights and duties between the two parties: "Allegiance is the right of the magistrate, and protection the right of the people." (See further Chapter 4.) Furthermore, in accordance with the paradigm of the people's two bodies, he differentiated between **natural and artificial persons**: "Natural persons are such as the God of nature formed us; artificial are such as are created and devised by human laws for the purposes of society and government, which are called corporations or bodies politic." The liberal component of Blackstone's otherwise largely republican and conservative approach can be seen, for example, in the way he treats the relative duties an individual has toward society. As **John Stuart Mill** (1806–1873) would later insist, he claimed that private vices are not to be punished by laws, so long as they do not affect society (**the harm principle**).

Blackstone agreed that what holds the people together is the government, or more specifically, the relationship between the people and the magistrates (rulers), yet this does not place him automatically in the classical liberal camp, for at least three reasons: first, because the focus of his theory was not, as in Hobbes or Locke (Chapter 3), the social contract, but the political contract between the rulers and the ruled. Second, because he still conceived of the people as a hierarchically structured community. For him, as for the Puritans (Chapter 4) or for John Adams (Chapter 5), differences in ranks and honors were beneficial to the well functioning of the whole. And third, because even if he agreed that "the supposition of law [. . .] is, that neither the king nor either house of parliament (collectively taken) is capable of doing any wrong," under extraordinary circumstances, "the law feels itself incapable of furnishing any adequate remedy. [. . .] [T]he *prudence* of the times must provide new remedies upon new emergencies." It was an argument that would be fully embraced by the Patriots (Chapter 5). Yet, as we shall see, prudence and virtue are notably absent from the classical liberal approach, as they contradict basic egalitarian premises.

Even though, as a Whig, he was seated across the aisle from Blackstone (a Tory) in the British Parliament, **Edmund Burke** (1729–1797) agreed with and supported most of Blackstone's understandings of the people and of the proper balance between the three branches of the government. He was, by all measures, a fascinating character. Edward Gibbon, a British historian, described Burke as "the most eloquent and rational madman I ever knew."[5] Born in Dublin, Ireland, to a Catholic mother

---

[5] E. Gibbon, *"Letter 556", Private Letters of Edward Gibbon*, edited by R. E. Prothero (London: Murray, 1896).

and an Anglican father and proud of his Irish heritage, Burke never failed to identify himself as an Englishman; for him, as for Blackstone, the nation and the people were both politically, not ethnically or religiously, defined. He started his early education in a Quaker school and continued it in a Protestant college in Dublin and a Jesuit college in France, which caused hardcore Anglicans to suspect him of Catholic sympathies.

Like Blackstone, Burke's mixture of liberalism and conservatism made him attractive in the eyes of many Americans, as did the fact that he was sympathetic to the claims of the American colonists (though he thought the independence of the colonies was hurting both sides). He claimed that "a state without the means of some change is without the means of its conservation. Without such means it might even risque the loss of that part of the constitution which it wished the most religiously to preserve." Throughout British history, from Magna Carta to the Declaration of Rights after the Glorious Revolution of 1688, he saw an almost uninterrupted effort to protect the rights and the liberties of Englishmen. (Thomas Jefferson, among other founders, initially made the same arguments in order to protect the rights of the colonists.) And yet, he claimed, this was not an "antiquarian" approach, but a philosophical one; not considered in the abstract, but deeply embedded in the country's traditions: "By adhering in this manner and on those principles to our forefathers, we are guided not by the superstition of antiquarians, but by the spirit of philosophic analogy."

The refusal to apply abstract philosophical principles to an extremely complex reality led him to take a vigorous stance against the French Revolution, warning, from its very beginning, that this approach would end in a bloodbath. He was proven right in this respect, but his position resulted in the splitting of the Whig Party (into Old and New Whigs) – much like the founders, who were at odds when it came to interpreting the French Revolution. Paradoxically, since both Burke and the American founders perceived parties as factions acting against the republican public good, it was **the beginning of the party systems** on both sides of the Atlantic (Chapter 8).

As we shall see throughout this volume, history has its own ironies when it comes to unintended consequences.

CLASSICAL REPUBLICANISM

Aristotle *The Politics*[6]

Book 1

Every state is a community of some kind, and every community is established with   1
a view to some good; for everyone always acts in order to obtain that which they
think good. But, if all communities aim at some good, the state or political community, which is the highest of all, and which embraces all the rest, aims at good in
a greater degree than any other, and at the highest good. [. . .]

He who thus considers things in their first growth and origin, whether a state or   2
anything else, will obtain the clearest view of them. In the first place there must be
a union of those who cannot exist without each other; namely, of male and female,
that the race may continue (and this union which is formed, not of choice, but
because, in common with other animals and with plants, mankind have a natural
desire to leave behind them an image of themselves), and of natural ruler and subject,
that both may be preserved. For that which can foresee by the exercise of mind is by
nature intended to be lord and master, and that which can with its body give effect to
such foresight is a subject, and by nature a slave; hence master and slave have the
same interest. Now nature has distinguished between the female and the slave. For
she is not niggardly, like the smith who fashions the Delphian knife for many uses;
she makes each thing for a single use, and every instrument is best made when
intended for one and not for many uses. But among barbarians no distinction is made
between women and slaves, because there is no natural ruler among them: they are
a community of slaves, male and female. Wherefore the poets say, "It is meet that
Hellenes should rule over barbarians";[7] as if they thought that the barbarian and the
slave were by nature one.

Out of these two relationships the first thing to arise is the family, and Hesiod is
right when he says, "First house and wife and an ox for the plough,"[8] for the ox is the
poor man's slave. The family is the association established by nature for the supply
of men's everyday wants, and the members of it are called by Charondas, "companions of the cupboard," and by Epimenides the Cretan, "companions of the manger."
But when several families are united, and the association aims at something more
than the supply of daily needs, the first society to be formed is the village. And the
most natural form of the village appears to be that of a colony from the family,
composed of the children and grandchildren, who are said to be "suckled with the
same milk." And this is the reason why Hellenic states were originally governed by
kings; because the Hellenes were under royal rule before they came together, as the
barbarians still are. Every family is ruled by the eldest, and therefore in the colonies
of the family the kingly form of government prevailed because they were of the same

---

[6] Aristotle, *The Politics*, translated by B. Jowett, edited by S. Everson (Cambridge: Cambridge
University Press, 1996), pp. 11–14, 27–8, 61–5, 69–74, 76–8, 120–2.
[7] Euripides, *Iphigenia in Aulis* 1400.   [8] Hesiod, *Works and Days* 405.

blood. As Homer says: "Each one gives law to his children and to his wives."[9] For they lived dispersedly, as was the manner in ancient times. That is why men say that the Gods have a king, because they themselves either are or were in ancient times under the rule of a king. For they imagine not only the forms of the Gods but their ways of life to be like their own.

When several villages are united in a single complete community, large enough to be nearly or quite self-sufficing, the state comes into existence, originating in the bare needs of life, and continuing in existence for the sake of a good life. And therefore, if the earlier forms of society are natural, so is the state, for it is the end of them, and the nature of a thing is its end. For what each thing is when fully developed, we call its nature, whether we are speaking of a man, a horse, or a family. Besides, the final cause and end of a thing is the best, and to be self-sufficing is the end and the best.

Hence it is evident that the state is a creation of nature, and that man is by nature a political animal. And he who by nature and not by mere accident is without a state, is either a bad man or above humanity; he is like the "Tribeless, lawless, heartless one,"[10] whom Homer denounces – the natural outcast is forthwith a lover of war; he may be compared to an isolated piece at draughts.

Now, that man is more of a political animal than bees or any other gregarious animals is evident. Nature, as we often say, makes nothing in vain, and man is the only animal who has the gift of speech. And whereas mere voice is but an indication of pleasure or pain, and is therefore found in other animals (for their nature attains to the perception of pleasure and pain and the intimation of them to one another, and no further), the power of speech is intended to set forth the expedient and inexpedient, and therefore likewise the just and the unjust. And it is a characteristic of man that he alone has any sense of good and evil, of just and unjust, and the like, and the association of living beings who have this sense makes a family and a state.

Further, the state is by nature clearly prior to the family and to the individual, since the whole is of necessity prior to the part; for example, if the whole body be destroyed, there will be no foot or hand, except homonymously, as we might speak of a stone hand; for when destroyed the hand will be no better than that. But things are defined by their function and power; and we ought not to say that they are the same when they no longer have their proper quality, but only that they are homonymous. The proof that the state is a creation of nature and prior to the individual is that the individual, when isolated, is not self-sufficing; and therefore he is like a part in relation to the whole. But he who is unable to live in society, or who has no need because he is sufficient for himself must be either a beast or a god: he is no part of a state. A social instinct is implanted in all men by nature, and yet he who first founded the state was the greatest of benefactors. For man, when perfected, is the best of animals, but, when separated from law and justice, he is the worst of all; since armed injustice is the more dangerous, and he is equipped at birth with arms, meant to be used by intelligence and excellence, which he may use for the worst ends. That is why, if he has not excellence, he is the most unholy and the most savage of animals,

---

[9] Homer, *Odyssey* 9.114–15.   [10] Homer, *Iliad* 9.63.

and the most full of lust and gluttony. But justice is the bond of men in states; for the administration of justice, which is the determination of what is just, is the principle of order in political society. [. . .]

Of household management we have seen that there are three parts – one is the rule of a master over slaves, which has been discussed already, another of a father, and the third of a husband. A husband and father, we saw, rules over wife and children, both free, but the rule differs, the rule over his children being a royal, over his wife a constitutional rule. For although there may be exceptions to the order of nature, the male is by nature fitter for command than the female, just as the elder and full-grown is superior to the younger and more immature. But in most constitutional states the citizens rule and are ruled by turns, for the idea of a constitutional state implies that the natures of the citizens are equal, and do not differ at all. Nevertheless, when one rules and the other is ruled we endeavour to create a difference of outward forms and names and titles of respect, which may be illustrated by the saying of Amasis about his foot-pan.[11] The relation of the male to the female is always of this kind. The rule of a father over his children is royal, for he rules by virtue both of love and of the respect due to age, exercising a kind of royal power. And therefore Homer has appropriately called Zeus "father of Gods and men"[12] because he is the king of them all. For a king is the natural superior of his subjects, but he should be of the same kin or kind with them, and such is the relation of elder and younger, of father and son. [. . .]

Book 3

He who would inquire into the essence and attributes of various kinds of government must first of all determine what a state is. At present this is a disputed question. Some say that the state has done a certain act; others, not the state, but the oligarchy or the tyrant. And the legislator or statesman is concerned entirely with the state, a government being an arrangement of the inhabitants of a state. But a state is composite, like any other whole made up of many parts – these are the citizens, who compose it. It is evident, therefore, that we must begin by asking, Who is the citizen, and what is the meaning of the term? For here again there may be a difference of opinion. He who is a citizen in a democracy will often not be a citizen in an oligarchy. Leaving out of consideration those who have been made citizens, or who have obtained the name of citizen in any other accidental manner, we may say, first, that a citizen is not a citizen because he lives in a certain place, for resident aliens and slaves share in the place; nor is he a citizen who has legal rights to the extent of suing and being sued; for this right may be enjoyed under the provisions of a treaty. Resident aliens in many places do not possess even such rights completely, for they are obliged to have a patron, so that they do but imperfectly participate in the community, and we call them citizens only in a qualified sense, as we might apply the term to children who are too young to be on the register, or to old men who have been relieved from state duties. Of these we do not say quite simply that they are citizens,

---

[11] Herodotus, 2.172.   [12] Homer, *Iliad* 1.544.

but add in the one case that they are not of age, and in the other, that they are past the age, or something of that sort; the precise expression is immaterial, for our meaning is clear. Similar difficulties to those which I have mentioned may be raised and answered about disfranchised citizens and about exiles. But the citizen whom we are seeking to define is a citizen in the strictest sense, against whom no such exception can be taken, and his special characteristic is that he shares in the administration of justice, and in offices. Now of offices some are discontinuous, and the same persons are not allowed to hold them twice, or can only hold them after a fixed interval; others have no limit of time – for example, the office of juryman or member of the assembly. It may, indeed, be argued that these are not magistrates at all, and that their functions give them no share in the government. But surely it is ridiculous to say that those who have the supreme power do not govern. Let us not dwell further upon this, which is a purely verbal question; what we want is a common term including both juryman and member of the assembly. Let us, for the sake of distinction, call it "indefinite office," and we will assume that those who share in such office are citizens. This is the most comprehensive definition of a citizen, and best suits all those who are generally so called.

But we must not forget that things of which the underlying principles differ in kind, one of them being first, another second, another third, have, when regarded in this relation, nothing, or hardly anything, worth mentioning in common. Now we see that governments differ in kind, and that some of them are prior and that others are posterior; those which are faulty or perverted are necessarily posterior to those which are perfect. (What we mean by perversion will be hereafter explained.) The citizen then of necessity differs under each form of government; and our definition is best adapted to the citizen of a democracy; but not necessarily to other states. For in some states the people are not acknowledged, nor have they any regular assembly, but only extraordinary ones; and law-suits are distributed by sections among the magistrates. At Lacedaemon, for instance, the Ephors determine suits about contracts, which they distribute among themselves, while the elders are judges of homicide, and other causes are decided by other magistrates. A similar principle prevails at Carthage; there certain magistrates decide all causes. We may, indeed, modify our definition of the citizen so as to include these states. In them it is the holder of a definite, not an indefinite office, who is juryman and member of the assembly, and to some or all such holders of definite offices is reserved the right of deliberating or judging about some things or about all things. The conception of the citizen now begins to clear up.

He who has the power to take part in the deliberative or judicial administration of any state is said by us to be a citizen of that state; and, speaking generally, a state is a body of citizens sufficing for the purposes of life. [. . .]

3   [. . .] It is further asked: When are men, living in the same place, to be regarded as a single city – what is the limit? Certainly not the wall of the city, for you might surround all Peloponnesus with a wall. Babylon, we may say, is like this, and every city that has the compass of a nation rather than a city; Babylon, they say, had been taken for three days before some part of the inhabitants became aware of the fact. This difficulty may, however, with advantage be deferred to another occasion; the

statesman has to consider the size of the state, and whether it should consist of more than one race or not.

Again, shall we say that while the race of inhabitants remains the same, the city is also the same, although the citizens are always dying and being born, as we call rivers and fountains the same, although the water is always flowing away and more coming? Or shall we say that the generations of men, like the rivers, are the same, but that the state changes? For, since the state is a partnership, and is a partnership of citizens in a constitution, when the form of the government changes, and becomes different, then it may be supposed that the state is no longer the same, just as a tragic differs from a comic chorus, although the members of both may be identical. And in this manner we speak of every union or composition of elements as different when the form of their composition alters; for example, a scale containing the same sounds is said to be different, accordingly as the Dorian or the Phrygian mode is employed. And if this is true it is evident that the sameness of the state consists chiefly in the sameness of the constitution, and it may be called or not called by the same name, whether the inhabitants are the same or entirely different. It is quite another question, whether a state ought or ought not to fulfil engagements when the form of government changes.

There is a point nearly allied to the preceding: Whether the excellence of a good   4
man and a good citizen is the same or not. But before entering on this discussion, we must certainly first obtain some general notion of the excellence of the citizen. Like the sailor, the citizen is a member of a community. Now, sailors have different functions, for one of them is a rower, another a pilot, and a third a look-out man, a fourth is described by some similar term; and while the precise definition of each individual's excellence applies exclusively to him, there is, at the same time, a common definition applicable to them all. For they have all of them a common object, which is safety in navigation. Similarly, one citizen differs from another, but the salvation of the community is the common business of them all. This community is the constitution; the excellence of the citizen must therefore be relative to the constitution of which he is a member. If, then, there are many forms of government, it is evident that there is not one single excellence of the good citizen which is perfect excellence. But we say that the good man is he who has one single excellence which is perfect excellence. Hence it is evident that the good citizen need not of necessity possess the excellence which makes a good man. [. . .]

Having determined these questions, we have next to consider whether there is only   6
one form of government or many, and if many, what they are, and how many, and what are the differences between them.

A constitution is the arrangement of magistracies in a state, especially of the highest of all. The government is everywhere sovereign in the state, and the constitution is in fact the government. For example, in democracies the people are supreme, but in oligarchies, the few; and, therefore, we say that these two constitutions also are different: and so in other cases.

First, let us consider what is the purpose of a state, and how many forms of rule there are by which human society is regulated. We have already said, in the first part of this treatise, when discussing household management and the rule of a master, that man is by nature a political animal. And therefore, men, even when they do not require one another's help, desire to live together; not but that they are also brought together by their common interests in so far as they each attain to any measure of well-being. This is certainly the chief end, both of individuals and of states. And mankind meet together and maintain the political community also for the sake of mere life (in which there is possibly some noble element so long as the evils of existence do not greatly overbalance the good). And we all see that men cling to life even at the cost of enduring great misfortune, seeming to find in life a natural sweetness and happiness. [...]

And so in politics: when the state is framed upon the principle of equality and likeness, the citizens think that they ought to hold office by turns. Formerly, as is natural, everyone would take his turn of service; and then again, somebody else would look after his interest, just as he, while in office, had looked after theirs. But nowadays, for the sake of the advantage which is to be gained from the public revenues and from office, men want to be always in office. One might imagine that the rulers, being sickly, were only kept in health while they continued in office; in that case we may be sure that they would be hunting after places. The conclusion is evident: that governments which have a regard to the common interest are constituted in accordance with strict principles of justice, and are therefore true forms; but those which regard only the interest of the rulers are all defective and perverted forms, for they are despotic, whereas a state is a community of freemen.

7   Having determined these points, we have next to consider how many forms of government there are, and what they are; and in the first place what are the true forms, for when they are determined the perversions of them will at once be apparent. The words constitution and government have the same meaning, and the government, which is the supreme authority in states, must be in the hands of one, or of a few, or of the many. The true forms of government, therefore, are those in which the one, or the few, or the many, govern with a view to the common interest; but governments which rule with a view to the private interest, whether of the one, or of the few, or of the many, are perversions. For the members of a state, if they are truly citizens, ought to participate in its advantages. Of forms of government in which one rules, we call that which regards the common interest, kingship; that in which more than one, but not many, rule, aristocracy; and it is so called, either because the rulers are the best men, or because they have at heart the best interests of the state and of the citizens. But when the many administer the state for the common interest, the government is called by the generic name – a constitution. And there is a reason for this use of language. One man or a few may excel in excellence; but as the number increases it becomes more difficult for them to attain perfection in every kind of excellence, though they may in military excellence, for this is found in the masses. Hence in a constitutional government the fighting-men have the supreme power, and those who possess arms are the citizens.

Of the above-mentioned forms, the perversions are as follows: – of kingship, tyranny; of aristocracy, oligarchy; of constitutional government, democracy. For tyranny is a kind of monarchy which has in view the interest of the monarch only;

oligarchy has in view the interest of the wealthy; democracy, of the needy: none of them the common good of all. [. . .]

Let us begin by considering the common definitions of oligarchy and democracy, 9 and what is oligarchical and democratic justice. For all men cling to justice of some kind, but their conceptions are imperfect, and they do not express the whole idea. For example, justice is thought by them to be, and is, equality – not, however, for all, but only for equals. And inequality is thought to be, and is, justice; neither is this for all, but only for unequals. When the persons are omitted, then men judge erroneously. The reason is that they are passing judgement on themselves, and most people are bad judges in their own case. And whereas justice implies a relation to persons as well as to things, and a just distribution, as I have already said in the *Ethics*,[13] implies the same ratio between the persons and between the things, they agree about the equality of the things, but dispute about the equality of the persons, chiefly for the reason which I have just given – because they are bad judges in their own affairs; and secondly, because both the parties to the argument are speaking of a limited and partial justice, but imagine themselves to be speaking of absolute justice. For the one party, if they are unequal in one respect, for example wealth, consider themselves to be unequal in all; and the other party, if they are equal in one respect, for example free birth, consider themselves to be equal in all. But they leave out the capital point. For if men met and associated out of regard to wealth only, their share in the state would be proportioned to their property, and the oligarchical doctrine would then seem to carry the day. It would not be just that he who paid one mina should have the same share of a hundred minae, whether of the principal or of the profits, as he who paid the remaining ninety-nine. But a state exists for the sake of a good life, and not for the sake of life only: if life only were the object, slaves and brute animals might form a state, but they cannot, for they have no share in happiness or in a life based on choice. Nor does a state exist for the sake of alliance and security from injustice, nor yet for the sake of exchange and mutual intercourse; for then the Tyrrhenians and the Carthaginians, and all who have commercial treaties with one another, would be the citizens of one state. True, they have agreements about imports, and engagements that they will do no wrong to one another, and written articles of alliance. But there are no magistracies common to the contracting parties; different states have each their own magistracies. Nor does one state take care that the citizens of the other are such as they ought to be, nor see that those who come under the terms of the treaty do no wrong or wickedness at all, but only that they do no injustice to one another. Whereas, those who care for good government take into consideration political excellence and defect. Whence it may be further inferred that excellence must be the care of a state which is truly so called, and not merely enjoys the name: for without this end the community becomes a mere alliance which differs only in place from alliances of which the members live apart; and law is only a convention, "a surety to one another of justice," as the sophist Lycophron says, and has no real power to make the citizens good and just. [. . .]

---

[13] *Nicomachean Ethics* 5.3.

11   [...] The principle that the multitude ought to be in power rather than the few best might seem to be solved and to contain some difficulty and perhaps even truth. For the many, of whom each individual is not a good man, when they meet together may be better than the few good, if regarded not individually but collectively, just as a feast to which many contribute is better than a dinner provided out of a single purse. For each individual among the many has a share of excellence and practical wisdom, and when they meet together, just as they become in a manner one man, who has many feet, and hands, and senses, so too with regard to their character and thought. Hence the many are better judges than a single man of music and poetry; for some understand one part, and some another, and among them they understand the whole. There is a similar combination of qualities in good men, who differ from any individual of the many, as the beautiful are said to differ from those who are not beautiful, and works of art from realities, because in them the scattered elements are combined, although, if taken separately, the eye of one person or some other feature in another person would be fairer than in the picture. Whether this principle can apply to every democracy, and to all bodies of men, is not clear. Or rather, by heaven, in some cases it is impossible to apply; for the argument would equally hold about brutes; and wherein, it will be asked, do some men differ from brutes? But there may be bodies of men about whom our statement is nevertheless true. And if so, the difficulty which has been already raised, and also another which is akin to it – viz. what power should be assigned to the mass of freemen and citizens, who are not rich and have no personal merit – are both solved. There is still a danger in allowing them to share the great offices of state, for their folly will lead them into error, and their dishonesty into crime. But there is a danger also in not letting them share, for a state in which many poor men are excluded from office will necessarily be full of enemies. The only way of escape is to assign to them some deliberative and judicial functions. For this reason, Solon and certain other legislators give them the power of electing to offices, and of calling the magistrates to account, but they do not allow them to hold office singly. When they meet together their perceptions are quite good enough, and combined with the better class they are useful to the state (just as impure food when mixed with what is pure sometimes makes the entire mass more wholesome than a small quantity of the pure would be), but each individual, left to himself, forms an imperfect judgement. On the other hand the popular form of government involves certain difficulties. In the first place, it might be objected that he who can judge of the healing of a sick man would be one who could himself heal his disease, and make him whole – that is, in other words, the physician; and so in all professions and arts. As, then, the physician ought to be called to account by physicians, so ought men in general to be called to account by their peers. But physicians are of three kinds: – there is the ordinary practitioner, and there is the master physician, and thirdly the man educated in the art: in all arts there is such a class; and we attribute the power of judging to them quite as much as to professors of the art. Secondly, does not the same principle apply to elections? For a right election can only be made by those who have knowledge; those who know geometry, for example, will choose a geometrician rightly, and those who know how to steer, a pilot; and, even if there be some occupations and arts in which private persons share in the ability to choose, they

certainly cannot choose better than those who know. So that, according to this argument, neither the election of magistrates, nor the calling of them to account, should be entrusted to the many. Yet possibly these objections are to a great extent met by our old answer, that if the people are not utterly degraded, although individually they may be worse judges than those who have special knowledge, as a body they are as good or better. Moreover, there are some arts whose products are not judged of solely, or best, by the artists themselves, namely those arts whose products are recognized even by those who do not possess the art; for example, the knowledge of the house is not limited to the builder only; the user, or, in other words, the master, of the house will actually be a better judge than the builder, just as the pilot will judge better of a rudder than the carpenter, and the guest will judge better of a feast than the cook. [. . .]

Book 5

[. . .] Here then, so to speak, are opened the very springs and fountains of revolution;   1
and hence arise two sorts of changes in governments; the one affecting the constitution, when men seek to change from an existing form into some other, for example, from democracy into oligarchy, and from oligarchy into democracy, or from either of them into constitutional government or aristocracy, and conversely; the other not affecting the constitution, when, without disturbing the form of government, whether oligarchy, or monarchy, or another, they try to get the administration into their own hands. Further, there is a question of degree; an oligarchy, for example, may become more or less oligarchical, and a democracy more or less democratic; and in like manner the characteristics of the other forms of government may be more or less strictly maintained. Or the revolution may be directed against a portion of the constitution only, e.g., the establishment or overthrow of a particular office: as at Sparta it is said that Lysander attempted to overthrow the monarchy, and King Pausanias, the Ephoralty. At Epidamnus, too, the change was partial. For instead of phylarchs or heads of tribes, a council was appointed; but to this day the magistrates are the only members of the ruling class who are compelled to go to the Heliaea when an election takes place, and the office of the single archon was another oligarchical feature. Everywhere inequality is a cause of revolution, but an inequality in which there is no proportion – for instance, a perpetual monarchy among equals; and always it is the desire of equality which rises in rebellion. [. . .]

In considering how dissensions and political revolutions arise, we must first of all   2
ascertain the beginnings and causes of them which affect constitutions generally. They may be said to be three in number; and we have now to give an outline of each. We want to know (1) what is the feeling? (2) what are the motives of those who make them? (3) whence arise political disturbances and quarrels? The universal and chief cause of this revolutionary feeling has been already mentioned; viz., the desire of equality, when men think that they are equal to others who have more than themselves; or, again, the desire of inequality and superiority, when conceiving themselves to be superior they think that they have not more but the same or less than their inferiors; pretensions which may and may not be just. Inferiors revolt in order that

they may be equal, and equals that they may be superior. Such is the state of mind which creates revolutions. The motives for making them are the desire of gain and honour, or the fear of dishonour and loss; the authors of them want to divert punishment or dishonour from themselves or their friends. The causes and reasons of revolutions, whereby men are themselves affected in the way described, and about the things which I have mentioned, viewed in one way may be regarded as seven, and in another as more than seven. Two of them have been already noticed; but they act in a different manner, for men are excited against one another by the love of gain and honour – not, as in the case which I have just supposed, in order to obtain them for themselves, but at seeing others, justly or unjustly, engrossing them. Other causes are insolence, fear, excessive predominance, contempt, disproportionate increase in some part of the state; causes of another sort are election intrigues, carelessness, neglect about trifles, dissimilarity of elements.

Polybius *Histories*[14]

Book 1

1   Had the praise of History been passed over by former Chroniclers it would perhaps have been incumbent upon me to urge the choice and special study of records of this sort, as the readiest means men can have of correcting their knowledge of the past. But my predecessors have not been sparing in this respect. They have all begun and ended, so to speak, by enlarging on this theme: asserting again and again that the study of History is in the truest sense an education, and a training for political life; and that the most instructive, or rather the only, method of learning to bear with dignity the vicissitudes of fortune is to recall the catastrophes of others. It is evident, therefore, that no one need think it his duty to repeat what has been said by many, and said well. Least of all myself: for the surprising nature of the events which I have undertaken to relate is in itself sufficient to challenge and stimulate the attention of everyone, old or young, to the study of my work. Can anyone be so indifferent or idle as not to care to know by what means, and under what kind of polity, almost the whole inhabited world was conquered and brought under the dominion of the single city of Rome, and that too within a period of not quite fifty-three years? Or who again can be so completely absorbed in other subjects of contemplation or study, as to think any of them superior in importance to the accurate understanding of an event for which the past affords no precedent. [. . .]

4   There is this analogy between the plan of History and the marvellous spirit of the age with which I have to deal. Just as Fortune made almost all the affairs of the world incline in one direction, and forced them to converge upon one and the same point; so it is my task as an historian to put before my readers a compendious view of the part played by Fortune in bringing about the general catastrophe. It was this peculiarity

[14] *The Histories of Polybius: Translated from the Text of F. Hultsch*, edited and translated by E. S. Shuckburgh (London: Macmillan and Co., 1889).

which originally challenged my attention, and determined me on undertaking this work. And combined with this was the fact that no writer of our time has undertaken a general history. Had any one done so my ambition in this direction would have been much diminished. But, in point of fact, I notice that by far the greater number of historians concern themselves with isolated wars and the incidents that accompany them: while as to a general and comprehensive scheme of events, their date, origin, and catastrophe, no one as far as I know has undertaken to examine it. I thought it, therefore, distinctly my duty neither to pass by myself, nor allow anyone else to pass by, without full study, a characteristic specimen of the dealings of Fortune at once brilliant and instructive in the highest degree. For fruitful as Fortune is in change, and constantly as she is producing dramas in the life of men, yet never assuredly before this did she work such a marvel, or act such a drama, as that which we have witnessed. [. . .]

Book 6

[. . .] Now it is undoubtedly the case that most of those who profess to give us   3
authoritative instruction on this subject distinguish three kinds of constitutions, which they designate kingship, aristocracy, democracy. But in my opinion the question might fairly be put to them, whether they name these as being the *only* ones, or as the *best*. In either case I think they are wrong. For it is plain that we must regard as the *best* constitution that which partakes of all these three elements. And this is no mere assertion, but has been proved by the example of Lycurgus, who was the first to construct a constitution – that of Sparta – on this principle. Nor can we admit that these are the *only* forms: for we have had before now examples of absolute and tyrannical forms of government, which, while differing as widely as possible from kingship, yet appear to have some points of resemblance to it; on which account all absolute rulers falsely assume and use, as far as they can, the title of king. Again there have been many instances of oligarchical governments having in appearance some analogy to aristocracies, which are, if I may say so, as different from them as it is possible to be. The same also holds good about democracy.

I will illustrate the truth of what I say. We cannot hold every absolute government   4
to be a kingship, but only that which is accepted voluntarily, and is directed by an appeal to reason rather than to fear and force. Nor again is every oligarchy to be regarded as an aristocracy; the latter exists only where the power is wielded by the justest and wisest men selected on their merits. Similarly, it is not enough to constitute a democracy that the whole crowd of citizens should have the right to do whatever they wish or propose. But where reverence to the gods, succour of parents, respect to elders, obedience to laws, are traditional and habitual, in such communities, if the will of the majority prevail, we may speak of the form of government as a democracy.

So then we enumerate six forms of government, – the three commonly spoken of which I have just mentioned, and three more allied forms, I mean despotism, oligarchy and mob-rule. The first of these arises without artificial aid and in the natural order of events. Next to this, and produced from it by the aid of art and adjustment, comes kingship; which degenerating into the evil form allied to it, by which I mean tyranny, both are once more destroyed and aristocracy produced. Again the latter being in the course of nature perverted to oligarchy, and the people passionately avenging the unjust acts of their rulers, democracy comes into existence; which again by its violence and contempt of law becomes sheer mob-rule.

No clearer proof of the truth of what I say could be obtained than by a careful observation of the natural origin, genesis, and decadence of these several forms of government. For it is only by seeing distinctly how each of them is produced that a distinct view can also be obtained of its growth, zenith, and decadence, and the time, circumstance, and place in which each of these may be expected to recur. This method I have assumed to be especially applicable to the Roman constitution, because its origin and growth have from the first followed natural causes. [...]

10   For the present I will make a brief reference to the legislation of Lycurgus for such a discussion is not at all alien to my subject. That statesman was fully aware that all those changes which I have enumerated come about by an undeviating law of nature; and reflected that every form of government that was unmixed, and rested on one species of power, was unstable; because it was swiftly perverted into that particular form of evil peculiar to it and inherent in its nature. For just as rust is the natural dissolvent of iron, wood-worms and grubs to timber, by which they are destroyed without any external injury, but by that which is engendered in themselves; so in each constitution there is naturally engendered a particular vice inseparable from it: in kingship it is absolutism; in aristocracy it is oligarchy; in democracy lawless ferocity and violence; and to these vicious states all these forms of government are, as I have lately shown, inevitably transformed.

Lycurgus, I say, saw all this, and accordingly combined together all the excellences and distinctive features of the best constitutions, that no part should become unduly predominant, and be perverted into its kindred vice; and that, each power being checked by the others, no one part should turn the scale or decisively outbalance the others; but that, by being accurately adjusted and in exact equilibrium, the whole might remain long steady like a ship sailing close to the wind. The royal power was prevented from growing insolent by fear of the people, which had also assigned to it an adequate share in the constitution. The people in their turn were restrained from a bold contempt of the kings by fear of the Gerusia: the members of which, being selected on grounds of merit, were certain to throw their influence on the side of justice in every question that arose; and thus the party placed at a disadvantage by its conservative tendency was always strengthened and supported by the weight and influence of the Gerusia. The result of this combination has been that the Lacedaemonians retained their freedom for the longest period of any people with which we are acquainted. [...]

11   [...] As for the Roman constitution, it had three elements, each of them possessing sovereign powers: and their respective share of power in the whole state had been regulated with such a scrupulous regard to equality and equilibrium, that no one could say for certain, not even a native, whether the constitution as a whole were an aristocracy or democracy or despotism. And no wonder: for if we confine our observation to the power of the Consuls we should be inclined to

regard it as despotic; if on that of the Senate, as aristocratic; and if finally one looks at the power possessed by the people it would seem a clear case of a democracy. [...]

[...] I must now show how each of these several parts can, when they choose, 15 oppose or support each other. The Consul, then, when he has started on an expedition [...] is to all appearance absolute in the administration of the business in hand; still he has need of the support both of people and Senate, and, without them, is quite unable to bring the matter to a successful conclusion. For it is plain that he must have supplies sent to his legions from time to time; but without a decree of the Senate they can be supplied neither with corn, nor clothes, nor pay, so that all the plans of a commander must be futile, if the Senate is resolved either to shrink from danger or hamper his plans. And again, whether a Consul shall bring any undertaking to a conclusion or no depends entirely upon the Senate: for it has absolute authority at the end of a year to send another Consul to supersede him, or to continue the existing one in his command. [...]

As for the people, the Consuls are pre-eminently obliged to court their favour, however distant from home may be the field of their operations; for it is the people, as I have said before, that ratifies, or refuses to ratify, terms of peace and treaties; but most of all because when laying down their office they have to give an account of their administration before it. Therefore in no case is it safe for the Consuls to neglect either the Senate or the goodwill of the people.

As for the Senate, which possesses the immense power I have described, in the first 16 place it is obliged in public affairs to take the multitude into account, and respect the wishes of the people; and it cannot put into execution the penalty for offences against the republic, which are punishable with death, unless the people first ratify its decrees. Similarly even in matters which directly affect the senators, – for instance, in the case of a law diminishing the Senate's traditional authority, or depriving senators of certain dignities and offices, or even actually cutting down their property, – even in such cases the people have the sole power of passing or rejecting the law. But most important of all is the fact that, if the Tribunes interpose their veto, the Senate not only are unable to pass a decree, but cannot even hold a meeting at all, whether formal or informal. Now, the Tribunes are always bound to carry out the decree of the people, and above all things to have regard to their wishes: therefore, for all these reasons the Senate stands in awe of the multitude, and cannot neglect the feelings of the people.

In like manner the people on its part is far from being independent of the Senate, 17 and is bound to take its wishes into account both collectively and individually. For contracts, too numerous to count, are given out by the censors in all parts of Italy for the repairs or construction of public buildings; there is also the collection of revenue from many rivers, harbours, gardens, mines, and land – everything, in a word, that comes under the control of the Roman government: and in all these the people at large are engaged; so that there is scarcely a man, so to speak, who is not interested either as a contractor or as being employed in the works. [...]

Now over all these transactions the Senate has absolute control. It can grant an extension of time; and in case of unforeseen accident can relieve the contractors from a portion of their obligation, or release them from it altogether, if they are absolutely unable to fulfil it. And there are many details in which the Senate can inflict great hardships, or, on the other hand, grant great indulgences to the contractors: for in every case the appeal is to it. But the most important point of all is that the judges are taken from its members in the majority of trials, whether public or private, in which the charges are heavy. Consequently, all citizens are much at its mercy; and being alarmed at the uncertainty as to when they may need its aid, are cautious about resisting or actively opposing its will. And for a similar reason men do not rashly resist the wishes of the Consuls, because one and all may become subject to their absolute authority on a campaign.

18   The result of this power of the several estates for mutual help or harm is a union sufficiently firm for all emergencies, and a constitution than which it is impossible to find a better. For whenever any danger from without compels them to unite and work together, the strength which is developed by the State is so extraordinary, that everything required is unfailingly carried out by the eager rivalry shown by all classes to devote their whole minds to the need of the hour, and to secure that any determination come to should not fail for want of promptitude; while each individual works, privately and publicly alike, for the accomplishment of the business in hand. Accordingly, the peculiar constitution of the State makes it irresistible, and certain of obtaining whatever it determines to attempt.

Nay, even when these external alarms are past, and the people are enjoying their good fortune and the fruits of their victories, and, as usually happens, growing corrupted by flattery and idleness, show a tendency to violence and arrogance, – it is in these circumstances, more than ever, that the constitution is seen to possess within itself the power of correcting abuses. For when any one of the three classes becomes puffed up, and manifests an inclination to be contentious and unduly encroaching, the mutual interdependency of all the three, and the possibility of the pretensions of any one being checked and thwarted by the others, must plainly check this tendency: and so the proper equilibrium is maintained by the impulsiveness of the one part being checked by its fear of the other. [. . .]

47   [. . .] To my mind, then, there are two things fundamental to every state, in virtue of which its powers and constitution become desirable or objectionable. These are customs and laws. Of these the desirable are those which make men's private lives holy and pure, and the public character of the state civilised and just. The objectionable are those whose effect is the reverse. As, then, when we see good customs and good laws prevailing among certain people, we confidently assume that, in consequence of them, the men and their civil constitution will be good also, so when we see private life full of covetousness, and public policy of injustice, plainly we have reason for asserting their laws, particular customs, and general constitution to be bad. [. . .]

56   [. . .] But the most important difference for the better which the Roman commonwealth appears to me to display is in their religious beliefs. For I conceive that what in other nations is looked upon as a reproach, I mean a scrupulous fear of the gods, is the very thing which keeps the Roman commonwealth together. To such an extraordinary height is this carried among them, both in private and public business, that nothing could exceed it. Many people might think this unaccountable; but in my opinion their object is to use it as a check upon the common people. If it were

possible to form a state wholly of philosophers, such a custom would perhaps be unnecessary. But seeing that every multitude is fickle, and full of lawless desires, unreasoning anger, and violent passion, the only resource is to keep them in check by mysterious terrors and scenic effects of this sort. Wherefore, to my mind, the ancients were not acting without purpose or at random, when they brought in among the vulgar those opinions about the gods, and the belief in the punishments in Hades: much rather do I think that men nowadays are acting rashly and foolishly in rejecting them. This is the reason why, apart from anything else, Greek statesmen, if entrusted with a single talent, though protected by ten checking-clerks, as many seals, and twice as many witnesses, yet cannot be induced to keep faith: whereas among the Romans, in their magistracies and embassies, men have the handling of a great amount of money, and yet from pure respect to their oath keep their faith intact. And, again, in other nations it is a rare thing to find a man who keeps his hands out of the public purse, and is entirely pure in such matters: but among the Romans it is a rare thing to detect a man in the act of committing such a crime.

Book 12

[...] Well, I quite agree that in such writings truth should be the first consideration: 12
and, in fact, somewhere in the course of my work I have said "that as in a living body, when the eyes are out, the whole is rendered useless, so if you take truth from history what is left is but an idle tale." [...]

The special province of history is, first, to ascertain what the actual words used   25b
were; and secondly, to learn why it was that a particular policy or argument failed or succeeded. For a bare statement of an occurrence is interesting indeed, but not instructive: but when this is supplemented by a statement of cause, the study of history becomes fruitful. For it is by applying analogies to our own circumstances that we get the means and basis for calculating the future; and for learning from the past when to act with caution, and when with greater boldness, in the present. [...]

[...] History and the science of medicine are alike in this respect, that both may be   25d
divided broadly into three departments; and therefore those who study either must approach them in three ways. For instance, the three departments of medicine are the rhetorical, the dietetic, and the surgical and pharmaceutical. [...] [25e] In the same way the science of genuine history is threefold: first, the dealing with written documents and the arrangement of the material thus obtained; second, topography, the appearance of cities and localities, the description of rivers and harbours, and, speaking generally, the peculiar features of seas and countries and their relative distances; thirdly, political affairs. Now, as in the case of medicine, it is the last branch that many attach themselves to, owing to their preconceived opinions on the subject. And the majority of writers bring to the undertaking no spirit of fairness at all: nothing but dishonesty, impudence and unscrupulousness. Like vendors of drugs, their aim is to catch popular credit and favour, and to seize every opportunity of enriching themselves. About such writers it is not worthwhile to say more.

But some of those who have the reputation of approaching history in a reasonable   25f
spirit are like the theoretical physicians. They spend all their time in libraries, and

acquire generally all the learning which can be got from books, and then persuade themselves that they are adequately equipped for their task. Yet in my opinion they are only partially qualified for the production of genuine history. To inspect ancient records indeed, with the view of ascertaining the notions entertained by the ancients of certain places, nations, polities and events, and of understanding the several circumstances and contingencies experienced in former times, is useful; for the history of the past directs our attention in a proper spirit to the future, if a writer can be found to give a statement of facts as they really occurred. But to persuade one's self [...] that such ability in research is sufficient to enable a man to describe subsequent transactions with success is quite foolish. It is as though a man were to imagine that an inspection of the works of the old masters would enable him to become a painter and a master of the art himself.

25g   It is in fact as impossible to write well on the operations in a war, if a man has had no experience of actual service, as it is to write well on politics without having been engaged in political transactions and vicissitudes. And when history is written by the book-learned, without technical knowledge, and without clearness of detail, the work loses all its value. For if you take from history its element of practical instruction, what is left of it has nothing to attract and nothing to teach. [...]

28   [...] Plato says that "human affairs will not go well until either philosophers become kings or kings become philosophers. So I should say that history will never be properly written, until either men of action undertake to write it (not as they do now, as a matter of secondary importance; but, with the conviction that it is their most necessary and honourable employment, shall devote themselves through life exclusively to it), or historians become convinced that practical experience is of the first importance for historical composition. Until that time arrives there will always be abundance of blunders in the writings of historians. [...]

LIBERAL CONSERVATISM

William Blackstone *Commentaries on the Laws of England* (1765/1770)[15]

Book I Of the Rights of Persons

Chapter 1   Of the Absolute Rights of Individuals

§160   **Objects of the Law: Rights and Wrongs.** – The objects of the laws of England are so very numerous and extensive, that, in order to consider them with any tolerable ease and perspicuity, it will be necessary to distribute them methodically under proper and distinct heads; avoiding as much as possible divisions too large and

---

[15] Sir W. Blackstone, *Commentaries on the Laws of England. In Four Books* (Philadelphia: J. B. Lippincott Company, 1893). Paragraph numbering is based on the edition by W. C. Jones (San Francisco: Bancroft Whitney Company, 1915). Footnotes have been omitted due to space constraints.

comprehensive on the one hand, and too trifling and minute on the other; both of which are equally productive of confusion.

Now, as municipal law is a rule of civil conduct, commanding what is right, and prohibiting what is wrong; or as Cicero, and after him our Bracton, have expressed it, sanctio justa, jubens honesta et prohibens contraria, it follows that the primary and principal object of the law are rights and wrongs. In the prosecution, therefore, of these commentaries, I shall follow this very simple and obvious division; and shall, in the first place, consider the rights that are commanded, and secondly the wrongs that are forbidden, by the laws of England.

Division of rights and wrongs. – Rights are, however, liable to another subdivision; being either, first, those which concern and are annexed to the persons of men, and are then called jura personarum, or the rights of persons; or they are, secondly, such as a man may acquire over external objects, or things unconnected with his person, which are styled jura rerum, or the rights of things. Wrongs also are divisible into, first, private wrongs, which, being an infringement merely of particular rights, concern individuals only, and are called civil injuries; and, secondly, public wrongs, which, being a breach of general and public rights, affect the whole community, and are called crimes and misdemeanors. [...] §161

Rights of persons. – We are now first to consider the rights of persons, with the means of acquiring and losing them. §163

Now the rights of persons that are commanded to be observed by the municipal law are of two sorts: first, such as are due from every citizen, which are usually called civil duties; and, secondly, such as belong to him, which is the more popular acceptation of rights or jura. Both may indeed be comprised in this latter division; for, as all social duties are of a relative nature, at the same time that they are due from one man, or set of men, they must also be due to another. But I apprehend it will be more clear and easy to consider many of them as duties required from, rather than as rights belonging to, particular persons. Thus, for instance, allegiance is usually, and therefore most easily, considered as the duty of the people, and protection as the duty of the magistrate; and yet they are reciprocally the rights as well as duties of each other. Allegiance is the right of the magistrate, and protection the right of the people.

a. Division of persons. – Persons also are divided by the law into either natural persons, or artificial. Natural persons are such as the God of nature formed us; artificial are such as are created and devised by human laws for the purposes of society and government, which are called corporations or bodies politic. §164

b. Division of rights of persons: absolute and relative. – The rights of persons considered in their natural capacities are also of two sorts, absolute and relative. Absolute, which are such as appertain and belong to particular men, merely as individuals or single persons: relative, which are incident to them as members of society, and standing in various relations to each other. The first, that is, absolute rights, will be the subject of the present chapter. §165

(1) Absolute rights. – By the absolute rights of individuals, we mean those which are so in their primary and strictest sense; such as would belong to their persons merely in a state of nature, and which every man is entitled to enjoy, whether out of society or in it. But with regard to the absolute duties, which man is bound to perform §166 considered as a mere individual, it is not to be expected that any human municipal law should at all explain or enforce them. For the end and intent of such laws being only to regulate the behaviour of mankind, as they are members of society, and stand in various relations to each other, they have consequently no concern with any other but social or relative duties. Let a man therefore be ever so abandoned in his principles, or vicious in his practice, provided he keeps his wickedness to himself, and does not offend against the rules of public decency, he is out of the reach of human laws. But if he makes his vices public, though they be such as seem principally to affect himself, (as drunkenness, or the like,) then they become, by the bad example they set, of pernicious effects to society; and therefore it is then the business of human laws to correct them. Here the circumstance of publication is what alters the nature of the case. Public sobriety is a relative duty, and therefore enjoined by our laws; private sobriety is an absolute duty, which, whether it be performed or not, human tribunals can never know; and therefore they can never enforce it by any civil sanction. But, with respect to rights, the case is different. Human laws define and enforce as well those rights which belong to a man considered as an individual, as those which belong to him considered as related to others.

§167   **(a) Protections of absolute rights.** – For the principal aim of society is to protect individuals in the enjoyment of those absolute rights, which were vested in them by the immutable laws of nature, but which could not be preserved in peace without that mutual assistance and intercourse which is gained by the institution of friendly and social communities. Hence it follows, that the first and primary end of human laws is to maintain and regulate these absolute rights of individuals. Such rights as are social and relative result from, and are posterior to, the formation of states and societies: so that to maintain and regulate these is clearly a subsequent consideration. And, therefore, the principal view of human laws is, or ought always to be, to explain, protect, and enforce such rights as are absolute, which in themselves are few and simple: and then such rights as are relative, which, arising from a variety of connections, will be far more numerous and more complicated. These will take up a greater space in any code of laws, and hence may appear to be more attended to – though in reality they are not – than the rights of the former kind. Let us therefore proceed to examine how far all laws ought, and how far the laws of England actually do, take notice of these absolute rights, and provide for their lasting security. [. . .]

Chapter 2   Of the Parliament

§201   **Relations of persons: public and private.** – We are next to treat of the rights and duties of persons, as they are members of society, and stand in various relations to each other. These relations are either public or private: and we will first consider those that are public.

§202   **Government.** – The most universal public relation, by which men are connected together, is that of government; namely, as governors or governed; or, in other words, as magistrates and people. Of magistrates, some also are supreme, in whom the sovereign power of the state resides; others are subordinate, deriving all their authority from the supreme magistrate, accountable to him for their conduct, and acting in an inferior secondary sphere.

1. Departments of Government. – In all tyrannical governments, the supreme magistracy, or the right of both making and of enforcing the laws, is vested in one and the same man, or one and the same body of men; and wherever these two powers are united together, there can be no public liberty. The magistrate may enact tyrannical laws, and execute them in a tyrannical manner, since he is possessed, in quality of dispenser of justice, with all the power which he, as legislator, thinks proper to give himself. But, where the legislative and executive authority are in distinct hands, the former will take care not to entrust the latter with so large a power as may tend to the subversion of its own independence, and therewith of the liberty of the subject. With us, therefore, in England, this supreme power is divided into two branches; the one legislative, to wit, the parliament, consisting of king, lords, and commons; the other executive, consisting of the king alone. It will be the business of this chapter to consider the British parliament, in which the legislative power, and (of course) the supreme and absolute authority of the state, is vested by our constitution. [...]

§203

(1) The crown. – It is highly necessary for preserving the balance of the constitution, that the executive power should be a branch, though not the whole, of the legislative. The total union of them, we have seen, would be productive of tyranny; the total disjunction of them, for the present, would in the end produce the same effects, by causing that union against which it seems to provide. The legislative would soon become tyrannical, by making continual encroachments, and gradually assuming to itself the rights of the executive power. Thus the long parliament of Charles the First, while it acted in a constitutional manner, with the royal concurrence, redressed many heavy grievances, and established many salutary laws. But when the two houses assumed the power of legislation, in exclusion of the royal authority, they soon after assumed likewise the reins of administration; and, in consequence of these united powers, overturned both church and state, and established a worse oppression than any they pretended to remedy. To hinder therefore any such encroachments, the king is himself a part of the parliament: and as this is the reason of his being so, very properly therefore the share of legislation, which the constitution has placed in the crown, consists in the power of rejecting rather than resolving; this being sufficient to answer the end proposed. For we may apply to the royal negative, in this instance, what Cicero observes of the negative of the Roman tribunes, that the crown has not any power of doing wrong, but merely of preventing wrong from being done. The crown cannot begin of itself any alterations in the present established law; but it may approve or disapprove of the alterations suggested and consented to by the two houses. The legislative therefore cannot abridge the executive power of any rights which it now has by law, without its own consent; since the law must perpetually stand as it now does, unless all the powers will agree to alter it. And herein indeed consists the true excellence of the English government, that all the parts of it form a mutual check upon each other. In the legislature, the people are a check upon the nobility, and the nobility a check upon the people, by the mutual privilege of rejecting what the other has resolved: while the king is a check upon both, which preserves the executive power from encroachments. And this very

§213

executive power is again checked and kept within due bounds by the two houses, through the privilege they have of inquiring into, impeaching, and punishing the conduct (not indeed of the king, which would destroy his constitutional independence; but, which is more beneficial to the public) of his evil and pernicious counsellors. Thus every branch of our civil polity supports and is supported, regulates and is regulated, by the rest: for the two houses naturally drawing in two directions of opposite interest, and the prerogative in another still different from them both, they mutually keep each other from exceeding their proper limits; while the whole is prevented from separation and artificially connected together by the mixed nature of the crown, which is a part of the legislative, and the sole executive magistrate. Like three distinct powers in mechanics, they jointly impel the machine of government in a direction different from what either, acting by itself, would have done; but at the same time in a direction partaking of each, and formed out of all; a direction which constitutes the true line of the liberty and happiness of the community. [. . .]

§216   **(c) Rank and honors in a state.** – The distinction of rank and honours is necessary in every well-governed state, in order to reward such as are eminent for their services to the public in a manner the most desirable to individuals, and yet without burden to the community; exciting thereby an ambitious yet laudable ardour, and generous emulation, in others: and emulation, or virtuous ambition, is a spring of action, which, however dangerous or invidious in a mere republic, or under a despotic sway, will certainly be attended with good effects under a free monarchy, where, without destroying its existence, its excesses may be continually restrained by that superior power, from which all honour is derived. Such a spirit, when nationally diffused, gives life and vigour to the community; it sets all the wheels of government in motion, which, under a wise regulator, may be directed to any beneficial purpose; and thereby every individual may be made subservient to the public good, while he principally means to promote his own particular views. [. . .]

§220   **(4) Consent of all parts of parliament.** – These are the constituent parts of a parliament; the king, the lords spiritual and temporal, and the commons. Parts, of which each is so necessary, that the consent of all three is required to make any new law that shall bind the subject. Whatever is enacted for law by one, or by two only, of the three, is no statute; and to it no regard is due, unless in matters relating to their own privileges. For though, in the times of madness and anarchy, the commons once passed a vote, "that whatever is enacted or declared for law by the commons in parliament assembled hath the force of law; and all the people of this nation are concluded thereby, although the consent and concurrence of the king or house of peers be not had thereto"; yet, when the constitution was restored in all its forms, it was particularly enacted by statute 13 Car. II. c. 1, that if any person shall maliciously or advisedly affirm that both or either of the houses of parliament have any legislative authority without the king, such person shall incur all the penalties of a praemunire. [. . .]

§222   **(1) Supreme power of parliament.** – [. . .] It must be owned that Mr. Locke, and other theoretical writers, have held, that "there remains still inherent in the people a supreme power to remove or alter the legislative, when they find the legislative act contrary to the trust reposed in them; for, when such trust is abused, it is thereby forfeited, and devolves to those who gave it." But however just this conclusion may be in theory, we cannot practically adopt it, nor take any legal steps for carrying it into execution, under any dispensation of government at present actually existing. For this devolution of power, to the people at large, includes in it a dissolution of the whole form of government established by that people; reduces all the members to their original state of equality; and, by annihilating the sovereign power, repeals all positive laws whatsoever before enacted. No human laws will therefore suppose a case, which at once must destroy all law, and compel men to build afresh upon a new foundation; nor will they make provision for so desperate an event, as must render all legal provisions ineffectual. So long therefore as the English constitution lasts, we may venture to affirm, that the power of parliament is absolute and without control. [...]

(2) In election of members. – Next, with regard to the election of knights, §232 citizens, and burgesses; we may observe that herein consists the exercise of the democratical part of our constitution: for in a democracy there can be no exercise of sovereignty but by suffrage, which is the declaration of the people's will. In all democracies, therefore, it is of the utmost importance to regulate by whom, and in what manner, the suffrages are to be given. And the Athenians were so justly jealous of this prerogative, that a stranger who interfered in the assemblies of the people, was punished by their laws with death; because such a man was esteemed guilty of high treason, by usurping those rights of sovereignty to which he had no title. In England, where the people do not debate in a collective body, but by representation, the exercise of his sovereignty consists in the choice of representatives. The laws have therefore very strictly guarded against usurpation or abuse of this power, by many salutary provisions; which may be reduced to these three points, 1. The qualifications of the electors. 2. The qualifications of the elected. 3. The proceedings at elections.

(a) Qualifications of the electors. – As to the qualifications of the electors. The §233 true reason of requiring any qualification, with regard to property, in voters, is to exclude such persons as are in so mean a situation that they are esteemed to have no will of their own. If these persons had votes, they would be tempted to dispose of them under some undue influence or other. This would give a great, an artful, or a wealthy man, a larger share in elections than is consistent with general liberty. If it were probable that every man would give his vote freely and without influence of any kind, then, upon the true theory and genuine principles of liberty, every member of the community, however poor, should have a vote in electing those delegates, to whose charge is committed the disposal of his property, his liberty, and his life. But, since that can hardly be expected in persons of indigent fortunes, or such as are under the immediate dominion of others, all popular states have been obliged to establish certain qualifications; whereby some, who are suspected to have no will of their own, are excluded from voting, in order to set other individuals, whose wills may be supposed independent, more thoroughly upon a level with each other.

And this constitution of suffrages is framed upon a wiser principle, with us, than either of the methods of voting, by centuries or by tribes, among the Romans. In the method by centuries, instituted by Servius Tullius, it was principally property, and not numbers, that turned the scale: in the method by tribes, gradually introduced by the tribunes of the people, numbers only were regarded, and property entirely overlooked. Hence the laws passed by the former method had usually too great a tendency to aggrandize the patricians or rich nobles; and those by the latter had too much of a levelling principle. Our constitution steers between the two extremes. Only such are entirely excluded, as can have no will of their own: there is hardly a free agent to be found, who is not entitled to a vote in some place or other in the kingdom. Nor is comparative wealth or property, entirely disregarded in elections; for though the richest man has only one vote at one place, yet, if his property be at all diffused, he has probably a right to vote at more places than one, and therefore has many representatives. This is the spirit of our constitution: not that I assert it is in fact quite so perfect as I have here endeavoured to describe it; for, if any alteration might be wished or suggested in the present frame of parliaments, it should be in favour of a more complete representation of the people. [...]

§253   **(3) Dissolution of Parliament. (a) By the king's will.** – A dissolution is the civil death of the parliament; and this may be effected three ways: 1. By the king's will, expressed either in person or by representation; for, as the king has the sole right of convening the parliament, so also it is a branch of the royal prerogative that he may (whenever he pleases) prorogue the parliament for a time, or put a final period to its existence. If nothing had a right to prorogue or dissolve a parliament but itself, it might happen to become perpetual. And this would be extremely dangerous, if at any time it should attempt to encroach upon the executive power: as was fatally experienced by the unfortunate king Charles the First, who having unadvisedly passed an act to continue the parliament then in being till such time as it should please to dissolve itself, at last fell a sacrifice to that inordinate power, which he himself had consented to give them. It is therefore extremely necessary that the crown should be empowered to regulate the duration of these assemblies, under the limitations which the English constitution has prescribed: so that, on the one hand, they may frequently and regularly come together, for the despatch of business, and redress of grievances; and may not, on the other, even with the consent of the crown, be continued to an inconvenient or unconstitutional length.

§254   **(b) By demise of the crown.** – 2. A parliament may be dissolved by the demise of the crown. This dissolution formerly happened immediately upon the death of the reigning sovereign: for he being considered in law as the head of the parliament, (caput principium et finis,) that failing, the whole body was held to be extinct. But, the calling a new parliament immediately on the inauguration of the successor being found inconvenient, and dangers being apprehended from having no parliament in being in case of a disputed succession, it was enacted by the statutes 7 & 8 W. III. c. 15, and 6 Anne, c. 7, that the parliament in being shall continue for six months after the death of any king or queen, unless sooner prorogued or dissolved by the successor: that, if the parliament be, at the time of the king's death, separated by adjournment or prorogation, it shall, notwithstanding, assemble immediately; and that, if no parliament is then in being, the members of the last parliament shall assemble, and be again a parliament.

§255   **(c) By lapse of time.** – 3. Lastly, a parliament may be dissolved or expire by length of time. For, if either the legislative body were perpetual, or might last for the life of the prince who convened them, as formerly; and were so to be supplied, by occasionally filling the vacancies with new representatives: in these cases, if it were once corrupted, the evil would be past all remedy; but when different bodies succeed each other, if the people see cause to disapprove of the present, they may rectify its faults in the next. A legislative assembly, also, which is sure to be separated again, (whereby its members will themselves become private men, and subject to the full extent of the laws which they have enacted for others,) will think themselves bound, in interest as well as duty, to make only such laws as are good. The utmost extent of time that the same parliament was allowed to sit, by the statute 6 W. and M. c. 2, was three years; after the expiration of which, reckoning from the return of the first summons, the parliament was to have no longer continuance. But, by the statute 1 Geo. I. st. 2, c. 38, (in order, professedly, to prevent the great and continued expenses of frequent elections, and the violent heats and animosities consequent thereupon, and for the peace and security of the government, then just recovering from the late rebellion,) this term was prolonged to seven years: and, what alone is an instance of the vast authority of parliament, the very same house, that was chosen for three years, enacted its own continuance for seven. So that, as our constitution now stands, the parliament must expire, or die a natural death, at the end of every seventh year, if not sooner dissolved by the royal prerogative.

Edmund Burke

Speech to the Electors of Bristol (November 3, 1774)[16]

[...] I am sorry I cannot conclude without saying a word on a topic touched upon by my worthy colleague. I wish that topic had been passed by at a time when I have so little leisure to discuss it. But since he has thought proper to throw it out, I owe you a clear explanation of my poor sentiments on that subject.

He tells you that "the topic of instructions has occasioned much altercation and uneasiness in this city"; and he expresses himself (if I understand him rightly) in favour of the coercive authority of such instructions.

Certainly, gentlemen, it ought to be the happiness and glory of a representative to live in the strictest union, the closest correspondence, and the most unreserved communication with his constituents. Their wishes ought to have great weight with him; their opinion, high respect; their business, unremitted attention. It is his duty to sacrifice his repose, his pleasures, his satisfactions, to theirs; and above all, ever, and in all cases, to prefer their interest to his own. But his unbiassed opinion, his mature judgment, his enlightened conscience, he ought not to sacrifice to you, to any man, or to any set of men living. These he does not derive from your pleasure; no, nor from the law and the constitution. They are a trust from Providence, for the abuse of which he is deeply answerable. Your representative owes you, not his industry only,

---

[16] Retrieved from http://press-pubs.uchicago.edu/founders/documents/v1ch13s7.html.

but his judgment; and he betrays, instead of serving you, if he sacrifices it to your opinion.

My worthy colleague says, his will ought to be subservient to yours. If that be all, the thing is innocent. If government were a matter of will upon any side, yours, without question, ought to be superior. But government and legislation are matters of reason and judgment, and not of inclination; and what sort of reason is that, in which the determination precedes the discussion; in which one set of men deliberate, and another decide; and where those who form the conclusion are perhaps three hundred miles distant from those who hear the arguments?

To deliver an opinion, is the right of all men; that of constituents is a weighty and respectable opinion, which a representative ought always to rejoice to hear; and which he ought always most seriously to consider. But *authoritative* instructions; *mandates* issued, which the member is bound blindly and implicitly to obey, to vote, and to argue for, though contrary to the clearest conviction of his judgment and conscience, – these are things utterly unknown to the laws of this land, and which arise from a fundamental mistake of the whole order and tenor of our constitution.

Parliament is not a *congress* of ambassadors from different and hostile interests; which interests each must maintain, as an agent and advocate, against other agents and advocates; but parliament is a *deliberative* assembly of *one* nation, with *one* interest, that of the whole; where, not local purposes, not local prejudices, ought to guide, but the general good, resulting from the general reason of the whole. You choose a member indeed; but when you have chosen him, he is not member of Bristol, but he is a member of *parliament*. If the local constituent should have an interest, or should form an hasty opinion, evidently opposite to the real good of the rest of the community, the member for that place ought to be as far, as any other, from any endeavour to give it effect. I beg pardon for saying so much on this subject. I have been unwillingly drawn into it; but I shall ever use a respectful frankness of communication with you. Your faithful friend, your devoted servant, I shall be to the end of my life: a flatterer you do not wish for. [...]

Speech on Conciliation with America (March 22, 1775)[17]

[...] The proposition is peace. Not peace through the medium of war; not peace to be hunted through the labyrinth of intricate and endless negotiations; not peace to arise out of universal discord, fomented from principle, in all parts of the empire; not peace to depend on the juridical determination of perplexing questions, or the precise marking the shadowy boundaries of a complex government. It is simple peace, sought in its natural course and in its ordinary haunts.

Let the colonies always keep the idea of their civil rights associated with your government – they will cling and grapple to you, and no force under heaven will be of power to tear them from their allegiance. But let it be once understood that your government may be one thing and their privileges another, that these two things may exist without any mutual relation – the cement is gone, the cohesion is loosened, and

[17] From *The Works of Edmund Burke*, Vol. I (London: George Bell & Sons, 1902), pp. 442–9.

everything hastens to decay and dissolution. As long as you have the wisdom to keep the sovereign authority of this country as the sanctuary of liberty, the sacred temple consecrated to our common faith, wherever the chosen race and sons of England worship freedom, they will turn their faces towards you. The more they multiply, the more friends you will have, the more ardently they love liberty, the more perfect will be their obedience. Slavery they can have anywhere. It is a weed that grows in every soil. They may have it from Spain, they may have it from Prussia. But until you become lost to all feeling of your true interest and your natural dignity, freedom they can have from none but you. This is the commodity of price, of which you have the monopoly. This is the true Act of Navigation, which binds to you the commerce of the colonies, and through them secures to you the wealth of the world. Deny them this participation of freedom, and you break that sole bond which originally made, and must still preserve, the unity of the empire. Do not entertain so weak an imagination as that your registers and your bonds, your affidavits and your suffer-ances, your cockets and your clearances, are what form the great securities of your commerce. Do not dream that your Letters of office, and your instructions, and your suspending clauses are the things that hold together the great contexture of this mysterious whole. These things do not make your government. Dead instruments, passive tools as they are, it is the spirit of the English communion that gives all their life and efficacy to them. It is the spirit of the English constitution which, infused through the mighty mass, pervades, feeds, unites, invigorates, vivifies every part of the empire, even down to the minutest member.

Is it not the same virtue which does every thing for us here in England? Do you imagine, then, that it is the Land-Tax Act which raises your revenue? that it is the annual vote in the Committee of Supply, which gives you your army? or that it is the Mutiny Bill which inspires it with bravery and discipline? No! surely, no! It is the love of the people; it is their attachment to their government, from the sense of the deep stake they have in such a glorious institution, which gives you your army and your navy, and infuses into both that liberal obedience without which your army would be a base rabble and your navy nothing but rotten timber.

All this, I know well enough, will sound wild and chimerical to the profane herd of those vulgar and mechanical politicians who have no place among us: a sort of people who think that nothing exists but what is gross and material, and who, therefore, far from being qualified to be directors of the great movement of empire, are not fit to turn a wheel in the machine. But to men truly initiated and rightly taught, these ruling and master principles, which in the opinion of such men as I have mentioned have no substantial existence, are in truth everything, and all in all. Magnanimity in politics is not seldom the truest wisdom; and a great empire and little minds go ill together. If we are conscious of our situation, and glow with zeal to fill our places as becomes our station and ourselves, we ought to auspicate all our public proceedings on America with the old warning of the Church, *Sursum corda*! We ought to elevate our minds to the greatness of that trust to which the order of Providence has called us. By adverting to the dignity of this high calling, our ancestors have turned a savage wilderness into a glorious empire, and have made the most extensive and the only honorable conquests, not by destroying, but by promoting the wealth, the number, the happiness of the human race. Let us get an American revenue as we have got an American empire. English privileges have made it all that it is; English privileges alone will make it all it can be.

Reflections on the Revolution in France (1790)[18]

[...] Circumstances (which with some gentlemen pass for nothing) give in reality to every political principle its distinguishing colour, and discriminating effect. The circumstances are what render every civil and political scheme beneficial or noxious to mankind. Abstractedly speaking, government, as well as liberty, is good; yet could I, in common sense, ten years ago, have felicitated France on her enjoyment of a government (for she then had a government) without enquiry what the nature of that government was, or how it was administered? Can I now congratulate the same nation upon its freedom? Is it because liberty in the abstract may be classed amongst the blessings of mankind, that I am seriously to felicitate a madman, who has escaped from the protecting restraint and wholesome darkness of his cell, on his restoration to the enjoyment of light and liberty? Am I to congratulate an highwayman and murderer, who has broke prison, upon the recovery of his natural rights? This would be to act over again the scene of the criminals condemned to the gallies, and their heroic deliverer, the metaphysic Knight of the Sorrowful Countenance. [...]

A state without the means of some change is without the means of its conservation. Without such means it might even risque [*sic*] the loss of that part of the constitution which it wished the most religiously to preserve. The two principles of conservation and correction operated strongly at the two critical periods of the Restoration and Revolution, when England found itself without a king. At both those periods the nation had lost the bond of union in their antient edifice; they did not, however, dissolve the whole fabric. On the contrary, in both cases they regenerated the deficient part of the old constitution through the parts which were not impaired. They kept these old parts exactly as they were, that the part recovered might be suited to them. They acted by the ancient organized states in the shape of their old organization, and not by the organic *moleculae* of a disbanded people. [...]

Our oldest reformation is that of Magna Charta. You will see that Sir Edward Coke, that great oracle of our law, and indeed all the great men who follow him, to Blackstone, are industrious to prove the pedigree of our liberties. They endeavour to prove, that the antient charter, the Magna Charta of King John, was connected with another positive charter from Henry I. and that both the one and the other were nothing more than a re-affirmance of the still more antient standing law of the kingdom. In the matter of fact, for the greater part, these authors appear to be in the right; perhaps not always: but if the lawyers mistake in some particulars, it proves my position still the more strongly; because it demonstrates the powerful

---

[18] E. Burke, *Revolutionary Writings: Reflections on the Revolution in France and the First Letter on a Regicide Peace*, edited by I. Hampsher-Monk (Cambridge: Cambridge University Press, 2014), pp. 8, 23, 32–6, 38–9, 59–62.

prepossession towards antiquity, with which the minds of all our lawyers and legislators, and of all the people whom they wish to influence, have been always filled; and the stationary policy of this kingdom in considering their most sacred rights and franchises as an *inheritance*.

In the famous law of the 3rd of Charles I. called the *Petition of Right*, the parliament says to the king, "Your subjects have *inherited* this freedom," claiming their franchises, not on abstract principles as the "rights of men," but as the rights of Englishmen, and as a patrimony derived from their forefathers. Selden, and the other profoundly learned men, who drew this petition of right, were as well acquainted, at least, with all the general theories concerning the "rights of men," as any of the discoursers in our pulpits, or on your tribune; full as well as Dr. Price, or as the Abbé Seyes. But, for reasons worthy of that practical wisdom which superseded their theoretic science, they preferred this positive, recorded, *hereditary* title to all which can be dear to the man and the citizen, to that vague speculative right, which exposed their sure inheritance to be scrambled for and torn to pieces by every wild litigious spirit. [. . .]

You will observe, that from Magna Charta to the Declaration of Right, it has been the uniform policy of our constitution to claim and assert our liberties, as an *entailed inheritance* derived to us from our forefathers, and to be transmitted to our posterity; as an estate specially belonging to the people of this kingdom without any reference whatever to any other more general or prior right. By this means our constitution preserves an unity in so great a diversity of its parts. We have an inheritable crown; an inheritable peerage; and an house of commons and a people inheriting privileges, franchises, and liberties, from a long line of ancestors.

This policy appears to me to be the result of profound reflection; or rather the happy effect of following nature, which is wisdom without reflection, and above it. A spirit of innovation is generally the result of a selfish temper and confined views. People will not look forward to posterity, who never look backward to their ancestors. Besides, the people of England well know, that the idea of inheritance furnishes a sure principle of conservation, and a sure principle of transmission; without at all excluding a principle of improvement. It leaves acquisition free; but it secures what it acquires. Whatever advantages are obtained by a state proceeding on these maxims, are locked fast as in a sort of family settlement; grasped as in a kind of mortmain[19] forever. By a constitutional policy, working after the pattern of nature, we receive, we hold, we transmit our government and our privileges, in the same manner in which we enjoy and transmit our property and our lives. The institutions of policy, the goods of fortune, the gifts of Providence, are handed down, to us and from us, in the same course and order. [. . .] Thus, by preserving the method of nature in the conduct of the state, in what we improve we are never wholly new; in what we retain we are never wholly obsolete. By adhering in this manner and on those principles to our forefathers, we are guided not by the superstition of antiquarians, but by the spirit of philosophic analogy. In this choice of inheritance we have given to our frame of

---

[19] Norman French, literally "dead hand," a kind of feudal property right which could not be sold or alienated at will (so related to entailment). A way of establishing a persisting property right in a corporation or other legally fictive person for the same purpose.

polity the image of a relation in blood; binding up the constitution of our country with our dearest domestic ties; adopting our fundamental laws into the bosom of our family affections; keeping inseparable, and cherishing with the warmth of all their combined and mutually reflected charities, our state, our hearths, our sepulchres, and our altars.

Through the same plan of a conformity to nature in our artificial institutions, and by calling in the aid of her unerring and powerful instincts, to fortify the fallible and feeble contrivances of our reason, we have derived several other, and those no small benefits, from considering our liberties in the light of an inheritance. Always acting as if in the presence of canonized forefathers, the spirit of freedom, leading in itself to misrule and excess, is tempered with an awful gravity. This idea of a liberal descent inspires us with a sense of habitual native dignity, which prevents that upstart insolence almost inevitably adhering to and disgracing those who are the first acquirers of any distinction. By this means our liberty becomes a noble freedom. It carries an imposing and majestic aspect. It has a pedigree and illustrating ancestors. It has its bearings and its ensigns armorial. It has its gallery of portraits; its monumental inscriptions; its records, evidences, and titles. We procure reverence to our civil institutions on the principle upon which nature teaches us to revere individual men; on account of their age; and on account of those from whom they are descended. All your sophisters cannot produce any thing better adapted to preserve a rational and manly freedom than the course that we have pursued, who have chosen our nature rather than our speculations, our breasts rather than our inventions, for the great conservatories and magazines of our rights and privilege. [...]

Compute your gains: see what is got by those extravagant and presumptuous speculations which have taught your leaders to despise all their predecessors, and all their contemporaries, and even to despise themselves, until the moment in which they became truly despicable. By following those false lights, France has bought undisguised calamities at a higher price than any nation has purchased the most unequivocal blessings! France has bought poverty by crime! France has not sacrificed her virtue to her interest; but she has abandoned her interest, that she might prostitute her virtue. All other nations have begun the fabric of a new government, or the reformation of an old, by establishing originally, or by enforcing with greater exactness some rites or other of religion. All other people have laid the foundations of civil freedom in severer manners, and a system of a more austere and masculine morality. France, when she let loose the reins of regal authority, doubled the licence, of a ferocious dissoluteness in manners, and of an insolent irreligion in opinions and practices; and has extended through all ranks of life, as if she were communicating some privilege, or laying open some secluded benefit, all the unhappy corruptions that usually were the disease of wealth and power. This is one of the new principles of equality in France. [...]

Far am I from denying in theory; full as far is my heart from withholding in practice, (if I were of power to give or to withhold,) the real rights of men. In denying their false claims of right, I do not mean to injure those which are real, and are such as their pretended rights would totally destroy. If civil society be made for the advantage of man, all the advantages for which it is made become his right. It is an institution of beneficence; and law itself is only beneficence acting by a rule. Men have a right to live by that rule; they have a right to justice; as between their fellows, whether their fellows are in politic function or in ordinary occupation. They have a right to the fruits of their industry; and to the means of making their industry fruitful. They have a right to the acquisitions of their parents; to the nourishment and improvement of their offspring; to instruction in life, and to consolation in death. Whatever each man can separately do, without trespassing upon others, he has a right to do for himself; and he has a right to a fair portion of all which society, with all its combinations of skill and force, can do in his favour. [In this partnership all men have equal rights; but not to equal things. He that has but five shillings in the partnership, has as good a right to it, as he that has five hundred pound has to his larger proportion. But he has not a right to an equal dividend in the product of the joint stock; and] as to the share of power, authority, and direction which each individual ought to have in the management of the state, that I must deny to be amongst the direct original rights of man in civil society; for I have in my contemplation the civil social man, and no other. It is a thing to be settled by convention.

If civil society be the offspring of convention, that convention must be its law. That convention must limit and modify all the descriptions of constitution which are formed under it. Every sort of legislative, judicial, or executory power are its creatures. They can have no being in any other state of things; and how can any man claim, under the conventions of civil society, rights which do not so much as suppose its existence? Rights which are absolutely repugnant to it? One of the first motives to civil society, and which becomes one of its fundamental rules, is, that *no man should be judge in his own cause.* By this each person has at once divested himself of the first fundamental right of uncovenanted man, that is, to judge for himself, and to assert his own cause. He abdicates all right to be his own governor. He inclusively, in a great measure, abandons the right of self-defence, the first law of nature. Men cannot enjoy the rights of an uncivil and of a civil state together. That he may obtain justice he gives up his right of determining what it is in points the most essential to him. That he may secure some liberty, he makes a surrender in trust of the whole of it.

Government is not made in virtue of natural rights, which may and do exist in total independence of it; and exist in much greater clearness, and in a much greater degree of abstract perfection: but their abstract perfection is their practical defect. By having a right to every thing they want every thing. Government is a contrivance of human wisdom to provide for human *wants.* Men have a right that these wants should be provided for by this wisdom. Among these wants is to be reckoned the want, out of civil society, of a sufficient restraint upon their passions. Society requires not only that the passions of individuals should be subjected, but that even in the mass and body as well as in the individuals, the inclinations of men should frequently be thwarted, their will controlled, and their passions brought into subjection. This can only be done *by a power out of themselves*; and not, in the exercise of its function, subject to that will and to those passions which it is its office to bridle and subdue. In this sense the restraints on men, as well as their liberties, are to be reckoned among their rights. But as the liberties and the restrictions vary with times and circumstances, and admit of infinite modifications, they cannot be settled upon any abstract rule; and nothing is so foolish as to discuss them upon that principle.

The moment you abate any thing from the full rights of men, each to govern himself, and suffer any artificial positive limitation upon those rights, from that moment the whole organization of government becomes a consideration of convenience. This it is which makes the constitution of a state, and the due distribution of its powers, a matter of the most delicate and complicated skill. It requires a deep knowledge of human nature and human necessities, and of the things which facilitate or obstruct the various ends which are to be pursued by the mechanism of civil institutions. The state is to have recruits to its strength, and remedies to its distempers. What is the use of discussing a man's abstract right to food or to medicine? The question is upon the method of procuring and administering them. In that deliberation I shall always advise to call in the aid of the farmer and the physician, rather than the professor of metaphysics.

The science of constructing a commonwealth, or renovating it, or reforming it, is, like every other experimental science, not to be taught *a priori*. Nor is it a short experience that can instruct us in that practical science; because the real effects of moral causes are not always immediate; but that which in the first instance is prejudicial may be excellent in its remoter operation; and its excellence may arise even from the ill effects it produces in the beginning. The reverse also happens; and very plausible schemes, with very pleasing commencements, have often shameful and lamentable conclusions. In states there are often some obscure and almost latent causes, things which appear at first view of little moment, on which a very great part of its prosperity or adversity may most essentially depend. The science of government being therefore so practical in itself, and intended for such practical purposes, a matter which requires experience, and even more experience than any person can gain in his whole life, however sagacious and observing he may be, it is with infinite caution that any man ought to venture upon pulling down an edifice which has answered in any tolerable degree for ages the common purposes of society, or on building it up again, without having models and patterns of approved utility before his eyes. [...]

3 Liberalism

The People "Are"

There is truth in the saying "ideas can go viral," but not only because they can spread fast. Like any resilient microorganism, they can also lie more or less dormant for centuries or even millennia, waiting for favorable conditions, as was the case for classical liberalism. Some of its versions, like the Hobbesian theory that justice is nothing but a convention, hence that there is no actual foundation for right and wrong but what the majority decides, were already embraced by the sophists of ancient Greece.[1] After all, it is impossible to deny that opinions about what is to be rewarded and what to be punished vary dramatically across cultures and across time. Aren't the various laws about, say, slavery, the death penalty, homosexuality, or polygamy throughout history proof enough that right and wrong depend on social conventions? Other elements of classical liberalism, like the state of nature or natural rights, were to be found in different versions throughout the next centuries.[2]

Yet it took almost two millennia until these ideas found a fertile ground for blooming and spreading, crafting a *Weltanschauung* of their own, different from classical republicanism. This favorable context was made possible by some crucial events that marked the transition from medievalism to early modernity, no matter how disputable these labels are. The first one was the appearance of firearms in Europe. This was the **democratization of warfare**. The second major development was the "printing revolution." This was the **democratization of knowledge**. Last but not least came the **Reformation**,[3] which in some ways represented the **democratization of Christianity**.[4] All of these contributed to a new *Weltanschauung*, more egalitarian and more centered on the individual.

Yet remember that, despite being a comprehensive world view, a *Weltanschauung* is by no means a neatly coherent theoretical approach to the world, but rather a composite of many different strains, and one has to look behind the surface in order to identify the similarities. **Hobbes**'s theory appears on first sight entirely

---

[1] Compare also Gorgias's exposition of the opinion of the majority on the origins of justice, in Book 2 of Plato's *Republic*, with Hobbes's position.

[2] For a detailed discussion on the differences between the classic and the modern natural right theory, see L. Strauss, *Natural Right and History* (Chicago: Chicago University Press, 1965).

[3] Started by **Martin Luther** (1483–1546), the Reformation represented the second major schism in the Christian Church, after the Schism between the Catholic (Western) Church and the Orthodox (Eastern) Church in 1054. The Protestants, as they came to be known, opposed the corruption of the Catholic Church, its hierarchy, and its sacraments. See Chapter 4.

[4] See Alexis de Tocqueville on what he calls "the democratic revolution." Tocqueville, *Democracy in America*, Vol. 1, introduction.

different from **Locke**'s. The former believed that justice is a convention (the **anti-foundationalist** position), the latter that the laws of nature distinguish between right and wrong (the **foundationalist** position). Still, their respective theoretical frameworks share many essential features, which came to be known as the **social contract theory**, switching the emphasis from the people apprehended as an organic whole to the people as a collection of individuals, from <u>reason</u> to <u>will</u>, and from <u>public</u> to <u>private</u> good. Neither **Montesquieu** nor **Hume** embraced the social contract theory. Yet they were both liberals in that they believed that the state is meant to protect, *as much as possible*, the right of individuals to pursue their lives as they see fit, while refusing to fully embrace a theory centered on abstract individuals, overlooking the unicity of each person.

These latter approaches would not have been pleasing to **Thomas Hobbes** (1588–1679) for they remained open to interpretation and thus to disagreements and arguments. His declared ambition was to be the first to inaugurate a "true" political science, one that would be as free of disagreements as the science of mathematics. After all, no one disputes that $2 + 3 = 5$. In order to do so, he parted with the <u>organic</u> vision of the state and replaced it with a fully <u>artificial</u> and <u>instrumental</u> one. The advantage of a man-made creation is that there are no surprises. A "natural" dog, for example, can get rabies and bite you; a robot dog will never do such a thing, nor will it stain your carpet. Hobbes's **Leviathan**, i.e. the state, is supposed to be as reliable as a robot. How can this be done? By turning the entire classical *Weltanschauung* upside down. Even if people disagree about what is good, they can agree about what is bad – death.

In his autobiography, Hobbes recounted that on the day of his birth in 1588, his mother learned that the Spanish Armada had set sail to attack England. This news so terrified her that she went into labor prematurely, and thus, he wrote, "fear and I were born twins together." Being close to the royalist circles at the end of 1640, before the **English Civil War** erupted, he was, according to his own confession, "the first to flee for my life."[5] In France he became the tutor of the beheaded king's son, Charles II, and he returned to England only after the restoration of the monarchy. These biographical details are telling for his philosophical approach, which is centered on the <u>fear of death</u> and the <u>right to self-preservation</u>. Considering how long he lived in one of the bloodiest periods of English history, one could say that he managed quite successfully to apply this theory to his own life.

Hobbes wrote during a time when, in England, the religious conflicts between Catholics and Protestants were further complicated by the emergence of the **Anglican Church** (Chapter 4). But once religious authority began to be challenged, *all* authority – including political authority – came to be disputed. Hobbes attempted to recreate political power on a new, indisputable basis by starting from scratch. One must posit, argued Hobbes, a **state of nature** in which there is <u>no authority</u>

---

[5] The English Civil War pitted the supporters of the Parliament and supporters of the king, the Royalists, against each other. It eventually ended with the victory of the Parliamentary party and the beheading of Charles I. Oliver Cromwell (1599–1658) led the Parliament's armies against King Charles and ruled the British Isles as Lord Protector from 1653 until his death in 1658. After his death, Charles II was recalled to the throne.

whatsoever, and men are born <u>equal</u> and <u>free</u>, endowed with *all* <u>natural rights</u>. It sounds great, right? Think again. Precisely because they are equal and free, with no authority to declare what is right and what is wrong, each individual has all rights to take advantage of any other individual, including the right to kill. Far from being a paradise, this state is insufferable, because it is <u>the war of all against all</u>, and the life of man, as he famously put it, is "solitary, poor, nasty, brutish, and short."

In order to escape this condition and ensure their self-preservation, individuals have no other option but to consent <u>unanimously</u> to resign their rights into the hands of the **majority**. From now on, all decisions are to be made by the majority, since counting wills, unlike discussing reasons, is indisputable. The majority decides who the **sovereign** should be. It can be one (a <u>monarchy</u>), a few (an <u>aristocracy</u>), or even many (a <u>democracy</u>). If Hobbes is partial toward monarchy, it is because he finds it more efficient, yet his system is meant to apply to all types of regimes. The defining feature of the sovereign is **the unity of the will**. There cannot be any separation of powers, for *by definition sovereignty cannot be limited or divided*. If the sovereign is made from more than one person, the majority rule applies again in order to decide that **one will**.

It is the sovereign who decides what is right and what is wrong. Hence, the sovereign can do no wrong. Unlike the case of the classical political contract between the ruler and the ruled, Hobbes's sovereign does not promise anything; it is not part of any contract and therefore cannot be held responsible for anything. Rebellion against the sovereign is thus absurd. It is not simply "suicidal," for the sovereign is the "head" that keeps together this whole artificial body, absent which individuals would return to the ghastly state of nature. It is also like rebelling against oneself, since each and every single individual has willingly entered the social contract aware of the fact that from that point on the decisions of the majority will be his or her own.

Born and raised as a Puritan (Chapter 4), **John Locke** (1632–1704) took Hobbes's main theoretical framework and improved upon it, in order to respond to **Sir Robert Filmer**'s (*c.*1588–1653) *Patriarcha*. Locke's *Two Treatises on Government* had two purposes: first, to refute Filmer's claim that the authority of the kings comes from God via the patriarchs of the Old Testament and, second, to propose his own theory of the social contract, but with some major twists.

Locke wrote in a different context than Hobbes, around the time of the **Glorious Revolution** of 1688, which replaced James II with King William and Queen Mary and, by asserting the supremacy of the Parliament, transformed England into the first **constitutional monarchy**. Because Locke published his *Two Treatises* a year later and dedicated his book to Prince William, it was initially assumed that he wrote it in order to justify the right of the people to revolt against a tyrannical king and to justify the pre-eminence of the Parliament. In fact, he wrote it some eight years before the Glorious Revolution. It is also worth noting that, when justifying the removal of James II from the throne, the Parliament did not make appeal to the <u>social contract theory</u>, but to the breaking of the <u>political compact</u> between the ruler and the people. As we shall see, there is a reason for that: while Locke's theory allows for the change of government, *the social contract itself, unlike the political one, cannot be broken*.

One may change the rulers (i.e. the representatives), but one cannot alter the theoretical framework that makes them possible.

Like Hobbes, Locke starts by positing the existence of a **state of nature** in which men are born <u>equal</u>, <u>free</u>, and endowed with <u>natural rights</u>. Yet, unlike Hobbes, Locke argues that even in the state of nature men have the ability to know the **laws of nature**, thus to distinguish between right and wrong. As a result, as he puts it, "though this be a state of liberty, yet it is not a state of license." The few that break these laws of nature by committing crimes can be <u>lawfully</u> punished. Furthermore, even if God has given the Earth "to mankind in common," private property is possible even in the state of nature, for by working to acquire something, man "hath mixed his labour with, and joined to it something that is his own." In short, unlike Hobbes's, Locke's state of nature seems a rather pleasant one. Everything is plentiful, there are only a few "bad apples," and the <u>invention of money</u> gives everyone the opportunity to increase their property. So why abandon the state of nature and create a commonwealth?

Locke's answer is simple: the state of nature is <u>insecure</u>, having three main <u>deficiencies</u>. The first one is that, while people agree *in general* upon the laws of nature, they disagree when it comes to *particulars*. Consider this: people generally agree with the commandment "thou shall not kill," yet they disagree about the death penalty, abortion, or euthanasia. The second deficiency follows from the first one: the lack of an impartial arbitrator to solve such disagreements. Last but not least, the lack of sufficient executive power to punish the transgressors makes the state of nature an insecure one. So, in order to protect <u>life, liberty, and property</u>, individuals decide to leave the state of nature and to enter a social compact.

From this point onwards, Locke follows Hobbes's template. Individuals unanimously consent to entrust their rights to the hands of the **majority** and to accept the majority's decisions as their own. The majority then decides what form of government they want – a monarchy, an aristocracy, or a democracy. The distinction between the three forms of government depends on who has been entrusted with the **legislative power** – the one, the few, or the many – for the legislative power is *supreme*. It is not *sovereign*, however, because Locke believed in the <u>separation of powers</u> in order to prevent arbitrary decisions. According to his theory, not only can the executive be removed by the legislative if it fails to properly fulfill its duties, but the legislative itself can be replaced by the majority of the people if it fails to perform according to the **trust** put in its hands. Unlike in Hobbes's theory, the change of government does not imply a return to the state of nature. The majority still retains the power to elect a new government. They have *entrusted* their rights; they did not simply *give them away*. I may *entrust* someone with managing my money, but it is still *my* money, and I can change the manager if I am displeased with its management. One may argue that, according to Locke's theory, nowadays we "rebel" in every election, for the majority may choose to replace the executive, the legislative, or both. Whence does this loss of trust in our elected representatives come? This is a question worth pondering.

Charles-Louis de Secondat, Baron de La Brède et de Montesquieu (1689–1755) was one of the Frenchmen who admired England, especially for recently having established a constitutional monarchy and for its separation of powers. He lived in England for almost two years and got to know not just its institutions, but its people and its mores as well. After traveling to many countries, from Austria and Italy to Hungary, he concluded that, even if any system of laws in any given country appears at first sight to be the result of a series of historical accidents, this apparent chaos can become comprehensible using the right approach. This is what he tried to do in his most important work, *The Spirit of Laws*. Beyond the immense variety of laws, their *spirit* can be discovered if one looks at how they are adapted "to the people for whom they are framed, [...] to the nature and principle of each government, [...] to the climate of each country, to the quality of its soil, to its situation and extent, to the principal occupation of the natives, [...] to the religion of the inhabitants, to their inclinations, riches, numbers, commerce, manners, and customs."

Like Locke, Montesquieu believed that liberty is not a state of license: "Liberty is the right to do everything the laws permit; and if one citizen could do what they forbid, he would no longer have liberty because the others would likewise have this same power." He also believed that "the spirit of commerce brings with it the spirit of frugality, economy, moderation, work, wisdom, tranquility, order, and rule. Thus, as long as this spirit continues to exist, the wealth it produces has no bad effect." Like Locke, he was a firm believer in the separation of powers as a defense against tyranny, yet he did not embrace the supremacy of the legislative as Locke did. Instead, he argued that any power, including the legislative one, can become abusive. Thus, "power must check power by the arrangement of things." It was a lesson that the Americans would learn by doing, after crafting their first state constitutions (Chapter 6).

Montesquieu managed to combine some major liberal tenets with some equally important republican and even conservative ones. Like Aristotle, he believed that democracies can be corrupted either by the "spirit of inequality" or by the "spirit of extreme equality." Both extremes are pernicious. He also believed that democracy relies mainly on the virtue of its citizens, who ought to have "a constant preference of public to private interest," and who must want to distinguish themselves in the service of their country. This, he argued, is not a natural impulse of men, but instead "a self-renunciation, which is ever arduous and painful," thus requiring "the whole power of education." Such emphasis on personal virtue and on sacrifice for the common good, together with his plea for incremental reforms in order to make each regime more liberal and more protective of individual rights and liberties, places Montesquieu in the category of a **conservative liberal**. This *theoretical* mixture of liberalism with republicanism resonated with the Americans' own *practical* experience, so they quoted him frequently as the final authority on various topics, from checks and balances to the advantages of a federation in combining "all the internal advantages of republican government and the external force of monarchy."

A different combination of the liberal and republican *Weltanschauungen* made the **Scottish Enlightenment** another successful theoretical approach throughout the American founding. It was taught and promoted in the first American universities, thus shaping the education of generations to come – and **David Hume** (1711–1776) was one of its main exponents. Like Montesquieu, he believed that, behind historical accidents, there are underlying causes that can be discovered, and – like Hobbes – that politics can be made a science as rigorous as mathematics. Because of his **naturalistic** and **skeptic** approach, some have labeled him a liberal and others a conservative. Some considered him too much of a Whig, while others thought him too much of a Tory, yet Hume himself, like most of the founders, found factionalism and partisanship detrimental. He confessed that "My views of *things* are more conformable to Whig principles; my representations of *persons* to Tory prejudices."

Hume claimed that the disputes between Tories and Whigs were fueled by the misinterpretation of the "philosophical" or "speculative" principles that each party promoted without fully understanding them. After all, as he boldly claimed in his *Treatise on Human Nature*, "reason is and ought only to be the slave of the passions," yet passions can be misguided by poor reasoning about the object of the desire and about the means to attain it.

On the one hand, he argued, one finds those who believe that all governments are the Deity's will, and thus revolting against them amounts to "little less than sacrilege" even if they become tyrannical; on the other hand, there are thinkers who find the source of authority in the consent of the people and in some original compact. Both sides are simultaneously right and wrong. The former is right in that the whole universe can be said to run according to the plan of the Deity, but wrong in failing to understand that the vehicles of this plan are humans. The latter are also right in claiming that originally men were more or less equal and that they had to consent to some form of government necessary to regulate their relationship to one another, but wrong in denying the present day's reality in favor of some abstract theory. Justice and property are, Hobbes claimed, <u>artificial</u> creations, yet they can also be called <u>natural</u> insofar as no society can exist absent them. They appear with <u>necessity</u> in any society. Furthermore, <u>selfishness</u> is a driving force for all human actions, but so is <u>pity or love</u> toward other human beings. The **state of nature** is but an abstraction, a myth, but a useful one, for teaching us what <u>scarcity</u> and unchecked <u>selfishness</u> would produce, and the **Golden Age** is another attractive myth for teaching us that under the ideal condition of <u>abundancy</u> and <u>love</u>, no government or system of justice would be necessary.

Such pragmatism, combining revolutionary ideas with a respect for tradition, proved attractive for many of the founders, although not all of them. Thomas Jefferson, for example, forbade Hume's *History of England* at the University of Virginia, fearing that it would spread "toryism," i.e. conservatism, despite Hume's support for American independence. Yet one may argue that the history of the founding has vindicated at least his suggestion that two different *Weltanschauungen* can be both right and wrong at the same time.

CLASSICAL LIBERALISM

Thomas Hobbes *The Leviathan* (1651)[6]

The Introduction

NATURE (the Art whereby God hath made and governes the world) is by the *Art* of man, as in many other things, so in this also imitated, that it can make an Artificial Animal: For seeing life is but a motion of Limbs, the begining whereof is in some principall part within; why may we not say, that all *Automata* (Engines that move themselves by springs and wheeles as doth a watch) have an artificial life? For what is the *Heart*, but a *Spring*; and the *Nerves*, but so many *Strings*; and the *Joynts*, but so many *Wheels*, giving motion to the whole Body, such as was intended by the Artificer? *Art* goes yet further, imitating that Rational and most excellent worke of Nature, *Man*. For by Art is created that great LEVIATHAN called a COMMON-WEALTH, or STATE, (in latine CIVITAS) which is but an Artificial Man; though of greater stature and strength than the Natural, for whose protection and defence it was intended; and in which, the *Soveraignty* is an Artificial *Soul*, as giving life and motion to the whole body; The *Magistrates*, and other *Officers* of Judicature and Execution, artificial *Joynts*; *Reward* and *Punishment* (by which fastned to the seat of the Soveraignty, every joynt and member is moved to performe his duty) are the *Nerves*, that do the same in the Body Natural; The *Wealth* and *Riches* of all the particular members, are the *Strength*; *Salus Populi* (the *peoples safety*) its *Business*; *Counsellours*, by whom all things needfull for it to know, are suggested unto it, are the *Memory*; *Equity* and *Lawes*, an artificial *Reason* and *Will*; *Concord*, *Health*; *Sedition*, *Sickness*; and *Civil War*, *Death*. Lastly, the *Pacts* and *Covenants*, by which the parts of this Body Politique were at first made, set together, and united, resemble that *Fiat*, or the *Let us make man*, pronounced by God in the Creation.

Part I Of Man

Chapter XIII   Of the Natural Condition of Man as Concerning Their Felicity and Misery

Nature hath made men so equal, in the faculties of body, and mind; as that though there bee found one man sometimes manifestly stronger in body, or of quicker mind then another; yet when all is reckoned together, the difference between man, and man, is not so considerable, as that one man can thereupon claim to himself any benefit, to which another may not pretend, as well as he. For as to the strength of body, the weakest has strength enough to kill the strongest, either by secret machination, or by confederacy with others, that are in the same danger with himself. [...]

From this equality of ability, ariseth equality of hope in the attaining of our Ends. And therefore if any two men desire the same thing, which neverthelesse they cannot both enjoy, they become enemies; and in the way to their End, (which is principally their own conservation, and sometimes their delectation only,) endeavour to destroy,

---

[6] T. Hobbes, *Leviathan, or The Matter, Form, and Power of a Common-Wealth Ecclesiastical and Civil* (London: Andrew Crooke, 1651), pp. 1, 60–5, 85–92, 94–5, 109, 111–13.

or subdue one an other. And from hence it comes to passe, that where an Invader hath no more to feare, than an other mans single power; if one plant, sow, build, or possesse a convenient Seat, others may probably be expected to come prepared with forces united, to dispossesse, and deprive him, not only of the fruit of his labour, but also of his life, or liberty. And the Invader again is in the like danger of another.

And from this diffidence of one another, there is no way for any man to secure himself, so reasonable, as Anticipation; that is, by force, or wiles, to master the persons of all men he can, so long, till he see no other power great enough to endanger him: And this is no more than his own conservation requireth, and is generally allowed. Also because there be some, that taking pleasure in contemplating their own power in the acts of conquest, which they pursue farther than their security requires; if others, that otherwise would be glad to be at ease within modest bounds, should not by invasion increase their power, they would not be able, long time, by standing only on their defence, to subsist. And by consequence, such augmentation of dominion over men, being necessary to a mans conservation, it ought to be allowed him. [...]

Hereby it is manifest, that during the time men live without a common Power to keep them all in awe, they are in that condition which is called Warre; and such a warre, as is of every man, against every man. For WARRE, consisteth not in Battel onely, or the act of fighting; but in a tract of time, wherein the Will to contend by Battel is sufficiently known: and therefore the notion of *Time*, is to be considered in the nature of Warre; as it is in the nature of Weather. For as the nature of Foule weather, lyeth not in a shower or two of rain; but in an inclination thereto of many days together: So the nature of War, consisteth not in actuall fighting; but in the known disposition thereto, during all the time there is no assurance to the contrary. All other time is PEACE.

Whatsoever therefore is consequent to a time of Warre, where every man is Enemy to every man; the same is consequent to the time, wherein men live without other security, than what their own strength, and their own invention shall furnish them withal. In such condition, there is no place for industry; because the fruit thereof is uncertain: and consequently no Culture of the Earth; no Navigations, nor use of the commodities that may be imported by Sea; no commodious Building; no Instruments of moving, and removing such things as require much force; no Knowledge of the face of the Earth; no account of Time; no Arts; no Letters; no Society; and which is worst of all, continual fear, and danger of violent death; And the life of man, solitary, poore, nasty, brutish, and short. [...]

To this war of every man against every man, this also is consequent; that nothing can be Unjust. The notions of Right and Wrong, Justice and Injustice have there no place. Where there is no common Power, there is no Law: where no Law, no Injustice. Force, and Fraud, are in warre the two Cardinal vertues. Justice, and Injustice are none of the Faculties neither of the Body, nor Mind. If they were, they might be in a man that were alone in the world, as well as his Senses, and Passions. They are Qualities, that relate to men in Society, not in Solitude. It is consequent also to the same condition, that there be no Propriety, no Dominion, no *Mine* and *Thine* distinct; but onely that to be every mans that he can get; and for so long, as he can keep it. And thus much for the ill condition, which man by meer Nature is actually placed in; though with a possibility to come out of it, consisting partly in the Passions, partly in his Reason.

Chapter XIV   Of the First and Second Natural Laws, and of Contracts

The RIGHT OF NATURE, which Writers commonly call *Jus Naturale*, is the Liberty each man hath, to use his own power, as he will himself, for the preservation of his own Nature; that is to say, of his own Life; and consequently, of doing any thing, which in his own Judgement, and Reason, hee shall conceive to be the aptest means thereunto.

By LIBERTY, is understood, according to the proper signification of the word, the absence of externall Impediments: which Impediments, may oft take away part of a mans power to do what he would; but cannot hinder him from using the power left him, according as his judgement, and reason shall dictate to him.

A LAW OF NATURE, (*Lex Naturalis*,) is a Precept, or general Rule, found out by Reason, by which a man is forbidden to do, that, which is destructive of his life, or taketh away the means of preserving the same; and to omit, that, by which he thinketh it may be best preserved. For though they that speak of this subject, use to confound *Jus*, and *Lex*, *Right* and *Law*: yet they ought to be distinguished; because RIGHT, consisteth in liberty to do, or to forbear; Whereas LAW, determineth, and bindeth to one of them: so that Law, and Right, differ as much, as Obligation, and Liberty; which in one and the same matter are inconsistent.

And because the condition of Man, (as hath been declared in the precedent Chapter) is a condition of War of every one against every one; in which case every one is governed by his own Reason; and there is nothing he can make use of, that may not be a help unto him, in preserving his life against his enemyes; It followeth, that in such a condition, every man has a Right to every thing: even to one anothers body. And therefore, as long as this natural Right of every man to every thing endureth, there can be no security to any man, (how strong or wise soever he be,) of living out the time, which Nature ordinarily alloweth men to live. And consequently it is a precept, or general rule of Reason, *That every man, ought to endeavour Peace, as farre as he has hope of obtaining it; and when he cannot obtain it, that he may seek, and use, all helps, and advantages of Warre.* The first branch, of which Rule, containeth the first, and Fundamental Law of Nature; which is, *To seek Peace, and follow it.* The Second, the summe of the Right of Nature; which is, *By all means we can, to defend our selves.*

From this Fundamental Law of Nature, by which men are commanded to endeavour Peace, is derived this second Law; *That a man be willing, when others are so too, as far-forth, as for Peace, and defence of himself he shall think it necessary, to lay down this right to all things; and be contented with so much liberty against other men, as he would allow other men against himselfe.* [. . .]

Part II Of Commonwealth

Chapter XVII   Of the Causes, Generation, and Definition of a Commonwealth

The final Cause, End, or Design of men, (who naturally love Liberty, and Dominion over others,) in the introduction of that restraint upon themselves, (in which wee see them live in Common-wealths,) is the foresight of their own preservation, and of a more contented life thereby; that is to say, of getting themselves out from that miserable condition of War, which is necessarily consequent (as hath been shewn) to the natural Passions of men, when there is no visible Power to keep them in awe, and tye them by fear of punishment to the performance of their Covenants, and observation of these Lawes of Nature set down in the 14th. and 15th. Chapters.

For the Laws of Nature (as *Justice, Equity, Modesty, Mercy,* and (in summe) *doing to others, as wee would be done to,*) of themselves, without the terrour of some Power, to cause them to be observed, are contrary to our naturall Passions, that carry us to Partiality, Pride, Revenge, and the like. And Covenants, without the Sword, are but Words, and of no strength to secure a man at all. Therefore notwithstanding the Laws of Nature, (which every one hath then kept, when he has the will to keep them, when he can do it safely,) if there be no Power erected, or not great enough for our security; every man will and may lawfully rely on his own strength and art, for caution against all other men. [...]

It is true, that certain living creatures, as Bees, and Ants, live sociably one with another, (which are therefore by *Aristotle* numbred amongst Political creatures;) and yet have no other direction, than their particular judgements and appetites; nor speech, whereby one of them can signifie to another, what he thinks expedient for the common benefit: and therefore some man may perhaps desire to know, why Mankind cannot do the same. To which I answer,

First, that men are continually in competition for Honour and Dignity, which these creatures are not; and consequently amongst men there ariseth on that ground, Envy and Hatred, and finally Warre; but amongst these not so.

Secondly, that amongst these creatures, the Common good differeth not from the Private; and being by nature enclined to their private, they procure thereby the common benefit. But man, whose Joy consisteth in comparing himself with other men, can relish nothing but what is eminent.

Thirdly, that these creatures, having not (as man) the use of reason, do not see, nor think they see any fault, in the administration of their common businesse: whereas amongst men, there are very many, that think themselves wiser, and abler to govern the Publique, better than the rest; and these strive to reforme and innovate, one this way, another that way; and thereby bring it into Distraction and Civil War.

Fourthly, that these creatures, though they have some use of voice, in making knowne to one another their desires, and other affections; yet they want that art of words, by which some men can represent to others, that which is Good, in the likenesse of Evil; and Evil, in the likenesse of Good; and augment, or diminish the apparent greatnesse of Good and Evil; discontenting men, and troubling their Peace at their pleasure.

Fiftly, irrational creatures cannot distinguish betweene *Injury,* and *Dammage*; and therefore as long as they be at ease, they are not offended with their fellowes: whereas Man is then most troublesome, when he is most at ease: for then it is that he loves to shew his Wisdome, and controul the Actions of them that governe the Common-wealth.

Lastly, the agreement of these creatures is Natural; that of men, is by Covenant only, which is Artificial: and therefore it is no wonder if there be somewhat else required (besides Covenant) to make their Agreement constant and lasting; which is a Common Power, to keep them in awe, and to direct their actions to the Common Benefit.

The only way to erect such a Common Power, as may be able to defend them from the invasion of Forreigners, and the injuries of one another, and thereby to secure them in such sort, as that by their own industrie, and by the fruits of the Earth, they may nourish themselves and live contentedly; is, to confer all their power and strength upon one Man, or upon one Assembly of men, that may reduce all their Wills, by plurality of voices, unto one Will: which is as much as to say, to appoint one man, or Assembly of men, to bear their Person; and every one to own, and acknowledge himself to be Author of whatsoever he that so beareth their Person, shall Act, or cause to be Acted, in those things which concern the Common Peace and Safety; and therein to submit their Wills, every one to his Will, and their Judgements, to his Judgment. This is more than Consent, or Concord; it is a reall Unity of them all, in one and the same Person, made by Covenant of every man with every man, in such manner, as if every man should say to every man, *I Authorise and give up my Right of Governing myself, to this Man, or to this Assembly of men, on this condition, that thou give up thy Right to him, and Authorise all his Actions in like manner*. This done, the Multitude so united in one Person, is called a COMMON-WEALTH, in Latine CIVITAS. This is the Generation of that great LEVIATHAN, or rather (to speake more reverently) of that *Mortal God*, to which wee owe under the *Immortal God*, our peace and defence. For by this Authoritie, given him by every particular man in the Common-wealth, he hath the use of so much Power and Strength conferred on him, that by terrour thereof, he is enabled to perform the wills of them all, to Peace at home, and mutuall aid against their enemies abroad. And in him consisteth the Essence of the Common-wealth; which (to define it,) is *One Person, of whose Acts a great Multitude, by mutual Covenants one with another, have made themselves every one the Author, to the end he may use the strength and means of them all, as he shall think expedient, for their Peace and Common Defence*.

And he that carryeth this Person, as called SOVERAIGN, and said to have *Soveraign Power*; and every one besides, his SUBJECT.

The attaining to this Soveraign Power, is by two ways. One, by Natural force; as when a man maketh his children, to submit themselves, and their children to his government, as being able to destroy them if they refuse, or by War subdueth his enemies to his will, giving them their lives on that condition. The other, is when men agree amongst themselves, to submit to some Man, or Assembly of men, voluntarily, on confidence to be protected by him against all others. This later, may be called a Political Common-wealth, or Common-wealth by *Institution*; and the former, a Common-wealth by *Acquisition*. And first, I shall speak of a Common-wealth by Institution.

Chapter XVIII   Of the Rights of Soveraigns by Institution

A *Common-wealth* is said to be *Instituted*, when a *Multitude* of men do Agree, and *Covenant, every one, with every one*, that to whatsoever *Man*, or *Assembly of Men*, shall be given by the major part, the *Right* to *Present* the Person of them all, (that is to say, to be their Representative;) every one, as well he that *Voted For It*, as he that *Voted Against It*, shall *Authorise* all the Actions and Judgements, of that Man, or Assembly of men, in the same manner, as if they were his own, to the end, to live peaceably amongst themselves, and be protected against other men.

From this Institution of a Common-wealth are derived all the *Rights*, and *Faculties* of him, or them, on whom the Soveraign Power is conferred by the consent of the People assembled.

First, because they Covenant, it is to be understood, they are not obliged by former Covenant to any thing repugnant hereunto. And Consequently they that have already Instituted a Common-wealth, being thereby bound by Covenant, to own the Actions, and Judgements of one, cannot lawfully make a new Covenant, amongst themselves, to be obedient to any other, in any thing whatsoever, without his permission. And therefore, they that are subjects to a Monarch, cannot without his leave cast off Monarchy, and return to the confusion of a disunited Multitude; nor transfer their Person from him that beareth it, to another Man, or other Assembly of men: for they are bound, every man to every man, to Own, and be reputed Author of all, that he that already is their Soveraign, shall do, and judge fit to be done: so that any one man dissenting, all the rest should break their Covenant made to that man, which is injustice: and they have also every man given the Soveraignty to him that beareth their Person; and therefore if they depose him, they take from him that which is his own, and so again it is injustice. [...]

Secondly, Because the Right of bearing the Person of them all, is given to him they make Soveraign, by Covenant only of one to another, and not of him to any of them; there can happen no breach of Covenant on the part of the Soveraign; and consequently none of his Subjects, by any pretence of forfeiture, can be freed from his Subjection. That he which is made Soveraign maketh no Covenant with his Subjects before-hand, is manifest; because either he must make it with the whole multitude, as one party to the Covenant; or he must make a several Covenant with every man. With the whole, as one party, it is impossible; because as yet they are not one Person: and if he make so many several Covenants as there be men, those Covenants after he hath the Soveraignty are void, because what act soever can be pretended by any one of them for breach thereof, is the act both of himself, and of all the rest, because done in the Person, and by the Right of every one of them in particular. [...]

Fourthly, because every Subject is by this Institution Author of all the Actions, and Judgements of the Soveraign Instituted; it follows, that whatsoever he doth, it can be no injury to any of his Subjects; nor ought he to be by any of them accused of Injustice. For he that doth any thing by authority from another, doth therein no injury to him by whose authority he acteth: But by this Institution of a Common-wealth, every particular man is Author of all the Soveraigne doth; and consequently he that complaineth of injury from his Soveraign, complaineth of that whereof he himself is Authour; and therefore ought not to accuse any man but himself; no nor himself of injury; because to do injury to ones self, is impossible. It is true that they that have Soveraign power, may commit Iniquity; but not injustice, or Injury in the proper signification. [...]

Seventhly, is annexed to the Soveraignty, the whole power of prescribing the Rules, whereby every man may know, what Goods he may enjoy, and what Actions he may do, without being molested by any of his fellow Subjects: And this is it men call *Propriety*. For before constitution of Soveraign Power (as hath already been shewn) all men had right to all things; which necessarily causeth Warre: and therefore this *Propriety*, being necessary to Peace, and depending on Soveraign Power, is the Act of the Power, in order to the publique peace. These Rules of Propriety (or *Meum* and *Tuum*) and of *Good, Evil, Lawful* and *Unlawful* in the actions of Subjects, are the Civil Laws; that is to say, the Laws of each Common-wealth in particular; though the name of Civil Law be now restrained to the antient Civil Laws of the City of *Rome*; which being the head of a great part of the World, her Laws at that time were in these parts the Civil Law.

Eightly, is annexed to the Soveraignty, the Right of Judicature; that is to say, of hearing and deciding all controversies, which may arise concerning Law, either Civil, or natural, or concerning Fact. For without the decision of Controversies, there is no protection of one Subject, against the injuries of another; the Laws concerning *Meum* and *Tuum* are in vaine; and to every man remaineth, from the natural and necessary appetite of his own conservation, the right of protecting himself by his private strength, which is the condition of War; and contrary to the end for which every Common-wealth is instituted.

Chapter XIX   Of the Several Kinds of Common-Wealths by Institution, and of Succession to the Soveraigne Power

The difference of Common-wealths, consisteth in the difference of the Soveraign, or the Person representative of all and every one of the Multitude. And because the Soveraignty is either in one Man, or in an Assembly of more than one; and into that Assembly either Every man hath right to enter, or not every one, but certain men distinguished from the rest; it is manifest, there can be but Three kinds of Common-wealth. For the Representative must needs be One man, or More: and if more, then it is the Assembly of All, or but of a Part. When the Representative is One man, then is the Common-wealth a MONARCHY: when an Assembly of All that will come together, then it is a DEMOCRACY, or Popular Common-wealth: when an Assembly of a Part only, then it is called an ARISTOCRACY. Other kind of Common-wealth there can be none: for either One, or More, or All must have the Soveraign Power (which I have shewn to be indivisible) entire.

There be other names of Government, in the Histories, and books of Policy; as *Tyranny*, and *Oligarchy*: But they are not the names of other Formes of Government, but of the same Formes misliked. For they that are discontented under *Monarchy*, call it *Tyranny*; and they that are displeased with *Aristocracy*, called it *Oligarchy*: so also, they which find themselves grieved under a *Democracy*, call it *Anarchy*, (which signifies want of Government;) and yet I think no man believes, that want of Government, is any new kind of Government: nor by the same reason ought they to believe, that the Government is of one kind, when they like it, and another, when they mislike it, or are oppressed by the Governours. [. . .]

Chapter XXI   Of the Liberty of Subjects

[...] The Liberty of a Subject, lyeth therefore only in those things, which in regulating their actions, the Soveraign hath praetermitted; such as is the Liberty to buy, and sell, and otherwise contract with one another; to choose their own aboad, their own diet, their own trade of life, and institute their children as they themselves think fit; & the like.

Neverthelesse we are not to understand, that by such Liberty, the Soveraign Power of life, and death, is either abolished, or limited. For it has been already shewn, that nothing the Soveraign Representative can doe to a Subject, on what pretence soever, can properly be cald Injustice, or Injury; because every Subject is Author of every act the Soveraign doth; so that he never wanteth Right to any thing, otherwise, than as he himself is the Subject of God, and bound thereby to observe the laws of Nature. And therefore it may, and doth often happen in Common-wealths, that a Subject may be put to death, by the command of the Soveraign Power; and yet neither doe the other wrong. [...]

First therefore, seeing Soveraignty by Institution, is by Covenant of every one to every one; and Soveraignty by Acquisition, by Covenants of the Vanquished to the Victor, or Child to the Parent; It is manifest, that every Subject has Liberty in all those things, the right whereof cannot by Covenant be transferred. I have shewn before in the 14. Chapter, that Covenants, not to defend a mans own body, are voyd. Therefore,

If the Soveraign command a man (though justly condemned,) to kill, wound, or mayme himself; or not to resist those that assault him; or to abstain from the use of food, ayre, medicine, or any other thing, without which he cannot live; yet hath that man the Liberty to disobey.

If a man be interrogated by the Soveraign, or his Authority, concerning a crime done by himself, he is not bound (without assurance of Pardon) to confess it; because no man (as I have shewn in the same Chapter) can be obliged by Covenant to accuse himself.

Again, the Consent of a Subject to Soveraign Power, is contained in these words, *I Authorise, or take upon me, all his actions*; in which there is no restriction at all, of his own former natural Liberty: For by allowing him to *kill me*, I am not bound to kill my self when he commands me. 'Tis one thing to say *Kill me, or my fellow, if you please*; another thing to say, *I will kill my self, or my fellow*. It followeth therefore, that

No man is bound by the words themselves, either to kill himselfe, or any other man; And consequently, that the Obligation a man may sometimes have, upon the Command of the Soveraign to execute any dangerous, or dishonourable Office, dependeth not on the Words of our Submission; but on the Intention; which is to be understood by the End thereof. When therefore our refusall to obey, frustrates the End for which the Soveraignty was ordained; then there is no Liberty to refuse: otherwise there is. [...]

As for other Liberty, they depend on the Silence of the Law. In cases where the Soveraign hath prescribed no rule, there the Subject hath the liberty to do, or forbear, according to his own discretion. And therefore such Liberty is in some places more, and in some less; and in some times more, in other times lesse, according as they that have the Soveraignty shall think most convenient. As for Example, there was a time, when in *England* a man might enter in to his own Land, (and dispossesse such as wrongfully possessed it,) by force. But in after-times, that Liberty of Forcible Entry, was taken away by a Statute made (by the King) in Parliament. And in some places of the world, men have the Liberty of many wives: in other places, such Liberty is not allowed. [...]

John Locke *Second Treatise of Government* (1689)[7]

Chapter II Of the State of Nature

To understand Political Power aright, and derive it from its Original, we must consider, what State all Men are naturally in, and that is, a *State of perfect Freedom* to order their Actions, and dispose of their Possessions and Persons, as they think fit, within the bounds of the Law of Nature, without asking leave, or depending upon the Will of any other Man.   §4

A *State* also *of Equality*, wherein all the Power and Jurisdiction is reciprocal, no one having more than another; there being nothing more evident, than that Creatures of the same species and rank, promiscuously born to all the same advantages of Nature, and the use of the same Faculties, should also be equal one amongst another, without Subordination or Subjection, unless the Lord and Master of them all should, by any manifest Declaration of his Will, set one above another, and confer on him, by an evident and clear Appointment, an undoubted Right to Dominion and Sovereignty. [...]

But tho this be *a State of Liberty*, yet *it is not a State of Licence*: tho Man in that State have an uncontroulable Liberty to dispose of his Person or Possessions, yet he has not Liberty to destroy himself, or so much as any Creature in his Possession, but where some nobler use than its bare Preservation calls for it. The *State of Nature* has a Law of Nature to govern it, which obliges every one: And Reason, which is that Law, teaches all Mankind, who will but consult it, that being all *equal and independent*, no one ought to harm another in his Life, Health, Liberty, or Possession. [...]   §6

And that all Men may be restrained from invading others Rights, and from doing hurt to one another, and the Law of Nature be observed, which willeth the Peace and *Preservation of all Mankind*, the *Execution* of the Law of Nature is, in that State, put into every Man's hands, whereby every one has a right to punish the Transgressors of that Law to such a degree as may hinder its Violation. For the *Law of Nature* would, as all other Laws that concern Men in this World, be in vain, if there were no body that in the State of Nature had a *Power to execute* that Law, and thereby preserve the Innocent and restrain Offenders. And if any one in the State of Nature may punish another for any Evil he has done, every one may do so. For in that *State of perfect Equality*, where naturally   §7

---

[7] J. Locke, *Two Treatises of Government*, 5th ed. (London: Bettesworth, 1728), pp. 145–8, 154–5, 160–2, 173–5, 206–8, 223, 225–32, 239–41, 284–6, 289, 292–4, 307–8.

there is no Superiority or Jurisdiction of one over another, what any may do in Prosecution of that Law, every one must needs have a Right to do.

§8   And thus, in the State of Nature, *one Man comes by a Power over another*; but yet no absolute or arbitrary Power, to use a Criminal, when he has got him in his hands, according to the passionate Heats, or boundless Extravagancy of his own Will; but only to retribute to him, so far as calm Reason and Conscience dictate, what is proportionate to his Transgression, which is so much as may serve for *Reparation* and *Restraint*. For these two are the only reasons, why one Man may lawfully do harm to another, which is that we call *Punishment*. In transgressing the Law of Nature, the Offender declares himself to live by another Rule than that of Reason and common Equity, which is that measure God has set to the Actions of Men, for their mutual security; and so he becomes dangerous to Mankind, the Tie, which is to secure them from Injury and Violence, being slighted and broken by him. [...] And in the Case, and upon this Ground, *every Man hath a Right to punish the Offender, and be Executioner of the Law of Nature.* [...]

Chapter III Of the State of War

§17   And hence it is, that he who attempts to get another Man into his absolute Power, does thereby *put himself into a State of War* with him; it being to be understood as a Declaration of a Design upon his Life. For I have reason to conclude, that he who would get me into his Power without my Consent, would use me as he pleased, when he had got me there, and destroy me too, when he had a fancy to it: for no body can desire to *have me in his absolute Power*, unless it be to compel me by Force to that, which is against the Right of my Freedom, *i.e.* make me a Slave. To be free from such Force is the only Security of my Preservation; and Reason bids me look on him, as an Enemy to my Preservation, who would take away that *Freedom,* which is the Fence to it; so that he who makes an *Attempt to enslave* me, thereby puts himself into a State of War with me. He that in the State of Nature *would take away the Freedom* that belongs to any one in that State, must necessarily be supposed to have a Design to take away every thing else, that *Freedom* being the Foundation of all the rest: As he that in the state of Society would take away the *Freedom* belonging to those of that Society or Commonwealth, must be supposed to design to take away from them every thing else, and so be looked on as *in a state of War*.

§18   This makes it lawful for a Man to *kill a Thief*, who has not in the least hurt him, nor declared any design upon his Life, any farther than by the use of Force, so to get him in his Power, as to take away his Money, or what he pleases from him: because using force, where he has no Right, to get me into his Power, let his pretence be what it will, I have no Reason to suppose, that he, who would *take away my Liberty*, would not, when he had me in his Power, take away every thing else. And therefore it is lawful for me to treat him as one who has put *himself into a State of War* with me, *i.e.* kill him if I can; for to that Hazard does he justly expose himself, whoever introduces a State of War, and is *Aggressor* in it.

And here we have the plain *Difference between the state of Nature and the state of* §19
War, which however some men have confounded, are as far distant, as a state of
Peace, good Will, mutual Assistance, and Preservation, and a State of enmity,
Malice, Violence, and mutual Destruction are one from another. Men living together
according to Reason, without a common Superior on Earth, with Authority to judge
between them, is *properly the state of Nature*. But force, or a declared Design of
Force upon the Person of another, where there is no common Superior on Earth to
appeal to for relief, *is the State of War*. [...]

Chapter V Of Property

Tho the Earth, and all inferior Creatures, be common to all Men, yet every Man has §27
a *Property* in his own *Person*: This no body has any Right to but himself. The *Labour*
of his Body, and the *Work* of his Hands, we may say, are properly his. Whatsoever
then he removes out of the State that Nature hath provided, and left it in, he hath
mixed his *Labour* with, and joined to it something that is his own, and thereby makes
it his *Property*. It being by him removed from the common State Nature hath placed it
in, it hath by this *Labour* something annexed to it, that excludes the common Right of
other Men. For this *Labour* being the unquestionable Property of the Labourer, no
Man but he can have a right to what that is once joined to, at least where there is
enough, and as good left in common for others.

He that is nourished by the Acorns he pick'd up under an Oak, or the Apples he §28
gathered from the Trees in the Wood, has certainly appropriated them to himself: No
body can deny but the nourishment is his. I ask then, When did they begin to be his?
When he digested, or when he eat, or when he boiled, or when he brought them
home, or when he pick'd them up? And 'tis plain, if the first gathering made them not
his, nothing else could. That *Labour* put a Distinction between them and common:
that added something to them more than Nature, the common Mother of all, had
done; and so they became his private Right. [...]

It will perhaps be objected to this, That if gathering the Acorns, or other Fruits of §31
the Earth, &c. makes a Right to them, then any one may *ingross* as much as he will.
To which I answer, Not so: The same Law of Nature, that does by this means give us
Property, does also *bound* that *Property* too. *God has given us all things richly*,
1 Tim. 6. 17. is the Voice of Reason confirmed by Inspiration. But how far has he
given it us *to enjoy*? As much as any one can make use of to any Advantage of Life
before it spoils; so much he may by his Labour fix a Property in: Whatever is beyond
this, is more than his share, and belongs to others. Nothing was made by God for Man
to spoil or destroy. [...]

The greatest part of *things really useful* to the Life of Man, and such as the §46
necessity of subsisting made the first Commoners of the World look after, as it doth
the *Americans* now, *are* generally things *of short duration*; such as, if they are not
consumed by use, will decay and perish of themselves: Gold, Silver, and Diamonds,
are things that Fancy or Agreement hath put the Value on, more than real Use, and the
necessary Support of Life. [...] If he would give his Nuts for a piece of Metal,
pleased with its Colour; or exchange his Sheep for Shells, or Wool for a sparkling

Pebble or a Diamond, and keep those by him all his Life he invaded not the Right of others, he might heap up as much of these durable things as he pleased; the *exceeding of the bounds of* his *just Property* not lying in the largeness of his Possession, but the perishing of any thing uselesly in it.

§47   And thus *came in the use of Money*, some lasting thing that Men might keep without spoiling, and that by mutual Consent Men would take in exchange for the truly useful, but perishable supports of Life. [...]

§50   But since Gold and Silver, being little useful to the Life of Man in proportion to Food, Raiment, and Carriage, has its *Value* only from the consent of men, whereof *Labour* yet *makes*, in great part, *the Measure*, it is plain, that Men have agreed to a disproportionate and unequal *Possession of the Earth*, they having by a tacit and voluntary consent, found out a Way how a Man may fairly possess more Land than he himself can use the Product of, by receiving in Exchange for the overplus Gold and Silver, which may be hoarded up without Injury to any one; these Metals not spoiling or decaying in the hands of the Possessor. This partage of things in an inequality of private Possessions, men have made practicable out of the bounds of Society, and without Compact, only by putting a Value on Gold and Silver, and tacitly agreeing in the use of Money. For in Governments the Laws regulate the Right of Property, and the possession of Land is determined by positive Constitutions.

Chapter VIII Of the Beginning of Political Societies

§95   Men being, as has been said, by Nature, all free, equal, and independent, no one can be put out of this Estate, and subjected to the Political Power of another, without his own Consent. The only way whereby any one divests himself of his natural Liberty, and puts on the *Bonds of Civil Society*, is by agreeing with other Men to join and unite into a Community, for their comfortable, safe, and peaceable living one amongst another, in a secure Enjoyment of their Properties, and a greater Security against any, that are not of it. This any number of Men may do, because it injures not the Freedom of the rest; they are left as they were in the Liberty of the state of Nature. When any number of men have so *consented to make one Community or Government*, they are thereby presently incorporated, and make *one Body politick*, wherein the *Majority* have a Right to act and conclude the rest. [...]

§97   And thus every Man, by consenting with others to make one Body politick under one Government, puts himself under an Obligation, to every one of that Society, to submit to the determination of the *Majority*, and to be concluded by it; or else this *original Compact*, whereby he with others incorporates into *one Society*, would signify nothing, and be no Compact, if he be left free, and under no other Ties than he was in before in the state of Nature. For what appearance would there be of any Compact; what new Engagement, if he were no farther tied by any Decrees of the Society, than he himself thought fit, and did actually consent to? This would be still as great a Liberty, as he himself had before his Compact, or any one else in the state of Nature hath, who may submit himself, and consent to any Acts of it if he thinks fit.

§98   For if *the consent of the Majority* shall not in reason be received as *the Act of the whole*, and conclude every individual, nothing but the consent of every individual can make any thing to be the act of the whole: But such a consent is next to impossible ever to be had, if we consider the Infirmities of Health, and Avocations of Business, which in a number, though much less than that of a Commonwealth, will necessarily keep many away from the publick Assembly. To which if we add the variety of Opinions, and contrariety of Interests, which unavoidably happen in all Collections of Men, the coming into Society upon such Terms would be only like *Cato*'s coming into the Theatre, only to go out again. Such a Constitution as this, would make the mighty *Leviathan* of a shorter duration, than the feeblest Creatures; and not let it outlast the day it was born in: Which cannot be suppos'd, till we can think, that rational Creatures should desire and constitute Societies only to be dissolved. For where the *Majority* cannot conclude the rest, there they cannot act as one Body, and consequently will be immediately dissolved again. [...]

Every Man being, as has been shewed, *naturally free*, and nothing being able to put   §119
him into Subjection to any Earthly Power, but only his own Consent, it is to be considered, what shall be understood to be *a sufficient Declaration of a* Man's *Consent, to make him subject* to the Laws of any Government. There is a common Distinction of an express and a tacit Consent, which will concern our present Case. No Body doubts but an express *Consent*, of any man, entring into any Society, makes him a perfect Member of that Society, a Subject of that Government. The difficulty is, what ought to be look'd upon as a *tacit Consent*, and how far it binds, *i.e.* how far any one shall be looked on to have consented, and thereby submitted to any Government, where he has made no Expressions of it at all. And to this I say, that every Man that hath any Possessions, or Enjoyment, of any part of the Dominions of any Government, doth thereby give his *tacit Consent*, and is as far forth obliged to Obedience to the Laws of that Government, during such Enjoyment, as any one under it; whether this his Possession be of Land, to him and his Heirs for ever, or a Lodging only for a Week; or whether it be barely travelling freely on the Highway; and in effect, it reaches as far as the very being of any one within the Territories of that Government. [...]

But submitting to the Laws of any Country, living quietly, and enjoying Privileges   §122
and Protection under them, *makes not a Man a Member of that Society*: This is only a local Protection and Homage due to and from all those, who, not being in a state of War, come within the Territories belonging to any Government, to all parts whereof the Force of its Laws extends. But this no more *makes a Man a Member of that Society*, a perpetual Subject of that Commonwealth, than it would make a Man a Subject to another, in whose Family he found it convenient to abide for some time; tho, whilst he continued in it, he were obliged to comply with the Laws, and submit to the Government he found there. And thus we see, that *Foreigners*, by living all their Lives under another Government, and enjoying the Privileges and Protection of it, tho they are bound, even in Conscience, to submit to its Administration, as far forth as any Denison; yet do not thereby come to be *Subjects or Members of that Commonwealth*. Nothing can make any Man so, but his actually entering into it by positive Engagement, and express Promise and Compact. This is that which I think concerning the beginning of Political Societies, and that *Consent which makes any one a Member* of any Commonwealth. [...]

Chapter IX On the Ends of Political Society and Government

§124   The great and *chief End*, therefore, of Mens uniting into Commonwealths, and putting themselves under Government, *is the Preservation of their Property*. To which in the state of Nature there are many things wanting.

First, There wants an *establish'd*, settled, known *Law*, received and allowed by common consent to be the Standard of Right and Wrong, and the common Measure to decide all Controversies between them. For tho the Law of Nature be plain and intelligible to all rational Creatures; yet men being biassed by their Interest, as well as ignorant for want of Study of it, are not apt to allow of it as a Law binding to them, in the application of it to their particular Cases.

§125   *Secondly*, In the state of Nature there wants *a known and indifferent Judge*, with Authority to determine all Differences according to the established Law. For every one in that state being both Judge and Executioner of the Law of Nature, Men being partial to themselves, Passion and Revenge is very apt to carry them too far, and with too much Heat, in their own Cases; as well as Negligence, and Unconcernedness, to make them too remiss in other Mens.

§126   *Thirdly*, In the state of Nature there often wants *Power* to back and support the Sentence when right, and to *give* it due *Execution*. They who by any Injustice offended, will seldom fail, where they are able, by Force to make good their Injustice; such Resistance many times makes the Punishment dangerous, and frequently destructive, to those who attempt it.

§127   [. . .] 'Tis this makes them so willingly give up every one his single Power of punishing, to be exercised by such alone, as shall be appointed to it amongst them; and by such Rules as the Community, or those authorized by them to that purpose, shall agree on. And in this we have the original *Right and Rise* of both *the Legislative and Executive Power*, as well as of the Governments, and Societies themselves.

§128   For in the State of Nature, to omit the Liberty he has of innocent Delights, a Man has two Powers.

The first is to do whatsoever he thinks fit for the preservation of himself, and others within the permission of the *Law of Nature*: by which Law common to them all, he and all the rest of *Mankind are one Community*, make up one Society, distinct from all other Creatures. And were it not for the Corruption and Vitiousness of degenerate Men, there would be no need of any other; no necessity that men should separate from this great and natural Community, and by positive agreements combine into smaller and divided Associations.

The other Power a Man has in the state of Nature, is the *power to punish the Crimes* committed against that Law. Both these he gives up, when he joins in a private, if I may so call it, or particular Politic Society, and incorporates into any Commonwealth, separate from the rest of Mankind.

§129   The first *Power,* viz. *of doing whatsoever he thought for the preservation of himself*, and the rest of Mankind, *he gives up* to be regulated by Laws made by the Society, so far forth as the preservation of himself, and the rest of that Society shall require; which Laws of the Society in many things confine the liberty he had by the Law of Nature.

Secondly, the *Power of punishing* he wholly *gives up*, and engages his natural §130
force, (which he might before employ in the Execution of the Law of Nature, by his
own single Authority, as he thought fit) to assist the executive Power of the Society,
as the Law thereof shall require. For being now in a new State, wherein he is to enjoy
many Conveniencies, from the Labour, Assistance, and Society of others in the same
Community, as well as Protection from its whole Strength; he is to part also with as
much of his natural Liberty, in providing for himself, as the Good, Prosperity, and
Safety of the Society shall require: which is not only necessary, but just; since the
other Members of the Society do the like.

Chapter X Of the Forms of the Commonwealth

The Majority having, as has been shew'd, upon Mens first uniting into Society, the §132
whole Power of the Community naturally in them, may employ all that Power in
making Laws for the Community from time to time, and Executing those Laws by
Officers of their own appointing; and then the Form of the Government is a perfect
Democracy: Or else may put the power of making Laws into the hands of a few
select Men, and their Heirs or Successors; and then it is an *Oligarchy*: or else into
the hands of one Man, and then it is a *Monarchy*: If to him and his Heirs, it is an
hereditary Monarchy: If to him only for Life, but upon his Death the Power only
of nominating a Successor to return to them; an *Elective Monarchy*. And so
accordingly of these the Community may make compounded and mixed Forms
of Government, as they think good. And if the legislative Power be at first given
by the Majority to one or more persons only for their Lives, or any limited time,
and then the Supream [*sic*] to revert to them again; when it is so reverted, the
Community may dispose of it again anew into what hands they please, and so
constitute a new Form of Government. [. . .]

Chapter XI Of the Extent of the Legislative Power

The great end of Mens entring into Society, being the enjoyment of their §134
Properties in Peace and Safety, and the great instrument and means of that being
the Laws establish'd in that Society; the *first and fundamental positive Law* of all
Commonwealths, *is the establishing of the Legislative* Power; as the *first and
fundamental natural Law*, which is to govern even the Legislative it self, *is the
preservation of the Society*, and (as far as will consist with the publick good) of
every Person in it. This *Legislative* is not only *the supreme Power* of the
Commonwealth, but sacred and unalterable in the hands where the Community
have once placed it; nor can any Edict of any body else, in what Form soever
conceived, or by what Power soever backed, have the force and obligation of
a *Law*, which has not its *Sanction from* that *Legislative,* which the Publick has
chosen and appointed. For without this the Law could not have that, which is
absolutely necessary to its being a *Law, the consent of the Society*, over whom no
Body can have a Power to make Laws, but by their own Consent, and by Authority
received from them. [. . .]

§142   These are the *Bounds* which the Trust that is put in them by the Society, and the Law of God and Nature, have *set to the Legislative* Power of every Commonwealth, in all Forms of Government.

First, They are to govern by *promulgated establish'd Laws*, not to be varied in particular Cases, but to have one rule for Rich and Poor, for the Favourite at Court, and the Countryman at Plough.

Secondly, These *Laws* also ought to be designed *for* no other end ultimately, but *the good of the People.*

Thirdly, They must *not raise Taxes* on the *Property of the People, without the Consent of the People*, given by themselves, or their Deputies. And this properly concerns only such Governments where the *Legislative* is always in being, or at least where the People have not reserv'd any part of the Legislative to Deputies, to be from time to time chosen by themselves.

Fourthly, The *Legislative* neither must *nor can transfer the Power of making Laws* to any body else, or place it any where, but where the People have.

Chapter XII Of the Legislative, Executive, and Federative Power of the Commonwealth

§143   The *Legislative* Power is that, which has a right *to direct, how the Force of the Commonwealth* shall be employ'd for preserving the Community and the Members of it. But because those Laws which are constantly to be Executed, and whose force is always to continue, may be made in a little time; therefore there is no need, that the *Legislative* should be always in Being, not having always business to do. And because it may be too great a temptation to human Frailty, apt to grasp at Power, for the same Persons who have the Power of making Laws, to have also in their hands the Power to execute them, whereby they may exempt themselves from Obedience to the Laws they make, and suit the Law, both in its making, and execution, to their own private advantage, and thereby come to have a distinct interest from the rest of the Community, contrary to the end of Society and Government: Therefore in well order'd Commonwealths, where the good of the whole is so considered, as it ought, the *Legislative* Power is put into the hands of divers Persons, who, duly assembled, have by themselves, or jointly with others, a Power to make Laws, which when they have done, being separated again, they are themselves subject to the Laws they have made; which is a new and near Tie upon them, to take care, that they make them for the public good.

§144   But because the Laws, that are at once, and in a short time made, have a constant and lasting force, and need a *perpetual Execution*, or an attendance thereunto: Therefore 'tis necessary there should be a *Power always in being*, which should see to the *Execution* of the Laws that are made, and remain in Force. And thus the *Legislative* and *Executive Power* come often to be separated. [...]

Chapter XIX Of the Dissolution of Government

§211   He that will with any clearness speak of the *Dissolution of Government*, ought in the first place to distinguish between the *Dissolution of the Society* and the *Dissolution of the Government.* That which makes the Community, and brings men out of the loose State of Nature, into *one Politick Society*, is the Agreement which every one has with the rest to incorporate, and act as one Body, and so be one distinct Commonwealth. The usual, and almost only way whereby *this Union is dissolved*, is the Inroad of Foreign Force making a Conquest upon them. For in that Case, (not being able to maintain and support themselves, as *one intire* and *independent Body*) the Union belonging to that Body which consisted therein, must necessarily cease, and so every one return to the state he was in before, with a Liberty to shift for himself, and provide for his own Safety, as he thinks fit, in some other Society. When the *Society is dissolved*, 'tis certain the Government of that Society cannot remain. [. . .]

Besides this over-turning from without, *Governments are dissolved from within*, §212

First, When the *Legislative* is *altered*. [. . .] This *is the Soul that gives Form, Life, and Unity*, to the Commonwealth: From hence the several Members have their mutual Influence, Sympathy, and Connexion: And therefore when the *Legislative* is broken, or *dissolved*, Dissolution and Death follows. [. . .] When any one or more shall take upon them to make Laws, whom the People have not appointed so to do, they make Laws without Authority, which the People are not therefore bound to obey; by which means they come again to be out of Subjection, and may constitute to themselves a *new Legislative*, as they think best, being in full liberty to resist the Force of those, who without Authority would impose any thing upon them. Every one is at the disposure of his own Will, when those who had by the Delegation of the Society, the declaring of the publick Will, are excluded from it, and others usurp the Place, who have no such Authority or Delegation. [. . .]

In these and the like Cases, *when the Government is dissolved*, the People are at §220 liberty to provide for themselves, by erecting a new Legislative, differing from the other, by the change of Persons, or Form, or both, as they shall find it most for their Safety and Good. For the *Society* can never, by the Fault of another, lose the native and original Right it has to preserve it self, which can only be done by a settled Legislative, and a fair and impartial Execution of the Laws made by it. [. . .]

There is therefore, secondly, another way whereby *Governments are dissolved*, §221 and that is, when the Legislative, or the Prince either of them act contrary to their Trust.

First, The *Legislative acts against the Trust* reposed in them, when they endeavour to invade the Property of the Subject, and to make themselves, or any part of the Community, Masters, or arbitrary Disposers of the Lives, Liberties, or Fortunes of the People. [. . .]

But 'twill be said, this *Hypothesis* lays a *ferment for* frequent *Rebellion*. To which §224 I Answer,

First, No more than any other *Hypothesis*. For when the *People* are made miserable, and find themselves *exposed to the ill usage of arbitrary Power*, cry up their Governors, as much as you will, for Sons of *Jupiter*; let them be Sacred and Divine, descended, or authoriz'd from Heaven; give them out for whom or what you please, the same will happen. *The People generally ill treated*, and contrary to Right, will be ready upon any occasion to ease themselves of a Burden that sits heavy upon them. They will wish, and seek for the Opportunity, which in the Change, Weakness and

Accidents of human Affairs, seldom delays long to offer it self. He must have lived but a little while in the World, who has not seen Examples of this in his time; and he must have read very little, who cannot produce Examples of it in all sorts of Governments in the World. [...]

§225   *Secondly*, I answer, such *Revolutions happen* not upon every little Mismanagement in public Affairs. *Great Mistakes* in the ruling part, many wrong and inconvenient Laws, and all the *slips* of human Frailty, will be *borne by the People* without Mutiny or Murmur. But if a long train of Abuses, Prevarications and Artifices, all tending the same way, make the Design visible to the People, and they cannot but feel, what they lie under, and see, whither they are going; 'tis not to be wonder'd, that they should then rouze themselves, and endeavour to put the Rule into such hands which may secure to them the Ends for which Government was at first erected [...].

§226   *Thirdly*, I answer, That *this Doctrine* of a Power in the People of providing for their Safety anew, by a new Legislative, when their Legislators have acted contrary to their Trust, by invading their Property, is *the best Fence against Rebellion*, and the probablest Means to hinder it. For *Rebellion* being an Opposition, not to Persons, but Authority, which is founded only in the Constitutions and Laws of the Government; those, whoever they be, who by Force break thro', and by Force justify their Violation of them, are truly and properly *Rebels*. For when Men, by entering into Society and Civil Government, have excluded Force, and introduced Laws for the preservation of Property, Peace, and Unity amongst themselves; those who set up Force again, in opposition to the Laws, do *rebellare*, that is, bring back again the state of War, and are properly Rebels: Which they who are in Power, (by the pretence they have to Authority, the Temptation of Force they have in their hands, and the Flattery of those about them) being likeliest to do; the properest way to prevent the Evil, is to shew them the Danger and Injustice of it, who are under the greatest Temptation to run into it. [...]

§243   To conclude, The *Power that every Individual gave the Society*, when he entered into it, can never revert to the Individuals again, as long as the Society lasts, but will always remain in the Community; because without this, there can be no Community, no Commonwealth, which is contrary to the original Agreement: So also when the Society hath placed the Legislative in any Assembly of Men, to continue in them and their Successors, with Direction and Authority for providing such Successors, *the Legislative can never revert to the People* whilst that Government lasts: Because having provided a Legislative with Power to continue for ever, they have given up their Political Power to the Legislative, and cannot resume it. But if they have set Limits to the Duration of their Legislative, and made this supreme Power in any Person, or Assembly, only temporary: Or else, when by the Miscarriages of those in Authority, it is forfeited; upon the Forfeiture, or at the Determination of the Time set, *it reverts to the Society*, and the People have a Right to act as Supreme, and continue the Legislative in themselves; or erect a new Form, or under the old Form place it in new Hands, as they think good.

CONSERVATIVE LIBERALISM

Baron de Montesquieu *The Spirit of the Laws* (1748)[8]

Book V That the Laws Given by the Legislator Should Be Relative to the Principle of the Government

Chapter 6　How Laws Should Sustain Frugality in Democracy

[...] Certainly, when democracy is founded on commerce, it may very well happen that individuals have great wealth, yet that the mores are not corrupted. This is because the spirit of commerce brings with it the spirit of frugality, economy, moderation, work, wisdom, tranquility, order, and rule. Thus, as long as this spirit continues to exist, the wealth it produces has no bad effect. The ill comes when an excess of wealth destroys the spirit of commerce; one sees the sudden rise of the disorders of inequality which had not made themselves felt before.

In order for the spirit of commerce to be maintained, the principal citizens must engage in commerce themselves; this spirit must reign alone and not be crossed by another; all the laws must favor it; these same laws, whose provisions divide fortunes in proportion as commerce increases them, must make each poor citizen comfortable enough to be able to work as the others do and must bring each rich citizen to a middle level such that he needs to work in order to preserve or to acquire.

In a commercial republic, the law giving all children an equal portion in the inheritance of the fathers is very good. In this way, whatever fortune the father may have made, his children, always less rich than he, are led to flee luxury and work as he did. I speak only of commercial republics, because, for those that are not, the legislator has to make many other regulations. [...]

Book VIII On the Corruption of the Principles of the Three Governments

Chapter 20　Consequence of the Preceding Chapter

If the natural property of small states is to be governed as republics, that of medium-sized ones, to be subject to a monarch, and that of large empires to be dominated by a despot, it follows that, in order to preserve the principles of the established government, the state must be maintained at the size it already has and that it will change its spirit to the degree to which its boundaries are narrowed or extended. [...]

Book IX On the Laws in Their Relation with Defensive Force

Chapter 1　How Republics Provide for Their Security

If a republic is small, it is destroyed by a foreign force; if it is large, it is destroyed by an internal vice.

---

[8] Montesquieu, *The Spirit of the Laws*, translated by A. M. Cohler, B. C. Miller, and H. S. Stone (Cambridge and New York: Cambridge University Press, 1989), pp. 48, 126, 131–2, 154–62, 164, 187–94, 197–200, 202–4, 338–9.

This dual drawback taints democracies and aristocracies equally, whether they are good or whether they are bad. The ill is in the thing itself; there is no form that can remedy it.

Thus, it is very likely that ultimately men would have been obliged to live forever under the government of one alone if they had not devised a kind of constitution that has all the internal advantages of republican government and the external force of monarchy. I speak of the federal republic.

This form of government is an agreement by which many political bodies consent to become citizens of the larger state that they want to form. It is a society of societies that make a new one, which can be enlarged by new associates that unite with it. [...]

This sort of republic, able to resist external force, can be maintained at its size without internal corruption: the form of this society curbs every drawback. [...]

Composed of small republics, it enjoys the goodness of the internal government of each one; and, with regard to the exterior, it has, by the force of the association, all the advantages of large monarchies. [...]

Book XI On the Laws Which Establish Political Liberty, with Regard to the Constitution

Chapter 1   General Idea

I distinguish the laws that form political liberty in its relation with the constitution from those that form it in its relation with the citizen. The first are the subject of the present book; I shall discuss the second in the next book. [...]

Chapter 3   What Liberty Is

It is true that in democracies the people seem to do what they want, but political liberty in no way consists in doing what one wants. In a state, that is, in a society where there are laws, liberty can consist only in having the power to do what one should want to do and in no way being constrained to do what one should not want to do.

One must put oneself in mind of what independence is and what liberty is. Liberty is the right to do everything the laws permit; and if one citizen could do what they forbid, he would no longer have liberty because the others would likewise have this same power.

Chapter 4   Continuation of the Same Subject

Democracy and aristocracy are not free states by their nature. Political liberty is found only in moderate governments. But it is not always in moderate states. It is present only when power is not abused, but it has eternally been observed that any man who has power is led to abuse it; he continues until he finds limits. Who would think it! Even virtue has need of limits.

So that one cannot abuse power, power must check power by the arrangement of things. A constitution can be such that no one will be constrained to do the things the law does not oblige him to do or be kept from doing the things the law permits him to do. [...]

Chapter 6   On the Constitution of England

In each state there are three sorts of powers: legislative power, executive power over the things depending on the right of nations, and executive power over the things depending on civil right.

By the first, the prince or the magistrate makes laws for a time or for always and corrects or abrogates those that have been made. By the second, he makes peace or war, sends or receives embassies, establishes security, and prevents invasions. By the third, he punishes crimes or judges disputes between individuals. The last will be called the power of judging, and the former simply the executive power of the state.

Political liberty in a citizen is that tranquility of spirit which comes from the opinion each one has of his security, and in order for him to have this liberty the government must be such that one citizen cannot fear another citizen.

When legislative power is united with executive power in a single person or in a single body of the magistracy, there is no liberty, because one can fear that the same monarch or senate that makes tyrannical laws will execute them tyrannically.

Nor is there liberty if the power of judging is not separate from legislative power and from executive power. If it were joined to legislative power, the power over the life and liberty of the citizens would be arbitrary, for the judge would be the legislator. If it were joined to executive power, the judge could have the force of an oppressor.

All would be lost if the same man or the same body of principal men, either of nobles, or of the people, exercised these three powers: that of making the laws, that of executing public resolutions, and that of judging the crimes or the disputes of individuals. [...]

The power of judging should not be given to a permanent senate but should be exercised by persons drawn from the body of the people at certain times of the year in the manner prescribed by law to form a tribunal which lasts only as long as necessity requires.

In this fashion the power of judging, so terrible among men, being attached neither to a certain state nor to a certain profession, becomes, so to speak, invisible and null. Judges are not continually in view; one fears the magistracy, not the magistrates. [...]

though tribunals should not be fixed, judgments should be fixed to such a degree that they are never anything but a precise text of the law. If judgments were the individual opinion of a judge, one would live in this society without knowing precisely what engagements one has contracted.

Further, the judges must be of the same condition as the accused, or his peers, so that he does not suppose that he has fallen into the hands of people inclined to do him violence. [...]

As, in a free state, every man, considered to have a free soul, should be governed by himself, the people as a body should have legislative power; but, as this is impossible in large states and is subject to many drawbacks in small ones, the people must have their representatives do all that they themselves cannot do.

One knows the needs of one's own town better than those of other towns, and one judges the ability of one's neighbors better than that of one's other compatriots. Therefore, members of the legislative body must not be drawn from the body of the nation at large; it is proper for the inhabitants of each principal town to choose a representative from it.

The great advantage of representatives is that they are able to discuss public business. The people are not at all appropriate for such discussions; this forms one of the great drawbacks of democracy.

It is not necessary that the representatives, who have been generally instructed by those who have chosen them, be instructed about each matter of business in particular, as is the practice in the Diets of Germany. It is true that, in their way, the word of the deputies would better express the voice of the nation; but it would produce infinite delays and make each deputy the master of all the others, and on the most pressing occasions the whole force of the nation could be checked by a caprice. [. . .]

In choosing a representative, all citizens in the various districts should have the right to vote except those whose estate is so humble that they are deemed to have no will of their own. [. . .]

In a state there are always some people who are distinguished by birth, wealth, or honors; but if they were mixed among the people and if they had only one voice like the others, the common liberty would be their enslavement and they would have no interest in defending it, because most of the resolutions would be against them. Therefore, the part they have in legislation should be in proportion to the other advantages they have in the state, which will happen if they form a body that has the right to check the enterprises of the people, as the people have the right to check theirs.

Thus, legislative power will be entrusted both to the body of the nobles and to the body that will be chosen to represent the people, each of which will have assemblies and deliberations apart and have separate views and interests. [. . .]

The nobility should be hereditary. In the first place, it is so by its nature; and, besides, it must have a great interest in preserving its prerogatives, odious in themselves, and which, in a free state, must always be endangered.

But, as a hereditary power could be induced to follow its particular interests and forget those of the people, in the things about which one has a sovereign interest in corrupting, for instance, in the laws about levying silver coin, it must take part in legislation only through its faculty of vetoing and not through its faculty of enacting.

I call the right to order by oneself, or to correct what has been ordered by another, the *faculty of enacting*. I call the right to render null a resolution taken by another the *faculty of vetoing*, which was the power of the tribunes of Rome. And, although the one who has the faculty of vetoing can also have the right to approve, this approval is no more than a declaration that one does not make use of one's faculty of vetoing, and it derives from that faculty.

The executive power should be in the hands of a monarch, because the part of the government that almost always needs immediate action is better administered by one than by many, whereas what depends on legislative power is often better ordered by many than by one. [. . .]

It would be useless for the legislative body to be convened without interruption. That would inconvenience the representatives and besides would overburden the executive power, which would not think of executing, but of defending its prerogatives and its right to execute.

In addition, if the legislative body were continuously convened, it could happen that one would do nothing but replace the deputies who had died with new deputies; and in this case, if the legislative body were once corrupted, the ill would be without remedy. When various legislative bodies follow each other, the people, holding a poor opinion of the current legislative body, put their hopes, reasonably enough, in the one that will follow; but if the legislative body were always the same, the people, seeing it corrupted, would expect nothing further from its laws; they would become furious or would sink into indolence.

The legislative body should not convene itself. For a body is considered to have a will only when it is convened; and if it were not convened unanimously, one could not identify which part was truly the legislative body, the part that was convened or the one that was not. For if it had the right to prorogue itself, it could happen that it would never prorogue itself; this would be dangerous in the event that it wanted to threaten executive power. Besides, there are some times more suitable than others for convening the legislative body; therefore, it must be the executive power that regulates, in relation to the circumstances it knows, the time of the holding and duration of these assemblies.

If the executive power does not have the right to check the enterprises of the legislative body, the latter will be despotic, for it will wipe out all the other powers, since it will be able to give to itself all the power it can imagine.

But the legislative power must not have the reciprocal faculty of checking the executive power. For, as execution has the limits of its own nature, it is useless to restrict it; besides, executive power is always exercised on immediate things. And the power of the tribunes in Rome was faulty in that it checked not only legislation but even execution; this caused great ills.

But if, in a free state, legislative power should not have the right to check executive power, it has the right and should have the faculty to examine the manner in which the laws it has made have been executed [. . .].

Here, therefore, is the fundamental constitution of the government of which we are speaking. As its legislative body is composed of two parts, the one will be chained to the other by their reciprocal faculty of vetoing. The two will be bound by the executive power, which will itself be bound by the legislative power.

The form of these three powers should be rest or inaction. But as they are constrained to move by the necessary motion of things, they will be forced to move in concert. [. . .]

Book XII Of the Laws That Form Political Liberty, as Relative to the Citizen

Chapter 1   The Idea of This Book

It is not enough to treat political liberty in its relation to the constitution; it must be shown in its relation to the citizen.

I have said that, in the former instance, liberty is formed by a certain distribution of the three powers, but in the latter it must be considered with a different idea in view. It consists in security or in one's opinion of one's security.

It can happen that the constitution is free and that the citizen is not. The citizen can be free and the constitution not. In these instances, the constitution will be free by right and not in fact; the citizen will be free in fact and not by right.

Only the disposition of the laws, and especially of the fundamental laws, forms liberty in its relation to the constitution. But, in the relation to the citizen, mores, manners, and received examples can give rise to it and certain civil laws can favor it, as we shall see in the present book.

Further, as in most states liberty is more hampered, countered, or beaten down than is required by their constitutions, it is well to speak of the particular laws that, in each constitution, can aid or run counter to the principle of the liberty of which each government can admit.

Chapter 2   On the Liberty of the Citizen

Philosophical liberty consists in the exercise of one's will or, at least (if all systems must be mentioned), in one's opinion that one exerts one's will. Political liberty consists in security or, at least, in the opinion one has of one's security.

This *security* is never more attacked than by public or private accusations. Therefore, the citizen's liberty depends principally on the goodness of the criminal laws. [...]

When the innocence of the citizens is not secure, neither is liberty. [...]

Liberty can be founded only on the practice of this knowledge, and in a state that had the best possible laws in regard to it, a man against whom proceedings had been brought and who was to be hung the next day would be freer than is a pasha in Turkey. [...]

Chapter 4   That Liberty Is Favored by the Nature of Penalties, and by Their Proportion

It is the triumph of liberty when criminal laws draw each penalty from the particular nature of the crime. All arbitrariness ends; the penalty does not ensue from the legislator's capriciousness but from the nature of the thing, and man does not do violence to man.

There are four sorts of crimes. Those of the first kind run counter to religion; those of the second, to mores; those of the third, to tranquility; those of the fourth, to the security of the citizens. The penalties inflicted should derive from the nature of each of these kinds.

I include in the class of crimes concerning religion only those that attack it directly, such as all cases of simple sacrilege. For crimes of disturbing the exercise of religion are of the nature of those that run counter to the tranquility or the security of the citizens and should be shifted to these classes.

In order for the penalty against simple sacrilege to be drawn from the nature of the thing, it should consist in the deprivation of all the advantages given by religion: expulsion from the temples; deprivation of the society of the faithful for a time or forever; shunning the presence of the sacrilegious; execration, detestation, and exorcism.

In the things that disturb the tranquility or security of the state, hidden actions are a concern of human justice. But in those that wound the divinity, where there is no public action, there is no criminal matter; it is all between the man and god who knows the measure and the time of his vengeance. For if the magistrate, confusing things, even searches out hidden sacrilege, he brings an inquisition to a kind of action where it is not necessary; he destroys the liberty of citizens by arming against them the zeal of both timid and brash consciences.

The ill came from the idea that the divinity must be avenged. But one must make divinity honored, and one must never avenge it. Indeed, if one were guided by the latter idea, where would punishments end? If men's laws are to avenge an infinite being, they will be ruled by his infinity and not by the weakness, ignorance, and caprice of human nature. [...]

The second class is of crimes against the mores: these are the violation of public or individual continence, that is, of the police concerning how one should enjoy the pleasures associated with the use of one's senses and with corporal union. The penalties for these crimes should also be drawn from the nature of the thing. Deprivation of the advantages that society has attached to the purity of mores, fines, shame, the constraint to hide oneself, public infamy, and expulsion from the town and from society; finally, all the penalties within the correctional jurisdiction suffice to repress the temerity of the two sexes. Indeed, these things are founded less on wickedness than on forgetting or despising oneself.

Here it is a question only of crimes that involve mores alone, not of those that also run counter to public security, such as kidnapping and rape, which are of the fourth kind.

The crimes of the third class are those that run counter to the citizens' tranquility, and the penalties for them should be drawn from the nature of the thing and relate to that tranquility, such as deprivation, exile, corrections, and other penalties that restore men's troubled spirits and return them to the established order.

I restrict crimes against tranquility to the things that are a simple breach of police; the ones that, while disturbing tranquility, attack security at the same time, should be put in the fourth class.

The penalties for these last crimes are what are called punishments. They are a kind of retaliation, which causes the society to refuse to give security to a citizen who has deprived or has wanted to deprive another of it. This penalty is derived from the nature of the thing and is drawn from reason and from the sources of good and evil. A citizen deserves death when he has violated security so far as to take or to attempt to take a life. The death penalty is the remedy, as it were, for a sick society.

When one violates security with respect to goods there can be reasons for the penalty to be capital; but it would perhaps be preferable, and it would be more natural, if the penalty for crimes committed against the security of goods were punished by the loss of goods. And that ought to be so, if fortunes were common or equal; but as those who have no goods more readily attack the goods of others, the corporal penalty has had to replace the pecuniary penalty.

All that I say is drawn from nature and is quite favorable to the citizen's liberty.

Chapter 5   On Certain Accusations in Particular Need of Moderation and Prudence

Important maxim: one must be very circumspect in the pursuit of magic and of heresy. Accusation of these two crimes can offend liberty in the extreme and be the source of infinite tyrannies if the legislator does not know how to limit it. For, as it does not bear directly on the actions of a citizen, but rather on the idea one has of his character, the accusation becomes dangerous in proportion to the people's ignorance, and from that time, a citizen is always in danger because the best conduct in the world, the purest morality, and the practice of all one's duties do not guarantee one from being suspected of these crimes. [...]

I have not said here that heresy must not be punished; I say that one must be very circumspect in punishing it. [...]

Chapter 7   On the Crime of High Treason

The laws of China decide that whoever lacks respect for the emperor should be punished by death. As they do not define what lack of respect is, anything can furnish a pretext for taking the life of whomever one wants and for exterminating whatever family one wants.

Vagueness in the crime of high treason is enough to make government degenerate into despotism. I shall treat the subject at length in the Book "On the composition of the laws." [...]

Chapter 11   On Thoughts

A certain Marsyas dreamed he cut the throat of Dionysius. Dionysius had him put to death, saying that Marsyas would not have dreamed it at night if he had not thought it during the day. This was a great tyranny; for, even if he had thought it, he had not attempted it. Laws are charged with punishing only external actions.

Chapter 12   On Indiscreet Speech

Nothing makes the crime of high treason more arbitrary than when indiscreet speech becomes its material. Discourse is so subject to interpretation, there is so much difference between indiscretion and malice and so little in the expressions they use, that the law can scarcely subject speech to a capital penalty, unless it declares explicitly which speech is subject to it.

Speech does not form a *corpus delicti*: it remains only an idea. Most frequently it has no meaning in itself but rather in the tone in which it is spoken. Often when repeating the same words, one does not express the same meaning; the meaning depends on the link the words have with other things. Silence sometimes expresses more than any speech. Nothing is so equivocal. How, then, can one make speech a crime of high treason? Wherever this law is established, not only is there no longer liberty, there is not even its shadow. [. . .]

I do not intend to diminish the indignation one should have against those who want to stigmatize the glory of their prince, but I do say that if one wants to moderate despotism, punishing with a simple correction will suit these occasions better than an accusation of high treason, which is always terrible, even to the innocent.

Actionable acts are not an everyday occurrence; they may be observed by many people: a false accusation over facts can easily be clarified. The words that are joined to an act take on the nature of that action. Thus a man who goes into the public square to exhort the subjects to revolt becomes guilty of high treason, because the speech is joined to the act and participates in it. It is not speech that is punished but an act committed in which speech is used. Speech becomes criminal only when it prepares, when it accompanies, or when it follows a criminal act. Everything is turned upside down if speech is made a capital crime instead of being regarded as the sign of a capital crime. [. . .]

Chapter 13   On Writings

Writings contain something more permanent than speech, but when they do not prepare the way for high treason, they are not material to the crime of high treason. [. . .]

Satirical writings are scarcely known in despotic states, where dejection on the one hand and ignorance on the other produce neither the talent nor the will to write them. In democracy, they are not prevented, for the very reason that they are prohibited in the government of one alone. As they are usually composed against powerful people, they flatter the spitefulness of the people who govern in a democracy. In a monarchy, they are prohibited, but they have been made an object of police rather than of crime. They can amuse the general spitefulness, console malcontents, reduce envy of those in high positions, give the people the patience to suffer, and make them laugh about their sufferings. [. . .]

Chapter 18   How Dangerous It Is in Republics to Punish Excessively the Crime of High Treason

When a republic has destroyed those who want to upset it, one must hasten to put an end to vengeances, penalties, and even rewards.

One cannot inflict great punishments, and consequently, make great changes, without putting a great power into the hands of a few citizens. It is better then, in this case, to pardon many than to punish many, to exile few than to exile many, to leave men their goods than to multiply confiscations. On the pretext of avenging the republic, one would establish the tyranny of the avengers. It is not a question of destroying the one who dominates but of destroying domination. One must return as quickly as possible to the ordinary pace of government where the laws protect all and are armed against no one. [...]

Chapter 19   How the Usage of Liberty Is Suspended in a Republic

There are, in the states where one sets the most store by liberty, laws that violate it for a single person in order to keep it for all. Such are what are called *bills of attainder* in England. They are related to those laws of Athens that were enacted against an individual provided they were made by the vote of six thousand citizens. They are related to those laws made in Rome against individual citizens, which were called *privileges*. They were made only in the great estates of the people. But, however the people made them, Cicero wanted them abolished, because the force of the law consists only in its being enacted for everyone. I admit, however, that the usage of the freest peoples that ever lived on earth makes me believe that there are cases where a veil has to be drawn, for a moment, over liberty, as one hides the statues of the gods.

Book XX On the Laws in Their Relation to Commerce, Considered in Its Nature and Its Distinction

Chapter 1   On Commerce

[...] Commerce cures destructive prejudices, and it is an almost general rule that everywhere there are gentle mores, there is commerce and that everywhere there is commerce, there are gentle mores.

Therefore, one should not be surprised if our mores are less fierce than they were formerly. Commerce has spread knowledge of the mores of all nations everywhere; they have been compared to each other, and good things have resulted from this.

One can say that the laws of commerce perfect mores for the same reason that these same laws ruin mores. Commerce corrupts pure mores, and this was the subject of Plato's complaints; it polishes and softens barbarous mores, as we see every day.

Chapter 2   On the Spirit of Commerce

The natural effect of commerce is to lead to peace. Two nations that trade with each other become reciprocally dependent; if one has an interest in buying, the other has an interest in selling, and all unions are founded on mutual needs.

But, if the spirit of commerce unites nations, it does not unite individuals in the same way. We see that in countries where one is affected only by the spirit of commerce, there is traffic in all human activities and all moral virtues; the smallest things, those required by humanity, are done or given for money.

The spirit of commerce produces in men a certain feeling for exact justice, opposed on the one hand to banditry and on the other to those moral virtues that make it so that one does not always discuss one's own interests alone and that one can neglect them for those of others. [...]

David Hume *Political Essays* (1772)

That Politics May Be Reduced to a Science[9]

It is a question with several, whether there be any essential difference between one form of government and another? and, whether every form may not become good or bad, according as it is well or ill administered? Were it once admitted, that all governments are alike, and that the only difference consists in the character and conduct of the governors, most political disputes would be at an end, and all *Zeal* for one constitution above another, must be esteemed mere bigotry and folly. But, though a friend to moderation, I cannot forbear condemning this sentiment, and should be sorry to think, that human affairs admit of no greater stability, than what they receive from the casual humours and characters of particular men. [...]

So great is the force of laws, and of particular forms of government, and so little dependence have they on the humours and tempers of men, that consequences almost as general and certain may sometimes be deduced from them, as any which the mathematical sciences afford us. [...]

But in order to prove more fully, that politics admit of general truths, which are invariable by the humour or education either of subject or sovereign, it may not be amiss to observe some other principles of this science, which may seem to deserve that character. [...]

There is an observation in Machiavel, with regard to the conquests of Alexander the Great, which, I think, may be regarded as one of those eternal political truths, which no time nor accidents can vary. It may seem strange, says that politician, that such sudden conquests, as those of Alexander, should be possessed so peaceably by his successors, and that the Persians, during all the confusions and civil wars among the Greeks, never made the smallest effort towards the recovery of their former independent government. To satisfy us concerning the cause of this remarkable event, we may consider, that a monarch may govern his subjects in two different ways. He may either follow the maxims of the eastern princes, and stretch his authority so far as to leave no distinction of rank among his subjects, but what proceeds immediately from himself; no advantages of birth; no hereditary honours and possessions; and, in a word, no credit among the people, except from his commission alone. Or a monarch may exert his power after a milder manner, like other European princes; and leave other sources of honour, beside his smile and favour: Birth, titles, possessions, valour, integrity, knowledge, or great and fortunate achievements. In the former species of government, after a conquest, it is impossible ever to shake off the yoke; since no one possesses, among the people, so much personal credit and authority as to begin such an enterprize: Whereas, in the latter, the least misfortune, or discord among the victors, will encourage the vanquished to take arms, who have leaders ready to prompt and conduct them in every undertaking. [...]

[9] D. Hume, *Essays and Treatises on Several Subjects, Vol. I: Essays Moral, Political, and Literary* (Edinburgh: Printed for Bell & Bradfute, etc., 1825), pp. 12–26.

Of the Original Contract[10]

As no party, in the present age, can well support itself without a philosophical or speculative system of principles, annexed to its political or practical one, we accordingly find, that each of the factions, into which this nation is divided, has reared up a fabric of the former kind, in order to protect and cover that scheme of actions which it pursues. The people being commonly very rude builders, especially in this speculative way, and more especially still, when actuated by party zeal; it is natural to imagine, that their workmanship must be a little unshapely, and discover evident marks of that violence and hurry in which it was raised. The one party, by tracing up government to the Deity, endeavour to render it so sacred and inviolate, that it must be little less than sacrilege, however tyrannical it may become, to touch or invade it in the smallest article. The other party, by founding government altogether on the consent of the People, suppose that there is a kind of *original contract*, by which the subjects have tacitly reserved the power of resisting their sovereign, when ever they find themselves aggrieved by that authority, with which they have, for certain purposes, voluntarily entrusted him. These are the speculative principles of the two parties; and these too are the practical consequences deduced from them. [...]

That the Deity is the ultimate author of all government, will never be denied by any, who admit a general providence, and allow, that all events in the universe are conducted by a uniform plan, and directed to wise purposes. As it is impossible for the human race to subsist, at least in any comfortable or secure state, without the protection of government; this institution must certainly have been intended by that beneficent Being, who means the good of all his creatures: And as it has universally, in fact, taken place, in all countries, and all ages, we may conclude, with still greater certainty, that it was intended by that omniscient Being, who can never be deceived by any event or operation. But since he gave rise to it, not by any particular or miraculous interposition, but by his concealed and universal efficacy, a sovereign cannot, properly speaking, be called his vicegerent in any other sense than every power or force, being derived from him, may be said to act by his commission. Whatever actually happens is comprehended in the general plan or intention of Providence; nor has the greatest and most lawful prince any more reason, upon that account, to plead a peculiar sacredness or inviolable authority, than an inferior magistrate, or even an usurper, or even a robber and a pyrate. The same divine superintendant, who, for wise purposes, invested a Titus or a Trajan with authority, did also, for purposes, no doubt, equally wise, though unknown, bestow power on a Borgia or an Angria. The same causes, which gave rise to the sovereign power in every state, established likewise every petty jurisdiction in it, and every limited authority. A constable, therefore, no less than a king, acts by a divine commission, and possesses an indefeasible right.

When we consider how nearly equal all men are in their bodily force, and even in their mental powers and faculties, till cultivated by education; we must necessarily allow, that nothing but their own consent could at first associate them together, and

---

[10] Hume, *Essays and Treatises on Several Subjects, Vol. I*, pp. 444–66.

subject them to any authority. The people, if we trace government to its first origin in the woods and desarts, are the source of all power and jurisdiction, and voluntarily, for the sake of peace and order, abandoned their native liberty, and received laws from their equal and companion. The conditions, upon which they were willing to submit, were either expressed, or were so clear and obvious, that it might well be esteemed superfluous to express them. If this, then, be meant by the *original contract*, it cannot be denied, that all government is, at first, founded on a contract, and that the most ancient rude combinations of mankind were formed chiefly by that principle. In vain are we asked in what records this charter of our liberties is registered. It was not written on parchment, nor yet on leaves or barks of trees. It preceded the use of writing and all the other civilized arts of life. But we trace it plainly in the nature of man, and in the equality, or something approaching equality, which we find in all the individuals of that species. The force, which now prevails, and which is founded on fleets and armies, is plainly political, and derived from authority, the effect of established government. A man's natural force consists only in the vigour of his limbs, and the firmness of his courage; which could never subject multitudes to the command of one. Nothing but their own consent, and their sense of the advantages resulting from peace and order, could have had that influence.

Yet even this consent was long very imperfect, and could not be the basis of a regular administration. The chieftain, who had probably acquired his influence during the continuance of war, ruled more by persuasion than command; and till he could employ force to reduce the refractory and disobedient, the society could scarcely be said to have attained a state of civil government. No compact or agreement, it is evident, was expressly formed for general submission; an idea far beyond the comprehension of savages: Each exertion of authority in the chieftain must have been particular, and called forth by the present exigencies of the case: The sensible utility, resulting from his interposition, made these exertions become daily more frequent; and their frequency gradually produced an habitual, and, if you please to call it so, a voluntary, and therefore precarious, acquiescence in the people.

But philosophers, who have embraced a party (if that be not a contradiction in terms) are not contented with these concessions. They assert, not only that government in its earliest infancy arose from consent or rather the voluntary acquiescence of the people; but also that, even at present, when it has attained full maturity, it rests on no other foundation. They affirm, that all men are still born equal, and owe allegiance to no prince or government, unless bound by the obligation and sanction of a *promise*. And as no man, without some equivalent, would forego the advantages of his native liberty, and subject himself to the will of another; this promise is always understood to be conditional, and imposes on him no obligation, unless he meet with justice and protection from his sovereign. These advantages the sovereign promises him in return; and if he fail in the execution, he has broken, on his part, the articles of engagement, and has thereby freed his subject from all obligations to allegiance. Such, according to these philosophers, is the foundation of authority in every government; and such the right of resistance, possessed by every subject.

But would these reasoners look abroad into the world, they would meet with nothing that, in the least, corresponds to their ideas, or can warrant so refined and philosophical a system. On the contrary, we find every where princes who claim their subjects as their property, and assert their independent right of sovereignty, from conquest or succession. We find also every where subjects who acknowledge this right in their prince, and suppose themselves born under obligations of obedience to a certain sovereign, as much as under the ties of reverence and duty to certain parents. [. . .] Obedience or subjection becomes so familiar, that most men never make any enquiry about its origin or cause, more than about the principle of gravity, resistance, or the most universal laws of nature. Or if curiosity ever move them, as soon as they learn that they themselves and their ancestors have, for several ages, or from time immemorial, been subject to such a form of government or such a family; they immediately acquiesce, and acknowledge their obligation to allegiance. [. . .] It is strange, that an act of the mind, which every individual is supposed to have formed, and after he came to the use of reason too, otherwise it could have no authority; that this act, I say, should be so much unknown to all of them, that, over the face of the whole earth, there scarcely remain any traces or memory of it. [. . .]

Almost all the governments, which exist at present, or of which there remains any record in history, have been founded originally, either on usurpation or conquest, or both, without any pretence of a fair consent or voluntary subjection of the people. When an artful and bold man is placed at the head of an army or faction, it is often easy for him, by employing, sometimes violence, sometimes false pretences, to establish his dominion over a people a hundred times more numerous than his partisans. [. . .]

But where no force interposes, and election takes place; what is this election so highly vaunted? It is either the combination of a few great men, who decide for the whole, and will allow of no opposition; or it is the fury of a multitude, that follow a seditious ringleader, who is not known, perhaps, to a dozen among them, and who owes his advancement merely to his own impudence, or to the momentary caprice of his fellows.

Are these disorderly elections, which are rare too, of such mighty authority as to be the only lawful foundation of all government and allegiance? [. . .]

It is in vain to say, that all governments are or should be at first founded on popular consent, as much as the necessity of human affairs will admit. This favours entirely my pretension. I maintain, that human affairs will never admit of this consent, seldom of the appearance of it; but that conquest or usurpation, that is, in plain terms, force, by dissolving the ancient governments, is the origin of almost all the new ones, which were ever established in the world. And that in the few cases where consent may seem to have taken place, it was commonly so irregular, so confined, or so much intermixed either with fraud or violence, that it cannot have any great authority.

My intention here is not to exclude the consent of the people from being one just foundation of government where it has place. It is surely the best and most sacred of any. I only contend, that it has very seldom had place in any degree, and never almost in its full extent. And that therefore some other foundation of government must also be admitted.

Were all men possessed of so inflexible a regard to justice, that of themselves, they would totally abstain from the properties of others; they had for ever remained in a state of absolute liberty, without subjection to any magistrate or political society: But this is a state of perfection of which human nature is justly deemed incapable. Again, were all men possessed of so perfect an understanding, as always to know their own interests, no form of government had ever been submitted to, but what was established on consent, and was fully canvassed by every member of the society: But this state of perfection is likewise much superior to human nature. [. . .]

When a new government is established, by whatever means, the people are commonly dissatisfied with it, and pay obedience more from fear and necessity, than from any idea of allegiance or of moral obligation. The prince is watchful and jealous, and must carefully guard against every beginning or appearance of insurrection. Time, by degrees, removes all these difficulties, and accustoms the nation to regard, as their lawful or native princes, that family which, at first they considered as usurpers or foreign conquerors. In order to found this opinion, they have no recourse to any notion of voluntary consent or promise, which, they know, never was, in this case, either expected or demanded. The original establishment was formed by violence, and submitted to from necessity. The subsequent administration is also supported by power, and acquiesced in by the people, not as a matter of choice, but of obligation. They imagine not, that their consent gives their prince a title: But they willingly consent, because they think, that, from long possession, he has acquired a title, independent of their choice or inclination.

Should it be said, that, by living under the dominion of a prince which one might leave, every individual has given a tacit consent to his authority, and promised him obedience; it may be answered, that such an implied consent can only have place, where a man imagines, that the matter depends on his choice. But where he thinks (as all mankind do who are born under established governments) that by his birth he owes allegiance to a certain prince or certain form of government; it would be absurd to infer a consent or choice, which he expressly, in this case, renounces and disclaims. [. . .]

The truest *tacit* consent of this kind, that is ever observed, is when a foreigner settles in any country, and is beforehand acquainted with the prince, and government, and laws, to which he must submit: Yet is his allegiance, though more voluntary, much less expected or depended on, than that of a natural born subject. On the contrary, his native prince still asserts a claim to him. And if he punish not the renegade, when he seizes him in war with his new prince's commission; this clemency is not founded on the municipal law, which in all countries condemns the prisoner; but on the consent of princes, who have agreed to this indulgence, in order to prevent reprisals. [. . .]

But as human society is in perpetual flux, one man every hour going out of the world, another coming into it, it is necessary, in order to preserve stability in government, that the new brood should conform themselves to the established constitution, and nearly follow the path which their fathers, treading in the footsteps of theirs, had marked out to them. Some innovations must necessarily have place in every human institution; and it is happy where the enlightened genius of the age give these a direction to the side of reason, liberty, and justice: But violent innovations no individual is entitled to make: They are even dangerous to be attempted by the legislature: More ill than good is ever to be expected from them: And if history affords examples to the contrary, they are not to be drawn into precedent, and are only to be regarded as proofs, that the science of politics affords few rules, which will not admit of some exception, and which may not sometimes be controuled by fortune and accident. [...]

But would we have a more regular, at least a more philosophical, refutation of this principle of an original contract or popular consent; perhaps, the following observations may suffice.

All *moral* duties may be divided into two kinds. The *first* are those, to which men are impelled by a natural instinct or immediate propensity, which operates on them, independent of all ideas of obligation, and of all views, either to public or private utility. Of this nature are, love of children, gratitude to benefactors, pity to the unfortunate. When we reflect on the advantage which results to society from such humane instincts, we pay them the just tribute of moral approbation and esteem: But the person actuated by them feels their power and influence antecedent to any such reflection.

The *second* kind of moral duties are such as are not supported by any original instinct of nature, but are performed entirely from a sense of obligation, when we consider the necessities of human society, and the impossibility of supporting it, if these duties were neglected. It is thus *justice*, or a regard to the property of others, *fidelity*, or the observance of promises, become obligatory, and acquire an authority over mankind. For as it is evident that every man loves himself better than any other person, he is naturally impelled to extend his acquisitions as much as possible; and nothing can restrain him in this propensity but reflection and experience, by which he learns the pernicious effects of that licence, and the total dissolution of society which must ensue from it. His original inclination, therefore, or instinct, is here checked and restrained by a subsequent judgment or observation.

The case is precisely the same with the political or civil duty of *allegiance*, as with the natural duties of justice and fidelity. Our primary instincts lead us, either to indulge ourselves in unlimited freedom, or to seek dominion over others; and it is reflection only which engages us to sacrifice such strong passions to the interests of peace and public order. A small degree of experience and observation suffices to teach us, that society cannot possibly be maintained without the authority of magistrates, and that this authority must soon fall into contempt, where exact obedience is not paid to it. The observation of these general and obvious interests is the source of all allegiance, and of that moral obligation, which we attribute to it.

What necessity, therefore, is there to found the duty of *allegiance* or obedience to magistrates on that of *fidelity*, or a regard to promises, and to suppose, that it is the consent of each individual, which subjects him to government; when it appears, that both allegiance and fidelity stand precisely on the same foundation, and are both submitted to by mankind, on account of the apparent interests and necessities of human society? We are bound to obey our sovereign, it is said, because we have given a tacit promise to that purpose. But why are we bound to observe our promise? It must here be asserted, that the commerce and intercourse of mankind, which are of such mighty advantage, can have no security where men pay no regard to their engagements. In like manner, may it be said, that men could not live at all in society, at least in a civilized society, without laws, and magistrates and judges, to prevent the encroachments of the strong upon the weak, of the violent upon the just and equitable. The obligation to allegiance being of like force and authority with the obligation to fidelity, we gain nothing by resolving the one into the other. The general interests or necessities of society are sufficient to establish both.

If the reason be asked of that obedience, which we are bound to pay to government, I readily answer, *because society could not otherwise subsist*; and this answer is clear and intelligible to all mankind. Your answer is, *because we should keep our word*. But besides, that no body, till trained in a philosophical system, can either comprehend or relish this answer, besides this, I say, you find yourself embarrassed, when it is asked, *why we are bound to keep our word*? Nor can you give any answer, but what would immediately, without any circuit, have accounted for our obligation to allegiance.

But *to whom is allegiance due*? *And who is our lawful sovereign*? This question is often the most difficult of any, and liable to infinite discussions. When people are so happy, that they can answer, *Our present sovereign, who inherits, in a direct line, from ancestors, that have governed us for many ages*: This answer admits of no reply, even though historians, in tracing up to the remotest antiquity, the origin of that royal family, may find, as commonly happens, that its first authority was derived from usurpation and violence. [...]

In an absolute government, when there is no legal prince, who has a title to the throne, it may safely be determined to belong to the first occupant. Instances of this kind are but too frequent, especially in the eastern monarchies. When any race of princes expires, the will or destination of the last sovereign will be regarded as a title. [...] The general bond of obligation, which binds us to government, is the interest and necessities of society; and this obligation is very strong. The determination of it to this or that particular prince, or form of government, is frequently more uncertain and dubious. Present possession has considerable authority in these cases, and greater than in private property; because of the disorders which attend all revolutions and changes of government.

We shall only observe, before we conclude, that though an appeal to general opinion may justly, in the speculative sciences of metaphysics, natural philosophy, or astronomy, be deemed unfair and inconclusive, yet in all questions with regard to morals, as well as criticism, there is really no other standard, by which any controversy can ever be decided. And nothing is a clearer proof, that a theory of this kind is erroneous, than to find, that it leads to paradoxes, repugnant to the common sentiments of mankind, and to the practice and opinion of all nations and all ages. The doctrine, which founds all lawful government on an *original contract*, or consent of the people, is plainly of this kind; nor has the most noted of its partisans, in prosecution of it, scrupled to affirm, *that absolute monarchy is inconsistent with civil society, and so can be no form of civil government at all, and that the supreme power in a state cannot take from any man, by taxes and impositions, any part of his property, without his own consent or that of his representatives*. What authority any moral reasoning can have, which leads into opinions so wide of the general practice of mankind, in every place but this single kingdom, it is easy to determine. [...]

Of Passive Obedience[11]

In the former essay, we endeavoured to refute the *speculative* systems of politics advanced in this nation; as well the religious system of the one party, as the philosophical of the other. We come now to examine the *practical* consequences deduced by each party, with regard to the measures of submission due to sovereigns.

As the obligation to justice is founded entirely on the interests of society, which require mutual abstinence from property, in order to preserve peace among mankind; it is evident, that, when the execution of justice would be attended with very pernicious consequences, that virtue must be suspended, and give place to public utility, in such extraordinary and such pressing emergencies. The maxim, *fiat Justitia et ruat Cœlum*, let justice be performed, though the universe be destroyed, is apparently false, and by sacrificing the end to the means, shews a preposterous idea of the subordination of duties. What governor of a town makes any scruple of burning the suburbs, when they facilitate the approaches of the enemy? Or what general abstains from plundering a neutral country, when the necessities of war require it, and he cannot otherwise subsist his army? The case is the same with the duty of allegiance; and common sense teaches us, that, as government binds us to obedience only on account of its tendency to public utility, that duty must always, in extraordinary cases, when public ruin would evidently attend obedience, yield to the primary and original obligation. *Salus populi suprema Lex*, the safety of the people is the supreme law. This maxim is agreeable to the sentiments of mankind in all ages. [...]

Resistance, therefore, being admitted in extraordinary emergencies, the question can only be among good reasoners, with regard to the degree of necessity, which can justify resistance, and render it lawful or commendable. And here I must confess, that I shall always incline to their side, who draw the bond of allegiance very close, and consider an infringement of it as the last refuge in desperate cases, when the public is in the highest danger from violence and tyranny. For besides the mischiefs of a civil war, which commonly attends insurrection, it is certain, that, where a disposition to rebellion appears among any people, it is one chief cause of tyranny in the rulers, and forces them into many violent measures which they never would have embraced, had every one been inclined to submission and obedience. [...]

Besides, we must consider, that as obedience is our duty in the common course of things, it ought chiefly to be inculcated; nor can any thing be more preposterous than an anxious care and solicitude in stating all the cases in which resistance may be allowed. In like manner, though a philosopher reasonably acknowledges, in the course of an argument, that the rules of justice may be dispensed with in cases of urgent necessity; what should we think of a preacher or casuist, who should make it his chief study to find out such cases, and enforce them with all the vehemence of argument and eloquence? Would he not be better employed in inculcating the general doctrine, than in displaying the particular exceptions, which we are, perhaps, but too much inclined, of ourselves, to embrace and to extend? [...]

---

[11] Hume, *Essays and Treatises on Several Subjects, Vol. I*, pp. 467–71.

4 The Puritans

The Bi-Dimensional Covenant

The Puritans who arrived in the New World in the 1620s and the 1630s were not the first British colonists, as the colony of Virginia had been founded in 1607 as a commercial enterprise. These Puritans were no political theorists; they were, nevertheless, concerned about politics, but only because politics was supposed to serve their religious purposes. In Tocqueville's words, "they tore themselves away from the pleasures of home in obedience to a purely intellectual need. They braved the inevitable miseries of exile because they wished to ensure the victory of *an idea*."[1] This idea was a very ambitious one – to create perfect theologico-political communities in which the *invisible* would be made *visible* in this world. As *A Platform of Church Discipline* stipulated, "*Saints by calling* must have a *visible political union* among themselves, or else they are not yet a *particular* church." In other words, the Puritans wanted to bridge the gap between the world of transcendence and the world of immanence, and thus between religion and politics.

This conversion of the invisible into the visible was supposed to start with the individual. Each aspiring member of these theologico-political communities had to demonstrate his or her "authenticity" during the pre-conversion phase by *publicly* confessing their innermost sinful thoughts, and these inner struggles needed to be authenticated by "the visible saints." Furthermore, absent a superior authority to serve as judge, the selection of the "pillars of the church" relied on reciprocal scrutiny and detailed interrogations. Long before social media and the voluntary disclosure of one's private life to the public, Big Brother took the form of many small "brothers."

What fueled their religious drive was the peculiar position of the **Anglican Church**. Upset by the refusal of the pope to grant him a divorce, **King Henry VIII** had started the so-called **English Reformation** with the **Act of Supremacy** of 1534, which made him the head of the Church of England. Nevertheless, after declaring the separation from the Vatican, King Henry maintained both the hierarchy and the sacraments of the Catholic Church. Thus, the Anglican Church was from the very beginning neither fully Catholic nor fully Protestant, which for those who wanted to "purify" the Church of all its "papist" remnants was deeply disturbing. These religious dissenters clashed with the hierarchy of the Anglican Church and came to be labeled Puritans.

---

[1] Tocqueville, *Democracy in America*, p. 37 (emphasis in the original).

Fleeing religious persecution, some of them moved to the Netherlands and eventually came to decide that the New World offered them not only a safe haven (literally), by being so far away from all the powers that be, but also the opportunity to build, from scratch, voluntary communities dedicated to the same religious aim and upholding the same moral standards. However, they were not the only ones looking for new beginnings and new opportunities. Back then, the East Coast was the Wild West, where everything was possible. People crossed the Atlantic for a variety of reasons, not necessarily religious ones, yet the religious make-up of each colony ended up influencing its evolution. Composed mainly of **Anglicans** looking for economic profit, **Virginia** eventually had a culture and a constitution different from, say, **Pennsylvania**, founded by the **Quaker William Penn**, or from **Massachusetts**, made up mainly of **Puritans** and **Pilgrims** (Chapter 6). Consequently, when painting the founding with too broad a brush, one overlooks some important nuances.

For example, the famous *Mayflower Compact*, which created the foundation for the **Plymouth Colony** (eventually to be incorporated into the **Massachusetts Bay Colony**), was not technically a **compact**, but rather a **covenant**: *"we covenant and combine ourselves together into a civil body politic."* Nowadays, the differences between a contract, a compact, and a covenant appear insignificant, but back then they carried specific connotations. The <u>contract</u> was understood as a legally enforced agreement between two or more people; the <u>compact</u> was meant to create a tight-knit community; the <u>covenant</u> did the same, only in the presence of a higher witness/ authority (usually God or a king, or both, as in the case of the *Mayflower Compact*). "Put another way, a document which is a covenant can, by simply removing the reference to higher authority, be changed into a compact."[2]

Furthermore, the *Mayflower Compact* (or rather Covenant) was signed by the **Pilgrims** (not the Puritans) who were heading for Virginia, but ended up in what came to be known as Plymouth, Massachusetts; thus, under no jurisdiction whatso- ever, they were forced by necessity *to found* a new political authority, as did the ***Inhabitants upon the Piscataqua River***. The difference between the Pilgrims and the Puritans was that the former were so appalled by what they perceived as the corruption of the Anglican Church that they formally declared their separation from the Church of England. Thus, they were also known as **Separatists**. In practice though, when both the Pilgrims and the Puritans found themselves alone in the New World, thousands of miles away from their original source of political and religious authority, such formalities mattered less, and they became rather indistinguishable. Thus, from now on we will call them simply Puritans.

In terms of numbers, by today's standards, the Puritans were far from impressive. What came to be known as the **Great Migration** of the 1630s amounted to a little more than 20,000 people, scattered along the East Coast. Their ideas, however, would prove powerful enough to shape the entire American founding. As Tocqueville put it, as "[i]n a manner of speaking, the whole man already lies

---

[2] D. S. Lutz, "The Evolution of Covenant Form and Content as the Basis for Early American Political Culture" in D. J. Elazar (ed.), *The Covenant in the Nineteenth Century: The Decline of an American Tradition* (Lanham, MD: Rowman and Littlefield, 1994), p. 39.

swaddled in his cradle," so "[e]very people bears the marks of its origins" – and, according to him, the American people's origins were to be found in Puritan New England, not because it was the only "ingredient," but because it proved to be the most important. "The civilization of New England was like a bonfire on a hilltop, which, having spread its warmth to its immediate vicinity, tinges even the distant horizon with its glow."[3]

As mentioned in the Introduction, what made the Puritans exceptional was their particular understanding of covenants, and the ways they chose to implement them in this world. As David A. Weir observed, New England was a "covenanted society" in which everything revolved around one covenant or another.[4] Besides the distinctions they made between the *covenant of works*, the *covenant of grace*, and the *covenant of justification*, the Puritans managed – for a while – to juggle at the same time three others, loosely related to the first ones: the covenant of each individual with God (the *inward covenant* "betwixt God and the soul only"), the *church covenant* (the *visible* one), and *the covenant of each church with God*. While the church covenant resembled in its horizontality the **social contract theory**, by creating a religious community with an accepted government from the free accord of its individual members, the vertical covenant of each church with God was modeled after the classic, medieval **political contract** between the people, as a hierarchical *universitas*, and its rulers.

Yet since the same logic applied not just to the heavenly governance but to worldly governments as well, it opened the door for the right of a community – political or religious – to justly replace its rulers. As seen, for example, in the ***Providence Agreement***, to drop any religious reference when creating a new political community, by consenting to the will of the majority, was an easy step. Nevertheless, such a subjection "in active and passive obedience" to the will of the majority did not automatically imply either the rejection of the corporatist apprehension of the people, or the denial of a certain hierarchy of merits. As stipulated in ***A Platform of Church Discipline***, "A church being free, cannot become subject to any [one] but by a free election; yet when such a people do choose any to be over them in the Lord, then do they become subject, and most willingly submit to their ministry in the Lord, whom they have chosen." Thus, both the **liberal** apprehension of the people, as a collection of equal individuals, on the one hand, and the **republican** understanding of the people as a corporate and hierarchically structured whole, on the other hand, came to be *practically* acknowledged throughout the settlements of New England. Therefore, "American Puritanism managed to combine the traditional and the radical, the voluntary and the authoritarian, as well as a host of other diametrically opposed impulses, into one organic whole that apparently thrived on its own internal conflicts."[5] This organic vision of different callings for each of its members is well

---

[3] Tocqueville, *Democracy in America*, pp. 31, 36.

[4] D. A. Weir, *Early New England : A Covenanted Society* (Cambridge: William B. Eerdmans, 2005). Imagine how outrageous the Puritans would have found Hobbes's claim that one cannot make covenants with God or beasts, for one party does not understand the terms.

[5] S. Foster, *Their Solitary Way: The Puritan Social Ethic in the First Century of Settlement in New England* (New Haven and London: Yale University Press, 1971), p. xvi.

captured in the writings of **William Perkins** (1558–1602), long before the Great Migration began.

The same rationale by which the *inner* covenant was supposed to be reflected by the *church* covenant informed not only the covenants among persons, but also the ones among different *political bodies*. As seen in *The Fundamental Orders of Connecticut* (1639), people from different towns and congregations did "associate and conjoin [. . .] to be as one Public State or Commonwealth." This **Confederation** served a double purpose: "to maintain and preserve the liberty and purity of the Gospel," but also to regulate "civil affairs" according to a detailed set of "Laws, Rules, Orders and Decrees." Each town was to elect two deputies, who in turn would participate in elections during the twice-yearly General Assemblies.

The **English Civil War** gave impetus to the formation of an even more significant confederation, one that a century later would come to inspire the first Constitution of the United States, namely the *Articles of Confederation and Perpetual Union*. Largely forgotten nowadays, *The Articles of Confederation of the United Colonies of New England*, signed by Massachusetts, New Plymouth, Connecticut, and New Haven, represented a huge step forward in the creation of the United States as we know it today (Chapters 5 and 6).[6]

Each Plantation or Jurisdiction, *regardless of its size and population*, enjoyed equal representation by two Commissioners, since the people from each colony were apprehended as equal, like individuals entering a covenant, despite their different capabilities. Undeniably, the document introduced features that would be imitated by all future attempts to unite the colonies. Harry M. Ward identified several essential features of this Confederation: (1) representation by whole states; (2) equal votes for each state; (3) two delegates from each state; (4) a national forum; (5) power to make treatises with foreign states; (6) war powers, such as declaring war and calling into service of the "Country" the militia of the states; (7) regulatory powers, though without enforcement mechanisms; (8) oversight of Indian affairs of the colonies; (9) a watchdog for the common welfare; (10) an entrenchment of conservative interests among the majority of its members.[7]

John Winthrop (1587/8–1649) was one of the people who promoted this political arrangement years before it became a reality. In 1638, Winthrop's explanation for postponing the confederation was "another plot the old serpent had against us, by sowing jealousies and differences between us and our friends at Connecticut, and also Plymouth."[8] This is an observation worth remembering, as it reveals a perennial problem: *the connection between the cultural identity and the political identity is a two-way street*. On the one hand, people sharing a common <u>cultural</u> identity – ethnic, racial, religious, linguistic, and the like – aspire to create their own political communities meant to protect these identities. Yet, on the other hand, <u>politically</u> created communities tend to create their own culture, despite ethnic, racial, religious,

---

[6] Founded by dissenters such as Roger Williams and Anne Hutchinson, Rhode Island was excluded from the start, its government being considered anarchical and heretical.

[7] H. M. Ward, *The United Colonies of New England, 1643–90* (New York: Vantage Press, 1961), pp. 379–80.

[8] Quoted in Ward, *The United Colonies*, p. 51.

or linguistic similarities. It was a conundrum faced not only by the first colonists, but also by the generations to come.

Winthrop was one of the leading figures in the founding of the Massachusetts Bay Colony; he was elected eighteen times as governor or lieutenant-governor. As such, he became acutely aware of the difficulties involved in answering "[t]he great questions that have troubled the *country*, [namely] the authority of the magistrates and the liberty of the people" (***Little Speech on Liberty***). Even before setting foot in the New World, in his ***Model of Christian Charity***, he laid out many of what would become the defining features of the theologico-political Puritan communities, like the organic vision of a community bonded by love, entering into a covenant with God in order to become "a city upon a hill." "The eyes of all people are upon us."

For Winthrop, *both love and liberty are twofold*. The *outward* love is propelled by "the variety and difference of the creatures" so that "every man might have need of others. And from hence they might be all knit together in the bonds of brotherly affection." The *inward* love, on the contrary, is based upon similitude, "for the ground of love is an apprehension of some resemblance in the things loved. [...] So a mother loves her child, because she thoroughly conceives a resemblance of herself in it. Thus it is between the members of Christ; each discerns, by the work of the Spirit, his own Image and resemblance in another, and therefore cannot but love him as he loves himself." "There is also a twofold liberty," one natural, shared with beasts, which is "incompatible and inconsistent with authority," and one "civil or federal," the moral liberty which is "the proper end and object of authority," one in which the magistrates, being called (elected) by the people have their authority from God. Without acknowledging it, no community is possible.

By contemporary standards, John Winthrop would appear a **radical-conservative**, but by the standards of his time he was considered a **moderate** (hence his repeated re-election). In **Samuel Willard**'s (1640–1707) words, he had the character of a good ruler. For example, though he disagreed with **Roger Williams**, Winthrop warned him about the decision to banish Williams from the colony in the middle of the winter, thus saving his life and – unintentionally – helping to create what eventually became the colony of Rhode Island.

Roger Williams (1603–1683) had strong separatist views and would not accept any congregation that refused to repudiate their ties with the Church of England. As a result, he declined the position of teacher offered by the Boston congregation; the Salem congregation withdrew its offer for the same reasons, and he found Plymouth's Pilgrims insufficiently separatist, so he returned to Salem and started preaching as an unofficial assistant to Pastor Skelton. After Skelton's death, Williams was offered the position of formal pastor of the congregation, and he began openly preaching the separation of civil affairs from spiritual ones.

The detail often left out of this well-known picture, however, is that Williams's concerns with the separation of church and state, in modern parlance, was not meant to protect the state from religious interferences – rather the opposite. The aim was to protect the Church from state interference, as was the practice in Massachusetts. "Roger Williams's assertion of toleration came not from a political and constitutional scruple but from a conception of the spiritual life so exalted that he could not see it contaminated by earthly compulsion."[9] This contradicted the views of mainstream Puritans like **Nathaniel Ward** (1578–1652): "He that is willing to tolerate any Religion, or discrepant way of Religion, besides his own, unless it be in matters meerly indifferent, either doubts of his own, or is not sincere in it." Not surprisingly, Williams, more Puritan than the Puritans, eventually became disappointed by all churches, yet through this development he started the process of both democratization and religious fragmentation.

Such twists of fate and faith, literally speaking, can be easily understood once one considers "the flexibility of covenant theory and practice," which can "explain, therefore, the various highways and byways that the covenant concept and the various forms of Puritanism took." The emphasis on the vertical or on the horizontal dimension of the covenant made all the difference when it came to compromise, as Williams came to experience first-hand. "Providence had a reputation for being one of the most argumentative plantations in New England, and within a period of ten years it signed at least five more civil covenants in an attempt to draw its various factions together."[10]

John Cotton (1585–1682) was no friend of Roger Williams, with whom he had heated exchanges. He found Williams's insistence on the separation between church and state too extreme, yet he also opposed **Presbyterianism** for being too hierarchical. Instead, he militated for **Congregationalism**, which allowed every church (congregation) the right to control its affairs independently.[11] Even so, this support for the decentralization of church governance did not make him a supporter of democracy, of which he wrote, "Democracy I do not conceive that ever God did ordain as a fit government either for church or commonwealth." But once again, once spelled out, ideas take on a life of their own and can have unintended consequences. The "democratic revolution" started in New England almost at the very beginning of the colonization and, as Tocqueville put it, "[e]veryone played a part: those who strove to ensure democracy's success as well as those who never dreamt of serving it; those who fought for it as well as those who declared themselves its enemies."[12]

John Wise (1652–1725) is the perfect exemplification of this development. Unlike Cotton, he believed Congregationalism was proof that God wanted democracy to rule both churches and governments. After acknowledging God's wisdom, he moved swiftly from Divine Laws to Natural and Human Laws. "It is certain Civil Government in General, is a very Admirable Result of Providence, and an Incomparable Benefit to Man-kind, yet must needs be acknowledged to be the Effect of Human Free-Compacts and not of Divine Institution." Like Locke, he agreed that "The Internal Native Liberty of Mans Nature [...] does not consist in a loose and ungovernable Freedom, or in unbounded Licence of Acting." Every man "must be acknowledged equal to every Man."

---

[9] P. Miller, *The New England Mind* (Boston: Beacon Press, 1961), p. 454.

[10] Weir, *Early New England*, pp. 223, 103.

[11] Because of the peculiar situation of the Anglican Church, the beheading of Charles I, after the English Civil War, implied literally the beheading of the Church as well. Thus, the question arose as to who was now in charge: the bishops and archbishops (**Episcopalians**), the Elders (**Presbyterians**), or the congregation (**Congregationalists**)? Centuries later, this debate still persists today.

[12] Tocqueville, *Democracy in America*, p. 6.

Even if Aristotle suggested that "'Nothing is more suitable to Nature, than that those who Excel in Understanding and Prudence, should Rule and Controul those who are less happy in those Advantages' [...] there is room for an Answer. That it would be the greatest absurdity to believe, that Nature actually Invests the Wise with a Sovereignty over the weak [...] for that no Sovereignty can be Established, unless some Humane Deed, or Covenant Precede."

Thus, both the **social compact** and the following **political compacts** were needed to legitimize the "rule and control of those who exceed in understanding and prudence to rule over those who are less happy in those advantages."

After opposing the taxation of the colonists by the British and leading a rebellion against what he perceived as unfair taxation, John Wise was considered by many the forefather of the American Revolutionary War. Yet it was less his actions and more his furtherance of the people's two bodies and the respective social and political contract theories that provided the Patriots with the much-needed ideological ammunition in the years to come.

EXAMPLES OF COMPACTS AND FIRST CONSTITUTIONS

The Mayflower Compact (1620)[13]

In the name of God, Amen. We, whose names are underwritten, the loyall subjects of our dread soveraigne Lord, King James, by the Grace of God, of Great Britain, Franc, and Ireland king, defender of the faith, etc.

Haveing undertaken, for the glorie of God, and advancemente of the Christian faith, and the honour of our king and countrie, a voyage to plant the first colonie in the Northerne parts of Virginia, doe by these presents solemnly and mutualy in the presence of God, and one another, covenant and combine our selves togeather into a civill body politick, for our better ordering and preservation, and furtherance of the ends aforesaid; and by vertue hearof to enacte, constitute, and frame, shuch just and equall lawes, ordinances, acts, constitutions, and offices, from time to time, as shall be thought most meete and convenient for the generall good of the Colonie, unto which we promise all due submission and obedience. In witnes whereof we have hereunder subscribed our names at Cape-Codd the 11 of November, in the year of the raigne of our souveraigne lord, King James, of England, France, and Ireland, the eighteenth, and of Scotland the fifty-fourth. Anno Dom. 1620.

Covenant of the First Church in Charlestown-Boston (July 30, 1630)[14]

In the name of our Lord Jesus Christ, and in obedience to his holy will and divine ordinance, we whose names are hereunder written, being by his most wise and good providence brought together in this part of America in the Bay of Massachusetts, and desirous to unite ourselves into one congregation or church under the Lord Jesus Christ our Head, in such sort as becomes all those whom he has redeemed and sanctified to himself,

[We] do hereby solemnly and religiously, as in his most holy presence, promise and bind ourselves to walk in all our ways according to the rule of the gospel, and in all sincere conformity to his holy ordinances, and in mutual love and respect each to other, so near as God shall give us grace.

The Providence Agreement (August 20, 1637)[15]

We whose names are hereunder, desirous to inhabit in the town of Providence, do promise to subject ourselves in active and passive obedience to all such orders or

---

[13] From W. Bradford, *History of Plymouth Plantation, 1620–1647*, Vol. I (Boston: Houghton Mifflin, 1912), pp. 190–1.

[14] From L. Woolsey Bacon, *The Story of the Churches: The Congregationalists* (New York: The Baker & Taylor Co., 1904), pp. 47–8.

[15] From C. Evans, "Oaths of Allegiance in Colonial New England," *Proceedings of the American Antiquarian Society*, 31 (1921), p. 424.

agreements as shall be made for the public good of the body in an orderly way, by the major consent of present inhabitants, masters of families, incorporated together in a Towne fellowship, and others whom they shall admit unto them only in civil things.

The Fundamental Orders of Connecticut (1639)[16]

For as much as it hath pleased Almighty God by the wise disposition of his divine providence so to order and dispose of things that we the Inhabitants and Residents of Windsor, Hartford and Wethersfield are now cohabiting and dwelling in and upon the River of Connectecotte and the lands thereunto adjoining; and well knowing where a people are gathered together the word of God requires that to maintain the peace and union of such a people there should be an orderly and decent Government established according to God, to order and dispose of the affairs of the people at all seasons as occasion shall require; do therefore associate and conjoin ourselves to be as one Public State or Commonwealth; and do for ourselves and our successors and such as shall be adjoined to us at any time hereafter, enter into Combination and Confederation together, to maintain and preserve the liberty and purity of the Gospel of our Lord Jesus which we now profess, as also, the discipline of the Churches, which according to the truth of the said Gospel is now practiced amongst us; as also in our civil affairs to be guided and governed according to such Laws, Rules, Orders and Decrees as shall be made, ordered, and decreed as followeth:

1   It is Ordered, sentenced, and decreed, that there shall be yearly two General Assemblies or Courts, the one the second Thursday in April, the other the second Thursday in September following; the first shall be called the Court of Election, wherein shall be yearly chosen from time to time, so many Magistrates and other public Officers as shall be found requisite: Whereof one to be chosen Governor for the year ensuing and until another be chosen, and no other Magistrate to be chosen for more than one year: provided always there be six chosen besides the Governor, which being chosen and sworn according to an Oath recorded for that purpose, shall have the power to administer justice according to the Laws here established, and for want thereof, according to the Rule of the Word of God; which choice shall be made by all that are admitted freemen and have taken the Oath of Fidelity, and do cohabit within this Jurisdiction having been admitted Inhabitants by the major part of the Town wherein they live or the major part of such as shall be then present.

2   It is Ordered, sentenced, and decreed, that the election of the aforesaid Magistrates shall be in this manner: every person present and qualified for choice shall bring in (to the person deputed to receive them) one single paper with the name of him written in it whom he desires to have Governor, and that he that hath the greatest number of papers shall be Governor for that year. And the rest of the Magistrates or public officers to be chosen in this manner: the Secretary for the time being shall first read the names of all

---

[16] From F. Newton Thorpe, *The Federal and State Constitutions, Colonial Charters, and Other Organic Laws of the States, Territories, and Colonies Now or Heretofore Forming the United States of America* (Washington, DC: Government Printing Office, 1909) via the Avalon Project, https://avalon .law.yale.edu/.

that are to be put to choice and then shall severally nominate them distinctly, and every one that would have the person nominated to be chosen shall bring in one single paper written upon, and he that would not have him chosen shall bring in a blank; and every one that hath more written papers than blanks shall be a Magistrate for that year; which papers shall be received and told by one or more that shall be then chosen by the court and sworn to be faithful therein; but in case there should not be six chosen as aforesaid, besides the Governor, out of those which are nominated, than he or they which have the most writen papers shall be a Magistrate or Magistrates for the ensuing year, to make up the aforesaid number. [...]

4   It is Ordered, sentenced, and decreed, that no person be chosen Governor above once in two years, and that the Governor be always a member of some approved Congregation, and formerly of the Magistracy within this Jurisdiction; and that all the Magistrates, Freemen of this Commonwealth. [...]

5   It is Ordered, sentenced, and decreed, that to the aforesaid Court of Election the several Towns shall send their deputies, and when the Elections are ended they may proceed in any public service as at other Courts. Also the other General Court in September shall be for making of laws, and any other public occasion, which concerns the good of the Commonwealth. [...]

7   It is Ordered, sentenced, and decreed, that after there are warrants given out for any of the said General Courts, the Constable or Constables of each Town, shall forthwith give notice distinctly to the inhabitants of the same, in some public assembly or by going or sending from house to house, that at a place and time by him or them limited and set, they meet and assemble themselves together to elect and choose certain deputies to be at the General Court then following to agitate the affairs of the Commonwealth; which said deputies shall be chosen by all that are admitted Inhabitants in the several Towns and have taken the oath of fidelity; provided that none be chosen a Deputy for any General Court which is not a Freeman of this Commonwealth. [...]

8   It is Ordered, sentenced, and decreed, that Windsor, Hartford, and Wethersfield shall have power, each Town, to send four of their Freemen as their deputies to every General Court; and Whatsoever other Town shall be hereafter added to this Jurisdiction, they shall send so many deputies as the Court shall judge meet, a reasonable proportion to the number of Freemen that are in the said Towns being to be attended therein; which deputies shall have the power of the whole Town to give their votes and allowance to all such laws and orders as may be for the public good, and unto which the said Towns are to be bound. [...]

Combination of the Inhabitants upon the Piscataqua River for Government (1641)[17]

Whereas sundry Mischiefs and Inconveniences have befallen us, and more and greater may, in regard of want of Civil Government, his gracious Majesty having settled no order for us, to our knowledge, we whose names are underwritten, being

---

[17] From E. Hazard (ed.), *Historical Collections: Consisting of State Papers, and Other Authentic Documents*, Vol. I (Philadelphia: T. Dobson, 1792), pp. 484–7.

Inhabitants upon the River of Pascataqua have voluntarily agreed to combine ourselves into a body Politick, that we may the more comfortably enjoy the Benefit of his Majesty's Laws, and do hereby actually engage ourselves to submit to his Royal Majesty's Laws, together with all such Laws as shall be concluded by a major part of the Freemen of our Society, in Case they be not repugnant to the laws of England, and administered in behalf of his Majesty. And this we have mutually promised, and engaged to do, and so to continue till his excellent Majesty shall give other orders concerning us. In witness whereof We have hereunto set our hands, October 22. In the 16th year of the Reign of our Sovereign Lord, Charles by the grace of God, King of Great Britain, France and Ireland, Defender of the Faith, etc.

The Articles of Confederation of the United Colonies of New England (May 19, 1643)[18]

The Articles of Confederation between the Plantations under the Government of the Massachusetts, the Plantations under the Government of New Plymouth, the Plantations under the Government of Connecticut, and the Government of New Haven with the Plantations in Combination therewith:

Whereas we all came into these parts of America with one and the same end and aim, namely, to advance the Kingdom of our Lord Jesus Christ and to enjoy the liberties of the Gospel in purity with peace; and whereas in our settling (by a wise providence of God) we are further dispersed upon the sea coasts and rivers than was at first intended, so that we can not according to our desire with convenience communicate in one government and jurisdiction; and whereas we live encompassed with people of several nations and strange languages which hereafter may prove injurious to us or our posterity. And forasmuch as the natives have formerly committed sundry Insolence and outrages upon several Plantations of the English and have of late combined themselves against us: and seeing by reason of those sad distractions in England which they have heard of, and by which they know vie [*sic*] are hindered from that humble way of seeking advice, or reaping those comfortable fruits of protection, which at other times we might well expect. We therefore do conceive it our bounder [*sic*] duty, without delay to enter into a present Consociation amongst ourselves, for mutual help and strength in all our future concernments: That, as in nation and religion, so in other respects, we be and continue one according to the tenor and true meaning of the ensuing articles: Wherefore it is fully agreed and concluded by and between the parties or Jurisdictions above named, and they jointly and severally do by these presents agree and conclude that they all be and henceforth be called by the name of the United Colonies of New England.   1

The said United Colonies for themselves and their posterities do jointly and severally hereby enter into a firm and perpetual league of friendship and amity for offence and defence, mutual advice and succor upon all just occasions both for   2

[18] From Newton Thorpe, *The Federal and State Constitutions*, via the Avalon Project, https://avalon .law.yale.edu/.

preserving and propagating the truth and liberties of the Gospel and for their own mutual safety and welfare.

3   It is further agreed that the Plantations which at present are or hereafter shall be settled within the limits of the Massachusetts shall be forever under the Massachusetts and shall have peculiar jurisdiction among themselves in all cases as an entire body, and that Plymouth, Connecticut, and New Haven shall each of them have like peculiar jurisdiction and government within their limits; and in reference to the Plantations which already are settled, or shall hereafter be erected, or shall settle within their limits respectively; provided no other Jurisdiction shall hereafter be taken in as a distinct head or member of this Confederation, nor shall any other Plantation or Jurisdiction in present being, and not already in combination or under the jurisdiction of any of these Confederates, be received by any of them; nor shall any two of the Confederates join in one Jurisdiction without consent of the rest, which consent to be interpreted as is expressed in the sixth article ensuing.

4   It is by these Confederates agreed that the charge of all just wars, whether offensive or defensive, upon what part or member of this Confederation soever they fall, shall both in men, provisions and all other disbursements be borne by all the parts of this Confederation in different proportions according to their different ability in manner following, namely, that the Commissioners for each Jurisdiction from time to time, as there shall be occasion, bring a true account and number of all their males in every Plantation, or any way belonging to or under their several Jurisdictions, of what quality or condition soever they be, from sixteen years old to threescore, being inhabitants there. And that according to the different numbers which from time to time shall be found in each Jurisdiction upon a true and just account, the service of men and all charges of the war be borne by the poll: each Jurisdiction or Plantation being left to their own just course and custom of rating themselves and people according to their different estates with due respects to their qualities and exemptions amongst themselves though the Confederation take no notice of any such privilege: and that according to their different charge of each Jurisdiction and Plantation the whole advantage of the war (if it please God so to bless their endeavors) whether it be in lands, goods, or persons, shall be proportionately divided among the said Confederates. [. . .]

6   It is also agreed, that for the managing and concluding of all Stairs [sic] and concerning the whole Confederation two Commissioners shall be chosen by and out of each of these four Jurisdictions: namely, two for the Massachusetts, two for Plymouth, two for Connecticut, and two for New Haven, being all in Church-fellowship with us, which shall bring full power from their several General Courts respectively to hear, examine, weigh, and determine all affairs of our war, or peace, leagues, aids, charges, and numbers of men for war, division of spoils and whatsoever is gotten by conquest, receiving of more Confederates for Plantations into combination with any of the Confederates, and all things of like nature, which are the proper concomitants or consequents of such a Confederation for amity, offense, and defence: not intermeddling with the government of any of the Jurisdictions, which by the third article is preserved entirely to themselves. But if these eight Commissioners when they meet shall not all agree yet it [is] concluded that any six of the eight agreeing shall have power to settle and determine the business in question. But if six do not

agree, that then such propositions with their reasons so far as they have been debated, be sent and referred to the four General Courts; namely, the Massachusetts, Plymouth, Connecticut, and New Haven; and if at all the said General Courts the business so referred be concluded, then to be prosecuted by the Confederates and all their members. It is further agreed that these eight Commissioners shall meet once every year besides extraordinary meetings (according to the fifth article) to consider, treat, and conclude of all affairs belonging to this Confederation, which meeting shall ever be the first Thursday in September. And that the next meeting after the date of these presents, which shall be accounted the second meeting, shall be at Boston in the Massachusetts, the third at Hartford, the fourth at New Haven, the fifth at Plymouth, the sixth and seventh at Boston; and then Hartford, New Haven, and Plymouth, and so [i]n course successively, if in the meantime some middle place be not found out and agreed on, which may be commodious for all the Jurisdictions.

It is further agreed that at each meeting of these eight Commissioners, whether   7 ordinary or extraordinary, they or six of them agreeing as before, may choose their President out of themselves whose office work shall be to take care and direct for order and a comely carrying on of all proceedings in the present meeting: but he shall be invested with no such power or respect, as by which he shall hinder the propounding or progress of any business, or any way cast the scales otherwise than in the precedent article is agreed.

It is also agreed that the Commissioners for this Confederation hereafter at their   8 meetings, whether ordinary or extraordinary, as they may have commission or opportunity, do endeavor to frame and establish agreements and orders in general cases of a civil nature, wherein all the Plantations are interested, for preserving of peace among themselves, for preventing as much as may be all occasion of war or differences with others, as about the free and speedy passage of justice in every Jurisdiction, to all the Confederates equally as to their own, receiving those that remove from one Plantation to another without due certificate, how all the Jurisdictions may carry it towards the Indians, that they neither grow insolent nor be injured without due satisfaction, lest war break in upon the Confederates through such miscarriages. It is also agreed that if any servant run away from his master into any other of these confederated Jurisdictions, that in such case, upon the ceritficate [sic] of one magistrate in the Jurisdiction out of which the said servant fled, or upon other due proof; the said servant shall be delivered, either to his master, or any other that pursues and brings such certificate or proof. [. . .]

And for that the justest wars may be of dangerous consequence, especially to the   9 smaller Plantations in these United Colonies, it is agreed that neither the Massachusetts, Plymouth, Connecticut, nor New Haven, nor any of the members of them, shall at any time hereafter begin, undertake, or engage themselves, or this Confederation, or any part thereof in any war whatsoever (sudden exigencies, with the necessary consequents thereof excepted), which are also to be moderated as much as the case will permit, without the consent and agreement of the forementioned eight Commissioners, or at least six of them, as in the sixth article is provided: and that no charge be required of any of the Confederates, in case of a defensive war, till the said Commissioners have met, and approved the justice of the war, and have agreed upon the sum of money to be levied, which sum is then to be paid by the several Confederates in proportion according to the fourth article. [. . .]

11   It is further agreed that if any of the Confederates shall hereafter break any of these present articles, or be any other ways injurious to any one of the other Jurisdictions; such breach of agreement or injury shall be duly considered and ordered by the Commissioners for the other Jurisdictions, that both peace and this present Confederation may be entirely preserved without violation. [. . .]

At a meeting of the Commissioners for the Confederation held at Boston the 7th of September, it appearing that the General Court of New Plymouth and the several townships thereof have read, considered, and approved these Articles of Confederation, as appeareth by commission of their General Court bearing date the 29th of August, 1643, to Mr. Edward Winslow and Mr. William Collier to ratify and confirm the same on their behalf: we therefore, the Commissioners for the Massachusetts, Connecticut, and New Haven, do also from our several Governments subscribe unto them.

PURITAN WRITINGS

William Perkins *A Treatise of the Vocations* (1605)[19]

[. . .] A vocation or calling is a certain kind of life, ordained and imposed on man by God, for the common good.

First of all I say, it is a certain condition or kind of life: that is, a certain manner of leading our lives in this world. For example, the life of a king is to spend his time in the governing of his subjects, and that is his calling; and the life of a subject is to live in obedience to the Magistrate, and that is his calling. The state and condition of a Minister is to lead his life in preaching the Gospel and word of God, and that is his calling. A master of a family is to lead his life in the government of his family, and that is his calling. In a word, that particular and honest manner of conversation to which every man is called and set apart, that is (I say) his calling.

Now, in every calling we must consider two causes. First, the efficient and author of it. Secondly, the final and proper end of it. The author of every calling is God Himself; and therefore Paul says, "As God has called every man, let him walk," verse 17. And for this reason, this order and manner of living in this world is called a Vocation, because every man is to live as he is called by God. [. . .]

The final cause or end of every calling, I note in the last words of the description: For the common good; that is, for the benefit and good estate of mankind. In man's body there are sundry parts and members, and every one has its several use and office, which it performs not for itself, but for the good of the whole body – as the office of the eye is to see, of the ear to hear, and the foot to go. Now all societies of men are bodies; a family is a body; so is every particular church a body; and the

---

[19] W. Perkins, *The Works of That Famous and Worthy Minister of Christ in the University of Cambridge Mr. William Perkins*, Vol. I (London: Legatt, 1635), pp. 750–79.

commonwealth also. And in these bodies there are several members, which are men walking in several callings and offices, the execution of which must tend to the happy and good estate of the rest – indeed, the good of all men everywhere, as much as possible. The common good of men stands in this: not only that they live, but that they live well, in righteousness and holiness; and consequently in true happiness. And to attain this, God has ordained and disposed all callings, and in His providence he has designed the persons to bear them. Here then we must in general know that he abuses his calling, whoever he is, if he is against the end of that calling, if he employs it for himself, and seeks wholly his own by it, and not the common good. And that common saying, Every man for himself, and God for us all, is wicked, and is directly against the end of every calling or honest kind of life.

Edward Johnson *The Wonder-Working Providence of Sions Saviour in New England* (1628)[20]

Chapter II The Commission of The People of Christ Shipped for New England, and First of Their Gathering into Churches

[. . .] At your landing see you observe the Rule of his Word, for neither larger nor stricter Commission can hee give by any, and therefore at first filling the land wither you are sent, with diligence, search out the mind of God both in planting and continuing Church and civill Government, but be sure they be distinct, yet agreeing and helping the one to the other; Let the matter and forme of your Churches be such as were in the Primitive Times (before Antichrists Kingdom prevailed) plainly poynted out by Christ and his Apostles, in most of their Epistles, to be neither Nationall nor Provinciall, but gather together in Covenant of such a number as might ordinarily meete together in one place, and built of such living stones as outwardly appeare Saints by calling. You are to ordaine Elders in every Church, make you use of such as Christ hath indued with the best gifts to that end, their call to Office shall be mediate from you, but their authority and commission shall be immediate from Christ revealed in his word [. . .]

Chapter IV How the People in Christs Churches Are to Behave Themselves

Now you his People, who are pickt out by his provide[nce] to passe this Westerne Ocean for this honourable service, beware you call not weake ones to Office in this honorable Army, nor Novices, lest they be lifted up by pride. [. . .] Abuse not the free and full liberty Christ hath given you in making choyce of your own Officers, and consent in admitting into his Churches, and casting out such Members as walke disorderly; you are to walke in all humility, lest in injoyment of such freedom as you formerly have not exercised, you exceed the bounds of modesty, and instead of having your moderation knowne to all, your imbecility, and self-exaltation bee discovered by many. In admission of others into

---

[20] E. Johnson, *The Wonder-Working Providence* (New York: Charles Scribner's Sons, 1910), pp. 25–32.

Church society, remember your selves were once Aliens from the Covenant of Grace, and in Excommunication, consider how your selves have been also tempted: in sincerity and singleness of heart, let your words be few, do nothing [to] be had in high esteeme among me; And think it no imputation of a weake discerning to be followe[r]s of those are set over you in the Lord as they follow Christ; Let your Profession outstrip your Confession, for seeing you are to be set as lights upon a Hill more obvious than the highest Mountaine in the World [...]

John Winthrop

A Model of Christian Charity (1630)

God Almighty in His most holy and wise providence, hath so disposed of the condition of mankind, as in all times some must be rich, some poor, some high and eminent in power and dignity; others mean and in submission.

The Reason Hereof

1st Reason. First to hold conformity with the rest of His world, being delighted to show forth the glory of his wisdom in the variety and difference of the creatures, and the glory of His power in ordering all these differences for the preservation and good of the whole, and the glory of His greatness, that as it is the glory of princes to have many officers, so this great king will have many stewards, counting himself more honored in dispensing his gifts to man by man, than if he did it by his own immediate hands.

2nd Reason. Secondly, that He might have the more occasion to manifest the work of his Spirit: first upon the wicked in moderating and restraining them, so that the rich and mighty should not eat up the poor, nor the poor and despised rise up against and shake off their yoke. Secondly, in the regenerate, in exercising His graces in them, as in the great ones, their love, mercy, gentleness, temperance etc., and in the poor and inferior sort, their faith, patience, obedience etc.

3rd Reason. Thirdly, that every man might have need of others, and from hence they might be all knit more nearly together in the bonds of brotherly affection. From hence it appears plainly that no man is made more honorable than another or more wealthy etc., out of any particular and singular respect to himself, but for the glory of his Creator and the common good of the creature, Man. [...]

There are two rules whereby we are to walk one towards another: Justice and Mercy. These are always distinguished in their act and in their object, yet may they both concur in the same subject in each respect; as sometimes there may be an occasion of showing mercy to a rich man in some sudden danger or distress, and also doing of mere justice to a poor man in regard of some particular contract, etc.

There is likewise a double Law by which we are regulated in our conversation towards another. In both the former respects, the Law of Nature and the Law of Grace (that is, the moral law or the law of the gospel) to omit the rule of justice as not properly belonging to this purpose otherwise than it may fall into consideration in some particular cases. By the first of these laws, Man as he was enabled so withal is commanded to love his neighbor as himself. Upon this ground stands all the precepts of the moral law, which concerns our dealings with men. To apply this to the works of mercy, this law requires two things. First, that every man afford his help to another in every want or distress. Secondly, that he perform this out of the same affection which makes him careful of his own goods, according to the words of our Savior (from Matthew 7:12), whatsoever ye would that men should do to you. This was practiced by Abraham and Lot in entertaining the angels and the old man of Gibea.

The law of Grace or of the Gospel hath some difference from the former (the law of nature), as in these respects: First, the law of nature was given to Man in the estate of innocence. This of the Gospel in the estate of regeneracy. Secondly, the former propounds one man to another, as the same flesh and image of God. This as a brother in Christ also, and in the communion of the same Spirit, and so teacheth to put a difference between Christians and others. Do good to all, especially to the household of faith. Upon this ground the Israelites were to put a difference between the brethren of such as were strangers, though not of the Canaanites.

Thirdly, the Law of Nature would give no rules for dealing with enemies, for all are to be considered as friends in the state of innocence, but the Gospel commands love to an enemy. Proof: If thine enemy hunger, feed him; "Love your enemies . . . Do good to them that hate you" (Matt. 5:44).

This law of the Gospel propounds likewise a difference of seasons and occasions. There is a time when a Christian must sell all and give to the poor, as they did in the Apostles' times. There is a time also when Christians (though they give not all yet) must give beyond their ability, as they of Macedonia (2 Cor. 8). Likewise, community of perils calls for extraordinary liberality, and so doth community in some special service for the church.

Lastly, when there is no other means whereby our Christian brother may be relieved in his distress, we must help him beyond our ability rather than tempt God in putting him upon help by miraculous or extraordinary means. This duty of mercy is exercised in the kinds: giving, lending and forgiving (of a debt). [. . .]

The definition which the Scripture gives us of love is this: Love is the bond of perfection. First it is a bond or ligament. Secondly, it makes the work perfect. There is no body but consists of parts and that which knits these parts together, gives the body its perfection, because it makes each part so contiguous to others as thereby they do mutually participate with each other, both in strength and infirmity, in pleasure and pain. To instance in the most perfect of all bodies: Christ and his Church make one body. The several parts of this body considered a part before they were united, were as disproportionate and as much disordering as so many contrary qualities or elements, but when Christ comes, and by his spirit and love knits all these parts to himself and each to other, it is become the most perfect and best proportioned body in the world (Eph. 4:15–16). Christ, by whom all the body being knit together by every joint for the furniture thereof, according to the effectual power which is in the measure of every perfection of parts, a glorious body without spot or wrinkle; the ligaments hereof being Christ, or his love, for Christ is love (1 John 4:8). So this definition is right. Love is the bond of perfection.

From hence we may frame these conclusions:

First of all, true Christians are of one body in Christ (1 Cor. 12). Ye are the body of Christ and members of their part. All the parts of this body being thus united are made so contiguous in a special relation as they must needs partake of each other's strength and infirmity; joy and sorrow, weal and woe. If one member suffers, all suffer with it, if one be in honor, all rejoice with it.

Secondly, the ligaments of this body which knit together are love.

Thirdly, no body can be perfect which wants its proper ligament.

Fourthly, All the parts of this body being thus united are made so contiguous in a special relation as they must needs partake of each other's strength and infirmity, joy and sorrow, weal and woe. (1 Cor. 12:26) If one member suffers, all suffer with it; if one be in honor, all rejoice with it.

Fifthly, this sensitivity and sympathy of each other's conditions will necessarily infuse into each part a native desire and endeavor, to strengthen, defend, preserve and comfort the other. To insist a little on this conclusion being the product of all the former, the truth hereof will appear both by precept and pattern. 1 John 3:16, "We ought to lay down our lives for the brethren." Gal. 6:2, "Bear ye one another's burden's and so fulfill the law of Christ." [. . .]

The third consideration is concerning the exercise of this love, which is twofold, inward or outward. The outward hath been handled in the former preface of this discourse. From unfolding the other we must take in our way that maxim of philosophy, "simile simili gaudet," or like will to like; for as of things which are turned with disaffection to each other, the ground of it is from a dissimilitude or arising from the contrary or different nature of the things themselves; for the ground of love is an apprehension of some resemblance in the things loved to that which affects it. This is the cause why the Lord loves the creature, so far as it hath any of his Image in it; He loves his elect because they are like Himself, He beholds them in His beloved son.

So a mother loves her child, because she thoroughly conceives a resemblance of herself in it. Thus it is between the members of Christ; each discerns, by the work of the Spirit, his own Image and resemblance in another, and therefore cannot but love him as he loves himself. Now when the soul, which is of a sociable nature, finds anything like to itself, it is like Adam when Eve was brought to him. She must be one with himself. This is flesh of my flesh (saith he) and bone of my bone. So the soul conceives a great delight in it; therefore she desires nearness and familiarity with it. She hath a great propensity to do it good and receives such content in it. [. . .]

If any shall object that it is not possible that love shall be bred or upheld without hope of requital, it is granted; but that is not our cause; for this love is always under reward. It never gives, but it always receives with advantage:

First in regard that among the members of the same body, love and affection are reciprocal in a most equal and sweet kind of commerce.

Secondly, in regard of the pleasure and content that the exercise of love carries with it, as we may see in the natural body. The mouth is at all the pains to receive and mince the food which serves for the nourishment of all the other parts of the body; yet it hath no cause to complain; for first the other parts send back, by several passages, a due proportion of the same nourishment, in a better form for the strengthening and comforting the mouth. Secondly, the labor of the mouth is accompanied with such pleasure and content as far exceeds the pains it takes. So is it in all the labor of love among Christians. The party loving, reaps love again, as was showed before, which the soul covets more then all the wealth in the world.

Thirdly, nothing yields more pleasure and content to the soul then when it finds that which it may love fervently; for to love and live beloved is the soul's paradise both here and in heaven. In the State of wedlock there be many comforts to learn out of the troubles of that condition; but let such as have tried the most, say if there be any sweetness in that condition comparable to the exercise of mutual love.

From the former considerations arise these conclusions:

First, this love among Christians is a real thing, not imaginary.

Secondly, this love is as absolutely necessary to the being of the body of Christ, as the sinews and other ligaments of a natural body are to the being of that body.

Thirdly, this love is a divine, spiritual, nature; free, active, strong, courageous, permanent; undervaluing all things beneath its proper object and of all the graces, this makes us nearer to resemble the virtues of our heavenly father.

Fourthly, it rests in the love and welfare of its beloved. For the full certain knowledge of those truths concerning the nature, use, and excellency of this grace, that which the holy ghost hath left recorded, 1 Cor. 13, may give full satisfaction, which is needful for every true member of this lovely body of the Lord Jesus, to work upon their hearts by prayer, meditation continual exercise at least of the special influence of this grace, till Christ be formed in them and they in him, all in each other, knit together by this bond of love.

It rests now to make some application of this discourse, by the present design, which gave the occasion of writing of it. Herein are four things to be propounded; first the persons, secondly, the work, thirdly the end, fourthly the means.

First, for the persons. We are a company professing ourselves fellow members of Christ, in which respect only, though we were absent from each other many miles, and had our employments as far distant, yet we ought to account ourselves knit together by this bond of love and live in the exercise of it, if we would have comfort of our being in Christ. [. . .]

Secondly for the work we have in hand. It is by a mutual consent, through a special overvaluing providence and a more than an ordinary approbation of the churches of Christ, to seek out a place of cohabitation and consortship under a due form of government both civil and ecclesiastical. In such cases as this, the care of the public must oversway all private respects, by which, not only conscience, but mere civil policy, doth bind us. For it is a true rule that particular estates cannot subsist in the ruin of the public.

Thirdly, the end is to improve our lives to do more service to the Lord; the comfort and increase of the body of Christ, whereof we are members, that ourselves and posterity may be the better preserved from the common corruptions of this evil world, to serve the Lord and work out our salvation under the power and purity of his holy ordinances.

Fourthly, for the means whereby this must be effected. They are twofold, a conformity with the work and end we aim at. These we see are extraordinary, therefore we must not content ourselves with usual ordinary means. Whatsoever we did, or ought to have done, when we lived in England, the same must we do, and more also, where we go. That which the most in their churches maintain as truth in profession only, we must bring into familiar and constant practice; as in this duty of love, we must love brotherly without dissimulation, we must love one another with a pure heart fervently. We must bear one another's burdens. We must not look only on our own things, but also on the things of our brethren. [. . .]

Thus stands the cause between God and us. We are entered into covenant with Him for this work. We have taken out a commission. The Lord hath given us leave to draw our own articles. We have professed to enterprise these and those accounts, upon these and those ends. We have hereupon besought Him of favor and blessing. Now if the Lord shall please to hear us, and bring us in peace to the place we desire, then hath He ratified this covenant and sealed our commission, and will expect a strict performance of the articles contained in it; but if we shall neglect the observation of these articles which are the ends we have propounded, and, dissembling with our God, shall fall to embrace this present world and prosecute our carnal intentions, seeking great things for ourselves and our posterity, the Lord will surely break out in wrath against us, and be revenged of such a people, and make us know the price of the breach of such a covenant.

[. . .] So shall we keep the unity of the spirit in the bond of peace. The Lord will be our God, and delight to dwell among us, as His own people, and will command a blessing upon us in all our ways, so that we shall see much more of His wisdom, power, goodness and truth, than formerly we have been acquainted with. We shall find that the God of Israel is among us, when ten of us shall be able to resist a thousand of our enemies; when He shall make us a praise and glory that men shall say of succeeding plantations, "may the Lord make it like that of New England." *For we must consider that we shall be as a city upon a hill. The eyes of all people are upon us. So that if we shall deal falsely with our God in this work we have undertaken, and so cause Him to withdraw His present help from us, we shall be made a story and a by-word through the world.* We shall open the mouths of enemies to speak evil of the ways of God, and all professors for God's sake. We shall shame the faces of many of God's worthy servants, and cause their prayers to be turned into curses upon us till we be consumed out of the good land whither we are going. [. . .]

A Defense of an Order of Court (1637)[21]

A Declaration of the Intent and Equity of the Order made at the last Court, to this effect, that none should be received to inhabit within this Jurisdiction but such as should be allowed by some of the Magistrates.

---

[21] Excerpt taken from T. Hutchinson (ed.), *A Collection of Original Papers Relative to the History of the Colony of Massachusetts-Bay* (Boston: Thomas and John Fleet, 1769), pp.67–71. In 1636, the General Court of the Massachusetts Bay Colony (the legislative assembly for the colony) barred the admission

For clearing of such scruples as have arisen about this order, it is to be considered, first, what is the essential form of a common weal or body politics such as this is, which I conceive to be this: The consent of a certain company of people, to cohabitate together, under one government for their mutual safety and welfare.

In this description all these things do concur to the wellbeing of such a body, 1. Persons, 2. Place, 3. Content, 4. Government or Order, 5. Welfare.

It is clearly agreed, by all, that the care and safety and welfare was the original cause or occasion of common weals and of many families subjecting themselves to rulers and laws; for no man has lawful power over another, but by birth or consent, so likewise, by the law of property, no man can have just interest in that which belong to another, without his consent.

From the premise will arise these conclusions.

1. No common weal can be founded but by free consent.
2. The persons so incorporating have a public and relative interest each in other, and in the place of their cohabitation and goods, and laws, etc. and in all the means of their welfare so as none other can claim privilege with them but by free consent.
3. The nature of such an incorporation ties every member thereof to seek out and entertain all means that may conduce to the welfare of the body, and to keep off whatever does appear to tend to their damage.
4. The welfare of the whole is [not] to be put to apparent hazard for the advantage of any particular members.

From these conclusions I thus reason.

1. If we here be a corporation established by free consent, if the place of our cohabitation be our own, then no man has right to come into us etc. without our consent.
2. If no man has right to our lands, our government privileges, etc. but by our consent, then it is reason we should take notice of before we confer any such upon them.
3. If we are bound to keep off whatever appears to tend to our ruin or damage, then may we lawfully refuse to receive such whose dispositions suit not with ours and whose society (we know) will be hurtful to us, and therefore it is lawful to take knowledge of all men before we receive them.
4. The churches take liberty (as lawfully they may) to receive or reject at their discretion; yea particular towns make orders to the like effect. Why then should the common weal be denied the like liberty and the whole more restrained than any part?
5. If it be sin in us to deny some men place, etc. among us, then it is because of some right they have to this place, etc. for to deny a man that which he has no right unto is neither sin nor injury.
6. If strangers have right to our houses or lands, etc. then it is either of justice or of mercy; if of justice let them plead, and we shall know what to answer: but if it be only in way of mercy, or by the rule of hospitality, etc then I answer 1st, A man is not a fit object of mercy except he be in misery. 2nd, We are not bound to exercise mercy to others to the ruin of ourselves. 3rd, There are few that stand in need of

of any new colonists without the approval of the magistrates. Winthrop, governor of the colony, issues this statement justifying the court order.

mercy at their first coming hither. As for hospitality, that rule does not bind further than for some present occasion, not for continual residence.

7. A family is a little commonwealth, and a commonwealth is a great family. Now as a family is not bound to entertain all comers, no not every good man (otherwise than by way of hospitality) no more is a commonwealth. [. . .]

9. The rule of the Apostle, John 2.10, is, that such as come and bring not the true doctrine with them should not be received to house, and by the same reason not into the common weal. [. . .]

Little Speech on Liberty (1645)[22]

I suppose something may be expected from me upon this charge that is befallen me, which moves me to speak now to you; yet I intend not to intermeddle in the proceedings of the court, or with any of the persons concerned therein. Only I bless God that I see an issue of this troublesome business. I also acknowledge the justice of the court, and, for mine own part, I am well satisfied, I was publicly charged, and I am publicly and legally acquitted, which is all I did expect or desire. And though this be sufficient for my justification before men, yet not so before the God who hath seen so much amiss in my dispensations (and even in this affair) as calls me to be humble. For to be publicly and criminally charged in this court is matter of humiliation (and I desire to make a right use of it), notwithstanding I be thus acquitted. If her father had spit in her face (saith the Lord concerning Miriam), should she not have been ashamed seven days? Shame had lien upon her, whatever the occasion had been. I am unwilling to stay you from your urgent affairs, yet give me leave (upon this special occasion) to speak a little more to this assembly.

It may be of some good use to inform and rectify the judgments of some of the people, and may prevent such distempers as have arisen amongst us. The great questions that have troubled the country are about the authority of the magistrates and the liberty of the people. It is yourselves who have called us to this office, and, being called by you, we have our authority from God, in way of an ordinance, such as hath the image of God eminently stamped upon it, the contempt and violation whereof hath been vindicated with examples of divine vengeance. I entreat you to consider that, when you choose magistrates, you take them from among yourselves, men subject to like passions as you are. Therefore, when you see infirmities in us, you should reflect upon your own, and that would make you bear the more with us, and not be severe censurers of the failings of your magistrates, when you have continual experience of the like infirmities in yourselves and others. We account him a good servant who breaks not his covenant. The covenant between you and us is the oath you have taken of us, which is to this purpose, that we shall govern you and judge your causes by the rules of God's laws and our own, according to our best skill. When you agree with a workman to build you a ship or house, etc., he undertakes as well for his skill as for his faithfulness; for it is his profession, and you pay him for

[22] In J. Winthrop, *The History of New England, from 1630 to 1649*, Vol. II (Boston: Little Brown and Company, 1853), pp. 228–30.

both. But, when you call one to be a magistrate, he doth not profess nor undertake to have sufficient skill for that office, nor can you furnish him with gifts, etc., therefore you must run the hazard of his skill and ability. But if he fail in faithfulness, which by his oath he is bound unto, that he must answer for. If it fall out that the case be clear to common apprehension, and the rule clear also, if he transgress here, the error is not in the skill, but in the evil of the will: it must be required of him. But if the case be doubtful, or the rule doubtful, to men of such understanding and parts as your magistrates are, if your magistrates should err here, yourselves must bear it.

For the other point concerning liberty, I observe a great mistake in the country about that. There is a twofold liberty, natural (I mean as our nature is now corrupt) and civil or federal. The first is common to man with beasts and other creatures. By this, man as he stands in relation to man simply, hath liberty to do what he lists: it is a liberty to evil as well as to good. This liberty is incompatible and inconsistent with authority, and cannot endure the least restraint of the most just authority. The exercise and maintaining of this liberty makes men grow more evil, and in time to be worse than brute beasts: *omnes sumus licentia deteriores*. This is that great enemy of truth and peace, that wild beast, which all the ordinances of God are bent against, to restrain and subdue it.

The other kind of liberty I call civil or federal; it may also be termed moral, in reference to the covenant between God and man, in the moral law, and the politic covenants and constitutions, amongst men themselves. This liberty is the proper end and object of authority, and cannot subsist without it; and it is a liberty to that only which is good, just, and honest. This liberty you are to stand for, with the hazard (not only of your goods, but) of your lives, if need be. Whatsoever crosseth this is not authority, but a distemper thereof. This liberty is maintained and exercised in a way of subjection to authority; it is of the same kind of liberty wherewith Christ hath made us free. The woman's own choice makes such a man her husband; yet, being so chosen, he is her lord, and she is to be subject to him, yet in a way of liberty, not of bondage; and a true wife accounts her subjection her honor and freedom, and would not think her condition safe and free but in her subjection to her husband's authority. Such is the liberty of the church under the authority of Christ, her king and husband; his yoke is so easy and sweet to her as a bride's ornaments; and if through frowardness or wantonness, etc., she shake it off, at any time, she is at no rest in her spirit until she take it up again; and whether her lord smiles upon her, and embraceth her in his arms, or whether he frowns, or rebukes, or smites her, she apprehends the sweetness of his love in all, and is refreshed, supported, and instructed by every such dispensation of his authority over her. On the other side, ye know who they are that complain of this yoke and say, let us break their bands, etc., we will not have this man to rule over us. Even so, brethren, it will be between you and your magistrates. If you stand for your natural corrupt liberties, and will do what is good in your own eyes, you will not endure the least weight of authority, but will murmur, and oppose, and be always striving to shake off that yoke; but if you will be satisfied to enjoy such civil and lawful liberties, such as Christ allows you, then will you quietly and cheerfully submit unto that authority which is set over you, in all the administrations of it, for your good. Wherein, if we fail at any time, we hope we shall be willing (by God's assistance) to hearken to good advice from any of you, or in any other way of God; so shall your liberties be preserved, in upholding the honor and power of authority amongst you.

John Cotton *Letter to Lord Say and Seal* (1636)[23]

Right honourable,

[...] Your Lordships advertisement touching the civill state of this colony, as they doe breath forth your singular wisdome, and faithfulness, and tender care of the peace, so wee have noe reason to misinterprite, or undervalue your Lordships eyther directions, or intentions therein. I know noe man under heaven (I speake in Gods feare without flattery) whose counsell I should rather depend upon, for the wise administration of a civill state according to God, than upon your Lordship, and such confidence have I (not in you) but in the Lords presence in Christ with you, that I should never feare to betrust a greater commonwealth than this (as much as in us lyeth) under such a *perpetuâ dictaturâ* as your lordship should prescribe. For I nothing doubt, but that eyther your Lordship would prescribe all things according to the rule, or be willing to examine againe, and againe, all things according to it. I am very apt to believe [...] that the word, and scriptures of God doe conteyne a short *upoluposis*, or platforme, not onely of theology, but also of other sacred sciences [...] attendants, and hand maids thereunto, which he maketh ethicks, eoconomicks, politicks, church-government, prophecy, academy. It is very suitable to Gods all-sufficient wisdome, and to the fulnes and perfection of Holy Scriptures, not only to prescribe perfect rules for the right ordering of a private mans soule to everlasting blessednes with himselfe, but also for the right ordering of a mans family, yea, of the commonwealth too, so farre as both of them are subordinate to spiritual ends, and yet avoide both the churches usurpation upon civill jurisdictions, *in ordine ad spiritualia*, and the commonwealths invasion upon ecclesiasticall administrations, *in ordine* to civill peace, and conformity to the civill state. Gods institutions (such as the government of church and of commonwealth be) may be close and compact, and coordinate one to another, and yet not confounded. God hath so framed the state of church government and ordinances, that they may be compatible to any commonwealth, though never so much disordered in his frame. But yet when a commonwealth hath liberty to mould his owne frame (*scripturae plenitudinem adoro*) I conceyve the scripture hath given full direction for the right ordering of the same, and that, in such sort as may best mainteyne the *euexia* of the church. Mr. Hooker doth often quote a saying out of Mr. Cartwright (though I have not read it in him) that noe man fashioneth his house to his hangings, but his hangings to his house. It is better that the commonwealth be fashioned to the setting forth of Gods house, which is his church: than to accommodate the church frame to the civill state. Democracy, I do not conceyve that ever God did ordeyne as a fitt government eyther for church or commonwealth. If the people be governors, who shall be governed? As for monarchy, and aristocracy, they are both of them clearly approved, and directed in scripture, yet so as referreth the soveraigntie to himselfe, and setteth up Theocracy in both, as the best forme of government in the commonwealth, as well as in the church.

The law, which your Lordship instanceth in [that none shall be chosen to magistracy among us, but a church member] was made and enacted before I came into the countrey; but I have hitherto wanted sufficient light to plead against it. 1st. The rule

---

[23] From T. Hutchinson (ed.), *The History of the Colony of Massachusetts-Bay*, Vol. I (Boston: Thomas and John Fleet, 1764), pp. 496–501.

that directeth the choice of supreame governors, is of like aequitie and weight in all magistrates, that one of their brethren (not a stranger) should be set over them. [...] Your Lordship's feare, that this will bring in papal excommunicatjon, is iust, and pious; but let your Lordship be pleased againe to consider whether the consequence be necessary. *Turpius ejicitur quam non admittitur*: non-membership may be a iust cause of nonadmission to the place of magistracy, but yet, ejection out of his membership will not be a iust cause of ejecting him out of his magistracy. A godly woman, being to make choice of an husband, may iustly refuse a man that is eyther cast out of church fellowship, or is not yet receyved into it, but yet, when shee is once given to him, shee may not reject him then, for such defect. [...]

When your Lordship doubteth, that this corse will draw all things under the determination of the church, *in ordine ad spiritualia* (seeing the church is to determine who shall be members, and none but a member may have to doe in the government of a commonwealth) be pleased (I pray you) to conceyve, that magistrates are neyther chosen to office in the church, nor doe governe by directions from the church, but by civill lawes, and those enacted in generall corts, and executed in corts of iustice, by the governors and assistants. In all which, the church (as the church) hath nothing to doe: onely, it prepareth fitt instruments both to rule, and to choose rulers, which is no ambition in the church, nor dishonor to the commonwealth, the apostle, on the contrary, thought it a great dishonor and reproach to the church of Christ, if it were not able to yield able judges to heare and determine all causes amongst their brethren. i. Cor, 6. i. to 5. which place alone seemeth to me fully to decide this question: for it plainely holdeth forth this argument: It is a shame to the church to want able judges of civill matters and an audacious act in any church member voluntarily to go for judgment, other where than before the saints (as v. i.) then it will be noe arrogance nor folly in church members, nor preiudice to the commonwealth, if voluntarily they never choose any civill judges but from amongst the saints, such as church members are called to be. [...]

But your Lordship doubteth, that if such a rule were necessary, then the church estate and the best ordered commonwealth in the world were not compatible. But let not your Lordship so conceyve. For, the church submitteth it selfe to all the lawes and ordinances of men, in what commonwealth soever they come to dwell. But it is one thing, to submit unto what they have noe calling to reforme: another thing, voluntarily to ordeyne a forme of government, which to the best discerning of many of us (for I speake not of myselfe) is expressly contrary to rule. Nor neede your Lordship feare (which yet I speake with submission to your Lordships better judgment) that this corse will lay such a foundation, as nothing but a mere democracy can be built upon it. Bodine confesseth, that though it be status popularis, where a people choose their owne governors; yet the government is not a democracy, if it be administred, not by the people, but by the governors, whether one (for then it is a monarchy, though elective) or by many, for then (as you know) it is aristocracy. In which respect it is, that church government is iustly denyed (even by Mr. Robinson) to be democratical, though the people choose their owne officers and rulers.

Nor neede wee feare, that this course will, in time, cast the commonwealth into distractions, and popular confusions. For (under correction) these three things doe not undermine, but doe mutually and strongly mainteyne one another (even those three which wee principally aime at) authority in magistrates, liberty in people, purity in the church. Purity, preserved in the church, will preserve well ordered liberty in the people, and both of them establish well-ballanced authority in the magistrates. God is the author of all these three, and neyther is himselfe the God of confusion, nor are his wayes the wayes of confusion, but of peace.

What our brethren (magistrates or ministers, or lead-ing freeholders) will answer to the rest of the propositions, I shall better understand before the gentlemans returne from Connecticutt, who brought them over. Mean while, two of the principall of them, the generall cort hath already condescended unto. 1. In establishing a standing councell, who, during their lives, should assist the governor in managing the chiefest affayres of this little state. They have chosen, for the present, onely two (Mr. Winthrope and Mr. Dudley) not willing to choose more, till they see what further better choyse the Lord will send over to them, that so they may keep an open doore, for such desireable gentlemen as your Lordship mentioneth. 2. They have graunted the governor and assistants a negative voyce, and reserved to the freemen the like liberty also. Touching other things, I hope to give your Lordship further account, when the gentleman returneth. [...]

Now the Lord Jesus Christ (the prince of peace) keepe and bless your Lordship, and dispose of all your times and talents to his best advantage: and let the covenant of his grace and peace rest upon your honourable family and posterity, throughout all generations.

Thus, humbly craving pardon for my boldnesse and length, I take leave and rest, Your Honours to serve in Christ Jesus,

J. C.

Roger Williams *The Bloody Tenent of Persecution* (1644)[24]

Reply to the Aforesaid Answer of Mr. Cotton. In a Conference between Truth and Peace.

Chapter VI

Peace. The next distinction concerneth the manner of persons holding forth the aforesaid practices, not only the weightier duties of the law, but points of doctrine and worship less principal: "Some," saith he [John Cotton], "hold them forth in a meek and peaceable way; some with such arrogance and impetuousness, as of itself tendeth to the disturbance of civil peace."

Truth. In the examination of this distinction we shall discuss,

First, what is civil peace (wherein we shall vindicate thy name the better),

Secondly, what it is to hold forth a doctrine, or practice, in this impetuousness or arrogancy.

---

[24] R. Williams, *The Bloudy Tenent of Persecution for Cause of Conscience Discussed, and Mr. Cotton's Letter Examined and Answered* (London: J. Haddon, 1848).

First, for civil peace, what is it but *pax civitatis*, the peace of the city, whether an English city, Scotch, or Irish city, or further abroad, French, Spanish, Turkish city, &c.

Thus it pleased the Father of lights to define it, Jer. 24:7, *Pray for the peace of the city*; which peace of the city, or citizens, so compacted in a civil way of union, may be entire, unbroken, safe, &c., notwithstanding so many thousands of God s people, the Jews, were there in bondage, and would neither be constrained to the worship of the city Babel, nor restrained from so much of the worship of the true God as they then could practice, as is plain in the practice of the three worthies, Shadrach, Meshach, and Abednego, as also of Daniel, Dan. iii. and Dan. vi. the peace of the city or kingdom being a far different peace from the peace of the religion, or spiritual worship, maintained and professed of the citizens. This peace of their (worship which worship also in some cities being God's people various) being a false peace, God s people were and ought to be nonconformitants, not daring either to be restrained from the true, or constrained to false worship; and yet without breach of the civil or city peace, properly so called.

Peace. Hence it is that so many glorious and flourishing cities of the world maintain their civil peace; yea, the very Americans and wildest pagans keep the peace of their towns or cities, though, neither in one nor the other can any man prove a true church of God in those places, and consequently no spiritual and heavenly peace. The peace spiritual, whether true or false, being of a higher and far different nature from the peace of the place or people, being merely and essentially civil and human.

Truth. Oh! how lost are the sons of men in this point! To illustrate this: – the church, or company of worshippers whether true or false, is like unto a body or college of physicians in a city like unto a corporation, society, or company of East India or Turkey merchants, or any other society or company in London; which companies may hold their courts, keep their records, hold disputations, and in matters concerning their society may dissent, divide, break into schisms and factions, sue and implead each other at the law, yea, wholly break up and dissolve into pieces and nothing, and yet the peace of the city not be in the least measure impaired or disturbed; because the essence or being of the city, and so the well being and peace thereof, is essentially distinct from those particular societies; the city courts, city laws, city punishments distinct from theirs. The city was before them, and stands absolute and entire when such a corporation or society is taken down. For instance further, the city or civil state of Ephesus was essentially distinct from the Spiritual worship of Diana in the city, or of the whole city. Again, the church of Christ in Ephesus, which were God's people, converted and called out from the worship of that city unto Christianity, or worship of God in Christ, was distinct from both. [. . .]

Chapter IX

Peace. It will here be said, whence then ariseth civil dissensions and uproars about matters of religion?

Truth. [...] Breach of civil peace may arise when false and idolatrous practices are held forth, and yet no breach of civil peace from the doctrine or practice, or the manner of holding forth, but from that wrong and preposterous way of suppressing, preventing, and extinguishing such doctrines or practices by weapons of wrath and blood, whips, stocks, imprisonment, banishment, death, &c.; by which men commonly are persuaded to convert heretics, and to cast out unclean spirits, which only the finger of God can do, that is, the mighty power of the Spirit in the word.

Hence the town is in an uproar, and the country takes the alarum to expel that fog or mist of error, heresy, blasphemy, as is supposed, with swords and guns. Whereas it is light alone, even light from the bright shining Sun of Righteousness, which is able, in the souls and consciences of men, to dispel and scatter such fogs and darkness. [...]

Chapter XLV

Truth. [...] [T]o batter down idolatry, false worship, heresy, schism, blindness, hardness, out of the soul and spirit, it is vain, improper, and unsuitable to bring those weapons which are used by persecutors, stocks, whips, prisons, swords, gibbets, stakes, &c., (where these seem to prevail with some cities or kingdoms, a stronger force sets up again, what a weaker pulled down); but against these spiritual strongholds in the souls of men, spiritual artillery and weapons are proper, which are mighty through God to subdue and bring under the very thought to obedience, or else to bind fast the soul with chains of darkness, and lock it up in the prison of unbelief and hardness to eternity.

I observe that as civil weapons are improper in this business, and never able to effect aught in the soul: so although they were proper, yet they are unnecessary ; for if, as the Spirit here saith, and the answerer grants, spiritual weapons in the hand of church officers are able and ready to take vengeance on all disobedience, that is, able and mighty, sufficient and ready for the Lord's work, either to save the soul, or to kill the soul of whomsoever be the party or parties opposite; in which respect I may again remember that speech of Job, How hast thou helped him that hath no power? Job xxvi. 2. [...]

Chapter L

Peace. Which is the third argument against the civil magistrates' power in spiritual and soul matters out of this scripture, Rom. xiii?

Truth. [...] We find four sorts of swords mentioned in the New Testament. First, the sword of persecution, which Herod stretched forth against James, Acts xii. 1, 2. Secondly, the sword of God's Spirit, expressly said to be the word of God, Ephes. vi. A sword of two edges, carried in the mouth of Christ, Rev. i., which is of strong and mighty operation, piercing between the bones and the marrow, between the soul and the spirit, Heb. iv. Thirdly, the great sword of war and destruction, given to him that rides that terrible red horse of war, so that he takes peace from the earth, and men kill one another, as is most lamentably true in the slaughter of so many hundred thousand souls within these few years in several parts of Europe, our own and others. None of these three swords are intended in this scripture [Romans 7]. Therefore, fourthly, there is a civil sword, called the sword of civil justice, which being of a material, civil nature, for the defence of persons, estates, families, liberties of a city or civil state, and the suppressing of uncivil or injurious persons or actions, by such civil punishment, it cannot, according to its utmost reach and capacity, now under Christ, when all nations are merely civil, without any such typical, holy respect upon them, as was upon Israel, a national church I say, cannot extend to spiritual and soul-causes, spiritual and soul-punishment, which be longs to that spiritual sword with two edges, the soul-piercing, in soul-saving, or soul-killing, the word of God. [...]

Chapter LXXIII

[...]

Truth. I answer, in this joint confession of the answerer with Luther, to wit, that the government of the civil magistrate extendeth no further than over the bodies and goods of their subjects, not over their souls: who sees not what a clear testimony from his own mouth and pen is given, to wit, that either the spiritual and church estate, the preaching of the word, and the gathering of the church, the baptism of it, the ministry, government, and administrations thereof, belong to the civil body of the common-weal, that is, to the bodies and goods of men, which seems monstrous to imagine? Or else that the civil magistrate cannot, without exceeding the bounds of his office, meddle with those spiritual affairs? [...]

Chapter XCII

[...]

Truth. I infer (as before hath been touched) that the sovereign, original, and foundation of civil power lies in the people, (whom they must needs mean by the civil power distinct from the government set up.) And if so, that a people may erect and establish what form of government seems to them most meet for their civil condition. It is evident that such governments as are by them erected and established, have no more power, nor for no longer time, than the civil power, or people consenting and agreeing, shall betrust them with. This is clear not only in reason, but in the experience of all commonweals, where the people are not deprived of their natural freedom by the power of tyrants.

Chapter CXXVI

[...]

Truth. [...] The result of all this: the church of Christ is the ship, wherein the prince – if a member, for otherwise the case is altered – is a passenger. In this ship the officers and governors, such as are appointed by the Lord Jesus, they are the chief, and in those respects above the prince himself, and are to be obeyed and submitted to in their works and administrations, even before the prince himself.

In this respect every Christian in the church, man or woman, if of more knowledge and grace of Christ, ought to be to be of higher esteem, concerning religion and Christianity, than all the princes in the world who have either none or less grace or knowledge of Christ: although in civil things all civil reverence, honour, and obedience ought to be yielded by all men.

Nathaniel Ward *The Simple Cobler of Aggawam in America* (1646/7)[25]

[...] If the devill might have his free option, I believe he would ask nothing else, but liberty to enfranchize all false Religions, and to embondage the true; nor should he need: It is much to bee feared, that laxe Tolerations upon State pretences and planting necessities, will be the next subtle Stratagem he will spread, to distate the Truth of God and supplant the peace of the Churches. Tolerations in things tolerable, exquisitely drawn out by the lines of the Scripture, and pensill of the Spirit, are the sacred favours of Truth, the due latitudes of Love, the faire Compartments of Christian fraternity: but irregular dispensations, dealt forth by the facilities of men, are the frontiers of errour, the redoubts of Schisme, the perillous irritaments of carnall and spirituall enmity. [...]

To tell a practicall lye, is a great sin, but yet transient; but to set up a Theoricall untruth, is to warrant every lye that lies from its root to the top of every branch it hath, which are not a few. [...]

Concerning Tolerations I may further assert.

That Persecution of True Religion, and Toleration of false, are the *Jannes* and *Jambres* to the Kingdome of Christ, whereof the last is farre the worst. [...]

He that is willing to tolerate any Religion, or discrepant way of Religion, besides his own, unlesse it be in matters meerly indifferent, either doubts of his own, or is not sincere in it.

He that is willing to tolerate any unsound Opinion, that his own may also be tolerated, though never so sound, will for a need hang Gods Bible at the Devils girdle.

Every Toleration of false Religions, or Opinions hath as many Errours and sins in it, as all the false Religions and Opinions it tolerates, and one sound one more.

That State that will give Liberty of Conscience in matters of Religion, must give Liberty of Conscience and Conversation in their Morall Laws, or else the Fiddle will be out of tune, and some of the strings cracke.

---

[25] N. Ward, *The Simple Cobler of Aggawam in America* (Boston: James Munroe and Co., 1848), pp. 4–6, 8–9.

He that will rather make an irreligious quarrell with other Religions, then try the truth of his own by valuable Arguments, and peaceable Sufferings; either his Religion, or himselfe is irreligious.

Experience will teach Churches and Christians, that it is farre better to live in a State united, though a little Corrupt, then in a State, whereof some Part is incorrupt, and all the rest divided.

I am not altogether ignorant of the eight Rules given by Orthodox Divines about giving Tolerations, yet with their favour I dare affirme,

That there is no Rule given by God for any State to give an Affirmative Toleration to any false Religion, or Opinion whatsoever; they must connive in some cases, but may not concede in any. [. . .]

John Cotton, Richard Mather, and Ralph Partridge *A Platform of Church Discipline* (1649)[26]

Chapter I Of the Form of Church Government; and That It Is One, Immutable, and Prescribed in the Word

Ecclesiastical polity, or church government or discipline, is nothing else but that form   1
and order that is to be observed in the church of Christ upon earth, both for the constitution of it, and all the administrations that therein are to be performed.

Church government is considered in a double respect, either in regard of the parts   2
of government themselves, or necessary circumstances thereof. The parts of government are prescribed in the word, because the Lord Jesus Christ, the King and Lawgiver in his church, is no less faithful in the house of God, than was Moses, who from the Lord delivered a form and pattern of government to the children of Israel in the Old Testament; and the holy Scriptures are now also so perfect as they are able to make the man of God perfect, and thoroughly furnished unto every good work; and therefore doubtless to the well-ordering of the house of God. [. . .]

Chapter II Of the Nature of the Catholic Church in General, and in Special of a Particular Visible Church

This militant church is to be considered as invisible and visible. Invisible, in respect   3
to their relation, wherein they stand to Christ as a body unto the head, being united unto him by the Spirit of God and faith in their hearts. Visible, in respect of the profession of their faith, in their persons, and in particular churches. [. . .]

The members of the militant visible church, considered either as not yet in church   4
order, or walking according to the church order of the gospel. In order, and so besides the spiritual union and communion common to all believers, they enjoy moreover an union and communion ecclesiastical-political. [. . .]

[26] In Congregational Churches in Massachusetts, *The Cambridge Platform of Church Discipline* (Boston: Perkins & Whipple, 1850), pp. 49–85.

6   A congregational church is by the institution of Christ a part of the militant visible church, consisting of a company of saints by calling, united into one body by an holy covenant, for the publique worship of God, and the mutual edification of one another in the fellowship of the Lord Jesus. [. . .]

Chapter IV Of the Form of a Visible Church, and of Church Covenant

1   Saints by calling must have a visible political union among themselves, or else they are not yet a particular church, as those similitudes hold forth, which the Scripture makes use of to shew the nature of particular churches; as a body, a building, house, hands, eyes, feet and other members, must be united, or else (remaining separate) are not a body. Stones, timber, though squared, hewn and polished, are not an house, until they are compacted and united; so saints or believers in judgment of charity, are not a church unless orderly knit together. [. . .]

3   This form is the visible covenant, agreement, or consent, whereby they give up themselves unto the Lord, to the observing of the ordinances of Christ together in the same society, which is usually called the church covenant: For we see not otherwise how members can have church-power over one another mutually. The comparing of each particular church to a city, and unto a spouse, seemeth to conclude not only a form, but that that form is by way of covenant. The covenant, as it was that which made the family of Abraham and children of Israel to be a church and people unto God, so is it that which now makes the several societies of Gentile believers to be churches in these days.

4   This voluntary agreement, consent or covenant (for all these are here taken for the same) although the more express and plain it is, the more fully it puts us in mind of our mutual duty; and stirreth us up to it, and leaveth less room for the questioning of the truth of the church-estate of a company of professors, and the truth of member-ship of particular persons; yet we conceive the substance of it is kept where there is real agreement and consent of a company of faithful persons to meet constantly together in one congregation, for the public worship of God, and their mutual edification; which real agreement and consent they do express by their constant practice in coming together for the public worship of God and by their religious subjection unto the ordinances of God there; the rather, if we do consider how Scripture-covenants have been entered into, not only expressly by word of mouth, but by sacrifice, by handwriting and seal; and also sometimes by silent consent, without any writing or expression of words at all. [. . .]

Chapter VIII Of the Election of Church Officers

2   Calling unto office is either immediate, by Christ himself, such was the call of the apostles and prophets; this manner of calling ended with them, as hath been said: or mediate, by the church.

3   It is meet that, before any be ordained or chosen officers, they should first be tried and proved; because hands are not suddenly to be laid upon any, and both elders and deacons must be of both honest and good report.

The things in respect of which they are to be tried, are those gifts and virtues which the scripture requireth in men that are to be elected unto such places, viz. that elders must be blameless, sober, apt to teach, and endued with such other qualifications as are laid down, 1 Tim. iii. 2; Tit. i. 6 to 9. Deacons to be fitted as is directed, Acts vi. 3; 1 Tim. iii. 8 to 11. [...]   4

A church being free, cannot become subject to any but by a free election; yet when such a people do choose any to be over them in the Lord, then do they become subject, and most willingly submit to their ministry in the Lord, whom they have chosen.   6

And if the church have power to choose their officers and ministers then, in case of manifest unworthiness and delinquency, they have power also to depose them: for to open and shut, to choose and refuse, to constitute in office, and to remove from office, are acts belonging to the same power. [...]   7

Chapter IX Of Ordination, and Imposition of Hands

[...] The essence and substance of the outward calling of an ordinary officer in the church does not consist in his ordination, but in his voluntary and free election by the church, and his accepting of that election; whereupon is founded that relation between pastor and flock, between such a minister and such a people. Ordination does not constitute an officer, nor give him the essentials of his office. [...]   2

Chapter X Of the Power of the Church and Its Presbyter

This government of the church is a mixt government, and so hath been acknow-ledged, long before the term of independency was heard of. In respect of Christ, the head and king of the church, and the sovereign power residing in him, and exercised by him, it is a monarchy; in respect of the body or brotherhood of the church, and power from Christ granted unto them it resembles a democracy; in respect of the presbytery and power committed unto them, it is an aristocracy. [...]   3

Church government or rule is placed by Christ in the officers of the church, who are therefore called rulers, while they rule with God; yet, in case of maladministra-tion, they are subject to the power of the church, as hath been said before. The Holy Ghost frequently, yea always, where it mentioneth church rule and church govern-ment, ascribeth it to elders; whereas the work and duty of the people is expressed in the phrase of obeying their elders, and submitting themselves unto them in the Lord. So as it is manifest that an organic or complete church is a body politic, consisting of some that are governors, and some that are governed in the Lord. [...]   7

From the promises, namely, that the ordinary power of government belonging only to the elders, power of privilege remaining with the brotherhood, (as the power of judgment in matters of censure and power of liberty in matters of liberty,) it followeth, that in an organic church, and right administration, all church acts proceed after the manner of a mixt administration, so as no church act can be consummated or perfected without the consent of both. [...]   11

Chapter XIII Of Church Members, Their Removal from One Church to Another, and of Recommendation and Dismissal

1   Church members may not remove or depart from the church, and so one from another as they please, nor without just and weighty cause, but ought to live and dwell together; forasmuch as they are commanded not to forsake the assembling of themselves together. Such departure tends to the dissolution and ruin of the body, as the pulling of stones and pieces of timber from the building, and of members from the natural body, tend to the destruction of the whole.

2   It is therefore the duty of church members, in such times and places, where counsel may be had, to consult with the church whereof they are members about their removal, that, accordingly, they having their approbation, may be encouraged, or otherwise desist. They who are joined with consent, should not depart without consent, except forced thereunto. [. . .]

Chapter XVII Of the Civil Magistrate's Power in Matters Ecclesiastical

2   Church-government stands in no opposition to civil government of commonwealths, nor any way intrencheth upon the authority of civil magistrates in their jurisdictions; nor any whit weakeneth their hands in governing, but rather strengtheneth them, and furthereth the people in yielding more hearty and conscionable obedience to them, whatsoever some ill affected persons to the ways of Christ have suggested, to alienate the affections of kings and princes from the ordinances of Christ; as if the kingdom of Christ in his church could not rise and stand, without the falling and weakening of their government, which is also of Christ, whereas the contrary is most true, that they may both stand together and flourish, the one being helpful unto the other, in their distinct and due administrations.

Samuel Willard *The Character of a Good Ruler* (1694)[27]

[. . .] For tho', had ma n kept his first state, the Moral Image Concreated in him, consisting in, *Knowledg*, *Righteousness*, and *True Holiness*, would have maintained him in a perfect understanding of, and Spontaneous Obedience to the whole duty incumbent on him, without the need of civil Laws to direct him, or a civil Sword to lay compulsion on him; and it would have been the true Golden Age, which the Heathen *Mythologists* are to Fabulous about. Yet even then did the All-Wise God Ordain Orders of Superiority and Inferiority among men, and required all *Honour* to be paid accordingly. But since the unhappy Fall hath Robbed man of that perfection, and filled his heart with perverse and rebellious principles, tending to the Subversion of all Order and the reducing of the World to a *Chaos*; necessity requires, and the Political happiness of a People is concerned in the establishment of Civil

---

[27] From S. Willard, *The Character of a Good Ruler* (Boston, 1694), included in P. Miller and T. H. Johnson, *The Puritans: A Sourcebook on Their Writings* (Mineola: Dover, 2001 [1938]), pp. 250–6.

Government. The want of it hath ever been pernicious, and attended on with miserable Circumstances. When there was no Governour in *Israel*, but every mail did what he would, what horrible outrages, were then perpetrated, though Holy and Zealous *Phinehas* was at that time the High-Priest? and we ourselves have had a Specimen of this in the short *Anarchy* accompanying our late *Revolution*. Gods Wisdom therefore, and his goodness is to be adored in that he hath laid in such a relief for the Children of men, against the mischief which would otherwise devour them; and engraven an inclination on their heart, generally to comply with it. But this notwithstanding, mens sins may put a curse into their Blessings, & render their remedy to be not better, possibly worse than the Malady. Government is to prevent and cure the disorders that are apt to break forth among the Societies of men; and to promote the civil peace and prosperity of such a people, as well as to suppress impiety, and nourish Religion. For this end there are to be both *Rulers*, and such as are to be *Ruled* by them: and the Weal or Wo of a People mainly depends on the qualifications of those Rulers, by whom we are to be Governed. [...]

Doctrine

It is of highest Consequence, that Civil Rulers should be Just Men, and such as Rule in the Fear of God [...]

Civil Rulers are all such as are in the exercise of a rightful Authority over others. These do not all of them stand in one equal Rank, nor are alike influential into Government. There are Supream and Subordinate Powers: and of these also there are some who have a *Legislative*, others an *Executive* Power in their Hands; which two, though they may sometimes meet in the same persons, yet are in themselves things of a different Nature. There are *Superiour Magistrates* in Provinces, and such as are of *Council* with them, and *Assembly men*, the *Representatives* of the People. There are *Judges* in Courts, *Superiour* and *Inferiour*, *Justices* of the *Peace* in their several Precincts: and in each of these Orders there Resides a measure of Authority.

Now, that all these may be Just, it is firstly required, that they have a Principle of Moral Honesty in them, and Swaying of them: that they Love Righteousness, and Hate Iniquity: that they be Men of Truth, Exod. 18. 21. for every man will act in his Relation, according to the Principle that Rules in him: so that an Unrighteous man will be an Unrighteous Ruler, so far as he hath an Opportunity.

They must also be acquainted with the Rules of Righteousness; they must know what is just, and what is Unjust, be Able Men, Exod. 18. 21. For, though men may know and not do, yet without Knowledge the Mind cannot be good. Ignorance is a Foundation for Error, and will likely produce it, when the man applies himself to act: and if he do right at any time, it is but by guess, which is a very poor Commendation. [...]

Finally, he [the civil ruler] must be one who prefers the publick Benefit above all private and separate Interests whatsoever. Every man in his place, owes himself to the good of the whole; and if he doth not so devote himself, he is unjust: and he who either to advance himself, or to be Revenged on another, will push on Injurious Laws, or pervert the true Intention of such as are in Force, is an unjust man: and he who is under the influence of a Narrow Spirit, will be ready to do so, as occasion offers. [...]

It then follows that we enquire of what great moment or consequence it is that these should be such: and there is a three-fold respect in which the high importance of it is to be discovered by us.

1   In respect to the Glory of God. Civil Rulers are God's Vicegerents here upon earth; hence they are sometimes honoured with the title of Gods, *Psal.* 82:6. *I have said ye are Gods*. Government is God's Ordinance; and those that are Vested with it, however *mediately* introduced into it, have their rightful authority from him, Prov. 8:15,16. *By me Kings Reign, and Princes Decree Justice. By me Princes Rule, and Nobles, even all the Judges of the Earth*, and they that are from him, should be for him, and ought to seek the Honour of him who is *King of Kings, and Lord of Lords* [...]

2   In regard to the weal of the People over whom they Rule. A People are not made for Rulers, But Rulers for a People. It is indeed an Honour which God puts upon some above others, when he takes them from among the People, and sets them up to Rule over them, but it is for the Peoples sake, and the Civil felicity of them is the next end of Civil Policy; and the happiness of Rulers is bound up with theirs in it. Nor can any wise men in authority think themselves happy in the Misery of their Subjects, to whom they either are or should be as Children are to their Fathers: We have the Benefit of Government expressed, 1. *Tim.* 2:2 *a quiet Life and peaceable, in all Godliness and honesty.* and it lies especialy with Rulers, under God, to make a People Happy or Miserable. When men can enjoy their Liberties and Rights without molestation or oppression; when they can live without fear of being born down by their more Potent Neighbours; when they are secured against Violence, and may be Righted against them that offer them any injury, without fraud; and are encouraged to serve God in their own way, with freedom, and without being imposed upon contrary to the Gospel precepts; now are they an happy People. But this is to be expected from none other but men just and Pious: they that are otherwise, will themselves be oppressours, and they that are influenced by them, and dependent on them, will adde to the grievance. [...]

3   With Reference to Rulers themselves. It is, as we before Observed, a Dignity put upon them, to be preferred to Government over their Brethren; to have the oversight, not of Beasts, but of Men. But as there is a great Trust devolved on them, so there is an answerable Reckoning which they must be called unto: And however they are settled in Authority by men, yet GOD, who Rules over all, hath put them in only *Durante Bene Plecito*: they are upon their good Behaviour; they are Stewards, and whensoever GOD pleaseth, He will call for a Reckoning, and put them out. *God sets up, and he pulls down*; and he hath a respect to men's Carriages in his dealings with them. [...] And although God doth not always peculiarly put a Brand in this World upon Impious and Unjust Rulers, yet there is a Tribunal before which they must stand e're long as other men; only their Account will be so much the more Fearful, and Condemnation more Tremendous, by how much they have neglected to take their greater advantages to Glorify God, and abused their Power to His Dishonour, by which they had a fairer opportunity than other men.

John Wise *A Vindication of the Government of New England Churches* (1717)[28]

Demonstration II

Chapter II

I Shall disclose several Principles of Natural Knowledge; plainly discovering the Law of Nature; or the true sentiments of Natural Reason, with Respect to Mans Being and Government. And in this Essay I shall peculiarly confine the discourse to two heads, *viz.*

I. Of the Natural [in distinction to the Civil] and then,
II. Of the Civil Being of Man. [. . .]

I shall consider Man in a state of Natural Being, as a Free-Born Subject under the Crown of Heaven, and owing Homage to none but God himself. It is certain Civil Government in General, is a very Admirable Result of Providence, and an Incomparable Benefit to Man-kind, yet must needs be acknowledged to be the Effect of Humane Free-Compacts and not of Divine Institution; it is the Produce of Mans Reason, of Humane and Rational Combinations, and not from any direct Orders of Infinite Wisdom, in any positive Law wherein is drawn up this or that Scheme of Civil Government. Government [says the Lord *Warrington*] is necessary – in that no Society of Men can subsist without it; and that Particular Form of Government is necessary which best suits the Temper and Inclination of a People. Nothing can be Gods Ordinance, but what he has particularly Declared to be such; there is no particularly [*sic*] Form of Civil Government described in Gods Word, neither does Nature prompt it. The Government of the *Jews* was changed five Times. Government is not formed by Nature, as other Births or Productions; If it were, it would be the same in all Countries; because Nature keeps the same Method, in the same thing, in all Climates. [. . .]

The Prime Immunity in Mans State, is that he is most properly the Subject of the Law of Nature. He is the Favourite Animal on Earth; in that this Part of Gods Image, *viz.* Reason is Congenate with his Nature, wherein by a Law Immutable, Instampt upon his Frame, God has provided a Rule for Men in all their Actions, obliging each one to the performance of that which is Right, not only as to Justice, but likewise as to all other Moral Vertues, the which is nothing but the Dictate of Right Reason founded in the Soul of Man. [. . .] But moreover, the foundation of the Law of Nature with relation to Government, may be thus Discovered. *scil.* Man is a Creature extremely desirous of his own Preservation; of himself he is plainly Exposed to many Wants, unable to secure his own safety, and Maintenance without the Assistance of his fellows; and he is also able of returning Kindness by the furtherance of mutual Good; But yet Man is often found to be Malicious, Insolent, and easily Provoked, and as powerful in Effecting mischief, as he is ready in designing it. Now that such

---

[28] J. Wise, *Vindication of the Government of New England Churches* (Boston: N. Boone, 1717), pp. 32–70.

a Creature may be Preserved, it is necessary that he be Sociable; that is, that he be capable and disposed to unite himself to those of his own species, and to Regulate himself towards them, that they may have no fair Reason to do him harm; but rather incline to promote his Interests, and secure his Rights and Concerns. This then is a Fundamental Law of Nature, that every Man as far as in him lies, do maintain a Sociableness with others, agreeable with the main end and disposition of humane Nature in general. For this is very apparent, that Reason and Society render Man the most potent of all Creatures. And Finally, from the Principles of Sociableness it follows as a fundamental Law of Nature, that Man is not so Wedded to his own Interest, but that he can make the Common good the mark of his Aim: And hence he becomes Capacitated to enter into a Civil State by the Law of Nature; for without this property in Nature, *viz.* Sociableness, which is for Cementing of parts, every Government would soon moulder and dissolve.

2   The Second Great Immunity of Man is an Original Liberty Instampt upon his Rational Nature. He that intrudes upon this Liberty, Violates the Law of Nature. [...] Which Liberty may be briefly Considered, Internally as to his Mind, and Externally as to his Person.

   i. The Internal Native Liberty of Mans Nature in general implies, a faculty of Doing or Omitting things according to the Direction of his Judgment. But in a more special meaning, this Liberty does not consist in a loose and ungovernable Freedom, or in an unbounded Licence of Acting. Such Licence is disagreeing with the condition and dignity of Man, and would make Man of a lower and meaner Constitution then Bruit Creatures; who in all their Liberties are kept under a better and more Rational Government, by their Instincts. [...] So that the true Natural Liberty of Man, such as really and truely agrees to him, must be understood, as he is Guided and Restrained by the Tyes of Reason, and Laws of Nature; all the rest is Brutal, if not worse.
   ii. Mans External Personal, Natural Liberty, Antecedent to all Humane parts, or Alliances must also be considered. And so every Man must be conceived to be perfectly in his own Power and disposal, and not to be controuled by the Authority of any other. And thus every Man, must be acknowledged equal to every Man, since all Subjection and all Command are equally banished on both sides; and considering all Men thus at Liberty, every Man has a Prerogative to Judge for himself, *viz.* What shall be most for his Behoove, Happiness and Well-being.

3   The Third Capital Immunity belonging to Mans Nature, is an equality amongst Men; Which is not to be denied by the Law of Nature, till Man has Resigned himself with all his Rights for the sake of a Civil State; and then his Personal Liberty and Equality is to be cherished, and preserved to the highest degree, as will consist with all just distinctions amongst Men of Honour, and shall be agreeable with the publick Good. [...]

There be many popular, or plausible Reasons that greatly Illustrate this Equality, *viz.* that we all Derive our Being from one stock, the same Common Father of humane Race. [...] And also that our Bodies are Composed of matter, frail, brittle, and lyable to be destroyed by thousand Accidents; we all owe our Existence to the same Method of propagation. The Noblest Mortal in his Entrance on to the Stage of Life, is not distinguished by any pomp or of passage from the lowest of Mankind; and our Life hastens to the same General Mark: Death observes no Ceremony, but Knocks as loud at the Barriers of the Court, as at the Door of the Cottage. [. . .] And though as *Hensius*, Paraphrases upon *Aristotle's* Politicks to this Purpose. *viz. Nothing is more suitable to Nature, then that those who Excel in Understanding and Prudence, should Rule and Controul those who are less happy in those Advantages, &c.* Yet we must note, that there is room for an Answer, *scil*. That it would be the greatest absurdity to believe, that Nature actually Invests the Wise with a Sovereignity over the weak; or with a Right of forcing them against their Wills; for that no Sovereignty can be Established, unless some Humane Deed, or Covenant Precede. [. . .]

To consider Man in a Civil State of Being; wherein we shall observe the great II difference betwen a Natural, and Political State; for in the latter State many Great disproportions appear, or at least many obvious distinctions are soon made amongst Men; which Doctrine is to be laid open under a few heads.

Every Man considered in a Natural State, must be allowed to be Free, and at his 1 own dispose; yet to suit Mans Inclinations to Society; And in a peculiar manner to gratify the necessity he is in of publick Rule and Order, he is Impelled to enter into a Civil Community; and Divests himself of his Natural Freedom, and puts himself under Government; which amongst other things Comprehends the Power of Life and Death over Him; together with Authority to Injoyn him some things to which he has an utter Aversation, and to prohibit him other things, for which he may have as strong an Inclination; so that he may be often under this Authority, obliged to Sacrifice his Private, for the Publick Good. So that though Man is inclined to Society, yet he is driven to a Combination by great necessity. For that the true and leading Cause of forming Governments, and yielding up Natural Liberty, and throwing Mans Equality into a Common Pile to be new Cast by the Rules of fellowship; was really and truly to guard themselves against the Injuries Men were lyable to Interchangeably; for none so Good to Man, as Man, and yet none a greater Enemy. So that,

The first Humane Subject and Original of Civil Power is the People. For as they 2 have a Power every Man over himself in a Natural State, so upon a Combination they can and do bequeath this Power unto others; and settle it according as their united discretion shall Determine. For that this is very plain, that when the Subject of Sovereign Power is quite Extinct, that Power returns to the People again. And when they are free, they may set up what species of Government they please; or if they rather incline to it, they may subside into a State of Natural Being, if it be plainly for the best. [. . .]

The formal Reason of Government is the Will of a Community, yielded up and 3 surrendered to some other Subject, either of one particular Person, or more, Conveyed in the following manner.

Let us conceive in our Mind a multitude of Men, all Naturally Free & Equal; going about voluntarily, to Erect themselves into a new Common-Wealth. Now their

Condition being such, to bring themselves into a Politick Body, they must needs Enter into divers Covenants.

  i. They must Interchangeably each Man Covenant to joyn in one lasting Society, that they may be capable to concert the measures of their safety, by a Publick Vote.
 ii. A Vote or Decree must then nextly pass to set up some Particular speecies of Government over them. And if they are joyned in their first Compact upon absolute Terms to stand to the Decision of the first Vote concerning the Species of Government: Then all are bound by the Majority to acquiesce in that particular Form thereby settled, though their own private Opinion, incline them to some other Model.
iii. After a Decree has specified the Particular form of Government, then there will be need of a New Covenant, whereby those on whom Sovereignty is conferred, engage to take care of the Common Peace, and Welfare. And the Subjects on the other hand, to yield them faithful Obedience. In which Covenant is Included that Submission and Union of Wills, by which a State may be conceived to be but one Person. So that the most proper Definition of a Civil State, is this. *viz.* A Civil State is a Compound Moral Person. whose Will [United by those Covenants before passed] is the Will of all; to the end it may Use, and Apply the strength and riches of Private Persons towards maintaining the Common Peace, Security, and Well-being of all. Which may be conceived as tho' the whole State was now become but one Man; in which the aforesaid Covenants may be supposed under Gods Providence, to be the Divine Fiat, Pronounced by God, let us make Man. And by way of resemblance the aforesaid Being may be thus Anatomized.

  1. The Sovereign Power is the Soul infused, giving Life and Motion to the whole Body.
  2. Subordinate Officers are the Joynts by which the Body moves.
  3. Wealth and Riches are the Strength.
  4. Equity and Laws are the Reason.
  5. Councellors the Memory.
  6. Salus Populi, or the Happiness of the People, is the End of its Being; or main Business to be attended and done.
  7. Concord amongst the Members, and all Estates, is the Health.
  8. Sedition is Sickness, and Civil War Death.

4   The Parts of Sovereignty may be considered: So,

  i. As it Prescribes the Rule of Action: It is rightly termed Legislative Power.
 ii. As it determines the Controversies of Subjects by the Standard of those Rules. So is it justly Termed Judiciary Power.
iii. As it Arms the Subjects against Foreigners, or forbids Hostility, so its called the Power of Peace and War.
 iv. As it takes in Ministers for the discharge of Business, so it is called the Right of Appointing Magistrates. So that all great Officers and Publick Servants, must needs owe their Original to the Creating Power of Sovereignty. [...]

The Chief End of Civil Communities, is, that Men thus conjoyned, may be secured   5
against the Injuries, they are lyable to from their own Kind. For if every Man could
secure himself singly; It would be great folly for him, to Renounce his Natural
Liberty, in which every Man is his own King and Protector

The Sovereign Authority besides that it inheres in every State as in a Common and   6
General Subject. So farther according as it resides in some One Person, or in
a Council [consisting of some Select Persons, or of all the Members of
a Community] as in a proper and particular Subject, so it produceth different
Forms of Common-wealths, *viz.* Such as are either simple and regular, or mixt. [. . .]

  i. A Democracy, which is when the Sovereign Power is Lodged in a Council
     consisting of all the Members, and where every Member has the Priviledge of
     a Vote. [. . .] A democracy is then Erected, when a Number of Free Persons, do
     Assemble together, in Order to enter into a Covenant for Uniting themselves in
     a Body: And such a Preparative Assembly hath some appearance already of
     a Democracy; it is a Democracy in *Embrio* properly in this Respect, that every
     Man hath the Priviledge freely to deliver his Opinion concerning the Common
     Affairs. Yet he who dissents from the Vote of the Majority, is not in the least
     obliged by what they determine, till by a second Covenant, a Popular Form be
     actually Established; for not before then can we call it a Democratical
     Government, *viz.* Till the Right of Determining all matters relating to the publick
     Safety, is actually placed in a General Assembly of the whole People; or by their
     own Compact and Mutual Agreement, Determine themselves the proper Subject
     for the Exercise of Sovereign Power. [. . .]
 ii. The Second Species of Regular Government, is an Aristocracy; and this is said
     then to be Constituted when the People, or Assembly United by a first Covenant,
     and having thereby cast themselves into the first Rudiments of a State; do then by
     Common Decree, Devolve the Sovereign Power, on a Council consisting of
     some Select Members; and these having accepted of the Designation, are then
     properly invested with Sovereign Command; and then an Aristocracy is formed.
iii. The Third Species of a Regular Government, is a Monarchy which is settled
     when the Sovereign Power is confered on some one worthy Person. It differs
     from the former, because a Monarch who is but one Person in Natural, as well as
     in Moral account. [. . .]

It is very plain [allowing me to speak Emblematically] the Primitive Constitution
of the Churches was a Democracy. [. . .] The End of all good Government is to
Cultivate Humanity, and Promote the happiness of all, and the good of every Man in
all his Rights, his Life, Liberty, Estate, Honour, &c. without injury or abuse done to
any. Then certainly it cannot easily be thought, that a company of Men, that shall
enter into a voluntary Compact, to hold all Power in their own hands, thereby to use
and improve their united force, wisdom, riches and strength for the Common and
Particular good of every Member, as is the Nature of a Democracy; I say it cannot be
that this sort of Constitution, will so readily furnish those in Government with an
appetite, or disposition to prey upon each other, or imbezle the common Stock; as
some Particular Persons may be apt to do when set off, and Intrusted with the same

Power. And moreover this appears very Natural, that when the aforesaid Government or Power, settled in all, when they have Elected certain capable Persons to Minister in their affairs, and the said Ministers remain accountable to the Assembly; these Officers must needs be under the influence of many wise cautions from their own thoughts [as well as under confinement by their Commission] in their whole Administration: And from thence it must needs follow that they will be more apt, and inclined to steer Right for the main Point, *viz*. The peculiar good, and benefit of the whole, and every particular Member fairly and sincerely. And why may not these stand for very Rational Pleas in Church Order?

For certainly if Christ has settled any form of Power in his Church he has done it for his Churches safety, and for the Benefit of every Member: Then he must needs be presumed to have made choice of that Government as should least Expose his People to Hazard, either from the fraud, or Arbitrary measures of particular Men. And it is as plain as day light, there is no Species of Government like a Democracy to attain this End. There is but about two steps from an Aristocracy, to a Monarchy, and from thence but one to a Tyranny; an able standing force, and an Ill-Nature, *Ipso facto*, turns an absolute Monarch into a Tyrant; this is obvious among the Roman *Caesars*, and through the World. And all these direful Transmutations are easier in Church affairs [from the different Qualities of things] then in Civil States. For what is it that cunning and learned Men can't make the World swallow as an Article of their Creed, if they are once invested with an Uncontroulable Power, and are to be the standing Oratours to Mankind in matters of Faith and Obedience? [. . .]

1   Three Particulars; or so many golden Maxims, securing the Honour of Congregational Churches.

Particular 1. That the People or Fraternity under the Gospel, are the first Subject of Power; or else Religion sinks the Dignity of Humane Nature into a baser Capacity with relation to Ecclesiastical, then it is in, in a Natural State of being with relation to Civil Government.

Particular 2. That a Democracy in Church or State, is a very honourable and regular Government according to the Dictates of Right Reason. And therefore,

Particular 3. That these Churches of New-England, in their ancient Constitution of Church Order; it being a Democracy, are manifestly Justified and Defended by the Law & Light of Nature.

[. . .] Whatever the Power is, the several Delegates must from the nature of the Government they derive from, be equal sharers in it. Democratical States, in their Representative Body can make but one House, because they have but one Subject of Supream Power in their Nature, and therefore their Delegates, let them be who or what they may be, are under equal Trust; so that none can justly claim Superiority over their Fellows, or pretend to a higher power in their Suffrage. Indeed, in such Kingdoms, where the Sovereign Power is distributed and settled in divers Subjects, that the ballance of Power may be more Even, for the safety of the whole, and of all parts under all Acts of Sovereign Power: From such a Settlement of Power, there arises several distinct States in the same Government, which when Convened as one Subject of Sovereign Power, they make different Houses in their Grand Sessions; and so one House or State can Negative another. But in every distinct House of these States, the Members are equal in their Vote, the most Ayes makes the Affirmative Vote, and most No's the Negative: They don't weigh the intellectual furniture, or other distinguishing Qualifications of the several Voters in the Scales of the Golden Rule of Fellowship; they only add up the Ayes, and the No's, and so determine the Suffrage of the House.

Suggested Readings

William Perkins, *The Works of That Famous and Worthie Minister of Christ, in the Universitie of Cambridge, M.W. Perkins*, 3 vols. (London: I. Legatt, 1603).

Anne Hutchinson, "The Examination of Mrs. Anne Hutchinson at the Court at Newton (1637)" in D. D. Hall (ed.), *The Antinomian Controversy, 1636–1638: A Documentary History* (Durham, NC: Duke University Press, 1990), pp. 311–48.

John Cotton, *The Pouring Out of the Seven Vials* (London, 1642).

Urian Oakes, *New-England Pleaded with* . . . (Cambridge: Printed by Samuel Green, 1673).

Nathaniel Hawthorne, *The Scarlet Letter* (London: David Bogue, 1851).

5 Independence

The Negative Founding

As a religious movement, Puritanism was extinct by the time of the First Great Awakening (1740). Its strength, i.e. the emphasis on the "purity" of its identity, also hastened its demise. As the case of Roger Williams demonstrates, dissenters – either banished or self-banished – had plenty of opportunities to move and create their own communities, with their own "people." The strictly controlled Puritan communities became impossible to maintain, and compromises had to be made. This rapid *theological* fragmentation destroyed the theologico-political communities, leaving them with just one side of the binomen, namely the *political* one. From then on individuals would no longer define themselves in terms of their belonging to a particular church, but rather in terms of their belonging to a particular political community, i.e. their respective towns, counties, and colonies. Yet the foundational double helix of the people's two bodies proved helpful for the colonists' arguments during the Imperial Debate and the Revolutionary War.

According to some scholars, what was awakened in 1740 was nothing less than "the spirit of American democracy."[1] Christianity became democratic, reshaped "by common people who molded it in their own image."[2] It was the discovery of religious populism, but not everyone embraced this development. For many of the **Old Lights**, the idea that the people are a mere collection of equal individuals to be guided by the majority of votes was deeply disturbing. They were worried that "[t]he elective dictatorship of the wise and virtuous could give way to the still more formidable dictatorship of the many."[3]

Jonathan Mayhew (1720–1766) was one of them. As a firm <u>foundationalist</u> he argued that, since "the truth and right have a real existence in nature, independent of the sentiments and practices of men, they do not necessarily follow the multitude or the major part." The idea that truth was just a social convention determined by a majority vote (the <u>anti-foundationalist</u> perspective) was abhorrent to him, for "the multitude may do evil, and the many judge falsely."[4] Unsurprisingly, Mayhew conceived of "the people" as a well-structured whole. In his famous ***Discourse Concerning Unlimited Submission and Non-Resistance to the Higher Powers***,

---

[1] A. Heimert and P. Miller (eds.), *The Great Awakening: Documents Illustrating the Crisis and Its Consequences* (Indianapolis and New York: The Bobbs-Merrill Company, 1967), p. lxi.

[2] N. O. Hatch, *The Democratization of American Christianity* (New Haven: Yale University Press, 1989), p. 9.

[3] Foster, *Their Solitary Way*, p. 168.

[4] Quoted in Heimert and Miller (eds.), *The Great Awakening*, p. 576.

upon the occasion of the centennial of the execution of Charles I, he alluded to a political compact between the rulers and the ruled. He argued not just for the *right* of "the whole body politic" to rebel, but for their *duty* to do so whenever the ruler became a tyrant. Otherwise, "'tis treason against common sense; 'tis treason against God." Yet, the fact that Mayhew was a Patriot who vehemently opposed the Stamp Act, allegedly coined the phrase "no taxation without representation," and urged common action among the colonies in the famous sermon *The Snare Broken* cannot be directly related to his anti-populist views. Both the corporatist apprehension of the people and the idea of individuals enjoying inalienable rights played important roles in the move toward independence, and in the process some people changed sides.

For example, **Daniel Leonard** (1740–1829) originally opposed what he perceived as an abuse of power by the British Parliament directed against the colonists, and he did so from a **liberal** perspective. In a letter from 1773, he argued that men enter civil society "to prevent that confusion and bloodshed which would inevitably take place were each individual left to judge in his own case and take by the strong hand what should appear to him satisfactory," but also to protect their freedom and property. Like Locke, for the Leonard of 1773, civil society "is nothing more than *the union of a multitude of people* who agree to live in subjection to [. . .] any power having legislative authority." Therefore, "every lawful government under heaven are extremely watchful in ascertaining and protecting the right of private property." Abusing this power amounted to robbery; by attempting to tax the colonists, the Parliament had violated the "most sacred bonds of human society." Yet, after the **First Continental Congress** (1774), the same Daniel Leonard became concerned by the real possibility that the colonies would declare their independence from Great Britain. Like many other **Loyalists**, he believed resistance to abusive measures, petitions and the like, were legitimate, but declaring independence was unjustifiable and extreme. For the Loyalists, the fact that the infamous **Stamp Act** of 1765 was repealed in 1766 was proof that resistance was effective.

In a letter from 1775, Leonard (under the pseudonym **Massachusettensis**) changed his tune, switching from a largely **liberal** to a mainly **republican** stance. There was "little real cause" for revolting. The British constitution was so admired because it combines the principles of monarchy, aristocracy, and democracy, but it does so because of the sovereignty attributed to the king in Parliament. Denying the authority of the Parliament amounted to denying the very principle of the <u>mixed constitution</u> that was universally admired, by getting rid of the aristocratic (House of Lords) and the democratic elements (House of Commons) embedded in it. Furthermore, Leonard denied the argument that the Americans were not represented in Parliament, by claiming that all British subjects were *virtually* represented. Hence, by refusing to acknowledge the authority of the Parliament, the colonies would become different countries, losing even the ties that connect them to each other.

The distinction between **virtual** and **actual representation** occupied the Imperial Debate for a while, as seen, for example, in the writings of **Daniel Dulany** (1722–1797) at the beginning of the Stamp Act crisis. "Whether, therefore, upon the whole matter, the imposition of the Stamp Duties is a proper exercise of constitutional authority, or not, depends upon the single question, Whether the Commons of Great-

Britain are virtually the representatives of the Commons of America, or not." The answer, for Dulany, was evidently in the negative. While he agreed that the non-electors from Great Britain were virtually represented in the Parliament, since "[t]he interests [. . .] of the non-electors, the electors, and the representatives, are individually the same; to say nothing of the connection among neighbours, friends, and relations," he argued that the same does not apply to non-voting colonists. First, because if the British non-electors were not taxed by the Parliament, they would not be taxed at all, while the colonists are taxed twice – once by their local legislatures and once by the Parliament. Second, because even though "the interests of England and the colonies are allied, and an injury to the colonies produced into all its consequences, will eventually affect the mother country; yet, these consequences being generally remote, are not at once foreseen; they do not immediately alarm the fears, and engage the passions of the English electors."

Nevertheless, in the long run, the well-known cry, "No taxation without representation!" (Johnathan Mayhew), lost its appeal, and Dulany would end up in the Loyalist camp, like Leonard. The reason for abandoning this line of argumentation was simple: relatively early in the debate, the colonists realized that, even if they were allowed to send their own representatives to the Parliament, the most likely scenario would be that even these representatives would become estranged from the colonial interests, because of the sheer distance that separated them. But more importantly, such representatives would always remain a minority, unable to defend the colonial interests in the British legislature. The only solution left was to deny the authority of the Parliament over the colonies entirely, and to revive the importance of the royal charters. In other words, while agreeing with the **liberal** view that people are a multitude held together by their legislatures – the social contract theory – they also agreed with the **republican** view that, as a corporation, people made political compacts with their rulers (in this case, the people from each colony with the king).

In the main, this was **John Adams**'s argument. Adams (1735–1826) eventually became the framer of the constitution of Massachusetts (Chapter 6) and the second President of the United States under the new Constitution, but he was also the first president to not be re-elected after his first term in office. This may have had something to do with his disinterest in the fickleness of public opinion, as demonstrated by his legal defense of the British soldiers involved in the (in)famous **Boston Massacre** (1770), in which five colonists had died. As a lawyer who believed in the presumption of innocence, he successfully defended the British soldiers despite the anti-British sentiments of the day. Yet, this did not prevent him from being among the fiercest supporters of colonial independence.

Under the pseudonym **Novanglus**, Adams engaged in a long exchange of arguments with the Loyalist Daniel Leonard (**Massachusettensis**), whom he referred to as "this rhetorical magician." In a direct reply to Leonard's arguments, he agreed that "two supreme and independent authorities cannot exist in the same state," but arrived at a radically different conclusion: "Therefore, I contend, that our provincial legislatures are the only supreme authorities in our colonies." He applied the same reasoning to invert another of Leonard's arguments: "If the colonies are not subject to the authority of parliament, Great Britain and the colonies must be distinct states," claimed Leonard. Adams replied that "There is no need of being startled at this consequence. It is very harmless. There is no absurdity at all in it. *Distinct states may be united under one king.*"

As a result of this new type of argument, in which the only connection with the British Empire was through the political compacts between each colony and the king, the colonists raised the king to an importance that would have been hard to conceive for the Whigs just a few years prior. As late as 1775, **Alexander Hamilton** (*c.*1755–1804) argued that the monarch "is under no temptation to purchase the favour of one part of his dominion, at the expense of another; but it is his interest to treat them all, upon the same footing. Very different is the case with regard to the Parliament. The Lords and Commons both, have a private and separate interest to pursue."[5] Metaphors about "the paternal Care of the Monarch" and "his Paternal Goodness" abounded at the beginning of the 1770s.

Such a development was baffling for many British. **Lord North** (1732–1792) argued that

> if he understood the meaning of the words Whig and Tory [. . .] he conceived that it was characteristic of Whiggism to gain for the people as much as possible, while the aim of Toryism was to increase the [royal] prerogative. That in the present case, the administration contended for the right of parliament, while the Americans talked about their belonging to the crown. Their language therefore was that of Toryism.[6]

Nevertheless, it was a relatively short idyll. It is difficult to pinpoint the precise date when the honeymoon between the Patriots and the king ended, since it occurred at different times in different places for different people. As late as July 1775, while rejecting the Parliament's offer of peace and reconciliation (which made moot the taxation issue and made clear to everyone that this was a disagreement of principles), Congress extended the Olive Branch Petition to the king.

Unlike the many colonists who embraced the principle of the social compact inside the colonies, but not in their relationships with Great Britain, **Jonathan Boucher** (1738–1804) found Locke's theory both inconsistent and pernicious for any government. Born in England, Boucher was an Anglican preacher, a teacher, and a philologist. He also opposed the Stamp Act, which he judged "oppressive, impolitic and illegal," but considered the threat of rebellion not just a mistake, but a sin. "Obedience to Government is every man's duty, because it is every man's interest: but it is particularly incumbent on Christians, [. . .] and therefore, when Christians are disobedient to human ordinances, they are also disobedient to God." Despite his many references to Christianity and Scripture, most of Boucher's arguments against rebellion were of a philosophical nature.

According to him, even if one accepts that the end of government is "the common good of mankind," it does not follow that "government must therefore have been

---

[5] A. Hamilton, *The Farmer Refuted: or, A More Impartial and Comprehensive View of the Disputes between Great-Britain and the Colonies* (New York: James Rivington, 1775), p. 18.

[6] Quoted in E. Nelson, "Patriot Royalism: The Stuart Monarchy in American Political Thought, 1769–75," *The William and Mary Quarterly*, 68:4 (2011), p. 535. For a more developed argument, see E. Nelson, *The Royalist Revolution: Monarchy and the American Founding* (Cambridge, MA: The Belknap Press of Harvard University Press, 2014), pp. 80–97.

instituted by common consent," as the **liberal** theory stated. The logic of the argument is but an appearance: "In no instance have mankind ever yet agreed as to what is, or is not, 'the common good.' [. . .] The premises, therefore, that 'common good is matter of common feeling,' being false, the consequence drawn from it, viz. that government was instituted by 'common consent,' is of course equally false." Boucher goes on to attack every single premise of Locke's theory, beginning with the principle of equality, the requirement of unanimous consent for the creation of civil society, and the acceptance of the majority principle, either implicitly or even explicitly. "The same principle of equality that exempts him from being governed without his own consent, clearly entitles him to recall and resume that consent whenever he sees fit; and he alone has a right to judge when and for what reasons it may be resumed." Since the principle of the majority is determined by law, "[a] right of resistance, therefore, for which Mr. Locke contends, is incompatible with the duty of submitting to the determination of 'the majority,' for which he also contends." Because of his support for the monarchy, Jonathan Boucher was eventually forced to flee back to England, despite his long-time friendship with none other than **George Washington**. Boucher never wavered in his views of the American Revolution, nor in his appreciation of Washington, to whom he dedicated his book *A View of the Causes and Consequences of the American Revolution* (1797). It goes to show that people can disagree in both theory and practice, yet remain friends and respect each other.

Compared to Boucher, **Thomas Paine** (1737–1809) stood at the opposite end of the political spectrum. Although he was the main contributor in changing the meaning of "republicanism" into "anti-monarchism," he was neither a classical republican nor a classical liberal. He was a revolutionary who used and mixed different types of arguments in order to convince as many people as possible to rebel against Great Britain. And he was good at it; even John Adams, far from being an admirer of Paine, acknowledged that "without the pen of the author of *Common Sense*, the sword of Washington would have been raised in vain." As soon as he arrived in the colonies in 1774, he declared that "[a]s Britain hath not manifested the least inclination towards a compromise, we may be assured that no terms can be obtained worthy the acceptance of the Continent, or any ways equal to the expence of blood and treasure we have been already put to."[7]

The publication of *Common Sense* in January 1776 was serendipitous. It happened the day (January 10) after news reached the colonies that in his speech in Parliament on October 26, 1775, the king had declared the colonies to be in open rebellion and had rejected the Olive Branch Petition. Paine's booklet became an instant success; in the first three months, it sold an estimated 100,000 copies, with as many as 500,000 sold by the end of the Revolutionary War, and it was crucial in tipping colonial public opinion in favor of independence. Though a firm believer in the Enlightenment, Paine also acknowledged that some thoughts may not *yet* be fashionable, for "*time makes more converts than reason.*" Nevertheless, he insisted that at stake was not just the future of the

[7] T. Paine, "Thoughts on the Present State of American Affairs," in *The Writings of Thomas Paine*, Vol. I: *1774–1779* (Indianapolis: Liberty Fund, 1774), p. 93.

American colonies, but of the whole world. Britain was waging war not just against the colonists, but against "the natural rights of all Mankind."

The entire tract is a mixture of republican, liberal, and Puritan arguments (although he was a deist), thus appealing to multiple audiences. Paine began by claiming that government is a necessary evil (man is social by nature, but not political), because of the Fall and the ensuing corruption ("the lost badge of innocence"). **Direct democracy**, as in Aristotle's time, was the first form of government, but, as the number of people increased, **representative democracy** became the second-best system (compare this with Madison in Chapter 7). Nevertheless, it must be a **descriptive representation**, one which mirrors the composition of the "whole body" of the people and the "common interest." The idea of descriptive representation remains popular even today and assumes that only if one belongs to a given group – professional, ethnic, racial, religious, gender, and so forth – can one properly understand and represent its interests.

Paine attacked the much-praised mixed constitution of Britain, arguing, on the one hand, that it was too complicated, making it impossible to assign either blame or responsibility. Yet, on the other hand, he also claimed that, far from being a real republican mixed constitution, it was, in effect, dominated by two tyrannical principles (monarchy and aristocracy). He went on by concentrating his criticisms on monarchy, playing on the anti-Catholic sentiments of his audience ("monarchy [. . .] is the popery of government"), and concluded by building the case for American independence as soon as possible, as "our duty to mankind at large, as well as to ourselves." The last part was permeated by a sentiment of urgency; it was now or never. "Youth is the seed-time of good habits as well in nations as in individuals. It might be difficult, if not impossible, to form the Continent into one government half a century hence. The vast variety of interests, occasioned by an increase of trade and population, would create confusion. Colony would be against colony."

Paine's approach proved successful, for some six months later the **Declaration of Independence** was signed. Penned mostly by Thomas Jefferson, the Declaration did more than make a reconciliation with Great Britain impossible. Since it was already agreed that the only connection between the colonies and Britain was through the political compact between the people of each colony and the king, King George III became "the perfect scapegoat" almost overnight.[8] Although this feature was largely ignored in the first years after its adoption, the Declaration of Independence managed to depict the king as the main culprit of all colonial infringements on corporatist rights, all the while reaffirming that "consanguinity" and the "Ties of our common Kindred" do not matter when "it becomes necessary for one People to dissolve the Political Bands which have connected them with another."[9]

The Loyalist **Peter Oliver** (1713–1791) continued to be baffled even years later, while acknowledging the exceptionality of the event: "The Revolt of North America,

---

[8] G. Stourzh, *From Vienna to Chicago and Back: Essays on Intellectual History and Political Thought in Europe and America* (Chicago: University of Chicago Press, 2010 [1970]), p. 25.

[9] B. A. Shain (ed.), *The Declaration of Independence in Historical Context: American State Papers, Petitions, Proclamations and Letters of the Delegates in the First National Congress* (New Haven and London: Yale University Press, 2014).

from their Allegiance to & Connection with the Parent State, seems to be as striking a Phaenomenon, in the political World, as hath appeared for many Ages past; & perhaps it is a singular one." He was proven right, even if for the wrong reasons. What mattered in the long run was less the victory of the Patriots in the Revolutionary War, and more their victory in the war of ideas.

Jonathan Mayhew

A Discourse Concerning Unlimited Submission and Non-Resistance to the Higher Powers: With Some Reflections on the Resistance Made to King Charles I. (1750)[10]

[...] The apostle's doctrine, in the passage thus explained [Romans 13:1–8], concerning the office of civil rulers, and the duty of subjects, may be summed up in the following observations; *viz.* That the end of magistracy is the good of civil society, *as such*:

That civil rulers, as such, are the ordinance and ministers of god; it being by his permission and providence that any bear rule; and agreeable to his will, that there should be some persons vested with authority in society, for the well-being of it: That which is here said concerning civil rulers, extends to all of them in common: it relates indifferently to monarchical, republican and aristocratical government; and to all other forms which truly answer the sole end of government, the happiness of society; and to all the different degrees of authority in any particular state; to inferior officers no less than to the supreme:

That disobedience to civil rulers in the due exercise of their authority; is not merely a *political sin*, but an heinous offence against God and *religion*:

That the true ground and reason of our obligation to be subject to the higher powers, is the usefulness of magistracy (when properly exercised) to human society, and its subserviency to the general welfare: [...]

And lastly, that those civil rulers to whom the apostle injoins subjection, are the persons *in possession*; *the powers that be*; those who are *actually* vested with authority.

There is one very important and interesting point which remains to be inquired into; namely, the *extent* of that subjection *to the higher powers*, which is here enjoined as a duty upon all christians. Some have thought it warrantable and glorious, to disobey the civil powers in certain circumstances; and, in cases of very great and general oppression, when humble remonstrances fail of having any effect; and when the publick welfare cannot be otherwise provided for and secured, to rise unanimously even against the sovereign himself, in order to redress their grievances; to vindicate their natural and legal rights: to break the yoke of tyranny, and free themselves and posterity from inglorious servitude and ruin. It is upon this principle that many royal oppressors have been driven from their thrones into banishment; and many slain by the hands of their subjects. [...] It was upon this principle, that king *Charles* I, was beheaded before his own banqueting house. It was upon this principle, that king *James* II. was made to fly that country which he aim'd at enslaving: And upon this principle was that revolution brought about, which has been so fruitful of happy consequences to *Great-Britain*. [...] Now whether we are obliged to yield such an absolute submission to our prince; or whether disobedience and resistance

---

[10] J. Mayhew, *A Discourse Concerning Unlimited Submission and Non-Resistance to the Higher Powers: With Some Reflections on the Resistance Made to King Charles I.* (Boston: D. Fowle, 1750), pp. 9–13, 20–3, 29–30, 35–40, 44–6.

may not be justifiable in some cases, notwithstanding any thing in the passage before us, is an inquiry in which we are all concerned; and this is the inquiry which is the main design of the present discourse. [...]

And if we attend to the nature of the argument with which the apostle here inforces the duty of submission to *the higher powers*, we shall find it to be such an one as concludes not in favor of submission to all who bear the *title* of rulers, in common; but only, to those who *actually* perform the duty of rulers, by exercising a reasonable and just authority, for the good of human society. This is a point which it will be proper to enlarge upon; because the question before us turns very much upon the truth or falshood of this position. It is obvious, then, in general, that the civil rulers whom the apostle here speaks of, and obedience to whom he presses upon christians as a duty, are *good rulers*, such as are, in the exercise of their office and power, benefactors to society. [...] It is manifest that this character and description of rulers, agrees only to such as are rulers in fact, as well as in name: to such as govern well, and act agreeably to their office. And the apostle's argument for submission to rulers, is wholly built and grounded upon a presumption that they do in fact answer this character; and is of no force at all upon supposition of the contrary. If *rulers are a terror to good works, and not to the evil*; if they are not *ministers for good to society*, but for evil and distress, by violence and oppression; if they *execute wrath upon* sober, peaceable persons, who do their duty as members of society; and suffer rich and honourable knaves to escape with impunity; if, instead of *attending continually upon* the good work of advancing the publick welfare, they *attend* only upon the gratification of their own lust and pride and ambition, to the destruction of the public welfare; if this be the case, it is plain that the apostle's argument for submission does not reach them; they are not the same, but different persons from those whom he characterizes; and who must be obeyed according to his reasoning. [...] If those who bear the title of civil rulers, do not perform the duty of civil rulers, but act directly counter to the sole end and design of their office; if they injure and oppress their subjects, instead of defending their rights and doing them good; they have not the least pretence to be honored, obeyed and rewarded, according to the apostle's argument. For his reasoning, in order to show the duty of subjection to the *higher powers*, is, as was before observed, built wholly upon the supposition, that they do, *in fact*, perform the duty of rulers. [...]

I now add, farther, that the apostle's argument is so far from proving it to be the duty of people to obey, and submit to, such rulers as act in contradiction to the public good, and so to the design of their office, that it proves *the direct contrary*. [...] If it be our duty, for example, to obey our king merely for this reason, that he rules for the public welfare, (which is the only argument the apostle makes use of) it follows, by a parity of reason, that when he turns tyrant, and makes his subjects his prey to devour and to destroy, instead of his charge to defend and cherish, we are bound to throw off our allegiance to him, and to resist; and that according to the tenor of the apostle's argument in this passage. Not to discontinue our allegiance, in this case, would be to join with the sovereign in promoting the slavery and misery of that society, the welfare of which, we ourselves, as well as our sovereign, are indispensably obliged to secure and promote, as far as in us lies. It is true the apostle puts no case of such a tyrannical prince; but by his grounding his argument for submission wholly upon the good of civil society; it is plain he implicitly authorises, and even requires us to make resistance, whenever this shall be necessary to the public safety and happiness. [...]

But then, if unlimited submission and passive obedience to the *higher powers*, in all possible cases, be not a duty, it will be asked, "How far are we obliged to submit? If we may innocently disobey and resist in some cases, why not in all? Where shall we stop? What is the measure of our duty? This doctrine tends to the total dissolution of civil government; and to introduce such scenes of wild anarchy and confusion, as are more fatal to society than the worst of tyranny." [...]

[Footnote in the original text:] We may very safely assert these two things in general, without undermining government: one is, That no civil rulers are to be obeyed when they enjoin things that are inconsistent with the commands of god: All such disobedience is lawful and glorious; particularly, if persons refuse to comply with any *legal establishment of religion.* [...] Another thing that may be asserted with equal truth and safety, is, That no government is to be submitted to, at the *expence* of that which is the *sole end* of all government, – the common good and safety of society. Because, to submit in this case, if it should ever happen, would evidently be to set up the *means* as more valuable, and above, the *end*: than which there cannot be a greater solecism and contradiction. The only reason of the institution of civil government; and the only rational ground of submission to it, is the common safety and utility. If therefore, in any case, the common safety and utility would not be promoted by submission to government, but the contrary, there is no ground or motive for obedience and submission, but, for the contrary.

Whoever considers the nature of civil government must, indeed, be sensible that a great degree of *implicit confidence*, must unavoidably be placed in those that bear rule: this is implied in the very notion of authority's being originally a *trust*, committed by the people, to those who are vested with it, as all just and righteous authority is; all besides, is mere lawless force and usurpation; neither god nor nature, having given any man a right of dominion over any society, independently of that society's approbation, and consent to be governed by him. – Now as all men are fallible, it cannot be supposed that the public affairs of any state, should be always administered in the best manner possible, even by persons of the greatest wisdom and integrity. Nor is it sufficient to legitimate disobedience to the *higher powers* that they are not so administred; or that they are, in some instances, very ill-managed; for upon this principle, it is scarcely supposeable that any government at all could be supported, or subsist. Such a principle manifestly tends to the dissolution of government; and to throw all things into confusion and anarchy. – But it is equally evident, upon the other hand, that those in authority may abuse their *trust* and power *to such a degree*, that neither the law of reason, nor of religion, requires, that any obedience or submission should be paid to them; but, on the contrary, that they should be totally *discarded*; and the authority which they were before vested with, transferred to others, who may exercise it more to those good purposes for which it is given. – Nor is this principle, that resistance to the *higher powers*, is, in some extraordinary cases, justifiable, so liable to abuse, as many persons seem to apprehend it. For although there will be always some petulant, querulous men, in every state – men of factious, turbulent and carping dispositions, – glad to lay hold of any trifle to justify and legitimate their caballing against their rulers, and other seditious practices; yet there are, comparatively speaking, but few men of this *contemptible character*. It does not appear but that mankind, in general, have a disposition to be as submissive and passive and tame under government as they ought to be. [...] Till people find themselves greatly abused and oppressed by their governors, they are not apt to complain; and whenever they do, in fact, find themselves thus abused and oppressed, they must be stupid not to complain. To say that subjects in general are not proper judges when their governors oppress them, and play the tyrant; and when they defend their rights, administer justice impartially, and promote the public welfare, is as great *treason* as ever man uttered; 'tis treason, not against one *single* man, but the state; against the whole body politic; 'tis treason against mankind; 'tis treason against common sense; 'tis treason against God. [...] The people know for what end they set up, and maintain, their governors; and they are the proper judges when they execute their trust as they ought to do it; when their prince exercises an equitable and paternal authority over them; when from a prince and common father, he exalts himself into a tyrant; when from subjects and children, he degrades them into the class of slaves; plunders them, makes them his prey, and unnaturally sports himself with their lives and fortunes—— [End of footnote.]

A people, really oppressed to a great degree by their sovereign, cannot well be insensible when they are so oppressed. [...] For a nation thus abused to arise unanimously, and to resist their prince, even to the dethroning him, is not criminal; but a reasonable way of vindicating their liberties and just rights; it is making use of the means, and the only means, which god has put into their power, for mutual and self-defence. And it would be highly criminal in them, not to make use of this means. It would be stupid tameness, and unaccountable folly, for whole nations to suffer *one* unreasonable, ambitious and cruel man, to wanton and riot in their misery. And in such a case it would, of the two, be more rational to suppose, that they did NOT *resist*, than that they who did, would *receive to themselves damnation*. [...]

The next question which naturally arises, is, whether the resistance which was made to the king [Charles I] by the parliament was properly rebellion or not? The answer to which is plain, that it was not; but a most righteous and glorious stand, made in defence of the natural and legal rights of the people, against the unnatural and illegal encroachments of arbitrary power. Nor was this a rash and too sudden opposition. The nation had been patient under the oppressions of the crown, even to longsuffering; – for a course of many years; and there was no rational hope of redress in any other way – Resistance was absolutely necessary in order to preserve the nation from slavery, misery and ruin. And who so proper to make this resistance as the lords and commons – the whole representative body of the people; – guardians of the public welfare; and each of which was, in point of legislation, vested with an equal, coordinate power, with that of the crown? [...]

[Footnote in the original text:] The king, in his coronation oath, swears to exercise only such a power as the constitution gives him: And the subject, in the oath of allegiance, swears only to obey him in the exercise of such a power. The king is as much bound by his oath, not to infringe the legal rights of the people, as the people are bound to yield subjection to him. From whence it follows, that as soon as the prince sets himself up above law, he loses the king in the tyrant: he does to all intents and purposes, unking himself, by acting out of, and beyond, that sphere which the constitution allows him to move in. And in such cases, he has no more right to be obeyed, than any inferior officer who acts beyond his commission. The subjects obligation to allegiance then ceases of course: and to resist him, is no more rebellion, than to resist any foreign invader. There is an essential difference betwixt government and tyranny; at least under such a constitution as the english. The former consists in ruling according to law and equity; the latter, in ruling contrary to law and equity, So also, there is an essential difference betwixt resisting a tyrant, and rebellion; The former is a just and reasonable self-defence; the latter consists in resisting a prince whose administration is just and legal; and this is what denominates it a crime. [...]

The Snare Broken (Sermon; 1766)

[...] Having rendered our devout thanks to God, whose kingdom ruleth over all, and sung his high praises; permit me now, my friends and brethren, with unfeigned love to my country, to congratulate you on that interesting event [Parliament's repeal of the Stamp Act on March 18, 1766], which is the special occasion of this solemnity: An event, as I humbly conceive, of the utmost importance to the whole British empire, whose peace and prosperity we ought ardently to desire; and one, very peculiarly affecting the welfare of these colonies. Believe me, I lately took no inconsiderable part with you in your grief, and gloomy apprehensions, on account of a certain parliamentary act, which you supposed ruinous in its tendency to the American plantations, and, eventually, to Great-Britain. I now partake no less in your common joy, on account of the repeal of that act; whereby these colonies are emancipated from a slavish, inglorious bondage; are re-instated in the enjoyment of their ancient rights and privileges, and a foundation is laid for lasting harmony between Great-Britain and them, to their mutual advantage. [...]

[I]t shall now be taken for granted, that as we were free-born, never made slaves by the right of conquest in war, if there be indeed any such right, nor sold as slaves in any open lawful market, for money, so we have a natural right to our own, till we have freely consented to part with it, either in person, or by those whom *we* have appointed to represent, and to act for us.

It shall be taken for granted, that this natural right is declared, affirmed and secured to us, as we are British subjects, by Magna Charta; all acts contrary to which, are said to be *ipso facto* null and void: And, that this natural, constitutional right has been further confirmed to most of the plantations by particular subsequent royal charters, taken in their obvious sense; the legality and authority of which charters was never once denied by either house of Parliament; but implicitly at least acknowledged, ever since they were respectively granted, till very lately. [...]

It shall, therefore, be taken for granted, that the colonies had great reason to petition and remonstrate against a late act of Parliament, as being an infraction of these rights, and tending directly to reduce us to a state of slavery. [. . .]

It is taken for granted, that as the surprising, unexampled growth of these colonies, to the extension of his majesty's dominion, and prodigious advantage of Britain in many respects, has been chiefly owing, under God, to the liberty enjoyed here; so the infraction thereof in two such capital points as those before referred to, would undoubtedly discourage the trade, industry and population of the colonies, by rendering property insecure and precarious; would soon drain them of all their little circulating money; would put it absolutely out of their power to purchase British commodities, force them into manufactures of their own, and terminate, if not in the ruin, yet in the very essential detriment of the mother-country.

It shall, therefore, also be taken for granted, that altho' the colonies could not justly claim an exclusive right of taxing themselves, and the right of being tried by juries; yet they had great reason to remonstrate against the act aforesaid on the footing of inexpedience, the great hardship, and destructive tendency of it; as a measure big with mischief to Britain, as well as to themselves; and promoted at first, perhaps, only by persons who were real friends to neither. [. . .]

To excite our gratitude to God the more effectually, let us consider the greatness of our late danger and of our deliverance: Let us take a brief retrospective view of the perplexed, wretched state, in which these colonies were, a few months ago, compared with the joyful and happy condition, in which they are at present, by the removal of their chief grievances. [. . .]

[T]hey, as we generally suppose, are really slaves to all intents and purposes, who are obliged to labor and toil only for the benefit of others; or, which comes to the same thing, the fruit of whose labour and industry may be lawfully taken from them without their consent, and they justly punished if they refuse to surrender it on demand, or apply it to other purposes than those, which their masters, of their mere grace and pleasure, see fit to allow. Nor are there many American understandings acute enough to distinguish any material difference between this being done by a single person, under the title of an absolute monarch, and done by a far-distant legislature consisting of many persons, in which they are not represented; and the members whereof, instead of feeling, and sharing equally with them in the burden thus imposed, are eased of their own in proportion to the greatness and weight of it. It may be questioned, whether the ancient Greeks or Romans, or any other nation in which slavery was allowed, carried their idea of it much further than this. So that our late apprehensions, and universal consternation, on account of ourselves and posterity, were far, very far indeed, from being groundless. For what is there in this world more wretched, than for those who were born free, and have a right to continue so, to be made slaves themselves, and to think of leaving a race of slaves behind them; even though it be to masters, confessedly the most humane and generous in the world? Or what wonder is it, if after groaning with a low voice for a while, to no purpose, we at length groaned so loudly, as to be heard more than three thousand miles; and to be pitied throughout Europe, wherever it is not hazardous to mention even the name of liberty, unless it be to reproach it, as only another name for sedition, faction or rebellion. [. . .]

The repeal, the repeal has at once, in a good measure, restored things to order, and composed our minds, by removing the chief ground of our fears. The course of justice between man and man is no longer obstructed; commerce lifts up her head, adorned with golden tresses, pearls and precious stones. All things that went on right before, are returning gradually to their former course; those that did not, we have reason to hope, will go on better now; almost every person you meet, wears the smiles of contentment and joy; and even our slaves rejoice, as tho' they had received their manumission. Indeed, all the lovers of liberty in Europe, in the world, have reason to rejoice; the cause is in some measure common to them and us. Blessed revolution! glorious change! [. . .]

[T]he duty of subjects to kings, and to all that are in authority, is frequently to be inculcated by the ministers of the gospel, if they will follow the example of the apostles in this respect. And the present occasion seems particularly proper to remind you of that important duty; since we have now before us a recent and memorable proof of his majesty's moderation, his attention to the welfare of his people, and readiness, so far as in him lies according to the constitution, to redress their grievances, on reasonable and humble complaint. If any persons among us have taken it unkindly, that his majesty should have given his royal assent to an act, which they think was an infraction of those liberties and privileges, to which they were justly intitled; and if the usual tide and fervor of their loyal affection is in any degree abated on that account; yet, surely, the readiness which his majesty has shewn to hear and redress his people's wrongs, ought to give a new spring, an additional vigor to their loyalty and obedience. Natural parents, thro' human frailty, and mistakes about facts and circumstances, sometimes *provoke their children to wrath*, tho' they tenderly love them, and sincerely desire their good. But what affectionate and dutiful child ever harboured resentment on any such account, if the grievance was removed, on a dutiful representation of it? [. . .] I shall make no application of this, any farther than to remind you, that British kings are the political fathers of their people, and the people their children; the former are not tyrants, or even masters; the latter are not slaves, or even servants.

Let me farther exhort you to pay due respect in all things to the British Parliament; the Lords and Commons being two branches of the supreme legislative over all his majesty's dominions. The right of parliament to superintend the general affairs of the colonies, to direct, check or controul them, seems to be supposed in their charters; all which, I think, while they grant the power of legislation, limit the exercise of it to the enacting such laws as are not contrary to the laws of England, or Great-Britain; so that our several legislatures are subordinate to that of the mother-country, which extends to and over all the king's dominions: At least, so far as to prevent any parts of them from doing what would be either destructive to each other, or manifestly to the ruin of Britain. It might be of the most dangerous consequence to the mother-country, to relinquish this supposed authority or right, which, certainly, has all along been recognized by the colonies; or to leave them dependent on the crown only, since, probably, within a century, the subjects in them will be more than thrice as numerous as those of Great-Britain and Ireland. And, indeed, if the colonies are properly parts of the British empire, as it is both their interest and honor to be, it seems absurd to deny, that they are subject to the highest authority therein, or not bound to yield obedience to it. I hope there are very few people, if any, in the colonies, who have the least inclination to renounce the general jurisdiction of Parliament over them, whatever we may think of the particular right of taxation. If, in any particular cases, we should think our selves hardly treated, laid under needless and unreasonable restrictions, or curtailed of any liberties or privileges, which other our fellow subjects in common enjoy; we have an undoubted right to complain, and, by humble and respectful, tho' not abject and servile petitions, to seek the redress of such supposed grievances. The colonists are men, and need not be afraid to assert the natural rights of men; they are British subjects, and may justly claim the common rights, and all the privileges of such, with plainness and freedom. And from what has lately occurred, there is reason to hope, that the Parliament will ever hereafter be willing to hear and grant our just requests; especially if any grievances should take place, so great, so general and alarming, as to unite all the colonies in petitioning for redress, as with one voice. The humble united prayers of three or four million loyal subjects, so connected with Great Britain, will not be thought unworthy of a serious attention; especially when seconded by such spirited resolutions and conduct of the American merchants, as they have lately given an example of. Humble petitions, so enforced, always carry great weight with them; and, if just and reasonable, will doubtless meet with a suitable return, as in the late instance; since Great Britain can scarce subsist without the trade of her colonies, which will be still increasing. And an equitable, kind treatment of them, on her part, will firmly bind them to her by the threefold cord of duty, interest and filial affection; such an one as the wise man says, is not easily broken: This would do more, far more to retain the colonies in due subjection, than all the fleets or troops she would think proper to send for that purpose.

[. . .] Let us highly reverence the supreme authority of the British empire, which to us is the highest, under that of heaven. Let us, as much as in us lies, cultivate harmony and brotherly love between our fellow subjects in Britain and ourselves. We shall doubtless find our account in this at last, much more than in a contrary way of proceeding. There are no other people on earth, that so "naturally care for us." We are connected with them by the strongest ties; in some measure by blood; for look but a century or two back, and you will find their ancestors and ours, in a great measure the same persons, tho' their posterity is now so divided. We are strongly connected with them by a great commercial intercourse, by our common language, by our common religion as protestants, and by being subjects of the same king, whom God long preserve and prosper, while his enemies are cloathed with shame.

 [. . .] Let none suspect that, because I thus urge the duty of cultivating a close harmony with our mother-country, and a dutiful submission to the king and Parliament, our chief grievances being redressed, I mean to disswade people from having a just concern for their own rights, or legal, constitutional privileges. History, one may presume to say, affords no example of any nation, country or people long free, who did not take some care of themselves; and endeavour to guard and secure their own liberties. Power is of a grasping, encroaching nature, in all beings. [. . .] Power aims at extending itself, and operating according to mere will, where-ever it meets with no ballance, check, controul or opposition of any kind. For which reason it will always be necessary, as was said before, for those who would preserve and perpetuate their liberties, to guard them with a wakeful attention; and in all righteous, just and prudent ways, to oppose the first encroachments on them. [...]

Daniel Dulany *Considerations on the Propriety of Imposing Taxes in the British Colonies, for the Purpose of Raising a Revenue, by Act of Parliament* (October 1765)[11]

IN the constitution of England, the three principal forms of government, monarchy, aristocracy, and democracy, are blended together in certain proportions; but each of these orders, in the exercise of the legislative authority, hath its peculiar department, from which the others are excluded. In this division, the granting of supplies, or laying taxes, is deemed to be the province of the House of Commons, as the representative of the people. [...]

This observation being considered, it will undeniably appear, that, in framing the late Stamp Act, the Commons acted in the character of representative of the colonies. They assumed it as the principle of that measure, and the propriety of it must therefore stand, or fall, as the principle is true or false: For the preamble sets forth, that the Commons of Great-Britain had resolved to give and grant the several rates and duties imposed by the act; but what right had the Commons of Great-Britain to be thus munificent at the expence of the Commons of America? – To give property not belonging to the giver, and without the consent of the owner, is such evident and flagrant injustice, in ordinary cases, that few are hardy enough to avow it; and, therefore, when it really happens, the fact is disguised and varnished over by the most plausible pretences the ingenuity of the giver can suggest. – But it is alledged that there is a virtual, or implied, representation of the colonies springing out of the constitution of the British government: And it must be confessed on all hands, that, as the representation is not actual, it is virtual, or it doth not exist at all; for no third kind of representation can be imagined. The colonies claim the privilege, which is common to all British subjects, of being taxed only with their consent given by their representatives, and all the advocates for the Stamp Act admit this claim. Whether, therefore, upon the whole matter, the imposition of the Stamp Duties is a proper exercise of constitutional authority, or not, depends upon the single question, Whether the Commons of Great-Britain are virtually the representatives of the Commons of America, or not.

The advocates for the Stamp Act admit, in express terms, that "the colonies do not choose members of Parliament," but they assert that "the colonies are virtually represented in the same manner with the non-electors resident in Great-Britain."

How have they proved this position? Where have they defined, or precisely explained what they mean by the expression, virtual representation? As it is the very hinge upon which the rectitude of the taxation turns, something more

---

[11] D. Dulany, *Considerations on the Propriety of Imposing Taxes in the British Colonies, for the Purpose of Raising Revenue, by Act of Parliament*, 2nd ed. (Annapolis: Jonas Green, 1795), pp. 5–8, 10–11, 14–15, 48.

satisfactory than mere assertion, more solid than a form of expression, is necessary; for, how can it be seriously expected, that men, who think themselves injuriously affected in their properties and privileges, will be convinced and reconciled by a fanciful phrase, the meaning of which can't be precisely ascertained by those who use it, or properly applied to the purpose for which it hath been advanced? [. . .]

I shall undertake to disprove the supposed similarity of situation, whence the same kind of representation is deduced, of the inhabitants of the colonies, and of the British non-electors; and, if I succeed, the notion of a virtual representation of the colonies must fail, which, in truth, is a mere cobweb, spread to catch the unwary, and intangle the weak. I would be understood: I am upon a question of propriety, not of power; and, though some may be inclined to think it is to little purpose to discuss the one, when the other is irresistible, yet are they different considerations; and, at the same time I invalidate the claim upon which it is founded, I may very consistently recommend a submission to the law, whilst it endures. [. . .]

Lessees for years, copyholders, proprietors of the public funds, inhabitants of Birmingham, Leeds, Halifax, and Manchester, merchants of the city of London, or members of the corporation of the East-India Company, are, as such, under no personal incapacity to be electors; for they may acquire the right of election, and there are *actually* not only a considerable number of electors in each of the classes of lessees for years, etc. but in many of them, if not all, even Members of Parliament. The interests, therefore, of the non-electors, the electors, and the representatives, are individually the same; to say nothing of the connection among neighbours, friends, and relations. The security of the non-electors against oppression, is, that their oppression will fall also upon the electors and the representatives. The one can't be injured, and the other indemnified.

Further, if the non-electors should not be taxed by the British Parliament, they would not be taxed *at all*; and it would be iniquitous as well as a solecism, in the political system, that they should partake of all the benefits resulting from the imposition, and application of taxes, and derive an immunity from the circumstance of not being qualified to vote. Under this constitution then, a double or virtual representation may be reasonably supposed. The electors, who are inseparably connected in their interests with the non-electors, may be justly deemed to be the representatives of the non-electors, at the same time they exercise their personal privilege in the right of election; and the members chosen, therefore, the representatives of both. This is the only rational explanation of the expression, virtual representation. None has been advanced by the assertors of it, and their meaning can only be inferred from the instances, by which they endeavour to elucidate it, and no other meaning can be stated, to which the instances apply. [. . .]

The situation of the non-electors in England – their capacity to become electors – their inseparable connection with those who are electors, and their representatives – their security against oppression resulting from this connection, and the necessity of imagining a double or virtual representation, to avoid iniquity and absurdity, have been explained – the inhabitants of the colonies are, as such, incapable of being electors, the privilege of election being exerciseable only in person, and therefore if every inhabitant of America had the requisite freehold, not one could vote, but upon the supposition of his ceasing to be an inhabitant of America, and becoming a resident of Great-Britain, a supposition which would be impertinent, because it shifts the question – should the colonies not be taxed by parliamentary impositions, their respective legislatures have a regular, adequate, and constitutional authority to tax them, and, therefore, there would not necessarily be an iniquitous and absurd exemption, from their not being represented by the House of Commons.

[. . .] It is indeed true, that the interests of England and the colonies are allied, and an injury to the colonies produced into all its consequences, will eventually affect the mother country; yet, these consequences being generally remote, are not at once foreseen; they do not immediately alarm the fears, and engage the passions of the English electors; the connection between a freeholder of Great-Britain, and a British American being deducible only thro' a train of reasoning, which few will take the trouble, or can have opportunity, if they have capacity, to investigate; wherefore, the relation between the British Americans, and the English electors, is a knot too infirm to be relied on as a competent security, especially against the force of a present, counteracting expectation of relief.

If it would have been a just conclusion, that the colonies being exactly in the same situation with the non-electors of England, and therefore represented in the same manner; it ought to be allowed, that the reasoning is solid, which, after having evinced a total dissimilarity of situation, infers, that their representation is different.

If the commons of Great-Britain have no right by the constitution, to GIVE AND GRANT property not belonging to themselves or others, without their consent actually or virtually given – If the claim of the colonies not to be taxed without their consent, signified by their representatives, is well founded, if it appears that the colonies are not actually represented by the commons of Great-Britain, and that the notion of a double or virtual representation, doth not with any propriety apply to the people of America; then the principle of the Stamp Act, must be given up as indefensible on the point of representation, and the validity of it rested upon the power which they who framed it, have to carry it into execution.

[. . .] Now, under favour, I conceive [. . .] it may be satisfactorily and easily proved, that the subordination and dependence of the colonies may be preserved, and the supreme authority of the mother country be firmly supported, and yet the principle of representation, and the right of the British House of Commons flowing from it, to give and grant the property of the commons of America, be denied.

The colonies are dependent upon Great-Britain, and the supreme authority vested in the King, Lords, and Commons, may justly be exercised to secure, or preserve their dependence, whenever necessary for that purpose. This authority results from, and is implied in the idea of the relation subsisting between England and her colonies; for, considering the nature of human affections, the inferior is not to be trusted with providing regulations to prevent his rising to an equality with his superior. But, though the right of the superior to use the proper means for preserving the subordination of his inferior is admitted, yet it does not necessarily follow, that he has a right to seize the property of his inferior when he pleases, or to command him in every thing; since, in the degrees of it, there may very well exist a dependence and inferiority, without absolute vassalage and slavery. In what the superior may rightfully controul, or compel, and in what the inferior ought to be at liberty to act without controul or compulsion, depends upon the nature of the dependence, and the degree of the subordination; and, these being ascertained, the measure of obedience, and submission, and the extent of the authority and superintendence will be settled. When powers, compatible with the relation between the superior and inferior, have, by express compact, been granted to, and accepted by, the latter, and have been, after that compact, repeatedly recognized by the former. [...]

By their constitutions of government, the colonies are empowered to impose internal taxes. This power is compatible with their dependence, and hath been expressly recognized by British ministers and the British Parliament, upon many occasions; and it may be exercised effectually without striking at, or impeaching, in any respect, the superintendence of the British Parliament. May not then the line be distinctly and justly drawn between such acts as are necessary, or proper, for preserving or securing the dependence of the colonies, and such as are *not* necessary or proper for that very important purpose; and would moreover destroy the fundamental and necessary principle of constitutional liberty? [...]

Not only, "as a friend to the colonies," but as an inhabitant having my all at stake upon their welfare, I desire an "exemption from taxes imposed without my consent" [...] I value it as one of the dearest privileges I enjoy: I acknowledge dependence on Great-Britain, but I can perceive a degree of it without slavery, and I disown all other. I do not expect that the interests of the colonies will be considered by some men, but in subserviency to other regards. The effects of luxury, and venality, and oppression, posterity may perhaps experience, and SUFFICIENT FOR THE DAY WILL BE THE EVIL THEREOF.

Daniel Leonard

To All Nations of Men (published in the *Massachusetts Spy*, November 18, 1773)[12]

To all Nations of Men, dwelling upon the face of the whole Earth, especially those of GREAT-BRITAIN and Ireland, more especially the Inhabitants of British North-America, and particularly those of the Massachusetts-Bay in New England.

MEN, BRETHREN and FATHERS,

It is indispensable to the well-being of civil society that every member thereof should have a sure and righteous rule of action in every occurence of life; and also that upon the observance of this rule he should be happy and secure from the molestation and disturbance of all men; municipal law, which is no more than the law of nature applied to man in society, having for its principal objects, the freedom of the person, conscience, and security of the subject in his property. And men enter into society for no other end than to place the execution of those laws in the hands of such as they

---

[12] D. Leonard, "To All Nations of Men" in C. Hyneman and D. Lutz (eds.), *American Political Writing during the Founding Era: 1760–1805*, Vol. I (Indianapolis: Liberty Fund, 1983), pp. 209–16.

esteem worthy to be entrusted with them; and to defend themselves, their laws and properties against foreign invasions. They do this in the first place to prevent that confusion and bloodshed which would inevitably take place were each individual left to judge in his own case and take by the strong hand what should appear to him satisfactory. Civil society then (to use the words of a celebrated author) is nothing more than the union of a multitude of people who agree to live in subjection to a sovereign (i.e. any power having legislative authority) in order to find through his protection and care that happiness to which they Naturally Aspire. This is equally true whatever self governing community it is applied to, whether to the smallest principality in Germany, the weakest colony in America or the Kingdom of Great-Britain, France or Muscovy. Thus we see what forms a state and can easily perceive what are the duties both of rulers and people; viz. rulers must afford them *that protection whereby they may surely attain that felicity they naturally aspire to* – The people then should take care not to transgress the laws of society, which being formed by the wisest and best of their own body, must undoubtedly be intended at least, for the promotion and security of the public happiness.

[. . .] The laws both of nature and nations, as well as those of every free state, indeed of every lawful government under heaven are extremely watchful in ascertaining and protecting the right of private property. So great is the regard of the law for private property, that it will not authorize the least violation of it, unless applied to the detriment of the Society. – That men have a natural right to retain their justly acquired property, or dispose of it as they please without injuring others, is a proposition that has never been controverted to my knowledge: That they should lose this right by entering society is repugnant to common sense and the united voice of every writer of reputation upon the subject. All agree that no man can be justly deprived of his property without his consent in person or by his representative, unless he has forfeited it by the breach of the laws of his country to the enaction of which he consented.

All demands upon our purse, on other terms, are illegal; and put into execution robbery; if the demand be made sword in hand, the crime is still more attrocious; "*it is robbery with murderous intention!*" Can any one dispute the justice of one sentence of the above propositions? or admitting them, can they excuse the British parliament, from the violation of these most sacred bonds of human society? Have they not actually invaded the freedom of our persons pretending to bind us by laws to which our consent was never so much as asked? Have they not demanded our money at the point of the bayonet and mouth of the cannon? Have they not utterly subverted the free constitution of our state by making our extreme magistrate a mere dependent on the minister of Great Britain, and thus destroyed all confidence of the body politic in the head? Have they not further interfered with our civil policy and intruded a set of officers upon us, entirely independent of the supreme power of the province constituting that most dangerous and intolerable evil that ever was felt by a people; that source of civil discord, treasons and murders an *imperium in imperio*, which constitutes the house whose fate the breath of conscience has pronounced, viz. "*it cannot stand!*" Have they not further, to defeat all prospect of our relieving ourselves by the free course of the laws of the land, held out a bribe to our supreme executive, and doubly corrupted the council, whose duty it is to *see the commonwealth suffer no injury*? Are we not by these several most intolerable encroachments, these injurious interferences into the civil polity of our state, cut off from all hopes of relief from courts of law, and even from our high court of parliament, which the aforesaid omnipotent parliament of Great-Britain have by a late resolve, rendered, or endeavored to render as useless as a King of the Romans? For if one supreme legislative body, in which the whole continent of America have not a single voice, have power to make laws which shall be binding upon us in all cases whatsoever, rights, liberties, legislative powers, under such absolute suspending, dispensing, establishing annihilating power as this, are meer shadows, Jack o'lanterns serving only to mislead and engulph us.

There can be no doubt but it is fit, and perfectly consistent with the principle of all laws human and divine, to resist robbers, murderers and subverters of the government of free states, whether these crimes are committed by individuals or nations, or more properly a despotism endeavouring to establish itself over the most free and happy nation on the globe. The only question is, whether it be prudent to risque resistance.

To this I answer we must be sure that we have a good cause; and I think of this we are certain. We may then safely venture it with that God who loves righteousness and hates oppression; who has made it our indispensable duty to *preserve our own lives and the lives of others*, more especially our brethren of the same community. Under his protection we shall be safe while we walk in his commandments, and by his all powerful assistance one may chase a thousand, and two put ten thousand to flight.

It is highly probable our oppressors will withdraw their hand when they find our resolution, and consider how fatal it must be to themselves to drive things to extremity. Great-Britain at war with her colonies would be in the condition of a trunk deprived of its members. Besides the foundation of the dispute being an effort of her ministers to *diminish the sovereignty of so great a number of free self governing states*, and erect an absolute despotism over them, must give umbrage to every other power in Europe, this being an open violation of the law of nations, and punishable [. . .].

In recapitulation of the foregoing, please to attend to the few plain Propositions following, viz.

I. That men naturally have a right to life, liberty, and the possession and disposal of their property, in such wise as to injure none other.

II. That the same is true in society, with this difference that whereas in a state of nature each judged for himself, what was just or injurious, in society he submits to indifferent arbiters.

III. That all demands upon us for any part of our substance not warranted by our own consent or the judgment of our peers are robbery with murderous intention.

IV. That on these principles, the administration of Great-Britain are justly chargeable with this complicated crime.

V. That it is fit, and perfectly consistent with the principle of all laws human and divine, to resist robbers, murderers, and subverters of the constitution of our country.

VI. That both legislative and executive powers in this province being corrupted, the partizans of our oppressive plunderers and murderers are screened from public justice.

VII. That this corruption of public justice with regard to these internal enemies, and the deprivation of the people from the application of it for their own safety, naturally throws us back into a state of nature, with respect to them, whereby our natural right of self defence, and revenge returns.

VIII. That life, personal liberty, and private property, when employed to the detriment or destruction of society, where constitutional provisions cannot be applied, are forfeited into the hands of any, who have public spirit enough to take them.

IX. That Jurors who are the sole and only judges of fact and law; and at present our only security against tyranny are bound by the true interest of all law, the public security to acquit any persons who may be brought before them, for cutting off or destroying the life and property of the invaders of our liberties, from this alone consideration, viz. *That the law of the land cannot be applied to our relief.*

These are matters of the last importance, and demand the serious consideration of every man who values his freedom or his life, (the latter being but of very precarious tenure when the former is ravished) and if the foregoing propositions are founded in truth on the principles of natural justice and the security of human welfare, adopt them, and act in conformity to them; if not reject them, and substitute something better in their stead. Demonstrate that the domination of law, according to the caprice of their own arbitrary will, to the destruction of all laws, constitutions and injunctions, human and divine, is *lawful government*; and that the subject though certain to be stripped of liberty and property at pleasure; thrown into a bastile to weep out a life of anguish and distress; exposed to all the miseries of cold, hunger and confinement, may be happier than were our noble, free and generous ancestors, and *none will be a more zealous and determined tory, than MASSACHUSETTENSIS.*

Letter in the Massachusetts Gazette (January 9, 1775)[13]

To the Inhabitants of the Province of Massachusetts-Bay.
MY DEAR COUNTRYMEN.

[...] Perhaps the whole story of empire does not furnish another instance of a forcible opposition to government with so much specious and so little real cause, with such apparent probability without any possibility of success. The stamp-act gave the alarm. [...] I intend to consider the acts of the British government, which

---

[13] From *Massachusettensis: or A Series of Letters, Containing a Faithful State of Many Important and Striking Facts, Which Laid the Foundation of the Present Troubles in the Colony of Massachusetts-Bay* (Boston: J. Mathews, 1776), pp. 37–44.

are held up as the principal grievance, and enquire whether Great-Britain is chargeable with injustice in any one of them; but must first ask your attention to the authority of parliament. I suspect many of our politicians are wrong in their first principle, in denying that the constitutional authority of parliament extends to the colonies; if so, it must not be wondered at, that their whole fabric is so ruinous: I shall not travel through all the arguments that have been adduced, for and against this question, but attempt to reduce the substance of them to a narrow compass, after having taken a cursory view of the British constitution.

The security of the people from internal rapacity and violence, and from foreign invasion, is the end and design of government. The simple forms of government are monarchy, aristocracy and democracy, that is, where the authority of the state is vested in *one*, a *few*, or the *many*. Each of these species of government has advantages peculiar to itself, and would answer the ends of government, were the persons, intrusted with the authority of the state, always guided themselves by unerring wisdom and public virtue; but rulers are not always exempt from the weakness and depravity, which make government necessary to society. Thus monarchy is apt to rush headlong into tyranny, aristocracy to beget faction and multiplied usurpation, and democracy to degenerate into tumult, violence and anarchy. A government, formed upon these three principles in due proportion, is the best calculated to answer the ends of government, and to endure. Such a government is the British constitution, consisting of King, Lords and Commons, which at once includes the principal excellencies, and excludes the principal defects of the other kinds of government. It is allowed, both by Englishmen and foreigners, to be the most perfect system that the wisdom of ages has produced. The distributions of power are so just, and the proportions so exact, as at once to support and controul each other. An Englishman glories in being subject to and protected by such a government.

The colonies are a part of the British empire. The best writers upon the law of nations tell us, that when a nation takes possession of a distant country, and settles there, that country, though separated from the principal establishment or mother-country, naturally becomes a part of the state, equal with its ancient possessions. Two supreme or independent authorities cannot exist in the same state. It would be what is called *imperium in imperio*, and the height of political absurdity. The analogy between the political and human body is great. Two independent authorities in a state would be like two distinct principles of volition and action in the human body, dissenting, opposing, and destroying each other. If then we are a part of the British empire, we must be subject to the supreme power of the state, which is vested in the estates of parliament, notwithstanding each of the colonies have legislative and executive powers of their own, delegated or granted to them for the purposes of regulating their own internal police, which are subordinate, and must necessarily be subject, to the checks, controul and regulation of the supreme authority.

This doctrine is not new; but the denial of it is. It is beyond a doubt that it was the sense both of the parent country and our ancestors, that they were to remain subject to parliament; it is evident from the charter itself, and this authority has been exercised by parliament, from time to time, almost ever since the first settlement of the country, and has been expressly acknowledged by our provincial legislatures. It is not less our interest than our duty to continue subject to the authority of parliament, which will be more fully considered hereafter. The principal argument against the authority is this; the Americans are entitled to all the privileges of an englishman; it is the privilege of an englishman to be exempt from all laws that he does not consent to in person, or by representative; the Americans are not represented in parliament, and therefore are exempt from acts of parliament, or, in other words, not subject to its authority. This appears specious; but leads to such absurdities as demonstrate its fallacy. If the colonies are not subject to the authority of parliament, Great-Britain and the colonies must be distinct states, as completely so as England and Scotland were before the union, or as Great-Britain and Hanover are now. The colonies in that case will owe no allegiance to the imperial crown, and perhaps not to the person of the King; as the title to the crown is derived from an act of parliament, made since the settlement of this province, which act respects the imperial crown only. Let us wave this difficulty, and suppose allegiance due from the colonies to the person of the king of Great Britain; he then appears in a new capacity, as king of America, or rather, in several new capacities, as king of Massachusetts, king of Rhode-Island, king of Connecticut, &c. &c. For, if our connection with Great Britain, by the parliament, be dissolved, we shall have none among ourselves; but each colony will become as distinct from the others, as England was from Scotland before the union. Some have supposed, that each state having one and the same person for its king, it is a sufficient connection: Were he an absolute monarch, it might be; but, in a mixed government, it is no union at all. For, as the king must govern each state by its parliament, those several parliaments would pursue the particular interest of its own state; and however well disposed the king might be to pursue a line of interest that was common to all, the checks and controul, that he would meet with, would render it impossible. If the king of Great-Britain has really these new capacities, they ought to be added to his titles; and then another difficulty will arise, the prerogatives of these new crowns have never been defined or limited. Is the monarchical part of the several provincial constitutions to be nearer, or more remote from absolute monarchy, in an inverted ratio to each one's approaching to, or receding from a republic? But let us suppose the same prerogatives inherent in the several American crowns, as are in the imperial crown of Great-Britain; where shall we find the British constitution, that we all agree we are entitled to? We shall seek for it in vain in our provincial assemblies. They are but faint sketches of the estates of parliament. The houses of representatives or burgesses have not all the powers of the house of commons: in the charter governments they have no more than what is expressly granted by their several charters. The first charters, granted to this province, did not impower the assembly to tax the people at all. Our council-boards are as destitute of the constitutional authority of the house of lords, as their several members are of the noble independence and splendid appendages of peerage. [...] Thus, the supposition of our being independent states, or exempt from the authority of parliament, destroys the very idea of our having a British constitution. The provincial constitutions, considered as subordinate, are generally well adapted to those purposes of government, for which they were intended, that is, to regulate the internal police of the several colonies; but, having no principle of stability within themselves, tho' they may support themselves in moderate times, they would be merged by the violence of turbulent ones. The several colonies would become wholly monarchical or wholly republican, were it not for the checks, controuls, regulations and supports, of the supreme authority of the empire. Thus, the argument that is drawn from their first principle of our being entitled to English liberties, destroys the principle itself; it deprives us of the bill of rights, and all the benefits resulting from the revolution, of English laws, and of the British constitution. [...]

Allegiance and protection are reciprocal. It is our highest interest to continue a part of the British empire; and equally our duty to remain subject to the authority of parliament. Our own internal police may generally be regulated by our provincial legislatures; but, in national concerns, or where our own assemblies do not answer the ends of government, with respect to ourselves, the ordinances or interposition of the great council of the nation is necessary. In this case, the major must rule the minor. After many more centuries shall have rolled away, long after we, who are now bustling upon the stage of life, shall have been received to the bosom of mother earth, and our names are forgotten; the colonies may be so far increased as to have the balance of wealth, numbers, and power in their favour. The good of the empire may then make it necessary to fix the seat of government here; and some future George, equally the friend of mankind with him who now sways the British scepter, may cross the Atlantic, and rule Great Britain by an American parliament.

MASSACHUSETTENSIS

John Adams *Novanglus, Essay VII* (February 6, 1775)[14]

Addressed to the Inhabitants of the Colony of Massachusetts Bay

Our rhetorical magician [Daniel Leonard], in his paper of January the 9th, continues to *wheedle*: [...] After a long discourse, which has nothing in it but what has been answered already, he comes to a great subject indeed, the British constitution; and undertakes to prove, that "the authority of parliament extends to the colonies."

Why will not this writer state the question fairly? The whigs allow that, from the necessity of a case not provided for by common law, and to supply a defect in the British dominions, which there undoubtedly is, if they are to be governed only by that law, America has all along consented, still consents, and ever will consent, that parliament, being the most powerful legislature in the dominions, should regulate the trade of the dominions. This is founding the authority of parliament to regulate our trade, upon *compact* and *consent* of the colonies, not upon any principle of common or statute law; not upon any original principle of the English constitution; not upon the principle that parliament is the supreme and sovereign legislature over them in all cases whatsoever. The question is not, therefore, whether the authority of parliament

---

[14] J. Adams, "Novanglus, Essay VII" in C. F. Adams (ed.), *The Works of John Adams*, Vol. IV (Boston: Little, Brown and Co., 1856), pp. 99–121.

extends to the colonies in any case, for it is admitted by the whigs, that it does in that of commerce; but whether it extends in all cases. [. . .]

Then we are told, "that the colonies are a part of the British empire." [. . .] If the English parliament were to govern us, where did they get the right, without our consent, to take the Scottish parliament into a participation of the government over us [Acts of Union between England and Scotland in 1707]? When this was done, was the American share of the democracy of the constitution consulted? If not, were not the Americans deprived of the benefit of the democratical part of the constitution? And is not the democracy as essential to the English constitution as the monarchy or aristocracy? [. . .]

If a new constitution was to be formed for the whole British dominions, and a supreme legislature coextensive with it, upon the general principles of the English constitution, an equal mixture of monarchy, aristocracy, and democracy, let us see what would be necessary. England has six millions of people, we will say; America had three. England has five hundred members in the house of commons, we will say; America must have two hundred and fifty. Is it possible she should maintain them there, or could they at such a distance know the state, the sense, or exigencies of their constituents? Ireland, too, must be incorporated, and send another hundred or two of members. The territory in the East Indies and West India Islands must send members. And after all this, every navigation act, every act of trade must be repealed. America, and the East and West Indies, and Africa too, must have equal liberty to trade with all the world, that the favored inhabitants of Great Britain have now. Will the ministry thank Massachusettensis for becoming an advocate for such a union, and incorporation of all the dominions of the King of Great Britain? Yet, without such a union, a legislature which shall be sovereign and supreme in all cases whatsoever, and coextensive with the empire, can never be established upon the general principles of the English constitution which Massachusettensis lays down, namely, – an equal mixture of monarchy, aristocracy, and democracy. Nay, further, in order to comply with this principle, this new government, this mighty colossus, which is to bestride the narrow world, must have a house of lords, consisting of Irish, East and West Indian, African, American, as well as English and Scottish noblemen; for the nobility ought to be scattered about all the dominions, as well as the representatives of the commons. If in twenty years more America should have six millions of inhabitants, as there is a boundless territory to fill up, she must have five hundred representatives. Upon these principles, if in forty years she should have twelve millions, a thousand; and if the inhabitants of the three kingdoms remain as they are, being already full of inhabitants, what will become of your supreme legislative? It will be translated, crown and all, to America. This is a sublime system for America. It will flatter those ideas of independency which the tories impute to them, if they have any such, more than any other plan of independency that I have ever heard projected. [. . .]

I agree, that "two supreme and independent authorities cannot exist in the same state," any more than two supreme beings in one universe; and, therefore, I contend, that our provincial legislatures are the only supreme authorities in our colonies. Parliament, notwithstanding this, may be allowed an authority supreme and sovereign over the ocean, which may be limited by the banks of the ocean, or the bounds of our charters; our charters give us no authority over the high seas. Parliament has our consent to assume a jurisdiction over them. And here is a line fairly drawn between the rights of Britain and the rights of the colonies, namely, the banks of the ocean, or low-water mark; the line of division between common law, and civil or maritime law. [...]

"If, then, we are a part of the British empire, we must be subject to the supreme power of the state, which is vested in the estates in parliament."

Here, again, we are to be conjured out of our senses by the magic in the words "British empire," and "supreme power of the state." But, however it may sound, I say we are not a part of the British empire; because the British government is not an empire. [...] It is a limited monarchy. If Aristotle, Livy, and Harrington knew what a republic was, the British constitution is much more like a republic than an empire. They define a republic to be a government of laws, and not of men. If this definition be just, the British constitution is nothing more nor less than a republic, in which the king is first magistrate. This office being hereditary, and being possessed of such ample and splendid prerogatives, is no objection to the government's being a republic, as long as it is bound by fixed laws, which the people have a voice in making, and a right to defend. [...]

The question should be, whether we are a part of the kingdom of Great Britain. This is the only language known in English laws. We are not then a part of the British kingdom, realm, or state; and therefore the supreme power of the kingdom, realm, or state is not, upon these principles, the supreme power of us. That "supreme power over America is vested in the estates in parliament," is an affront to us; for there is not an acre of American land represented there; there are no American estates in parliament. [...]

"If the colonies are not subject to the authority of parliament, Great Britain and the colonies must be distinct states, as completely so as England and Scotland were before the union, or as Great Britain and Hanover are now." There is no need of being startled at this consequence. It is very harmless. There is no absurdity at all in it. Distinct states may be united under one king. And those states may be further cemented and united together by a treaty of commerce. This is the case. We have, by our own express consent, contracted to observe the Navigation Act, and by our implied consent, by long usage and uninterrupted acquiescence, have submitted to the other acts of trade, however grievous some of them may be. This may be compared to a treaty of commerce, by which those distinct states are cemented together, in perpetual league and amity. And if any further ratifications of this pact or treaty are necessary, the colonies would readily enter into them, provided their other liberties were inviolate.

The only proposition in all this writer's long string of pretended absurdities, which he says follows from the position that we are distinct states, is this: – That "as the king must govern each state by its parliament, those several parliaments would pursue the particular interest of its own state; and however well disposed the king might be to pursue a line of interest that was common to all, the checks and control that he would meet with would render it impossible." Every argument ought to be allowed its full weight; and therefore candor obliges me to acknowledge, that here lies all the difficulty that there is in this whole controversy. There has been, from first to last, on both sides of the Atlantic, an idea, an apprehension, that it was necessary there should be some superintending power, to draw together all the wills, and unite all the strength of the subjects in all the dominions, in case of war, and in the case of trade. The necessity of this, in case of trade, has been so apparent, that, as has often been said, we have consented that parliament should exercise such a power. In case of war, it has by some been thought necessary. But in fact and experience, it has not been found so. What though the proprietary colonies, on account of disputes with the proprietors, did not come in so early to the assistance of the general cause in the last war as they ought, and perhaps one of them not at all? The inconveniences of this were small, in comparison of the absolute ruin to the liberties of all which must follow the submission to parliament, in all cases, which would be giving up all the popular limitations upon the government. These inconveniences fell chiefly upon New England. She was necessitated to greater exertions; but she had rather suffer these again and again than others infinitely greater. However, this subject has been so long in contemplation, that it is fully understood now in all the colonies; so that there is no danger, in case of another war, of any colony's failing of its duty.

But, admitting the proposition in its full force, that it is absolutely necessary there should be a supreme power, coextensive with all the dominions, will it follow that parliament, as now constituted, has a right to assume this supreme jurisdiction? By no means.

A union of the colonies might be projected, and an American legislature; for, if America has three millions of people, and the whole dominions, twelve millions, she ought to send a quarter part of all the members to the house of commons; and, instead of holding parliaments always at Westminster, the haughty members for Great Britain must humble themselves, one session in four, to cross the Atlantic, and hold the parliament in America. [. . .]

That a representation in parliament is impracticable, we all agree; but the consequence is, that we must have a representation in our supreme legislatures here. This was the consequence that was drawn by kings, ministers, our ancestors, and the whole nation, more than a century ago, when the colonies were first settled, and continued to be the general sense until the last peace; and it must be the general sense again soon, or Great Britain will lose her colonies. [. . .]

"It is our highest interest to continue a part of the British empire; and equally our duty to remain subject to the authority of parliament," says Massachusettensis.

We are a part of the British dominions, that is, of the King of Great Britain, and it is our interest and duty to continue so. It is equally our interest and duty to continue subject to the authority of parliament, in the regulation of our trade, as long as she shall leave us to govern our internal policy, and to give and grant our own money, and no longer.

This letter concludes with an agreeable flight of fancy. The time may not be so far off, however, as this writer imagines, when the colonies may have the balance of numbers and wealth in their favor. But when that shall happen, if we should attempt to rule her by an American parliament, without an adequate representation in it, she will infallibly resist us by her arms.

Jonathan Boucher *On Civil Liberty, Passive Obedience, and Non-Resistance* (1775)[15]

Stand fast, therefore, in the liberty wherewith Christ hath made us free.

(Galatians 5:1)

[...] Obedience to Government is every man's duty, because it is every man's interest: but it is particularly incumbent on Christians, because (in addition to its moral fitness) it is enjoined by the positive commands of God: and therefore, when Christians are disobedient to human ordinances, they also disobedient to God. If the form of government under which the good providence of God has been pleased to place us be mild and free, it is our duty to enjoy it with gratitude and with thankfulness; and, in particular, to be careful not to abuse it by licentiousness. If it be less indulgent and less liberal than in reason it ought to be, still it is our duty not to disturb and destroy the peace of the community, by becoming refractory and rebellious subjects, and resisting the ordinances of God. However humiliating such acquiescence may seem to men of warm and eager minds, the wisdom of God in having made it our duty is manifest. For, as it is the natural temper and bias of the human mind to be impatient under restraint, it was wise and merciful in the blessed Author of our religion not to add any new impulse to the natural force of this prevailing propensity, but, with the whole weight of his authority, altogether to discountenance every tendency to disobedience. [...]

It is laid down in this sermon, as a settled maxim that the end of government is "the common good of mankind." I am not sure that the position itself is indisputable; but, if it were, it would by no means follow that, "this common good being matter of common feeling, government must therefore have been instituted by common consent." There is an appearance of logical accuracy and precision in this statement; but it is only an appearance. The position is vague and loose; and the assertion is made without an attempt to prove it. [...] In no instance have mankind ever yet agreed as to what is, or is not, "the common good." A form or mode of government cannot be named, which these "common feelings" and "common consent," the sole arbiters, as it seems, of "common good," have not, at one time or another, set up and established, and again pulled down and reprobated. What one people in one age have concurred in establishing as the "common good," another in another age have voted to be mischievous and big with ruin. The premises, therefore, that "the common good is matter of common feeling," being false, the consequence drawn from it, viz. that government was instituted by "common consent," is of course equally false.

---

[15] From J. Boucher, *A View of the Causes and Consequences of the American Revolution; in Thirteen Discourses, Preached in North America between the Years 1763 and 1775* (London: G. G. and J. Robinson, 1797), pp. 507–8, 512–18, 552, 554–9.

This popular notion, that government was originally formed by the consent or by a compact of the people, rests on, and is supported by, another similar notion, not less popular, nor better founded. This other notion is, that the whole human race is born equal; and that no man is naturally inferior, or, in any respect, subjected to another; and that he can be made subject to another only by his own consent. The position is equally ill-founded and false both in its premises and conclusions. [. . .] Man differs from man in every thing that can be supposed to lead to supremacy and subjection, as one star differs from another star in glory. It was the purpose of the Creator, that man should be social: but, without government, there can be no society; nor, without some relative inferiority and superiority, can there be any government. [. . .] If (according to the idea of the advocates of this chimerical scheme of equality) no man could rightfully be compelled to come in and be a member even of a government to be formed by a regular compact, but by his own individual consent; it clearly follows, from the same principles, that neither could he rightfully be made or compelled to submit to the ordinances of any government already formed, to which he has not individually or actually consented. On the principle of equality, neither his parents, nor even the vote of a majority of the society, (however virtuously and honourably that vote might be obtained,) can have any such authority over any man. Neither can it be maintained that acquiescence implies consent; because acquiescence may have been extorted from impotence or incapacity. Even an explicit consent can bind a man no longer than he chooses to be bound. The same principle of equality that exempts him from being governed without his own consent, clearly entitles him to recall and resume that consent whenever he sees fit; and he alone has a right to judge when and for what reasons it may be resumed.

[. . .] Mr. Locke indeed says, that, "by consenting with others to make one body-politic under government, a man puts himself under an obligation to every one of that society to submit to the determination of the majority, and to be concluded by it." [. . .] [b]ut, on the principles of the system now under consideration, before Mr. Locke or any of his followers can have authority to say that it actually is the case, it must be stated and proved that every individual man, on entering into the social compact, did first consent, and declare his consent, to be concluded and bound in all cases by the vote of the majority. [. . .] Mr. Locke himself afterwards disproves his own position respecting this supposed obligation to submit to the "determination of the majority," when he argues that a right of resistance still exists in the governed: for, what is resistance but a recalling and resuming the consent heretofore supposed to have been given, and in fact refusing to submit to the "determination of the majority?" It does not clearly appear what Mr. Locke exactly meant by what he calls "the determination of the majority:" but the only rational and practical public manner of declaring "the determination of the majority," is by law: the laws, therefore, in all countries, even in those that are despotically governed, are to be regarded as the declared "determination of a majority" of the members of that community; because, in such cases, even acquiescence only must be looked upon as equivalent to a declaration. A right of resistance, therefore, for which Mr. Locke contends, is incompatible with the duty of submitting to the determination of "the majority," for which he also contends.

It is indeed impossible to carry into effect any government which, even by compact, might be framed with this reserved right of resistance. Accordingly there is no record that any such government ever was so formed. If there had, it must have carried the seeds of it's decay in it's very constitution. [. . .]

Mr. Locke, like many inferior writers, when defending resistance, falls into inconsistencies, and is at variance with himself. "Rebellion being," as he says, "an opposition not to persons, but to authority, which is founded only in the constitution and laws of the government, those, whoever they be, who by force break through, and by force justify their violation of them, are truly and properly rebels." To this argument no one can object: but it should be attended to, that, in political consider-ation, it is hardly possible to dissociate the ideas of authority in the abstract from persons vested with authority. To resist a person legally vested with authority, is, I conceive, to all intents and purposes, the same thing as to resist authority. Nothing, but it's success, could have rescued the revolution from this foul imputation, had it not been for the abdication. Accordingly this great event has always hung like a mill-stone on the necks of those who must protest against rebellions; whilst yet their system of politics requires that they should approve of resistance, and the revolution. [. . .]

Be it (for the sake of argument) admitted, that the government under which till now you have lived happily, is, most unaccountably, all at once become oppressive and severe; did you, of yourselves, make the discovery? No: I affirm, without any apprehension of being contradicted, that you are acquainted with these oppressions only from the report of others. For what, then, (admitting you have a right to resist in any case,) are you now urged to resist and rise against those whom you have hitherto always regarded (and certainly not without reason) as your nursing fathers and nursing mothers? Often as you have already heard it repeated without expressing any disapprobation, I assure myself it will afford you no pleasure to be reminded, that it is on account of an insignificant duty on tea, imposed by the British Parliament; and which, for aught we know, may or may not be constitutionally imposed; but which, we well know, two thirds of the people of America can never be called on to pay. Is it the part of an understanding people, of loyal subjects, or of good Christians, instantly to resist and rebel for a cause so trivial? O my brethren, consult your own hearts, and follow your own judgments! and learn not your "measures of obedience" from men who weakly or wickedly imagine there can be liberty unconnected with law – and whose aim it is to drive you on, step by step, to a resistance which will terminate, if it does not begin, in rebellion! On all such trying occasions, learn the line of conduct which it is your duty and interest to observe, from our Constitution itself: which, in this particular, is a fair transcript or exemplification of the ordinance of God. Both the one and the other warn you against resistance: but you are not forbidden either to remonstrate or to petition. And can it be humiliating to any man, or any number of men, to ask, when we have but to ask and it shall be given? Is prayer an abject duty; or do men ever appear either so great, or so amiable, as when they are modest and humble? However meanly this privilege of petitioning may be regarded by those who claim every thing as a right, they are challenged to shew an instance, in which it has failed, when it ought to have succeeded. If, however, our grievances, in any point of view, be of such moment as that other means of obtaining redress should be judged expedient, happily we enjoy those means. In a certain sense, some considerable portion of legislation is still in our own hands. We are supposed to have chosen "fit and able" persons to represent us in the great council of our country: and they only can constitutionally interfere either to obtain the enacting of what is right, or the repeal of what is wrong. If we, and our fellow-subjects, have been conscientiously faithful in the discharge of our duty, we can have no reason to doubt that our delegates will be equally faithful in the discharge of theirs. Our Provincial Assemblies, it is true, are but one part of our Colonial Legislature: they form, however, that part which is the most efficient. If the present general topic of complaint be, in their estimation, well founded, and a real and great grievance, what reason have you to imagine that all the Assemblies on the Continent will not concur and be unanimous in so representing it? [...]

If you think the duty of three pence a pound upon tea, laid on by the British Parliament, a grievance, it is your duty to instruct your members to take all the constitutional means in their power to obtain redress: if those means fail of success, you cannot but be sorry and grieved; but you will better bear your disappointment, by being able to reflect that it was not owing to any misconduct of your own. And, what is the whole history of human life, public or private, but a series of disappointments? It might be hoped that Christians would not think it grievous to be doomed to submit to disappointments and calamities, as their Master submitted, even if they were as innocent. His disciples and first followers shrunk from no trials nor danger. Treading in the steps of him who, when he was reviled, blessed, and when he was persecuted, suffered it, they willingly laid down their lives, rather than resist some of the worst tyrants that ever disgraced the annals of history. [...]

Thomas Paine *Common Sense* (1776)[16]

[...] The cause of America is, in a great measure, the cause of all mankind. Many circumstances have, and will arise, which are not local, but universal, and through which the principles of all lovers of mankind are affected, and in the event of which, their affections are interested. The laying a country desolate with fire and sword, declaring war against the natural rights of all mankind, and extirpating the defenders thereof from the face of the earth, is the concern of every man to whom nature hath given the power of feeling; of which class, regardless of party censure, is THE AUTHOR.

I. Of the Origin and Design of Government in General

Some writers have so confounded society with government, as to leave little or no distinction between them; whereas they are not only different, but have different origins. Society is produced by our wants and government by our wickedness; the

---

[16] T. Paine, *Common Sense* (Philadelphia: W. and T. Bradford, 1776).

former promotes our happiness positively by uniting our affections, the latter negatively by restraining our vices. The one encourages intercourse, the other creates distinctions. The first is a patron, the last a punisher.

Society in every state is a blessing, but government, even in its best state, is but a necessary evil; in its worst state an intolerable one: for when we suffer, or are exposed to the same miseries by a government, which we might expect in a country without government, our calamity is heightened by reflecting that we furnish the means by which we suffer. Government, like dress, is the badge of lost innocence; the palaces of kings are built upon the ruins of the bowers of paradise. For were the impulses of conscience clear, uniform and irresistibly obeyed, man would need no other law-giver; but that not being the case, he finds it necessary to surrender up a part of his property to furnish means for the protection of the rest; and this he is induced to do by the same prudence which in every other case advises him, out of two evils to choose the least. Wherefore, security being the true design and end of government, it unanswerably follows that whatever form thereof appears most likely to ensure it to us, with the least expence and greatest benefit, is preferable to all others.

In order to gain a clear and just idea of the design and end of government, let us suppose a small number of persons settled in some sequestered part of the earth, unconnected with the rest; they will then represent the first peopling of any country, or of the world. In this state of natural liberty, society will be their first thought. A thousand motives will excite them thereto; the strength of one man is so unequal to his wants, and his mind so unfitted for perpetual solitude, that he is soon obliged to seek assistance and relief of another, who in his turn requires the same. Four or five united would be able to raise a tolerable dwelling in the midst of a wilderness, but one man might labour out the common period of life without accomplishing any thing; when he had felled his timber he could not remove it, nor erect it after it was removed; hunger in the mean time would urge him to quit his work, and every different want would call him a different way. Disease, nay even misfortune, would be death; for, though neither might be mortal, yet either would disable him from living, and reduce him to a state in which he might rather be said to perish than to die.

Thus necessity, like a gravitating power, would soon form our newly arrived emigrants into society, the reciprocal blessings of which would supersede, and render the obligations of law and government unnecessary while they remained perfectly just to each other; but as nothing but Heaven is impregnable to vice, it will unavoidably happen that in proportion as they surmount the first difficulties of emigration, which bound them together in a common cause, they will begin to relax in their duty and attachment to each other: and this remissness will point out the necessity of establishing some form of government to supply the defect of moral virtue.

Some convenient tree will afford them a State House, under the branches of which the whole Colony may assemble to deliberate on public matters. It is more than probable that their first laws will have the title only of Regulations and be enforced by no other penalty than public disesteem. In this first parliament every man by natural right will have a seat.

But as the Colony encreases, the public concerns will encrease likewise, and the distance at which the members may be separated, will render it too inconvenient for all of them to meet on every occasion as at first, when their number was small, their habitations near, and the public concerns few and trifling. This will point out the convenience of their consenting to leave the legislative part to be managed by a select number chosen from the whole body, who are supposed to have the same concerns at stake which those have who appointed them, and who will act in the same manner as the whole body would act were they present. If the colony continue encreasing, it will become necessary to augment the number of representatives, and that the interest of every part of the colony may be attended to, it will be found best to divide the whole into convenient parts, each part sending its proper number: and that the ELECTED might never form to themselves an interest separate from the ELECTORS, prudence will point out the propriety of having elections often: because as the ELECTED might by that means return and mix again with the general body of the ELECTORS in a few months, their fidelity to the public will be secured by the prudent reflection of not making a rod for themselves. And as this frequent interchange will establish a common interest with every part of the community, they will mutually and naturally support each other, and on this, (not on the unmeaning name of king,) depends the STRENGTH OF GOVERNMENT, AND THE HAPPINESS OF THE GOVERNED. [. . .]

Absolute governments, (tho' the disgrace of human nature) have this advantage with them, they are simple; if the people suffer, they know the head from which their suffering springs; know likewise the remedy; and are not bewildered by a variety of causes and cures. But the constitution of England is so exceedingly complex, that the nation may suffer for years together without being able to discover in which part the fault lies; some will say in one and some in another, and every political physician will advise a different medicine.

I know it is difficult to get over local or long standing prejudices, yet if we will suffer ourselves to examine the component parts of the English Constitution, we shall find them to be the base remains of two ancient tyrannies, compounded with some new Republican materials.

First. – The remains of Monarchical tyranny in the person of the King.

Secondly. – The remains of Aristocratical tyranny in the persons of the Peers.

Thirdly. – The new Republican materials, in the persons of the Commons, on whose virtue depends the freedom of England.

The two first, by being hereditary, are independent of the People; wherefore in a CONSTITUTIONAL SENSE they contribute nothing towards the freedom of the State.

To say that the constitution of England is an UNION of three powers, reciprocally CHECKING each other, is farcical; either the words have no meaning, or they are flat contradictions.

First. – That the King is not to be trusted without being looked after; or in other words, that a thirst for absolute power is the natural disease of monarchy.

Secondly. – That the Commons, by being appointed for that purpose, are either wiser or more worthy of confidence than the Crown.

But as the same constitution which gives the Commons a power to check the King by withholding the supplies, gives afterwards the King a power to check the Commons, by empowering him to reject their other bills; it again supposes that the King is wiser than those whom it has already supposed to be wiser than him. A mere absurdity! [...]

That the crown is this overbearing part in the English constitution needs not be mentioned, and that it derives its whole consequence merely from being the giver of places and pensions is self-evident; wherefore, though we have been wise enough to shut and lock a door against absolute Monarchy, we at the same time have been foolish enough to put the Crown in possession of the key. [...]

III. Thoughts on the Present State of American Affairs

[...] The sun never shone on a cause of greater worth. 'Tis not the affair of a city, a county, a province, or a kingdom; but of a continent – of at least one eighth part of the habitable globe. 'Tis not the concern of a day, a year, or an age; posterity are virtually involved in the contest, and will be more or less affected even to the end of time, by the proceedings now. Now is the seed-time of continental union, faith and honor. The least fracture now will be like a name engraved with the point of a pin on the tender rind of a young oak; the wound would enlarge with the tree, and posterity read it in full grown characters. [...]

As much has been said of the advantages of reconciliation, which, like an agreeable dream, has passed away and left us as we were, it is but right that we should examine the contrary side of the argument, and inquire into some of the many material injuries which these colonies sustain, and always will sustain, by being connected with and dependant on Great Britain. To examine that connection and dependance, on the principles of nature and common sense, to see what we have to trust to, if separated, and what we are to expect, if dependant.

I have heard it asserted by some, that as America has flourished under her former connection with Great Britain, the same connection is necessary towards her future happiness, and will always have the same effect. Nothing can be more fallacious than this kind of argument. We may as well assert that because a child has thrived upon milk, that it is never to have meat, or that the first twenty years of our lives is to become a precedent for the next twenty. But even this is admitting more than is true; for I answer roundly, that America would have flourished as much, and probably much more, had no European power taken any notice of her. The commerce by which she hath enriched herself are the necessaries of life, and will always have a market while eating is the custom of Europe.

But she has protected us, say some. That she hath engrossed us is true, and defended the continent at our expense as well as her own, is admitted; and she would have defended Turkey from the same motive, viz. for the sake of trade and dominion.

Alas! we have been long led away by ancient prejudices and made large sacrifices to superstition. We have boasted the protection of Great Britain, without considering, that her motive was interest not attachment; and that she did not protect us from our enemies on our account; but from her enemies on her own account, from those who had no quarrel with us on any other account, and who will always be our enemies on the same account. [...]

I challenge the warmest advocate for reconciliation to show a single advantage that this continent can reap by being connected with Great Britain. I repeat the challenge; not a single advantage is derived. Our corn will fetch its price in any market in Europe, and our imported goods must be paid for, buy them where we will.

But the injuries and disadvantages which we sustain by that connection, are without number; and our duty to mankind at large, as well as to ourselves, instruct us to renounce the alliance: because, any submission to, or dependence on, Great Britain, tends directly to involve this continent in European wars and quarrels, and set us at variance with nations who would otherwise seek our friendship, and against whom we have neither anger nor com-plaint. As Europe is our market for trade, we ought to form no partial connection with any part of it. It is the true interest of America to steer clear of European contentions, which she never can do, while, by her dependence on Britain, she is made the make-weight in the scale of British politics. [...]

Every thing that is right or reasonable pleads for separation. The blood of the slain, the weeping voice of nature cries, 'Tis time to part. Even the distance at which the Almighty hath placed England and America is a strong and natural proof that the authority of the one over the other, was never the design of heaven. The time likewise at which the continent was discovered, adds weight to the argument, and the manner in which it was peopled, encreases the force of it. The Reformation was preceded by the discovery of America: As if the Almighty graciously meant to open a sanctuary to the persecuted in future years, when home should afford neither friendship nor safety. [...]

As to government matters, 'tis not in the power of Britain to do this continent justice: the business of it will soon be too weighty and intricate to be managed with any tolerable degree of convenience, by a power so distant from us, and so very ignorant of us; for if they cannot conquer us, they cannot govern us. To be always running three or four thousand miles with a tale or a petition, waiting four or five months for an answer, which, when obtained, requires five or six more to explain it in, will in a few years be looked upon as folly and childishness. There was a time when it was proper, and there is a proper time for it to cease.

Small islands not capable of protecting themselves are the proper objects for government to take under their care; but there is something absurd, in supposing a Continent to be perpetually governed by an island. In no instance hath nature made the satellite larger than its primary planet; and as England and America, with respect to each other, reverse the common order of nature, it is evident that they belong to different systems. England to Europe: America to itself. [...]

IV. Of the Present Ability of America

[...] The infant state of the Colonies, as it is called, so far from being against, is an argument in favour of independence. We are sufficiently numerous, and were we more so we might be less united. 'Tis a matter worthy of observation that the more a country is peopled, the smaller their armies are. In military numbers, the ancients far exceeded the moderns; and the reason is evident, for trade being the consequence of population, men became too much absorbed thereby to attend to anything else. Commerce diminishes the spirit both of patriotism and military defence. And history sufficiently informs us that the bravest achievements were always accomplished in the non-age of a nation. With the increase of commerce England hath lost its spirit. The city of London, notwithstanding its numbers, submits to continued insults with the patience of a coward. The more men have to lose, the less willing are they to venture. The rich are in general slaves to fear, and submit to courtly power with the trembling duplicity of a spaniel.

Youth is the seed-time of good habits as well in nations as in individuals. It might be difficult, if not impossible, to form the Continent into one government half a century hence. The vast variety of interests, occasioned by an increase of trade and population, would create confusion. Colony would be against colony. Each being able would scorn each other's assistance; and while the proud and foolish gloried in their little distinctions the wise would lament that the union had not been formed before. Wherefore the present time is the true time for establishing it. The intimacy which is contracted in infancy, and the friendship which is formed in misfortune, are of all others the most lasting and unalterable. Our present union is marked with both these characters; we are young, and we have been distressed; but our concord hath withstood our troubles, and fixes a memorable era for posterity to glory in.

The present time, likewise, is that peculiar time which never happens to a nation but once, viz., the time of forming itself into a government. Most nations have let slip the opportunity, and by that means have been compelled to receive laws from their conquerors, instead of making laws for themselves. First, they had a king, and then a form of government; whereas the articles or charter of government should be formed first, and men delegated to execute them afterwards; but from the errors of other nations let us learn wisdom, and lay hold of the present opportunity – TO BEGIN GOVERNMENT AT THE RIGHT END. [...]

Peter Oliver *Origin & Progress of the American Rebellion to the Year 1776, in a Letter to a Friend* (1781)[17]

SIR!

The Revolt of *North America*, from their Allegiance to & Connection with the Parent State, seems to be as striking a Phaenomenon, in the political World, as hath appeared for many Ages past; & perhaps it is a *singular* one. For, by adverting to the historick Page, we shall find no Revolt of Colonies, whether under the *Roman* or any other State, but what originated from severe Oppressions, derived from the supreme Head of the State, or from those whom he had entrusted as his Substitutes to be Governors of his Provinces. In such Cases, the Elasticity of human Nature hath been exerted, to throw off the Burdens which the Subject hath groaned under; & in most of the Instances which are recorded in History, human Nature will still justify those Efforts.

[17] P. Oliver, *Origin and Progress of the American Rebellion: A Tory View*, edited by D. Adair and J. A. Schutz (Stanford: Stanford University Press, 1961), pp. 3–9. (Footnotes have been omitted.)

But for a Colony, wch. had been nursed, in its Infancy, with the most tender Care & Attention; which had been indulged with every Gratification that the most froward Child could wish for; which had even bestowed upon it such Liberality, which its Infancy & Youth could not *think* to ask for; which had been repeatedly saved from impending Destruction, sometimes by an Aid unsought – at other times by Assistance granted to them from their own repeated humble Supplications; for such Colonies to plunge into an unnatural Rebellion, & in the Reign of a Sovereign, too, whose publick Virtues had announced him to be the Father of his Country, & whose private Virtues had distinguished him as an Ornament of ye. human Species this surely, to an attentive Mind, must strike with some Degree of Astonishment; & such a Mind would anxiously wish for a Veil to throw over the Nakedness of human Nature.

The Rebellion in *America* hath been a Subject of as great Speculation, & of as much Altercation in *great Britain*, as any Topick whatever which hath agitated the Mind of an Englishman since the Year *1641*, & I am perswaded that few Subjects are so little understood. Liberty is the darling Idea of an Englishman, & there is so much Magic in the bare Sound of the Word, that the Discord of Licentiousness very seldom vibrates on the Ear. The Distinction between natural Liberty & civil Liberty is too seldom adverted to. Therefore, when in the former State there seems to be an Infringement, Mankind make[s] a Party to resent the Affront offered to an Individual; & in the latter State, an inattentive Mind, regardless of that Distinction, is too apt to suffer the latter to be absorbed in the former; and hence arise many Evils which Society are incident to, and which induce Anarchy & every Species of Confusion. Whereas, by drawing the Line between them, & casting our Eye on each Side of it, we shall view different Prospects; & unbiassed Reason will soon determine the Boundaries by which each of them are to be limited.

In a State of Nature, where she unbosoms herself to all her Offspring, he that first seizes an Object, adapted to satiate his natural Wants, hath as much Right to enjoy it as any other Individual of her Creation. But as Mankind increased, her Productions lessened in Proportion; so that where there was a Deficiency in her Efforts, human Aid stepped in, to supply them, by adding to her Fertility. It may be said, that by extending their Researches, Mankind would have explored Territory sufficient to have satiated all their Wants – true! But who of this Number should be obliged to migrate? Every one, in his natural State, had an equal Right to remain on that Spot which he had occupied; but then, if Numbers chose to reside in a Community they would, of Course, appropriate particular Soils for their own Improvement; & as different Passions operated, they would create to themselves artificial Wants, which they would chuse to defend as well as supply; hence would arise Encroachments upon Property. For, as Mankind are not constituted of like Tempers & Passions, some who were of a more indolent & indulging Make would claim a Right to Support, from the Labors of the more active & industrious. Consequently, such a Conduct would meet with Opposition. This Opposition would create Strife, War & Bloodshed; & these would necessarily terminate in what is, with the greatest Propriety, termed civil Government. This hath been the Fact from the earliest Ages to the present Era, & the Reasons on which it is founded are too irresistable to admit of a Doubt, that the same Causes will ever produce the same Effects. Here then a State of natural Liberty must end; & a State of civil Liberty must commence.

As to a State of natural Liberty's existing, for any Length of Duration, it is perfectly ideal; & that there is any such State of Existence now, among the human Species remains at present to be proved. If we were to search for it, the most probable Path to take would be to explore the *Wilds of America*, but here we should search in vain. For every Part, which the boldest Adventurer hath as yet explored, hath discovered no Nation but among whom the Footsteps of civil Liberty may be traced by stronger or weaker Impressions. These happy Tribes, as I chuse to term them, enjoy civil Government in certain Degrees, though different in the Modes of it. They have their Kings & wise Men of Council, their *Sachems* & *Sagamores*, on whom they rely for their Conduct; & their great Confidence in them supplys, in many Instances, the deficiency of the written Laws of more refined Nations. They have a Religion of their own, which, to the eternal Disgrace of many Nations who boast of Politeness, is more influential on their Conduct than that of those who hold them in so great Contempt. As in the earliest Ages of the World, so among those Tribes, they adhere to Tradition for their Conduct, in the more important Scenes of Life.

Since then we shall find, after the most critical Researches, that a mere State of *Natural* Liberty, amongst *Plato's* two legged rational Animals, is not at present existant, nor ever did exist for any Length of Time. Let us then advert to a State of *civil* Liberty, to which the former as naturally gravitates as heavy Bodies do to the Centre of the Earth; and we shall find, that whoever changes from the former to the latter, must part with some Priviledges, real or imaginary, which he enjoyed in that, in order to obtain greater Advantages in this. In the former Situation, he was exposed to the cruel Resentment of every one who imagined himself to be offended by him. His Hand perhaps would be against every Man, & every Mans Hand against him. His ideal Property would be unsafe; & his Life as unsafe as his Property; but, by stepping into the social State, he hath secured both. But then he must not expect to reap all the Advantages to himself, without deriving some Advantage to the Society which he hath connected himself with. He must part with that Power which he was formerly in Possession of, of appropriating every Thing to his own Use wch. he may first happen to stumble upon; in Exchange for which, he is to recieve the joint Force of the Community in defending him in any Property he may, now, or in future, possess agreeable to the Rules of that Community which he associates with. He must part with the Right of private Revenge which he claimed in his State of Nature, & submit it to publick Vengeance; unless, where he is drove by his Enemy, to defend his Life & Property, into such a Situation which obliges him to recur to a State of Nature for his own Security; & in this Case, the Laws of the most civilized Nations will justifie him, because he was, at that Time, in the ineligible State, of being out of their Protection.

He must go further still. He must abate of that self sufficiency which he had imbibed in the simple State of Nature, of doing what was right in his own Eyes; & submit his private Opinion to the publick Judgement of the many, confiding in their united Sense, as of more Authority than the Sentiments of any Individual. Nay, he must also consent to the Opinion of the *Majority* of the Society, be it never so small a Majority. Otherwise, he may introduce a Principle on which may be founded such

Dissentions as would be destructive of the very Existence of such a Society; for this Majority, be it ever so small, might have a Preponderance of Weight to resist the Force of any Opposition that might be thrown into the opposite Scale; the Consequences of which, it requires no great Sagacity to foresee. [. . .]

But here steps in a Maxim; which hath had a most powerfull Operation on the Minds of some who have set out in the political Race, vizt. *"that no Man can be said to be free, 'who hath not a Vote in enacting the Laws by which he is to be governed, or in giving his Consent to the imposing Taxes to which he is to contribute his Share."* This Maxim hath been advanced by some theoretick Writers on Government, who were an Honor to human Nature: but Theory & Practice often differ. The metaphy[si]cian often fails in his Dogmas, through want of a thorough Investigation of the human Mind. The Philosopher misses it also, at particular Times, for even that great Philosophical Luminary, *Sr. Isaac Newton*, whom, as Mr. *Pope* expresses himself, the Angelick Orders shew to each other as we lower Beings shew an Ape. Even Sr. *Isaac* hath had some of his Principles controverted & disproved; & why? but because neither are infallible. For there is such a Progression in Knowledge, that the Limits of the human Mind & its Duration are too contracted, fully to investigate the Process of Nature.

Let us now see what the Consequence of the foregoing Maxim, taken strictly, must be – supposing, as in Great Britain, there are several Millions to be governed, & each Individual is to give his Consent to every Vote to be passed by this collective Body. Where will be found a *Blackheath* large enough for them to assemble upon in full Synod? Or, when assembled, how long a Time must it take for the Sound of every Proposal to reverberate in its full Weight? I think it may be readily answered, that it would take such a Length of Time, that each Individual would be a Governor without having any one Subject to govern; starving at the same Time, either for Want of Bread, or for Want of Work to earn Bread with. But it may be said, let the united Body chuse those in whom they can confide to represent them in Council, & suffer this Body, or a Majority of it, to govern the whole Community. This certainly is the only or best Method that human Wisdom hath ever yet invented, or probably ever will invent, to secure the greatest Freedom to Society; but even here, it cannot be without its Objections, according to the Strictness of the aforesaid Maxim. For if the Person, whom fifty of us should depute to act for us, should act & vote our Minds, yet, if ten more Representatives of five hundred Men should outvote the one whom the fifty deputed, & pass a Law to tax me against my Consent; or the Consent of him who may represent me, how can I be said to be free? Or supposing that I am absent, or sick, when the Choice of a Representative may come on, so that I have lost my Vote for him, how can I be said to enjoy Freedom, when I am taxed without my Consent? Nay, even supposing that the Representative, whom I might have voted for, should have declared in publick Assembly that I ought to be taxed. These, added to many similar Instances that might be adduced to prove the same Consequences, must convince a rational Mind that there is no such Object as perfect Freedom to be attained, untill the Constitution of human Nature is changed; & such a Mind will be satisfied with the Lot assigned to it by the Author of Nature, & be contented, after its strictest

Researches, to sit down under the Shadow of the english System of Government, so much applauded by Foreigners.

But, even in this Government, much the greater Number are unrepresented. For in the original Deposit of the Power of making Laws for the publick Safety, it was provided, that the Major Part of those who were to establish the Laws should govern the minor Part. This major Part hath delineated the Qualifications of Voters for Representation, so that there is such a Constitution formed, which, to make Innovations upon, might endanger the whole Superstructure. Innovations have been tried, & the Building hath fallen to Ruin, & remained in that State, untill a Set of wiser Architects hath erected the present on the Ruins of the old one – Perfection in any Thing human is not to be expected. The nearer the Approach to it is, the better *Perfection is what ne'er was, nor is, nor e'er will be* – There is a publick Confidence due from us to our Legislators. If they err, for to err is human, & they err ignorantly, all just Allowances ought be given to them, untill we can convince them, by Reason, of what is right. If they err wilfully, it will soon be in our Power to remove them; but it is not probable, that so large a Body of the Community shou'd unite in pulling down the Building, because they must know, that on the Destruction of it, they, like Samson, must be buried in its Ruins.

The Declaration of Independence (July 4, 1776)

The unanimous Declaration of the thirteen united States of America:

When in the Course of human events it becomes necessary for one people to dissolve the political bands which have connected them with another and to assume among the powers of the earth, the separate and equal station to which the Laws of Nature and of Nature's God entitle them, a decent respect to the opinions of mankind requires that they should declare the causes which impel them to the separation.

We hold these truths to be self-evident, that all men are created equal, that they are endowed by their Creator with certain unalienable Rights, that among these are Life, Liberty and the pursuit of Happiness. – That to secure these rights, Governments are instituted among Men, deriving their just powers from the consent of the governed, – That whenever any Form of Government becomes destructive of these ends, it is the Right of the People to alter or to abolish it, and to institute new Government, laying its foundation on such principles and organizing its powers in such form, as to them shall seem most likely to effect their Safety and Happiness. Prudence, indeed, will dictate that Governments long established should not be changed for light and transient causes; and accordingly all experience hath shewn that mankind are more disposed to suffer, while evils are sufferable than to right themselves by abolishing the forms to which they are accustomed. But when a long train of abuses and usurpations, pursuing invariably the same Object evinces a design to reduce them under absolute Despotism, it is their right, it is their duty, to throw off such Government, and to provide new Guards for their future security. – Such has been the patient sufferance of these

Colonies; and such is now the necessity which constrains them to alter their former Systems of Government. The history of the present King of Great Britain is a history of repeated injuries and usurpations, all having in direct object the establishment of an absolute Tyranny over these States. To prove this, let Facts be submitted to a candid world.

He has refused his Assent to Laws, the most wholesome and necessary for the public good.

He has forbidden his Governors to pass Laws of immediate and pressing import-ance, unless suspended in their operation till his Assent should be obtained; and when so suspended, he has utterly neglected to attend to them.

He has refused to pass other Laws for the accommodation of large districts of people, unless those people would relinquish the right of Representation in the Legislature, a right inestimable to them and formidable to tyrants only.

He has called together legislative bodies at places unusual, uncomfortable, and distant from the depository of their Public Records, for the sole purpose of fatiguing them into compliance with his measures.

He has dissolved Representative Houses repeatedly, for opposing with manly firmness his invasions on the rights of the people.

He has refused for a long time, after such dissolutions, to cause others to be elected, whereby the Legislative Powers, incapable of Annihilation, have returned to the People at large for their exercise; the State remaining in the mean time exposed to all the dangers of invasion from without, and convulsions within.

He has endeavoured to prevent the population of these States; for that purpose obstructing the Laws for Naturalization of Foreigners; refusing to pass others to encourage their migrations hither, and raising the conditions of new Appropriations of Lands.

He has obstructed the Administration of Justice by refusing his Assent to Laws for establishing Judiciary Powers.

He has made Judges dependent on his Will alone for the tenure of their offices, and the amount and payment of their salaries.

He has erected a multitude of New Offices, and sent hither swarms of Officers to harass our people and eat out their substance.

He has kept among us, in times of peace, Standing Armies without the Consent of our legislatures.

He has affected to render the Military independent of and superior to the Civil Power.

He has combined with others to subject us to a jurisdiction foreign to our constitution, and unacknowledged by our laws; giving his Assent to their Acts of pretended Legislation:

For quartering large bodies of armed troops among us:

For protecting them, by a mock Trial from punishment for any Murders which they should commit on the Inhabitants of these States:

For cutting off our Trade with all parts of the world:

For imposing Taxes on us without our Consent:

For depriving us in many cases, of the benefit of Trial by Jury:

For transporting us beyond Seas to be tried for pretended offences:

For abolishing the free System of English Laws in a neighbouring Province, establishing therein an Arbitrary government, and enlarging its Boundaries so as to render it at once an example and fit instrument for introducing the same absolute rule into these Colonies:

For taking away our Charters, abolishing our most valuable Laws and altering fundamentally the Forms of our Governments:

For suspending our own Legislatures, and declaring themselves invested with power to legislate for us in all cases whatsoever.

He has abdicated Government here, by declaring us out of his Protection and waging War against us.

He has plundered our seas, ravaged our coasts, burnt our towns, and destroyed the lives of our people.

He is at this time transporting large Armies of foreign Mercenaries to compleat the works of death, desolation, and tyranny, already begun with circumstances of Cruelty & Perfidy scarcely paralleled in the most barbarous ages, and totally unworthy the Head of a civilized nation.

He has constrained our fellow Citizens taken Captive on the high Seas to bear Arms against their Country, to become the executioners of their friends and Brethren, or to fall themselves by their Hands.

He has excited domestic insurrections amongst us, and has endeavoured to bring on the inhabitants of our frontiers, the merciless Indian Savages whose known rule of warfare, is an undistinguished destruction of all ages, sexes and conditions.

In every stage of these Oppressions We have Petitioned for Redress in the most humble terms: Our repeated Petitions have been answered only by repeated injury. A Prince, whose character is thus marked by every act which may define a Tyrant, is unfit to be the ruler of a free people.

Nor have We been wanting in attentions to our British brethren. We have warned them from time to time of attempts by their legislature to extend an unwarrantable jurisdiction over us. We have reminded them of the circumstances of our emigration and settlement here. We have appealed to their native justice and magnanimity, and we have conjured them by the ties of our common kindred to disavow these usurpations, which would inevitably interrupt our connections and correspondence. They too have been deaf to the voice of justice and of consanguinity. We must, therefore, acquiesce in the necessity, which denounces our Separation, and hold them, as we hold the rest of mankind, Enemies in War, in Peace Friends.

We, therefore, the Representatives of the united States of America, in General Congress, Assembled, appealing to the Supreme Judge of the world for the rectitude of our intentions, do, in the Name, and by Authority of the good People of these Colonies, solemnly publish and declare, That these united Colonies are, and of Right ought to be Free and Independent States, that they are Absolved from all Allegiance to the British Crown, and that all political connection between them and the State of Great Britain, is and ought to be totally dissolved; and that as Free and Independent

States, they have full Power to levy War, conclude Peace, contract Alliances, establish Commerce, and to do all other Acts and Things which Independent States may of right do. – And for the support of this Declaration, with a firm reliance on the protection of Divine Providence, we mutually pledge to each other our Lives, our Fortunes, and our sacred Honor.

Suggested Readings

Nathaniel Blyfield, *An Account of the Late Revolution in England* (London: Ric. Chiswell, 1689).

James Otis, *The Rights of the British Colonies Asserted and Proved* (Boston: Edes & Gill, 1764).

Daniel Dulany, *Considerations on the Propriety of Imposing Taxes in the British Colonies for the Purpose of Raising a Revenue, by Act of Parliament* (Annapolis: Jonas Green, 1765).

John Dickinson, "Letters from a Farmer in Pennsylvania" [1767–1768] in F. McDonald (ed.), *Empire and Nation: Letters from a Farmer in Pennsylvania (John Dickinson). Letters from the Federal Farmer (Richard Henry Lee)* (Indianapolis: Liberty Fund, 1999).

Silas Downer, *A Discourse at the Dedication of the Tree of Liberty* (Providence: John Waterman, 1768).

Thomas Jefferson, *A Summary View of the Rights of British America* (Williamsburg: Clementina Rind, 1774).

6 The Positive Founding (I)

One People or Several Peoples?

Asserting their independence from Britain was just the first step for the colonists. They were no longer part of the British people, but who were they? The question to be solved next was whether there was one or many American peoples. It proved to be, in many respects, a much harder question to answer, both in theory and in practice, and it started already before Independence was declared. As we have seen in Chapter 4, the first attempt to confederate was made by the Puritans of New England. It took longer than John Winthrop would have wanted for an agreement to be reached, but once created, the Articles of Confederation of the United Colonies, despite all of their shortcomings, built a confederation that lasted half a century and enjoyed more than thirty years of peace – no small feat considering all the vagaries it had to endure both internally and externally.

The experiment demonstrated that, despite their differences, the peoples of the American colonies could eventually combine themselves into one body; it was not an easy task, but not an impossible one either. In the following years, several other plans of union were devised, sometimes by Great Britain and sometimes by the colonists themselves, only to be rejected either by the Crown, which saw in them an attempt to undermine its authority, or by the colonies, which were unwilling to sacrifice their much cherished autonomy.

When on May 23, 1774, the New York Committee suggested to the Boston Committee of Correspondence that a congress of deputies from all colonies should be called without delay to pass "some unanimous resolutions formed in this fatal emergency," they knew the difficulty of the task ahead.[1] The prospect of "unanimous resolutions" was further complicated not only by the differences between the New England colonies, the Middle colonies, and the Southern colonies, but also by the fact that "colonial nationalism," for lack of a better term, was by then so deeply ingrained as to make unanimity almost impossible.

> Each delegate thought of his own colony as his country, as an independent nation in its dealing with England and with its neighbors, with whom relations were often as not unfriendly. It is this simple fact that is too often overlooked. Instead of lamenting the absence of "national feeling," one must recognize that it was there in an intense

---

[1] In H. P. Johnston (ed.), *The Correspondence and Public Papers of John Jay*, Vol. I (New York: G. P. Putnam's Sons, 1890), p. 13.

form, but in the form that is illustrated by the attitude of John Adams when he wrote of Massachusetts Bay as "our country."[2]

After debating whether the colonies should have more votes depending on the size of their population or if they should be considered as equal corporate entities, the delegates to the **First Continental Congress** (1774), like the Puritans a century before them, accepted the idea that, as corporations, each colony should have an equal vote. **The Declaration and Resolves** of the First Continental Congress read "That the inhabitants of the English colonies in North-America, by *the immutable laws of nature, the principles of the English constitution, and the several charters or compacts*, have the following RIGHTS [...]." It was a declaration neither fully republican nor fully liberal; neither fully conservative nor fully revolutionary.

The First Continental Congress officially ended on October 26, 1774, and the Second opened May 10, 1775. Formally, it stayed in existence until it became the permanent organ of the newly created national government under the **Articles of Confederation**, although the use of the title "**Continental Congress**" persisted throughout the Confederation period, until the second Constitution went into effect in 1789. It was a period of dramatic shifts in opinions. Even as the evolutions of 1775 and 1776 pushed the delegates closer and closer to accepting the idea of a union, their fears about the impossibility of bridging the divisions between the colonies grew stronger. As John Adams observed in a **Letter to Joseph Hawley**, "I dread the Consequences of this Dissimilitude of Character, and without the Utmost Caution on both sides [the New England colonies and the Southern ones, respectively], and the most considerate Forbearance with one another and prudent Condescention on both sides, they will certainly be fatal."

Not discouraged by these intercolonial differences and tensions, and always on the lookout for a feasible compromise, Benjamin Franklin presented a draft of the "**Articles of Confederation and Perpetual Union [between] the Several Colonies**" to Congress on July 21, 1775, carefully stipulating that "each colony shall enjoy and retain as much as it may think fit of its own present Laws, Customs, Rights, Privileges [...]." Nevertheless, the "Power and Duty" of the General Congress would extend not only to "Determining on War and Peace" but also to "the Settling [of] all Disputes and Differences between Colony and Colony [...]."[3] Unfortunately, the timing was not right. Congress postponed its discussion for almost six months, only to reject it on January 16, 1776.

Meanwhile, despite the vagaries of war, there was a more pressing matter at hand – framing the new state constitutions. John Adams proved his pragmatism when, on June 3, 1776, he wrote in a **Letter to Patrick Henry** (1736–1799):[4]

> [T]he natural Course and order of Things, was this – for every Colony to institute a Government – for all the Colonies to confederate, and define the Limits of the Continental Constitution – then to declare the Colonies a sovereign State, or

---

[2] M. Jensen, *The Articles of Confederation: An Interpretation of the Social-Constitutional History of the American Revolution, 1774–1781* (Madison: University Wisconsin Press, 1970), p. 56.

[3] W. C. Ford (ed.), *Journal of the Continental Congress*, Vol. II (Washington, DC: Government Printing Office, 1905), pp. 194–9.

[4] For more on Patrick Henry, see Chapter 7.

a Number of confederated Sovereign States [. . .]. But I fear We cannot proceed systematically, and that We Shall be obliged to declare ourselves independent States before We confederate [. . .]

Ironically, **Richard Henry Lee** (1732–1794), who would eventually end up in the Antifederalist camp (Chapter 7), wondered if a single plan proposed by Congress should not be submitted to all colonies for their approval, in order to reinforce a sense of unity. Eventually, Congress refused to impose a certain form of state constitution, yet in May 1776 it passed two **Resolutions** demanding each colony "to adopt such government as shall, in the opinion of the representatives of the people, best conduce to the happiness and safety of their constituents in particular, and America in general."

Even before the **Declaration of Independence**, four legislatures – New Hampshire, South Carolina, New Jersey, and Virginia – adopted "provisional" constitutions, while also expressing their "earnest desire" to reconcile with Great Britain and to put an end to "the present unhappy and unnatural contest with Great Britain."[5] They considered themselves "the full and free representations of the people." Two other legislatures, from Connecticut and Rhode Island, did not even think that a new constitution was necessary, since the nullification of the charters by the king did not affect the desire of the people to live by them. The practice did not last long, and two questions remained to be addressed: first, whether the legislature was still representative of the people in a matter as fundamental as the establishment of a constitution, and second, whether the same legislature had the right to approve such a constitution in the name of the people. Eventually, the answers in both cases would turn out to be negative.

On the first matter, **Thomas Young** (1731–1777), organizer of the **Boston Tea Party** and co-drafter of the first **Constitution of Pennsylvania**, distinguished between the "supreme delegate power" of elected representatives and the "supreme constituent power" of the people: "They are the supreme constituent power, and of course their immediate Representatives are the supreme delegate power; and as soon as the delegate power gets too far out of the hands of the constituent power, a tyranny is in some degree established."[6] On the matter of popular ratification, the positions were even stronger. According to the Puritan legacy, the selected natural aristocracy was entitled to draft the constitution, but the power to approve it belonged exclusively "to the inhabitants at large."

As early as May 1776, a **Letter from the Town of Pittsfield to the House of Representatives of Massachusetts Bay** argued that, once King George had broken his contract, the people of the colonies "have fallen into a state of nature," hence the entire government had to be started "from scratch." In agreement with the basic tenets of **Lockean liberalism**, the inhabitants of Pittsfield agreed that "the first step to be taken by a people in such a state for the enjoyment or restoration of civil government among them is the formation of a fundamental constitution as the basis and ground-work of legislation." Yet, according to the **Puritan** tradition of the people's two bodies, they also agreed

---

[5] South Carolina Constitution of 1776; New Hampshire Constitution of 1776.

[6] An open letter dated April 11, 1777, 'To the Inhabitants of Vermont, a Free and Independent State . . . ', quoted in W. P. Adams, *The First American Constitutions: Republican Ideology and the Making of the State Constitutions in the Revolutionary Era*, translated by Rita and Robert Kimber (Chapel Hill: University of North Carolina Press, 1980), p. 65.

that "a representative body *may form, but cannot impose* said fundamental constitution upon a people, as they, being but servants of the people, cannot be greater than their masters, and must be responsible to them." The natural aristocracy is better qualified to draft the constitution, but the people *at large* had a <u>duty</u> to *approve* it.

The delegates to the **Virginia Convention**, held in Williamsburg from May 6 to July 6, 1776, did not consider it necessary to involve the people at large in any phase of the process. The Convention, dominated by wealthy planters, both discussed and approved the new constitution. The delegates agreed in principle that the legislative power should be divided between a House of Delegates and a Senate and also that "the legislative, executive, and judiciary department, shall be separate and distinct, so that neither exercise the powers properly belonging to the other." Nevertheless, it left most of the powers in the hands of the legislative, in charge of electing the Governor and his Privy Council, but also the "Judges of the Supreme Court of Appeals, and General Court, Judges in Chancery, Judges of Admiralty, Secretary, and the Attorney-General." Thus, the separation of powers remained more or less an empty phrase.

A few years later, in his **Notes on the State of Virginia**, Thomas Jefferson pointed out its shortcomings, but also found an excuse for them: it was a period of trial and error. "[W]e were new and unexperienced in the science of government. It was the first too which was formed in the whole United States. No wonder then that time and trial have discovered very capital defects in it." According to Jefferson, the formal separation of the legislative power into two branches had failed "to introduce the influence of different interests or different principles." "The senate," he argued, "is, by its constitution, too homogeneous with the house of delegates. Being chosen by the same electors, at the same time, and out of the same subjects, the choice falls of course on men of the same description." But even more concerning for him was the excessive power placed in the hands of this homogeneous legislative.

> All the powers of government, legislative, executive, and judiciary, result to the legislative body. The concentrating these in the same hands is precisely the definition of despotic government. It will be no alleviation that these powers will be exercised by a plurality of hands, and not by a single one. 173 despots would surely be as oppressive as one.

The Convention also adopted the first **Bill of Rights** – a practice that would be followed by other state constitutions, and would later become a matter of contention during the debates between the Federalists and the Antifederalists (Chapter 7). Yet, being framed mainly from an **aristocratic-republican** perspective, the **Virginia Bill of Rights** asserted that "all men are *equally free* and independent, and have certain inherent rights." There was no mention of men being "free *and* equal." John Adams was among the few aware of this distinction. When drafting the Bill of Rights for Massachusetts in 1780, he suggested that the key phrase read "equally free and independent." "But the constitutional convention decided to follow the wording of the Declaration of Independence more closely and declared, 'All men are born free and equal.' No one seemed to feel that there was a significant difference between 'equally free and independent' and 'free and equal.'"[7]

---

[7] Adams, *The First American Constitutions*, p. 175.

Meanwhile, in **Pennsylvania**, the pendulum swung decisively in favor of one of the people's two bodies – the egalitarian one. *The Alarm: or, An Address to the People of Pennsylvania on the Late Resolve of Congress* asked the most important question: "Who are, or who are not, the proper persons to be entrusted with carrying the said Resolve into execution [. . .]?" And since the Congress had asked the states to craft new constitutions "on the Authority of the People," it followed that the existing legislative, i.e. the House of Assembly, was not up to the task. A different body of representatives was needed to draft the new form of government, one in which "the persons delegated with proper powers to form a plan of government, ought to possess the entire confidence of the people." And so it was. The Pennsylvania **constitutional convention** that met in Philadelphia on July 15, 1776 completely replaced the old government, elected Benjamin Franklin as its president, and drafted the most radically democratic state constitution of all.

The **Constitution of Pennsylvania** was the first to expand the electoral franchise to all men paying taxes, thus dropping property requirements, and also the only one establishing a unicameral legislative. It was the embodiment of what may be labeled **popular republicanism**. The fact that all inequalities, either of wealth or of power, including the powers of the elected representatives, were suspicious almost by default explains why the constitution starts with what amounts to a Bill of Rights meant to protect individuals against any possible abuses. It also explains why there was no provision for a governor. Instead, the executive function was assured by an elected Executive Council which, together with the legislative, elected a president and a vice president. The judiciary was also under the control of the legislative; judges could be revoked by the legislative for misbehavior. The constitution also provided for a Council of Censors to meet every seven years in order to review the constitutionality of the laws. Furthermore, the constitution specified that "all bills of public nature shall be printed for the consideration of the people, before they are read in general assembly the last time for debate and amendment; and, except on occasions of sudden necessity, shall not be passed into laws until the next session of assembly."

Such **popular radicalism** raised many concerns. In his *Four Letters to the People of Pennsylvania*, **Benjamin Rush** (1746–1813), a physician who came to be considered "the father of American psychiatry," criticized the constitution for lodging "the supreme, absolute, and uncontrouled power of the whole State [. . .] in the hands of one body of men. Had it been lodged in the hands of one man, it would have been less dangerous to the safety and liberties of the community." Following in the footsteps of **classical republicanism**, he argued that imposing an abstract equality on the people would eventually destroy precisely what it was intended to protect. "I agree, that we have no artificial distinctions of men into noblemen and commoners among us, but it ought to be remarked, that superior degrees of industry and capacity [. . .] have introduced natural distinctions of rank in Pennsylvania, as certain and general as the artificial distinctions of men in Europe." Absent a bicameral legislative, Rush argued, "The men of middling property and poor men can never be safe in a mixed representation with the men of over-grown property." Maintaining the proper balance between the people's two bodies required "the opposite and different duties of the different representations of the people."

John Adams could not but agree. As the mastermind behind the **Constitution of Massachusetts**, he tried his best to introduce a system of checks and balances that would ensure such a dual representation. As we have seen in a **Letter from the Town of Pittsfield**, according to the Puritan tradition, the people agreed that a representative body should be in charge of framing the constitution, but also demanded that "the people at large" ought to approve it and have a right to amend it. In 1778, almost the entire adult male population of Massachusetts had an opportunity not only to vote on the draft of the new constitution but also to propose amendments to it – something unprecedented in the history of modern constitutionalism.

The Constitution of Massachusetts proved a success, being the only one of the early state constitutions that introduced a real system of **checks and balances** both between the two houses of the legislative and between the legislative, executive, and judicial powers, in an attempt to rein in the unavoidable corruption of human nature. It was an example of **moral republicanism**.[8] It was also the constitution that, in its preamble, captured the paradigm of the people's two bodies best. As explained later by John Quincy Adams,

> Thus when in the Constitution of the Commonwealth of Massachusetts, it is said that the body politic is formed by a social compact in which the *whole people* covenants with each citizen and each citizen with the *whole people*, the words *whole people* in the first part of the sentence, have not the same meaning as they have in the second. In the first part they mean the portion of the people *capable* of contracting for the whole and with the whole – in the second, they mean the sum of total human beings bound by and included in the compact.[9]

Not surprisingly, the Constitution of Massachusetts eventually became the template for the second Constitution of the United States (Chapter 7). In the meantime, amid these state constitutional debates, attempts to agree upon a national constitution continued.

It took more than a year and three different drafts before the delegates to the Continental Congress agreed on the **Articles of Confederation**. The main challenge was not the factional divisions between the large and the small states, nor between the three political subcultures – moralistic in New England, individualistic in the Middle Atlantic states, and traditionalistic in the South.[10] Rather, what was at stake was the same confrontation that had played out in the state constitutional conventions between the principle of corporate representation and the principle of numerical majorities. The issue could be rephrased as a question of orthography. If, in the Declaration of Independence, the spelling of "united States" was with a lower-case "u," ought not the first federal constitution redress the balance by capitalizing "Union"? Some of the delegates agreed, among them John Adams, who claimed

---

[8] P. Abbott, *Political Thought in America: Conversations and Debates* (Long Grove, IL: Waveland Press, 2010).

[9] Lecture delivered at the Franklin Lyceum on November 25, 1842.

[10] D. J. Elazar, *American Federalism: A View from the States* (New York: Thomas Y. Crowell, 1972); C. C. Jillson, "Political Culture and the Pattern of Congressional Politics under the Articles of Confederation," *Publius*, 18:1 (1988), pp. 10, 26.

that the aim of the confederation was "to form us, like separate parcels of metal, into one common mass. We shall no longer retain our separate individuality."[11]

Most of the delegates from the small states begged to differ, and the lower-case "u" in the "united States in Congress assembled" makes it easy to conclude that the latter camp ultimately carried the day. But this inference would completely disregard the fact that with each of the three drafts the unity of the states was pushed further. In effect, a closer reading of the Articles reveals that some of the most familiar parts of the future Constitution – such as the Supremacy Clause, the Privileges and Immunities Clause, and the Full Faith and Credit Clause – were directly inspired by the Articles of Confederation. Nevertheless, focusing solely on the corporatist understanding of the people of each state, the first constitution was short-lived. A more balanced representation of the people's two bodies was needed, and it would be found during the **Philadelphia Convention**.

[11] Quoted in T. Jefferson, "Notes on Debates" in P. L. Ford (ed.), *The Writings of Thomas Jefferson*, Vol. I (New York: G. P. Putnam's Sons, 1892–1899), p. 45.

John Adams

Letter to Joseph Hawley (November 25, 1775)[12]

[...] We cannot Suddenly alter the Temper, Principles, opinions or Prejudices of Men. The Characters of Gentlemen in the four New England Colonies, differ as much from those in the others, as that of the Common People differs, that is as much as several distinct Natures almost. Gentlemen, Men of sense, or any Kind of Education in the other Colonies are much fewer in Proportion than in N. England. Gentlemen in the other Colonies, have large Plantations of slaves, and the common People among them are very ignorant and very poor. These Gentlemen are accustomed, habituated to higher Notions of themselves and the Distinction between them and the common People, than We are, and an instantaneous alteration of the Character of a Colony, and that Temper and those sentiments which, its Inhabitants imbibed with their Mothers Milk, and which have grown with their Growth and strengthend with their Strength, cannot be made without a Miracle. I dread the Consequences of this Dissimilitude of Character, and without the Utmost Caution on both sides, and the most considerate Forbearance with one another and prudent Condescention on both sides, they will certainly be fatal. An alteration of the Southern Constitutions, which must certainly take Place if this War continues will gradually, bring all the Continent nearer and nearer to each other in all Respects. But this is the Most Critical Moment, We have yet seen. [...]

Thoughts on Government (1776)[13]

My dear Sir,

If I was equal to the task of forming a plan for the government of a colony, I should be flattered with your request, and very happy to comply with it; because as the divine science of politicks is the science of social happiness, and the blessings of society depend entirely on the constitutions of government, which are generally institutions that last for many generations, there can be no employment more agreeable to a benevolent mind, than a research after the best.

> Pope flattered tyrants too much when he said,
> "For forms of government let fools contest,
> That which is best administered is best."

Nothing can be more fallacious than this: But poets read history to collect flowers not fruits – they attend to fanciful images, not the effects of social institutions. Nothing is more certain from the history of nations, and the nature of man,

---

[12] *Founders Online*, National Archives, https://founders.archives.gov/documents/Adams/06-03-02-0169. Original source: *The Adams Papers*, Papers of John Adams, Vol. III: *May 1775–January 1776*, edited by R. J. Taylor (Cambridge, MA: Harvard University Press, 1979), pp. 316–17.

[13] *Founders Online*, National Archives, https://founders.archives.gov/documents/Adams/06-04-02-0026-0004. Original source: *The Adams Papers*, Papers of John Adams, Vol. IV, *February–August 1776*, edited by R. J. Taylor (Cambridge, MA: Harvard University Press, 1979), pp. 86–93.

than that some forms of government are better fitted for being well administered than others.

WE ought to consider, what is the end of government, before we determine which is the best form. Upon this point all speculative politicians will agree, that the happiness of society is the end of government, as all Divines and moral Philosophers will agree that the happiness of the individual is the end of man. From this principle it will follow, that the form of government, which communicates ease, comfort, security, or in one word happiness to the greatest number of persons, and in the greatest degree, is the best.

ALL sober enquiries after truth, ancient and modern, Pagan and Christian, have declared that the happiness of man, as well as his dignity consists in virtue. Confucius, Zoroaster, Socrates, Mahomet, not to mention authorities really sacred, have agreed in this.

IF there is a form of government then, whose principle and foundation is virtue, will not every sober man acknowledge it better calculated to promote the general happiness than any other form?

FEAR is the foundation of most governments; but is so sordid and brutal a passion, and renders men, in whose breasts it predominates, so stupid, and miserable, that Americans will not be likely to approve of any political institution which is founded on it.

HONOR is truly sacred but holds a lower rank in the scale of moral excellence than virtue. Indeed the former is but a part of the latter, and consequently has not equal pretensions to support a frame of government productive of human happiness.

THE foundation of every government is some principle or passion in the minds of the people. The noblest principles and most generous affections in our nature then, have the fairest chance to support the noblest and most generous models of government.

A MAN must be indifferent to the sneers of modern Englishmen to mention in their company the names of Sidney, Harrington, Locke, Milton, Nedham, Neville, Burnet, and Hoadley. No small fortitude is necessary to confess that one has read them. The wretched condition of this country, however, for ten or fifteen years past, has frequently reminded me of their principles and reasonings. They will convince any candid mind, that there is no good government but what is Republican. That the only valuable part of the British constitution is so; because the very definition of a Republic, is "an Empire of Laws, and not of men." That, as a Republic is the best of governments, so that particular arrangement of the powers of society, or in other words that form of government, which is best contrived to secure an impartial and exact execution of the laws, is the best of Republics.

OF Republics, there is an inexhaustable variety, because the possible combinations of the powers of society, are capable of innumerable variations.

As good government, is an empire of laws, how shall your laws be made? In a large society, inhabiting an extensive country, it is impossible that the whole should assemble, to make laws: The first necessary step then, is, to depute power from the many, to a few of the most wise and good. But by what rules shall you chuse your Representatives? Agree upon the number and qualifications of persons, who shall have the benefit of choosing, or annex this priviledge to the inhabitants of a certain extent of ground.

THE principal difficulty lies, and the greatest care should be employed in constituting this Representative Assembly. It should be in miniature, an exact portrait of the people at large. It should think, feel, reason, and act like them. That it may be the interest of this Assembly to do strict justice at all times, it should be an equal representation, or in other words equal interest among the people should have equal interest in it. Great care should be taken to effect this, and to prevent unfair, partial, and corrupt elections. Such regulations, however, may be better made in times of greater tranquility than the present, and they will spring up of themselves naturally, when all the powers of government come to be in the hands of the people's friends. At present it will be safest to proceed in all established modes to which the people have been familiarised by habit.

A REPRESENTATION of the people in one assembly being obtained, a question arises whether all the powers of government, legislative, executive, and judicial, shall be left in this body? I think a people cannot be long free, nor ever happy, whose government is in one Assembly. My reasons for this opinion are as follow.

1. A SINGLE Assembly is liable to all the vices, follies and frailties of an individual. Subject to fits of humour, starts of passion, flights of enthusiasm, partialities of prejudice, and consequently productive of hasty results and absurd judgments: And all these errors ought to be corrected and defects supplied by some controuling power.
2. A SINGLE Assembly is apt to be avaricious, and in time will not scruple to exempt itself from burthens which it will lay, without compunction, on its constituents.
3. A SINGLE Assembly is apt to grow ambitious, and after a time will not hesitate to vote itself perpetual. This was one fault of the long parliament, but more remarkably of Holland, whose Assembly first voted themselves from annual to septennial, then for life, and after a course of years, that all vacancies happening by death, or otherwise, should be filled by themselves, without any application to constituents at all.
4. A REPRESENTATIVE Assembly, altho' extremely well qualified, and absolutely necessary as a branch of the legislature, is unfit to exercise the executive power, for want of two essential properties, secrecy and dispatch.
5. A REPRESENTATIVE Assembly is still less qualified for the judicial power; because it is too numerous, too slow, and too little skilled in the laws.
6. BECAUSE a single Assembly, possessed of all the powers of government, would make arbitrary laws for their own interest, execute all laws arbitrarily for their own interest, and adjudge all controversies in their own favour.

BUT shall the whole power of legislation rest in one Assembly? Most of the foregoing reasons apply equally to prove that the legislative power ought to be more complex – to which we may add, that if the legislative power is wholly in one Assembly, and the executive in another, or in a single person, these two powers will oppose and enervate upon each other, until the contest shall end in war, and the whole power, legislative and executive, be usurped by the strongest.

THE judicial power, in such case, could not mediate, or hold the balance between the two contending powers, because the legislative would undermine it. And this shews the necessity too, of giving the executive power a negative upon the legislative, otherwise this will be continually encroaching upon that.

TO avoid these dangers let a distant Assembly be constituted, as a mediator between the two extreme branches of the legislature, that which represents the people and that which is vested with the executive power.

LET the Representative Assembly then elect by ballot, from among themselves or their constituents, or both, a distinct Assembly, which for the sake of perspicuity we will call a Council. It may consist of any number you please, say twenty or thirty, and should have a free and independent exercise of its judgment, and consequently a negative voice in the legislature.

THESE two bodies thus constituted, and made integral parts of the legislature, let them unite, and by joint ballot choose a Governor, who, after being stripped of most of those badges of domination called prerogatives, should have a free and independent exercise of his judgment, and be made also an integral part of the legislature. This I know is liable to objections, and if you please you may make him only President of the Council, as in Connecticut: But as the Governor is to be invested with the executive power, with consent of Council, I think he ought to have a negative upon the legislative. If he is annually elective, as he ought to be, he will always have so much reverence and affection for the People, their Representatives and Councillors, that although you give him an independent exercise of his judgment, he will seldom use it in opposition to the two Houses, except in cases the public utility of which would be conspicuous, and some such cases would happen.

IN the present exigency of American affairs, when by an act of Parliament we are put out of the royal protection, and consequently discharged from our allegiance; and it has become necessary to assume government for our immediate security, the Governor, Lieutenant-Governor, Secretary, Treasurer, Commissary, Attorney-General, should be chosen by joint Ballot, of both Houses. And these and all other elections, especially of Representatives, and Councillors, should be annual, there not being in the whole circle of the sciences, a maxim more infallible than this, "Where annual elections end, there slavery begins." [. . .]

This will teach them the great political virtues of humility, patience, and moderation, without which every man in power becomes a ravenous beast of prey.

THIS mode of constituting the great offices of state will answer very well for the present, but if, by experiment, it should be found inconvenient, the legislature may at its leisure devise other methods of creating them, by elections of the people at large, as in Connecticut, or it may enlarge the term for which they shall be chosen to seven years, or three years, or for life, or make any other alterations which the society shall find productive of its ease, its safety, its freedom, or in one word, its happiness.

A ROTATION of all offices, as well as of Representatives and Councillors, has many advocates, and is contended for with many plausible arguments. It would be attended no doubt with many advantages, and if the society has a sufficient number of suitable characters to supply the great number of vacancies which would be made by such a rotation, I can see no objection to it. These persons may be allowed to serve for three years, and then excluded three years, or for any longer or shorter term. [. . .]

THE Governor should have the command of the militia, and of all your armies. The power of pardons should be with the Governor and Council.

JUDGES, Justices and all other officers, civil and military, should be nominated and appointed by the Governor, with the advice and consent of Council, unless you choose to have a government more popular; if you do, all officers, civil and military, may be chosen by joint ballot of both Houses, or in order to preserve the independence and importance of each House, by ballot of one House, concurred by the other. Sheriffs should be chosen by the freeholders of counties – so should Registers of Deeds and Clerks of Counties. [. . .]

THE dignity and stability of government in all its branches, the morals of the people and every blessing of society, depends so much upon an upright and skillful administration of justice, that the judicial power ought to be distinct from both the legislative and executive, and independent upon both, that so it may be a check upon both, as both should be checks upon that. The Judges therefore should always be men of learning and experience in the laws, of exemplary morals, great patience, calmness, coolness and attention. Their minds should not be distracted with jarring interests; they should not be dependant upon any man or body of men. To these ends they should hold estates for life in their offices, or in other words their commissions should be during good behaviour, and their salaries ascertained and established by law. For misbehaviour the grand inquest of the Colony, the House of Representatives, should impeach them before the Governor and Council, where they should have time and opportunity to make their defence, but if convicted should be removed from their offices, and subjected to such other punishment as shall be thought proper. [. . .]

A CONSTITUTION, founded on these principles, introduces knowledge among the People, and inspires them with a conscious dignity, becoming Freemen. A general emulation takes place, which causes good humour, sociability, good manners, and good morals to be general. That elevation of sentiment, inspired by such a government, makes the common people brave and enterprizing. That ambition which is inspired by it makes them sober, industrious and frugal. You will find among them some elegance, perhaps, but more solidity; a little pleasure, but a great deal of business – some politeness, but more civility. If you compare such a country with the regions of domination, whether Monarchial or Aristocratical, you will fancy yourself in Arcadia or Elisium.

IF the Colonies should assume governments separately, they should be left entirely to their own choice of the forms, and if a Continental Constitution should be formed, it should be a Congress, containing a fair and adequate Representation of the Colonies, and its authority should sacredly be confined to these cases, viz. war, trade, disputes between Colony and Colony, the Post-Office, and the unappropriated lands of the Crown, as they used to be called.

THESE Colonies, under such forms of government, and in such a union, would be unconquerable by all the Monarchies of Europe.

YOU and I, my dear Friend, have been sent into life, at a time when the greatest law-givers of antiquity would have wished to have lived. How few of the human race have ever enjoyed an opportunity of making an election of government more than of air, soil, or climate, for themselves or their children. When! Before the present epocha, had three millions of people full power and a fair opportunity to form and establish the wisest and happiest government that human wisdom can contrive? I hope you will avail yourself and your country of that extensive learning and indefatigable industry which you possess, to assist her in the formations of the happiest governments, and the best character of a great People. [...]

Letter to Patrick Henry (June 3, 1776)[14]

[...] I, esteam it an Honour and an Happiness, that my opinion So often co-incides with yours. It has ever appeared to me, that the natural Course and order of Things, was this – for every Colony to institute a Government – for all the Colonies to confederate, and define the Limits of the Continental Constitution – then to declare the Colonies a sovereign State, or a Number of confederated Sovereign States – and last of all to form Treaties with foreign Powers. But I fear We cannot proceed systematically, and that We Shall be obliged to declare ourselves independant States before We confederate, and indeed before all the Colonies have established their Governments.

It is now pretty clear, that all these Measures will follow one another in a rapid Succession, and it may not perhaps be of much Importance, which is done first. [...]

Your Intimation that the session of your Representative Body would be long gave me great Pleasure, because We all look up to Virginia for Examples and in the present Perplexities, Dangers and Distresses of our Country it is necessary that the Supream Councils of the Colonies should be almost constantly Sitting. Some Colonies are not sensible of this and they will certainly Suffer for their Indiscretion. Events of such Magnitude as those which present themselves now in such quick Succession, require constant Attention and mature Deliberation. [...]

---

[14] *Founders Online,* National Archives, https://founders.archives.gov/documents/Adams/06-04-02-0102. Original source: *The Adams Papers*, Papers of John Adams, Vol. IV, pp. 234–5.

Resolutions of the Second Continental Congress (May 1776)

May 10, 1776

Resolved, That it be recommended to the respective assemblies and conventions of the United Colonies, where no government sufficient to the exigencies of their affairs have been hitherto established, to adopt such government as shall, in the opinion of the representatives of the people, best conduce to the happiness and safety of their constituents in particular, and America in general.

May 15, 1776

The Congress took into consideration the draught of the preamble brought in by the committee [John Adams, Edward Rutledge, Richard Henry Lee], which was agreed to as follows:

Whereas his Britannic Majesty, in conjunction with the lords and commons of Great Britain, has, by a late act of Parliament, excluded the inhabitants of these United Colonies from the protection of his crown; And whereas, no answer, whatever, to the humble petitions of the colonies for redress of grievances and reconciliation with Great Britain, has been or is likely to be given; but, the whole force of that kingdom, aided by foreign mercenaries, is to be exerted for the destruction of the good people of these colonies; And whereas, it appears absolutely irreconcilable to reason and good Conscience, for the people of these colonies now to take the oaths and affirmations necessary for the support of any government under the crown of Great Britain, and it is necessary that the exercise of every kind of authority under the said crown should be totally suppressed, and all the powers of government exerted, under the authority of the people of the colonies, for the preservation of internal peace, virtue, and good order, as well as for the defence of their lives, liberties, and properties, against the hostile invasions and cruel depredations of their enemies; therefore, resolved, &c.

Ordered, That the said preamble, with the resolution passed the 10th instant, be published.

VIRGINIA

Constitution of Virginia (June 29, 1776)

Whereas George the third, King of Great Britain and Ireland, and elector of Hanover, heretofore intrusted with the exercise of the kingly office in this government, hath endeavoured to prevent, the same into a detestable and insupportable tyranny, by putting his negative on laws the most wholesome and necessary for the public good:

> By denying his Governors permission to pass laws of immediate and pressing importance, unless suspended in their operation for his assent, and, when so suspended neglecting to attend to them for many years:
>
> By refusing to pass certain other laws, unless the persons to be benefited by them would relinquish the inestimable right of representation in the legislature:
>
> By dissolving legislative Assemblies repeatedly and continually, for opposing with manly firmness his invasions of the rights of the people:
>
> When dissolved, by refusing to call others for a long space of time, thereby leaving the political system without any legislative head: [...]
>
> By answering our repeated petitions for redress with a repetition of injuries: And finally, by abandoning the helm of government and declaring us out of his allegiance and protection.

By which several acts of misrule, the government of this country, as formerly exercised under the crown of Great Britain, is TOTALLY DISSOLVED.

We therefore, the delegates and representatives of the good people of Virginia, having maturely considered the premises, and viewing with great concern the deplorable conditions to which this once happy country must be reduced, unless some regular, adequate mode of civil polity is speedily adopted, and in compliance with a recommendation of the general Congress, do ordain and declare the future form of government of Virginia to be as followeth:

The legislative, executive, and judiciary department, shall be separate and distinct, so that neither exercise the powers properly belonging to the other: nor shall any person exercise the powers of more than one of them, at the same time; except that the Justices of the County courts shall be eligible to either House of Assembly.

The legislative shall be formed of two distinct branches, who, together, shall be a complete Legislature. They shall meet once, or oftener, every year, and shall be called, The General Assembly of Virginia. One of these shall be called, The House of Delegates, and consist of two Representatives, to be chosen for each county, and for the district of West-Augusta, annually, of such men as actually reside in, and are freeholders of the same, or duly qualified according to law, and also of one Delegate or Representative, to be chosen annually for the city of Williamsburgh, and one for the borough of Norfolk, and a Representative for each of such other cities and boroughs, as may hereafter be allowed particular representation by the legislature; but when any city or borough shall so decrease, as that the number of persons, having right of suffrage therein, shall have been, for the space of seven Years successively, less than half the number of voters in some one county in Virginia, such city or borough thenceforward shall cease to send a Delegate or Representative to the Assembly.

The other shall be called The Senate, and consist of twenty-four members, of whom thirteen shall constitute a House to proceed on business; for whose election, the different counties shall be divided into twenty-four districts; and each county of the respective district, at the time of the election of its Delegates, shall vote for one Senator, who is actually a resident and freeholder within the district, or duly qualified according to law, and is upwards of twenty-five years of age [...]. To keep up this Assembly by rotation, the districts shall be equally divided into four classes and numbered by lot. At the end of one year after the general election, the six members, elected by the first division, shall be displaced, and the vacancies thereby occasioned supplied from such class or division, by new election, in the manner aforesaid. This rotation shall be applied to each division, according to its number, and continued in due order annually.

The right of suffrage in the election of members for both Houses shall remain as exercised at present; and each House shall choose its own Speaker, appoint its own officers, settle its own rules of proceeding, and direct writs of election, for the supplying intermediate vacancies.

All laws shall originate in the House of Delegates, to be approved of or rejected by the Senate, or to be amended, with consent of the House of Delegates; except money-bills, which in no instance shall be altered by the Senate, but wholly approved or rejected.

A Governor, or chief magistrate, shall be chosen annually by joint ballot of both Houses (to be taken in each House respectively) deposited in the conference room; [...] who shall not continue in that office longer than three years successively; nor be eligible, until the expiration of four years after he shall have been out of that office. An adequate, but moderate salary shall be settled on him, during his continuance in office; and he shall, with the advice of a Council of State, exercise the executive powers of government, according to the laws of this Commonwealth; and shall not, under any presence, exercise any power or prerogative, by virtue of any law, statute or custom of England. [...]

A Privy Council, or Council of State, consisting of eight members, shall be chosen, by joint ballot of both Houses of Assembly, either from their own members or the people at large, to assist in the administration of government. They shall annually choose, out of their own members, a President, who, in case of death, inability, or absence of the Governor from the government, shall act as Lieutenant-Governor. Four members shall be sufficient to act, and their advice and proceedings shall be entered on record, and signed by the members present, (to any part whereof, any member may enter his dissent) to be laid before the General Assembly, when called for by them. [...] A sum of money, appropriated to that purpose, shall be divided annually among the members, in proportion to their attendance; and they shall be incapable, during their continuance in office, of sitting in either House of Assembly. [...]

The Delegates for Virginia to the Continental Congress shall be chosen annually, or superseded in the mean time, by joint ballot of both Houses of Assembly. [...]

The Governor may embody the militia, with the advice of the Privy Council; and when embodied, shall alone have the direction of the militia, under the laws of the country.

The two Houses of Assembly shall, by joint ballot, appoint Judges of the Supreme Court of Appeals, and General Court, Judges in Chancery, Judges of Admiralty, Secretary, and the Attorney-General, to be commissioned by the Governor, and continue in office during good behaviour. In case of death, incapacity, or resignation, the Governor, with the advice of the Privy Council, shall appoint persons to succeed in office, to be approved or displaced by both Houses. These officers shall have fixed and adequate salaries, and, together with all others, holding lucrative offices, and all ministers of the gospel, of every denomination, be incapable of being elected members of either House of Assembly or the Privy Council. [. . .]

The Governor, when he is out of office, and others, offending against the State, either by mal-administration, corruption, or other means, by which the safety of the State may be endangered, shall be impeachable by the House of Delegates. Such impeachment to be prosecuted by the Attorney-General, or such other person or persons, as the House may appoint in the General Court, according to the laws of the land. If found guilty, he or they shall be either forever disabled to hold any office under government, or be removed from such office pro tempore, or subjected to such pains or penalties as the laws shall direct. [. . .]

Thomas Jefferson *Notes on the State of Virginia* (1781/82)[15]

Query XIII The Constitution of the State, and Its Several Charters?

[. . .] This constitution was formed when we were new and unexperienced in the science of government. It was the first too which was formed in the whole United States. No wonder then that time and trial have discovered very capital defects in it.

1   The majority of the men in the state, who pay and fight for its support, are unrepresented in the legislature, the roll of freeholders intitled to vote, not including generally the half of those on the roll of the militia, or of the tax-gatherers.

2   Among those who share the representation, the shares are very unequal. Thus the county of Warwick, with only one hundred fighting men, has an equal representation with the county of Loudon, which has 1746. So that every man in Warwick has as much influence in the government as 17 men in Loudon. [. . .]

3   The senate is, by its constitution, too homogeneous with the house of delegates. Being chosen by the same electors, at the same time, and out of the same subjects, the choice falls of course on men of the same description. The purpose of establishing different houses of legislation is to introduce the influence of different interests or different principles. Thus in Great-Britain it is said their constitution relies on the

---

[15] T. Jefferson, *Notes on the State of Virginia* (London: John Stockdale, 1787), pp.192, 194–205.

house of commons for honesty, and the lords for wisdom; which would be a rational reliance if honesty were to be bought with money, and if wisdom were hereditary. In some of the American states the delegates and senators are so chosen, as that the first represent the persons, and the second the property of the state. But with us, wealth and wisdom have equal chance for admission into both houses. We do not therefore derive from the separation of our legislature into two houses, those benefits which a proper complication of principles is capable of producing, and those which alone can compensate the evils which may be produced by their dissensions.

All the powers of government, legislative, executive, and judiciary, result to the   4 legislative body. The concentrating these in the same hands is precisely the definition of despotic government. It will be no alleviation that these powers will be exercised by a plurality of hands, and not by a single one. 173 despots would surely be as oppressive as one. Let those who doubt it turn their eyes on the republic of Venice. As little will it avail us that they are chosen by ourselves; An elective despotism was not the government we fought for; but one which should not only be founded on free principles, but in which the powers of government should be so divided and balanced among several bodies of magistracy, as that no one could transcend their legal limits, without being effectually checked and restrained by the others. For this reason that convention, which passed the ordinance of government, laid its foundation on this basis, that the legislative, executive and judiciary departments should be separate and distinct, so that no person should exercise the powers of more than one of them at the same time. But no barrier was provided between these several powers. The judiciary and executive members were left dependant on the legislative, for their subsistence in office, and some of them for their continuance in it. If therefore the legislature assumes executive and judiciary powers, no opposition is likely to be made; nor, if made, can it be effectual; because in that case they may put their proceedings into the form of an act of assembly, which will render them obligatory on the other branches. They have accordingly, in many instances, decided rights which should have been left to judiciary controversy: and the direction of the executive, during the whole time of their session, is becoming habitual and familiar. And this is done with no ill intention. The views of the present members are perfectly upright. When they are led out of their regular province, it is by art in others, and inadvertence in themselves. And this will probably be the case for some time to come. But it will not be a very long time. Mankind soon learn to make interested uses of every right and power which they possess, or may assume. The public money and public liberty, intended to have been deposited with three branches of magistracy, but found inadvertently to be in the hands of one only, will soon be discovered to be sources of wealth and dominion to those who hold them; distinguished too by this tempting circumstance, that they are the instrument, as well as the object of acquisition. [. . .] Nor should our assembly be deluded by the integrity of their own purposes, and conclude that these unlimited powers will never be abused, because themselves are not disposed to abuse them. They should look forward to a time, and that not a distant one, when corruption in this, as in the country from which we derive our origin, will have seized the heads of government, and be spread by them through the body of the people; when they will purchase the voices of the people, and make them pay the price. Human nature is the same on every side of the Atlantic, and will be alike influenced by the same causes. The time to guard against corruption and tyranny, is before they shall have gotten hold on us. It is better to keep the wolf out of the fold, than to trust to drawing his teeth and talons after he shall have entered. To render these considerations the more cogent, we must observe in addition,

5   That the ordinary legislature may alter the constitution itself. [. . .] [A]t the annual election in April 1776, a convention for the year was chosen. Independance, and the establishment of a new form of government, were not even yet the objects of the people at large. One extract from the pamphlet called Common Sense had appeared in the Virginia papers in February, and copies of the pamphlet itself had got into a few hands. But the idea had not been opened to the mass of the people in April, much less can it be said that they had made up their minds in its favor. So that the electors of April 1776 [. . .] not thinking of independance and a permanent republic, could not mean to vest in these delegates powers of establishing them, or any authorities other than those of the ordinary legislature. So far as a temporary organization of government was necessary to render our opposition energetic, so far their organization was valid. But they received in their creation no powers but what were given to every legislature before and since. They could not therefore pass an act transcendant to the powers of other legislatures. If the present assembly pass any act, and declare it shall be irrevocable by subsequent assemblies, the declaration is merely void, and the act repealable, as other acts are. So far, and no farther authorized, they organized the government by the ordinance entitled a Constitution or Form of government. It pretends to no higher authority than the other ordinances of the same session; it does not say, that it shall be perpetual; that it shall be unalterable by other legislatures; that it shall be transcendant above the powers of those, who they knew would have equal power with themselves. Not only the silence of the instrument is a proof they thought it would be alterable, but their own practice also: for this very convention, meeting as a House of Delegates in General Assembly with the new Senate in the autumn of that year, passed acts of assembly in contradiction to their ordinance of government; and every assembly from that time to this has done the same. I am safe therefore in the position, that the constitution itself is alterable by the ordinary legislature. [. . .] The other states in the Union have been of opinion, that to render a form of government unalterable by ordinary acts of assembly, the people must delegate persons with special powers. They have accordingly chosen special conventions to form and fix their governments. The individuals then who maintain the contrary opinion in this country, should have the modesty to suppose it possible that they may be wrong and the rest of America right. But if there be only a possibility of their being wrong, if only a plausible doubt remains of the validity of the ordinance of government, is it not better to remove that doubt, by placing it on a bottom which none will dispute? If they be right, we shall only have the unnecessary trouble of meeting once in convention. If they be wrong, they expose us to the hazard of having no fundamental rights at all. True it is, this is no time for deliberating on forms of government. While an enemy is within our bowels, the first object is to expel him. But when this shall be done, when peace shall be established, and leisure given us for intrenching within good forms, the rights for which we have bled, let no man be

found indolent enough to decline a little more trouble for placing them beyond the reach of question. [...]

PENNSYLVANIA

The Alarm: or, An Address to the People of Pennsylvania on the Late Resolve of Congress (Anonymous, Philadelphia, 1776)[16]

The long continued injuries and insults, which the Continent of America hath sustained from the cruel power of the British Court, and the disadvantages, which the several provinces in the mean time labour under from the want of a permanent form of government, by which they might in a proper constitutional manner of their own, afford protection to themselves, have at length risen to such an height, as to make it appear necessary to the Honourable Continental Congress to issue a Resolve, recommending it to the several Colonies to take up and establish new governments "on the authority of the people," in lieu of those old ones which were established on the authority of the Crown.

This, Fellow Countrymen, is the situation we now stand in, and the matter for your immediate consideration, is simply this: Who are, or who are not, the proper persons to be entrusted with carrying the said Resolve into execution, in what is the most eligible mode of authorizing such persons? for unless they have the full authority of the people for the especial purpose, any government modelled by them will not stand.

Men of interested view and dangerous designs may tell you, The House of Assembly: But be not deceived by the tinkling of a name, for either such an House does not now exist, or if it does exist, it is by an unconstitutional power, for as the people have not yet, by any public act of theirs, transferred to them any new authority necessary to qualify them agreeable to the sense and expression of Congress, which says, "on the Authority of the People," they consequently have none other than what is either immediately derived from, or conveyed to them in consequence of, the royal charter of our enemy, and this, saith the Honourable Congress, "should be totally suppressed." [...] The power from which the new authority is to be derived, is the only power which can properly suppress the old one. Thus, Fellow Countrymen, you are called upon by the standing law of nature and reason, and by the sense of the Honourable Congress, to assert your natural rights, by entering your protest against the authority of the present House of Assembly, in order that a new government, founded "on the authority of the people," may be established. [...]

In this situation, what is to be done? The union of the Colonies is not only our glory, but our protection, and altho' the House of Assembly hath outwitted itself, it

---

[16] *The Alarm: or, An Address to the People of Pennsylvania on the Late Resolve of Congress* (Philadelphia: Henry Miller, 1776).

is no reason that the Province should: Wherefore, in order to restore ourselves to our former Continental rank, which we lost in Congress by not being represented in that resolve; and in order, likewise, that the people of this province may be put into a proper capacity of carrying the said resolve of Congress into execution, we must refer to the second term mentioned therein, viz. Conventions, for, even admitting that the present House of Assembly was a proper body, yet, the people may choose which they please, for both are mentioned [in Congress's resolution]. [...]

Fellow countrymen, it must occur with the fullest force of conviction to every honest, thinking man, that the persons delegated with proper powers to form a plan of government, ought to possess the entire confidence of the people. They should be men having no false bias from old prejudices, no interest distinct or separate from the body of the people; in short, they should be a very different sort of men to what many of the present House of Assembly are. They should be men, likewise, invested with powers to form a plan of government only, and not to execute it after it is framed; for nothing can be a greater violation of reason and natural rights, than for men to give authority to themselves: And on this ground, likewise, the House of Assembly is again disqualified. [...]

We are now arrived at a period from which we are to look forward as a legal people. The Resolve of Congress, grounded on the justest foundation, hath recommended it to us, to establish a regular plan of legal government, and the means which they have recommended for that purpose, are, either by Assemblies or Conventions. Conventions, my Fellow Countrymen, are the only proper bodies to form a Constitution, and Assemblies are the proper bodies to make Laws agreeable to that constitution. – This is a just distinction. Let us begin right, and there is no [fear] but, under the providence of God, we shall end well. When the tyrant James the Second, king of Britain, abdicated the government, that is, ran away therefrom, or rather, was driven away by the just indignation of the people, the situation of England was like what America is now; and in that state a Convention was chosen, to settle the new or reformed plan of government, before any Parliament could presume to sit; and this is what is distinguished in history by the name of the Revolution. – Here, my Countrymen, is our precedent: A precedent which is worthy of imitation. We need no other – we can have no better. [...]

Having thus clearly stated the case for your consideration, we leave you to the exercise of your own reason, to determine whether the present House of Assembly, under all the disqualification, inconsistencies, prejudices and private interests herein mentioned, is a proper body to be entrusted with the extensive powers necessary for forming or reforming a government agreeable to the Resolve and Recommendation of Congress. Or whether a Convention, chosen fairly and openly for that express purpose, consisting, as has been before mentioned, of at least One Hundred members, of known reputation for wisdom, virtue and impartiality, is not a far more probable, nay the only possible, method for securing the just Rights of the people, and posterity.

Constitution of Pennsylvania (September 1, 1776)[17]

WHEREAS all government ought to be instituted and supported for the security and protection of the community as such, and to enable the individuals who compose it to enjoy their natural rights, and the other blessings which the Author of existence has bestowed upon man; and whenever these great ends of government are not obtained, the people have a right, by common consent to change it, and take such measures as to them may appear necessary to promote their safety and happiness. AND WHEREAS the inhabitants of this common-wealth have in consideration of protection only, heretofore acknowledged allegiance to the king of Great Britain; and the said king has not only withdrawn that protection, but commenced, and still continues to carry on, with unabated vengeance, a most cruel and unjust war against them, employing therein, not only the troops of Great Britain, but foreign mercenaries, savages and slaves, for the avowed purpose of reducing them to a total and abject submission to the despotic domination of the British parliament, with many other acts of tyranny, (more fully set forth in the declaration of Congress) whereby all allegiance and fealty to the said king and his successors, are dissolved and at an end, and all power and authority derived from him ceased in these colonies. AND WHEREAS it is absolutely necessary for the welfare and safety of the inhabitants of said colonies, that they be henceforth free and independent States, and that just, permanent, and proper forms of government exist in every part of them, derived from and founded on the authority of the people only, agreeable to the directions of the honourable American Congress. We, the representatives of the freemen of Pennsylvania, in general convention met, for the express purpose of framing such a government, confessing the goodness of the great Governor of the universe (who alone knows to what degree of earthly happiness mankind may attain, by perfecting the arts of government) in permitting the people of this State, by common consent, and without violence, deliberately to form for themselves such just rules as they shall think best, for governing their future society, and being fully convinced, that it is our indispensable duty to establish such original principles of government, as will best promote the general happiness of the people of this State, and their posterity, and provide for future improvements, without partiality for, or prejudice against any particular class, sect, or denomination of men whatever, do, by virtue of the authority vested in us by our constituents, ordain, declare, and establish, the following Declaration of Rights and Frame of Government, to be the CONSTITUTION of this commonwealth, and to remain in force therein forever, unaltered, except in such articles as shall hereafter on experience be found to require improvement, and which shall by the same authority of the people, fairly delegated as this frame of government directs, be amended or improved for the more effectual obtaining and securing the great end and design of all government, herein before mentioned.

---

[17] Newton Thorpe, *The Federal and State Constitutions*, via the Avalon Project, https://avalon .law.yale.edu/.

A Declaration of the Rights of the Inhabitants of the Commonwealth or State of Pennsylvania

I   That all men are born equally free and independent, and have certain natural, inherent and inalienable rights, amongst which are, the enjoying and defending life and liberty, acquiring, possessing and protecting property, and pursuing and obtaining happiness and safety.

II   That all men have a natural and unalienable right to worship Almighty God according to the dictates of their own consciences and understanding: And that no man ought or of right can be compelled to attend any religious worship, or erect or support any place of worship, or maintain any ministry, contrary to, or against, his own free will and consent: Nor can any man, who acknowledges the being of a God, be justly deprived or abridged of any civil right as a citizen, on account of his religious sentiments or peculiar mode of religious worship: And that no authority can or ought to be vested in, or assumed by any power whatever, that shall in any case interfere with, or in any manner controul, the right of conscience in the free exercise of religious worship.

III   That the people of this State have the sole, exclusive and inherent right of governing and regulating the internal police of the same.

IV   That all power being originally inherent in, and consequently derived from, the people; therefore all officers of government, whether legislative or executive, are their trustees and servants, and at all times accountable to them.

V   That government is, or ought to be, instituted for the common benefit, protection and security of the people, nation or community; and not for the particular emolument or advantage of any single man, family, or sort of men, who are a part only of that community, and that the community hath an indubitable, unalienable and indefeasible right to reform, alter, or abolish government in such manner as shall be by that community judged most conducive to the public weal.

VI   That those who are employed in the legislative and executive business of the State, may be restrained from oppression, the people have a right, at such periods as they may think proper, to reduce their public officers to a private station, and supply the vacancies by certain and regular elections.

VII   That all elections ought to be free; and that all free men having a sufficient evident common interest with, and attachment to the community, have a right to elect officers, or to be elected into office.

VIII   That every member of society hath a right to be protected in the enjoyment of life, liberty and property, and therefore is bound to contribute his proportion towards the expence of that protection, and yield his personal service when necessary, or an equivalent thereto: But no part of a man's property can be justly taken from him, or applied to public uses, without his own consent, or that of his legal representatives: Nor can any man who is conscientiously scrupulous of bearing arms, be justly compelled thereto, if he will pay such equivalent, nor are the people bound by any laws, but such as they have in like manner assented to, for their common good.

IX   That in all prosecutions for criminal offences, a man hath a right to be heard by himself and his council, to demand the cause and nature of his accusation, to be confronted with the witnesses, to call for evidence in his favour, and a speedy public trial, by an impartial jury of the country, without the unanimous consent of which jury he cannot be found guilty; nor can he be compelled to give evidence against himself; nor can any man be justly deprived of his liberty except by the laws of the land, or the judgment of his peers.

That the people have a right to hold themselves, their houses, papers, and   X
possessions free from search and seizure, and therefore warrants without oaths or affirmations first made, affording a sufficient foundation for them, and whereby any officer or messenger may be commanded or required to search suspected places, or to seize any person or persons, his or their property, not particularly described, are contrary to that right, and ought not to be granted.

That in controversies respecting property, and in suits between man and man,   XI
the parties have a right to trial by jury, which ought to be held sacred.

That the people have a right to freedom of speech, and of writing, and publishing   XII
their sentiments; therefore the freedom of the press ought not to be restrained.

That the people have a right to bear arms for the defence of themselves and the   XIII
state; and as standing armies in the time of peace are dangerous to liberty, they ought not to be kept up; And that the military should be kept under strict subordination to, and governed by, the civil power. [. . .]

That all men have a natural inherent right to emigrate from one state to another that   XV
will receive them, or to form a new state in vacant countries, or in such countries as they can purchase, whenever they think that thereby they may promote their own happiness.

That the people have a right to assemble together, to consult for their common   XVI
good, to instruct their representatives, and to apply to the legislature for redress of grievances, by address, petition, or remonstrance.

Plan or Frame of Government for the Commonwealth or State of Pennsylvania

SECTION 1. The commonwealth or state of Pennsylvania shall be governed hereafter by an assembly of the representatives of the freemen of the same, and a president and council, in manner and form following——

SECT. 2. The supreme legislative power shall be vested in a house of representatives of the freemen of the commonwealth or state of Pennsylvania.

SECT. 3. The supreme executive power shall be vested in a president and council.

SECT. 4. Courts of justice shall be established in the city of Philadelphia, and in every county of this state. [. . .]

SECT. 6. Every freemen [*sic*] of the full age of twenty-one Years, having resided in this state for the space of one whole Year next before the day of election for representatives, and paid public taxes during that time, shall enjoy the right of an elector: Provided always, that sons of freeholders of the age of twenty-one years shall be intitled to vote although they have not paid taxes.

SECT. 7. The house of representatives of the freemen of this commonwealth shall consist of persons most noted for wisdom and virtue, to be chosen by the freemen of every city and county of this commonwealth respectively. And no person shall be elected unless he has resided in the city or county for which he shall be chosen two years immediately before the said election; nor shall any member, while he continues such, hold any other office, except in the militia. [...]

SECT. 9. The members of the house of representatives shall be chosen annually by ballot, by the freemen of the commonwealth, [...] and shall have power to choose their speaker, the treasurer of the state, and their other officers; sit on their own adjournments; prepare bills and enact them into laws; judge of the elections and qualifications of their own members; they may expel a member, but not a second time for the same cause; they may administer oaths or affirmations on examination of witnesses; redress grievances; impeach state criminals; grant charters of incorporation; constitute towns, boroughs, cities, and counties; and shall have all other powers necessary for the legislature of a free state or common-wealth: But they shall have no power to add to, alter, abolish, or infringe any part of this constitution.

SECT. 10. A quorum of the house of representatives shall consist of two-thirds of the whole number of members elected; and [...] shall each of them before they proceed to business take and subscribe, as well the oath or affirmation of fidelity and allegiance hereinafter directed, as the following oath or affirmation, viz:

I do swear (or affirm) that as a member of this assembly, I will not propose or assent to any bill, vote, or resolution, which shall appear to me injurious to the people; nor do or consent to any act or thing whatever, that shall have a tendency to lessen or abridge their rights and privileges, as declared in the constitution of this state; but will in all things conduct myself as a faithful honest representative and guardian of the people, according to the best of my judgment and abilities.

And each member, before he takes his seat, shall make and subscribe the following declaration, viz:

I do believe in one God, the creator and governor of the universe, the rewarder of the good and the punisher of the wicked. And I do acknowledge the Scriptures of the Old and New Testament to be given by Divine inspiration.

And no further or other religious test shall ever hereafter be required of any civil officer or magistrate in this State. [...]

SECT. 15. To the end that laws before they are enacted may be more maturely considered, and the inconvenience of hasty determinations as much as possible prevented, all bills of public nature shall be printed for the consideration of the people, before they are read in general assembly the last time for debate and amendment; and, except on occasions of sudden necessity, shall not be passed into laws until the next session of assembly; and for the more perfect satisfaction of the public, the reasons and motives for making such laws shall be fully and clearly expressed in the preambles. [...]

SECT. 19. For the present the supreme executive council of this state shall consist of twelve persons chosen in the following manner: The freemen of the city of

Philadelphia, and of the counties of Philadelphia, Chester, and Bucks, respectively, shall choose by ballot one person for the city, and one for each county aforesaid to serve for three years and no longer, at the time and place for electing representatives in general assembly. The freemen of the counties of Lancaster, York, Cumberland, and Berks, shall, in like manner elect one person for each county respectively, to serve as counsellors for two years and no longer. And the counties of Northampton, Bedford, Northumberland and Westmoreland, respectively, shall, in like manner, elect one person for each county, to serve as counsellors for one year, and no longer. And at the expiration of the time for which each counsellor was chosen to serve, the freemen of the city of Philadelphia, and of the several counties in this state, respectively, shall elect one person to serve as counsellor for three years and no longer; and so on every third year forever. By this mode of election and continual rotation, more men will be trained to public business, there will in every subsequent year be found in the council a number of persons acquainted with the proceedings of the foregoing Years, whereby the business will be more consistently conducted, and moreover the danger of establishing an inconvenient aristocracy will be effectually prevented. [...] The president and vice-president shall be chosen annually by the joint ballot of the general assembly and council, of the members of the council. Any person having served as a counsellor for three successive years, shall be incapable of holding that office for four years afterwards. [...]

SECT. 23. The judges of the supreme court of judicature shall have fixed salaries, be commissioned for seven years only, though capable of re-appointment at the end of that term, but removable for misbehaviour at any time by the general assembly; they shall not be allowed to sit as members in the continental congress, executive council, or general assembly, nor to hold any other office civil or military, nor to take or receive fees or perquisites of any kind. [...]

SECT. 35. The printing presses shall be free to every person who undertakes to examine the proceedings of the legislature, or any part of government. [...]

Benjamin Rush *Observations on the Present Government of Pennsylvania: In Four Letters to the People of Pennsylvania* (1777)[18]

Letter II

[...] In the second section, "the supreme legislature is vested in a 'single' House of Representatives of the Freemen of the Commonwealth." By this section we find, that the supreme, absolute, and uncontrouled power of the whole State is lodged in the hands of one body of men. Had it been lodged in the hands of one man, it would have been less dangerous to the safety and liberties of the community. Absolute power should never be trusted to man. It has perverted the wisest heads, and corrupted the

---

[18] B. Rush, *Observations on the Present Government of Pennsylvania: In Four Letters to the People of Pennsylvania* (Philadelphia: Styner and Cist, 1777), pp. 5, 7–9, 11–13, 15.

best hearts in the world. I should be afraid to commit my property, liberty and life to a body of angels for one whole year. The Supreme Being alone is qualified to possess supreme power over his creatures. It requires the wisdom and goodness of a Deity to controul, and direct it properly. [...]

I might go on further and shew, that all the dissentions of Athens and Rome, so dreadful in their nature, and so fatal in their consequences, originated in single Assemblies possessing all the power of those commonwealths; but this would be the business of a volume, and not of a single essay. – I shall therefore pass on, to answer the various arguments that have been used in Pennsylvania, in support of a single legislature.

1   We are told, that the perfection of everything consists in its simplicity, – that all mixtures in government are impurities, and that a single legislature is perfect, because it is simple. – To this I answer, that we should distinguish between simplicity in principles, and simplicity in the application of principles to practice. [...] A few simple elementary bodies compose all the matter of the universe, and yet how infinitely are they combined in the various forms and substances which they assume in the animal, vegetable, and mineral kingdoms. In like manner a few simple principles enter into the composition of all free governments. These principles are perfect security for property, liberty and life; but these principles admit of extensive combinations, when reduced to practice: – Nay more, they require them. A despotic government is the most simple government in the world, but instead of affording security to property, liberty or life, it obliges us to hold them all on the simple will of a capricious sovereign. I maintain therefore, that all governments are safe and free in proportion as they are compounded in a certain degree, and on the contrary, that all governments are dangerous and tyrannical in proportion as they approach to simplicity.

2   We are told by the friends of a single legislature, that there can be no danger of their becoming tyrannical, since they must partake of all the burdens they lay upon their constituents. Here we forget the changes that are made upon the head and heart by arbitrary power, and the cases that are recorded in history of annual Assemblies having refused to share with their constituents in the burdens which they had imposed upon them. If every elector in Pennsylvania is capable of being elected an assembly-man, then agreeably to the sixth section of the constitution, it is possible for an Assembly to exist who do not possess a single foot of property in the State, and who can give no other evidence of a common interest in, or attachment to, the community than having paid "public taxes," which may mean poor-taxes. Should this be the case, (and there is no obstacle in the constitution to prevent it) surely it will be in the power of such an Assembly to draw from the State the whole of its wealth in a few years, without contributing any thing further towards it than their proportion of the trifling tax necessary to support the poor. – But I shall shew in another place equal dangers from another class of men, becoming a majority in the Assembly.

3   We are told of instances of the House of Lords, in England, checking the most salutary laws, after they had passed the House of Commons, as a proof of the inconvenience of a compound legislature. I believe the fact to be true, but I deny its application in the present controversy. The House of Lords, in England, possess

privileges and interests, which do not belong to the House of Commons. Moreover, they derive their power from the crown and not from the people. No wonder therefore they consult their own interests, in preference to those of the People. In the State of Pennsylvania we wish for a council, with no one exclusive privilege, and we disclaim every idea of their possessing the smallest degree of power, but what is derived from the annual suffrages of the People, A body thus chosen could have no object in view but the happiness of their constituents. [. . .]

We have been told, that a legislative council or governor lays the foundation for   5 aristocratical and monarchical power in a community. However ridiculous this objection to a compound legislature may appear, I have more than once heard it mentioned by the advocates for a single Assembly. [. . .]

I cannot help commending the zeal that appears in my countrymen against the power of a King or a House of Lords. I concur with them in all their prejudices against hereditary titles, honour and power. History is little else than a recital of the follies and vices of kings and noblemen, and it is because I dread so much from them, that I wish to exclude them forever from Pennsylvania, for notwithstanding our government has been called a simple democracy, I maintain, that a foundation is laid in it for the most complete aristocracy that ever existed in the world.

In order to prove this assertion, I shall promise two propositions, which have never been controverted: First, where there is wealth, there will be power; and, secondly, the rich have always been an over-match for the poor in all contests for power.

These truths being admitted, I desire to know what can prevent our single representation being filled, in the course of a few years, with a majority of rich men? Say not, the people will not choose such men to represent them. The influence of wealth at elections is irresistible. It has been seen and felt in Pennsylvania, and I am obliged in justice to my subject to say, that there are poor men among us as prepared to be influenced, as the rich are prepared to influence them. The fault must be laid in both cases upon human nature. The consequence of a majority of rich men getting into the legislature is plain. Their wealth will administer fuel to the love of arbitrary power that is common to all men. The present Assembly have furnished them with precedents for breaking the Constitution. Farewell now to annual elections! Public emergencies will sanctify the most daring measures. The clamours of their constituents will be silenced with offices, bribes or punishments. An aristocracy will be established, and Pennsylvania will be inhabited like most of the countries in Europe, with only two sorts of animals, tyrants and slaves.

It has often been said, that there is but one rank of men in America, and therefore, that there should be only one representation of them in a government. I agree, that we have no artificial distinctions of men into noblemen and commoners among us, but it ought to be remarked, that superior degrees of industry and capacity, and above all, commerce, have introduced inequality of property among us, and these have introduced natural distinctions of rank in Pennsylvania, as certain and general as the artificial distinctions of men in Europe. This will ever be the case while commerce exists in this country. The men of middling property and poor men can never be safe in a mixed representation with the men of over-grown property. Their liberties can only be secured by having exact bounds prescribed to their power, in the fundamental principles of the Constitution. By a representation of the men of middling fortunes in one house, their whole strength is collected against the influence of wealth. Without such a representation, the violent efforts of individuals to oppose it would be divided and broken, and would want that system, which alone would enable them to check that lust for dominion which is always connected with opulence. The government of Pennsylvania therefore has been called most improperly a government for poor men. It carries in every part of it a poison to their liberties. It is impossible to form a government more suited to the nations and interests of rich men. [...]

9   But why all these arguments in favor of checks for the Assembly? The Constitution (says the single legislative-man) has provided no less than four for them. First, Elections will be annual. Secondly, The doors of the Assembly are to be always open. Thirdly, All laws are to be published for the consideration and assent of the people: And, Fourthly, The Council of Censors will punish, by their censures, all violations of the Constitution, and the authors of bad laws. I shall examine the efficacy of each of these checks separately.

I hope, for the peace of the state, that we shall never see a body of men in power more attached to the present Constitution than the present Assembly, and if, with all their affection for it, they have broken it in many articles, it is reasonable to suppose that future Assemblies will use the same freedoms with it. They may, if they chuse, abolish annual elections. They may tell their constituents that elections draw off the minds of the people from necessary labour; or, if a war should exist, they may shew the impossibility of holding elections when there is a chance of the militia being called into the field to oppose a common enemy: Or lastly, they may fetter elections with oaths in such a manner as to exclude nine-tenths of the electors from voting. Such stratagems for perpetual power will never want men nor a society of men to support them; for the Assembly possesses such a plenitude of power from the influence of the many offices of profit and honour that are in their gift, that they may always promise themselves support from a great part of the state. [...]

I shall take no notice of the delays of business, which must arise from publishing all laws for the consideration and assent of the people; but I beg to be informed how long they must be published before they are passed? For I take it for granted, that each county has a right to equal degrees of time to consider of the laws. In what manner are they to be circulated? How are the sentiments of the people, scattered over a county fifty or sixty miles in extent, to be collected? Whether by ballot, or by voting in a tumultuary manner? These are insurmountable difficulties in the way of the people at large acting as a check upon the Assembly. But supposing an attempt should be made to restrain the single legislature in this manner, are we sure the disapprobation of the people would be sufficient to put a negative upon improper or arbitrary laws? Would not the Assembly, from their partiality to their own proceedings, be apt to pass over the complaints of the people in silence? to neglect or refuse to enter their petitions or remonstrances upon their Journals? or to raise the hue and cry of a fostered junto upon them, as "tories" or "apostate whigs," or "an aristocratic faction?" [...]

I shall conclude my observations upon this part of the Constitution, by summing up the advantages of a compound or double legislature.

1. There is the utmost freedom in a compound legislature. The decisions of two legislative bodies cannot fail of coinciding with the wills of a great majority of the community.
2. There is safety in such a government, in as much as each body possesses a free and independant power, so that they mutually check ambition and usurpation in each other.
3. There is the greatest wisdom in such a government. Every act being obliged to undergo the revision and amendments of two bodies of men, is necessarily strained of every mixture of folly, passion, and prejudice.
4. There is the longest duration of freedom in such a government.
5. There is the most order in such a government. By order, I mean obedience to laws, subordination to magistrates, civility and decency of behaviour, and the contrary of every thing like mobs and factions.
6. Compound governments are most agreeable to human nature, inasmuch as they afford the greatest scope for the expansion of the powers and virtues of the mind. Wisdom, learning, experience, with the most extensive benevolence; the most unshaken firmness, and the utmost elevation of soul, are all called into exercise by the opposite and different duties of the different representations of the people.

Letter III

[...] It has been said often, and I wish the saying was engraven over the doors of every statehouse on the Continent, that "all power is derived from the people," but it has never yet been said that all power is seated in the people. Government supposes and requires a delegation of power: It cannot exist without it. And the idea of making the people at large judges of the qualifications necessary for magistrates, or judges of laws, or checks for Assemblies proceeds upon the supposition that mankind are all alike wise, and just, and have equal leisure. It moreover destroys the necessity for all government. What man ever made himself his own attorney? And yet this would not be more absurd than for the people at large to pretend to give up their power to a set of rulers, and afterwards reserve the right of making and of judging of all their laws themselves. Such a government is a monster in nature. It contains as many Governors, Assemblymen, Judges and Magistrates as there are freemen in the State, all exercising the same powers and at the same time. Happy would it be for us, if this monster was remarkable only for his absurdity; but, alas! he contains a tyrant in his bowels. All history shews us that the people soon grow weary of the folly and tyranny of one another. They prefer one to many masters, and stability to instability of slavery. They prefer a Julius Caesar to a Senate, and a Cromwell to a perpetual parliament. [...]

MASSACHUSETTS

Letter from the Town of Pittsfield to the House of Representatives of Massachusetts Bay (May 29, 1776)[19]

The petition and memorial of the town of Pittsfield in said Colony humbly showeth, – That they have the highest sense of the importance of civil and religious liberty, the destructive nature of tyranny and lawless power, and the absolute necessity of legal government to prevent anarchy and confusion. [...] We beg leave, therefore, to lay before your Honors our principles, real views, and designs in what we have hitherto done, and what object we are reaching after; with this assurance, that, if we have erred, it is through ignorance, and not bad intention. We beg leave, therefore, to represent that we have always been persuaded that the people are the fountain of power; that, since the dissolution of the power of Great Britain over these Colonies, they have fallen into a state of nature. That the first step to be taken by a people in such a state for the enjoyment or restoration of civil government among them is the formation of a fundamental constitution as the basis and ground-work of legislation; that the approbation, by the majority of the people, of this fundamental constitution is absolutely necessary to give life and being to it; that then, and not till then, is the foundation laid for legislation. We often hear of the fundamental constitution of Great Britain, which all political writers (except ministerial ones) set above the king, Lords, and Commons, which they cannot change; nothing short of the great rational majority of the people being sufficient for this. A representative body may form, but cannot impose said fundamental constitution upon a people, as they, being but servants of the people, cannot be greater than their masters, and must be responsible to them; that, if this fundamental constitution is above the whole legislature, the legislature certainly cannot make it; it must be the approbation of the majority which gives life and being to it. That said fundamental constitution has not been formed for this Province; the corner-stone is not yet laid, and whatever building is reared without a foundation must fall to ruins; that this can be instantly effected with the approbation of the Continental Congress; and law, subordination, and good government flow in better than their ancient channels in a few months' time; that, till this is done, we are but beating the air, and doing what will and must be undone afterwards, and all our labor is lost, and on divers reasons worse than lost; that a doctrine newly broached in this county by several of the justices newly created without the voice of the people, that the representatives of the people may form just what fundamental constitution they please, and impose it upon the people, and, however obnoxious to them, they can obtain no relief from it but by a new election; and, if our representatives should never see fit to give the people one that pleases them, there is no help for it, – appears to us to be the rankest kind of Toryism, the self-same monster we are now fighting against. These are some of the truths we firmly believe [...]. We beg leave further to represent, that we by no means object to the

---

[19] Excerpt from J. E. Adams Smith, *The History of Pittsfield (Berkshire County), Massachusetts ...* (Boston: Lee & Shepard, 1869), pp. 353–5.

most speedy institution of legal government through this Province, and that we are as earnestly desirous as any others of this great blessing. That, knowing the strong bias of human nature to tyranny and despotism, we have nothing else in view but to provide for posterity against the wanton exercise of power, which cannot otherwise be done than by the formation of a fundamental constitution. What is the fundamental constitution of this Province? What are the inalienable rights of the people? the power of the rulers? how often to be elected by the people, &c.? Have any of these things been as yet ascertained? Let it not be said by future posterity, that, in this great, this noble, this glorious contest, we made no provision against tyranny among ourselves. [...] We have heard much of government being founded in compact: what compact has been formed as the foundation of government in this Province? We beg leave further to represent, that we have undergone many grievous oppressions in this county, and that now we wish a barrier might be set up against such oppressions, against which we can have no security long till the foundation of government be well established. [...] We are determined to resist Great Britain to the last extremity, and all others who may claim a similar power over us. Yet we hold not to an *imperium imperio*; we will be determined by the majority. Your petitioners, therefore, beg leave to request that this honorable body would form a fundamental constitution for this Province, after leave is asked and obtained from the Honorable Continental Congress, and that said constitution be sent abroad for the approbation of the majority of the people of this Colony; that, in this way, we may emerge from a state of nature, and enjoy again the blessings of civil government. [...]

Constitution of Massachusetts (1780)

Preamble

The end of the institution, maintenance, and administration of government is to secure the existence of the body-politic, to protect it, and to furnish the individuals who compose it with the power of enjoying, in safety and tranquillity, their natural rights and the blessings of life; and whenever these great objects are not obtained the people have a right to alter the government, and to take measures necessary for their safety, prosperity, and happiness.

The body-politic is formed by a voluntary association of individuals; it is a social compact by which the whole people covenants with each citizen and each citizen with the whole people that all shall be governed by certain laws for the common good. It is the duty of the people, therefore, in framing a constitution of government, to provide for an equitable mode of making laws, as well as for an impartial interpretation and a faithful execution of them; that every man may, at all times, find his security in them.

We, therefore, the people of Massachusetts, acknowledging, with grateful hearts, the goodness of the great Legislator of the universe, in affording us, in the course of His providence, an opportunity, deliberately and peaceably, without fraud, violence, or surprise, of entering into an original, explicit, and solemn compact with each other, and of forming a new constitution of civil government for ourselves and posterity; and devoutly imploring His direction in so interesting a design, do agree upon, ordain, and establish the following declaration of rights and frame of government as the constitution of the commonwealth of Massachusetts.

Part the First

A Declaration of the Rights of the Inhabitants of the Commonwealth of Massachusetts

Article I. All men are born free and equal, and have certain natural, essential, and unalienable rights; among which may be reckoned the right of enjoying and defending their lives and liberties; that of acquiring, possessing, and protecting property; in fine, that of seeking and obtaining their safety and happiness.

Art. II. It is the right as well as the duty of all men in society, publicly and at stated seasons, to worship the Supreme Being, the great Creator and Preserver of the universe. And no subject shall be hurt, molested, or restrained, in his person, liberty, or estate, for worshipping God in the manner and season most agreeable to the dictates of his own conscience, or for his religious profession or sentiments, provided he doth not disturb the public peace or obstruct others in their religious worship.

Art. III. As the happiness of a people and the good order and preservation of civil government essentially depend upon piety, religion, and morality, and as these cannot be generally diffused through a community but by the institution of the public worship of God and of the public instructions in piety, religion, and morality: Therefore, To promote their happiness and to secure the good order and preservation of their government, the people of this commonwealth have a right to invest their legislature with power to authorize and require, and the legislature shall, from time to time, authorize and require, the several towns, parishes, precincts, and other bodies-politic or religious societies to make suitable provision, at their own expense, for the institution of the public worship of God and for the support and maintenance of public Protestant teachers of piety, religion, and morality in all cases where such provision shall not be made voluntarily.

And the people of this commonwealth have also a right to, and do, invest their legislature with authority to enjoin upon all the subjects an attendance upon the instructions of the public teachers aforesaid, at stated times and seasons, if there be any on whose instructions they can conscientiously and conveniently attend.

Provided, notwithstanding, That the several towns, parishes, precincts, and other bodies-politic, or religious societies, shall at all times have the exclusive right of electing their public teachers and of contracting with them for their support and maintenance. [...]

And every denomination of Christians, demeaning themselves peaceably and as good subjects of the commonwealth, shall be equally under the protection of the law; and no subordination of any sect or denomination to another shall ever be established by law.

Art. IV. The people of this commonwealth have the sole and exclusive right of governing themselves as a free, sovereign, and independent State, and do, and forever hereafter shall, exercise and enjoy every power, jurisdiction, and right which is not, or may not hereafter be, by them expressly delegated to the United States of America in Congress assembled.

Art. V. All power residing originally in the people, and being derived from them, the several magistrates and officers of government vested with authority, whether legislative, executive, or judicial, are the substitutes and agents, and are at all times accountable to them.

Art. VI. No man nor corporation or association of men have any other title to obtain advantages, or particular and exclusive privileges distinct from those of the community, than what rises from the consideration of services rendered to the public, and this title being in nature neither hereditary nor transmissible to children or descendants or relations by blood; the idea of a man born a magistrate, lawgiver, or judge is absurd and unnatural.

Art. VII. Government is instituted for the common good, for the protection, safety, prosperity, and happiness of the people, and not for the profit, honor, or private interest of any one man, family, or class of men; therefore the people alone have an incontestable, unalienable, and indefeasible right to institute government, and to reform, alter, or totally change the same when their protection, safety, prosperity, and happiness require it.

Art. VIII. In order to prevent those who are vested with authority from becoming oppressors, the people have a right at such periods and in such manner as they shall establish by their frame of government, to cause their public officers to return to private life; and to fill up vacant places by certain and regular elections and appointments.

Art. IX. All elections ought to be free; and all the inhabitants of this commonwealth, having such qualifications as they shall establish by their frame of government, have an equal right to elect officers, and to be elected, for public employments.

Art. X. Every individual of the society has a right to be protected by it in the enjoyment of his life, liberty, and property, according to standing laws. He is obliged, consequently, to contribute his share to expense of this protection; to give his personal service, or an equivalent, when necessary; but no part of the property of any individual can, with justice, be taken from him, or applied to public uses, without his own consent, or that of the representative body of the people. In fine, the people of this commonwealth are not controllable by any other laws than those to which their constitutional representative body have given their consent. And whenever the public exigencies require that the property of any individual should be appropriated to public uses, he shall receive a reasonable compensation therefor.

Art. XI. Every subject of the commonwealth ought to find a certain remedy, by having recourse to the laws, for all injuries or wrongs which he may receive in his person, property, or character. He ought to obtain right and justice freely, and without being obliged to purchase it; completely, and without any denial; promptly, and without delay, conformably to the laws.

Art. XII. No subject shall be held to answer for any crimes or no offence until the same is fully and plainly, substantially and formally, described to him; or be compelled to accuse, or furnish evidence against himself; and every subject shall have a right to produce all proofs that may be favorable to him; to meet the witnesses against him face to face, and to be fully heard in his defence by himself, or his counsel at his election. And no subject shall be arrested, imprisoned, despoiled, or deprived of his property, immunities, or privileges, put out of the protection of the law, exiled or deprived of his life, liberty, or estate, but by the judgment of his peers, or the law of the land. [...]

Art. XIV. Every subject has a right to be secure from all unreasonable searches and seizures of his person, his houses, his papers, and all his possessions. [...]

Art. XVI. The liberty of the press is essential to the security of freedom in a State; it ought not, therefore, to be restrained in this commonwealth.

Art. XVII. The people have a right to keep and to bear arms for the common defence. And as, in time of peace, armies are dangerous to liberty, they ought not to be maintained without the consent of the legislature; and the military power shall always be held in an exact subordination to the civil authority and be governed by it. [...]

Art. XIX. The people have a right, in an orderly and peaceable manner, to assemble to consult upon the common good; give instructions to their representatives, and to request of the legislative body, by the way of addresses, petitions, or remonstrances, redress of the wrongs done them, and of the grievances they suffer.

Art. XX. The power of suspending the laws, or the execution of the laws, ought never to be exercised but by the legislature, or by authority derived from it, to be exercised in such particular cases only as the legislature shall expressly provide for.

Art. XXI. The freedom of deliberation, speech, and debate, in either house of the legislature, is so essential to the rights of the people, that it cannot be the foundation of any accusation or prosecution, action or complaint, in any other court or place whatsoever. [...]

Art. XXIII. No subsidy, charge, tax, impost, or duties, ought to be established, fixed, laid, or levied, under any pretext whatsoever, without the consent of the people, or their representatives in the legislature. [...]

Art. XXVII. In time of peace, no soldier ought to be quartered in any house without the consent of the owner; and in time of war, such quarters ought not be made but by the civil magistrate, in a manner ordained by the legislature. [...]

Art. XXX. In the government of this commonwealth, the legislative department shall never exercise the executive and judicial powers, or either of them; the executive shall never exercise the legislative and judicial powers, or either of them; the judicial shall never exercise the legislative and executive powers, or either of them; to the end it may be a government of laws, and not of men.

Part the Second

The Frame of Government

The people inhabiting the territory formerly called the province of Massachusetts Bay do hereby solemnly and mutually agree with each other to form themselves into a free, sovereign, and independent body-politic or State, by the name of the commonwealth of Massachusetts.

Chapter I   Legislative Power

Section I   The General Court

Article I. The department of legislation shall be formed by two branches, a senate and house of representatives; each of which shall have a negative on the other. [...]

Art. II. No bill or resolve of the senate or house of representatives shall become a law, and have force as such, until it shall have been laid before the governor for his revisal; and if he, upon such revision, approve thereof, he shall signify his approbation by signing the same. But if he have any objection to the passing such bill or resolve, he shall return the same, together with his objections thereto, in writing, to the senate or house of representatives, in whichsoever the same shall have originated, who shall enter the objections sent down by the governor, at large, on their records, and proceed to reconsider the said bill or resolve; but if, after such reconsideration, two-thirds of the said senate or house of representatives shall, notwithstanding the said objections, agree to pass the same, it shall, together with the objections, be sent to the other branch of the legislature, where it shall also be reconsidered, and if approved by two-thirds of the members present, shall have the force of law; but in all such cases, the vote of both houses shall be determined by yeas and nays; and the names of the persons voting for or against the said bill or resolve shall be entered upon the public records of the commonwealth. [...]

Art. III. The general court shall forever have full power and authority to erect and constitute judicatories and courts of record or other courts, to be held in the name of the commonwealth, for the hearing, trying, and determining of all manner of crimes, offences, pleas, processes, plaints, actions, matters, causes, and things whatsoever, arising or happening within the commonwealth, or between or concerning persons inhabiting or residing, or brought within the same; [...].

Art. IV. And further, full power and authority are hereby given and granted to the said general court from time to time, to make, ordain, and establish all manner of wholesome and reasonable orders, laws, statutes, and ordinances, directions and instructions, either with penalties or without, so as the same be not repugnant or contrary to this constitution, as they shall judge to be for the good and welfare of this commonwealth, and for the government and ordering thereof, and of the subjects of the same, and for the necessary support and defence of the government thereof; [. . .] and to impose and levy proportional and reasonable assessments, rates, and taxes, upon all the inhabitants of, and persons resident, and estates lying, within the said commonwealth; and also to impose and levy reasonable duties and excises upon any produce, goods, wares, merchandise, and commodities whatsoever, brought into, produced, manufactured, or being within the same; to be issued and disposed of by warrant, under the hand of the governor of this commonwealth, for the time being, with the advice and consent of the council, for the public service, in the necessary defence and support of the government of the said commonwealth, and the protection and preservation of the subjects thereof, according to such acts as are or shall be in force within the same. [. . .]

Section 2   Senate

Article I. There shall be annually elected, by the freeholders and other inhabitants of this commonwealth, qualified as in this constitution is provided, forty persons to be councillors and senators, for the year ensuing their election; to be chosen by the inhabitants of the districts into which the commonwealth may from time to time be divided by the general court for that purpose; and the general court, in assigning the numbers to be elected by the respective districts, shall govern themselves by the proportion of the public taxes paid by the said districts; and timely make known to the inhabitants of the commonwealth the limits of each district, and the number of councillors and senators to be chosen therein: *Provided*, That the number of such districts shall never be less than thirteen; and that no district be so large as to entitle the same to choose more than six senators. [. . .]

   Art. II. The senate shall be the first branch of the legislature; and the senators shall be chosen in the following manner, viz: There shall be a meeting on the first Monday in April, annually, forever, of the inhabitants of each town in the several counties of this commonwealth [. . .] and at such meetings every male inhabitant of twenty-one year of age and upwards, having a freehold estate of the value of sixty pounds, shall have a right to give in his vote for the senators for the district of which he is an inhabitant. And to remove all doubts concerning the meaning of the word "inhabitant," in this constitution, every person shall be considered as an inhabitant, for the purpose of electing and being elected into any office or place within this State, in that town, district, or plantation where he dwelleth or hath his home. [. . .]

   Art. VIII. The senate shall be a court, with full authority to hear and determine all impeachments made by the house of representatives, against any officer or officers of the commonwealth, for misconduct and maladministration in their offices; but, previous to the trial of every impeachment, the members of the senate shall, respectively, be sworn truly and impartially to try and determine the charge in question, according to the evidence. Their judgment, however, shall not extend further than to removal from office, and disqualification to hold or enjoy any place of honor, trust, or profit under this commonwealth; but the part so convicted shall be, nevertheless, liable to indictment, trial, judgment, and punishment, according to the laws of the land. [...]

Section 3   House of Representatives

Article I. There shall be, in the legislature of this commonwealth, a representation of the people, annually elected, and founded upon the principle of equality.

Art. II. And in order to provide for a representation of the citizens of this commonwealth, founded upon the principle of equality, every corporate town containing one hundred and fifty ratable polls, may elect one representative; every corporate town containing three hundred and seventy-five ratable polls, may elect two representatives; every corporate town containing six hundred ratable polls, may elect three representatives; and proceeding in that manner, making two hundred and twenty-five ratable polls the mean increasing number for every additional representative. [...]

Art. IV. Every male person being twenty-one years of age, and resident in any particular town in this commonwealth, for the space of one year next preceding, having a freehold estate within the same town, of the annual income of three pounds, or any estate of the value of sixty pounds, shall have a right to vote in the choice of a representative or representatives for the said town. [...]

Art. VI. The house of representatives shall be the grand inquest of this commonwealth; and all impeachments made by them shall be heard and tried by the senate.

Art. VII. All money bills shall originate in the house of representatives; but the senate may propose or concur with amendments, as on other bills. [...]

Art. X. The house of representatives shall be the judge of the returns, elections, and qualifications of its own members, as pointed out in the constitution; shall choose their own speaker, appoint their own officers, and settle the rules and order of proceeding in their own house. [...] And no member of the house of representatives shall be arrested, or held to bail on mesne process, during his going unto, returning from, or his attending the general assembly. [...]

Chapter II   Executive Power

Section I   Governor

Article I. There shall be a supreme executive magistrate, who shall be styled "The governor of the commonwealth of Massachusetts"; and whose title shall be "His Excellency."

Art. II. The governor shall be chosen annually; and no person shall be eligible to this office, unless, at the time of his election, he shall have been an inhabitant of this commonwealth for seven years next preceding; and unless he shall, at the same time, be seized, in his own right, of a freehold, within the commonwealth, of the value of one thousand pounds; and unless he shall declare himself to be of the Christian religion. [...]

Art. IV. The governor shall have authority, from time to time, at his discretion, to assemble and call together the councillors of this commonwealth for the time being; and the governor, with the said councillors, or five of them at least, shall and may, from time to time, hold and keep a council, for the ordering and directing the affairs of the commonwealth, agreeably to the constitution and the laws of the land. [...]

Art. VII. The governor of this commonwealth, for the time being, shall be the commander-in-chief of the army and navy, and of all the military forces of the State, by sea and land; and shall have full power, by himself or by any commander, or other officer or officers, from time to time, to train, instruct, exercise, and govern the militia and navy; and, for the special defence and safety of the commonwealth, to assemble in martial array, and put in warlike posture, the inhabitants thereof, and to lead and conduct them, and with them to encounter, repel, resist, expel, and pursue, by force of arms, as by sea as by land, within or within the limits of this commonwealth; and also to kill, slay, and destroy, if necessary, and conquer, by all fitting ways, enterprises, and means whatsoever, all and every such person and persons as shall, at any time hereafter, in a hostile manner, attempt or enterprise the destruction, invasion, detriment, or annoyance of this commonwealth; [...] and that the governor be intrusted with all these and other powers incident to the offices of captain-general and commander-in-chief, and admiral, to be exercised agreeably to the rules and regulations of the constitution and the laws of the land, and not otherwise. [...]

Art. VIII. The power of pardoning offences, except such as persons may be convicted of before the senate, by an impeachment of the house, shall be in the governor, by and with the advice of council [...].

Art. IX. All judicial officers, the attorney-general, the solicitor-general, all sheriffs, coroners, and registers of probate, shall be nominated and appointed by the governor, by and with the advice and consent of the council; and every such nomination shall be made by the governor, and made at least seven days prior to such appointment. [...]

Art. XIII. As the public good requires that the governor should not be under the undue influence of any of the members of the general court, by a dependence on them for his support; that he should, in all cases, act with freedom for the benefit of the public; that he should not have his attention necessarily diverted from that object to his private concerns; and that he should maintain the dignity of the commonwealth in the character of its chief magistrate, it is necessary that he should have an honorable stated salary, of a fixed and permanent value, amply sufficient for those purposes, and established by standing laws; and it shall be among the first acts of the general court, after the commencement of this constitution, to establish such salary by law accordingly.

Permanent and honorable salaries shall also be established by law for the justices of the supreme judicial court.

And if it shall be found that any of the salaries aforesaid, so established, are insufficient, they shall, from time to time, be enlarged, as the general court shall judge proper.

Section 2   Lieutenant-Governor

Article I. There shall be annually elected a lieutenant-governor of the commonwealth of Massachusetts, whose title shall be "His Honor"; and who shall be qualified, in point of religion, property, and residence in the commonwealth, in the same manner with the governor; [...].

Art. II. The governor, and in his absence the lieutenant-governor, shall be president of the council; but shall have no voice in council; and the lieutenant-governor shall always be a member of the council, except when the chair of the governor shall be vacant.

Art. III. Whenever the chair of the governor shall be vacant, by reason of his death, or absence from the commonwealth, or otherwise, the lieutenant-governor, for the time being, shall, during such vacancy perform all the duties incumbent upon the governor, and shall have and exercise all the powers and authorities which, by this constitution, the governor is vested with, when personally present.

Section 3   Council, and the Manner of Settling Elections by the Legislature

Article I. There shall be a council, for advising the governor in the executive part of the government, to consist of nine persons besides the lieutenant-governor, whom the governor, for the time being, shall have full power and authority, from time to time, at his discretion, to assemble and call together; and the governor, with the said councillors, or five of them at least, shall and may, from time to time, hold and keep a council, for the ordering and directing the affairs of the commonwealth, according to the laws of the land.

Art. II. Nine councillors shall be annually chosen from among the persons returned for councillors and senators, on the last Wednesday in May, by the joint ballot of the senators and representatives assembled in one room. [...]

Art. IV. Not more than two councillors shall be chosen out of any one district in this commonwealth. [...]

Chapter III   Judiciary Power

Article I. The tenure that all commission officers shall by law have in their offices shall be expressed in their respective commissions. All judicial officers, duly appointed, commissioned, and sworn, shall hold their offices during good behavior, excepting such concerning whom there is different provision made in this constitution: *Provided, nevertheless*, The governor, with consent of the council, may remove them upon the address of both houses of the legislature. [...]

THE ARTICLES OF CONFEDERATION

Thomas Jefferson

Notes of Proceedings in the Continental Congress, July 30–Aug. 1, 1776[20]

[...] The other article was in these words. "Art. xvii. In determining questions each colony shall have one vote."

[...] Mr. Chase observed that this article was the most likely to divide us of any one proposed in the draught then under consideration. That the larger colonies had threatened they would not confederate at all if their weight in congress should not be equal to the numbers of people they added to the confederacy; while the smaller ones declared against a union if they did not retain an equal vote for the protection of their rights. That it was of the utmost consequence to bring the parties together, as should we sever from each other, either no foreign power will ally with us at all, or the different states will form different alliances, and thus increase the horrors of those scenes of civil war and bloodshed which in such a state of separation & independance would render us a miserable people. That our importance, our interests, our peace required that we should confederate, and that mutual sacrifices should be made to effect a compromise of this difficult question. He was of [the] opinion [that] the smaller colonies would lose their rights, if they were not in some instances allowed an equal vote; and therefore that a discrimination should take place among the questions which would come before Congress. That the smaller states should be secured in all questions concerning life or liberty & the greater ones in all respecting property. He therefore proposed that in votes relating to money, the voice of each colony should be proportioned to the number of its inhabitants.

Dr. Franklin thought that the votes should be so proportioned in all cases. [...] Certainly if we vote equally we ought to pay equally; but the smaller states will hardly purchase the privilege at this price. That had he lived in a state where the representation, originally equal, had become unequal by time & accident he might have submitted rather than disturb government; but that we should be very wrong to set out in this practice when it is in our power to establish what is right. [...] He reprobated the original agreement of Congress to vote by colonies and therefore was for their voting in all cases according to the number of taxable.

Dr. Witherspoon opposed every alteration of the article. All men admit that a confederacy is necessary. Should the idea get abroad that there is likely to be no union among us, it will damp the minds of the people, diminish the glory of our struggle, & lessen its importance, because it will open to our view future prospects of war & dissension among ourselves. If an equal vote be refused, the smaller states will become vassals to the larger; & all experience has shown that the vassals &

---

[20] *Founders Online*, National Archives, https://founders.archives.gov/documents/Jefferson/01-01-02-0160. Original source: *The Papers of Thomas Jefferson*, Vol. I: *1760–1776*, edited by J. P. Boyd (Princeton: Princeton University Press, 1950), pp. 299–329.

subjects of free states are the most enslaved. He instanced the Helots of Sparta & the provinces of Rome. He observed that foreign powers discovering this blemish would make it a handle for disengaging the smaller states from so unequal a confederacy. That the colonies should in fact be considered as individuals; and that as such in all disputes they should have an equal vote. That they are now collected as individuals making a bargain with each other, & of course had a right to vote as individuals. [...] That in questions of war the smaller states were as much interested as the larger, & therefore should vote equally; and indeed that the larger states were more likely to bring war on the confederacy, in proportion as their frontier was more extensive. He admitted that equality of representation was an excellent principle, but then it must be of things which are co-ordinate; that is, of things similar & of the same nature: that nothing relating to individuals could ever come before Congress; nothing but what would respect colonies.

John Adams advocated the voting in proportion to numbers. He said that we stand here as the representatives of the people. That in some states the people are many, in others they are few; that therefore their vote here should be proportioned to the numbers from whom it comes. Reason, justice, & equity never had weight enough on the face of the earth to govern the councils of men. It is interest alone which does it, and it is interest alone which can be trusted. That therefore the interests within doors should be the mathematical representatives of the interests without doors. [...] It has been said we are independant individuals making a bargain together. The question is not what we are now, but what we ought to be when our bargain shall be made. The confederacy is to make us one individual only; it is to form us, like separate parcels of metal, into one common mass. We shall no longer retain our separate individuality, but become a single individual as to all questions submitted to the Confederacy. Therefore all those reasons which prove the justice & expediency of equal representation in other assemblies, hold good here. It has been objected that a proportional vote will endanger the smaller states. We answer that an equal vote will endanger the larger. Virginia, Pennsylvania, & Massachusets are the three greater colonies. Consider their distance, their difference of produce, of interests, & of manners, & it is apparent they can never have an interest or inclination to combine for the oppression of the smaller. That the smaller will naturally divide on all questions with the larger. Rhode isld. from its relation, similarity & intercourse will generally pursue the same objects with Massachusets; Jersey, Delaware & Maryland with Pennsylvania.

Mr. Wilson thought that taxation should be in proportion to wealth, but that representation should accord with the number of freemen. That government is a collection or result of the wills of all. That if any government could speak the will of all it would be perfect; and that so far as it departs from this it becomes imperfect, it has been said that Congress is a representation of states; not of individuals. I say that the objects of its care are all the individuals of the states. It is strange that annexing the name of "State" to ten thousand men, should give them an equal right with forty thousand. This must be the effect of magic, not of reason. As to those matters which are referred to Congress, we are not so many states; we are one large state. We lay aside our individuality whenever we come here.

Letter to John Adams (May 16, 1776)[21]

Dear Sir

Matters in our part of the continent are too much in quiet to send you news from hence. Our battalions for the Continental service were some time ago so far filled as rendered the recommendation of a draught from the militia hardly requisite, and the more so as in this country it ever was the most unpopular and impracticable thing that could be attempted. Our people even under the monarchical government had learnt to consider it as the last of all oppressions. I learn from our delegates that the Confederation is again on the carpet. A great and a necessary work, but I fear almost desperate. The point of representation is what most alarms me, as I fear the great and small colonies are bitterly determined not to cede. Will you be so good as to recollect the proposition I formerly made you in private and try if you can work it into some good to save our union? It was that any proposition might be negatived by the representatives of a majority of the people of America, or of a majority of the colonies of America. The former secures the larger the latter the smaller colonies. I have mentioned it to many here. The good whigs I think will so far cede their opinions for the sake of the Union, and others we care little for. The journals of congress not being printed earlier gives more uneasiness than I would ever wish to see produced by any act of that body, from whom alone I know our salvation can proceed. In our assembly even the best affected think it an indignity to freemen to be voted away life and fortune in the dark. [. . .] The esteem I have for you privately, as well as for your public importance will always render assurances of your health and happiness agreeable. I am Dear Sir Your friend & servt:
Th: Jefferson

The Articles of Confederation (1781)[22]

Articles of Confederation and perpetual Union between the States of New Hampshire, Massachusetts-bay, Rhode Island and Providence Plantations, Connecticut, New York, New Jersey, Pennsylvania, Delaware, Maryland, Virginia, North Carolina, South Carolina and Georgia.

Article I. The Stile of this confederacy shall be "The United States of America."

Article II. Each state retains its sovereignty, freedom, and independence, and every Power, Jurisdiction and right, which is not by this confederation expressly delegated to the United States, in Congress assembled.

Article III. The said states hereby severally enter into a firm league of friendship with each other, for their common defence, the security of their Liberties, and their mutual and general welfare, binding themselves to assist each other, against all force

---

[21] *Founders Online*, National Archives, https://founders.archives.gov/documents/Jefferson/01-02-02-0016. Original source: *The Papers of Thomas Jefferson*, Vol. II: *1777–18 June 1779*, edited by J. P. Boyd (Princeton: Princeton University Press, 1950), pp. 18–20.

[22] From C. C. Tansill (ed.), *Documents Illustrative of the Formation of the Union of the American States*, House Document No. 398 (Washington, DC: Government Printing Office, 1927), via the Avalon Project, https://avalon.law.yale.edu/.

offered to, or attacks made upon them, or any of them, on account of religion, sovereignty, trade, or any other pretence whatever.

Article IV. The better to secure and perpetuate mutual friendship and intercourse among the people of the different states in this union, the free inhabitants of each of these states, paupers, vagabonds and fugitives from justice excepted, shall be entitled to all privileges and immunities of free citizens in the several states; and the people of each state shall have free ingress and regress to and from any other state, and shall enjoy therein all the privileges of trade and commerce, subject to the same duties impositions and restrictions as the inhabitants thereof respectively, provided that such restriction shall not extend so far as to prevent the removal of property imported into any state, to any other state, of which the Owner is an inhabitant; provided also that no imposition, duties or restriction shall be laid by any state, on the property of the united states, or either of them. If any Person guilty of, or charged with treason, felony, – or other high misdemeanor in any state, shall flee from Justice, and be found in any of the united states, he shall, upon demand of the Governor or executive power, of the state from which he fled, be delivered up and removed to the state having jurisdiction of his offence. Full faith and credit shall be given in each of these states to the records, acts and judicial proceedings of the courts and magistrates of every other state.

Article V. For the more convenient management of the general interests of the united states, delegates shall be annually appointed in such manner as the legislature of each state shall direct, to meet in Congress on the first Monday in November, in every year, with a power reserved to each state, to recall its delegates, or any of them, at any time within the year, and to send others in their stead, for the remainder of the Year.

No state shall be represented in Congress by less than two, nor by more than seven Members; and no person shall be capable of being a delegate for more than three years in any term of six years; nor shall any person, being a delegate, be capable of holding any office under the united states, for which he, or another for his benefit receives any salary, fees or emolument of any kind.

Each state shall maintain its own delegates in a meeting of the states, and while they act as members of the committee of the states. In determining questions in the united states in Congress assembled, each state shall have one vote.

Freedom of speech and debate in Congress shall not be impeached or questioned in any Court, or place out of Congress, and the members of congress shall be protected in their persons from arrests and imprisonments, during the time of their going to and from, and attendance on congress, except for treason, felony, or breach of the peace.

Article VI. No state, without the Consent of the united states in congress assembled, shall send any embassy to, or receive any embassy from, or enter into any conference agreement, alliance or treaty with any King, prince or state; nor shall any person holding any office of profit or trust under the united states, or any of them, accept of any present, emolument, office or title of any kind whatever from any king, prince or foreign state; nor shall the united states in congress assembled, or any of them, grant any title of nobility.

No two or more states shall enter into any treaty, confederation or alliance whatever between them, without the consent of the united states in congress assembled, specifying accurately the purposes for which the same is to be entered into, and how long it shall continue.

No state shall lay any imposts or duties, which may interfere with any stipulations in treaties, entered into by the united states in congress assembled, with any king, prince or state, in pursuance of any treaties already proposed by congress, to the courts of France and Spain.

No vessels of war shall be kept up in time of peace by any state, except such number only, as shall be deemed necessary by the united states in congress assembled, for the defence of such state, or its trade; nor shall any body of forces be kept up by any state, in time of peace, except such number only, as in the judgment of the united states, in congress assembled, shall be deemed requisite to garrison the forts necessary for the defence of such state; but every state shall always keep up a well regulated and disciplined militia, sufficiently armed and accoutered, and shall provide and constantly have ready for use, in public stores, a due number of field pieces and tents, and a proper quantity of arms, ammunition and camp equipage. No state shall engage in any war without the consent of the united states in congress assembled, unless such state be actually invaded by enemies, or shall have received certain advice of a resolution being formed by some nation of Indians to invade such state, and the danger is so imminent as not to admit of a delay till the united states in congress assembled can be consulted [. . .].

Article VIII. All charges of war, and all other expences that shall be incurred for the common defence or general welfare, and allowed by the united states in congress assembled, shall be defrayed out of a common treasury, which shall be supplied by the several states in proportion to the value of all land within each state, granted to or surveyed for any Person, as such land and the buildings and improvements thereon shall be estimated according to such mode as the united states in congress assembled, shall from time to time direct and appoint. [. . .]

Article IX. The united states in congress assembled, shall have the sole and exclusive right and power of determining on peace and war, except in the cases mentioned in the sixth article – of sending and receiving ambassadors – entering into treaties and alliances, provided that no treaty of commerce shall be made whereby the legislative power of the respective states shall be restrained from imposing such imposts and duties on foreigners as their own people are subjected to, or from prohibiting the exportation or importation of any species of goods or commodities, whatsoever – of establishing rules for deciding in all cases, what captures on land or water shall be legal, [. . .] [of] appointing courts for the trial of piracies and felonies committed on the high seas and establishing courts for receiving and determining finally appeals in all cases of captures, provided that no member of congress shall be appointed a judge of any of the said courts.

The united states in congress assembled shall also be the last resort on appeal in all disputes and differences now subsisting or that hereafter may arise between two or more states concerning boundary, jurisdiction or any other cause whatever;

which authority shall always be exercised in the manner following. Whenever the legislative or executive authority or lawful agent of any State in controversy with another shall present a petition to Congress stating the matter in question and praying for a hearing, notice thereof shall be given by order of Congress to the legislative or executive authority of the other State in controversy, and a day assigned for the appearance of the parties by their lawful agents, who shall then be directed to appoint by joint consent, commissioners or judges to constitute a court for hearing and determining the matter in question: but if they cannot agree, Congress shall name three persons out of each of the United States, and from the list of such persons each party shall alternately strike out one, the petitioners beginning, until the number shall be reduced to thirteen; and from that number not less than seven, nor more than nine names as Congress shall direct, shall in the presence of Congress be drawn out by lot, and the persons whose names shall be so drawn or any five of them, shall be commissioners or judges, to hear and finally determine the controversy, so always as a major part of the judges who shall hear the cause shall agree in the determination: and if either party shall neglect to attend at the day appointed, without showing reasons, which Congress shall judge sufficient, or being present shall refuse to strike, the Congress shall proceed to nominate three persons out of each State, and the secretary of Congress shall strike in behalf of such party absent or refusing; and the judgement and sentence of the court to be appointed, in the manner before prescribed, shall be final and conclusive; and if any of the parties shall refuse to submit to the authority of such court, or to appear or defend their claim or cause, the court shall nevertheless proceed to pronounce sentence, or judgement, which shall in like manner be final and decisive, the judgement or sentence and other proceedings being in either case transmitted to Congress, and lodged among the acts of Congress for the security of the parties concerned.

[...] The united states in congress assembled shall have authority to appoint a committee, to sit in the recess of congress, to be denominated "A Committee of the States," and to consist of one delegate from each state; and to appoint such other committees and civil officers as may be necessary for managing the general affairs of the united states under their direction – to appoint one of their number to preside, provided that no person be allowed to serve in the office of president more than one year in any term of three years; to ascertain the necessary sums of money to be raised for the service of the united states, and to appropriate and apply the same for defraying the public expences to borrow money, or emit bills on the credit of the united states, transmitting every half year to the respective states an account of the sums of money so borrowed or emitted, – to build and equip a navy – to agree upon the number of land forces, and to make requisitions from each state for its quota, in proportion to the number of white inhabitants in such state; which requisition shall be binding, and thereupon the legislature of each state shall appoint the regimental officers, raise the men and cloth, arm and equip them in a soldier like manner, at the expence of the united states [...].

The united states in congress assembled shall never engage in a war, nor grant letters of marque and reprisal in time of peace, nor enter into any treaties or alliances, nor coin money, nor regulate the value thereof, nor ascertain the sums and expences necessary for the defence and welfare of the united states, or any of them, nor emit bills, nor borrow money on the credit of the united states, nor appropriate money, nor agree upon the number of vessels of war, to be built or purchased, or the number of land or sea forces to be raised, nor appoint a commander in chief of the army or navy, unless nine states assent to the same: nor shall a question on any other point, except for adjourning from day to day be determined, unless by the votes of a majority of the united states in congress assembled. [. . .]

Article XI. Canada acceding to this confederation, and joining in the measures of the united states, shall be admitted into, and entitled to all the advantages of this union: but no other colony shall be admitted into the same, unless such admission be agreed to by nine states. [. . .]

Article XIII. Every state shall abide by the determinations of the united states in congress assembled, on all questions which by this confederation are submitted to them. And the Articles of this confederation shall be inviolably observed by every state, and the union shall be perpetual; nor shall any alteration at any time hereafter be made in any of them; unless such alteration be agreed to in a congress of the united states, and be afterwards confirmed by the legislatures of every state.

And Whereas it hath pleased the Great Governor of the World to incline the hearts of the legislatures we respectively represent in congress, to approve of, and to authorize us to ratify the said articles of confederation and perpetual union. Know Ye that we the undersigned delegates, by virtue of the power and authority to us given for that purpose, do by these presents, in the name and in behalf of our respective constituents, fully and entirely ratify and confirm each and every of the said articles of confederation and perpetual union, and all and singular the matters and things therein contained: And we do further solemnly plight and engage the faith of our respective constituents, that they shall abide by the determinations of the united states in congress assembled, on all questions, which by the said confederation are submitted to them. And that the articles thereof shall be inviolably observed by the states we respectively represent, and that the union shall be perpetual.

Suggested Readings

Benjamin Franklin, "Albany Plan of Union" [1754] in L. W. Labaree (ed.), *The Papers of Benjamin Franklin*, Vol. V: *July 1, 1753, through March 31, 1755* (New Haven: Yale University Press, 1962), pp. 374–92.

Theophilus Parsons, "The Essex Result" [1778] in O. Handlin and M. Handlin (eds.), *The Popular Sources of Political Authority: Documents on the Massachusetts Constitution of 1780* (Cambridge, MA: The Belknap Press of Harvard University Press, 1966), pp. 324–40.

Phillips Payson, *A Sermon Preached before the Honorable Council, and the Honorable House of Representatives, of the State of Massachusetts-Bay* (Boston: John Gill, 1778).

John Adams, *A Defence of the Constitutions of Government of the United States* (London: C. Dilly, 1787–1788).

Bostonians, "Serious Questions Proposed to All Friends to the Rights of Mankind, with Suitable Answers" [1787] in C. S. Hyneman and D. Lutz (eds.), *American Political Writing during the Founding Era: 1760–1805*, 2 vols., Vol. I (Indianapolis: Liberty Fund, 1983), pp. 702–4.

7 The Positive Founding (II)

The People as One *and* Many

The Articles of Confederation were more than four years in the making and were in effect for only eight more. On September 17, 1787, thirty-nine people signed another document that began with the famous words "We the People." Years later, in the preface to his *Notes of Debates in the Federal Convention of 1787*, James Madison reminisced "that there never was an assembly of men, charged with a great and arduous trust, who were more pure in their motives."

Attempts to better the Articles of Confederation were already made weeks before the first constitution even went into effect, but none were successful. Peoples' loyalties and interests were too strong at the state level. Even so, the **First Founding** (Chapter 6) appeared to many to be defective, and afterwards they began looking "for a system that would avoid the inefficacy of a mere Confederacy, without passing into the opposite extreme of a consolidated government." The 1786 **Annapolis Convention**'s only accomplishment was that, in a bold move, it gambled on a second convention in Philadelphia. This latter one proved to be a different story. In the words of **David Ramsay**, "Heaven smiled on their deliberations and inspired their councils with a spirit of conciliations."[1]

There are several, more or less conflicting interpretations of the **Philadelphia Convention** (May 25–September 17, 1787), ranging from the ones that follow the laudatory remarks of Madison or Ramsay to the ones that echo **Patrick Henry**'s mistrust in the legality of the proceedings, captured by the now famous phrase "*I smell a rat!*" As he put it later, speaking to the **Virginia Ratifying Convention**, "I have the highest veneration for those gentlemen; but, sir, give me leave to demand [...] Who authorized them to speak the language of, 'We, the people,' instead of, 'We, the states'?" The phrase captures the crux of the matter well. Simply put, what was at stake was the very definition of the American people: Were they to be apprehended in their *corporate* capacity, at state level, or as a collection of individuals that happened to live in various states? The preamble of the Constitution never defines "the people" it so emphatically claims to be its author – and for cause.

While the vast majority of the delegates in Philadelphia agreed that the Confederation was defective and needed to be amended, not everyone felt prepared or even authorized to replace it with an entirely new set of principles. According to Madison's *Notes*, the first to "doubt whether the act of Congress recommending the

---

[1] David Ramsay (1749–1815) was not only a witness of (and a participant in) the American founding, but also one of the major historians of the period.

Convention [...] could authorize a discussion of a system founded on different principles from the federal Convention" was **General Pinckney** of South Carolina.[2]

It soon became clear that it was a threefold issue, as **William Paterson** of New Jersey explained.[3] From a legalistic perspective, he observed "that the articles of Confederation were [...] the proper basis of all the proceedings of the Convention. We ought to keep within its limits, or we should be charged by our Constituents with usurpation, [for] the people of America were sharp-sighted and not be deceived." From a practical perspective, he argued, the proposal to replace the Articles of Confederation was doomed to fail, because "[t]he idea of a national Government as contradistinguished from a federal one, never entered the mind of any of them, and to the public mind we must accommodate ourselves." Last, but not least, the issue was a theoretical one as well: Were the representatives from the states to *lead*, or to *follow* their constituencies? Paterson was clear on this point: "We must follow the people; the people will not follow us."

Quite a few of his fellow delegates begged to differ. Speaking the same day, **James Wilson** found an original way to appease the legalistic concerns, arguing that, "[w]ith regard to the *power of the Convention*, he conceived himself authorized to *conclude nothing*, but to be at liberty to *propose anything*."[4] From a practical perspective, "[w]ith regard to the sentiments of the people, he conceived it difficult to know precisely what they are. [...] He could not persuade himself that the State Government & Sovereignties were so much the idols of the people, nor a National Government so obnoxious to them, as some supposed."

Charles Pinckney's doubts were immediately alleviated by Wilson's distinction between "concluding" and "proposing," finding "the Convention authorized to go to any length in *recommending*, which they found necessary to remedy the evils which produced this Convention." **Alexander Hamilton** agreed wholeheartedly. The crisis, he contended in rather Machiavellian terms, "was too serious to *permit any scruples whatever* to prevail over the duty imposed on every man to contribute his efforts for the public safety and happiness. [...] To rely on & propose any plan adequate to these exigencies, merely because it was not clearly within our powers, would be *to sacrifice the mean to the end*." As **Elbridge Gerry** put it bluntly when the problem of ratification came up, "The rulers will either conform to, or influence the sense of the people."[5] Thanks to the *paradigm of the people's two bodies*, we are now better equipped to understand the delegates' ambivalence concerning the people: As in the Puritan tradition, the people qua multitude were not to be trusted with all the subtleties of devising a particular form of government. This was the role and the duty of the natural aristocracy, of the enlightened, who could rise above petty particular interests.

---

[2] Charles Cotesworth Pinckney (1746–1825), lawyer, politician, and diplomat. Unless specified otherwise, the following quotes are from James Madison's *Notes*.

[3] William Paterson (1745–1806) – sometimes spelled as Patterson, as does Madison in his *Notes* – was to serve as an Associate Justice of the US Supreme Court.

[4] James Wilson (1742–1798) was to serve as an Associate Justice of the US Supreme Court.

[5] Elbridge Gerry (1744–1814) was to serve as the fifth Vice President of the United States under President James Madison.

Still, another question remained: Were the people to be understood at the state level or at the national level? The **Virginia Plan** (also known as **the large states plan**), drafted by Madison, was the first to be proposed at the Convention and thus framed the debates to follow. It asked for a National Legislative elected based upon the population of each state, which was supposed to elect not only the members of the second branch of the legislative but also a National Executive and a National Judiciary. In contrast, the **New Jersey Plan** (also known as the **small states plan** or Paterson's Plan) demanded equal representation for the states, in a unicameral legislative, with a vetoless federal executive elected by the legislative, and a Supreme Court elected by the plural federal executive. Finally, the **New York Plan** (Hamilton's Plan) proposed that a Supreme Legislative be elected by the people for a three-year term, a Senate elected by electors (for life) designated by the people in each "district," and also a "Gouvernour"/president elected (for life) through the same procedure. This last proposal never got any real traction, but it arguably contributed to the debates by dramatically tipping the balance from the legislative to the executive.

In the end, after much back-and-forth among the delegates, the **Connecticut Plan** was accepted. It came to be known as the **Great Compromise**, mainly for giving some satisfaction to both the large states, by providing for proportional (numerical) representation in the House of Representatives, and the small states, by accepting equal representation for the states in the Senate. As **William Samuel Johnson** (1727–1819) observed during the debates, "in some respects, the states are to be considered in their political capacity, and, in others, as districts of individual citizens, *the two ideas* embraced on different sides, *instead of being opposed to each other, ought to be combined* – that in *one* branch the *people* ought to be represented, in the *other*, the *states*."

Indeed, one can look at it as a successful compromise for a variety of reasons, not the least for imposing a system of **checks and balances** among the legislative, the executive, and the judicial powers. Yet, even more important was the document's status as a *written* compromise between the two understandings of the people, qua corporation of corporations on the one hand, and qua collection of equal individuals on the other. By the same token, this compromise managed to combine both **classical republican** and **classical liberal** understandings of the people. In some respects, one could claim that the framers managed to recuperate and make permanent the Puritan legacy of the **bi-dimensional covenant** at a scale previously difficult to imagine. The new draft thus offered a compromise between "the people" and the "peoples" of the United States. As Gerry observed, "We were, however, in a peculiar situation. We were neither the same nation, nor different nations. We ought not, therefore, to pursue the one or the other of these ideas too closely. If no compromise should take place, what will be the consequence?"

Regrettably, alongside this much praised compromise, the new Constitution also accepted the infamous **Three-Fifths Compromise**, according to which slaves were to be counted as three-fifths of a person in determining the population of each state. On July 11, the delegates argued about this shameful rule in the general context of discussing the principle of representing people versus representing wealth. Wilson did not see on what principle the admission of blacks in the proportion of three-fifths could be explained. Are they admitted as Citizens? then why are they not admitted on an equality with White Citizens? are they admitted as property? then why is not other property admitted into [the] computation? These were difficulties however which he thought must be overruled by the necessity of compromise.

Considering the Southern intransigence, if there was to be a new Constitution at all and the Union was to be preserved, there was no other solution. Yet, unintentionally, by insisting on constitutional rules for both a census and a reapportionment, the Southern delegates contributed to the legitimization of the principle that representation actually followed population, not wealth. When the final version was signed by the thirty-nine delegates, another, longer political battle was already in the making – the battle for ratification.

The motion for unanimous ratification by the thirteen states was immediately struck down. The number of states required for ratification was more heavily debated, varying between a simple majority of seven states, to ten, only to be finally agreed at nine – yet another compromise. Most delegates felt like Wilson: "The House on fire must be extinguished, without a scrupulous regard to minority rights." But the problems were far from over; were the people properly represented by their state legislatures? Or were additional measures needed to give the people a voice? Since the people were acknowledged as "the fountain of power," Madison argued that "the new Constitution should be ratified [. . .] by the supreme authority of the people themselves." In the end, Congress asked the state legislatures to convey state ratifying conventions, and thus the theoretical battles between the Federalists and the Antifederalists began.

Even if outnumbered, the Federalists had a considerable strategic advantage in these battles. Unlike their opponents, they presented a unified front. A case in point is the Federalist Papers. Despite their initial major disagreements, their authors – James Madison, Alexander Hamilton, and **John Jay** – chose to sign a series of eighty-five articles and essays using the same pseudonym **Publius**.[6] These articles had a threefold purpose: (1) to expose the shortcomings of the existing constitution; (2) to denounce the vices that plagued small republics; (3) to emphasize the remedies provided by the new proposal, both in terms of its general principles and of its specific features.

For example, in **Federalist 10**, following the **republican** tradition, Madison expressed his concern that "the *public good* is disregarded in the conflicts of rival parties, and that measures are too often decided [. . .] by the superior force of an interested and overbearing majority." Since people will always have different interests, one could argue that the only options for preventing the emergence of factions would be either to destroy "the liberty which is essential to its existence" or to give "to every citizen the same opinions, the same passions, and the same interests." The first option is suicidal, the second one impossible. Hence, the emergence of factions is unavoidable. Yet, if one cannot prevent their causes, one can still control their dangerous effects.

---

[6] John Jay (1745–1829) was a Patriot who helped organizing the resistance. He was elected President of the Second Continental Congress and would become the first Chief Justice of the United States.

Here, Madison introduced a rather familiar distinction at that time, between a "democracy" (by which he understood <u>direct democracy</u>) and a "republic" (by which he understood <u>representative democracy</u>). Unlike **Thomas Paine** (Chapter 5), for whom direct democracy was the ideal and representative democracy only second best, Madison argued that the only way "to refine and enlarge the public views" is by electing a small number of representatives "whose wisdom may best discern the true interest of their country, and whose patriotism and love of justice will be least likely to sacrifice it to temporary or partial considerations." The second argument brought forward was highly original and counterintuitive: If one cannot *prevent* factions from emerging, one can set up a system that will allow them to *multiply*. In this way, they will cancel each other out, and no faction will become so powerful as to impose its interests upon the minorities.

Even if they used the same pseudonym in **The Federalist**, the differences, both stylistically and substantive, between Madison and Hamilton are relatively easy to discern. Of the two, Hamilton is the blunter. In **Federalist 15**, he did not mince his words: "The great and radical vice in the construction of the existing Confederation is in the principle of LEGISLATION for STATES or GOVERNMENTS, in their CORPORATE or COLLECTIVE CAPACITIES, and as contradistinguished from the INDIVIDUALS of which they consist" (capitalization in the original). Madison, on the other hand, was trying to maintain the balance between the American people apprehended at a national level, and the people as corporations at the state level (which he calls "federal"). In **Federalist 39**, he reassured his audience that both understandings of the people are equally acknowledged: "The proposed Constitution, therefore, is, in strictness, neither a national nor a federal Constitution, but a composition of both."

Their opponents, however, were not convinced by these arguments. They worried that, underneath all the reassurances, the supporters of the new Constitution were plotting to create a "consolidated government," which would threaten the freedom of the people. Hence, their unanimous insistence upon a **Bill of Rights**. The idea was initially rejected, mainly under the **liberal** premises of the **social contract theory**, according to which there is nothing to fear from elected representatives who can be removed whenever they abuse their powers. But since the opponents of the new Constitution were familiar with constitutions as **political compacts** between the corporate people and their rulers, they could not think otherwise about the new one. The political compact came with a built-in suspicion of any man in power. Eventually, under the threat of a new Constitutional Convention, the proposal came to be accepted by Congress in 1789 and went into effect in 1791.

It was a significant accomplishment, but in all other respects, the Federalists proved more successful – starting with the battle over words. They were victorious in labeling their opponents as Antifederalists, to the latter camp's understandable despair. According to the accepted meanings of the time, as seen in **Federalist 39**, the Federalists were actually Nationalists, while their opponents were the "true Federalists" – and they considered themselves as such. Nevertheless, the Nationalists managed to define themselves as the Federalists, and to label the Federalists as the … Antifederalists. As Frank Schechter observed as early as

1915, "it would be hard to conceive a more deft and sudden abduction of a valuable verbal party asset, a more skillful appropriation of the enemy's thunder, than that by which [. . .] the metamorphosis of the meaning of the word 'Federal' [. . .] under the pens of Nationalists of America was effected."[7]

But the Antifederalists' main disadvantage was their lack of unity in their criticism and in rallying behind an alternative constitution. Except for the absence of a Bill of Rights and the unconstitutionality of the new Constitution, they could not agree on anything else. Some were concerned about the provision for a standing army, others considered the Senate and even the House of Representatives too aristocratic. Some accused the new presidency of being too strong ("a new King"); others of being too weak when confronted with the Senate, etc.

Centinel,[8] for example, was worried "that the men of the greatest purity of intention may be made instruments of despotism in the hands of the artful and designing." The proposed constitution, he argued, would melt the people of all states into one despotic Empire in which the democratic principles would be overlooked. For him, despite its claim to contrary, the government molded upon the new Constitution "appears that it is devoid of all responsibility or accountability to the great body of the people, and that so far from being a regular balanced government, it would be in practice *a permanent* ARISTOCRACY" (original capitalization).

The **Federal Farmer** was another famous Antifederalist.[9] He agreed that "a federal government of some sort is necessary," yet disagreed with the new proposal for various reasons, not the least because the proposal failed to provide for a "full and equal representation of the people in the legislature." Like many Antifederalists, he believed in <u>descriptive representation</u>, one "which possesses the same interests, feelings, opinions, and views the people themselves would were they all assembled." Notice how, like Paine and unlike Madison, the Federal Farmer considers <u>representative democracy</u> to be second to <u>direct democracy</u>. Yet his main concern was the prospect of melting the peoples of each state into one single people. Madison's argument that both understandings of the people were acknowledged by the new Constitution did not convince the Federal Farmer. "Instead of being thirteen republics, under a federal head, it is clearly designed to make us one consolidated government."

The Antifederalist writing under the pseudonym **Brutus** instead focused his criticisms on the proposed role of the Supreme Court.[10] In his opinion, the Supreme Court would not only become the only branch of the government not

---

[7] F. I. Schechter, "The Early History of the Tradition of the Constitution," *The American Political Science Review*, 9 (1915), p. 714.

[8] The real author behind this pseudonym remains a subject of disagreement, but most historians suspect Samuel Bryan from Philadelphia (1759–1821).

[9] The most likely author is Richard Henry Lee (1732–1794), the first to formally call for the independence of the Colonies, signer of the Declaration of the Independence and of the Articles of Confederation, and one-year term President of the Continental Congress.

[10] The author was, most likely, Robert Yates (1738–1801). One of the earliest fighters for Independence, Yates was appointed, together with John Lansing Jr. (1754–1829) and Alexander Hamilton, to represent the state of New York at the Philadelphia Convention. But, unlike Hamilton, Yates and Lansing thought the new proposal was too radical, beyond the authority invested in them, and left the Convention. Eventually, he would become Chief Justice of the New York State Supreme Court.

subjected to the checks and balances principle, but also the one invested with a tremendous power over the other two branches. Considering the vagueness of the articles of the Constitution, he argued, the judges would be free to impose whatever interpretation of the Constitution and of the laws that would please them. Practically, their position "will enable them to mould the government, into almost any shape they please." In his opinion, the way in which the judges would tilt the balance of justice between the states and the central governments' powers was clearly formulated in the preamble of the new document: "In order to form a more perfect union [...]."

In the end, the new Constitution came to be ratified without solving the main conundrum: Who was "We, the people"?

DEBATES DURING THE PHILADELPHIA CONVENTION

James Madison *Notes of Debates in the Federal Convention of 1787*

Madison's Preface (*c.*1830/1836)

[...] In the internal administration of the states, a violation of contracts had become familiar, in the form of depreciated paper made a legal tender, of property substituted for money, of instalment laws, and of the occlusions of the courts of justice, although evident that all such interferences affected the rights of other states, relatively creditors, as well as citizens creditors within the state. Among the defects which had been severely felt, was want of a uniformity in cases requiring it, as laws of naturalization and bankruptcy; a coercive authority operating on individuals; and a guaranty of the internal tranquility of the states.

As a natural consequence of this distracted and disheartening condition of the Union, the federal authority had ceased to be respected abroad, and dispositions were shown there, particularly in Great Britain, to take advantage of its imbecility, and to speculate on its approaching downfall. At home, it had lost all confidence and credit; the unstable and unjust career of the states had also forfeited the respect and confidence essential to order and good government, involving a general decay of confidence and credit between man and man. It was found, moreover, that those least partial to popular government, or most distrustful of its efficacy, were yielding to anticipations, that, from an increase of the confusion, a government might result more congenial with their taste or their opinions; whilst those most devoted to the principles and forms of republics were alarmed for the cause of liberty itself, at stake in the American experiment, and anxious for a system that would avoid the inefficacy of a mere Confederacy, without passing into the opposite extreme of a consolidated government. It was known that there were individuals who had betrayed a bias towards monarchy, and there had always been some not unfavorable to a partition of the Union into several confederacies, either from a better chance of figuring on a sectional theatre, or that the sections would require stronger governments, or, by their hostile conflicts, lead to a monarchical consolidation. The idea of dismemberment had recently made its appearance in the newspapers.

Such were the defects, the deformities, the diseases, and the ominous prospects, for which the Convention were to provide a remedy, and which ought never to be overlooked in expounding and appreciating the constitutional charter, the remedy that was provided. [...]

Of the ability and intelligence of those who composed the Convention, the debates and proceedings may be a test; as the character of the work, which was the offspring of their deliberations, must be tested by the experience of the future, added to that of nearly half a century which has passed.

But, whatever may be the judgment pronounced on the competency of the architects of the Constitution, or whatever may be the destiny of the edifice prepared by them, I feel it a duty to express my profound and solemn conviction, derived from my intimate opportunity of observing and appreciating the views of the Convention, collectively and individually, that there never was an assembly of men, charged with a great and arduous trust, who were more pure in their motives, or more exclusively or anxiously devoted to the object committed to them, than were the members of the Federal Convention of 1787 to the object of devising and proposing a constitutional system which should best supply the defects of that which it was to replace, and best secure the permanent liberty and happiness of their country.

[While waiting for the Convention to formally begin, James Madison sketched out an initial proposal for revising the Articles of Confederation, which became known as the Virginia Plan. The proposal was presented by Edmund Randolph, the Governor of Virginia, on May 29.]

Wednesday, May 30

[. . .] The propositions of Mr. RANDOLPH which had been referred to the committee being taken up, he moved, on the suggestion of Mr. G. MORRIS, that the first of his propositions, – to wit: "Resolved, that the Articles of Confederation ought to be so corrected and enlarged, as to accomplish the objects proposed by their institution; namely, common defence, security of liberty, and general welfare," – should mutually be postponed, in order to consider the three following:

"1. That a union of the states merely federal will not accomplish the objects proposed by the Articles of Confederation – namely, common defence, security of liberty, and general welfare.
"2. That no treaty or treaties among the whole or part of the states, as individual sovereignties, would be sufficient.
"3. That a *national* government ought to be established, consisting of a supreme legislative, executive, and judiciary."

The motion for postponing was seconded by Mr. G. MORRIS, and unanimously agreed to.

Some verbal criticisms were raised against the first proposition, and it was agreed, on motion of Mr. BUTLER, seconded by Mr. RANDOLPH, to pass on to the third, which underwent a discussion, less, however, on its general merits than on the force and extent of the particular terms *national* and *supreme*. [. . .]

Gen. PINCKNEY expressed a doubt whether the act of Congress recommending the Convention, or the commissions of the deputies to it, would authorize a discussion of a system founded on different principles from the Federal Constitution.

Mr. GERRY seemed to entertain the same doubt.

Mr. GOUVERNEUR MORRIS explained the distinction between a federal and a *national supreme* government; the former being a mere compact resting on the good faith of the parties, the latter having a complete and *compulsive* operation. He contended, that in all communities there must be one supreme power, and one only.

Mr. MASON observed, not only that the present Confederation was deficient in not providing for coercion and punishment against delinquent states, but argued very cogently, that punishment could not, in the nature of things, be executed on the states collectively, and therefore that such a government was necessary as could directly operate on individuals, and would punish those only whose guilt required it. [. . .]

On the question, as moved by Mr. BUTLER, on the third proposition, it was resolved, in committee of the whole, "that a national government ought to be established, consisting of a supreme legislative, executive, and judiciary." [. . .]

The following resolution, being the second of those proposed by Mr. RANDOLPH, was taken up, viz.:

> "That the rights of suffrage in the national legislature ought to be proportioned to the quotas of contribution, or to the number of free inhabitants, as the one or the other rule may seem best in different cases."

Mr. MADISON, observing that the words *"or to the number of free inhabitants"* might occasion debates which would divert the committee from the general question whether the principle of representation should be changed, moved that they might be struck out.

Mr. KING observed, that the quotas of contribution, which would alone remain as the measure of representation, would not answer; because, waiving every other view of the matter, the revenue might hereafter be so collected by the general government that the sums respectively drawn from the states would not appear, and would besides be continually varying. [. . .]

Col. HAMILTON moved to alter the resolution so as to read, "that the rights of suffrage in the national legislature ought to be proportioned to the number of free inhabitants." Mr. SPAIGHT seconded the motion.

It was then moved that the resolution be postponed; which was agreed to.

Mr. RANDOLPH and Mr. MADISON then moved the following resolution: "That the rights of suffrage in the national legislature ought to be proportioned."

It was moved, and seconded, to amend it by adding, "and not according to the present system;" which was agreed to.

It was then moved and seconded to alter the resolution so as to read, "That the rights of suffrage in the national legislature ought not to be according to the present system."

It was then moved and seconded to postpone the resolution moved by Mr. Randolph and Mr. Madison; which being agreed to, –

Mr. Madison moved, in order to get over the difficulties, the following resolution: "That the equality of suffrage established by the Articles of Confederation ought not to prevail in the national legislature; and that an equitable ratio of representation ought to be substituted." This was seconded by Mr. GOUVERNEUR MORRIS, and, being generally relished, would have been agreed to; when

Mr. READ moved, that the whole clause relating to the point of representation be postponed; reminding the committee that the deputies from Delaware were restrained by their commission from assenting to any change of the rule of suffrage, and in case such a change should be fixed on, it might become their duty to retire from the Convention.

Mr. GOUVERNEUR MORRIS observed, that the valuable assistance of those members could not be lost without real concern; and that so early a proof of discord in the Convention as the secession of a state would add much to the regret; that the change proposed was, however, so fundamental an article in a national government, that it could not be dispensed with.

Mr. MADISON observed, that, whatever reason might have existed for the equality of suffrage when the union was a federal one among sovereign states, it must cease when a national government should be put into the place. In the former case, the acts of Congress depended so much for their efficacy on the coöperation of the states, that these had a weight, both within and without Congress, nearly in proportion to their extent and importance. In the latter case, as the acts of the general government would take effect without the intervention of the state legislatures, a vote from a small state would have the same efficacy and importance as a vote from a large one, and there was the same reason for different numbers of representatives from different states, as from counties of different extents within particular states. [...]

Thursday, May 31

In the committee of the whole on Mr. RANDOLPH'S resolutions, – the third resolution, "that the national legislature ought to consist of two branches," was agreed to without debate, or dissent, except that of Pennsylvania, – given probably from complaisance to Dr. Franklin, who was understood to be partial to a single house of legislation.

The fourth resolution, first clause, "that the members of the first branch of the national legislature ought to be elected by the people of the several states," being taken up, –

Mr. SHERMAN opposed the election by the people, insisting that it ought to be by the state legislatures. The people, he said, immediately, should have as little to do as may be about the government. They want information, and are constantly liable to be misled.

Mr. GERRY. The evils we experience flow from the excess of democracy. The people do not want virtue, but are the dupes of pretended patriots. In Massachusetts, it had been fully confirmed by experience, that they are daily misled into the most baneful measures and opinions, by the false reports circulated by designing men, and which no one on the spot can refute. [...] He had, he said, been too republican heretofore: he was still, however, republican, but had been taught by experience the danger of the levelling spirit.

Mr. MASON argued strongly for an election of the larger branch by the people. It was to be the grand depository of the democratic principle of the government. It was, so to speak, to be our House of Commons. It ought to know and sympathize with every part of the community, and ought therefore to be taken, not only from different parts of the whole republic, but also from different districts of the larger members of it; which had in several instances, particularly in Virginia, different interests and views arising from difference of produce, of habits, &c. &c. He admitted that we had been too democratic, but was afraid we should incautiously run into the opposite extreme. We ought to attend to the rights of every class of the people. [...]

Mr. WILSON contended strenuously for drawing the most numerous branch of the legislature immediately from the people. He was for raising the federal pyramid to a considerable altitude, and for that reason wished to give it as broad a basis as possible. No government could long subsist without the confidence of the people. In a republican government, this confidence was peculiarly essential. He also thought it wrong to increase the weight of the state legislatures by making them the electors of the national legislature. All interference between the general and local governments should be obviated as much as possible. On examination, it would be found that the opposition of states to federal measures had proceeded much more from the officers of the states than from the people at large.

Mr. MADISON considered the popular election of one branch of the national legislature as essential to every plan of free government. He observed, that, in some of the states, one branch of the legislature was composed of men already removed from the people by an intervening body of electors; that, if the first branch of the general legislature should be elected by the state legislatures, the second branch elected by the first, the executive by the second together with the first, and other appointments again made for subordinate purposes by the executive, the people would be lost sight of altogether, and the necessary sympathy between them and their rulers and officers too little felt. He was an advocate for the policy of refining the popular appointments by successive filtrations, but thought it might be pushed too far. [...]

Wednesday, June 6

In Committee of the Whole. – Mr. PINCKNEY, according to previous notice, and rule obtained, moved, "that the first branch of the national legislature be elected by the state legislatures, and not by the people"; contending that the people were less fit judges in such a case, and that the legislatures would be less likely to promote the adoption of the new government if they were to be excluded from all share in it. [...]

Col. MASON. Under the existing Confederacy, Congress represent the *states*, and not the *people* of the states; their acts operate on the *states*, not on the individuals. The case will be changed in the new plan of government. The people will be represented: they ought therefore to choose the representatives. The requisites in actual representation are, that the representatives should sympathize with their constituents; should think as they think, and feel as they feel; and that for these purposes they should be residents among them. Much, he said, had been alleged against democratic elections. He admitted that much might be said; but it was to be considered that no government was free from imperfections and evils; and that improper elections, in many instances, were inseparable from republican governments. But compare these with the advantage of this form, in favor of the rights of the people – in favor of human nature. He was persuaded there was a better chance for proper elections by the people, if divided into large districts, than by the state legislatures. [...]

Mr. MADISON considered an election of one branch, at least, of the legislature by the people immediately, as a clear principle of free government; and that this mode, under proper regulations, had the additional advantage of securing better representatives, as well as of avoiding too great an agency of the state governments in the general one. [...] The gentleman (Mr. Sherman) had admitted that, in a very small state, faction and oppression would prevail. It was to be inferred, then, that wherever these prevailed, the state was too small. Had they not prevailed in the largest as well as the smallest, though less than in the smallest? And were we not thence admonished to enlarge the sphere as far as the nature of the government would admit? This was the only defence against the inconveniences of democracy consistent with the democratic form of government. All civilized societies would be divided into different sects, factions, and interests, as they happened to consist of rich and poor, debtors and creditors, the landed, the manufacturing, the commercial interests, the inhabitants of this district or that district, the followers of this political leader or that political leader, the disciples of this religious sect or that religious sect. In all cases where a majority are united by a common interest or passion, the rights of the minority are in danger. [...] In a republican government, the majority, if united, have always an opportunity. The only remedy is, to enlarge the sphere, and thereby divide the community into so great a number of interests and parties, that, in the first place, a majority will not be likely, at the same moment, to have a common interest separate from that of the whole, or of the minority; and, in the second place, that, in case they should have such an interest, they may not be so apt to unite in the pursuit of it. It was incumbent on us, then, to try this remedy, and, with that view, to frame a republican system on such a scale, and in such a form, as will control all the evils which have been experienced.

Mr. DICKINSON considered it essential that one branch of the legislature should be drawn immediately from the people, and expedient that the other should be chosen by the legislatures of the states. This combination of the state governments with the national government was as politic as it was unavoidable. In the formation of the Senate, we ought to carry it through such a refining process as will assimilate it, as nearly as may be, to the House of Lords in England. [...]

On the question for electing the first branch by the state legislatures, as moved by Mr. PINCKNEY, it was negatived. [...]

Saturday, June 9

[...] Mr. PATTERSON [...] The idea of a national government, as contradistinguished from a federal one, never entered into the mind of any of them; and to the public mind we must accommodate ourselves. We have no power to go beyond the federal scheme; and if we had, the people are not ripe for any other. We must follow the people; the people will not follow us. The proposition could not be maintained, whether considered in reference to us as a nation, or as a confederacy. A confederacy supposes sovereignty in the members composing it, and sovereignty supposes equality. If we are to be considered as a nation, all state distinctions must be abolished, the whole must be thrown into hotchpot, and when an equal division is made, then there may be fairly an equality of representation. [...] He said there was no more reason that a great individual state, contributing much, should have more votes than a small one, contributing little, than that a rich individual citizen should have more votes than an indigent one. If the ratable property of A was to that of B as forty to one, ought A, for that reason, to have forty times as many votes as B? Such a principle would never be admitted; and, if it were admitted, would put B entirely at the mercy of A. [...] Give the large states an influence in proportion to their magnitude, and what will be the consequence? Their ambition will be proportionally increased, and the small states will have every thing to fear. [...] It has been said that, if a national government is to be formed so as to operate on the people, and not on the states, the representatives ought to be drawn from the people. But why so? May not a legislature, filled by the state legislatures, operate on the people who choose the state legislatures? Or may not a practicable coercion be found? He admitted that there was none such in the existing system. He was attached strongly to the plan of the existing Confederacy, in which the people choose their legislative representatives, and the legislatures their federal representatives. No other amendments were wanting than to mark the orbits of the states with due precision, and provide for the use of coercion, which was the great point. [...] He would not only oppose the plan here, but, on his return home, do every thing in his power to defeat it there.

Mr. WILSON [...] entered elaborately into the defence of a proportional representation, stating, for his first position, that, as all authority was derived from the people, equal numbers of people ought to have an equal number of representatives, and different numbers of people, different numbers of representatives. This principle had been improperly violated in the Confederation, owing to the urgent circumstances of the time. As to the case of A and B, stated by Mr. Patterson, he observed that, in districts as large as the states, the number of people was the best measure of their comparative wealth. Whether, therefore, wealth or numbers was to form the ratio, it would be the same. Mr. Patterson admitted persons, not property, to be the measure of suffrage. Are not the citizens of Pennsylvania equal to those of New Jersey? Does it require one hundred and fifty of the former to balance fifty of the latter? Representatives of different districts ought clearly to hold the same proportion to each other, as their respective constituents hold to each other. If the small states will not confederate on this plan, Pennsylvania, and he presumed some other states, would not confederate on any other. We have been told that, each state being sovereign, all are equal. So each man is naturally a sovereign over himself, and all men are therefore naturally equal. Can he retain this equality when he becomes a member of civil government? He cannot. As little can a sovereign state, when it becomes a member of a federal government. If New Jersey will not part with her sovereignty, it is vain to talk of government. A new partition of the states is desirable, but evidently and totally impracticable. [...]

Monday, June 11

In Committee of the Whole. – The clause concerning the rule of suffrage in the national legislature, postponed on Saturday, was resumed.

Mr. SHERMAN proposed, that the proportion of suffrage in the first branch should be according to the respective numbers of free inhabitants; and that in the second branch, or Senate, each state should have one vote and no more. He said, as the states would remain possessed of certain individual rights, each state ought to be able to protect itself; otherwise, a few large states will rule the rest. [. . .]

Mr. KING and Mr. WILSON, in order to bring the question to a point, moved, "that the right of suffrage in the first branch of the national legislature ought not to be according to the rule established in the Articles of Confederation, but according to some equitable ratio of representation." [. . .]

On the question for agreeing to Mr. King's and Mr. Wilson's motion, it passed in the affirmative. [. . .]

It was then moved by Mr. RUTLEDGE, seconded by Mr. BUTLER, to add to the words "equitable ratio of representation," at the end of the motion just agreed to, the words "according to the quotas of contribution." On motion of Mr. WILSON, seconded by Mr. PINCKNEY, this was postponed in order to add, after the words "equitable ratio of representation," the words following – "in proportion to the whole number of white and other free citizens and inhabitants of every age, sex, and condition, including those bound to servitude for a term of years, and three fifths of all other persons not comprehended in the foregoing description, except Indians not paying taxes, in each state" – this being the rule in the act of Congress, agreed to by eleven states, for apportioning quotas of revenue on the states, and requiring a census only every five, seven, or ten years.

Mr. GERRY thought property not the rule of representation. Why, then, should the blacks, who were property in the south, be, in the rule of representation, more than the cattle and horses of the north? [. . .]

[On June 13, the revised report on the Virginia Plan was issued. This report summarized the decisions made by the delegates in the first two weeks of the Convention. On June 15, in turn, the so-called New Jersey Plan was introduced by William Paterson.]

Saturday, June 16

[. . .] Mr. PATTERSON said, as he had on a former occasion given his sentiments on the plan proposed by Mr. Randolph, he would now, avoiding repetition as much as possible, give his reasons in favor of that proposed by himself. He preferred it because it accorded, – first, with the powers of the convention; secondly, with the sentiments of the people. If the Confederacy was radically wrong, let us return to our states, and obtain larger powers, not assume them ourselves. I came here not to speak my own sentiments, but the sentiments of those who sent me. Our object is not such a government as may be best in itself, but such a one as our constituents have authorized us to prepare, and as they will approve. If we argue the matter on the supposition that no confederacy at present exists, it cannot be denied that all the states stand on the footing of equal sovereignty. All, therefore, must concur before any can be bound. If a proportional representation be right, why do we not vote so here? If we argue on the fact that a federal compact actually exists, and consult the articles of it, we still find an equal sovereignty to be the basis of it. This is the nature of all treaties. What is unanimously done, must be unanimously undone. [...] If the sovereignty of the states is to be maintained, the representatives must be drawn immediately from the states, not from the people; and we have no power to vary the idea of equal sovereignty. [...]

Mr. Wilson [...] With *regard to the sentiments of the people*, he conceived it difficult to know precisely what they are. Those of the particular circle in which one moved were commonly mistaken for the general voice. He could not persuade himself that the state governments and sovereignties were so much the idols of the people, nor a national government so obnoxious to them, as some supposed. Why should a national government be unpopular? Has it less dignity? Will each citizen enjoy under it less liberty or protection? Will a citizen of *Delaware* be degraded by becoming a citizen of the *United States*? Where do the people look at present for relief from the evils of which they complain? Is it from an internal reform of their governments? No, sir. It is from the national councils that relief is expected. For these reasons, he did not fear that the people would not follow us into a national government; and it will be a further recommendation of Mr. Randolph's plan, that it is to be submitted to *them*, and not to the *legislatures*, for ratification. [...]

Mr. RANDOLPH [...] The true question is, whether we shall adhere to the federal plan, or introduce the national plan. The insufficiency of the former has been fully displayed by the trial already made. [...] We must resort, therefore, to a national *legislation over individuals*; for which Congress are unfit. To vest such power in them would be blending the legislative with the executive, contrary to the received maxim on this subject. If the union of these powers, heretofore, in Congress has been safe, it has been owing to the general impotency of that body. Congress are, moreover, not elected by the people, but by the legislatures, who retain even a power of recall. They have, therefore, no will of their own; they are a mere diplomatic body, and are always obsequious to the views of the states, who are always encroaching on the authority of the United States. [...] A national government alone, properly constituted, will answer the purpose; and he begged it to be considered that the present is the last moment for establishing one. After this select experiment, the people will yield to despair. [...]

Friday, June 29

In Convention. – Dr. JOHNSON. The controversy must be endless whilst gentlemen differ in the grounds of their arguments: those on one side considering the states as districts of people composing one political society, those on the other considering them as so many political societies. The fact is, that the states do exist as political societies, and a government is to be formed for them in their political capacity, as well as for the individuals composing them. Does it not seem to follow, that if the states, as such, are to exist, they must be armed with some power of self-defence? This is the idea of Col. Mason, who appears to have looked to the bottom of this matter. Besides the aristocratic and other interests, which ought to have the means of defending themselves, the states have their interests as such, and are equally entitled to like means. On the whole, he thought that as, in some respects, the states are to be considered in their political capacity, and, in others, as districts of individual citizens, the two ideas embraced on different sides, instead of being opposed to each other, ought to be combined – that in *one* branch the *people* ought to be represented, in the *other*, the *states*. [...]

Mr. ELLSWORTH moved, "that the rule of suffrage in the second branch be the same with that established by the Articles of Confederation." He was not sorry, on the whole, he said, that the vote just passed had determined against this rule in the first branch. He hoped it would become a ground of compromise with regard to the second branch. We were partly national, partly federal. The proportional representation in the first branch was conformable to the national principle, and would secure the large states against the small. An equality of voices was conformable to the federal principle, and was necessary to secure the small states against the large. He trusted that on this middle ground a compromise would take place. He did not see that it could on any other, and if no compromise should take place, our meeting would not only be in vain, but worse than in vain. [...]

[As the Convention entered its second full month of deliberations, it was decided that further consideration of the prickly question of how to apportion representatives in the legislature should be referred to a committee composed of one delegate from each of the eleven states that were present at that time. The "Grand Committee," as it has come to be known, presented its report on July 5, 1787.]

Thursday, July 5

In Convention. – Mr. GERRY delivered in, from the committee appointed on Monday last, the following Report [...]

"That the subsequent propositions be recommended to the Convention on condition that both shall be generally adopted.

"1. That, in the first branch of the legislature, each of the states now in the Union shall be allowed one member for every forty thousand inhabitants, of the description reported in the seventh resolution of the Committee of the whole House: that each state not containing that number shall be allowed one member: that all bills for raising or appropriating money, and for fixing the salaries of the officers of the government of the United States, shall originate in the first branch of the legislature, and shall not be altered or amended by the second branch; and that no money shall be drawn from the public treasury but in pursuance of appropriations to be originated in the first branch.

"2. That, in the second branch, each state shall have an equal vote." [...]

Mr. GOUVERNEUR MORRIS thought the form as well as the matter of the report objectionable. It seemed, in the first place, to render amendment impracticable. In the next place, it seemed to involve a pledge to agree to the second part, if the first should be agreed to. He conceived the whole aspect of it to be wrong. He came here as a representative of America; he flattered himself he came here in some degree as a representative of the whole human race; for the whole human race will be affected by the proceedings of this Convention. He wished gentlemen to extend their views beyond the present moment of time; beyond the narrow limits of place from which they derive their political origin. If he were to believe some things which he had heard, he should suppose that we were assembled to truck and bargain for our particular states. He cannot descend to think that any gentlemen are really actuated by these views. We must look forward to the effects of what we do. These alone ought to guide us. Much has been said of the sentiments of the people. They were unknown. They could not be known. All that we can infer is, that, if the plan we recommend be reasonable and right, all who have reasonable minds and sound intentions will embrace it, notwithstanding what had been said by some gentlemen. [...]

Mr. ELLSWORTH said, he had not attended the proceedings of the committee, but was ready to accede to the compromise they had reported. Some compromise was necessary; and he saw none more convenient or reasonable. [...]

Mr. GERRY. Though he had assented to the report in the committee, he had very material objections to it. We were, however, in a peculiar situation. We were neither the same nation, nor different nations. We ought not, therefore, to pursue the one or the other of these ideas too closely. If no compromise should take place, what will be the consequence? A secession, he foresaw, would take place; for some gentlemen seemed decided on it. Two different plans will be proposed, and the result no man could foresee. If we do not come to some agreement among ourselves, some foreign sword will probably do the work for us. [...]

Monday, July 23

[...] Col. MASON considered a reference of the plan to the authority of the people as one of the most important and essential of the resolutions. The legislatures have no power to ratify it. They are the mere creatures of the state constitutions, and cannot be greater than their creators. And he knew of no power in any of the constitutions – he knew there was no power in some of them – that could be competent to this object. Whither, then, must we resort? To the people, with whom all power remains that has not been given up in the constitutions derived from them. It was of great moment, he observed, that this doctrine should be cherished, as the basis of free government. Another strong reason was, that, admitting the legislatures to have a competent authority, it would be wrong to refer the plan to them, because succeeding legislatures, having equal authority, could undo the acts of their predecessors; and the national government would stand, in each state, on the weak and tottering foundation of an act of assembly. There was a remaining consideration, of some weight. In some of the states, the governments were not derived from the clear and undisputed authority of the people. This was the case in Virginia. Some of the best and wisest citizens considered the constitution as established by an assumed authority. A national constitution derived from such a source would be exposed to the severest criticisms. [...]

Mr. GERRY [...] Great confusion, he was confident, would result from a recurrence to the people. They would never agree on any thing. He could not see any ground to suppose, that the people will do what their rulers will not. The rulers will either conform to or influence the sense of the people. [...]

Mr. ELSEWORTH [...] The fact is, that we exist at present and we need not inquire how, as a federal society, united by a charter, one article of which is, that alterations therein may be made by the legislative authority of the states. It has been said, that, if the Confederation is to be observed, the states must *unanimously* concur in the proposed innovations. He would answer, that, if such were the urgency and necessity of our situation as to warrant a new compact among a part of the states, founded on the consent of the people, the same pleas would be equally valid in favor of a partial compact, founded on the consent of the legislatures. [...]

Mr. KING thought with Mr. Ellsworth that the legislatures had a competent authority, the acquiescence of the people of America in the Confederation being equivalent to a formal ratification by the people. He thought with Mr. Ellsworth, also, that the plea of necessity was as valid in the one case as the other. At the same time, he preferred a reference to the authority of the people, expressly delegated to conventions, as the most certain means of obviating all disputes and doubts concerning the legitimacy of the new Constitution, as well as the most likely means of drawing forth the best men in the states to decide on it. [...]

Mr. MADISON thought it clear that the legislatures were incompetent to the proposed changes. These changes would make essential inroads on the state constitutions; and it would be a novel and dangerous doctrine, that a legislature could change the constitution under which it held its existence. There might indeed be some constitutions within the Union, which had given a power to the legislature to concur in alterations of the federal compact. But there were certainly some which had not; and, in the case of these, a ratification must of necessity be obtained from the people. He considered the difference between a system founded on the legislatures only, and one founded on the people, to be the true difference between a *league* or *treaty*, and a *constitution*. [...]

THE FEDERALIST PAPERS[11]

(Published in the *Independent Journal*, the *New York Packet*, and *The Daily Advertiser* between October 1787 and April 1788.)

Federalist No. 10 (James Madison)

To the People of the State of New York:

AMONG the numerous advantages promised by a well-constructed Union, none deserves to be more accurately developed than its tendency to break and control the violence of faction. The friend of popular governments never finds himself

---

[11] From *The Federalist* (Washington, DC: Jacob Gideon, 1818).

so much alarmed for their character and fate, as when he contemplates their propensity to this dangerous vice. He will not fail, therefore, to set a due value on any plan which, without violating the principles to which he is attached, provides a proper cure for it. [...] The valuable improvements made by the American constitutions on the popular models, both ancient and modern, cannot certainly be too much admired; but it would be an unwarrantable partiality, to contend that they have as effectually obviated the danger on this side, as was wished and expected. Complaints are everywhere heard from our most considerate and virtuous citizens, equally the friends of public and private faith, and of public and personal liberty, that our governments are too unstable, that the public good is disregarded in the conflicts of rival parties, and that measures are too often decided, not according to the rules of justice and the rights of the minor party, but by the superior force of an interested and overbearing majority. [...] These must be chiefly, if not wholly, effects of the unsteadiness and injustice with which a factious spirit has tainted our public administrations.

By a faction, I understand a number of citizens, whether amounting to a majority or a minority of the whole, who are united and actuated by some common impulse of passion, or of interest, adversed to the rights of other citizens, or to the permanent and aggregate interests of the community.

There are two methods of curing the mischiefs of faction: the one, by removing its causes; the other, by controlling its effects.

There are again two methods of removing the causes of faction: the one, by destroying the liberty which is essential to its existence; the other, by giving to every citizen the same opinions, the same passions, and the same interests.

It could never be more truly said than of the first remedy, that it was worse than the disease. Liberty is to faction what air is to fire, an aliment without which it instantly expires. But it could not be less folly to abolish liberty, which is essential to political life, because it nourishes faction, than it would be to wish the annihilation of air, which is essential to animal life, because it imparts to fire its destructive agency.

The second expedient is as impracticable as the first would be unwise. As long as the reason of man continues fallible, and he is at liberty to exercise it, different opinions will be formed. As long as the connection subsists between his reason and his self-love, his opinions and his passions will have a reciprocal influence on each other; and the former will be objects to which the latter will attach themselves. The diversity in the faculties of men, from which the rights of property originate, is not less an insuperable obstacle to a uniformity of interests. The protection of these faculties is the first object of government. From the protection of different and unequal faculties of acquiring property, the possession of different degrees and kinds of property immediately results; and from the influence of these on the sentiments and views of the respective proprietors, ensues a division of the society into different interests and parties.

The latent causes of faction are thus sown in the nature of man; and we see them everywhere brought into different degrees of activity, according to the different circumstances of civil society. A zeal for different opinions concerning religion, concerning government, and many other points, as well of speculation as of practice; an attachment to different leaders ambitiously contending for pre-eminence and power; or to persons of other descriptions whose fortunes have been interesting to the human passions, have, in turn, divided mankind into parties, inflamed them with mutual animosity, and rendered them much more disposed to vex and oppress each other than to co-operate for their common good. So strong is this propensity of mankind to fall into mutual animosities, that where no substantial occasion presents itself, the most frivolous and fanciful distinctions have been sufficient to kindle their unfriendly passions and excite their most violent conflicts. But the most common and durable source of factions has been the various and unequal distribution of property. Those who hold and those who are without property have ever formed distinct interests in society. Those who are creditors, and those who are debtors, fall under a like discrimination. A landed interest, a manufacturing interest, a mercantile interest, a moneyed interest, with many lesser interests, grow up of necessity in civilized nations, and divide them into different classes, actuated by different sentiments and views. The regulation of these various and interfering interests forms the principal task of modern legisla-tion, and involves the spirit of party and faction in the necessary and ordinary operations of the government. [. . .]

The inference to which we are brought is, that the CAUSES of faction cannot be removed, and that relief is only to be sought in the means of controlling its EFFECTS.

If a faction consists of less than a majority, relief is supplied by the republican principle, which enables the majority to defeat its sinister views by regular vote. It may clog the administration, it may convulse the society; but it will be unable to execute and mask its violence under the forms of the Constitution. When a majority is included in a faction, the form of popular government, on the other hand, enables it to sacrifice to its ruling passion or interest both the public good and the rights of other citizens. To secure the public good and private rights against the danger of such a faction, and at the same time to preserve the spirit and the form of popular government, is then the great object to which our inquiries are directed. Let me add that it is the great desideratum by which this form of government can be rescued from the opprobrium under which it has so long labored, and be recommended to the esteem and adoption of mankind.

By what means is this object attainable? Evidently by one of two only. Either the existence of the same passion or interest in a majority at the same time must be prevented, or the majority, having such coexistent passion or interest, must be rendered, by their number and local situation, unable to concert and carry into effect schemes of oppression. If the impulse and the opportunity be suffered to coincide, we well know that neither moral nor religious motives can be relied on as an adequate control. They are not found to be such on the injustice and violence of individuals, and lose their efficacy in proportion to the number combined together, that is, in proportion as their efficacy becomes needful.

From this view of the subject it may be concluded that a pure democracy, by which I mean a society consisting of a small number of citizens, who assemble and administer the government in person, can admit of no cure for the mischiefs of faction. A common passion or interest will, in almost every case, be felt by a majority of the whole; a communication and concert result from the form of government itself; and there is nothing to check the inducements to sacrifice the weaker party or an obnoxious individual. [...]

A republic, by which I mean a government in which the scheme of representation takes place, opens a different prospect, and promises the cure for which we are seeking. Let us examine the points in which it varies from pure democracy, and we shall comprehend both the nature of the cure and the efficacy which it must derive from the Union.

The two great points of difference between a democracy and a republic are: first, the delegation of the government, in the latter, to a small number of citizens elected by the rest; secondly, the greater number of citizens, and greater sphere of country, over which the latter may be extended.

The effect of the first difference is, on the one hand, to refine and enlarge the public views, by passing them through the medium of a chosen body of citizens, whose wisdom may best discern the true interest of their country, and whose patriotism and love of justice will be least likely to sacrifice it to temporary or partial considerations. Under such a regulation, it may well happen that the public voice, pronounced by the representatives of the people, will be more consonant to the public good than if pronounced by the people themselves, convened for the purpose. On the other hand, the effect may be inverted. Men of factious tempers, of local prejudices, or of sinister designs, may, by intrigue, by corruption, or by other means, first obtain the suffrages, and then betray the interests, of the people. [...]

The other point of difference is, the greater number of citizens and extent of territory which may be brought within the compass of republican than of democratic government; and it is this circumstance principally which renders factious combinations less to be dreaded in the former than in the latter. The smaller the society, the fewer probably will be the distinct parties and interests composing it; the fewer the distinct parties and interests, the more frequently will a majority be found of the same party; and the smaller the number of individuals composing a majority, and the smaller the compass within which they are placed, the more easily will they concert and execute their plans of oppression. Extend the sphere, and you take in a greater variety of parties and interests; you make it less probable that a majority of the whole will have a common motive to invade the rights of other citizens; or if such a common motive exists, it will be more difficult for all who feel it to discover their own strength, and to act in unison with each other. [...]

Hence, it clearly appears, that the same advantage which a republic has over a democracy, in controlling the effects of faction, is enjoyed by a large over a small republic, – is enjoyed by the Union over the States composing it. Does the advantage consist in the substitution of representatives whose enlightened views and virtuous sentiments render them superior to local prejudices and schemes of injustice? It will not be denied that the representation of the Union will be most likely to possess these requisite endowments. Does it consist in the greater security afforded by a greater variety of parties, against the event of any one party being able to outnumber and oppress the rest? In an equal degree does the increased variety of parties comprised within the Union, increase this security. Does it, in fine, consist in the greater obstacles opposed to the concert and accomplishment of the secret wishes of an unjust and interested majority? Here, again, the extent of the Union gives it the most palpable advantage.

The influence of factious leaders may kindle a flame within their particular States, but will be unable to spread a general conflagration through the other States. A religious sect may degenerate into a political faction in a part of the Confederacy; but the variety of sects dispersed over the entire face of it must secure the national councils against any danger from that source. A rage for paper money, for an abolition of debts, for an equal division of property, or for any other improper or wicked project, will be less apt to pervade the whole body of the Union than a particular member of it; in the same proportion as such a malady is more likely to taint a particular county or district, than an entire State.

In the extent and proper structure of the Union, therefore, we behold a republican remedy for the diseases most incident to republican government. And according to the degree of pleasure and pride we feel in being republicans, ought to be our zeal in cherishing the spirit and supporting the character of Federalists.

Federalist No. 15 (Alexander Hamilton)

To the People of the State of New York:

[. . .] It is true, as has been before observed that facts, too stubborn to be resisted, have produced a species of general assent to the abstract proposition that there exist material defects in our national system; but the usefulness of the concession, on the part of the old adversaries of federal measures, is destroyed by a strenuous opposition to a remedy, upon the only principles that can give it a chance of success. While they admit that the government of the United States is destitute of energy, they contend against conferring upon it those powers which are requisite to supply that energy. They seem still to aim at things repugnant and irreconcilable; at an augmentation of federal authority, without a diminution of State authority; at sovereignty in the Union, and complete independence in the members. They still, in fine, seem to cherish with blind devotion the political monster of an *imperium in imperio*. This renders a full display of the principal defects of the Confederation necessary, in order to show that the evils we experience do not proceed from minute or partial imperfections, but from fundamental errors in the structure of the building, which cannot be amended otherwise than by an alteration in the first principles and main pillars of the fabric.

The great and radical vice in the construction of the existing Confederation is in the principle of LEGISLATION for STATES or GOVERNMENTS, in their CORPORATE or COLLECTIVE CAPACITIES, and as contradistinguished from the INDIVIDUALS of which they consist. Though this principle does not run through all the powers delegated to the Union, yet it pervades and governs those on which the efficacy of the rest depends. Except as to the rule of appointment, the

United States has an indefinite discretion to make requisitions for men and money; but they have no authority to raise either, by regulations extending to the individual citizens of America. The consequence of this is, that though in theory their resolutions concerning those objects are laws, constitutionally binding on the members of the Union, yet in practice they are mere recommendations which the States observe or disregard at their option. [. . .]

There is nothing absurd or impracticable in the idea of a league or alliance between independent nations for certain defined purposes precisely stated in a treaty regulating all the details of time, place, circumstance, and quantity; leaving nothing to future discretion; and depending for its execution on the good faith of the parties. Compacts of this kind exist among all civilized nations, subject to the usual vicissitudes of peace and war, of observance and non-observance, as the interests or passions of the contracting powers dictate. In the early part of the present century there was an epidemical rage in Europe for this species of compacts, from which the politicians of the times fondly hoped for benefits which were never realized. With a view to establishing the equilibrium of power and the peace of that part of the world, all the resources of negotiation were exhausted, and triple and quadruple alliances were formed; but they were scarcely formed before they were broken, giving an instructive but afflicting lesson to mankind, how little dependence is to be placed on treaties which have no other sanction than the obligations of good faith, and which oppose general considerations of peace and justice to the impulse of any immediate interest or passion.

If the particular States in this country are disposed to stand in a similar relation to each other, and to drop the project of a general DISCRETIONARY SUPERINTENDENCE, the scheme would indeed be pernicious, and would entail upon us all the mischiefs which have been enumerated under the first head; but it would have the merit of being, at least, consistent and practicable. Abandoning all views towards a confederate government, this would bring us to a simple alliance offensive and defensive; and would place us in a situation to be alternate friends and enemies of each other, as our mutual jealousies and rivalships, nourished by the intrigues of foreign nations, should prescribe to us.

But if we are unwilling to be placed in this perilous situation; if we still will adhere to the design of a national government, or, which is the same thing, of a superintending power, under the direction of a common council, we must resolve to incorporate into our plan those ingredients which may be considered as forming the characteristic difference between a league and a government; we must extend the authority of the Union to the persons of the citizens, – the only proper objects of government.

Government implies the power of making laws. It is essential to the idea of a law, that it be attended with a sanction; or, in other words, a penalty or punishment for disobedience. If there be no penalty annexed to disobedience, the resolutions or commands which pretend to be laws will, in fact, amount to nothing more than advice or recommendation. This penalty, whatever it may be, can only be inflicted in two ways: by the agency of the courts and ministers of justice, or by military force; by the COERCION of the magistracy, or by the COERCION of arms. The first kind can evidently apply only to men; the last kind must of necessity, be employed against bodies politic, or communities, or States. It is evident that there is no process of a court by which the observance of the laws can, in the last resort, be enforced. Sentences may be denounced against them for violations of their duty; but these sentences can only be carried into execution by the sword. In an association where the general authority is confined to the collective bodies of the communities, that compose it, every breach of the laws must involve a state of war; and military execution must become the only instrument of civil obedience. Such a state of things can certainly not deserve the name of government, nor would any prudent man choose to commit his happiness to it. [...]

If, therefore, the measures of the Confederacy cannot be executed without the intervention of the particular administrations, there will be little prospect of their being executed at all. The rulers of the respective members, whether they have a constitutional right to do it or not, will undertake to judge of the propriety of the measures themselves. They will consider the conformity of the thing proposed or required to their immediate interests or aims; the momentary conveniences or inconveniences that would attend its adoption. All this will be done; and in a spirit of interested and suspicious scrutiny, without that knowledge of national circumstances and reasons of state, which is essential to a right judgment, and with that strong predilection in favor of local objects, which can hardly fail to mislead the decision. The same process must be repeated in every member of which the body is constituted; and the execution of the plans, framed by the councils of the whole, will always fluctuate on the discretion of the ill-informed and prejudiced opinion of every part. Those who have been conversant in the proceedings of popular assemblies; who have seen how difficult it often is, where there is no exterior pressure of circumstances, to bring them to harmonious resolutions on important points, will readily conceive how impossible it must be to induce a number of such assemblies, deliberating at a distance from each other, at different times, and under different impressions, long to co-operate in the same views and pursuits.

In our case, the concurrence of thirteen distinct sovereign wills is requisite, under the Confederation, to the complete execution of every important measure that proceeds from the Union. It has happened as was to have been foreseen. The measures of the Union have not been executed; the delinquencies of the States have, step by step, matured themselves to an extreme, which has, at length, arrested all the wheels of the national government, and brought them to an awful stand. Congress at this time scarcely possess the means of keeping up the forms of administration, till the States can have time to agree upon a more substantial substitute for the present shadow of a federal government. [...] Each State, yielding to the persuasive voice of immediate interest or convenience, has successively withdrawn its support, till the frail and tottering edifice seems ready to fall upon our heads, and to crush us beneath its ruins.

PUBLIUS.

Federalist No. 39 (James Madison)

To the People of the State of New York:

[. . .] The first question that offers itself is, whether the general form and aspect of the government be strictly republican. It is evident that no other form would be reconcilable with the genius of the people of America; with the fundamental principles of the Revolution; or with that honorable determination which animates every votary of freedom, to rest all our political experiments on the capacity of mankind for self-government. If the plan of the convention, therefore, be found to depart from the republican character, its advocates must abandon it as no longer defensible.

What, then, are the distinctive characters of the republican form? [. . .] If we resort for a criterion to the different principles on which different forms of government are established, we may define a republic to be, or at least may bestow that name on, a government which derives all its powers directly or indirectly from the great body of the people, and is administered by persons holding their offices during pleasure, for a limited period, or during good behavior. It is ESSENTIAL to such a government that it be derived from the great body of the society, not from an inconsiderable proportion, or a favored class of it; otherwise a handful of tyrannical nobles, exercising their oppressions by a delegation of their powers, might aspire to the rank of republicans, and claim for their government the honorable title of republic. It is SUFFICIENT for such a government that the persons administering it be appointed, either directly or indirectly, by the people; and that they hold their appointments by either of the tenures just specified; otherwise every government in the United States, as well as every other popular government that has been or can be well organized or well executed, would be degraded from the republican character. [. . .]

On comparing the Constitution planned by the convention with the standard here fixed, we perceive at once that it is, in the most rigid sense, conformable to it. The House of Representatives, like that of one branch at least of all the State legislatures, is elected immediately by the great body of the people. The Senate, like the present Congress, and the Senate of Maryland, derives its appointment indirectly from the people. The President is indirectly derived from the choice of the people, according to the example in most of the States. Even the judges, with all other officers of the Union, will, as in the several States, be the choice, though a remote choice, of the people themselves, the duration of the appointments is equally conformable to the republican standard, and to the model of State constitutions. The House of Representatives is periodically elective, as in all the States; and for the period of two years, as in the State of South Carolina. The Senate is elective, for the period of six years; which is but one year more than the period of the Senate of Maryland, and but two more than that of the Senates of New York and Virginia. The President is to continue in office for the period of four years; [. . .]. The President of the United States is impeachable at any time during his continuance in office. The tenure by which the judges are to hold their places, is, as it unquestionably ought to be, that of good behavior. The tenure of the ministerial offices generally, will be a subject of legal regulation, conformably to the reason of the case and the example of the State constitutions.

Could any further proof be required of the republican complexion of this system, the most decisive one might be found in its absolute prohibition of titles of nobility, both under the federal and the State governments; and in its express guaranty of the republican form to each of the latter.

"But it was not sufficient," say the adversaries of the proposed Constitution, "for the convention to adhere to the republican form. They ought, with equal care, to have preserved the FEDERAL form, which regards the Union as a CONFEDERACY of sovereign states; instead of which, they have framed a NATIONAL government, which regards the Union as a CONSOLIDATION of the States." And it is asked by what authority this bold and radical innovation was undertaken? The handle which has been made of this objection requires that it should be examined with some precision.

[...] In order to ascertain the real character of the government, it may be considered in relation to the foundation on which it is to be established; to the sources from which its ordinary powers are to be drawn; to the operation of those powers; to the extent of them; and to the authority by which future changes in the government are to be introduced.

On examining the first relation, it appears, on one hand, that the Constitution is to be founded on the assent and ratification of the people of America, given by deputies elected for the special purpose; but, on the other, that this assent and ratification is to be given by the people, not as individuals composing one entire nation, but as composing the distinct and independent States to which they respectively belong. It is to be the assent and ratification of the several States, derived from the supreme authority in each State, the authority of the people themselves. The act, therefore, establishing the Constitution, will not be a NATIONAL, but a FEDERAL act.

That it will be a federal and not a national act, as these terms are understood by the objectors; the act of the people, as forming so many independent States, not as forming one aggregate nation, is obvious from this single consideration, that it is to result neither from the decision of a MAJORITY of the people of the Union, nor from that of a MAJORITY of the States. It must result from the UNANIMOUS assent of the several States that are parties to it, differing no otherwise from their ordinary assent than in its being expressed, not by the legislative authority, but by that of the people themselves. Were the people regarded in this transaction as forming one nation, the will of the majority of the whole people of the United States would bind the minority, in the same manner as the majority in each State must bind the minority; and the will of the majority must be determined either by a comparison of the individual votes, or by considering the will of the majority of the States as evidence of the will of a majority of the people of the United States. Neither of these rules have been adopted. Each State, in ratifying the Constitution, is considered as a sovereign body, independent of all others, and only to be bound by its own voluntary act. In this relation, then, the new Constitution will, if established, be a FEDERAL, and not a NATIONAL constitution.

The next relation is, to the sources from which the ordinary powers of government are to be derived. The House of Representatives will derive its powers from the people of America; and the people will be represented in the same proportion, and on the same principle, as they are in the legislature of a particular State. So far the government is NATIONAL, not FEDERAL. The Senate, on the other hand, will derive its powers from the States, as political and coequal societies; and these will be represented on the principle of equality in the Senate, as they now are in the existing Congress. So far the government is FEDERAL, not NATIONAL. The executive power will be derived from a very compound source. The immediate election of the President is to be made by the States in their political characters. The votes allotted to them are in a compound ratio, which considers them partly as distinct and coequal societies, partly as unequal members of the same society. The eventual election, again, is to be made by that branch of the legislature which consists of the national representatives; but in this particular act they are to be thrown into the form of individual delegations, from so many distinct and coequal bodies politic. From this aspect of the government it appears to be of a mixed character, presenting at least as many FEDERAL as NATIONAL features.

The difference between a federal and national government, as it relates to the OPERATION OF THE GOVERNMENT, is supposed to consist in this, that in the former the powers operate on the political bodies composing the Confederacy, in their political capacities; in the latter, on the individual citizens composing the nation, in their individual capacities. On trying the Constitution by this criterion, it falls under the NATIONAL, not the FEDERAL character; though perhaps not so completely as has been understood. In several cases, and particularly in the trial of controversies to which States may be parties, they must be viewed and proceeded against in their collective and political capacities only. So far the national countenance of the government on this side seems to be disfigured by a few federal features. But this blemish is perhaps unavoidable in any plan; and the operation of the government on the people, in their individual capacities, in its ordinary and most essential proceedings, may, on the whole, designate it, in this relation, a NATIONAL government.

But if the government be national with regard to the OPERATION of its powers, it changes its aspect again when we contemplate it in relation to the EXTENT of its powers. The idea of a national government involves in it, not only an authority over the individual citizens, but an indefinite supremacy over all persons and things, so far as they are objects of lawful government. Among a people consolidated into one nation, this supremacy is completely vested in the national legislature. Among communities united for particular purposes, it is vested partly in the general and partly in the municipal legislatures. In the former case, all local authorities are subordinate to the supreme; and may be controlled, directed, or abolished by it at pleasure. In the latter, the local or municipal authorities form distinct and independent portions of the supremacy, no more subject, within their respective spheres, to the general authority, than the general authority is subject to them, within its own sphere. In this relation, then, the proposed government cannot be deemed a NATIONAL one;

since its jurisdiction extends to certain enumerated objects only, and leaves to the several States a residuary and inviolable sovereignty over all other objects. [. . .]

If we try the Constitution by its last relation to the authority by which amendments are to be made, we find it neither wholly NATIONAL nor wholly FEDERAL. Were it wholly national, the supreme and ultimate authority would reside in the MAJORITY of the people of the Union; and this authority would be competent at all times, like that of a majority of every national society, to alter or abolish its established government. Were it wholly federal, on the other hand, the concurrence of each State in the Union would be essential to every alteration that would be binding on all. The mode provided by the plan of the convention is not founded on either of these principles. In requiring more than a majority, and principles. In requiring more than a majority, and particularly in computing the proportion by STATES, not by CITIZENS, it departs from the NATIONAL and advances towards the FEDERAL character; in rendering the concurrence of less than the whole number of States sufficient, it loses again the FEDERAL and partakes of the NATIONAL character.

The proposed Constitution, therefore, is, in strictness, neither a national nor a federal Constitution, but a composition of both. In its foundation it is federal, not national; in the sources from which the ordinary powers of the government are drawn, it is partly federal and partly national; in the operation of these powers, it is national, not federal; in the extent of them, again, it is federal, not national; and, finally, in the authoritative mode of introducing amendments, it is neither wholly federal nor wholly national.

PUBLIUS.

Federalist No. 44 (James Madison)

To the People of the State of New York:

[. . .] The SIXTH and last class [of provisions in favor of the federal authority] consists of the several powers and provisions by which efficacy is given to all the rest.

1   Of these the first is, the "power [of Congress] to make all laws which shall be necessary and proper for carrying into execution the foregoing powers, and all other powers vested by this Constitution in the government of the United States, or in any department or officer thereof."

Few parts of the Constitution have been assailed with more intemperance than this; yet on a fair investigation of it, no part can appear more completely invulnerable. Without the SUBSTANCE of this power, the whole Constitution would be a dead letter. [. . .]

If it be asked what is to be the consequence, in case the Congress shall misconstrue this part of the Constitution, and exercise powers not warranted by its true meaning, I answer, the same as if they should misconstrue or enlarge any other power vested in them; as if the general power had been reduced to particulars, and any one of these were to be violated; the same, in short, as if the State legislatures should violate the irrespective constitutional authorities. In the first instance, the success of the usurpation will depend on the executive and judiciary departments, which are to expound and give effect to the legislative acts; and in the last resort a remedy must be obtained from the people who can, by the election of more faithful representatives, annul the acts of the usurpers. The truth is, that this ultimate redress may be more confided in against unconstitutional acts of the federal than of the State legislatures, for this plain reason, that as every such act of the former will be an invasion of the rights of the latter, these will be ever ready to mark the innovation, to sound the alarm to the people, and to exert their local influence in effecting a change of federal representatives. There being no such intermediate body between the State legislatures and the people interested in watching the conduct of the former, violations of the State constitutions are more likely to remain unnoticed and unredressed.

"This Constitution and the laws of the United States which shall be made in   2 pursuance thereof, and all treaties made, or which shall be made, under the authority of the United States, shall be the supreme law of the land, and the judges in every State shall be bound thereby, anything in the constitution or laws of any State to the contrary notwithstanding."

The indiscreet zeal of the adversaries to the Constitution has betrayed them into an attack on this part of it also, without which it would have been evidently and radically defective. To be fully sensible of this, we need only suppose for a moment that the supremacy of the State constitutions had been left complete by a saving clause in their favor.

In the first place, as these constitutions invest the State legislatures with absolute sovereignty, in all cases not excepted by the existing articles of Confederation, all the authorities contained in the proposed Constitution, so far as they exceed those enumerated in the Confederation, would have been annulled, and the new Congress would have been reduced to the same impotent condition with their predecessors.

In the next place, as the constitutions of some of the States do not even expressly and fully recognize the existing powers of the Confederacy, an express saving of the supremacy of the former would, in such States, have brought into question every power contained in the proposed Constitution.

In the third place, as the constitutions of the States differ much from each other, it might happen that a treaty or national law, of great and equal importance to the States, would interfere with some and not with other constitutions, and would consequently be valid in some of the States, at the same time that it would have no effect in others.

In fine, the world would have seen, for the first time, a system of government founded on an inversion of the fundamental principles of all government; it would have seen the authority of the whole society every where subordinate to the authority of the parts; it would have seen a monster, in which the head was under the direction of the members.

"The Senators and Representatives, and the members of the several State legisla-   3 tures, and all executive and judicial officers, both of the United States and the several States, shall be bound by oath or affirmation to support this Constitution."

It has been asked why it was thought necessary, that the State magistracy should be bound to support the federal Constitution, and unnecessary that a like oath should be imposed on the officers of the United States, in favor of the State constitutions.

Several reasons might be assigned for the distinction. I content myself with one, which is obvious and conclusive. The members of the federal government will have no agency in carrying the State constitutions into effect. The members and officers of the State governments, on the contrary, will have an essential agency in giving effect to the federal Constitution. The election of the President and Senate will depend, in all cases, on the legislatures of the several States. And the election of the House of Representatives will equally depend on the same authority in the first instance; and will, probably, forever be conducted by the officers, and according to the laws, of the States. [...]
PUBLIUS.

Federalist No. 51 (James Madison)

To the People of the State of New York:

TO WHAT expedient, then, shall we finally resort, for maintaining in practice the necessary partition of power among the several departments, as laid down in the Constitution? The only answer that can be given is, that as all these exterior provisions are found to be inadequate, the defect must be supplied, by so contriving the interior structure of the government as that its several constituent parts may, by their mutual relations, be the means of keeping each other in their proper places. Without presuming to undertake a full development of this important idea, I will hazard a few general observations, which may perhaps place it in a clearer light, and enable us to form a more correct judgment of the principles and structure of the government planned by the convention.

In order to lay a due foundation for that separate and distinct exercise of the different powers of government, which to a certain extent is admitted on all hands to be essential to the preservation of liberty, it is evident that each department should have a will of its own; and consequently should be so constituted that the members of each should have as little agency as possible in the appointment of the members of the others. Were this principle rigorously adhered to, it would require that all the appointments for the supreme executive, legislative, and judiciary magistracies should be drawn from the same fountain of authority, the people, through channels having no communication whatever with one another. Perhaps such a plan of constructing the several departments would be less difficult in practice than it may in contemplation appear. Some difficulties, however, and some additional expense would attend the execution of it. Some deviations, therefore, from the principle must be admitted. [...]

It is equally evident, that the members of each department should be as little dependent as possible on those of the others, for the emoluments annexed to their offices. Were the executive magistrate, or the judges, not independent of the legislature in this particular, their independence in every other would be merely nominal.

But the great security against a gradual concentration of the several powers in the same department, consists in giving to those who administer each department the necessary constitutional means and personal motives to resist encroachments of the others. The provision for defense must in this, as in all other cases, be made commensurate to the danger of attack. Ambition must be made to counteract ambition. The interest of the man must be connected with the constitutional rights of the place. It may be a reflection on human nature, that such devices should be necessary to control the abuses of government. But what is government itself, but the greatest of all reflections on human nature? If men were angels, no government would be necessary. If angels were to govern men, neither external nor internal controls on government would be necessary. In framing a government which is to be administered by men over men, the great difficulty lies in this: you must first enable the government to control the governed; and in the next place oblige it to control itself. A dependence on the people is, no doubt, the primary control on the government; but experience has taught mankind the necessity of auxiliary precautions. [...]

But it is not possible to give to each department an equal power of self-defense. In republican government, the legislative authority necessarily predominates. The remedy for this inconveniency is to divide the legislature into different branches; and to render them, by different modes of election and different principles of action, as little connected with each other as the nature of their common functions and their common dependence on the society will admit. It may even be necessary to guard against dangerous encroachments by still further precautions. As the weight of the legislative authority requires that it should be thus divided, the weakness of the executive may require, on the other hand, that it should be fortified. An absolute negative on the legislature appears, at first view, to be the natural defense with which the executive magistrate should be armed. But perhaps it would be neither altogether safe nor alone sufficient. On ordinary occasions it might not be exerted with the requisite firmness, and on extraordinary occasions it might be perfidiously abused. May not this defect of an absolute negative be supplied by some qualified connection between this weaker department and the weaker branch of the stronger department, by which the latter may be led to support the constitutional rights of the former, without being too much detached from the rights of its own department? [...]

There are, moreover, two considerations particularly applicable to the federal system of America, which place that system in a very interesting point of view. *First.* In a single republic, all the power surrendered by the people is submitted to the administration of a single government; and the usurpations are guarded against by a division of the government into distinct and separate departments. In the compound republic of America, the power surrendered by the people is first divided between two distinct governments, and then the portion allotted to each subdivided among distinct and separate departments. Hence a double security arises to the rights of the people. The different governments will control each other, at the same time that each will be controlled by itself.

Second. It is of great importance in a republic not only to guard the society against the oppression of its rulers, but to guard one part of the society against the injustice of the other part. Different interests necessarily exist in different classes of citizens. If a majority be united by a common interest, the rights of the minority will be insecure. There are but two methods of providing against this evil: the one by creating a will in the community independent of the majority that is, of the society itself; the other, by comprehending in the society so many separate descriptions of citizens as will render an unjust combination of a majority of the whole very improbable, if not impracticable. The first method prevails in all governments possessing an hereditary or self-appointed authority. This, at best, is but a precarious security; because a power independent of the society may as well espouse the unjust views of the major, as the rightful interests of the minor party, and may possibly be turned against both parties. The second method will be exemplified in the federal republic of the United States. Whilst all authority in it will be derived from and dependent on the society, the society itself will be broken into so many parts, interests, and classes of citizens, that the rights of individuals, or of the minority, will be in little danger from interested combinations of the majority. [. . .]

ANTIFEDERALIST RESPONSES

Centinel *Letter I* (published in the *New York Journal*, October 5, 1787)

To the Freemen of Pennsylvania.

Friends, Countrymen and Fellow Citizens,

[. . .] The late convention have submitted to your consideration a plan of a new federal government – The subject is highly interesting to your future welfare – Whether it be calculated to promote the great ends of civil society, viz. the happiness and prosperity of the community; it behoves you well to consider, uninfluenced by the authority of names. Instead of that frenzy of enthusiasm, that has actuated the citizens of Philadelphia, in their approbation of the proposed plan, before it was possible that it could be the result of a rational investigation into its principles; it ought to be dispassionately and deliberately examined, and its own intrinsic merit the only criterion of your patronage. If ever free and unbiased discussion was proper or necessary, it is on such an occasion. – All the blessings of liberty and the dearest privileges of freemen, are now at stake and dependent on your present conduct. Those who are competent to the task of developing the principles of government, ought to be encouraged to come forward, and thereby the better enable the people to make a proper judgment; for the science of government is so abstruse, that few are able to judge for themselves: without such assistance the people are too apt to yield an implicit assent to the opinions of those characters, whose abilities are held in the highest esteem, and to those in whose integrity and patriotism they can confide: not considering that the love of domination is generally in proportion to talents, abilities, and superior acquire-ments; and that the men of the greatest purity of intention may be made instru-ments of despotism in the hands of the artful and designing. If it were not for the stability and attachment which time and habit gives to forms of government it would be in the power of the enlightened and aspiring few, if they should combine, at any time to destroy the best establishments, and even make the people the instruments of their own subjugation.

The late revolution having effaced in a great measure all former habits, and the present institutions are so recent, that there exists not that great reluctance to innovation, so remarkable in old communities, and which accords with reason, for the most comprehensive mind cannot foresee the full operation of material changes on civil polity; it is the genius of the common law to resist innovation.

The wealthy and ambitious, who in every community think they have a right to lord it over their fellow creatures, have availed themselves, very successfully, of this favorable disposition; for the people thus unsettled in their sentiments, have been prepared to accede to any extreme of government; all the distresses and difficulties they experience, proceeding from various causes, have been ascribed to the impotency of the present confederation, and thence they have been led to expect full relief from the adoption of the proposed system of government, and in the other event, immediately ruin and annihilation as a nation. [. . .]

To put the omnipotency of Congress over the state government and judicatories out of all doubt, the 6th article ordains that "this constitution and the laws of the United States which shall be made in pursuance thereof, and all treaties made, or which shall be made under the authority of the United States, shall be the supreme law of the land, and the judges in every state shall be bound thereby, any thing in the constitution or laws of any state to the contrary notwithstanding."

By these sections the all-prevailing power of taxation, and such extensive legislative and judicial powers are vested in the general government, as must in their operation, necessarily absorb the state legislatures and judicatories; and that such was in the contemplation of the framers of it, will appear from the provision made for such event, in another part of it; (but that, fearful of alarming the people by so great an innovation, they have suffered the forms of the separate governments to remain, as a blind.) By sect. 4th of the 1st article, "the times, places and manner of holding elections for senators and representatives, shall be prescribed in each state by the legislature thereof; but the Congress may at any time, by law, make or alter such regulations, except as to the place of chusing senators." The plain construction of which is, that when the state legislatures drop out of sight, from the necessary operation [of] this government, then Congress are to provide for the election and appointment of representatives and senators.

If the foregoing be a just comment – if the United States are to be melted down into one empire, it becomes you to consider, whether such a government, however constructed, would be eligible in so extended a territory; and whether it would be practicable, consistent with freedom? It is the opinion of the greatest writers, that a very extensive country cannot be governed on democratical principles, on any other plan, than a confederation of a number of small republics, possessing all the powers of internal government, but united in the management of their foreign and general concerns.

It would not be difficult to prove, that any thing short of despotism, could not bind so great a country under one government; and that whatever plan you might, at the first setting out, establish, it would issue in a despotism.

If one general government could be instituted and maintained on principles of freedom, it would not be so competent to attend to the various local concerns and wants, of every particular district, as well as the peculiar governments, who are nearer the scene, and possessed of superior means of information, besides, if the business of the whole union is to be managed by one government, there would not be time. Do we not already see, that the inhabitants in a number of larger states, who are remote from the seat of government, are loudly complaining of the inconveniencies and disadvantages they are subjected to on this account, and that, to enjoy the comforts of local government, they are separating into smaller divisions. [. . .]

Thus we see, the house of representatives, are on the part of the people to balance the senate, who I suppose will be composed of the *better sort*, the *well born*, etc. The number of the representatives (being only one for every 30,000 inhabitants) appears to be too few, either to communicate the requisite information, of the wants, local circumstances and sentiments of so extensive an empire, or to prevent corruption and undue influence, in the exercise of such great powers; the term for which they are to be chosen, too long to preserve a due dependence and accountability to their constituents; and the mode and places of their election not sufficiently ascertained, for as Congress have the control over both, they may govern the choice, by ordering the *representatives* of a *whole* state, to be *elected* in *one* place, and that too may be the most *inconvenient*.

The senate, the great efficient body in this plan of government, is constituted on the most unequal principles. The smallest state in the union has equal weight with the great states of Virginia, Massachusetts, or Pennsylvania – The Senate, besides its legislative functions, has a very considerable share in the Executive; none of the principal appointments to office can be made without its advice and consent. The term and mode of its appointment, will lead to permanency; the members are chosen for six years, the mode is under the control of Congress, and as there is no exclusion by rotation, they may be continued for life, which, from their extensive means of influence, would follow of course. The President, who would be a mere pageant of state, unless he coincides with the views of the Senate, would either become the head of the aristocratic junto in that body, or its minion, besides, their influence being the most predominant, could the best secure his re-election to office. And from his power of granting pardons, he might skreen from punishment the most treasonable attempts on liberties of the people, when instigated by the Senate.

From this investigation into the organization of this government, it appears that it is devoid of all responsibility or accountability to the great body of the people, and that so far from being a regular balanced government, it would be in practice *a permanent* ARISTOCRACY. [. . .]

Federal Farmer *Observations Leading to Fair Examination of the System of Government Proposed by the Late Convention; And to Several Essential and Necessary Alterations in It. In a Number of Letters from the Federal Farmer to the Republic (1787)*

I.

October 8, 1787.

Dear Sir,

My letters to you last winter, on the subject of a well balanced national government for the United States, were the result of free enquiry; when I passed from that subject to enquiries relative to our commerce, revenues, past administration, etc. I anticipated the anxieties I feel, on carefully examining the plan of government proposed by the convention. It appears to be a plan retaining some federal features; but to be the first important step, and to aim strongly to one consolidated government of the United States. It leaves the powers of government, and the representation of the people, so unnaturally divided between the general and state governments, that the operations of our system must be very uncertain. [...] A federal government of some sort is necessary. We have suffered the present to languish; and whether the confederation was capable or not originally of answering any valuable purposes, it is now but of little importance. I will pass by the men, and states, who have been particularly instrumental in preparing the way for a change, and, perhaps, for governments not very favourable to the people at large. A constitution is now presented which we may reject, or which we may accept, with or without amendments; and to which point we ought to direct our exertions, is the question. To determine this question, with propriety, we must attentively examine the system itself, and the probable consequences of either step. This I shall endeavour to do, so far as I am able, with candor and fairness; and leave you to decide upon the propriety of my opinions, the weight of my reasons, and how far my conclusions are well drawn. [...] The present moment discovers a new face in our affairs. Our object has been all along, to reform our federal system, and to strengthen our governments – to establish peace, order and justice in the community – but a new object now presents. The plan of government now proposed is evidently calculated totally to change, in time, our condition as a people. Instead of being thirteen republics, under a federal head, it is clearly designed to make us one consolidated government. Of this, I think, I shall fully convince you, in my following letters on this subject. This consolidation of the states has been the object of several men in this country for some time past. Whether such a change can ever be effected in any manner; whether it can be effected without convulsions and civil wars; whether such a change will not totally destroy the liberties of this country – time only can determine.

To have a just idea of the government before us, and to shew that a consolidated one is the object in view, it is necessary not only to examine the plan, but also its history, and the politics of its particular friends.

The confederation was formed when great confidence was placed in the voluntary exertions of individuals, and of the respective states; and the framers of it, to guard against usurpation, so limited and checked the powers, that, in many respects, they are inadequate to the exigencies of the union. We find, therefore, members of congress urging alterations in the federal system almost as soon as it was adopted. It was early proposed to vest congress with powers to levy an impost, to regulate trade, etc. but such was known to be the caution of the states in parting with power, that the vestment, even of these, was proposed to be under several checks and limitations. [. . .]

The conduct of several legislatures, touching paper money, and tender laws, has prepared many honest men for changes in government, which otherwise they would not have thought of – when by the evils, on the one hand, and by the secret instigations of artful men, on the other, the minds of men were become sufficiently uneasy, a bold step was taken, which is usually followed by a revolution, or a civil war. A general convention for mere commercial purposes was moved for – the authors of this measure saw that the people's attention was turned solely to the amendment of the federal system; and that, had the idea of a total change been started, probably no state would have appointed members to the convention. The idea of destroying, ultimately, the state government, and forming one consolidated system, could not have been admitted – a convention, therefore, merely for vesting in congress power to regulate trade was proposed. This was pleasing to the commercial towns; and the landed people had little or no concern about it. September, 1786, a few men from the middle states met at Annapolis, and hastily proposed a convention to be held in May, 1787, for the purpose, generally, of amending the confederation – this was done before the delegates of Massachusetts, and of the other states arrived – still not a word was said about destroying the old constitution, and making a new one – The states still unsuspecting, and not aware that they were passing the Rubicon, appointed members to the new convention, for the sole and express purpose of revising and amending the confederation – and, probably, not one man in ten thousand in the United States, till within these ten or twelve days, had an idea that the old ship was to be destroyed, and he put to the alternative of embarking in the new ship presented, or of being left in danger of sinking – The States, I believe, universally supposed the convention would report alterations in the confederation, which would pass an examination in congress, and after being agreed to there, would be confirmed by all the legislatures, or be rejected. [. . .]

The plan proposed appears to be partly federal, but principally however, calculated ultimately to make the states one consolidated government.

The first interesting question, therefore suggested, is, how far the states can be consolidated into one entire government on free principles. [. . .]

Independant of the opinions of many great authors, that a free elective government cannot be extended over large territories, a few reflections must evince, that one government and general legislation alone, never can extend equal benefits to all parts of the United States: Different laws, customs, and opinions exist in the different states, which by a uniform system of laws would be unreasonably invaded. The United States contain about a million of square miles, and in half a century will, probably, contain ten millions of people; and from the center to the extremes is about 800 miles.

Before we do away the state governments, or adopt measures that will tend to abolish them, and to consolidate the states into one entire government, several principles should be considered and facts ascertained: – These, and my examination into the essential parts of the proposed plan, I shall pursue in my next.

II.

October 9, 1787.

Dear Sir,

The essential parts of a free and good government are a full and equal representation of the people in the legislature, and the jury trial of the vicinage in the administration of justice – a full and equal representation, is that which possesses the same interests, feelings, opinions, and views the people themselves would were they all assembled – a fair representation, therefore, should be so regulated, that every order of men in the community, according to the common course of elections, can have a share in it – in order to allow professional men, merchants, traders, farmers, mechanics, etc. to bring a just proportion of their best informed men respectively into the legislature, the representation must be considerably numerous – We have about 200 state senators in the United States, and a less number than that of federal representatives cannot, clearly, be a full representation of this people, in the affairs of internal taxation and police, were there but one legislature for the whole union. The representation cannot be equal, or the situation of the people proper for one government only – if the extreme parts of the society cannot be represented as fully as the central – It is apparently impracticable that this should be the case in this extensive country – it would be impossible to collect a representation of the parts of the country five, six, and seven hundred miles from the seat of government.

Under one general government alone, there could be but one judiciary, one supreme and a proper number of inferior courts. I think it would be totally impracticable in this case to preserve a due administration of justice, and the real benefits of the jury trial of the vicinage [. . .]. I am not for bringing justice so near to individuals as to afford them any temptation to engage in law suits; though I think it one of the greatest benefits in a good government, that each citizen should find a court of justice within a reasonable distance, perhaps, within a day's travel of his home; so that, without great inconveniences and enormous expences, he may have the advantages of his witnesses and jury – it would be impracticable to derive these advantages from one judiciary – the one supreme court at most could only set in the centre of the union, and move once a year into the centre of the eastern and southern extremes of it – and, in this case, each citizen, on an average, would travel 150 or 200 miles to find this court – that, however, inferior courts might be properly placed in the different counties, and districts of the union, the appellate jurisdiction would be intolerable and expensive.

If it were possible to consolidate the states, and preserve the features of a free government, still it is evident that the middle states, the parts of the union, about the seat of government, would enjoy great advantages, while the remote states would experience the many inconveniences of remote provinces. Wealth, offices, and the benefits of government would collect in the centre: and the extreme states and their principal towns, become much less important. [...]

There are certain unalienable and fundamental rights, which in forming the social compact, ought to be explicitly ascertained and fixed – a free and enlightened people, in forming this compact, will not resign all their rights to those who govern, and they will fix limits to their legislators and rulers [...]. These rights should be made the basis of every constitution: and if a people be so situated, or have such different opinions that they cannot agree in ascertaining and fixing them, it is a very strong argument against their attempting to form one entire society, to live under one system of laws only. – I confess, I never thought the people of these states differed essentially in these respects; they having derived all these rights from one common source, the British systems; and having in the formation of their state constitutions, discovered that their ideas relative to these rights are very similar. However, it is now said that the states differ so essentially in these respects, and even in the important article of the trial by jury, that when assembled in convention, they can agree to no words by which to establish that trial, or by which to ascertain and establish many other of these rights, as fundamental articles in the social compact. If so, we proceed to consolidate the states on no solid basis whatever. [...]

In examining the proposed constitution carefully, we must clearly perceive an unnatural separation of these powers from the substantial representation of the people. The state governments will exist, with all their governors, senators, representatives, officers and expences; in these will be nineteen-twentieths of the representatives of the people; they will have a near connection, and their members an immediate intercourse with the people; and the probability is, that the state governments will possess the confidence of the people, and be considered generally as their immediate guardians.

The general government will consist of a new species of executive, a small senate, and a very small house of representatives. As many citizens will be more than three hundred miles from the seat of this government as will be nearer to it, its judges and officers cannot be very numerous, without making our governments very expensive. Thus will stand the state and the general governments, should the constitution be adopted without any alterations in their organization; but as to powers, the general government will possess all essential ones, at least on paper, and those of the states a mere shadow of power. And therefore, unless the people shall make some great exertions to restore to the state governments their powers in matters of internal police; as the powers to lay and collect, exclusively, internal taxes, to govern the militia, and to hold the decisions of their own judicial courts upon their own laws final, the balance cannot possibly continue long; but the state governments must be annihilated, or continue to exist for no purpose. [...]

III.

October 10, 1787

[...] Not sanguine in my expectations of a good federal administration, and satisfied, as I am, of the impracticability of consolidating the states, and at the same time of preserving the rights of the people at large, I believe we ought still to leave some of those powers in the state governments, in which the people, in fact, will still be represented – to define some other powers proposed to be vested in the general government, more carefully, and to establish a few principles to secure a proper exercise of the powers given it. It is not my object to multiply objections, or to contend about inconsiderable powers or amendments; I wish the system adopted with a few alterations; but those, in my mind, are essential ones [...].

First. As to the organization – the house of representatives, the democrative branch, as it is called, is to consist of 65 members: that is, about one representative for fifty thousand inhabitants, to be chosen biennially [...]. I have no idea that the interests, feelings, and opinions of three or four millions of people, especially touching internal taxation, can be collected in such a house. [...] The branches of the legislature are essential parts of the fundamental compact, and ought to be so fixed by the people, that the legislature cannot alter itself by modifying the elections of its own members. This, by a part of Art. 1. Sect. 4. the general legislature may do, it may evidently so regulate elections as to secure the choice of any particular description of men. [...] This is a very general and unguarded clause, and many evils may flow from that part which authorises the congress to regulate elections – Were it omitted, the regulations of elections would be solely in the respective states, where the people are substantially represented; and where the elections ought to be regulated, otherwise to secure a representation from all parts of the community, in making the constitution, we ought to provide for dividing each state into a proper number of districts, and for confining the electors in each district to the choice of some men, who shall have a permanent interest and residence in it; and also for this essential object, that the representative elected shall have a majority of the votes of those electors who shall attend and give their votes.

In considering the practicability of having a full and equal representation of the people from all parts of the union, not only distances and different opinions, customs, and views, common in extensive tracts of country, are to be taken into view, but many differences peculiar to Eastern, Middle, and Southern states. These differences are not so perceivable among the members of congress, and men of general information in the states, as among the men who would properly form the democratic branch. The Eastern states are very democratic, and composed chiefly of moderate freeholders; they have but few rich men and no slaves; the Southern states are composed chiefly of rich planters and slaves; they have but few moderate freeholders, and the prevailing influence, in them, is generally a dissipated aristocracy: The Middle states partake partly of the Eastern, and partly of the Southern character. [...]

VII.

December 31, 1787

[...] I shall proceed to consider further my principal position, viz. that there is no substantial representation of the people provided for in a government, in which the most essential powers, even as to the internal police of the country, are proposed to be lodged; and to propose certain amendments as to the representative branch: 1st, That there ought to be an increase of the numbers of representatives: And, 2dly, That the elections of them ought to be better secured.

The representation is unsubstantial and ought to be increased. [...] I am in a field where doctors disagree; and as to genuine representation, though no feature in government can be more important, perhaps, no one has been less understood, and no one that has received so imperfect a consideration by political writers. [...]

Where the people, or their representatives, make the laws, it is probable they will generally be fitted to the national character and circumstances, unless the representation be partial, and the imperfect substitute of the people. However, the people may be electors, if the representation be so formed as to give one or more of the natural classes of men in the society an undue ascendency over the others, it is imperfect; the former will gradually become masters, and the latter slaves. It is the first of all among the political balances, to preserve in its proper station each of these classes. We talk of balances in the legislature, and among the departments of government; we ought to carry them to the body of the people. [...] Each order must have a share in the business of legislation actually and efficiently. It is deceiving a people to tell them they are electors, and can chuse their legislators, if they cannot, in the nature of things, chuse men from among themselves, and genuinely like themselves. [...]

[A] small representation can never be well informed as to the circumstances of the people, the members of it must be too far removed from the people, in general, to sympathize with them, and too few to communicate with them: a representation must be extremely imperfect where the representatives are not circumstanced to make the proper communications to their constituents, and where the constituents in turn cannot, with tolerable convenience, make known their wants, circumstances, and opinions, to their representatives; where there is but one representative to 30,000, or 40,000 inhabitants, it appears to me, he can only mix, and be acquainted with a few respectable characters among his constituents, even double the federal representation, and then there must be a very great distance between the representatives and the people in general represented. [...]

Could we get over all our difficulties respecting a balance of interests and party efforts, to raise some and oppress others, the want of sympathy, information and intercourse between the representatives and the people, an insuperable difficulty will still remain, I mean the constant liability of a small number of representatives to private combinations; the tyranny of the one, or the licentiousness of the multitude, are, in my mind, but small evils, compared with the factions of the few. It is a consideration well worth pursuing, how far this house of representatives will be liable to be formed into private juntos, how far influenced by expectations of appointments and offices, how far liable to be managed by the president and senate, and how far the people will have confidence in them. To obviate difficulties on this head, as well as objections to the representative branch, generally, several observations have been made – these I will now examine, and if they shall appear to be unfounded, the objections must stand unanswered.

Robert Yates *Essays of Brutus No. XI* (published in the *New York Journal*, January 31, 1788)

The nature and extent of the judicial power of the United States, proposed to be granted by this constitution, claims our particular attention.

Much has been said and written upon the subject of this new system on both sides, but I have not met with any writer, who has discussed the judicial powers with any degree of accuracy. And yet it is obvious, that we can form but very imperfect ideas of the manner in which this government will work, or the effect it will have in changing the internal police and mode of distributing justice at present subsisting in the respective states, without a thorough investigation of the powers of the judiciary and of the manner in which they will operate. This government is a complete system, not only for making, but for executing laws. And the courts of law, which will be constituted by it, are not only to decide upon the constitution and the laws made in pursuance of it, but by officers subordinate to them to execute all their decisions. The real effect of this system of government, will therefore be brought home to the feelings of the people, through the medium of the judicial power. It is, moreover, of great importance, to examine with care the nature and extent of the judicial power, because those who are to be vested with it, are to be placed in a situation altogether unprecedented in a free country. They are to be rendered totally independent, both of the people and the legislature, both with respect to their offices and salaries. [...]

This part of the plan is so modelled, as to authorise the courts, not only to carry into execution the powers expressly given, but where these are wanting or ambiguously expressed, to supply what is wanting by their own decisions.

That we may be enabled to form a just opinion on this subject, I shall, in considering it,

1st. Examine the nature and extent of the judicial powers – and
2d. Enquire, whether the courts who are to exercise them, are so constituted as to afford reasonable ground of confidence, that they will exercise them for the general good. [...]

In article 3d, sect. 2d, it is said, "The judicial power shall extend to all cases in law and equity arising under this constitution, the laws of the United States, and treaties made, or which shall be made, under their authority, &c."

The first article to which this power extends, is, all cases in law and equity arising under this constitution.

What latitude of construction this clause should receive, it is not easy to say. At first view, one would suppose, that it meant no more than this, that the courts under the general government should exercise, not only the powers of courts of law, but also that of courts of equity, in the manner in which those powers are usually exercised in the different states. But this cannot be the meaning, because the next clause authorises the courts to take cognizance of all cases in law and equity arising under the laws of the United States; this last article, I conceive, conveys as much power to the general judicial as any of the state courts possess.

The cases arising under the constitution must be different from those arising under the laws, or else the two clauses mean exactly the same thing.

The cases arising under the constitution must include such, as bring into question its meaning, and will require an explanation of the nature and extent of the powers of the different departments under it.

This article, therefore, vests the judicial with a power to resolve all questions that may arise on any case on the construction of the constitution, either in law or in equity.

1st   They are authorised to determine all questions that may arise upon the meaning of the constitution in law. This article vests the courts with authority to give the constitution a legal construction, or to explain it according to the rules laid down for construing a law. – These rules give a certain degree of latitude of explanation. According to this mode of construction, the courts are to give such meaning to the constitution as comports best with the common, and generally received acceptation of the words in which it is expressed, regarding their ordinary and popular use, rather than their grammatical propriety. Where words are dubious, they will be explained by the context. The end of the clause will be attended to, and the words will be understood, as having a view to it; and the words will not be so understood as to bear no meaning or a very absurd one.

2d   The judicial are not only to decide questions arising upon the meaning of the constitution in law, but also in equity.

By this they are empowered, to explain the constitution according to the reasoning spirit of it, without being confined to the words or letter.

They [the courts of law] will give the sense of every article of the constitution, that may from time to time come before them. And in their decisions they will not confine themselves to any fixed or established rules, but will determine, according to what appears to them, the reason and spirit of the constitution. The opinions of the supreme court, whatever they may be, will have the force of law; because there is no power provided in the constitution, that can correct their errors, or controul their adjudications. From this court there is no appeal. And I conceive the legislature themselves, cannot set aside a judgment of this court, because they are authorised by the constitution to decide in the last resort. [. . .]

The judicial power will operate to effect, in the most certain, but yet silent and imperceptible manner, what is evidently the tendency of the constitution: – I mean, an entire subversion of the legislative, executive and judicial powers of the individual states. Every adjudication of the supreme court, on any question that may arise upon the nature and extent of the general government, will affect the limits of the state jurisdiction. In proportion as the former enlarge the exercise of their powers, will that of the latter be restricted.

That the judicial power of the United States, will lean strongly in favour of the general government, and will give such an explanation to the constitution, as will favour an extension of its jurisdiction, is very evident from a variety of considerations.

1st   The constitution itself strongly countenances such a mode of construction. Most of the articles in this system, which convey powers of any considerable importance, are conceived in general and indefinite terms, which are either equivocal, ambiguous, or which require long definitions to unfold the extent of their meaning. [...]

Not only will the constitution justify the courts in inclining to this mode of explaining it, but they will be interested in using this latitude of interpretation. Every body of men invested with office are tenacious of power; they feel interested, and hence it has become a kind of maxim, to hand down their offices, with all its rights and privileges, unimpared to their successors; the same principle will influence them to extend their power, and increase their rights; this of itself will operate strongly upon the courts to give such a meaning to the constitution in all cases where it can possibly be done, as will enlarge the sphere of their own authority. [...]   2d

Because they will have precedent to plead, to justify them in it. It is well known, that the courts in England, have by their own authority, extended their jurisdiction far beyond the limits set them in their original institution, and by the laws of the land. [...]   3d

When the courts will have a precedent before them of a court which extended its jurisdiction in opposition to an act of the legislature, is it not to be expected that they will extend theirs, especially when there is nothing in the constitution expressly against it? and they are authorised to construe its meaning, and are not under any controul?

This power in the judicial, will enable them to mould the government, into almost any shape they please. – The manner in which this may be effected we will hereafter examine.

Brutus.

Patrick Henry *"We the People"* or *"We the States"?* (delivered in the Virginia Ratifying Convention, June 4, 1788, on the Preamble and the First Two Sections of the First Article of the Federal Constitution)[12]

Mr. Chairman,

The public mind, as well as my own, is extremely uneasy at the proposed change of government. Give me leave to form one of the number of those who wish to be thoroughly acquainted with the reasons of this perilous and uneasy situation, and why we are brought hither to decide on this great national question. I consider myself as the servant of the people of this commonwealth, as a sentinel over their rights, liberty, and happiness. I represent their feelings when I say that they are exceedingly uneasy at being brought from that state of full security, which they enjoyed, to the present delusive appearance of things. A year ago, the minds of our citizens were at perfect repose. Before the meeting of the late federal Convention at Philadelphia, a general peace and a universal tranquillity prevailed in this country; but, since that period, they are exceedingly uneasy and disquieted. When I wished for an

[12] From B. Bailyn (ed.), *The Debate on the Constitution, Part Two* (New York: Library of America, 1993), p. 596.

appointment to this Convention, my mind was extremely agitated for the situation of public affairs. I conceived the republic to be in extreme danger. If our situation be thus uneasy, whence has arisen this fearful jeopardy? It arises from this fatal system; it arises from a proposal to change our government – a proposal that goes to the utter annihilation of the most solemn engagements of the states – a proposal of establishing nine states into a confederacy, to the eventual exclusion of four states. It goes to the annihilation of those solemn treaties we have formed with foreign nations.

The present circumstances of France, the good offices rendered us by that kingdom, require our most faithful and most punctual adherence to our treaty with her. We are in alliance with the Spaniards, the Dutch, the Prussians; those treaties bound us as thirteen states confederated together. Yet here is a proposal to sever that confederacy. Is it possible that we shall abandon all our treaties and national engagements? And for what? I expected to hear the reasons for an event so unexpected to my mind and many others. Was our civil polity, or public justice, endangered or sapped? Was the real existence of the country threatened, or was this preceded by a mournful progression of events? This proposal of altering our federal government is of a most alarming nature! Make the best of this new government – say it is composed by any thing but inspiration – you ought to be extremely cautious, watchful, jealous of your liberty; for, instead of securing your rights, you may lose them forever. If a wrong step be now made, the republic may be lost forever. If this new government will not come up to the expectation of the people, and they shall be disappointed, their liberty will be lost, and tyranny must and will arise. I repeat it again, and I beg gentlemen to consider, that a wrong step, made now, will plunge us into misery, and our republic will be lost.

It will be necessary for this Convention to have a faithful historical detail of the facts that preceded the session of the federal Convention, and the reasons that actuated its members in proposing an entire alteration of government, and to demonstrate the dangers that awaited us. If they were of such awful magnitude as to warrant a proposal so extremely perilous as this, I must assert, that this Convention has an absolute right to a thorough discovery of every circumstance relative to this great event. And here I would make this inquiry of those worthy characters who composed a part of the late federal Convention. I am sure they were fully impressed with the necessity of forming a great consolidated government, instead of a confederation. That this is a consolidated government is demonstrably clear; and the danger of such a government is, to my mind, very striking.

I have the highest veneration for those gentlemen; but, sir, give me leave to demand, What right had they to say, "We, the people"? My political curiosity, exclusive of my anxious solicitude for the public welfare, leads me to ask, Who authorized them to speak the language of, "We, the people," instead of, "We, the states"? States are the characteristics and the soul of a confederation. If the states be not the agents of this compact, it must be one great, consolidated, national government, of the people of all the states. I have the highest respect for those gentlemen who formed the Convention, and, were some of them not here, I would express some testimonial of esteem for them. America had, on a former occasion, put the utmost confidence in them – a confidence which was well placed; and I am sure, sir, I would give up any thing to them; I would cheerfully confide in them as my representatives. But, sir, on this great occasion, I would demand the cause of their conduct. Even from that illustrious man who saved us by his valor [George Washington], I would have a reason for his conduct: that liberty which he has given us by his valor, tells me to ask this reason; and sure I am, were he here, he would give us that reason. But there are other gentlemen here, who can give us this information.

The people gave them no power to use their name. That they exceeded their power is perfectly clear. It is not mere curiosity that actuates me: I wish to hear the real, actual, existing danger, which should lead us to take those steps, so dangerous in my conception. Disorders have arisen in other parts of America; but here, sir, no dangers, no insurrection or tumult have happened; every thing has been calm and tranquil. But, notwithstanding this, we are wandering on the great ocean of human affairs. I see no landmark to guide us. We are running we know not whither. Difference of opinion has gone to a degree of inflammatory resentment in different parts of the country, which has been occasioned by this perilous innovation. The federal Convention ought to have amended the old system; for this purpose they were solely delegated; the object of their mission extended to no other consideration. You must, therefore, forgive the solicitation of one unworthy member to know what danger could have arisen under the present Confederation, and what are the causes of this proposal to change our government.

Suggested Readings

Alexander Hamilton, James Madison, and John Jay, *The Federalist Papers*, especially Nos. 1, 9, 40, 47–9, 78, 84 (1787).

Noah Webster, *An Examination into the Leading Principles of the Federal Constitution* (Philadelphia: Richard Hall, 1787).

James Madison, "Letter to Thomas Jefferson (October 24, 1787)" and Jefferson's response "Letter to James Madison (December 20, 1787)" in R. A. Rutland, C. F. Hobson, W. M. E. Rachal, and F. J. Teute (eds.), *The Papers of James Madison*, Vol. X: *27 May 1787–3 March 1788* (Chicago: University of Chicago Press, 1977), pp. 205–20, 335–9. Both letters are also available at https://founders.archives.gov/.

Robert Yates, "Essays of Brutus," esp. Essays I and V [1787], in H. J. Storing (ed.), *The Anti-Federalist: Writings by Opponents of the Constitution* (Chicago: University of Chicago Press, 1981), pp. 103–98.

"Address of the Minority of the Pennsylvania Convention" in Nathaniel Breading, Eleazer Oswald, et al., *The Address and Reasons of Dissent of the Minority of the Convention, of the State of Pennsylvania, to Their Constituents* (Philadelphia: Printed by E. Oswald, 1787).

Thomas Jefferson, "Letter to James Madison (September 6, 1789)" in C. F. Hobson and R. A. Rutland (eds.), *The Papers of James Madison*, Vol. XII: *2 March 1789–20 January 1790 and supplement 24 October 1775–24 January 1789* (Charlottesville: University Press of Virginia, 1979), pp. 382–8.

8 The Whole and the Parties

When the ratification of the Constitution became a *fait accompli*, the Antifederalists acknowledged its legitimacy rather quickly. Case in point, a confession the young John Quincy Adams made in his diary when he received news that the Constitution had been ratified the day prior: "I have not been pleased with this system, and many acquaintances have long since branded me with the name of an anti-Federalist. But I am now converted though not convinced. I think it is my duty to submit without murmuring against what is not to be helped."[1] Yet, acknowledging the Constitution was one thing; agreeing upon its proper interpretation was an entirely different matter.

Some, like **John Marshall**[2] or **Daniel Webster**,[3] saw the Constitution as a compact agreed upon by the *American people* to form a nation. Others, like **Andrew Jackson**,[4] were sure that it was a compact between *the peoples of different states*. Even Thomas Jefferson, who thought that Jackson was "one of the most unfit men I know [for the presidency]," because "he has had very little respect for laws and constitutions," agreed with him on this interpretation.[5] Many years after he famously claimed in his **First Inaugural Address**, "We are all Republicans, we are all Federalists," the same Jefferson praised John Taylor's book, *Construction Construed*, as "the most effectual retraction of our government to its original principles which has ever yet been sent by heaven to our aid."[6] Yet, in this "heavenly" book, Taylor asserted that "the federal is not a national government; it is a league between nations." According to him, each state was a nation, and "*the natural rights of nations* [...] *are more universally recognized than the rights of individual men.*"[7] No future secessionist could have interpreted the Constitution in terms more radical than these.

---

[1] C. F. Adams (ed.), *Diary of John Quincy Adams* (Boston: Little Brown, 1903), p. 94.

[2] John Marshall (1755–1835) was the fourth Chief Justice of the United States (1801–1835). In this capacity, he expanded the powers of the Supreme Court, among others upholding the principle of **judicial review**.

[3] Daniel Webster's (1782–1852) successive party affiliations capture the survival of the Federalists' principles under different party labels: Federalist, National Republican, and Whig, respectively.

[4] Andrew Jackson (1767–1845) became a national hero after his victory in the Battle of New Orleans (1815). A Republican, initially, Jackson became the leader of the Democratic Party.

[5] Quoted in D. S. Brown (2016), *Moderates: The Vital Center of American Politics, from the Founding to Today* (Chapel Hill: University of North Carolina Press), p. 94.

[6] Thomas Jefferson to Archibald Thweatt, January 19, 1821, in P. L. Ford (ed.), *The Writings of Thomas Jefferson*, Vol. X (New York: G. P. Putnam's Sons, 1899), p. 184.

[7] J. Taylor, *Construction Construed and Constitutions Vindicated* (Richmond: Shepherd and Pollard, 1820), pp. 234, 171.

As the main theorist of republicanism and state rights, **John Taylor** (1753–1824) argued bluntly that there is no such thing as the American people. "Common consent is necessary to constitute a people, and no such consent, expressly or implied, can be shewn, by which all the inhabitants of the United States have ever constituted themselves into *one* people. *This could not have been effected without destroying every people constituted within each state*, as *one political being called a people* cannot exist within another."[8] Since the state constitutions claimed the sovereignty of their peoples – a claim never contested by the federal Constitution, which contained no reference to sovereignty whatsoever – it followed that any talk about one American people was both illegal and absurd.

Such a position was in complete opposition to the Federalists' own understanding of the people and of the Constitution. As Alexander Hamilton argued in his defense of the **First National Bank**, sovereignty belonged not to the states, but to the United States. Thus, "it is unquestionably incident to *sovereign power* to erect corporations, and consequently to that of the United States." The issue boiled down to the correct interpretation of the "**necessary and proper clause**" (Chapter 7). Hamilton argued that the narrow way in which Jefferson interpreted the words "necessary" and "proper" was fundamentally wrong. "It is certain that neither the grammatical nor popular sense of the term requires that construction." Years later, during the debates surrounding the creation of the **Second National Bank**, Chief Justice (and staunch Federalist) John Marshall used arguments similar to Hamilton's in justifying the constitutionality of the Bank in *McCulloch v. Maryland*. The quarrel between what came to be known as **loose constructionism** of the Constitution (a more flexible interpretation of its meaning) and **strict constructionism** (a narrower interpretation) is enduring in American constitutional thought.[9]

For a while, the authority and the popular support enjoyed by **George Washington** was enough to keep the tensions between Hamilton's and Jefferson's camps in check.[10] However, this didn't mean that Washington was not fully aware of the two camps, nor that he, in line with the **classical republican** tradition, was not concerned about the emergence of parties.[11] In his **Farewell Address**, he made an appeal to both the affections and the interests of all Americans to reinforce their sense of belonging, as citizens, to the same American people ("by birth or by choice"). In an almost prophetic tone, he noticed that "[i]n contemplating the causes which may disturb our Union, it occurs as matter of serious concern that any ground should have been furnished for characterizing parties by geographical discriminations, Northern and Southern, Atlantic and Western." Such parties, he argued, "are likely, in the course of time and things, to become potent engines, by which cunning, ambitious, and unprincipled men will be enabled to *subvert the power of the people*."

---

[8] Taylor, *Construction Construed*, p. 47 (emphasis added).

[9] The two interpretations are sometimes labeled "liberal" and "conservative," respectively, but by now we are better equipped to see why these are misnomers.

[10] George Washington (1732–1799) was the first President of the United States under the new Constitution. Some scholars, who also count the eight yearly presidents under the Articles of the Confederation, claim that he was, in fact, the ninth president.

[11] Remember the republican argument against factions, either as a majority or as a minority, from Aristotle to Madison.

Following in Washington's footsteps, all subsequent presidents – from John Adams to Andrew Jackson – emphasized the need for unity and for overcoming the party spirit. Despite their different convictions, they all warned against "the spirit of party, the spirit of intrigue, the profligacy of corruption, and the pestilence of foreign influence, which is the angel of destruction to elective governments" (John Adams).

The reality, however, moved further and further away from the presidential rhetoric. Even though, until the end of the eighteenth century, elections were not contested under party labels, newspapers did openly assume partisanship. Appeals continued to be made to the common good instead of sectional interests, but the rhetoric grew increasingly vicious during this period. Each side accused the other of being "a party," driven by particular interests, while denying themselves that same label. The **first party system** emerged before the end of the century, opposing **Federalists** – supporters of a strong central government and a strong executive (like Hamilton) – to **Republicans** – advocates for state and individual rights (like Jefferson).

All economic and particular interests aside, what was at stake was the proper interpretation of popular sovereignty; in other words, of the people's two bodies. One party, the Federalists, favored the vision of a corporatist *American people*, ruled by an aristocracy of merit. The Republicans, on the other hand, promoted a more egalitarian view of *peoples*, apprehended mainly at state level. The **French Revolution** served as a catalyst for accelerating the differentiation between the two camps.[12] The people's two bodies began to grow apart.

For the Federalists, the **Reign of Terror** that followed the enthusiastic support of the French Revolution was proof of the dangers of egalitarian populism.[13] As **Fisher Ames** put it,[14] "with the democrats *the people is a sovereign who can do no wrong*, even when he respects and spares no existing right, and whose voice, however obtained or however counterfeited, bears all the sanctity and all the force of a living divinity." For the Republicans, on the other hand, the Federalists' "aristocratic" attitude was proof of those pro-monarchical and even tyrannical inclinations against which the French people had justly rebelled. Jefferson openly opposed what he saw as an attempt by the Federalists at "monarchising" the Constitution. The Republican rhetoric was centered, instead, on the archetypal "yeoman," the small farmer cultivating his piece of land, self-sufficient, preserver and defender of republican values, in contrast to the corrupted "aristocracy of paper money," merchants and bankers producing no "visible wealth."

In his **First Inaugural Address**, making an appeal to both Federalists and Republicans, Thomas Jefferson combined liberal and republican principles,

---

[12] The French Revolution started in 1789, but its end date is still disputed among scholars. Ironically, the anti-monarchical Revolution was precipitated by the French monarchy's expensive yet essential support of the American Revolution.

[13] The exact periodization of the Reign of Terror is still disputed, but tens of thousands were beheaded by guillotine, in public executions, in a matter of just a few years.

[14] Fisher Ames (1758–1808) was a Federalist renowned for his oratorical skills. He was elected in the First Congress of the United States by defeating the famous Antifederalist, Samuel Adams, in 1789 and served until 1797.

appealing to "this sacred principle, that though the will of the majority is in all cases to prevail, that will to be rightful must be reasonable; that the minority possess their equal rights." He also pledged to support "state governments in all their rights, as the most competent administrations," and claimed commerce to be the handmaid of agriculture. John Taylor took the praise of agriculture even further: "The capacity of agriculture for affording luxuries to the body, is not less conspicuous than its capacity for affording luxuries to the mind." No mention of slave labor was made.

As the second President of the United States, **John Adams** fell somewhere between these two increasingly distinct camps. Not Federalist enough for the hardcore Federalists like Hamilton, he was no Republican either. The passage of the **Alien and Sedition Acts** by the Federalist Congress,[15] signed into law by Adams in 1798, was for the Republicans the confirmation that their fear of a despotic government was justified. The subsequent presidential victory of Jefferson and of the Republican Party signaled the beginning of the end for the Federalists. The Republicans came to dominate the political scene for more than two decades with very little opposition. These were the decades of the **Louisiana Purchase** (1803), which basically doubled the territory of the United States for a mere 15 million dollars,[16] and of increasing electoral franchise. In the end, the opposition to the Republican Party came not from the outside, but from within.

Capitalizing on his military successes, **Andrew Jackson** ran for presidency in 1824, winning a plurality of the popular and electoral vote. Yet, since no candidate won the majority, the final election was made in Congress, where the House of Representatives elected **John Quincy Adams**. Accusing Congress of a "corrupt bargain," the supporters of Jackson broke away from the Republican Party, forming the **Democratic Party**. In 1828, Jackson defeated John Quincy Adams in a landslide victory, by championing "the common man" against the powerful money interests that supported the **Second National Bank**.

One has, however, to be cautious of such enthusiastic labels as "the **Age of the Common Man**." Despite the unstoppable extension of the electoral franchise, not all people were as lucky as white, native-born men in seeing their rights expanded throughout the period. Women and free blacks, who, contrary to popular belief, were *not* formally prevented from voting in many states at the beginning of the 1790s, saw their rights restricted in the decades to follow. While in 1790 only Virginia, South Carolina, and Georgia explicitly reserved the right to vote to white males, by 1855 only five states – all of them in New England – allowed free blacks to vote on the same basis as whites. This was not a matter of "aristocrats," i.e. Federalists, versus "democrats," i.e. Republicans, but a strategic development. Since in the early 1800s women and free blacks tended to vote Federalist, the Republicans worked success-fully to deny both groups this right. As for Native Americans, in 1830, Jackson signed the **Indian Removal Act**, which resulted in the infamous **Trail of Tears**,

---

[15] The series of laws known collectively as the **Alien and Sedition Acts** included new powers to deport foreigners, as well as making it harder for new immigrants to vote. The Sedition Act stipulated that fines and imprisonment could be used against those who "write, print, utter, or publish [. . .] any false, scandalous and malicious writing" against the government.

[16] A little more than 300 million dollars in today's money.

forcefully relocating tens of thousands of Native Americans, resulting in thousands of deaths (Chapter 9).

The Jacksonian Democrats were also the first to acknowledge the existence of parties not only as a matter of fact, but also as a positive good, necessary for a healthy democratic system. As **Martin Van Buren** argued when orchestrating the split of the Republican Party[17] – while co-opting some of the former Federalists in the process – party attachments based upon "principles" offered "a complete antidote for sectional prejudices," which – as Washington was the first to warn – were the most threatening to the future of the Union. **Enos T. Throop** went a step further,[18] arguing that since *party spirit* is unavoidable, having it contained, softened, and educated inside *organized* parties is beneficial for the common good: "Thus, organized parties watch and scan each other's doings, the public mind is instructed by ample discussions of public measures, and acts of violence are restrained by the convictions of the people [. . .]."

Their wishes came to fruition sooner than Van Buren had probably anticipated; in his second bid for presidency in 1840, he was defeated by a Whig, **William Henry Harrison**.[19] Orchestrated mainly by **Henry Clay**, The Great Compromiser (Chapter 10), the **Whig Party** was a reaction to the perceived extremely populist and horizontal understanding of the people, promoted by Jackson for his own self-aggrandizement.[20] The Whigs' electoral successes marked the beginning of the **second party system**. While they depicted Jackson as a tyrannical king playing on the naivete of the masses, the Whigs were in turn depicted by their opponents as "aristocrats," even though they gathered support from a variety of groups, including the anti-elitist **Anti-Masonic Party**, abolitionists, moral reformers, and people upset by the Democrats' cruel treatment of Native Americans.

The Whigs supported the Second National Bank and a more corporate vision of the American people, transcending state loyalties. As Daniel Webster argued, even before the Whig Party came formally into existence, there were two competing visions of the Union. For the Democrats, the Union was just a convenient compact among states for the promotion of their particular interests, "a mere question of present and temporary expediency." In contrast, according to the **republican** tradition, Webster claimed, the central government ought not to be perceived as a necessary evil, created only to prevent even bigger ones, as the **liberal** understanding had it, but as a positive good. He asked rhetorically: "Whatever is positively beneficent, whatever is actively good [. . .] must all this be rejected and reprobated as a dangerous and obnoxious policy?"

---

[17] Martin Van Buren (1782–1862) was among the founders of the Democratic Party, and in 1836 he won the presidential race with the support of Andrew Jackson.

[18] Enos T. Throop (1784–1874) succeeded his lifelong friend, Martin Van Buren, as Governor of New York, and was one of the first theorists of the benefits of pluripartyism.

[19] Like Jackson, Harrison (1773–1841) capitalized on his military exploits, one of them being the victory against Tecumseh's Confederacy of tribes in the **Battle of Tippecanoe**, in 1811. He died of pneumonia or paratyphoid fever after only thirty-one days in office, beginning the legend of "Tecumseh's curse" (Chapter 9).

[20] The very label "Whigs" was derived from the English anti-monarchist party, portraying Jackson as "King Andrew."

Yet the emergence of the first and second party systems should not obscure the fact that, throughout the entire nineteenth century, there were other, smaller parties, competing with varying degrees of success for the second and the third place in any given electoral competition. Like meteorites, they burst into the American political scene, only to disintegrate in a matter of years, with their fragments assimilated by one of the two major players.

Such was, for example, the fate of the **Anti-Masonic Party**. Ignited by the mysterious disappearance of William Morgan, a former Mason who threatened to publish a book exposing the secrets of Freemasonry, this **single-issue party** grew rapidly, expanding its platform, and emerging as a more successful opposition to President Jackson than the feeble **National Republican Party** of John Quincy Adams.[21] For the Anti-Masons, Freemasons came to embody what they perceived as powers beyond people's control. Presenting themselves as the *people's party*, "principally composed of farmers and mechanics, as yet retaining too much of the blessed spirit of their ancestors tamely to submit under the thraldom of a privileged Order," they claimed to save the republic from this elitist secret society at the ballot box, "the constitutional tribunal established by the founders of this government for the redress of all great political evils and abuses." Nevertheless, in one of the many ironies of that tumultuous period, by the end of the 1830s, most of its members ended up joining the "aristocratic" Whig Party.

Yet such historical ironies were far from over. By the time the Whig Party was on the verge of disappearance in the 1850s, another populist party emerged ... from a secret society. The **American Party**, or the **Native American Party** (*sic*) was informally called the **Know Nothing Party**, because, when asked by outsiders about their organization, its members were instructed to say, "I know nothing." As previously mentioned, the expansion of the electoral franchise proved sometimes to be a double-edged sword. Populist rhetoric began making appeals to racial, ethnic, and religious discrimination. Electioneering was no longer possible unless one dressed and acted as "one of the people." The candidates, as numerous newspapers and campaign documents advertised them, were allegedly all "fresh from the loins of the people."[22]

The successive waves of Catholic immigrants (mostly Irish and German) became an easy target. Conspiracy theories claimed that the pope was trying to subjugate a country based upon Protestant (Puritan) values by the sheer force of immigrant numbers. As former President **Millard Fillmore** wrote, "The rights of native-born citizens are voted away by those who blindly follow their mercenary and selfish leaders," and "as a general rule, our country should be governed by American-born citizens."[23] **F. R. Anspach** also warned that non-native citizens would corrupt the American way of life, "since they are not actuated by those sentiments which thrill

---

[21] Andrew Jackson was openly a high-ranking Mason.

[22] D. Peart and A. I. P. Smith (2015), "Introduction" in D. Peart and A. I. P. Smith (eds.), *Practicing Democracy: Popular Politics in the United States from the Constitution to the Civil War* (Charlottesville and London: University of Virginia Press), p. 14.

[23] Millard Fillmore (1800–1874) was the last elected Whig president. Eventually, he joined the ranks of the Know Nothing Party and finished third in the presidential race of 1856.

the native bosom."[24] Eventually, the responsibility to remind the Americans that they were first and foremost a *political people* fell on the **new Republican Party** in general, and on **Abraham Lincoln** in particular (Chapter 10).

Meanwhile, however, many other people were "left behind," who did not find a place for themselves in any of the people's two political bodies – among them women, Native Americans, and African Americans.

---

[24] Frederick Rinehart Anspach (1815–1867) was an American Lutheran clergyman and author of several popular books.

THE FEDERALISTS

Alexander Hamilton *Opinion as to the Constitutionality of an Act to Establish a National Bank* (1791)[25]

[...] In entering upon the argument, it ought to be premised that the objections of the Secretary of State and Attorney General are founded on a general denial of the authority of the United States to erect corporations. The latter, indeed, expressly admits, that if there be anything in the bill which is not warranted by the Constitution, it is the clause of incorporation.

Now it appears to the Secretary of the Treasury that this general principle is inherent in the very definition of government, and essential to every step of progress to be made by that of the United States, namely: That every power vested in a government is in its nature sovereign, and includes, by force of the term, a right to employ all the means requisite and fairly applicable to the attainment of the ends of such power, and which are not precluded by restrictions and exceptions specified in the Constitution, or not immoral, or not contrary to the essential ends of political society. [...]

This general and indisputable principle puts at once an end to the abstract question, whether the United States have power to erect a corporation; that is to say, to give a legal or artificial capacity to one or more persons, distinct from the natural. For it is unquestionably incident to sovereign power to erect corporations, and consequently to that of the United States, in relation to the objects intrusted to the management of the government. [...]

To this mode of reasoning respecting the right of employing all the means requisite to the execution of the specified powers of the government, it is objected, that none but necessary and proper means are to be employed; and the Secretary of State maintains, that no means are to be considered as necessary but those without which the grant of the power would be nugatory. Nay, so far does he go in his restrictive interpretation of the word, as even to make the case of necessity which shall warrant the constitutional exercise of the power to depend on casual and temporary circumstances; an idea which alone refutes the construction. The expediency of exercising a particular power, at a particular time, must, indeed depend on circumstances, but the constitutional right of exercising it must be uniform and invariable, the same to-day as to-morrow. [...]

It is essential to the being of the national government, that so erroneous a conception of the meaning of the word necessary should be exploded.

It is certain that neither the grammatical nor popular sense of the term requires that construction. According to both, necessary often means no more than needful, requisite, incidental, useful, or conducive to. It is a common mode of expression to say, that it is necessary for a government or a person to do this or that thing, when nothing more is intended or understood, than that the interests of the government

---

[25] From P. L. Ford (ed.), *The Federalist: A Commentary on the Constitution of the United States by Alexander Hamilton, James Madison and John Jay* (New York: Henry Holt and Company, 1898).

or person require, or will be promoted by, the doing of this or that thing. The imagination can be at no loss for exemplifications of the use of the word in this sense. And it is the true one in which it is to be understood as used in the Constitution. [...]

To understand the word as the Secretary of State does, would be to depart from its obvious and popular sense, and to give it a restrictive operation, an idea never before entertained. It would be to give it the same force as if the word absolutely or indispensably had been prefixed to it.

The degree in which a measure is necessary, can never be a test of the legal right to adopt it; that must be a matter of opinion, and can only be a test of expediency. The relation between the measure and the end; between the nature of the mean employed toward the execution of a power, and the object of that power must be the criterion of constitutionality, not the more or less of necessity or utility. [...]

This restrictive interpretation of the word necessary is also contrary to this sound maxim of construction, namely, that the powers contained in a constitution of government, especially those which concern the general administration of the affairs of a country, its finances, trade, defense, etc., ought to be construed liberally in advancement of the public good. [...] The means by which national exigencies are to be provided for, national inconveniences obviated, national prosperity promoted, are of such infinite variety, extent, and complexity, that there must of necessity be great latitude of discretion in the selection and application of those means. Hence, consequently, the necessity and propriety of exercising the authorities intrusted to a government on principles of liberal construction. [...]

But while on the one hand the construction of the Secretary of State is deemed inadmissible, it will not be contended, on the other, that the clause in question gives any new or independent power. But it gives an explicit sanction to the doctrine of implied powers, and is equivalent to an admission of the proposition that the government, as to its specified powers and objects, has plenary and sovereign authority, in some cases paramount to the States; in others, co-ordinate with it. For such is the plain import of the declaration, that it may pass all laws necessary and proper to carry into execution those powers. [...]

The moment the literal meaning is departed from, there is a chance of error and abuse. And yet an adherence to the letter of its powers would at once arrest the motions of government. [...]

It leaves, therefore, a criterion of what is constitutional, and of what is not so. This criterion is the end, to which the measure relates as a mean. If the end be clearly comprehended within any of the specified powers, and if the measure have an obvious relation to that end, and is not forbidden by any particular provision of the Constitution, it may safely be deemed to come within the compass of the national authority. There is also this further criterion, which may materially assist the decision: Does the proposed measure abridge a pre-existing right of any State or of any individual? If it does not, there is a strong presumption in favor of its constitutionality, and slighter relations to any declared object of the Constitution may be permitted to turn the scale. [...]

A hope is entertained that it has, by this time, been made to appear, to the satisfaction of the President, that a bank has a natural relation to the power of collecting taxes – to that of regulating trade – to that of providing for the common defense and that, as the bill under consideration contemplates the government in the light of a joint proprietor of the stock of the bank, it brings the case within the provision of the clause of the Constitution which immediately respects the property of the United States.

Under a conviction that such a relation subsists, the Secretary of the Treasury, with all deference, conceives that it will result as a necessary consequence from the position that all the special powers of government are sovereign, as to the proper objects that the incorporation of a bank is a constitutional measure, and that the objections taken to the bill, in this respect, are ill-founded. [. . .]

George Washington *Farewell Address* (1796)

Friends and Citizens

The period for a new election of a citizen to administer the executive government of the United States being not far distant, and the time actually arrived when your thoughts must be employed in designating the person who is to be clothed with that important trust, it appears to me proper, especially as it may conduce to a more distinct expression of the public voice, that I should now apprise you of the resolution I have formed, to decline being considered among the number of those out of whom a choice is to be made.

I beg you, at the same time, to do me the justice to be assured that this resolution has not been taken without a strict regard to all the considerations appertaining to the relation which binds a dutiful citizen to his country; and that in withdrawing the tender of service, which silence in my situation might imply, I am influenced by no diminution of zeal for your future interest, no deficiency of grateful respect for your past kindness, but am supported by a full conviction that the step is compatible with both. [. . .]

Here, perhaps, I ought to stop. But a solicitude for your welfare, which cannot end but with my life, and the apprehension of danger, natural to that solicitude, urge me, on an occasion like the present, to offer to your solemn contemplation, and to recommend to your frequent review, some sentiments which are the result of much reflection, of no inconsiderable observation, and which appear to me all-important to the permanency of your felicity as a people. These will be offered to you with the more freedom, as you can only see in them the disinterested warnings of a parting friend, who can possibly have no personal motive to bias his counsel. Nor can I forget, as an encouragement to it, your indulgent reception of my sentiments on a former and not dissimilar occasion.

Interwoven as is the love of liberty with every ligament of your hearts, no recommendation of mine is necessary to fortify or confirm the attachment.

The unity of government which constitutes you one people is also now dear to you. It is justly so, for it is a main pillar in the edifice of your real independence, the support of your tranquility at home, your peace abroad; of your safety; of your prosperity; of that very liberty which you so highly prize. But as it is easy to foresee that, from different causes and from different quarters, much pains will be taken, many artifices employed to weaken in your minds the conviction of this truth; as this is the point in your political fortress against which the batteries of internal and external enemies will be most constantly and actively (though often covertly and insidiously) directed, it is of infinite moment that you should properly estimate the immense value of your national union to your collective and individual happiness; that you should cherish a cordial, habitual, and immovable attachment to it; accustoming yourselves to think and speak of it as of the palladium of your political safety and prosperity; watching for its preservation with jealous anxiety; discountenancing whatever may suggest even a suspicion that it can in any event be abandoned; and indignantly frowning upon the first dawning of every attempt to alienate any portion of our country from the rest, or to enfeeble the sacred ties which now link together the various parts.

For this you have every inducement of sympathy and interest. Citizens, by birth or choice, of a common country, that country has a right to concentrate your affections. The name of American, which belongs to you in your national capacity, must always exalt the just pride of patriotism more than any appellation derived from local discriminations. With slight shades of difference, you have the same religion, manners, habits, and political principles. You have in a common cause fought and triumphed together; the independence and liberty you possess are the work of joint counsels, and joint efforts of common dangers, sufferings, and successes.

But these considerations, however powerfully they address themselves to your sensibility, are greatly outweighed by those which apply more immediately to your interest. Here every portion of our country finds the most commanding motives for carefully guarding and preserving the union of the whole.

The North, in an unrestrained intercourse with the South, protected by the equal laws of a common government, finds in the productions of the latter great additional resources of maritime and commercial enterprise and precious materials of manufacturing industry. The South, in the same intercourse, benefiting by the agency of the North, sees its agriculture grow and its commerce expand. [. . .] The East, in a like intercourse with the West, already finds, and in the progressive improvement of interior communications by land and water, will more and more find a valuable vent for the commodities which it brings from abroad, or manufactures at home. The West derives from the East supplies requisite to its growth and comfort, and, what is perhaps of still greater consequence, it must of necessity owe the secure enjoyment of indispensable outlets for its own productions to the weight, influence, and the future maritime strength of the Atlantic side of the Union, directed by an indissoluble community of interest as one nation. [. . .]

In contemplating the causes which may disturb our Union, it occurs as matter of serious concern that any ground should have been furnished for characterizing parties by geographical discriminations, Northern and Southern, Atlantic and Western; whence designing men may endeavor to excite a belief that there is a real difference of local interests and views. One of the expedients of party to acquire influence within particular districts is to misrepresent the opinions and aims of other districts. You cannot shield yourselves too much against the jealousies and heartburnings which spring from these misrepresentations; they tend to render alien to each other those who ought to be bound together by fraternal affection. [. . .]

All obstructions to the execution of the laws, all combinations and associations, under whatever plausible character, with the real design to direct, control, counteract, or awe the regular deliberation and action of the constituted authorities, are destructive of this fundamental principle, and of fatal tendency. They serve to organize faction, to give it an artificial and extraordinary force; to put, in the place of the delegated will of the nation the will of a party, often a small but artful and enterprising minority of the community; and, according to the alternate triumphs of different parties, to make the public administration the mirror of the ill-concerted and incongruous projects of faction, rather than the organ of consistent and wholesome plans digested by common counsels and modified by mutual interests.

However combinations or associations of the above description may now and then answer popular ends, they are likely, in the course of time and things, to become potent engines, by which cunning, ambitious, and unprincipled men will be enabled to subvert the power of the people and to usurp for themselves the reins of government, destroying afterwards the very engines which have lifted them to unjust dominion. [. . .]

I have already intimated to you the danger of parties in the State, with particular reference to the founding of them on geographical discriminations. Let me now take a more comprehensive view, and warn you in the most solemn manner against the baneful effects of the spirit of party generally.

This spirit, unfortunately, is inseparable from our nature, having its root in the strongest passions of the human mind. It exists under different shapes in all governments, more or less stifled, controlled, or repressed; but, in those of the popular form, it is seen in its greatest rankness, and is truly their worst enemy.

The alternate domination of one faction over another, sharpened by the spirit of revenge, natural to party dissension, which in different ages and countries has perpetrated the most horrid enormities, is itself a frightful despotism. But this leads at length to a more formal and permanent despotism. The disorders and miseries which result gradually incline the minds of men to seek security and repose in the absolute power of an individual; and sooner or later the chief of some prevailing faction, more able or more fortunate than his competitors, turns this disposition to the purposes of his own elevation, on the ruins of public liberty.

Without looking forward to an extremity of this kind (which nevertheless ought not to be entirely out of sight), the common and continual mischiefs of the spirit of party are sufficient to make it the interest and duty of a wise people to discourage and restrain it.

It serves always to distract the public councils and enfeeble the public administration. It agitates the community with ill-founded jealousies and false alarms, kindles the animosity of one part against another, foments occasionally riot and insurrection. It opens the door to foreign influence and corruption, which finds a facilitated access to the government itself through the channels of party passions. Thus the policy and the will of one country are subjected to the policy and will of another.

There is an opinion that parties in free countries are useful checks upon the administration of the government and serve to keep alive the spirit of liberty. This within certain limits is probably true; and in governments of a monarchical cast, patriotism may look with indulgence, if not with favor, upon the spirit of party. But in those of the popular character, in governments purely elective, it is a spirit not to be encouraged. From their natural tendency, it is certain there will always be enough of that spirit for every salutary purpose. And there being constant danger of excess, the effort ought to be by force of public opinion, to mitigate and assuage it. A fire not to be quenched, it demands a uniform vigilance to prevent its bursting into a flame, lest, instead of warming, it should consume. [...]

John Adams *First Inaugural Address* (March 5, 1797)

[...] There may be little solidity in an ancient idea that congregations of men into cities and nations are the most pleasing objects in the sight of superior intelligences, but this is very certain, that to a benevolent human mind there can be no spectacle presented by any nation more pleasing, more noble, majestic, or august, than an assembly like that which has so often been seen in this and the other Chamber of Congress, of a Government in which the Executive authority, as well as that of all the branches of the Legislature, are exercised by citizens selected at regular periods by their neighbors to make and execute laws for the general good. Can anything essential, anything more than mere ornament and decoration, be added to this by robes and diamonds? Can authority be more amiable and respectable when it descends from accidents or institutions established in remote antiquity than when it springs fresh from the hearts and judgments of an honest and enlightened people? For it is the people only that are represented. It is their power and majesty that is reflected, and only for their good, in every legitimate government, under whatever form it may appear. The existence of such a government as ours for any length of time is a full proof of a general dissemination of knowledge and virtue throughout the whole body of the people. And what object or consideration more pleasing than this can be presented to the human mind? If national pride is ever justifiable or excusable it is when it springs, not from power or riches, grandeur or glory, but from conviction of national innocence, information, and benevolence.

In the midst of these pleasing ideas we should be unfaithful to ourselves if we should ever lose sight of the danger to our liberties if anything partial or extraneous should infect the purity of our free, fair, virtuous, and independent elections. If an election is to be determined by a majority of a single vote, and that can be procured by a party through artifice or corruption, the Government may be the choice of a party for its own ends, not of the nation for the national good. If that solitary suffrage can be obtained by foreign nations by flattery or menaces, by fraud or violence, by terror, intrigue, or venality, the Government may not be the choice of the American people, but of foreign nations. It may be foreign nations who govern us, and not we, the people, who govern ourselves; and candid men will acknowledge that in such cases choice would have little advantage to boast of over lot or chance. [. . .]

On this subject it might become me better to be silent or to speak with diffidence; but as something may be expected, the occasion, I hope, will be admitted as an apology if I venture to say that if a preference, upon principle, of a free republican government, formed upon long and serious reflection, after a diligent and impartial inquiry after truth; if an attachment to the Constitution of the United States, and a conscientious determination to support it until it shall be altered by the judgments and wishes of the people, expressed in the mode prescribed in it; if a respectful attention to the constitutions of the individual States and a constant caution and delicacy toward the State governments; if an equal and impartial regard to the rights, interest, honor, and happiness of all the States in the Union, without preference or regard to a northern or southern, an eastern or western, position, their various political opinions on unessential points or their personal attachments; if a love of virtuous men of all parties and denominations; if a love of science and letters and a wish to patronize every rational effort to encourage schools, colleges, universities, academies, and every institution for propagating knowledge, virtue, and religion among all classes of the people, not only for their benign influence on the happiness of life in all its stages and classes, and of society in all its forms, but as the only means of preserving our Constitution from its natural enemies, the spirit of sophistry, the spirit of party, the spirit of intrigue, the profligacy of corruption, and the pestilence of foreign influence, which is the angel of destruction to elective governments; if a love of equal laws, of justice, and humanity in the interior administration; if an inclination to improve agriculture, commerce, and manufacturers for necessity, convenience, and defense; if a spirit of equity and humanity toward the aboriginal nations of America, and a disposition to meliorate their condition by inclining them to be more friendly to us, and our citizens to be more friendly to them; if an inflexible determination to maintain peace and inviolable faith with all nations, and that system of neutrality and impartiality among the belligerent powers of Europe which has been adopted by this Government and so solemnly sanctioned by both Houses of Congress and applauded by the legislatures of the States and the public opinion, until it shall be otherwise ordained by Congress; if a personal esteem for the French nation, formed in a residence of seven years chiefly among them, and a sincere desire to preserve the friendship which has been so much for the honor and interest of both nations; if, while the conscious honor and integrity of the people of America and the internal sentiment of their own power and energies must be preserved, an earnest endeavor to investigate every just cause and remove every colorable pretense of complaint; if an intention to pursue by amicable negotiation a reparation for the injuries that have been committed on the commerce of our fellow-citizens by whatever nation, and if success can not be obtained, to lay the facts before the Legislature, that they may consider what further measures the honor and interest of the Government and its constituents demand; if a resolution to do justice as far as may depend upon me, at all times and to all nations, and maintain peace, friendship, and benevolence with all the world; if an unshaken confidence in the honor, spirit, and resources of the American people, on which I have so often hazarded my all and never been deceived; if elevated ideas of the high destinies of this country and of my own duties toward it, founded on a knowledge of the moral principles and intellectual improvements of the people deeply engraven on my mind in early life, and not obscured but exalted by experience and age; and, with humble reverence, I feel it to be my duty to add, if a veneration for the religion of a people who profess and call themselves Christians, and a fixed resolution to consider a decent respect for Christianity among the best recommendations for the public service, can enable me in any degree to comply with your wishes, it shall be my strenuous endeavor that this sagacious injunction of the two Houses shall not be without effect. [. . .]

Fisher Ames *The Dangers of American Liberty* (written 1805)[26]

[. . .] [W]e maintained that the federal Constitution, with all the bloom of youth and splendor of innocence, was gifted with immortality. For if time should impair its force, or faction tarnish its charms, the people, ever vigilant to discern its wants, ever powerful to provide for them, would miraculously restore it to the field, like some wounded hero of the epic, to take a signal vengeance on its enemies, or like Antaeus, invigorated by touching his mother earth, to rise the stronger for a fall.

There is of course a large portion of our citizens who will not believe, even on the evidence of facts, that any public evils exist, or are impending. They deride the apprehensions of those who foresee that licentiousness will prove, as it ever has proved, fatal to liberty. They consider her as a nymph, who need not be coy to keep herself pure, but that on the contrary, her chastity will grow robust by frequent scuffles with her seducers. They say, while a faction is a minority it will remain harmless by being outvoted; and if it should become a majority, all its acts, however profligate or violent, are then legitimate. For with the democrats the people is a sovereign who can do no wrong, even when he respects and spares no existing right, and whose voice, however obtained or however counterfeited, bears all the sanctity and all the force of a living divinity.

Where, then, it will be asked, in a tone both of menace and of triumph, can the people's danger lie, unless it be with the persecuted federalists? *They* are the partisans of monarchy, who propagate their principles in order, as soon as they have increased their sect, to introduce a king; for by this only avenue they foretell his approach. Is it possible the people should ever be their own enemies? [. . .]

Without pretending to define that liberty, which writers at length agree is incapable of any precise and comprehensive definition, all the European governments, except the British, admit a most formidable portion of arbitrary power; whereas, in America, no plan of government, without a large and preponderating commixture of democracy, can, for a moment, possess our confidence and attachment.

It is unquestionable, that the concern of the people in the affairs of such a government, tends to elevate the character and enlarge the comprehension, as

---

[26] From *The Works of Fisher Ames: Compiled by a Number of His Friends* (Boston: T. B. Wait & Co., 1809), pp. 379–437.

well as the enjoyments, of the citizens; and, supposing the government wisely constituted, and the laws steadily and firmly carried into execution, these effects, in which every lover of mankind must exult, will not be attended with a corresponding deprivation of the publick manners and morals. I have never yet met with an American of any party, who seemed willing to exclude the people from their temperate and well-regulated share of concern in the government. Indeed, it is notorious, that there was scarcely an advocate for the federal constitution, who was not anxious, from the first, to hazard the experiment of an unprecedented, and almost unqualified proportion of democracy, both in constructing and administering the government, and who did not rely with confidence, if not blind presumption, on its success. This is certain, the body of the federalists were always, and yet are essentially democratick in their political notions. The truth is, the American nation, with ideas and prejudices wholly democratick, undertook to frame, and expected tranquilly, and with energy and success, to administer a *republican* government.

It is, and ever has been my belief, that the federal constitution was as good, or nearly as good, as our country could bear; that the attempt to introduce a mixed monarchy was never thought of, and would have failed, if it had been made; and could have proved only an inveterate curse to the nation, if it had been adopted cheerfully, and even unanimously, by the people. Our materials for government were all democratick, and whatever the hazard of their combination may be, our Solons and Lycurguses in the convention had no alternative, nothing to consider, but how to combine them, so as to ensure the longest duration of the constitution, and the most favourable chance for the publick liberty in the event of those changes, which the frailty of the structure of government, the operation of time and accident, and the maturity and development of the national character were well understood to portend. [...]

The danger obviously was, that a species of government, in which the people choose all the rulers, and then, by themselves, or ambitious demagogues pretending to be the people, claim and exercise an effective control over what is called the government, would be found on trial no better than a turbulent, licentious democracy. The danger was, that their best interest would be neglected, their dearest rights violated, their sober reason silenced, and the worst passions of the worst men not only freed from legal restraint, but invested with publick power. The known propensity of a democracy is to licentiousness, which the ambitious call, and the ignorant believe to be liberty.

The great object, then, of political wisdom in framing our constitution, was to guard against licentiousness, that inbred malady of democracies, that deforms their infancy with grey hairs and decrepitude.

The federalists relied much on the efficiency of an independent judiciary, as a check on the hasty turbulences of the popular passions. They supposed the senate proceeding from the states, and chose for six years, would form a sort of balance to the democracy, and realise the hope, that a *federal republick of states might subsist.* [...]

It is needless to ask, how rational such hopes were, or how far experience has verified them. [...]

From these reflections the political observer will infer, that the American republic is impelled by the force of state ambition and of democratick licentiousness; and he will inquire, *which* of the two is our strongest propensity. Is the sovereign power to be contracted to a state centre? Is Virginia to be our Rome? and are we to be her Latin or Italian allies, like them to be emulous of the honour of our chains, on the terms of imposing them on Louisiana, Mexico, or Santa Fe? Or, are we to run the giddy circle of popular licentiousness, beginning in delusion, quickened by vice, and ending in wretchedness? [...]

It is undoubtedly a salutary labor, to diffuse among the citizens of a free state, as far as the thing is possible, a just knowledge of their publick affairs. But the difficulty of this task is augmented exactly in proportion to the freedom of the state; for the more free the citizens, the bolder and more profligate will be their demagogues, the more numerous and eccentric the popular errors, and the more vehement and pertinacious the passions that defend them.

Yet, as if there were neither vice nor passion in the world, one of the loudest of our boasts, one of the dearest of all the tenets of our creed is, that we are a sovereign people, *self-governed* – it would be nearer to the truth to say, self-conceived. For in what sense is it true, that any people, however free, are self-governed? If they have in fact no government, but such as comports with their every varying and often inordinate desires, then it is anarchy; if it counteracts those desires, it is compulsory. The individual, who is left to act according to his own humour, is not governed at all; and if any considerable number, and especially any combination of individuals, find or can place themselves in this situation, then the society is no longer free. For liberty obviously consists in the salutary restraint, and not in the uncontrolled indulgence of such humours. [...]

The essence and, in the opinion of many thousands not yet cured of their delusions, the *excellence* of democracy is, that it invests every citizen with an equal proportion of power. A state consisting of a million citizens has a million sovereigns, each of whom detests all other sovereignty but his own. This very boast implies as much of the spirit of turbulence and insubordination, as the utmost energy of any known regular government, even the most right, could keep in restraint. It also implies a state of agitation, that is justly terrible to all who love their ease, and of instability, that quenches the last hope of those who would transmit their liberty to posterity. [...]

If, then, all this is to happen, not from accident, not, as the shallow or base demagogues pretend, from the management of monarchists or aristocrats, but from the principles of democracy itself, as we have attempted to demonstrate, ought we not to consider democracy the worst of all governments, or if there be a worse, as the certain forerunner of that? What other form of civil rule among men so irresistibly tends to free vice from restraint, and to subject virtue to persecution? [...]

He is certainly a political novice or a hypocrite, who will pretend, that the antifederal opposition to the government is to be ascribed to the concern of the people for their liberties, rather than to the profligate ambition of their demagogues, eager for power, and suddenly alarmed by the imminent danger of losing it; demagogues, who, leading lives like Clodius, and with the maxims of Cato in their mouths, cherishing principles like Catiline, have acted steadily on a plan of usurpation like Cesar. Their labour for twelve years was to inflame and deceive; and their recompense, for the last four, has been to degrade and betray.

Any person who considers the instability of authority, that is not only derived from the multitude, but wanes or increases with the ever changing phases of their levity and caprice, will pronounce, that the federal government was from the first, and from its very nature and organization, fated to sink under the rivalship of state competitors for dominion.

THE REPUBLICANS

Thomas Jefferson

Letter to Elbridge Gerry (January 26, 1799)[27]

[...] I dothen with sincere zeal wish an inviolable preservation of our present federal constitution, according to the true sense in which it was adopted by the states, that in which it was advocated by it's [*sic*] friends, & not that which it's enemies apprehended, who therefore became it's enemies: and I am opposed to the monarchising it's features by the forms of it's administration, with a view to conciliate a first transition to a President & Senate for life, & from that to a hereditary tenure of these offices, & thus to worm out the elective principle. I am for preserving to the states the powers not yielded by them to the Union, & to the legislature of the Union it's constitutional share in the division of powers: and I am not for transferring all the powers of the states to the general government, & all those of that government to the Executive branch. I am for a government rigorously frugal & simple, applying all the possible savings of the public revenue to the discharge of the national debt: and not for a multiplication of officers & salaries merely to make partisans, & for increasing, by every device, the public debt, on the principle of it's being a public blessing. I am for relying, for internal defence, on our militia solely till actual invasion, and for such a naval force only as may protect our coasts and harbors from such depredations as we have experienced: and not for a standing army in time of peace which may overawe the public sentiment; nor for a navy which by it's own expenses and the eternal wars in which it will implicate us, will grind us with public burthens, & sink us under them. I am for free commerce with all nations, political connection with none, & little or no diplomatic establishment: and I am not for linking ourselves, by new treaties with the quarrels of Europe, entering that field of slaughter to preserve their balance, or joining in the confederacy of kings to war against the principles of liberty. I am for freedom of religion, & against all maneuvres to bring about a legal ascendancy of one sect over another: for freedom of the press, & against all violations of the constitution to silence by force & not by reason the complaints or criticisms, just or unjust, of our citizens against the conduct of their agents.

---

[27] Thomas Jefferson to Elbridge Gerry, January 26, 1799, in P. L. Ford (ed.), *The Writings of Thomas Jefferson*, Vol. IX (New York: G. P. Putnam's Sons, 1905), pp. 15–26.

and I am for encouraging the progress of science in all it's branches; and not for raising a hue and cry against the sacred name of philosophy, for awing the human mind, by stories of raw-head & bloody bones, to a distrust of it's own vision & to repose implicitly on that of others; to go backwards instead of forwards to look for improvement, to believe that government, religion, morality & every other science were in the highest perfection in ages of the darkest ignorance, and that nothing can ever be devised more perfect than what was established by our forefathers. To these I will add that I was a sincere well-wisher to the success of the French revolution, and still wish it may end in the establishment of a free & well-ordered republic: but I have not been insensible under the atrocious depredations they have committed on our commerce. The first object of my heart is my own country. In that is embarked my family, my fortune, & my own existence. I have not one farthing of interest, nor one fibre of attachment out of it, nor a single motive of preference of any one nation to another but in proportion as they are more or less friendly to us. but though deeply feeling the injuries of France, I did not think war the surest mode of redressing them. I did believe that a mission sincerely disposed to preserve peace, would obtain for us a peaceable & honorable settlement and retribution; & I appeal to you to say whether this might not have been obtained, if either of your colleagues had been of the same sentiment with yourself.——

These my friend are my principles; they are unquestionably the principles of the great body of our fellow citizens, and I know there is not one of them which is not yours also. In truth we never differed but on one ground, the funding system; and as from the moment of it's being adopted by the constituted authorities, I became religiously principled in the sacred discharge of it to the uttermost farthing, we are now united even on that single ground of difference. [...]

First Inaugural Address (March 4, 1801)

Called upon to undertake the duties of the first executive office of our country, I avail myself of the presence of that portion of my fellow-citizens which is here assembled to express my grateful thanks for the favor with which they have been pleased to look toward me, to declare a sincere consciousness that the task is above my talents, and that I approach it with those anxious and awful presentiments which the greatness of the charge and the weakness of my powers so justly inspire. [...]

During the contest of opinion through which we have passed the animation of discussions and of exertions has sometimes worn an aspect which might impose on strangers unused to think freely and to speak and to write what they think; but this being now decided by the voice of the nation, announced according to the rules of the Constitution, all will, of course, arrange themselves under the will of the law, and unite in common efforts for the common good. All, too, will bear in mind this sacred principle, that though the will of the majority is in all cases to prevail, that will to be rightful must be reasonable; that the minority possess their equal rights, which equal law must protect, and to violate would be oppression. Let us, then, fellow-citizens, unite with one heart and one mind. Let us restore to social intercourse that harmony and affection without which liberty and even life itself are but dreary things. And let us reflect that, having banished from our land that religious intolerance under which mankind so long bled and suffered, we have yet gained little if we countenance a political intolerance as despotic, as wicked, and capable of as bitter and bloody persecutions. During the throes and convulsions of the ancient world, during the agonizing spasms of infuriated man, seeking through blood and slaughter his long-lost liberty, it was not wonderful that the agitation of the billows should reach even this distant and peaceful shore; that this should be more felt and feared by some and less by others, and should divide opinions as to measures of safety. But every difference of opinion is not a difference of principle. We have called by different names brethren of the same principle. We are all Republicans, we are all Federalists. If there be any among us who would wish to dissolve this Union or to change its republican form, let them stand undisturbed as monuments of the safety with which error of opinion may be tolerated where reason is left free to combat it. I know, indeed, that some honest men fear that a republican government can not be strong, that this Government is not strong enough; but would the honest patriot, in the full tide of successful experiment, abandon a government which has so far kept us free and firm on the theoretic and visionary fear that this Government, the world's best hope, may by possibility want energy to preserve itself? I trust not. I believe this, on the contrary, the strongest Government on earth. I believe it the only one where every man, at the call of the law, would fly to the standard of the law, and would meet invasions of the public order as his own personal concern. Sometimes it is said that man can not be trusted with the government of himself. Can he, then, be trusted with the government of others? Or have we found angels in the forms of kings to govern him? Let history answer this question.

Let us, then, with courage and confidence pursue our own Federal and Republican principles, our attachment to union and representative government. Kindly separated by nature and a wide ocean from the exterminating havoc of one quarter of the globe; too high-minded to endure the degradations of the others; possessing a chosen country, with room enough for our descendants to the thousandth and thousandth generation; entertaining a due sense of our equal right to the use of our own faculties, to the acquisitions of our own industry, to honor and confidence from our fellow-citizens, resulting not from birth, but from our actions and their sense of them; enlightened by a benign religion, professed, indeed, and practiced in various forms, yet all of them inculcating honesty, truth, temperance, gratitude, and the love of man; acknowledging and adoring an overruling Providence, which by all its dispensations proves that it delights in the happiness of man here and his greater happiness hereafter – with all these blessings, what more is necessary to make us a happy and a prosperous people? Still one thing more, fellow-citizens – a wise and frugal Government, which shall restrain men from injuring one another, shall leave them otherwise free to regulate their own pursuits of industry and improvement, and shall not take from the mouth of labor the bread it has earned. This is the sum of good government, and this is necessary to close the circle of our felicities.

About to enter, fellow-citizens, on the exercise of duties which comprehend every-thing dear and valuable to you, it is proper you should understand what I deem the essential principles of our Government, and consequently those which ought to shape its Administration. I will compress them within the narrowest compass they will bear, stating the general principle, but not all its limitations. Equal and exact justice to all men, of whatever state or persuasion, religious or political; peace, commerce, and honest friendship with all nations, entangling alliances with none; the support of the State governments in all their rights, as the most competent administrations for our domestic concerns and the surest bulwarks against antirepublican tendencies; the preservation of the General Government in its whole constitutional vigor, as the sheet anchor of our peace at home and safety abroad; a jealous care of the right of election by the people – a mild and safe corrective of abuses which are lopped by the sword of revolution where peaceable remedies are unprovided; absolute acquiescence in the decisions of the majority, the vital principle of republics, from which is no appeal but to force, the vital principle and immediate parent of despotism; a well-disciplined militia, our best reliance in peace and for the first moments of war till regulars may relieve them; the supremacy of the civil over the military authority; economy in the public expense, that labor may be lightly burthened; the honest payment of our debts and sacred preservation of the public faith; encouragement of agriculture, and of commerce as its handmaid; the diffusion of information and arraignment of all abuses at the bar of the public reason; freedom of religion; freedom of the press, and freedom of person under the protection of the habeas corpus, and trial by juries impartially selected. These principles form the bright constellation which has gone before us and guided our steps through an age of revolution and reformation. The wisdom of our sages and blood of our heroes have been devoted to their attainment. They should be the creed of our political faith, the text of civic instruction, the touchstone by which to try the services of those we trust; and should we wander from them in moments of error or of alarm, let us hasten to retrace our steps and to regain the road which alone leads to peace, liberty, and safety. [...]

John Taylor *Arator* (1813)[28]

59. The Pleasure of Agriculture

In free countries, are more, and in enslaved, fewer, than the pleasures of most other employments. The reason of it is, that agriculture both from its nature, and also as being generally the employment of a great portion of a nation, cannot be united with power, considered as an exclusive interest. It must of course be enslaved, wherever despotism exists, and its masters will enjoy more pleasures in that case, than it can ever reach. On the contrary, where power is not an exclusive, but a general interest, agriculture can employ its own energies for the attainment of its own happiness.

Under a free government it has before it the inexhaustible sources of human pleasure, of fitting ideas to substances, and substances to ideas; and of a constant rotation of hope and fruition.

The novelty, frequency and exactness of accommodations between our ideas and operations, constitutes the most exquisite source of mental pleasure. Agriculture feeds it with endless supplies in the natures of soils, plants, climates, manures,

[28] J. Taylor, *Arator, Being a Series of Agricultural Essays, Practical and Political: In Sixty-One Numbers* (Georgetown: J. M. Carter, 1814), pp. 241–5.

instruments of culture and domestic animals. Their combinations are inexhaustible, the novelty of results is endless, discrimination and adaption are never idle, and an unsatiated interest receives gratification in quick succession.

Benevolence is so closely associated with this interest, that its exertion in numberless instances, is necessary to foster it. Liberality in supplying its labourers with the comforts of life, is the best sponsor for the prosperity of agriculture, and the practice of almost every moral virtue is amply remunerated in this world, whilst it is also the best surety for attaining the blessings of the next. [...]

With the pleasure of religion, agriculture unites those of patriotism, and among the worthy competitors for pre-eminence in the practice of this cardinal virtue, a profound author assigns a high station to him who has made two blades of grass grow instead of one; an idea capable of a signal amplification, by a comparison between a system of agriculture which doubles the fertility of a country, and a successful war which doubles its territory. By the first the territory itself is also substantially doubled, without wasting the lives, the wealth, or the liberty of the nation which has thus subdued sterility, and drawn prosperity from a willing source. By the second, the blood pretended to be enriched, is spilt; the wealth pretended to be increased, is wasted; the liberty said to be secured, is immolated to the patriotism of a victorious army; and desolation in every form is made to stalk in the glittering garb of false glory, throughout some neighboring country. [...]

The capacity of agriculture for affording luxuries to the body, is not less conspicuous than its capacity for affording luxuries to the mind; it being a science singularly possessing the double qualities of feeding with unbounded liberality, both the moral appetites of the one, and the physical wants of the other. [...] In short, by the exercise it gives both to the body and to the mind, it secures health and vigour to both; and by combining a thorough knowledge of the real affairs of life, with a necessity for investigating the arcana of nature, and the strongest invitations to the practice of morality, it becomes the best architect of a complete man.

If this eulogy should succeed in awakening the attention of men of science to a skilful practice of agriculture, they will become models for individuals, and guardians for national happiness. The discoveries of the learned will be practiced by the ignorant; and a system which sheds happiness, plenty and virtue all around, will be gradually substituted for one, which fosters vice, breeds want, and begets misery. [...]

John Quincy Adams *First Inaugural Address* (March 4, 1825)

In compliance with an usage coeval with the existence of our Federal Constitution, and sanctioned by the example of my predecessors in the career upon which I am about to enter, I appear, my fellow-citizens, in your presence and in that of Heaven to bind myself by the solemnities of religious obligation to the faithful performance of the duties allotted to me in the station to which I have been called.

In unfolding to my countrymen the principles by which I shall be governed in the fulfillment of those duties my first resort will be to that Constitution which I shall swear to the best of my ability to preserve, protect, and defend. That revered instrument enumerates the powers and prescribes the duties of the Executive Magistrate, and in its first words declares the purposes to which these and the whole action of the Government instituted by it should be invariably and sacredly devoted – to form a more perfect union, establish justice, insure domestic tranquillity, provide for the common defense, promote the general welfare, and secure the blessings of liberty to the people of this Union in their successive generations. Since the adoption of this social compact one of these generations has passed away. It is the work of our forefathers. Administered by some of the most eminent men who contributed to its formation, through a most eventful period in the annals of the world, and through all the vicissitudes of peace and war incidental to the condition of associated man, it has not disappointed the hopes and aspirations of those illustrious benefactors of their age and nation. It has promoted the lasting welfare of that country so dear to us all; it has to an extent far beyond the ordinary lot of humanity secured the freedom and happiness of this people. We now receive it as a precious inheritance from those to whom we are indebted for its establishment, doubly bound by the examples which they have left us and by the blessings which we have enjoyed as the fruits of their labors to transmit the same unimpaired to the succeeding generation. [. . .]

It is a source of gratification and of encouragement to me to observe that the great result of this experiment upon the theory of human rights has at the close of that generation by which it was formed been crowned with success equal to the most sanguine expectations of its founders. Union, justice, tranquillity, the common defense, the general welfare, and the blessings of liberty – all have been promoted by the Government under which we have lived. Standing at this point of time, looking back to that generation which has gone by and forward to that which is advancing, we may at once indulge in grateful exultation and in cheering hope. From the experience of the past we derive instructive lessons for the future. Of the two great political parties which have divided the opinions and feelings of our country, the candid and the just will now admit that both have contributed splendid talents, spotless integrity, ardent patriotism, and disinterested sacrifices to the formation and administration of this Government, and that both have required a liberal indulgence for a portion of human infirmity and error. The revolutionary wars of Europe, commencing precisely at the moment when the Government of the United States first went into operation under this Constitution, excited a collision of sentiments and of sympathies which kindled all the passions and imbittered the conflict of parties till the nation was involved in war and the Union was shaken to its center. This time of trial embraced a period of five and twenty years, during which the policy of the Union in its relations with Europe constituted the principal basis of our political divisions and the most arduous part of the action of our Federal Government. With the catastrophe in which the wars of the French Revolution terminated, and our own subsequent peace with Great Britain, this baneful weed of party strife was uprooted. From that time no difference of principle, connected either with the theory of government or with our intercourse with foreign nations, has existed or been called forth in force sufficient to sustain a continued combination of parties or to give more than wholesome animation to public sentiment or legislative debate. Our political creed is, without a dissenting voice that can be heard, that the will of the people is the source and the happiness of the people the end of all legitimate government upon earth; that the best security for the beneficence and the best guaranty against the abuse of power consists in the freedom, the purity, and the frequency of popular elections; that the General Government of the Union and the separate governments of the States are all sovereignties of limited powers, fellow-servants of the same masters, uncontrolled within their respective spheres, uncontrollable by encroachments upon each other; [. . .]. Ten years of peace, at home and abroad, have assuaged the animosities of political contention and blended into harmony the most discordant elements of public opinion. There still remains one effort of magnanimity, one sacrifice of prejudice and passion, to be made by the individuals throughout the nation who have heretofore followed the standards of political party. It is that of discarding every remnant of rancor against each other, of embracing as countrymen and friends, and of yielding to talents and virtue alone that confidence which in times of contention for principle was bestowed only upon those who bore the badge of party communion.

The collisions of party spirit which originate in speculative opinions or in different views of administrative policy are in their nature transitory. Those which are founded on geographical divisions, adverse interests of soil, climate, and modes of domestic life are more permanent, and therefore, perhaps, more dangerous. It is this which gives inestimable value to the character of our Government, at once federal and national. It holds out to us a perpetual admonition to preserve alike and with equal anxiety the rights of each individual State in its own government and the rights of the whole nation in that of the Union. Whatsoever is of domestic concernment, unconnected with the other members of the Union or with foreign lands, belongs exclusively to the administration of the State governments. Whatsoever directly involves the rights and interests of the federative fraternity or of foreign powers is of the resort of this General Government. The duties of both are obvious in the general principle, though sometimes perplexed with difficulties in the detail. To respect the rights of the State governments is the inviolable duty of that of the Union; the government of every State will feel its own obligation to respect and preserve the rights of the whole. The prejudices everywhere too commonly entertained against distant strangers are worn away, and the jealousies of jarring interests are allayed by the composition and functions of the great national councils annually assembled from all quarters of the Union at this place. Here the distinguished men from every section of our country, while meeting to deliberate upon the great interests of those by whom they are deputed, learn to estimate the talents and do justice to the virtues of each other. The harmony of the nation is promoted and the whole Union is knit together by the sentiments of mutual respect, the habits of social intercourse, and the ties of personal friendship formed between the representatives of its several parts in the performance of their service at this metropolis. [. . .]

THE DEMOCRATS

Martin Van Buren *Letter to Thomas Ritchie* (January 13, 1827)[29]

[In the letter, Van Buren discusses the possibility of holding a congressional caucus or a general convention of (a branch) of the Republican Party to nominate Andrew Jackson as presidential candidate and, thereby, to re-establish the two-party system.]

For myself I am not tenacious whether we have a congressional caucus or a general convention, so that we have either; the latter would remove the embarrassment of those who have or profess to have scruples, as to the former, would be fresher & perhaps more in unison with the spirit of the times, especially at the seat of the war Pensylvania & N. York. The following may, I think, justly be ranked among its probable advantages. First, It is the best and probably the only practicable mode of concentrating the entire vote of the opposition & of effecting what is of still greater importance, the substantial reorganization of the Old Republican Party.

2nd Its first result cannot be doubtful. Mr. Adams occupying the seat and being determined not to surrender it except "*in extremis*" will not submit his pretension to the convention. [. . .] I have long been satisfied that we can only get rid of the present, & restore a better state of things, by combining Genl. Jacksons personal popularity with the portion of old party feeling yet remaining. This sentiment is spreading, and wou'd of itself be sufficient to nominate him at the Convention.

3rd The call of such a convention, its exclusive Republican character, & the refusal of Mr. Adams and his friends to become parties to it, would draw anew the old Party lines & the subsequent contest would reestablish them; state nomination alone would fall far short of that object.

4th It would greatly improve the condition of the Republicans of the North & Middle States by substituting *party principle for personal preference* as one of the leading points in the contest. The location of the candidate would in a great degree, be merged in its consideration. Instead of the question being between a northern and Southern man, it would be whether or not the ties, which have heretofore bound together a great political party should be severed. The difference between the two questions would be found to be immense in the elective field. Altho' this is a mere party consideration, it is not on that account less likely to be effectual, considerations of this character not infrequently operate as efficiently as those which bear upon the most important questions of constitutional doctrine. Indeed Gen[era]l Jackson has been so little in public life, that it will be not a little difficult to contrast his opinions on great questions with those of Mr. Adams. [. . .]

5thly, It would place our Republican friends in New England on new and strong grounds. They would have to decide between an indulgence in sectional & personal feelings with an entire separation from their old political friends, on the one hand or acquiescence in the fairly expressed will of the party, on the other. In all the states the

---

[29] Retrieved from the Papers of Martin Van Buren Project, http://vanburenpapers.org/.

divisions between Republicans and Federalists is still kept up & cannot be laid aside whatever the leaders of the two parties may desire. [. . .]

6th Its effects would be highly salutary on your section of the union by the revival of old party distinctions. We must always have party distinctions and the old ones are the best of which the nature of the case admits. Political combinations between the inhabitants of the different states are unavoidable & the most natural & beneficial to the country is that between the planters of the South and the plain Republicans of the north. The country has once flourished under a party thus constituted & may again. It would take longer than our lives (even if it were practicable) to create new party feelings to keep those masses together. If the old ones are suppressed, Geographical divisions founded on local interests or, what is worse prejudices between free & slave holding states will inevitably take their place. Party attachment in former times furnished a complete antidote for sectional prejudices by producing counteracting feelings. It was not until that defence had been broken down that the clamour ag[ains]t Southern Influence and African Slavery could be made effectual in the North. Those in the South who assisted in producing the change are, I am satisfied, now deeply sensible of their errour. Every honest Federalist of the South therefore should (and would if he duly reflected upon the subject) prefer the revival of old party feelings to any other state of things he has a right to expect. Formerly, attacks upon Southern Republicans were regarded by those of the north as assaults upon their political brethren & resented accordingly. This all powerful sympathy has been much weakened, if not, destroyed by the amalgamating policy of Mr. Monroe. It can & ought to be revived and the proposed convention would be eminently service-able in effecting that object. The failure of the last caucus furnishes no argument ag[ains]t a convention nor would it against another caucus. The condition of things is essentially different. Then the South was divided, now it is united. Then we had several parties now we have in substance but two & for many other reasons.

Lastly, the effect of such an nomination on Gen[era]l Jackson could not fail to be considerable. His election, as the result of his military services without reference to party & so far as he alone is concerned, scarcely to principle, would be one thing. His election as the result of a combined and concerted effort of a political party, holding in the main, to certain tenets & opposed to certain prevailing principles, might be another and a far different thing. [. . .]

Enos T. Throop *Special Message to the Legislature* (New York, March 12, 1829)[30]

[Enos Throop succeeded Martin Van Buren as Governor of New York after Van Buren resigned to become Secretary of State in the cabinet of President Andrew Jackson. He delivered the following address on the occasion.]

[30] From C. Z. Lincoln (ed.), *Messages from the Governor*, Vol. III (Albany, NY: J. B. Lyon, 1909), pp. 274–6.

[...] I trust that you will not think it amiss, that I should be explicit with you in regard to another matter, to which direct reference is not usually made on occasions like the present. I allude to those political divisions which exist now, and have heretofore existed among us. Desiring to be fully understood by my fellow-citizens upon all points, and willing to abide by their decisions, I can see no reason why I should avoid an explanation of my sentiments upon a subject, which, every one knows, has a controlling influence over the conduct and deliberations of all our public functionaries.

However public opinion may be divided on the question, whether political parties are or are not desirable or beneficial in a government like ours, all sensible men must be convinced, and the experience of the world has shown, that they will prevail where there is the least degree of liberty of action on the part of public agents, or their constituents; and that they are more especially inseparable from a free government. The history of this republic demonstrates the truth of this position, and it is not desirable, in my opinion, that it should be otherwise.

Those party divisions which are based upon conflicting opinions in regard to the constitution of the government, or the measures of the administration of it, interest every citizen, and tend, inevitably, in the spirit of emulation and proselytism, to reduce many shades of opinion into two opposing parties. By the mutual concession of opinion, within the ranks of a party, acerbity of spirit is softened. Thus, organized parties watch and scan each other's doings, the public mind is instructed by ample discussions of public measures, and acts of violence are restrained by the convictions of the people, that the prevailing measures are the results of enlightened reason.

Diversity of opinion results from the infirmity of human judgment; and party spirit is but the passion with which opposing opinions are urged in the strife for the possession of power. As yet, our free institutions have not suffered from an indulgence in feelings of this character. We have, it is true, witnessed, in times past, a degree of party spirit, so highly excited as to alarm the fears of patriotic men for the integrity of the Union: but, at those periods, the compactness and harmony of our admirable system of government were not thoroughly understood, nor had the attachment of the people to it been fairly tested. Experience has proved, that its foundations are laid so deep in the affections of our citizens, and that its complicated machinery is so nicely adjusted, and so well adapted to its design, that it has an energy sufficient for its own preservation. The universal consciousness of these truths has tamed the spirit of party, and stationed it, as the vigilant watchman, over the conduct of those in power. No stronger proof of this position can be desired, than is furnished by the incidents of the election, through which we have just now passed. The excesses which characterized that struggle, were rebuked by the calm, orderly and dispassionate manner which marked the conduct of the people at the polls, in the discharge of their sacred functions as electors – a rebuke which, I have no doubt, will, at future elections, chasten the conduct of meretricious partizans, and bring down the temper of the paper contest to the manners of the times, and the sense of propriety manifested by the people themselves. [...]

I have said, and now repeat, that as yet, our invaluable institutions have suffered but little, if any thing, from the spirit of party, fiery and excited as at times it has been.

Political parties, at the present day, sobered by past experience, leave scope for the exercise of all the charities and courtesies of life, between opposing members. Their spirit does not enter into families to engender hate, nor into social and religious societies to create dissensions, and to produce bitter and destructive enmities. These are the offices of personal parties, whose spirit is overwrought passion, whose object of pursuit is vengeance, and whose ultimate end is civil disorders and cruel persecution. It is one of the peculiar benefits of a well regulated party spirit in a commonwealth, that it employs the passions actively in a milder mood, and thus shuts the door against faction. [...]

Andrew Jackson

First Inaugural Address (March 4, 1829)

Fellow-Citizens:

[...] As the instrument of the Federal Constitution it will devolve on me for a stated period to execute the laws of the United States, to superintend their foreign and their confederate relations, to manage their revenue, to command their forces, and, by communications to the Legislature, to watch over and to promote their interests generally. And the principles of action by which I shall endeavor to accomplish this circle of duties it is now proper for me briefly to explain.

In administering the laws of Congress I shall keep steadily in view the limitations as well as the extent of the Executive power trusting thereby to discharge the functions of my office without transcending its authority. [...]

In such measures as I may be called on to pursue in regard to the rights of the separate States I hope to be animated by a proper respect for those sovereign members of our Union, taking care not to confound the powers they have reserved to themselves with those they have granted to the Confederacy.

The management of the public revenue – that searching operation in all governments – is among the most delicate and important trusts in ours, and it will, of course, demand no inconsiderable share of my official solicitude. Under every aspect in which it can be considered it would appear that advantage must result from the observance of a strict and faithful economy. This I shall aim at the more anxiously both because it will facilitate the extinguishment of the national debt, the unnecessary duration of which is incompatible with real independence, and because it will counteract that tendency to public and private profligacy which a profuse expenditure of money by the Government is but too apt to engender. Powerful auxiliaries to the attainment of this desirable end are to be found in the regulations provided by the wisdom of Congress for the specific appropriation of public money and the prompt accountability of public officers.

With regard to a proper selection of the subjects of impost with a view to revenue, it would seem to me that the spirit of equity, caution and compromise in which the Constitution was formed requires that the great interests of agriculture, commerce, and manufactures should be equally favored, and that perhaps the only exception to this rule should consist in the peculiar encouragement of any products of either of them that may be found essential to our national independence.

Internal improvement and the diffusion of knowledge, so far as they can be promoted by the constitutional acts of the Federal Government, are of high importance.

Considering standing armies as dangerous to free governments in time of peace, I shall not seek to enlarge our present establishment, nor disregard that salutary lesson of political experience which teaches that the military should be held subordinate to the civil power. The gradual increase of our Navy, whose flag has displayed in distant climes our skill in navigation and our fame in arms; the preservation of our forts, arsenals, and dockyards, and the introduction of progressive improvements in the discipline and science of both branches of our military service are so plainly prescribed by prudence that I should be excused for omitting their mention sooner than for enlarging on their importance. But the bulwark of our defense is the national militia, which in the present state of our intelligence and population must render us invincible. As long as our Government is administered for the good of the people, and is regulated by their will; as long as it secures to us the rights of person and of property, liberty of conscience and of the press, it will be worth defending; and so long as it is worth defending a patriotic militia will cover it with an impenetrable aegis. [...]

The recent demonstration of public sentiment inscribes on the list of Executive duties, in characters too legible to be overlooked, the task of reform, which will require particularly the correction of those abuses that have brought the patronage of the Federal Government into conflict with the freedom of elections, and the counter-action of those causes which have disturbed the rightful course of appointment and have placed or continued power in unfaithful or incompetent hands. [...]

Seventh Annual Address (Washington, December 7, 1835)[31]

[...] It was supposed by those who established the Bank of the United States that from the credit given to it by the custody of the public moneys and other privileges and the precautions taken to guard against the evils which the country had suffered in the bankruptcy of many of the State institutions of that period we should derive from that institution all the security and benefits of a sound currency and every good end that was attainable under that provision of the Constitution which authorizes Congress alone to coin money and regulate the value thereof. But it is scarcely necessary now to say that these anticipations have not been realized.

After the extensive embarrassment and distress recently produced by the Bank of the United States, from which the country is now recovering, aggravated as they were by pretensions to power which defied the public authority, and which if acquiesced in by the people would have changed the whole character of our Government, every candid and intelligent individual must admit that for the

---

[31] From *A Compilation of the Messages and Papers of the Presidents*, Vol. III, Part 1: *Andrew Jackson, March 4, 1833 to March 4, 1837*, edited by J. D. Richardson (New York: Bureau of National Literature and Art, 1903).

attainment of the great advantages of a sound currency we must look to a course of legislation radically different from that which created such an institution. [...]

On this subject I am sure that I can not be mistaken in ascribing our want of success to the undue countenance which has been afforded to the spirit of monopoly. All the serious dangers which our system has yet encountered may be traced to the resort to implied powers and the use of corporations clothed with privileges, the effect of which is to advance the interests of the few at the expense of the many. We have felt but one class of these dangers exhibited in the contest waged by the Bank of the United States against the Government for the last four years. Happily they have been obviated for the present by the indignant resistance of the people, but we should recollect that the principle whence they sprung is an ever-active one, which will not fail to renew its efforts in the same and in other forms so long as there is a hope of success, founded either on the inattention of the people or the treachery of their representatives to the subtle progress of its influence. The bank is, in fact, but one of the fruits of a system at war with the genius of all our institutions – a system founded upon a political creed the fundamental principle of which is a distrust of the popular will as a safe regulator of political power, and whose great ultimate object and inevitable result, should it prevail, is the consolidation of all power in our system in one central government. Lavish public disbursements and corporations with exclusive privileges would be its substitutes for the original and as yet sound checks and balances of the Constitution – the means by whose silent and secret operation a control would be exercised by the few over the political conduct of the many by first acquiring that control over the labor and earnings of the great body of the people. Wherever this spirit has effected an alliance with political power, tyranny and despotism have been the fruit. If it is ever used for the ends of government, it has to be incessantly watched, or it corrupts the sources of the public virtue and agitates the country with questions unfavorable to the harmonious and steady pursuit of its true interests. [...]

Farewell Address (March 4, 1837)[32]

[...] The necessity of watching with jealous anxiety for the preservation of the Union was earnestly pressed upon his fellow-citizens by the Father of his Country in his Farewell Address. He has there told us that "while experience shall not have demonstrated its impracticability, there will always be reason to distrust the patriotism of those who in any quarter may endeavor to weaken its bands"; and he has cautioned us in the strongest terms against the formation of parties on geographical discriminations, as one of the means which might disturb our Union and to which designing men would be likely to resort.

The lessons contained in this invaluable legacy of Washington to his countrymen should be cherished in the heart of every citizen to the latest generation; and perhaps at no period of time could they be more usefully remembered than at the present

---

[32] From *A Compilation of the Messages and Papers of the Presidents*, Vol. III, Part 1: *Andrew Jackson, March 4, 1833 to March 4, 1837*, edited by J. D. Richardson.

moment; for when we look upon the scenes that are passing around us and dwell upon the pages of his parting address, his paternal counsels would seem to be not merely the offspring of wisdom and foresight, but the voice of prophecy, foretelling events and warning us of the evil to come. [...] We behold systematic efforts publicly made to sow the seeds of discord between different parts of the United States and to place party divisions directly upon geographical distinctions; to excite the *South* against the *North* and the *North* against the *South*, and to force into the controversy the most delicate and exciting topics – topics upon which it is impossible that a large portion of the Union can ever speak without strong emotion. Appeals, too, are constantly made to sectional interests in order to influence the election of the Chief Magistrate, as if it were desired that he should favor a particular quarter of the country instead of fulfilling the duties of his station with impartial justice to all; and the possible dissolution of the Union has at length become an ordinary and familiar subject of discussion. Has the warning voice of Washington been forgotten, or have designs already been formed to sever the Union? [...] The honorable feeling of State pride and local attachments finds a place in the bosoms of the most enlightened and pure. But while such men are conscious of their own integrity and honesty of purpose, they ought never to forget that the citizens of other States are their political brethren, and that however mistaken they may be in their views, the great body of them are equally honest and upright with themselves. Mutual suspicions and reproaches may in time create mutual hostility, and artful and designing men will always be found who are ready to foment these fatal divisions and to inflame the natural jealousies of different sections of the country. [...]

What have you to gain by division and dissension? Delude not yourselves with the belief that a breach once made may be afterwards repaired. If the Union is once severed, the line of separation will grow wider and wider, and the controversies which are now debated and settled in the halls of legislation will then be tried in fields of battle and determined by the sword. Neither should you deceive yourselves with the hope that the first line of separation would be the permanent one, and that nothing but harmony and concord would be found in the new associations formed upon the dissolution of this Union. [...]

It is true that cases may be imagined disclosing such a settled purpose of usurpation and oppression on the part of the Government as would justify an appeal to arms. These, however, are extreme cases, which we have no reason to apprehend in a government where the power is in the hands of a patriotic people. And no citizen who loves his country would in any case whatever resort to forcible resistance unless he clearly saw that the time had come when a freeman should prefer death to submission; for if such a struggle is once begun, and the citizens of one section of the country arrayed in arms against those of another in doubtful conflict, let the battle result as it may, there will be an end of the Union and with it an end to the hopes of freedom. The victory of the injured would not secure to them the blessings of liberty; it would avenge their wrongs, but they would themselves share in the common ruin. [...]

It is well known that there have always been those amongst us who wish to enlarge the powers of the General Government, and experience would seem to indicate that there is a tendency on the part of this Government to overstep the boundaries marked out for it by the Constitution. Its legitimate authority is abundantly sufficient for all the purposes for which it was created and its powers being expressly enumerated, there can be no justification for claiming anything beyond them. Every attempt to exercise power beyond these limits should be promptly and firmly opposed, for one evil example will lead to other measures still more mischievous; and if the principle of constructive powers or supposed advantages or temporary circumstances shall ever be permitted to justify the assumption of a power not given by the Constitution, the General Government will before long absorb all the powers of legislation, and you will have in effect but one consolidated government. From the extent of our country, its diversified interests, different pursuits, and different habits, it is too obvious for argument that a single consolidated government would be wholly inadequate to watch over and protect its interests; and every friend of our free institutions should be always prepared to maintain unimpaired and in full vigor the rights and sovereignty of the States and to confine the action of the General Government strictly to the sphere of its appropriate duties. [. . .]

But you must remember, my fellow-citizens, that eternal vigilance by the people is the price of liberty, and that you must pay the price if you wish to secure the blessing. It behooves you, therefore, to be watchful in your States as well as in the Federal Government. The power which the moneyed interest can exercise, when concentrated under a single head and with our present system of currency, was sufficiently demonstrated in the struggle made by the Bank of the United States. Defeated in the General Government, the same class of intriguers and politicians will now resort to the States and endeavor to obtain there the same organization which they failed to perpetuate in the Union; and with specious and deceitful plans of public advantages and State interests and State pride they will endeavor to establish in the different States one moneyed institution with overgrown capital and exclusive privileges sufficient to enable it to control the operations of the other banks. [. . .]

It is one of the serious evils of our present system of banking that it enables one class of society – and that by no means a numerous one – by its control over the currency, to act injuriously upon the interests of all the others and to exercise more than its just proportion of influence in political affairs. The agricultural, the mechanical, and the laboring classes have little or no share in the direction of the great moneyed corporations, and from their habits and the nature of their pursuits they are incapable of forming extensive combinations to act together with united force. [. . .] The planter, the farmer, the mechanic, and the laborer all know that their success depends upon their own industry and economy, and that they must not expect to become suddenly rich by the fruits of their toil. Yet these classes of society form the great body of the people of the United States; they are the bone and sinew of the country – men who love liberty and desire nothing but equal rights and equal laws, and who, moreover, hold the great mass of our national wealth, although it is distributed in moderate amounts among the millions of freemen who possess it. But with overwhelming numbers and wealth on their side they are in constant danger of losing their fair influence in the Government, and with difficulty maintain their just rights against the incessant efforts daily made to encroach upon them. [. . .]

THE WHIGS

Daniel Webster ("Webster–Hayne Debate")

First Speech on Foot's Resolution (January 20, 1830)[33]

[...] Sir, although I have felt quite indifferent about the passing of the resolution, yet opinions were expressed yesterday on the general subject of the public lands, and on some other subjects, by the gentleman from South Carolina, so widely different from my own, that I am not willing to let the occasion pass without some reply. [...]

As a reason for wishing to get rid of the public lands as soon as we could, and as we might, the honorable gentleman said, he wanted no permanent sources of income. He wished to see the time when the Government should not possess a shilling of permanent revenue. If he could speak a magical word, and by that word convert the whole capital into gold, the word should not be spoken. The administration of a fixed revenue, he said, only consolidates the Government, and corrupts the people! Sir, I confess I heard these sentiments uttered on this floor not without deep regret and pain.

I am aware that these, and similar opinions, are espoused by certain persons out of the capitol, and out of this Government; but I did not expect so soon to find them here. Consolidation! – that perpetual cry, both of terror and delusion – consolidation! Sir, when gentlemen speak of the effects of a common fund, belonging to all the States, as having a tendency to consolidation, what do they mean? Do they mean, or can they mean, any thing more than that the Union of the States will be strengthened, by whatever continues or furnishes inducements to the people of the States to hold together? If they mean merely this, then, no doubt, the public lands as well as every thing else in which we have a common interest, tends to consolidation; and to this species of consolidation every true American ought to be attached; it is neither more nor less than strengthening the Union itself. This is the sense in which the framers of the constitution use the word consolidation; and in which sense I adopt and cherish it. They tell us, in the letter submitting the constitution to the consideration of the country, that, "in all our deliberations on this subject, we kept steadily in our view that which appears to us the greatest interest of every true American – the consolidation of our Union – in which is involved our prosperity, felicity, safety; perhaps our national existence. This important consideration, seriously and deeply impressed on our minds, led each State in the Convention to be less rigid, on points of inferior magnitude, than might have been otherwise expected."

This, Sir, is General Washington's consolidation. This is the true constitutional consolidation. I wish to see no new powers drawn to the General Government; but I confess I rejoice in whatever tends to strengthen the bond that unites us, and encourages the hope that our Union may be perpetual. And, therefore, I cannot but feel regret at the expression of such opinions as the gentleman has avowed; because

---

[33] From *The Works of Daniel Webster*, 10th ed., Vol. III (Boston: Little, Brown and Company, 1857), pp. 248–69.

I think their obvious tendency is to weaken the bond of our connexion. I know that there are some persons in the part of the country from which the honorable member comes, who habitually speak of the Union in terms of indifference, or even of disparagement. The honorable member himself is not, I trust, and can never be, one of these. They significantly declare, that it is time to calculate the value of the Union; and their aim seems to be to enumerate, and to magnify all the evils, real and imaginary, which the Government under the Union produces.

The tendency of all these ideas and sentiments is obviously to bring the Union into discussion, as a mere question of present and temporary expediency; nothing more than a mere matter of profit and loss. The Union to be preserved, while it suits local and temporary purposes to preserve it; and to be sundered whenever it shall be found to thwart such purposes. Union, of itself, is considered by the disciples of this school as hardly a good. It is only regarded as a possible means of good; or on the other hand, as a possible means of evil. They cherish no deep and fixed regard for it, flowing from a thorough conviction of its absolute and vital necessity to our welfare. Sir, I deprecate and deplore this tone of thinking and acting. I deem far otherwise of the Union of the States; and so did the framers of the constitution themselves. What they said I believe; fully and sincerely believe, that the Union of the States is essential to the prosperity and safety of the States. I am a Unionist, and in this sense a National Republican. I would strengthen the ties that hold us together. Far, indeed, in my wishes, very far distant be the day, when our associated and fraternal stripes shall be severed asunder, and when that happy constellation under which we have risen to so much renown, shall be broken up, and be seen sinking, star after star, into obscurity and night! [. . .]

As I have already remarked, Sir, it was one among the reasons assigned by the honorable member for his wish to be rid of the public lands altogether, that the public disposition of them, and the revenues derived from them, tend to corrupt the people. This, Sir, I confess, passes my comprehension. These lands are sold at public auction, or taken up at fixed prices, to form farms and freeholds. Whom does this corrupt? According to the system of sales, a fixed proportion is everywhere reserved, as a fund for education. Does education corrupt? Is the schoolmaster a corrupter of youth? the spelling-book, does it break down the morals of the rising generation? and the Holy Scriptures, are they fountains of corruption? Or if, in the exercise of a provident liberality, in regard to its own property as a great landed proprietor, and to high purposes of utility towards others, the government gives portions of these lands to the making of a canal, or the opening of a road, in the country where the lands themselves are situated, what alarming and over whelming corruption follows from all this? Can there be nothing pure in government except the exercise of mere control? Can nothing be done without corruption, but the impositions of penalty and restraint? Whatever is positively beneficent, whatever is actively good, whatever spreads abroad benefits and blessings which all can see and all can feel, whatever opens channels of intercourse, augments population, enhances the value of property, and diffuses knowledge, – must all this be rejected and reprobated as a dangerous and obnoxious policy, hurrying us to the double ruin of a government, turned into despotism by the mere exercise of acts of beneficence, and of a people, corrupted, beyond hope of rescue, by the improvement of their condition? [...]

Second Speech on Foot's Resolution (January 26, 1830)[34]

[...] When the honorable member [Hayne] rose, in his first speech, I paid him the respect of attentive listening; and when he sat down, though surprised, and I must say even astonished, at some of his opinions, nothing was farther from my intention than to commence any personal warfare: and through the whole of the few remarks I made in answer, I avoided, studiously and carefully, every thing which I thought possible to be construed into disrespect. [...]

Since it does not accord with my views of justice and policy to give away the public lands altogether, as a mere matter of gratuity, I am asked by the honorable gentleman on what ground it is that I consent to vote them away in particular instances. How, he inquires, do I reconcile with these professed sentiments, my support of measures appropriating portions of the lands to particular roads, particular canals, particular rivers, and particular institutions of education in the West? This leads, Sir, to the real and wide difference in political opinion between the honorable gentleman and myself. On my part, I look upon all these objects as connected with the common good, fairly embraced in its object and its terms; he, on the contrary, deems them all, if good at all, only local good. This is our difference. The interrogatory which he proceeded to put, at once explains this difference. "What interest," asks he, "has South Carolina in a canal in Ohio?" Sir, this very question is full of significance. It develops the gentleman's whole political system; and its answer expounds mine. Here we differ. I look upon a road over the Alleghanies, a canal round the falls of the Ohio, or a canal or railway from the Atlantic to the Western waters, as being an object large and extensive enough to be fairly said to be for the common benefit. The gentleman thinks otherwise, and this is the key to his construction of the powers of the government. He may well ask what interest has South Carolina in a canal in Ohio. On his system, it is true, she has no interest. On that system, Ohio and Carolina are different governments, and different countries; connected here, it is true, by some slight and ill-defined bond of union, but in all main respects separate and diverse. On that system, Carolina has no more interest in a canal in Ohio than in Mexico. The gentleman, therefore, only follows out his own principles; he does no more than arrive at the natural conclusions of his own doctrines; he only announces the true results of that creed which he has adopted himself, and would persuade others to adopt, when he thus declares that South Carolina has no interest in a public work in Ohio.

Sir, we narrow-minded people of New England do not reason thus. Our notion of things is entirely different. We look upon the States, not as separated, but as united. We love to dwell on that union, and on the mutual happiness which it has so much promoted, and the common renown which it has so greatly contributed to acquire. In our contemplation, Carolina and Ohio are parts of the same country; States, united

---

[34] From *The Works of Daniel Webster*, 10th ed., Vol. III, pp. 270–342.

under the same General Government, having interests, common, associated, inter-mingled. In whatever is within the proper sphere of the constitutional power of this Government, we look upon the States as one. We do not impose geographical limits to our patriotic feeling or regard; we do not follow rivers and mountains, and lines of latitude, to find boundaries, beyond which public improvements do not benefit us. We who come here, as agents and representatives of these narrow-minded and selfish men of New England, consider ourselves as bound to regard, with equal eye, the good of the whole, in whatever is within our power of legislation. Sir, if a railroad or canal, beginning in South Carolina and ending in South Carolina, appeared to me to be of national importance and national magnitude, believing, as I do, that the power of government extends to the encouragement of works of that description, if I were to stand up here and ask, What interest has Massachusetts in a railroad in South Carolina? I should not be willing to face my constituents. These same narrow-minded men would tell me, that they had sent me to act for the whole country, and that one who possessed too little comprehension, either of intellect or feeling, one who was not large enough, both in mind and in heart, to embrace the whole, was not fit to be instructed with the interest of any part.

Sir, I do not desire to enlarge the powers of the government by unjustifiable construction, nor to exercise any not within a fair interpretation. But when it is believed that a power does exist, then it is, in my judgment, to be exercised for the general benefit of the whole. So far as respects the exercise of such a power, the States are one. It was the very object of the Constitution to create unity of interests to the extent of the powers of the general government. [...]

When I shall be found, Sir, in my place here in the Senate, or elsewhere, to sneer at public merit, because it happens to spring up beyond the little limits of my own State or neighborhood; when I refuse, for any such cause, or for any cause, the homage due to American talent, to elevated patriotism, to sincere devotion to liberty and the country; or, if I see an uncommon endowment of Heaven, if I see extraordinary capacity and virtue, in any son of the South, and if, moved by local prejudice or gangrened by State jealousy, I get up here to abate the tithe of a hair from his just character and just fame, may my tongue cleave to the roof of my mouth! [...]

When my eyes shall be turned to behold for the last time the sun in heaven, may I not see him shining on the broken and dishonored fragments of a once glorious Union; on States dissevered, discordant, belligerent; on a land rent with civil feuds, or drenched, it may be, in fraternal blood! Let their last feeble and lingering glance rather behold the gorgeous ensign of the republic, now known and honored through-out the earth, still full high advanced, its arms and trophies streaming in their original lustre, not a stripe erased or polluted, nor a single star obscured, bearing for its motto, no such miserable interrogatory as "What is all this worth?" nor those other words of delusion and folly, "Liberty first and Union afterwards"; but everywhere, spread all over in characters of living light, blazing on all its ample folds, as they float over the sea and over the land, and in every wind under the whole heavens, that other sentiment, dear to every true American heart, – Liberty and Union, now and for ever, one and inseparable!

THE ANTI-MASONIC PARTY

Proceedings of the Anti-Masonic Convention for the State of New York (1830)[35]

Resolutions

[...] And whereas it is the right and duty of every party explicitly to state the objects it proposes, and the principles it adopts in relation to the affairs of government: Therefore,

Resolved, That the anti-masonic republic party is opposed to the existence among this people of *all secret societies*, which by possibility may endanger the public peace, subsidize the public press, corrupt the legislative, overawe the executive, or obstruct the judicial department of government. That the society of free masons holding its meetings in secret, owing its perpetuity to oaths of mutual affiliation co-extensive with the limits of the nation, and yet capable of concentrating its power at any and all points of this Union, is by reason of its very organization liable to be perverted to purposes inconsistent with the public safety and welfare. That in the events which called the party into existence [the murder of William Morgan] we have proof that the society of free masons has broken the public peace, and with a high hand deprived the state of a citizen; that in the guarded and studious silence of the press throughout this Union on the subject of that outrage, we have proof that Free Masonry has subsidized the public press; that in the refusal of the House of Assembly to institute a legislative inquiry into the acts of the society of free masons in relation to that outrage, we have proof that the legislative department has been corrupted; that in the withholding of the acting governor of all positive aid in bringing to justice the actors in that profligate conspiracy, and in his recent denunciation of the same public feeling, which when a judge a hailed as "a pledge that our rights and liberties are destined to endure," we have proof that Freemasonry has made a timid executive subservient to her will – and that in the escape of the guilty conspirators by means of the masonic obligations of witnesses and jurors, we have fearful proof that Freemasonry has obstructed, defeated, and baffled the judiciary in the high exercise of its powers. That for these reasons the society of Freemasons ought to be abolished.

Resolved, That to the abolition of that Order throughout these United States the anti masonic republican party is pledged. [...] That we are impelled in the undertaking to abolish Free Masonry not by fiery excitement, or fanatic zeal, but by a deep sense of our responsibilities to perpetuate this government, the last hope of the friends of freedom throughout the world.

Resolved, That the anti masonic party, wherever organized, is principally composed of farmers and mechanics, as yet retaining too much of the blessed spirit of their ancestors tamely to submit under the thraldom of a privileged Order – too virtuous to be corrupted by the ambition for office and preferment – too steadfast to

[35] *Proceedings of the Anti-Masonic Convention for the State of New York: Held at Utica, August 11, 1830* (Utica: Printed by Wm. Williams, 1830), pp. 4–6, 7–9.

yield to temporary excitement. That the fact cannot be disguised, that the opposition it encounters is principally that of the office holders and office seekers in the cities, towns, and villages. That reposing its confidence upon the yeomanry of the land, and the merits of its principles, its success is certain; and that the attempt to arrest the party in its progress by traducing the character and motives of its members, is as futile as it is false and calumnious.

Resolved, That the ballot box is the constitutional tribunal established by the founders of this government for the redress of all great political evils and abuses; that to the ballot box we bring the question whether Free Masonry shall stand or fall, casting our votes for those who accord with us in opinion on this all important subject. [...]

Resolved, That the anti masonic republican party, while it invites the co-operation of all who love their country and value her institutions, expressly declares that it cannot yield support to any man for any office, who is not fearlessly and openly the opponent of Free Masonry, at all polls. [...]

Resolved, That the present administration of this state has proved itself entirely incompetent to all the following great and leading objects of government: The preservation of the funds and property of the state; the enforcing the demands of public justice; the securing the rights of citizens by equal legislation; the improving the moral condition of the people by necessary alteration in our jurisprudence; and the elevating the character, increasing the wealth, and developing the resources of the state, by means of internal improvement.

Resolved, That the attempt by the present administration, known as the Albany regency, to relieve the banks from the just proportion of the burthen of government, by imposing a tax upon the people, shows palpably their imbecility and gross injustice.

Resolved, That the attempt of the administration to levy a direct tax of more than three hundred thousand dollars, upon the people, to fill a treasury exhausted by its own improvidence and prodigality, justly calls forth the reprobation of the people.

Resolved, That the prosperity of the state of New York is identified with the policy of the protecting system, and works of internal improvement. That the present administration has deceived the people in relation to the former, while it has pursued the cruel policy of a stepmother towards the latter: That the Albany regency, in relation to the canals, have shown themselves incapable of appreciating their value, or pursuing the policy which will preserve them. [...]

Address

Since the dawn of the revolution, the United States have never witnessed a more interesting crisis. [...] The founders of our republic were men of wisdom and sagacity. They thought they had provided safeguards for the liberty they adored, and the independence they achieved, at every point, where human foresight could apprehend the approach of danger. Those unparalleled patriots, who in the estimation of royalty had sinned beyond forgiveness, *Samuel Adams* and *John Hancock*, to whom pardon was refused when it was proffered to all others, on condition of submission, imagined that they saw a lurking peril, in the secret conclaves of Free

Masonry. But the danger was too small or too distant to be perceived by the less acute and powerful optics of their contemporaries, and their prophetic forebodings were unheeded by a generation, happy in the enjoyment of unequalled freedom, and confident of its immortality. That generation has hardly gone, and the danger which those apostles of liberty discerned as by the power of inspiration, we have found increased to a magnitude that threatened the frustration of justice and the subversion of law. A vast effort has been made to shroud in mystery a transaction that now agitates this whole community. The story is as plain and simple as it is dreadful and alarming. Nearly four years ago, William Morgan was mysteriously absent from his family. His neighbors, obeying the impulse of sympathy, rallied to search for the lost man, and when they found he had been forcibly conveyed away, to detect and punish the malefactors who had feloniously stolen him from his country and his home, and as they soon apprehended, had deprived him of liberty or life. They were soon filled with unbounded astonishment, at finding themselves impeded at every step; that every effort was counteracted, and every exertion frustrated by the incessant activity of a portion of their fellow citizens. Alarm succeeded astonishment, when they discovered the appalling fact, that all concerned in the lawless deed, and all who labored to conceal the act, and its perpetrators, were members of a particular fraternity [...] And a people born to be free, rushed together to preserve the government of liberty and law, secured by the toil and wisdom of their fathers for the benefit of mankind. Unforeseen difficulties awaited them, and thickened as they progressed. The press, exultingly regarded as the proud palladium of liberty, proved recreant in its service. At the command of the "all powerful" Order, it uttered forth its thunders to blacken the character of its intended victim, and mark him for destruction [...] The implicated fraternity turned their batteries of defamation against every magistrate and public functionary who dared to perform his official duty. [...]

Dangers and difficulties are the proper stimulants of generous minds. Perils try the souls of men. The contest with the Order was vigorously maintained. New presses were erected, called into existence by the energies, and sustained by the exertions of a virtuous and indignant people.

[...] Notwithstanding all impediments, friends to the cause have multiplied as far and fast as information could be extended; and the anti masonic party, from a village meeting of a few neighbors, now probably numbers within its ranks, one fourth of the electors of this Union; and is now increasing with unprecedented rapidity. [...]

Only one resource remains to overthrow an institution that has proved superior to the law, and too powerful for our courts of justice – the power of public opinion. To that tribunal an appeal is made. The people are charged with the high responsibility of preserving the republican government which they inherited from their fathers, and transmitting it to posterity. To them is assigned the duty of its defence, against internal foes equally as against foreign hostility. The execution of that high trust depends upon the exercise of the elective franchise. By that alone can the people display their sovereignty, preserve the integrity of their political principles, and the purity of their government. Those who are satisfied of the dangers to be apprehended from Free Masonry, seek to overthrow the institution, by refusing to advance to offices of trust and responsibility, the *adhering* members of the fraternity. By this peaceful mode, they hope to bereave the Order of power and influence, and give to their fellow citizens a practical illustration of the impolicy and folly of attempting to uphold it. Claiming the right of bestowing their confidence where it can be safely reposed, they contemplate the removal of the dangers which threaten the existence of the government, by the lawful and peaceful exercise of the sovereign power of freemen. [...]

THE NATIVE AMERICAN PARTY

Millard Fillmore *Letter to Isaac Newton* (January 3, 1855)[36]

[Millard Fillmore was elected 12th vice president in 1848 and succeeded to the presidency in July 1850 upon the death of President Zachary Taylor. Formerly a member of the now near-defunct Whig Party, Fillmore was nominated as candidate for the presidency by the American Party's first and only National Nominating Convention in February 1856.]

[...] I return you many thanks for your information on the subject of politics. I am always happy to hear what is going forward; but, independently of the fact that I feel myself withdrawn from the political arena, I have been too much depressed in spirit to take an active part in the late elections. I contented myself with giving a silent vote for Mr. Ullman for governor.

While, however, I am an inactive observer of public events, I am by no means an indifferent one; and I may say to you, in the frankness of private friendship, I have for a long time looked with dread and apprehension at the corrupting influence which the contest for the foreign vote is exciting upon our elections. This seems to result from its being banded together, and subject to the control of a few interested and selfish leaders. Hence, it has been a subject of bargain and sale, and each of the great political parties of the country has been bidding to obtain it; and, as usual in all such contests, the party which is most corrupt is most successful. The consequence is, that it is fast demoralizing the whole country; corrupting the very fountains of political power; and converting the ballot-box, that great palladium of our liberty, into an unmeaning mockery, where the rights of native-born citizens are voted away by those who blindly follow their mercenary and selfish leaders. The evidence of this is found not merely in the shameless chaffering for the foreign vote at every election, but in the large disproportion of offices which are now held by foreigners, at home and abroad, as compared with our native citizens. Where is the true-hearted American whose cheek does not tingle with shame and mortification to see our highest and most coveted foreign missions filled by men of foreign birth, to the exclusion of native-born? Such appointments are a humiliating confession to the

---

[36] From J. R. Irelan, *History of the Life, Administration, and Times of Millard Fillmore: Trials and Compromises of Slavery and the Rise and Fall of the American Party* (Chicago: Fairbanks & Palmer Publishing Co., 1888), pp. 378–81.

crowned heads of Europe that a republican soil does not produce sufficient talent to represent a republican nation at a monarchical court. I confess that it seems to me, with all due respect to others, that, as a general rule, our country should be governed by American-born citizens. Let us give to the oppressed of every country an asylum and a home in our happy land; give to all the benefits of equal laws and equal protection; but let us at the same time cherish as the apple of our eye the great principles of Constitutional liberty, which few who have not had the good fortune to be reared in a free country know how to appreciate, and still less how to preserve.

Washington, in that inestimable legacy which he left to his country – his Farewell Address – has wisely warned us to beware of foreign influence as the most baneful foe of a Republican government. He saw it, to be sure, in a different light from that in which it now presents itself; but he knew that it would approach in all forms, and hence he cautioned us against the insidious wiles of its influence. Therefore, as well for our own sakes, to whom this invaluable inheritance of self-government has been left by our forefathers, as for the sake of the unborn millions who are to inherit this land – foreign and native – let us take warning of the Father of his Country, and do that we can to preserve our institutions from corruption, and our country from dishonor; but let this be done by the people themselves in their sovereign capacity, by making a proper discrimination in the selection of officers, and not by depriving any individual, native or foreign-born, of any Constitutional or legal right to which he is now entitled. [. . .]

F. R. Anspach *The Sons of the Sires; a History of the Rise, Progress, and Destiny of the American Party, and Its Probable Influence on the Next Presidential Election . . . By an American* (1855)[37]

[. . .] One of the leading dogmas of the new order is, that Americans should rule America. A principle so easily understood requires but little illustration; yet as it may wear an aspect of exclusiveness to some minds, it may not be inappropriate to offer a few considerations to show the justness of this article of their creed. Seeing that the government was managed in many instances by persons of foreign birth, who were reared under influences widely different from those under which the American mind matures, they believe that those men cannot sympathize with American interests, since they are not actuated by those sentiments which thrill the native bosom. To guard our country against a mal-administration of our laws, they hold the opinion that we shall most likely escape those evils that would militate against our prosperity, and be ruinous to our institutions, by elevating none but native born to official stations. That there is more or less danger in committing the government into the hands of adopted citizens, and that sad consequences either immediately or

---

[37] F. R. Anspach, *The Sons of the Sires; a History of the Rise, Progress, and Destiny of the American Party, and Its Probable Influence on the Next Presidential Election. To Which Is Added a Review of the Letter of the Hon. Henry A. Wise, against the Know-Nothings. By an American* (Philadelphia: Lippincott, Grambo & Co., 1855), pp. 41–4, 49–50, 57–8, 69–71.

remotely might be anticipated, is not an idea of recent growth. The framers of our constitution did not regard it in harmony with our interests or safety, to allow the eligibility of a foreigner to the Presidency of these United States. And if in the wisdom of those noble patriots, it would be impolitic and perilous to the peace of our country to select one of foreign birth to fill the chair of State, may we not, upon the same ground exclude them from all minor trusts? May we not urge the force of their example, as an irresistible argument as touching all other offices? Granted that the responsibility may be less and the ability of doing mischief comparatively circum-scribed in lower grades of office, still, if in the former there is reason to exclude them by a provisional act, there must be, though in a diminished degree, danger to trust them with any official stations.

That this maxim of the American party has been violently assailed we are fully aware, but that the wisdom and soundness of this policy has been disproved, we do not grant. [...] There are only four sources from which the opposers of the new order have attempted to draw their arguments against this dogma. From the instincts of humanity, from the teachings of reason, from the example of other nations, and the early practice of our government. The instincts of humanity only require us to afford them protection and to give them scope for the promotion of their happiness, and therefore none of its impulses or laws are contravened by this principle. The dictates of reason are manifestly in favor of it; and the example of other nations amply sustains the views of the American party. There is no other nation so recreant to its interests, as to allow aliens to bear a part in the administration of its government. Those indeed from whom our foreign population comes, do not even allow an expression of opinion concerning their laws and institutions, on the part of those who might wish to make their country a place of residence. Citizenship may not be obtained in many instances on any probation or at any price. And if there were no other ground upon which to defend the principle that Americans should rule America, the example of other nations would warrant the practice of this precaution-ary measure. [...]

Another dogma of the new order is, to protect American interests. [...] The first great duty is to preserve our glorious institutions in their purity. We are bound to transmit them to our posterity as we received them, untarnished and uncorrupted. If we do not guard them, who will? If Americans do not exercise "eternal vigilance which is the price of liberty," who will do it for us?[38] It is equally obvious, that in order to retain them as they are, the same influences, civil and moral, which have moulded the American character and made it what it is, must be kept alive and exerted upon the rising generation. What are these? Chiefly those connected with our educational institutions. Is there any danger that these influences may be weakened or counteracted? Most assuredly. And pray what or who would war against things so sacred, and so vitally associated with our very existence? I reply the papacy, French infidelity, German skepticism, and socialism have formed a tremendous combination against these very interests. [...]

---

[38] The expression "eternal vigilance is the price of liberty" has been spuriously attributed to Thomas Jefferson. There is no evidence that he ever said or wrote this expression or any of its variants, yet since the early nineteenth century Jefferson has frequently been referenced as its author.

Things were tending in that direction so palpably, as to call up the American party to stem the tide, and roll back the current of sympathy which was bearing our political leaders and our precious interests, to the unfathomable bosom of Holy Mother Rome. That power, ever ready for self-aggrandizement, looked with a wistful eye to the dominion of this broad land. The Mississippi valley would have made more than a second Italy. It would have been a magnificent seat for the sovereign Pontiff, and then it would have been not only far more beautiful and extensive than the states now subject to the triple crown, but it would have yielded such handsome revenues. The Pope of Rome could have made it quite convenient, to shift the seat of his dominion from the seven hills to that broad valley, seeing that he would not have broken the hearts of his people by leaving them. [...] And then, too, that noble stream – the father of rivers – would in point of majesty, have accorded much better with the boasted extent and magnificence of the Catholic Church, while it might have been a practical illustration by the filth gathered from afar and near, of the corruption of that mammoth mother of pollution. And while it would have been much more convenient for Arch John to go for his red cap, it would have been in all respects rather a desirable change from the narrow limits of the present papal sovereignty, to the possession of a country washed by the Atlantic and Pacific and filled with invaluable treasures. [...]

There are persons who object to a change in these statutes [laws relating to citizenship] on the ground that it would be unjust and oppressive to the better class of immigrants, to exclude them for a long period from the rights of citizenship, because some of their number are in an unfit state for such privileges. To this objection, I reply that it is not oppressive or unjust to guard the rights and blessings of the whole even if such a measure would in some instances seem to aggrieve the individual. It is the duty of every member of this great commonwealth of freemen, whether fully invested or not with the prerogatives of a citizen, to sacrifice his personal good for the good of the public, if the case is such that one or the other must suffer. [...]

The obligations which humanity imposes are more than met and discharged when we give him a place and a habitation, and extend over his person and his property the shield of our laws, that he may be secure in all his interests as a man. In many instances these men never enjoyed the right of suffrage in their native land, and hence there can be no sacrifice on their part if denied the privilege of voting for a longer term of years, because they never were in possession of the right anywhere, and therefore could not surrender it. [...]

Platform of the American Party, Adopted at the Session of the National Council (February 21, 1856)[39]

1st. An humble acknowledgment to the Supreme Being, for his protecting care vouchsafed to our fathers in their successful Revolutionary struggle, and

---

[39] From *Speeches of Millard Fillmore at New York, Newburgh, Albany, Rochester, Buffalo, etc.* (1856), p. 2.

hitherto manifested to us, their descendants, in the preservation of the liberties, the independence, and the union of these States.

2nd. The perpetuation of the Federal Union and Constitution, as the palladium of our civil and religious liberties, and the only sure bulwarks of American Independence.

3rd. Americans must rule America; and to this end native-born citizens should be selected for all State, Federal, and municipal offices of government employment, in preference to all others; nevertheless,

4th. Persons born of American parents residing temporarily abroad, should be entitled to all the rights of native-born citizens; but

5th. No person should be selected for political station (whether of native or foreign birth), who recognizes any allegiance or obligation of any description to any foreign prince, potentate, or power, or who refuses to recognize the Federal and State Constitutions (each within its sphere), as paramount to all other laws, as rules of political action. [...]

7th. The recognition of the right of native-born and naturalized citizens of the United States, permanently residing in any Territory thereof, to frame their Constitution and laws, and to regulate their domestic and social affairs in their own mode, subject only to the provisions of the Federal Constitution, with the privilege of admission into the Union whenever they have the requisite population for one Representative in Congress: Provided, always, that none but those who are citizens of the United States, under the Constitution and laws thereof, and who have a fixed residence in any such Territory, ought to participate in the formation of the Constitution, or in the enactment of laws for said Territory or State. [...]

9th. A change in the laws of naturalization, making a continued residence of twenty-one years, of all not heretofore provided for, an indispensable requisite for citizen ship hereafter, and excluding all paupers, and persons convicted of crime, from landing upon our shores; but no interference with the vested rights of foreigners.

10th. Opposition to any union between Church and State; no interference with religious faith or worship, and no test oaths for office. [...]

14th. Therefore, to remedy existing evils, and prevent the disastrous consequences otherwise resulting therefrom, we would build up the "American Party" upon the principles hereinbefore stated. [...]

Suggested Readings

Alexander Hamilton, "Report on the National Bank" [1790] in H. C. Syrett (ed.), *The Papers of Alexander Hamilton*, Vol. VII: *September 1790–January 1791* (New York: Columbia University Press, 1963), pp. 305–42.

Thomas Jefferson, "Opinion on the Constitutionality of the Bill for Establishing a National Bank" [1791] in P. L. Ford (ed.), *The Writings of Thomas Jefferson*, Vol. VI (New York: G. P. Putnam's Sons, 1904), pp. 197–204.

Alexander Hamilton, "Report on the Subject of Manufacturers" [1791] in H. C. Syrett (ed.), *The Papers of Alexander Hamilton*, Vol. X: *December 1791–January 1792* (New York: Columbia University Press, 1966), pp. 230–340.

Fisher Ames, "Speech on Jay's Treaty" (April 28, 1796), in *Annals of the Congress of the United States* (House of Representatives, 4th Congress, 1st Session), pp. 1239–64.

John Marshall, *McCulloch v. Maryland* (17 U.S. 316; 1819).

John Taylor, *An Inquiry into the Principles and Policy of the Government of the United States* (Fredericksburg: Green and Cady, 1814).

John Taylor, *Construction Construed and Constitutions Vindicated* (Richmond: Shepherd and Pollard, 1820).

Davy Crockett, "Speech on Electioneering," in *A Narrative of the Life of David Crockett* (New York: Nafis & Cornish, 1845).

Abraham Lincoln, "Letter to Joshua Speed (August 24, 1855), on the Know Nothing-Party," in J. G. Nicolay and J. Hay (eds.), *The Complete Works of Abraham Lincoln*, Vol. II (New York: Francis D. Tandy, 1905), pp. 281–7.

9 People That Were Left Behind

In order to make some sense of the tumultuous period that led up to the Civil War, one should consider, once more, the paradigm of the people's two bodies – the classical republican understanding of the people as a conceptual whole, built upon a differentiation of roles and virtues, and the classical liberal one, conceiving the people as a collection of equal individuals, ruled by the majority of wills.

If the American people were a corporate whole, as classical republicanism had it, why were so many members of this political body left behind? From the destitute dreams of a complete makeover of property laws, to individuals mistrusting all government, to Native Americans, women, and – last but not least – African Americans; what about *their* place and role in this political body? To stick with the corporeal metaphor, why were there so many pained "ghost members" in this body? How could a healthy *political* body deny the *political* existence of so many of its members? Not surprisingly, many sought to broaden or even transform the understanding of the people.

For these left-behind members, classical liberalism often appeared more attractive as a doctrine, by emphasizing the equality of all individuals and their natural rights, regardless of their race, gender, or beliefs. Yet, by the same token, liberal equality also implied submitting, as a minority, to the will of the majority. Moreover, liberal thinking insisted on representing abstract individuals and ignoring differences, while the republican corporatist view emphasized the representation of individuals qua members of a group – hence the need for <u>descriptive representation</u>, discussed in the previous chapters. Which argument should one choose?

As a minority – then and now – how one *practically* addresses these *theoretical* conundrums determines how one chooses between the different sets of strategies. One could, for example, feel that only a *complete and sudden* redress of all the grievances can restore the balance of justice. Let us label this the **all-or-nothing approach**, which is usually associated with **radical idealism**. Or, one could believe that a **step-by-step approach**, while more frustrating and slower, has a greater chance of success, as **conservative realists** tend to believe. Regardless of the strategy one chooses to embrace as a minority, an even bigger decision is the choice between **integration** and **segregation**, i.e. between emphasizing one's **equality** with the majority or emphasizing one's **difference** and particularity, with all the possible gradations in between. Since there is no magic formula or recipe for such decisions, they all have been tried in different combinations, with varying degrees of success.

Take the case of **Thomas Skidmore** (1790–1832). Co-founder of the **Working Men's Party** in 1829, Skidmore was a radical idealist, who followed an all-or-nothing approach. Labeled sometimes a socialist or even a proto-communist for vehemently arguing in favor of an equal redistribution of property (principally land), he would be better characterized, paradoxically, as a radical liberal, who inferred conclusions from Lockean principles that Locke himself would never have dreamed of. He disagreed with Jefferson's wording at the beginning of the Declaration of Independence: "We hold these truths to be self-evident; that all men are created equal; that they are endowed by their Creator with certain unalienable rights; that among these are life, liberty, and the *pursuit of happiness*" (Chapter 5). What displeased Skidmore was the Jeffersonian alteration of Locke's three fundamental rights for the protection of which men renounce the state of nature and enter civil society (Chapter 3): life, liberty, and *property*. "If, then, Mr. Jefferson, had made use of the word *property*, instead of '*the pursuit of happiness*,' I should have agreed with him."

Like Locke, Skidmore argued that one transforms common property into private property through one's labor, and that differences in the amount of work justify differences in the amount of property individuals can amass *during their lifetimes*. However, at this point Locke and Skidmore part ways. For the former, the right of inheritance was never questioned, unless the son wants to join a different government than his father; for the latter, inheritance was the source of all evils. A large inheritance allows one not to work a single day, yet to take advantage of the work of less fortunate inheritors, thus contradicting the very equation work = property. Simply put, Skidmore's proposal was to abolish all inheritance laws so that each generation could have a fresh and equal start. How this would *actually* work when people are born and die every day was of less concern.

Skidmore argued not only for giving equal amounts of property (land) to everyone, but also "the same rights of suffrage to the red man, the black man, and the white man." Yet, by the same logic, he denied Native Americans any special rights to their own land. "Do they hold it by deed from the Great Spirit? [...] Where is the record in marble?" In the end, Skidmore's radicalism did not serve him well. The same year that he was removed from the party he helped found, he created a new one called the **Agrarian Party**, or the **Original Working Men's Party**, but this split doomed the small hope of electoral success that the Working Men's Party had to begin with.

Another form of radical idealism, but one with no formal political ambitions, was the **transcendentalist movement**. It represented a peculiar mix of philosophical, religious, and scientific ideas, combined in such a way that anyone could find something in its teachings that resonated with them. In a nutshell, its members believed that men are naturally good, but they become corrupted by society and its antiquated institutions, false authorities, and politics. The only solution to "transcend" these false opinions was to become self-reliant, finding one's inner truth. "Society everywhere is in conspiracy against the manhood of every one of its members." If this sounds much like today's self-help books and motivational speakers, there may be a reason.

Ralph Waldo Emerson (1803–1882) was one of the founders of the transcendentalist movement, and he made a good living by delivering paid lectures all across the United States. All great men of the past, he argued, were great because they were non-conformists. They did not "capitulate to badges and names, to large societies and dead institutions," but chose to transform them. Instead of becoming yet another cog in the system, such great men become "the center of the movement, and compel the system to gyrate round it." His popular individualism mirrored in some ways the success of the preachers of the First Great Awakening a century before (Chapter 4).

Yet, for all his radical individualism and his enthusiasm for earth-shaking revolutions (like the French Revolution), Emerson also believed that real progress, while unstoppable, is rather slow. He was thus more on the side of the step-by-step approach. Like many conservatives, he claimed that most sudden changes are foolish, if they are not in accordance with the character of the citizens. The State is an artificial creation, "[b]ut politics rest on necessary foundations, and cannot be treated with levity." Hence, "the wise know that foolish legislation is a rope of sand, which perishes in the twisting; that the State must follow, and not lead the character and progress of the citizen." A wise leader would favor the flourishing of independent and freethinking individuals, "Hence, the less government we have, the better." On the contrary, corrupt leaders, even if charismatic (or possibly even more if so), "reap the rewards of the docility and zeal of the masses which they direct."

Emerson's distrust in any form of regimentation might explain his initial reluctance to join the abolitionist movement, despite his firm opposition to the institution of slavery. He suspected its supporters of being men of a single idea and of relying too much on systemic societal change and too little on individuals. Yet, as the Civil War approached, he became an increasingly vocal supporter of emancipation, to the extent that he accused Lincoln of placing the preservation of the Union ahead of the abolition of slavery (Chapter 10). Nevertheless, his "evolutionary" take led him also to believe that the "Anglo-Saxon race" remained at the top of the evolutionary ladder.

His younger disciple and friend, Henry David Thoreau (1817–1862), shared many of Emerson's ideas, but he was more radical and more impetuous than his master. His inclination for an all-or-nothing approach is evident when he takes his mentor's words a step further: "I heartily accept the motto, – 'That government is best which governs least'; and I should like to see it acted up to more rapidly and systematically. Carried out, it finally amounts to this, which also I believe – *'That government is best which governs not at all.'*" Because of these lines, taken out of context, he was often characterized as an anarchist. As a matter of fact, he believed in the power of civil disobedience to force dramatic changes in the government: "I ask for, not at once no government, but *at once* a better government."[1] Nevertheless, he understood civil disobedience to be both pacific non-resistance *and* forcible resistance; he therefore

---

[1] Not surprisingly, Thoreau had considerable influence on people like Mahatma Gandhi, John F. Kennedy, and Martin Luther King Jr.

wholeheartedly supported <u>radical abolitionist</u> **John Brown**, whose execution he compared with the crucifixion of Jesus Christ.[2]

Thoreau was no liberal, in that, like Madison, he believed that majorities can and often do become oppressive. If "a majority are permitted, and for a long period continue, to rule, [it] is not because they are most likely to be in the right, nor because this seems fairest to the minority, but because they are physically the strongest." Hence, "the only obligation which I have a right to assume, is to do at any time what I think right."

Thoreau took a more literal stance on Emerson's rather theoretical call for a return to nature and to a life in solitude. He built a small cabin on Emerson's lands near Walden Pond, and he spent over two years there, in quasi-reclusion. "Quasi," because the hut was only about a mile and a half from Emerson's family home, and he made frequent trips to town. On one of these trips he ran into a local tax collector who asked him to pay six years of delinquent poll taxes. Since he refused on principle, he spent one night in jail, before a mysterious benefactor paid off his debt. Yet that one night was enough to prompt Thoreau to write his famous essay on *Civil Disobedience*. Despite no immediate political consequences, the transcendentalists' idealism and belief in progress left an undeniable mark on American politics, proving, once again, that ideas do matter.

For Native Americans, the relationship between a minority and a majority was less theoretical and rather a matter of survival. After all, even if the Declaration of Independence referred to them as "the merciless Indian Savages," they were formally considered sovereign political bodies (nations), and as such several treaties were signed by Congress with various tribes under the Articles of Confederation. Art. I, § 8 of the Constitution likewise provided that "Congress shall have the power [...] to regulate commerce with foreign nations [...] *and* with Indian tribes." With stakes so high, different strategies of survival were attempted, yet, as in the case of the American states, the challenge was to decide whether or not their tribal identity was more important than their collective identity.

Tecumseh (1768–1813) was a Shawnee warrior leader who realized that the main weakness of his people was the lack of unity among the various tribes. He managed to create a multi-tribal confederation with the declared purpose of expelling settlers from the old Native American lands and to establish a unified Native American nation east of the Mississippi River, under British protection. His speeches were dominated by a sentiment of urgency; it was now or never. Many other tribes had already "vanished before the avarice and oppression of the white men, as snow before a summer sun. [...] Shall we calmly wait until they become so numerous that we will no longer be able to resist oppression?" Tecumseh's solution was "<u>all-or-nothing</u>". "War or extermination is now our only choice. Which do you choose?"

Not everyone agreed with Tecumseh. **Pushmataha** (*c.*1764–1824), one of the major Choctaw leaders, had the exact opposite opinion. He warned against "forming

---

[2] John Brown (1800–1859) was a fervent advocate of armed insurrection to abolish slavery. In October 1859, he led a raid on the federal armory at Harpers Ferry, intending to start a slave liberation movement. He seized the armory, but several people were killed or injured, and no slaves joined the rebellion. He was captured, tried for treason, and hanged.

rash and dangerous resolutions upon things of highest importance, through the instigations of others." Hence, Pushmataha opposed Tecumseh's radical idealism with <u>conservative realism</u>. He argued that not only would it be "unwise and inconsiderate" to start a war with no real hope of success, but also that it would be unjust and dishonorable to violate a "solemn" treaty. In the persisting conflicts between the British and the Americans, Pushmataha, unlike Tecumseh, supported the latter, so that the two leaders and their followers found themselves fighting on opposite sides during the **War of 1812** ("the Forgotten War").

In the end, Pushmataha's approach proved more successful – at least in the short term. In 1811, the Governor of the Indiana Territory and future president, William Henry Harrison, defeated the alliance of tribes under the leadership of Tecumseh and his brother **Tenkwatawa** (The Prophet, a charismatic religious figure). In the aftermath, Harrison burned down Prophetstown – a town created by the two brothers, along with more than 3,000 inhabitants from different tribes. It is said that this event led to <u>Tecumseh's curse</u>, according to which all presidents elected in a year ending in zero would die in office.[3] In 1812, Tecumseh's confederacy joined the British Army and remained loyal to the bitter end; on the other hand, Pushmataha joined the American forces, and after their victory managed to sign several treaties with the United States.

Yet Tecumseh's ideas were carried forward, and in 1821 a delegation of chiefs from several tribes traveled to Washington, DC. One member of the delegation was the Pawnee chief **Petalesharo** (*c.*1797–*c.*1836), whose reputation for having saved a Comanche girl from a human sacrifice ritual preceded him on the East Coast. His speech was meant to emphasize differences that ought to be acknowledged and respected: "The Great Spirit made us all – made my skin red, and yours white; he placed us on this earth, and intended that *we should live differently from each other*." Yet all of these efforts to find a solution were slow in bearing results; only in 1924, by adopting the **Indian Citizenship Act**, did Congress grant Native Americans the right to vote, and until 1957 some states still barred them from access to the polls.

The fight of women – a "Tribe more numerous and powerfull [*sic*] than all the rest," as Abigail Adams put it – for equal recognition took nearly as long. Women's electoral franchise was gained only in 1920, with the **19th Amendment**, but their battle began much earlier. **Abigail Adams** (1744–1818), the wife and closest confidante of John Adams, hoped initially that the issue would be solved by the time of the signing of the Declaration of Independence. She wrote to her husband, "I long to hear that you have declared an independancy [*sic*] – and by the way in the new Code of Laws which I suppose it will be necessary for you to make I desire you would Remember the Ladies, and be more generous and favourable to them than your ancestors." When her husband argued that this was not a realistic demand, given the many conflicting interests on the eve of Independence, she excused herself in a letter to **Mercy Otis**

---

[3] Harrison died after thirty days in office (elected 1840); 1860, Lincoln – assassinated; 1880, John Garfield – assassinated; 1890, William McKinley – assassinated; 1920, Warren G. Harding – died from a stroke; 1940, F. D. Roosevelt – died of natural causes; 1960, John F. Kennedy – assassinated; 1980, Ronald Reagan – "broke the curse" – survived an attempt to assassinate him.

Warren,[4] suggesting that there was only so much she could do on behalf of her gender. Overall, her attitude remained one of <u>conservative realism</u>.

Other pioneers of women's rights adopted a different strategy. Although she never set foot in the New World, the British **Mary Wollstonecraft** (1759–1797) inspired many American women to adopt a more <u>radical idealism</u>. It was her penchant for this approach that made her famous, once she published a rebuttal of Edmund Burke's *Reflections on the Revolution in France* (Chapter 2), entitled *A Vindication of the Rights of Woman*, in which she praised the French Revolution on a theoretical basis similar to Thomas Paine (Chapter 5). Even though, like Paine, her position became more nuanced after experiencing the Reign of Terror first-hand, her whole (and unfortunately short) life remained proof of the same <u>radical idealism</u>.

Wollstonecraft argued that if women appear more "innocent" (which "is but a civil term for weakness") than men, it is because they "are told from their infancy, and taught by the example of their mothers." She realized that an improved private education would not suffice, as "men and women must be educated, in a great degree, by the opinions and manners *of the society* they live in." Thus, the solution was a radical transformation of the whole society, on rational bases, like the French Revolution had promised. Until such conditions are met, "it cannot be demonstrated that woman is essentially inferior to man, because she has always been subjugated."

The American **Elizabeth Cady Stanton** (1815–1902) carried the torch even further. Besides her lifelong struggle for women's rights, she was involved in the temperance and abolitionist movements from her early years. When it came to women's rights, she was not satisfied with mere electoral franchise, even though she considered that "this right will secure all others." She was an <u>all-or-nothing</u> activist, as reflected in the **Seneca Falls Declaration of Sentiments and Resolutions**. Modeled after the Declaration of Independence, it formulated women's grievances in terms well known to American ears: "We hold these truths to be self-evident: that all men *and women* are created equal [. . .]." The tyrant was no longer King George, but man. "The history of mankind is a history of repeated injuries and usurpations on the part of man toward woman, having in direct object the establishment of an absolute tyranny over her."

Starting with men's refusing women the "inalienable right to electoral franchise," the document continues with an entire set of complaints, ranging from property rights to divorce, from equal access to education to equal access to the pulpit. Since an appeal to votes could not be made, the obvious recourse was an appeal to natural rights and to the respected figure of the British William Blackstone (Chapter 2). Yet, in the short run, this all-or-nothing approach proved less effective. Scared off by the sweeping demands, only 100 men and women from an audience of over 300 signed the Declaration and, faced with ridicule in subsequent press coverage, many chose to retract their signatures.

Stanton's approach put her in conflict with an old friend, **Frederick Douglass** (Chapter 10), as she opposed the passage of the 14th and 15th Amendments. She was

---

[4] Mercy Otis Warren (1728–1814) was one of the key figures of the founding era. She maintained a close relationship with many of the founders, and made her voice count. A poet and a playwright, she also published one of the earliest histories of the American Revolution.

revolted by the idea that "every type and shade of degraded, ignorant manhood should be enfranchised, before even the higher classes of womanhood should be admitted to the polls." In reply, Douglass argued that "with us, the matter is a question of life and death. [...] When women, because they are women, are hunted down [...]; when they are dragged from their houses and hung upon lamp-posts [...], when their children are not allowed to enter schools; then they will have an urgency to obtain the ballot equal to our own."

In retrospect it is difficult to understand how two old friends, both fighting for worthy causes, came to be at odds when reality forced them to choose sides. Yet, as we shall see in Chapter 10, Frederick Douglass came to the conclusion that the conservative realist approach tends to produce better results than the radical idealist one. The good news is that, in their final years, the fences between Stanton and Douglass came to be mended; maybe those between the two approaches can be as well.

THE WORKING MEN'S PARTY

Thomas Skidmore *The Rights of Men to Property* (1829)[5]

[The full title of Skidmore's book suggests the burden of his argument: *The Rights of Men to Property! Being a Proposition to Make It Equal among the Adults of the Present Generation: and to Provide Its Equal Transmission to Every Individual of Each Succeeding Generation on Arriving at the Age of Maturity.*]

There is no man of the least reflection, who has not observed, that the effect, in all ages and countries, of the possession of great and undue wealth, is, to allow those who possess it, to live on the labor of others. And yet there is no truth more readily, cheerfully, and universally acknowledged, than that the personal exertions of each individual of the human race, are exclusively and unalienably his own.

It would seem, then, to be no bad specimen of argument, to say, inasmuch as great wealth is an instrument which is uniformly used to extort from others, their property in their personal qualities and efforts – that it ought to be taken away from its possessor, on the same principle, that a sword or a pistol may be wrested from a robber, who shall undertake to accomplish the same effect, in a different manner.

One thing must be obvious to the plainest understanding; that as long as property is unequal; or rather, as long as it is so enormously unequal, as we see it at present, that those who possess it, will live on the labor of others, and themselves perform none, or if any, a very disproportionate share, of that toil which attends them as a condition of their existence, and without the performance of which, they have no just right to preserve or retain that existence, even for a single hour.

It is not possible to maintain a doctrine to the contrary of this position, without, at the same time, maintaining an absurdity no longer tolerated in enlightened countries; that a part, and that a very great part, of the human race, are doomed, of right, to the slavery of toil, while others are born, only to enjoy. [...]

There seem to be three things which have an intimate and inseparable connection with each other.

These are property, persons and rights.

Out of these materials are built, or ought to be built, all the governments in the world. These are all the necessary and proper elements of their constitution; and these being applied as they have been, have caused, in my estimation, more evil to mankind, than any one can pretend that governments have done good; and, being applied as they may be, will fulfil the destiny of man, by reversing the results of the past.

What, then, is property? I answer; the whole material world: just as it came from the hands of the Creator.

What are persons? The human beings, whom the same Creator placed, or formed upon it, as inhabitants.

---

[5] T. Skidmore, *The Rights of Men to Property* (New York: Burt Franklin, 1829), pp. 3–4, 32, 58–60, 119–21, 126–8, 130–2, 158–9, 269–70.

What are Rights? The title which each of the inhabitants of this Globe, has to partake of and enjoy equally with his fellows, its fruits and its productions. [...]

Mr. Jefferson speaks of the rights of man, in terms, which when they come to be investigated closely, appear to be very defective and equivocal. [...] "We hold these truths to be self-evident; that all men are created equal; that they are endowed by their Creator with certain unalienable rights; that among these are life, liberty, and the *pursuit of happiness*." These are his words in the declaration of American Independence.

Whoever looks over the face of the world, and surveys the population of all countries; our own, as well as any and every other; will see it divided in to rich and poor; into the hundred who have every thing, and the million who have nothing. If, then, Mr. Jefferson, had made use of the word *property*, instead of "*the pursuit of happiness*," I should have agreed with him. Then his language would have been clear and intelligible, and strictly conformable to natural right. For I hold, that man's natural right to *life* or *liberty*, is not more sacred or unalienable, than his right to property. But if property is to descend only to particular individuals from the previous generation, and if the many are born, having neither parents nor any one else, to give them property, equal in amount to that which the sons of the rich, receive, from their fathers and other testators, how is it established that they are created equal? In the pursuit of happiness, is property of no consequence? Can any one be as happy without property of any kind, as with it? Is even liberty and life to be preserved without it? Do we not every day, see multitudes, in order to acquire property, in the very pursuit of that happiness which Mr. Jefferson classes among the unalienable rights of man, obliged to sacrifice both liberty and health and often ultimately life, into the bargain? [...] If, then, even the rights of liberty and life, are so insecure and precarious, without property – how very essential to their preservation is it, that "the pursuit of happiness" – should be so construed, as to afford title to that, without which, the rights of life and liberty are but an empty name? [...]

The principle which the first of all governments in any country, and, indeed, every succeeding government, should adopt and practise, is this. In dividing that which is the equal and common property of all, the apportionments should be equal; and if it is concluded, as it will be, where men understand how best to pursue their own happiness, that a life-lease of property is better than any other, that will be the term preferred to every other. Then will every one understand that he has full liberty to use the materials of which, during his life-time, he is the master, in such a manner as, in his judgment, shall promote his own happiness. He will understand, too, that if the use which he shall make of them, shall be such as to meet, the approbation of those who come after him, they will be disposed to follow his example; but if not, that still the successor has a right to make such other use of the same, as to him shall seem good, with the knowledge that every other person coming after him, too, will be equally free. Society, thus organized, gives notice to all its members, that they are to use their own industry, with a view to their own happiness; and cannot be allowed, on any pretence whatever, whether of kindness or otherwise, to interfere with others in the same pursuit. Under these circumstances, then, no one would seek to acquire property for the purpose of making it an instrument (to be placed in the hands of children,) of domination over the children of other parents; and every one would be willing that all, in whatever age or generation they might appear, should have equal possession of the materials of the world, and, of course, of the means of assuring their own happiness.

If any thing can add force to these observations, it is, that as regards the prevailing ideas, as to who are and who are not successors to property, they are altogether founded in error. In a community where the soil, the equal and common property of all, should be divided equally, and the equal portions held by each member, for one year only, what member could say he had a successor? Is there any one on whom he could confer the right of occupying that which, by the death of his own tenure, he is compelled to vacate and abandon? Where the tenure extended to the term of ten years, who then would have a successor? If, indeed, there be any at all, the community itself is the successor; and there is no other. So also is the community the successor, and the sole successor, in the case where the government is so organized, that every member of it holds, property during his life. At his death, it returns to the community, and these, in duty to every member of which it is composed, yield to them, at the suitable age, their share of the common property, and secure to them its enjoyment during their lives. There is, therefore, no such thing, then, as Successor, in the meaning in which the word is received among men at the present day. It is only a misunderstanding of our rights that could have tolerated its use or existence among us. [. . .]

The truth is, all governments in the world, have begun wrong; in the *first appropriation* they have made, or suffered to be made, of the domain, over which they have exercised their power, and in the transmission of this domain to their posterity. Here are the two great and radical evils, that have caused all the misfortunes of man. These and these alone, have done the whole of it. I do not class among these misfortunes, the sufferings with which sickness afflicts him, because these have a natural origin; capable, however, of being nearly annihilated by good governments, but greatly aggravated by those that are bad.

If these remarks be true, there would seem, then, to be no remedy but by commencing anew. And is there any reason why we should not? That which is commenced in error and injustice, may surely be set right, when we know how to do it. There is *power* enough in the hands of the people of the State of New-York, or of any other State, to rectify any and every thing which requires it, when they shall see wherein the evil exists, and wherein lies the remedy. These two things it is necessary they should see, before they can possess the moral power and motive to act. I have succeeded, I think, in shewing [*sic*], for that is self-evident, that man's natural *right* to an equal portion of property, is indisputable. His artificial right, or right in society, is not less so. For it is not to be said that any power has any right to make our artificial rights unequal, any more than it has to make our natural rights unequal. And inasmuch as a man, in a state of nature, would have a right to resist, even to the extremity of death, his fellow, or his fellows, whatever might be their number, who should undertake to give him less of the property, common to all, than they take each to themselves; so also has man now, in society, the same right to resist a similar wrong done him. Thus, to day, if property had been made equal among all present, right would have taken place among them; but if to-morrow a new member appear, and provision be not made to give him a quantity substanly [*sic*] equal with all his fellows, injustice is done him, and if he had the power, he would have the perfect right, to dispossess all those who have monopolized to themselves not only their own shares, but his also. For it is not to be allowed, even to a majority to contravene equality, nor, of course, the right, even though it be of a single individual. And if, alone, he has not power sufficient to obtain his rights, and there be others, also, in like condition with him, they may unite their efforts, and thus accomplish it, if within their power. And, if this may be lawfully done, upon the supposition that yesterday, only, a government was made, and an equal enjoyment of property guaranteed to all, how much more proper is it when, unjust government existing, it has never been done at all. When the whole mass of people, as it were, ninety-nine out of every hundred, have never had this equal enjoyment, in any manner or shape, what ever? [. . .]

[T]here is no truth more indisputable than this; that the soil of any and every country, belongs wholly and equally to all who are found upon it; more especially so, if a majority of the people of of [*sic*] other nations do not object to it. It will serve little purpose to say that the Indians were, of right, the owners of the soil, exclusively, and that any transfer they should make to him who should negotiate with them, what is called a purchase is valid. The Indians themselves, (separate from the consent of other nations,) do not, and did not, own this whole country, unless it can be shown, that being divided equally among them, there was no more than their just and equal share, of the whole property of the globe. How this is, every one knows. Yet, still, if it be contended, that the Indians were nevertheless, the true owners of the soil; it must certainly, be, for some good reason. Let us enquire, (nor let it be said that on so important and interesting a subject as this, we can enquire too much) what that good reason may be. Is it because of their nativity? Is it in virtue of their being born upon it? This is a reason, which, if it is to have any force at all, can have it only when it is applicable to an individual. For nations, cannot be born. [. . .] The Indians themselves, never dreamed, that the country was so exclusively theirs, when the first discoverers came among them, that beings so much like themselves, might not partake of nature's bounties in the same equal manner with themselves; and only a mistaken avarice and superstition made them enemies. [. . .] If it be conceded, as I think it must be, that place of birth, cannot give title to the Indians, to the exclusive possession of this whole country, what other title is there? Do they hold it by deed from the Great Spirit? Where is the parchment that contains it? Where is the table of wax? Where is the record in marble? Is title engraved on the surface of the earth? Is it written on the face of the sun? In what other material, if there be any such, is his pleasure made known? Surely, if the right exist at all, there must be some means of ascertaining it, some memorial of its existence. [. . .]

I would give the same rights of suffrage to the red man, the black man, and the white man. [. . .] The same eternal and indissoluble rights, exist for all: "all men are created equal": and neither governments, nor others, have any right, so to speak, to *uncreate them.* The black man's right to suffrage, being a personal right, is as perfect as the white man's; and, so also is his right of property. But, if the present constitution existed, and the colored citizen were put in possession of his equal portion of the domain of the State, and all its personal effects, he would not have the same right to appear at the ballot boxes, as the white man. It is necessary that he should have such right; for elsewhere there is no power, but unlawful force, with which he may defend his property. Those who could go to the ballot-boxes, and put in their votes, could, by that very act, take it away from him, without his having a chance to make reprisal or resistance. It would be nonsense on the one hand to say, "this is your property"; and on the other, to tell him; "but you shall not have the same power to defend it, as belongs to another." Nor, can it be pretended, on any account, that what, some people call policy, should sanction the with-holding from the black man, the same right of suffrage, which is extended to the white man, by reason of the former existence of slavery among us. [...]

To all the free States particularly, will the principles of this Work extend, if they shall be found to be of any value to this. The extension of instruction, is now so general throughout the Union, that, if it be acceptable here [in New York], it is likely to be acceptable elsewhere; and particularly so, where the evil of slavery does not exist. And, even in the slave-holding States; the rights of the poor white man, in opposition to what are now considered as the rights of the rich white man, will not fail to be demanded and defended by the former, whenever this Work shall find its way to their understandings. They, as well as we, in our own State, will not fail to make inquiry, why it is, that one white man is better than another; why he should possess more houses, or lands, or negroes, than another; why wills are not as unjust there, as in other places? And, if no satisfactory answer can be given to the poor white man of the South, by his rich brother; what is to hinder him and his associates from doing as we can and may do here; that is, making a General Division of all property of the State wherein he lives, and taking the necessary measures to transmit it equally to posterity?

I go even further. I even believe that if it were possible, in any short time, for the poor white man of the South to renounce his prejudices against the slaves and to admit that it is no more consistent with *right*, that the slaves should be subservient to him, than it is for the poor white man, to be subservient to the rich one; that even the slaves, themselves, might at once be admitted to an equal participation with themselves. Those who have been at the South, know, that among the slaves, there are many, who would not willingly take their freedom, if it were given to them; and, for this reason; inasmuch, as they would have no property; they, therefore, think they could not support themselves. Such is the habit, which slavery has impressed upon their feelings, that they think they would fail of subsistence, if they had not a master. But, if, with freedom, they were presented with lands, and other property also; wherewith to obtain subsistence the case would be very different; and, nothing could intervene to create dissension or disturbance; if the whites, could prevail on their *own* feelings not to envy and oppose, this easy and natural method of extinguishing slavery, and its ten thousand attendant evils. To say that the whites are not capable of labor, would be no less than to say, that nature had made a mistake in creating them; by giving them wants in abundance, without the means of supplying them; and, would be just as true, as it would be, for our rich white man of the North, to say that *he*, too, could not labor; and, therefore, must have white men to labor for him, in every respect as good as himself!

Under present circumstances, however, I think, that such an event is impossible. [...]

AMERICAN TRANSCENDENTALISM

Ralph Waldo Emerson

Self-Reliance (1841)[6]

[...] To believe your own thought, to believe that what is true for you in your private heart is true for all men, – that is genius. Speak your latent conviction, and it shall be the universal sense; for the inmost in due time becomes the outmost, – and our first thought is rendered back to us by the trumpets of the Last Judgment. Familiar as the voice of the mind is to each, the highest merit we ascribe to Moses, Plato, and Milton is, that they set at naught books and traditions, and spoke not what men but what they thought. A man should learn to detect and watch that gleam of light which flashes across his mind from within, more than the lustre of the firmament of bards and sages. Yet he dismisses without notice his thought, because it is his. In every work of genius we recognize our own rejected thoughts: they come back to us with a certain alienated majesty. Great works of art have no more affecting lesson for us than this. They teach us to abide by our spontaneous impression with good-humored inflexibility then most when the whole cry of voices is on the other side. [...]

These are the voices which we hear in solitude, but they grow faint and inaudible as we enter into the world. Society everywhere is in conspiracy against the manhood of every one of its members. Society is a joint-stock company, in which the members agree, for the better securing of his bread to each shareholder, to surrender the liberty and culture of the eater. The virtue in most request is conformity. Self-reliance is its aversion. It loves not realities and creators, but names and customs.

Whoso would be a man must be a nonconformist. He who would gather immortal palms must not be hindered by the name of goodness, but must explore if it be goodness. Nothing is at last sacred but the integrity of your own mind. Absolve you to yourself, and you shall have the suffrage of the world. [...] No law can be sacred to me but that of my nature. Good and bad are but names very readily transferable to that or this; the only right is what is after my constitution, the only wrong what is against it. A man is to carry himself in the presence of all opposition, as if every thing were titular and ephemeral but he. I am ashamed to think how easily we capitulate to badges and names, to large societies and dead institutions. Every decent and well-spoken individual affects and sways me more than is right. I ought to go upright and vital, and speak the rude truth in all ways. [...]

---

[6] From R. W. Emerson, *Essays: First Series* (Boston: James Munroe & Co., 1850), pp. 37–80.

What I must do is all that concerns me, not what the people think. This rule, equally arduous in actual and in intellectual life, may serve for the whole distinction between greatness and meanness. It is the harder, because you will always find those who think they know what is your duty better than you know it. It is easy in the world to live after the world's opinion; it is easy in solitude to live after our own; but the great man is he who in the midst of the crowd keeps with perfect sweetness the independence of solitude. [...]

For nonconformity the world whips you with its displeasure. And therefore a man must know how to estimate a sour face. [...] It is easy enough for a firm man who knows the world to brook the rage of the cultivated classes. Their rage is decorous and prudent, for they are timid as being very vulnerable themselves. But when to their feminine rage the indignation of the people is added, when the ignorant and the poor are aroused, when the unintelligent brute force that lies at the bottom of society is made to growl and mow, it needs the habit of magnanimity and religion to treat it godlike as a trifle of no concernment. [...]

I hope in these days we have heard the last of conformity and consistency. Let the words be gazetted and ridiculous henceforward. Instead of the gong for dinner, let us hear a whistle from the Spartan fife. Let us never bow and apologize more. A great man is coming to eat at my house. I do not wish to please him; I wish that he should wish to please me. I will stand here for humanity, and though I would make it kind, I would make it true. Let us affront and reprimand the smooth mediocrity and squalid contentment of the times, and hurl in the face of custom, and trade, and office, the fact which is the upshot of all history, that there is a great responsible Thinker and Actor working wherever a man works; that a true man belongs to no other time or place, but is the centre of things. [...]

If we cannot at once rise to the sanctities of obedience and faith, let us at least resist our temptations; let us enter into the state of war, and wake Thor and Woden, courage and constancy, in our Saxon breasts. This is to be done in our smooth times by speaking the truth. Check this lying hospitality and lying affection. Live no longer to the expectation of these deceived and deceiving people with whom we converse. Say to them, O father, O mother, O wife, O brother, O friend, I have lived with you after appearances hitherto. Henceforward I am the truth's. Be it known unto you that henceforward I obey no law less than the eternal law. I will have no covenants but proximities. I shall endeavour to nourish my parents, to support my family, to be the chaste husband of one wife, – but these relations I must fill after a new and unprecedented way. I appeal from your customs. I must be myself. I cannot break myself any longer for you, or you. If you can love me for what I am, we shall be the happier. If you cannot, I will still seek to deserve that you should. I will not hide my tastes or aversions. [...] But so you may give these friends pain. Yes, but I cannot sell my liberty and my power, to save their sensibility. Besides, all persons have their moments of reason, when they look out into the region of absolute truth; then will they justify me, and do the same thing.

The populace think that your rejection of popular standards is a rejection of all standard, and mere antinomianism; and the bold sensualist will use the name of philosophy to gild his crimes. But the law of consciousness abides. There are two confessionals, in one or the other of which we must be shriven. You may fulfil your round of duties by clearing yourself in the *direct*, or in the *reflex* way. Consider whether you have satisfied your relations to father, mother, cousin, neighbour, town, cat, and dog; whether any of these can upbraid you. But I may also neglect this reflex standard, and absolve me to myself. I have my own stern claims and perfect circle. It denies the name of duty to many offices that are called duties. But if I can discharge its debts, it enables me to dispense with the popular code. If any one imagines that this law is lax, let him keep its commandment one day. [...]

Politics (1844)[7]

In dealing with the State, we ought to remember that its institutions are not aboriginal, though they existed before we were born: that they are not superior to the citizen: that every one of them was once the act of a single man: every law and usage was a man's expedient to meet a particular case: that they all are imitable, all alterable; we may make as good; we may make better. Society is an illusion to the young citizen. It lies before him in rigid repose, with certain names, men, and institutions, rooted like oak-trees to the centre, round which all arrange themselves the best they can. But the old statesman knows that society is fluid; there are no such roots and centres; but any particle may suddenly become the centre of the movement, and compel the system to gyrate round it, as every man of strong will, like Pisistratus, or Cromwell, does for a time, and every man of truth, like Plato, or Paul, does forever. But politics rest on necessary foundations, and cannot be treated with levity. Republics abound in young civilians, who believe that the laws make the city, that grave modifications of the policy and modes of living, and employments of the population, that commerce, education, and religion, may be voted in or out; and that any measure, though it were absurd, may be imposed on a people, if only you can get sufficient voices to make it a law. But the wise know that foolish legislation is a rope of sand, which perishes in the twisting; that the State must follow, and not lead the character and progress of the citizen; the strongest usurper is quickly got rid of; and they only who build on Ideas, build for eternity; and that the form of government which prevails, is the expression of what cultivation exists in the population which permits it. [...]

The same benign necessity and the same practical abuse appear in the parties into which each State divides itself, of opponents and defenders of the administration of the government. Parties are also founded on instincts, and have better guides to their own humble aims than the sagacity of their leaders. They have nothing perverse in their origin, but rudely mark some real and lasting relation. We might as wisely reprove the east wind, or the frost, as a political party, whose members, for the most part, could give no account of their position, but stand for the defence of those interests in which they find themselves. Our quarrel with them begins, when they quit this deep natural ground at the bidding of some leader, and, obeying personal considerations, throw themselves into the maintenance and defence of points, nowise belonging to their system. A party is perpetually corrupted by personality. Whilst we

[7] From R. W. Emerson, *Essays: Second Series* (Boston: James Munroe & Co., 1855), pp. 217–42.

absolve the association from dishonesty, we cannot extend the same charity to their leaders. They reap the rewards of the docility and zeal of the masses which they direct. Ordinarily, our parties are parties of circumstance, and not of principle; as, the planting interest in conflict with the commercial; the party of capitalists, and that of operatives; parties which are identical in their moral character, and which can easily change ground with each other, in the support of many of their measures. Parties of principle, as, religious sects, or the party of free-trade, of universal suffrage, of abolition of slavery, of abolition of capital punishment, degenerate into personalities, or would inspire enthusiasm. The vice of our leading parties in this country (which may be cited as a fair specimen of these societies of opinion) is, that they do not plant themselves on the deep and necessary grounds to which they are respectively entitled, but lash themselves to fury in the carrying of some local and momentary measure, nowise useful to the commonwealth. [...]

I do not for these defects despair of our republic. We are not at the mercy of any waves of chance. In the strife of ferocious parties, human nature always finds itself cherished, as the children of the convicts at Botany Bay are found to have as healthy a moral sentiment as other children. [...]

We must trust infinitely to the beneficent necessity which shines through all laws. Human nature expresses itself in them as characteristically as in statues, or songs, or railroads, and an abstract of the codes of nations would be a transcript of the common conscience. Governments have their origin in the moral identity of men. Reason for one is seen to be reason for another, and for every other. There is a middle measure which satisfies all parties, be they never so many, or so resolute for their own. Every man finds a sanction for his simplest claims and deeds in decisions of his own mind, which he calls Truth and Holiness. In these decisions all the citizens find a perfect agreement, and only in these; not in what is good to eat, good to wear, good use of time, or what amount of land, or of public aid, each is entitled to claim. This truth and justice men presently endeavor to make application of, to the measuring of land, the apportionment of service, the protection of life and property. Their first endeavors, no doubt, are very awkward. Yet absolute right is the first governor; or, every government is an impure theocracy. The idea, after which each community is aiming to make and mend its law, is, the will of the wise man. The wise man, it cannot find in nature, and it makes awkward but earnest efforts to secure his government by contrivance; as, by causing the entire people to give their voices on every measure; or, by a double choice to get the representation of the whole; or, by a selection of the best citizens; or, to secure the advantages of efficiency and internal peace, by confiding the government to one, who may himself select his agents. All forms of government symbolize an immortal government, common to all dynasties and independent of numbers, perfect where two men exist, perfect where there is only one man.

[...] If I put myself in the place of my child, and we stand in one thought, and see that things are thus or thus, that perception is law for him and me. We are both there, both act. But if, without carrying him into the thought, I look over into his plot, and, guessing how it is with him, ordain this or that, he will never obey me. This is the history of governments, – one man does something which is to bind another. A man who cannot be acquainted with me, taxes me; looking from afar at me, ordains that a part of my labor shall go to this or that whimsical end, not as I, but as he happens to fancy. Behold the consequence. Of all debts, men are least willing to pay the taxes. What a satire is this on government! Everywhere they think they get their money's worth, except for these.

Hence, the less government we have, the better, – the fewer laws, and the less confided power. The antidote to this abuse of formal Government, is, the influence of private character, the growth of the Individual; the appearance of the principal to supersede the proxy; the appearance of the wise man, of whom the existing government, is, it must be owned, but a shabby imitation. That which all things tend to educe, which freedom, cultivation, intercourse, revolutions, go to form and deliver, is character; that is the end of nature, to reach unto this coronation of her king. To educate the wise man, the State exists; and with the appearance of the wise man, the State expires. The appearance of character makes the State unnecessary. [...]

Antislavery Remarks at Worcester (August 3, 1849)[8]

[Emerson delivered this address at an anti-slavery gathering in Worcester, Massachusetts, which was held under the auspices of the Massachusetts Anti-Slavery Society.]

[...] I am accustomed to consider more the men than the abolitionists. It is perhaps the vice of my habit of speculation, that I am prone rather to consider the history of the race, the genius and energy of any nation, than to insist very much upon individual action. [...]

We are to rejoice in the march of events, in the sequence of the centuries, the progress of the great universal human, and shall I not say, divine, genius, which overpowers all our vices as well as our virtues, and turns our vices to the general benefit. I believe that the ardor of our virtuous enthusiasm in behalf of the slave, and of our indignation at his oppressor, naturally blinds us a little to the fate that is involved alike in our freedom, and in the slaveholding system at the South. [...]

The course of history is one everywhere. It is a constant progress of amelioration. Like the amelioration in the pear-tree, or apple-tree, so well-known to botanists. One must look to the planters of the South with the same feelings that he would regard the spider and the fly, the tiger and the deer. It is barbarism. The people are barbarous. They are still in the animal state. They are not accountable like those whose eyes have once been opened to a Christianity that makes a return to evil impossible. [...]

This progress of amelioration is very slow. Still we have gone forward a great way since that time. The people of the South are by their climate enervated. They have been demoralised by their vicious habits; still they are as innocent in their slaveholding as we are in our Norther vices. Yet it becomes essential, it becomes imperative, as man rises in the scale of civilization, as the ameliorating and expanding principles

[8] R. W. Emerson, "Antislavery Remarks at Worcester, 3 August 1849" in L. Gougeon and J. Myerson (eds.), *Emerson's Antislavery Writings* (New Haven: Yale University Press, 1995), pp. 47–50.

find effect in him; – it becomes as imperative that this institution should become discreditable, and should perish, as the old institutions which have gone before. [...]

Henry David Thoreau *Resistance to Civil Government, or Civil Disobedience* (1849)[9]

I HEARTILY accept the motto, – "That government is best which governs least"; and I should like to see it acted up to more rapidly and systematically. Carried out, it finally amounts to this, which also I believe – "That government is best which governs not at all"; and when men are prepared for it, that will be the kind of government which they will have. Government is at best but an expedient; but most governments are usually, and all governments are sometimes, inexpedient. The objections which have been brought against a standing army, and they are many and weighty, and deserve to prevail, may also at last be brought against a standing government. The standing army is only an arm of the standing government. The government itself, which is only the mode which the people have chosen to execute their will, is equally liable to be abused and perverted before the people can act through it. [...]

But, to speak practically and as a citizen, unlike those who call themselves no-government men, I ask for, not at once no government, but *at once* a better government. Let every man make known what kind of government would command his respect, and that will be one step toward obtaining it.

After all, the practical reason why, when the power is once in the hands of the people, a majority are permitted, and for a long period continue, to rule, is not because they are most likely to be in the right, nor because this seems fairest to the minority, but because they are physically the strongest. But a government in which the majority rule in all cases can not [*sic*] be based on justice, even as far as men understand it. Can there not be a government in which the majorities do not virtually decide right and wrong, but conscience? – in which majorities decide only those questions to which the rule of expediency is applicable? Must the citizen ever for a moment, or in the least degree, resign his conscience to the legislator? Why has every man a conscience, then? I think that we should be men first, and subjects afterward. It is not desirable to cultivate a respect for the law, so much as for the right. The only obligation which I have a right to assume, is to do at any time what I think right. [...] Law never made men a whit more just; and, by means of their respect for it, even the well-disposed are daily made the agents of injustice. A common and natural result of an undue respect for the law is, that you may see a file of soldiers, colonel, captain, corporal, privates, powder-monkeys and all, marching in admirable order over hill and dale to the wars, against their wills, aye, against their common sense and consciences, which makes it very steep marching indeed, and produces a palpitation of the heart. They have no doubt that it is a damnable business in which

---

[9] H. D. Thoreau, "Resistance to Civil Government" in E. P. Peabody (ed.), *Aesthetic Papers* (Boston and New York: The Editor & G. P. Putnam, 1849), pp. 189–211.

they are concerned; they are all peaceably inclined. Now, what are they? Men at all? or small movable forts and magazines, at the service of some unscrupulous man in power? [. . .]

The mass of men serve the State thus, not as men mainly, but as machines, with their bodies. They are the standing army, and the militia, jailers, constables, *posse comitatus*, &c. In most cases there is no free exercise whatever of the judgment or of the moral sense; but they put themselves on a level with wood and earth and stones; and wooden men can perhaps be manufactured that will serve the purpose as well. Such command no more respect than men of straw, or a lump of dirt. They have the same sort of worth only as horses and dogs. Yet such as these even are commonly esteemed good citizens. Others, as most legislators, politicians, lawyers, ministers, and office-holders, serve the state chiefly with their heads; and, as they rarely make any moral distinctions, they are as likely to serve the devil, without *intending* it, as God. A very few, as heroes, patriots, martyrs, reformers in the great sense, and *men*, serve the State with their consciences also, and so necessarily resist it for the most part; and they are commonly treated by it as enemies. [. . .]

How does it become a man to behave toward the American government today? I answer that he cannot without disgrace be associated with it. I cannot for an instant recognize that political organization as *my* government which is the *slave's* government also.

All men recognize the right of revolution; that is, the right to refuse allegiance to and to resist the government, when its tyranny or its inefficiency are great and unendurable. But almost all say that such is not the case now. [. . .] I say, [. . .] when a sixth of the population of a nation which has undertaken to be the refuge of liberty are slaves, and a whole country is unjustly overrun and conquered by a foreign army, and subjected to military law, I think that it is not too soon for honest men to rebel and revolutionize. What makes this duty the more urgent is that fact, that the country so overrun is not our own, but ours is the invading army.[10] [. . .]

All voting is a sort of gaming, like chequers or backgammon, with a slight moral tinge to it, a playing with right and wrong, with moral questions; and betting naturally accompanies it. The character of the voters is not staked. I cast my vote, perchance, as I think right; but I am not vitally concerned that that right should prevail. I am willing to leave it to the majority. Its obligation, therefore, never exceeds that of expediency. Even voting *for the right* is *doing* nothing for it. It is only expressing to men feebly your desire that it should prevail. A wise man will not leave the right to the mercy of chance, nor wish it to prevail through the power of the majority. There is but little virtue in the action of masses of men. When the majority shall at length vote for the abolition of slavery, it will be because they are indifferent to slavery, or because there is but little slavery left to be abolished by their vote. *They* will then be the only slaves. Only *his* vote can hasten the abolition of slavery who asserts his own freedom by his vote. [. . .] Oh for a man who is a *man*, and, as my neighbor says, has a bone in his back which you cannot pass your hand through! Our

[10] Thoreau is referring to the Mexican–American War (1846–1848).

statistics are at fault: the population has been returned too large. How many *men* are there to a square thousand miles in the country? Hardly one. [...]

Unjust laws exist: shall we be content to obey them, or shall we endeavor to amend them, and obey them until we have succeeded, or shall we transgress them at once? Men generally, under such a government as this, think that they ought to wait until they have persuaded the majority to alter them. They think that, if they should resist, the remedy would be worse than the evil. But it is the fault of the government itself that the remedy *is* worse than the evil. *It* makes it worse. Why is it not more apt to anticipate and provide for reform? Why does it not cherish its wise minority? Why does it cry and resist before it is hurt? Why does it not encourage its citizens to be on the alert to point out its faults, and *do* better than it would have them? [...]

One would think, that a deliberate and practical denial of its authority was the only offence never contemplated by government; else, why has it not assigned its definite, its suitable and proportionate penalty? [...] If the injustice is part of the necessary friction of the machine of government, let it go, let it go: perchance it will wear smooth, – certainly the machine will wear out. If the injustice has a spring, or a pulley, or a rope, or a crank, exclusively for itself, then perhaps you may consider whether the remedy will not be worse than the evil; but if it is of such a nature that it requires you to be the agent of injustice to another, then, I say, break the law. Let your life be a counter friction to stop the machine. What I have to do is to see, at any rate, that I do not lend myself to the wrong which I condemn. [...]

Under a government which imprisons any unjustly, the true place for a just man is also a prison. The proper place today, the only place which Massachusetts has provided for her freer and less desponding spirits, is in her prisons, to be put out and locked out of the State by her own act, as they have already put themselves out by their principles. It is there that the fugitive slave, and the Mexican prisoner on parole, and the Indian come to plead the wrongs of his race, should find them; on that separate, but more free and honorable ground, where the State places those who are not with her but against her, – the only house in a slave-state in which a free man can abide with honor. If any think that their influence would be lost there, and their voices no longer afflict the ear of the State, that they would not be as an enemy within its walls, they do not know by how much truth is stronger than error, nor how much more eloquently and effectively he can combat injustice who has experienced a little in his own person. Cast your whole vote, not a strip of paper merely, but your whole influence. A minority is powerless while it conforms to the majority; it is not even a minority then; but it is irresistible when it clogs by its whole weight. [...] If a thousand men were not to pay their tax-bills this year, that would not be a violent and bloody measure, as it would be to pay them, and enable the State to commit violence and shed innocent blood. This is, in fact, the definition of a peaceable revolution, if any such is possible. If the tax-gatherer, or any other public officer, asks me, as one has done, "But what shall I do?" my answer is, "If you really wish to do any thing, resign your office." When the subject has refused allegiance, and the officer has resigned his office, then the revolution is accomplished. [...]

I have paid no poll-tax for six years. I was put into a jail once on this account, for one night; and, as I stood considering the walls of solid stone, two or three feet thick, the door of wood and iron, a foot thick, and the iron grating which strained the light, I could not help being struck with the foolishness of that institution which treated me as if I were mere flesh and blood and bones, to be locked up. I wondered that it should have concluded at length that this was the best use it could put me to, and had never thought to avail itself of my services in some way. I saw that, if there was a wall of stone between me and my townsmen, there was a still more difficult one to climb or break through, before they could get to be as free as I was. I did nor for a moment feel confined, and the walls seemed a great waste of stone and mortar. I felt as if I alone of all my townsmen had paid my tax. They plainly did not know how to treat me, but behaved like persons who are underbred. In every threat and in every compliment there was a blunder; for they thought that my chief desire was to stand the other side of that stone wall. I could not but smile to see how industriously they locked the door on my meditations, which followed them out again without let or hindrance, and they were really all that was dangerous. As they could not reach me, they had resolved to punish my body; just as boys, if they cannot come at some person against whom they have a spite, will abuse his dog. I saw that the State was half-witted, that it was timid as a lone woman with her silver spoons, and that it did not know its friends from its foes, and I lost all my remaining respect for it, and pitied it.

Thus the state never intentionally confronts a man's sense, intellectual or moral, but only his body, his senses. It is not armed with superior wit or honesty, but with superior physical strength. I was not born to be forced. I will breathe after my own fashion. Let us see who is the strongest. [. . .]

When I came out of prison, – for some one interfered, and paid the tax, – I did not perceive that great changes had taken place on the common, such as he observed who went in a youth, and emerged a gray-headed man; and yet a change had to my eyes come over the scene, – the town, and State, and country, – greater than any that mere time could effect. I saw yet more distinctly the State in which I lived. I saw to what extent the people among whom I lived could be trusted as good neighbors and friends; that their friendship was for summer weather only; that they did not greatly purpose to do right; that they were a distinct race from me by their prejudices and superstitions, as the Chinamen and Malays are; that, in their sacrifices to humanity they ran no risks, not even to their property; that, after all, they were not so noble but they treated the thief as he had treated them, and hoped, by a certain outward observance and a few prayers, and by walking in a particular straight though useless path from time to time, to save their souls. This may be to judge my neighbors harshly; for I believe that most of them are not aware that they have such an institution as the jail in their village. [. . .]

I have never declined paying the highway tax, because I am as desirous of being a good neighbor as I am of being a bad subject; and, as for supporting schools, I am doing my part to educate my fellow-countrymen now. It is for no particular item in the tax-bill that I refuse to pay it. I simply wish to refuse allegiance to the State, to withdraw and stand aloof from it effectually. I do not care to trace the course of my dollar, if I could, till it buys a man, or a musket to shoot one with, – the dollar is innocent, – but I am concerned to trace the effects of my allegiance. In fact, I quietly declare war with the State, after my fashion, though I will still make use and get what advantages of her I can, as is usual in such cases. [. . .]

Is a democracy, such as we know it, the last improvement possible in government? Is it not possible to take a step further towards recognizing and organizing the rights of man? There will never be a really free and enlightened State, until the State comes to recognize the individual as a higher and independent power, from which all its own power and authority are derived, and treats him accordingly. I please myself with imagining a State at last which can afford to be just to all men, and to treat the individual with respect as a neighbor; which even would not think it inconsistent with its own repose, if a few were to live aloof from it, not meddling with it, nor embraced by it, who fulfilled all the duties of neighbors and fellow-men. A State which bore this kind of fruit, and suffered it to drop off as fast as it ripened, would prepare the way for a still more perfect and glorious State, which also I have imagined, but not yet anywhere seen.

SPEECHES BY NATIVE AMERICANS

Tecumseh *Speech before the Choctaws and Chickasaws (September 1811)*[11]

In view of questions of vast importance, have we met together in solemn council to-night. Nor should we here debate whether we have been wronged and injured, but by what measures we should avenge ourselves; for our merciless oppressors, having long since planned out their proceedings, are not about to make, but have and are still making attacks upon those of our race who have as yet come to no resolution. Nor are we ignorant by what steps, and by what gradual advances, the whites break in upon our neighbors. Imagining themselves to be still undiscovered, they show themselves the less audacious because you are insensible. The whites are already nearly a match for us all united, and too strong for any one tribe alone to resist; so that unless we support one another with our collective and united forces; unless every tribe unanimously combines to give a check to the ambition and avarice of the whites, they will soon conquer us apart and disunited, and we will be driven away from our native country and scattered as autumnal leaves before the wind.

But have we not courage enough remaining to defend our country and maintain our ancient independence? Will we calmly suffer the white intruders and tyrants to enslave us? Shall it be said of our race that we knew not how to extricate ourselves from the three most to be dreaded calamities – folly, inactivity, and cowardice? But what need is there to speak of the past? It speaks for itself and asks, "Where to-day is the Pequod? Where the Narragansetts, the Mohawks, Pocanokets, and many other once powerful tribes of our race?" They have vanished before the avarice and

---

[11] From H. B. Cushman, *History of the Choctaw, Chicksaw, and Natchez Indians* (Greenville, TX: Headlight Printing House, 1899), pp. 310–14.

oppression of the white men, as snow before a summer sun. In the vain hope of alone defending their ancient possessions, they have fallen in the wars with the white men. Look abroad over their once beautiful country, and what see you now? Naught but the ravages of the pale-face destroyers meet your eyes. So it will be with you Choctaws and Chickasaws! Soon your mighty forest trees, under the shade of whose wide spreading branches you have played in infancy, sported in boyhood, and now rest your wearied limbs after the fatigue of the chase, will be cut down to fence in the land which the white intruders dare to call their own. Soon, their broad roads will pass over the grave of your fathers, and the place of their rest will be blotted out forever. The annihilation of our race is at hand unless we unite in one common cause against the common foe. Think not, brave Choctaws and Chickasaws, that you can remain passive and indifferent to the common danger, and thus escape the common fate. Your people too, will soon be as falling leaves and scattering clouds before their blighting breath. You too will be driven away from your native land and ancient domains as leaves are driven before the wintry storms.

Sleep not longer, O Choctaws and Chickasaws in false security and delusive hopes. Our broad domains are fast escaping from our grasp. Every year our white intruders become more greedy [*sic*], exacting, oppressive, and overbearing. Every year contentions spring up between them and our people and when blood is shed we have to make atonement whether right or wrong, at the cost of the lives of our greatest chiefs, and the yielding up of large tracts of our lands. Before the pale-faces came among us, we enjoyed the happiness of unbounded freedom, and were acquainted with neither riches, wants, nor oppression. How is it now? Wants and oppressions are our lot; for are we not controlled in everything, and dare we move without asking, by your leave? Are we not being stripped day by day of the little that remains of our ancient liberty? Do they not even now kick and strike us as they do their black-faces? How long will it be before they will tie us to a post and whip us, and make us work for them in their corn fields as they do them? Shall we wait for that moment or shall we die fighting before submitting to such ignominy?

Have we not for years had before our eyes a sample of their designs, and are they not sufficient harbingers of their future determinations? Will we not soon be driven from our respective countries and the graves of our ancestors? Will not the bones of our dead be plowed up, and their graves be turned into fields? Shall we calmly wait until they become so numerous that we will no longer be able to resist oppression? Will we wait to be destroyed in our turn, without making an effort worthy of our race? Shall we give up our homes, our country, bequeathed to us by the Great Spirit, the graves of our dead, and everything that is dear and sacred to us, without a struggle? I know you will cry with me, Never! Never! Then let us by unity of action destroy them all, which we now can do, or drive them back whence they came. War or extermination is now our only choice. Which do you choose? I know your answer. Therefore, I now call on you, brave Choctaws and Chickasaws, to assist in the just cause of liberating our race from the grasp of our faithless invaders and heartless oppressors. The white usurpation in our common country must be stopped, or we, its rightful owners, be forever destroyed and wiped out as a race of people. I am now at the head of many warriors backed by the strong arm of English soldiers.

Choctaws and Chickasaws, you have too long borne with grievous usurpation inflicted by the arrogant Americans. Be no longer their dupes. If there be one here tonight who believes that his rights will not sooner or later, be taken from him by the avaricious American pale-faces, his ignorance ought to excite pity, for he knows little of the character of our common foe. And if there be one among you mad enough to undervalue the growing power of the white race among us, let him tremble in considering the fearful woes he will bring down upon our entire race, if by his criminal indifference he assists the designs of our common enemy against our common country. Then listen to the voice of duty, of honor, of nature, and of your endangered country. Let us form one body, one heart, and defend to the last warrior our country, our homes, our liberty, and the graces of ours fathers.

[. . .] They [the Americans] are people fond of innovations, quick to contrive and quick to put their schemes into effectual execution, no matter how great the wrong and injury to us; while we are content to preserve what we already have. Their design [is] to enlarge their possessions by taking yours in turn; and will you, can you longer dally, O Choctaws and Chickasaws? Do you imagine that people will not continue the longest in the enjoyment of peace who timely prepare to vindicate themselves, and manifest a determined resolution to do themselves right whenever they are wronged? Far otherwise. Then haste to the relief of our common cause, as by consanguinity of blood you are bound; lest the day be not far distant when you will be left single-handed and alone to the cruel mercy of our most inveterate foe.

Pushmataha *Response to Tecumseh's Call to Arms* (September 1811)[12]

It was not my design in coming here to enter into a disputation with any one. But I appear before you, my warriors and my people, not to throw in my plea against the accusations of Tecumseh; but to prevent your forming rash and dangerous resolutions upon things of highest importance, through the instigations of others. [. . .] Nor do I stand up before you tonight to contradict the many facts alleged against the American people or to raise my voice against them in useless accusations. The question before us now is not what wrongs they have inflicted upon our race, but what measures are best for us to adopt in regard to them; and though our race may have been unjustly treated and shamefully wronged by them, yet I shall not for that reason alone advise you to destroy them, unless it was just and expedient for you so to do; nor, would I advise you to forgive them, though worthy of your commiseration, unless I believe it would be to the interest of our common good. We should consult more in regard to our future welfare than our present. What people, my friends and countrymen, were so unwise and inconsiderate as to engage in a war of their own accord, when their own strength, and even with the aid of others, was judged unequal to the task? I well know causes often arise which force men to confront extremities, but, my countrymen, those causes do not now exist. Reflect,

---

[12] From Cushman, *History of the Choctaw, Chicksaw, and Natchez Indians*, pp. 315–18.

therefore, I earnestly beseech you, before you act hastily in this great matter, and consider with yourselves how greatly you will err if you injudiciously approve of and inconsiderately act upon Tecumseh's advice. Remember the American people are now friendly disposed towards us. [. . .] My friends and fellow countrymen! You now have no just cause to declare war against the American people, or wreak your vengeance upon them as enemies, since they have ever manifested feelings of friendship towards you. It is besides inconsistent with your national glory and with your honor, as a people to violate your solemn treaty; and a disgrace to the memory of your forefathers, to wage war against the American people merely to gratify the malice of the English.

The war, which you are now contemplating against the Americans, is a flagrant breach of justice, yea, a fearful blemish on your honor and also that of your fathers, and which you will find if you will examine it carefully and judiciously forbodes nothing but destruction to our entire race. [. . .] And though we will not permit ourselves to be made slaves, or, like inexperienced warriors, shudder at the thought of war, yet I am not so insensible and inconsistent to advise you to cowardly yield to the outrages of the whites, or wilfully connive at their unjust encroachments; but only not yet to have recourse to war, but to send ambassadors to our Great Father at Washington, and lay before him our grievances, without betraying too great eagerness for war, or manifesting any tokens of pusillanimity. [. . .]

Be not, I pray you, guilty of rashness, which I never as yet have known you to be; therefore, I implore you, while healing measures are in the election of us all, not to break the treaty, nor violate our pledge of honor, but to submit our grievances, whatever they may be, to the Congress of the United States, according to the articles of the treaty existing between us and the American people. [. . .]

Tecumseh *Speech before the Osages in Missouri* (Winter 1811–1812)[13]

Brothers. – We all belong to one family; we are all children of the Great Spirit; we walk in the same path; slake our thirst at the same spring; and now affairs of the greatest concern lead us to smoke the pipe around the same council fire!

Brothers. – We are friends; we must assist each other to bear our burdens. The blood of many of our fathers and brothers has run like water on the ground, to satisfy the avarice of the white men. We, ourselves, are threatened with a great evil; nothing will pacify them but the destruction of all the red men.

Brothers. – When the white men first set foot on our grounds, they were hungry; they had no place on which to spread their blankets, or to kindle their fires. They were feeble; they could do nothing for themselves. Our fathers commiserated their distress, and shared freely with them whatever the Great Spirit had given his red children. They gave them food when hungry, medicine when sick, spread skins for them to sleep on, and gave

[13] From J. D. Hunter, *Memoirs of a Captivity among the Indians of North America, from Childhood to Age Nineteen* (London: Longman, Hurst, Reese, Orme, and Brown, 1823), pp. 45–8.

them grounds, that they might hunt and raise corn. – Brothers, the white people are like poisonous serpents: when chilled, they are feeble and harmless; but invigorate them with warmth, and they sting their benefactors to death.

The white people came among us feeble; and now we have made them strong, they wish to kill us, or drive us back, as they would wolves and panthers.

Brothers. – The white men are not friends to the Indians: at first, they only asked for land sufficient for a wigwam; now, nothing will satisfy them but the whole of our hunting grounds, from the rising to the setting sun.

Brothers. – The white men want more than our hunting grounds; they wish to kill our warriors; they would even kill our old men, women, and little ones.

Brothers. – Many winters ago, there was no land; the sun did not rise and set: all was darkness. The Great Spirit made all things. He gave the white people a home beyond the great waters. He supplied these grounds with game, and gave them to his red children; and he gave them strength and courage to defend them.

Brothers. – My people wish for peace; the red men all wish for peace: but where the white people are, there is no peace for them, except it be on the bosom of our mother.

Brothers. – The white men despise and cheat the Indians; they abuse and insult them; they do not think the red men sufficiently good to live. The red men have borne many and great injuries; they ought to suffer them no longer. My people will not; they are determined on vengeance; they have taken up the tomahawk; they will make it fat with blood; they will drink the blood of the white people. [. . .]

Brothers. – If you do not unite with us, they will first destroy us, and then you will fall an easy prey to them. They have destroyed many nations of red men because they were not united, because they were not friends to each other.

Brothers. – The white people send runners amongst us; they wish to make us enemies, that they may sweep over and desolate our hunting grounds, like devastating winds, or rushing waters.

Brothers. – Our Great Father, over the great waters [the King of England], is angry with the white people, our enemies. He will send his brave warriors against them; he will send us rifles, and whatever else we want – he is our friend, and we are his children. [. . .]

Brothers. – We must be united; we must smoke the same pipe; we must fight each other's battles; and more than all, we must love the Great Spirit; he is for us; he will destroy our enemies, and make all his red children happy.

Petalesharo *Speech before the President of the United States (February 4, 1822)*[14]

[In February 1822, several chiefs from the Missouri Territory were brought by order of the government of the United States to Washington under the guidance of

---

[14] From J. Buchanan, *Sketches of the History, Manners, and Customs of the North American Indians with a Plan for Their Amelioration* (London: Black, Young, and Young, 1824), pp. 38–42.

Major O'Fallon. On the occasion, Pawnee chief Petalesharo (*c.*1797–*c.*1836) made the following address before President James Monroe.]

My Great Father: I have travelled a great distance to see you – I have seen you and my heart rejoices. I have heard your words – they have entered one ear and shall not escape the other, and I will carry them to my people as pure as they came from your mouth. [. . .]

The Great Spirit made us all – made my skin red, and yours white; he placed us on this earth, and intended that we should live differently from each other.

He made the whites to cultivate the earth, and feed on domestic animals; but he made us, red skins, to rove through the uncultivated woods and plains; to feed on wild animals; and to dress with their skins. He also intended that we should go to war – to take scalps – steal horses from and triumph over our enemies – cultivate peace at home, and promote the happiness of each other. I believe there no people of any color on this earth who do not believe in the Great Spirit – in rewards, and in punishments. We worship him, but we worship him not as you do. We differ from you in appearance and manners as well as in our customs; and we differ from you in our religion; we have no large houses as you have to worship the Great Spirit in; if we had them today, we should want others tomorrow, for we have not, like you, fixed habitation – we have no settled home except our villages, where we remain but two moons in twelve. We, like animals, rove through the country, whilst you whites reside between us and heaven; but still, my Great Father, we love the Great Spirit – we acknowledge the supreme power – our peace, our health, and our happiness depend upon him, and our lives belong to him – he made us and he can destroy us.

My Great Father: Some of your chiefs, as they are called [missionaries], have proposed to send some of their good people among us to change our habits, to make us work and live like the white people. I will not tell a lie – I am going to tell the truth. You love your country – your love your people – you love the manner in which they live, and you think your people brave. – I am like you, my Great Father, I love my country – I love my people – I love the manner in which we live, and think myself and [my] warriors brave. Spare me then, my Father; let me enjoy my country, and pursue my buffalo, and the beaver, and the other wild animals of our country, and I will trade their skins with your people. I have grown up, and lived thus long without work – I am in hopes you will suffer me to die without it. We have plenty of buffalo, beaver, deer and other wild animals – we have also an abundance of horses – we have every thing we want – we have plenty of land, if you will keep your people off of it. [. . .]

It is too soon, my Great Father, to send those good men among us. *We are not starving yet* – we wish you to permit us to enjoy the chase until the game of our country is exhausted – until the wild animals become extinct. Let us exhaust our present resources before you make toil and interrupt our happiness – let me continue to live as I have done, and after I have passed to the Good or Evil Spirit from off the wilderness of my present life, the subsistence of my children may become so precarious as to need and embrace the assistance of those good people.

There was a time when we did not know the whites – our wants were then fewer than they are now. They were always within our control – we had then seen nothing which we could not get. Before our intercourse with the *whites* (who have caused such destruction in our game), we could lie down to sleep, and when we awoke we would find the buffalo feeding around our camp – but now we are killing them for their skins, and feeding the wolves with their flesh, to make our children cry over their bones.

Here, My Great Father, is a pipe which I present you, as I am accustomed to present pipes to all the red skins in peace with us. It is filled with such tobacco as we were accustomed to smoke before we knew the white people. It is pleasant, and the spontaneous growth of the most remote parts of our country. I know that the robes, leggings, mockasins [*sic*], bear-claws, etc., are of little value to you, but we wish you to have them deposited and preserved in some conspicuous part of your lodge, so that when we are gone and the sod turned over our bones, if our children should visit this place, as we do now, they may see and recognize with pleasure the deposits of their fathers; and reflect on the times that are past.

THE WOMEN'S RIGHTS MOVEMENT

Abigail Adams

Letter to John Adams (November 27, 1775)[15]

[...] Col. Warren return[e]d last week to Plymouth, so that I shall not hear any thing from you till he goes back again which will not be till the last of this [next] month.

He Damp'd my Spirits greatly by telling me that the Court had prolonged your Stay an other month.[16] I was pleasing myself with the thoughts that you would soon be upon your return. Tis in vain to repine. I hope the publick will reap what I sacrifice.

I wish I knew what mighty things were fabricating. If a form of Gover[n]ment is to be established here what one will be assumed? Will it be left to our assemblies to chuse [*sic*] one? and will not many men have many minds? and shall we not run into Dissentions among ourselves?

I am more and more convinced that Man is a dangerous creature, and that power whether vested in many or a few is ever grasping, and like the grave cries give, give. The great fish swallow up the small, and he who is most strenuous for the Rights of the people, when vested with power, is as eager after the perogatives [*sic*] of Gover[n]ment. You tell me of degrees of perfection to which Humane Nature is

---

[15] *The Adams Papers*, Adams Family Correspondence, Vol. I: *December 1761–May 1776*, edited by L. H. Butterfield (Cambridge, MA: Harvard University Press, 1963), pp. 328–31.

[16] The Massachusetts House of Representatives had resolved that the commissions of the current delegates to the Continental Congress, including John Adams, were to be extended from the end of December to the end of January. Adams ended up being re-elected in January as well.

capable of arriving, and I believe it, but at the same time lament that our admiration should arise from the scarcity of the instances.

The Building up a Great Empire, which was only hinted at by my correspondent may now I suppose be realized even by the unbelievers. Yet will not ten thousand Difficulties arise in the formation of it? The Reigns [*sic*] of Gover[n]ment have been so long sla[c]k[e]ned, that I fear the people will not quietly submit to those restraints which are necessary for the peace, and security, of the community; if we seperate [*sic*] from Brittain, what Code of Laws will be established. How shall we be govern[e]d so as to retain our Liberties? Can any gover[n]ment be free which is not adminst[e]red by general stated Laws? Who shall frame these Laws? Who will give them force and energy? Tis true your Resolution[s] as a Body have heithertoo [*sic*] had the force of Laws. But will they continue to have?

When I consider these things and the prejudices of people in favour of Ancient customs and Regulations, I feel anxious for the fate of our Monarchy or Democracy or what ever is to take place. I soon get lost in a Labyrinth of perplexities, but whatever occurs, may justice and righteousness be the Stability of our times, and order arise out of confusion. Great difficulties may be surmounted, by patience and perseverance. [...]

Letter to John Adams (March 31, 1776)[17]

I wish you would ever write me a Letter half as long as I write you; and tell me if you may where your Fleet are gone? What sort of Defence Virginia can make against our common Enemy? Whether it is so situated as to make an able Defence? Are not the Gentry Lords and the common people vassals, are they not like the uncivilized Natives Brittain represents us to be? I hope their Riffel [*sic*] Men who have shewen [*sic*] themselves very savage and even Blood thirsty; are not a specimen of the Generality of the people. [...]

I have sometimes been ready to think that the passion for Liberty cannot be Eaquelly [*sic*] Strong in the Breasts of those who have been accustomed to deprive their fellow Creatures of theirs. Of this I am certain that it is not founded upon that generous and christian principal [*sic*] of doing to others as we would that others should do unto us. [...]

I long to hear that you have declared an independancy [*sic*] – and by the way in the new Code of Laws which I suppose it will be necessary for you to make I desire you would Remember the Ladies, and be more generous and favourable to them than your ancestors. Do not put such unlimited power into the hands of the Husbands. Remember all Men would be tyrants if they could. If perticuliar [*sic*] care and attention is not paid to the Laidies [*sic*] we are determined to foment a Rebel[l]ion, and will not hold ourselves bound by any Laws in which we have no voice, or Representation.

That your Sex are Naturally Tyrannical is a Truth so thoroughly established as to admit of no dispute, but such of you as wish to be happy willingly give up the harsh

---

[17] *The Adams Papers*, Adams Family Correspondence, Vol. I, pp. 369–71.

title of Master for the more tender and endearing one of Friend. Why then, not put it out of the power of the vicious and the Lawless to use us with cruelty and indignity with impunity. Men of Sense in all Ages abhor those customs which treat us only as the vassals of your Sex. Regard us then as Beings placed by providence under your protection and in immitation of the Supreem Being [*sic*] make use of that power only for our happiness.

Letter to Mercy Otis Warren (April 27, 1776)[18]

[. . .] I dare say he [John Adams] writes to no one unless to Portia oftner [*sic*] than to your Friend, because I know there is no one besides in whom he has an eaquel [*sic*] confidence.[19] His Letters to me have been generally short, but he pleads in Excuse the critical state of affairs and the Multiplicity of avocations and says further that he has been very Busy, and writ near ten Sheets of paper, about some affairs which he does not chuse [*sic*] to Mention for fear of accident.

He is very sausy [*sic*] to me in return for a List of Female Grievances which I transmitted to him. I think I will get you to join me in a petition to Congress. I thought it was very probable our wise Statesmen would erect a New Gover[n]ment and form a new code of Laws. I ventured to speak a word in behalf of our Sex, who are rather hardly dealt with by the Laws of England which gives such unlimitted [*sic*] power to the Husband to use his wife Ill.

I requested that our Legislators would consider our case and as all Men of Delicacy and Sentiment are averse to Excercising [*sic*] the power they possess, yet as there is a natural propensity in Humane Nature to domination, I thought the most generous plan was to put it out of the power of the Arbit[r]ary and tyranick to injure us with impunity by Establishing some Laws in our favour upon just and Liberal principals [*sic*].

I believe I even threat[e]ned fomenting a Rebellion in case we were not consider-[e]d, and assured him we would not hold ourselves bound by any Laws in which we had neither a voice, nor representation.

In return he tells me he cannot but Laugh at My Extrodonary [*sic*] Code of Laws. That he had heard their Struggle had loos[e]ned the bands of Gover[n]ment, that children and apprentices were dissabedient [*sic*], that Schools and Colledges [*sic*] were grown turbulant, that Indians slighted their Guardians, and Negroes grew insolent to their Masters. But my Letter was the first intimation that another Tribe more numerous and powerfull [*sic*] than all the rest were grown discontented. This is rather too coarse a complement, he adds, but that I am so sausy [*sic*] he won[']t blot it out.[20]

---

[18] *The Adams Papers*, Adams Family Correspondence, Vol. I, pp. 396–8.

[19] Portia was a pen name that Abigail Adams used during her adult years. "She first identified with Portia – the erudite and wise but long-suffering Roman wife of the great statesman Brutus – during the dark years of the Revolutionary War, but she retained the name after she had outlived her worst struggles. The imagery of wisdom, erudition, and humanity implicit in *Portia* satisfied her self-image" (E. B. Gelles, *Portia: The World of Abigail Adams* (Bloomington: Indiana University Press, 1992), p. xviii).

[20] Abigail reproduces John Adams's reply from April 14, 1776 almost verbatim.

So I have help'd the Sex abundantly, but I will tell him I have only been making trial of the Disintresstedness [*sic*] of his Virtue, and when weigh'd in the balance have found it wanting.

It would be bad policy to grant us greater power say they since under all the disadvantages we Labour we have the assendancy [*sic*] over their Hearts

And charm by accepting, by submitting sway.

I wonder Apollo and the Muses could not have indulged me with a poetical Genious. I have always been a votary to her charms but never could assend [. . .] Parnassus myself. [. . .]

Mary Wollstonecraft *A Vindication of the Rights of Woman* (1792)[21]

[. . .] To account for, and excuse the tyranny of man, many ingenious arguments have been brought forward to prove, that the two sexes, in the acquirement of virtue, ought to aim at attaining a very different character: or, to speak explicitly, women are not allowed to have sufficient strength of mind to acquire what really deserves the name of virtue. Yet it should seem, allowing them to have souls, that there is but one way appointed by providence to lead *mankind* to either virtue or happiness.

If then women are not a swarm of ephemeron triflers, why should they be kept in ignorance under the specious name of innocence? Men complain, and with reason, of the follies and caprices of our sex, when they do not keenly satirize our headstrong passions and groveling vices. Behold, I should answer, the natural effect of ignorance! The mind will ever be unstable that has only prejudices to rest on, and the current will run with destructive fury when there are no barriers to break its force. Women are told from their infancy, and taught by the example of their mothers, that a little knowledge of human weakness, justly termed cunning, softness of temper, *outward* obedience, and a scrupulous attention to a puerile kind of propriety, will obtain for them the protection of man; and should they be beautiful, every thing else is needless, for at least twenty years of their lives.

Thus Milton describes our first frail mother [Eve]; though when he tells us that women are formed for softness and sweet attractive grace, I cannot comprehend his meaning, unless, in the true Mahometan strain, he meant to deprive us of souls, and insinuate that we were beings only designed by sweet attractive grace, and docile blind obedience, to gratify the senses of man when he can no longer soar on the wing of contemplation. [. . .]

Men, indeed, appear to me to act in a very unphilosophical manner, when they try to secure the good conduct of women by attempting to keep them always in a state of childhood. Rousseau was more consistent when he wished to stop the progress of reason in both sexes; for if men eat of the tree of knowledge, women will come in for

[21] M. Wollstonecraft, *A Vindication of the Rights of Woman: With Strictures on Political and Moral Subjects*, 3rd ed. (London: J. Johnson, 1796), pp. 32–8, 49, 68–74.

a taste: but, from the imperfect cultivation which their understandings now receive, they only attain a knowledge of evil.

Children, I grant, should be innocent; but when the epithet is applied to men, or women, it is but a civil term for weakness. For if it be allowed that women were destined by Providence to acquire human virtues, and by the exercise of their understandings, that stability of character which is the firmest ground to rest our future hopes upon, they must be permitted to turn to the fountain of light, and not forced to shape their course by the twinkling of a mere satellite. [. . .]

In treating, therefore, of the manners of women, let us, disregarding sensual arguments [i.e. arguments emphasizing women's sensibility], trace what we should endeavour to make them in order to co-operate, if the expression be not too bold, with the Supreme Being.

By individual education, I mean – for the sense of the word is not precisely defined – such an attention to a child as will slowly sharpen the senses, form the temper, regulate the passions, as they begin to ferment, and set the understanding to work before the body arrives at maturity; so that the man may only have to proceed, not to begin, the important task of learning to think and reason.

To prevent any misconstruction, I must add, that I do not believe that a private education can work the wonders which some sanguine writers have attributed to it.[22] Men and women must be educated, in a great degree, by the opinions and manners of the society they live in. In every age there has been a stream of popular opinion that has carried all before it, and given a family character, as it were, to the century. It may then fairly be inferred, that, till society be differently constituted, much cannot be expected from education. It is, however, sufficient for my present purpose to assert, that, whatever effect circumstances have on the abilities, every being may become virtuous by the exercise of its own reason [. . .].

Consequently, the most perfect education, in my opinion, is such an exercise of the understanding as is best calculated to strengthen the body and form the heart; or, in other words, to enable the individual to attain such habits of virtue as will render it independent. In fact, it is a farce to call any being virtuous whose virtues do not result from the exercise of its own reason. This was Rousseau's opinion respecting men: I extend it to women, and confidently assert that they have been drawn out of their sphere by false refinement, and not by an endeavour to acquire masculine qualities. [. . .]

Let it not be concluded, that I wish to invert the order of things; I have already granted, that, from the constitution of their bodies, men seem to be designed by Providence to attain a greater degree of virtue. I speak collectively of the whole sex; but I see not the shadow of a reason to conclude that their virtues should differ in respect to their nature. In fact, how can they, if virtue has only one eternal standard? I must, therefore, if I reason consequentially, as strenuously maintain, that they have the same simple direction, as that there is a God. [. . .]

But avoiding, as I have hitherto done, any direct comparison of the two sexes collectively, or frankly acknowledging the inferiority of woman, according to the

---

[22] This seems to be another slap at Rousseau, who does not fare well in Wollstonecraft's evaluation.

present appearance of things, I shall only insist, that men have increased that inferiority till women are almost sunk below the standard of rational creatures. Let their faculties have room to unfold, and their virtues to gain strength, and then determine where the whole sex must stand in the intellectual scale. Yet, let it be remembered, that for a small number of distinguished women I do not ask a place. [. . .] [C]ultivate their minds, give them the salutary, sublime curb of principle, and let them attain conscious dignity by feeling themselves only dependent on God. Teach them, in common with man, to submit to necessity, instead of giving, to render them more pleasing, a sex to morals. [. . .]

These may be termed Utopian dreams. Thanks to that Being who impressed them on my soul, and gave me sufficient strength of mind to dare to exert my own reason, till becoming dependent only on him for the support of my virtue, I view with indignation, the mistaken notions that enslave my sex.

I love man as my fellow; but his sceptre real or usurped, extends not to me, unless the reason of an individual demands my homage; and even then the submission is to reason, and not to man. In fact, the conduct of an accountable being must be regulated by the operations of its own reason; or on what foundation rests the throne of God?

It appears to me necessary to dwell on these obvious truths, because females have been insulted, as it were; and while they have been stripped of the virtues that should clothe humanity, they have been decked with artificial graces, that enable them to exercise a short lived tyranny. Love, in their bosoms, taking place of every nobler passion, their sole ambition is to be fair, to raise emotion instead of inspiring respect; and this ignoble desire, like the servility in absolute monarchies, destroys all strength of character. Liberty is the mother of virtue, and if women are, by their very constitution, slaves, and not allowed to breathe the sharp invigorating air of freedom, they must ever languish like exotics, and be reckoned beautiful flaws in nature; let it also be remembered, that they are the only flaw.

As to the argument respecting the subjection in which the sex has ever been held, it retorts on man. [. . .] *Men* have submitted to superior strength, to enjoy with impunity the pleasure of the moment – *women* have only done the same, and therefore till it is proved that the courtier, who servilely resigns the birthright of a man, is not a moral agent, it cannot be demonstrated that woman is essentially inferior to man, because she has always been subjugated. [. . .]

Seneca Falls Declaration of Sentiments and Resolutions (1848)[23]

When, in the course of human events, it becomes necessary for one portion of the family of man to assume among the people of the earth a position different from that which they have hitherto occupied, but one to which the laws of nature and

[23] From "Chapter IV: New York" in E. Cady Stanton, S. B. Anthony, and M. Joslyn Gage (eds.), *History of Woman Suffrage*, Vol. 1: *1848–1861* (New York: Fowler and Wells, 1881), pp. 70–3.

of nature's God entitle them, a decent respect to the opinions of mankind requires that they should declare the causes that impel them to such a course.

We hold these truths to be self-evident: that all men and women are created equal; that they are endowed by their Creator with certain inalienable rights; that among these are life, liberty, and the pursuit of happiness; that to secure these rights governments are instituted, deriving their just powers from the consent of the governed. Whenever any form of government becomes destructive of these ends, it is the right of those who suffer from it to refuse allegiance to it, and to insist upon the institution of a new government, laying its foundation on such principles, and organizing its powers in such form, as to them shall seem most likely to effect their safety and happiness. Prudence, indeed, will dictate that governments long established should not be changed for light and transient causes; and accordingly all experience hath shown that mankind are more disposed to suffer, while evils are sufferable, than to right themselves by abolishing the forms to which they were accustomed. But when a long train of abuses and usurpations, pursuing invariably the same object evinces a design to reduce them under absolute despotism, it is their duty to throw off such government, and to provide new guards for their future security. Such has been the patient sufferance of the women under this government, and such is now the necessity which constrains them to demand the equal station to which they are entitled.

The history of mankind is a history of repeated injuries and usurpations on the part of man toward woman, having in direct object the establishment of an absolute tyranny over her. To prove this, let facts be submitted to a candid world.

He has never permitted her to exercise her inalienable right to the elective franchise.

He has compelled her to submit to laws, in the formation of which she had no voice.

He has withheld from her rights which are given to the most ignorant and degraded men – both natives and foreigners.

Having deprived her of this first right of a citizen, the elective franchise, thereby leaving her without representation in the halls of legislation, he has oppressed her on all sides.

He has made her, if married, in the eye of the law, civilly dead.

He has taken from her all right in property, even to the wages she earns.

He has made her, morally, an irresponsible being, as she can commit many crimes with impunity, provided they be done in the presence of her husband. In the covenant of marriage, she is compelled to promise obedience to her husband, he becoming, to all intents and purposes, her master – the law giving him power to deprive her of her liberty, and to administer chastisement.

He has so framed the laws of divorce, as to what shall be the proper causes, and in case of separation, to whom the guardianship of the children shall be given, as to be wholly regardless of the happiness of women – the law, in all cases, going upon a false supposition of the supremacy of man, and giving all power into his hands.

After depriving her of all rights as a married woman, if single, and the owner of property, he has taxed her to support a government which recognizes her only when her property can be made profitable to it.

He has monopolized nearly all the profitable employments, and from those she is permitted to follow, she receives but a scanty remuneration. He closes against her all the avenues to wealth and distinction which he considers most honorable to himself. As a teacher of theology, medicine, or law, she is not known.

He has denied her the facilities for obtaining a thorough education, all colleges being closed against her.

He allows her in Church, as well as State, but a subordinate position, claiming Apostolic authority for her exclusion from the ministry, and, with some exceptions, from any public participation in the affairs of the Church.

He has created a false public sentiment by giving to the world a different code of morals for men and women, by which moral delinquencies which exclude women from society, are not only tolerated, but deemed of little account in man.

He has usurped the prerogative of Jehovah himself, claiming it as his right to assign for her a sphere of action, when that belongs to her conscience and to her God.

He has endeavored, in every way that he could, to destroy her confidence in her own powers, to lessen her self-respect, and to make her willing to lead a dependent and abject life.

Now, in view of this entire disfranchisement of one-half the people of this country, their social and religious degradation – in view of the unjust laws above mentioned, and because women do feel themselves aggrieved, oppressed, and fraudulently deprived of their most sacred rights, we insist that they have immediate admission to all the rights and privileges which belong to them as citizens of the United States.

In entering upon the great work before us, we anticipate no small amount of misconception, misrepresentation, and ridicule; but we shall use every instrumentality within our power to effect our object. We shall employ agents, circulate tracts, petition the State and National legislatures, and endeavor to enlist the pulpit and the press in our behalf. We hope this Convention will be followed by a series of Conventions embracing every part of the country.

The following resolutions were discussed by Lucretia Mott, Thomas and Mary Ann McClintock, Amy Post, Catharine A. F. Stebbins, and others, and were adopted:

WHEREAS, The great precept of nature is conceded to be, that "man shall pursue his own true and substantial happiness." Blackstone in his Commentaries remarks, that this law of Nature being coeval with mankind, and dictated by God himself, is of course superior in obligation to any other. It is binding over all the globe, in all countries and at all times; no human laws are of any validity if contrary to this, and such of them as are valid, derive all their force, and all their validity, and all their authority, mediately and immediately, from this original; therefore,

Resolved, That such laws as conflict, in any way, with the true and substantial happiness of woman, are contrary to the great precept of nature and of no validity, for this is "superior in obligation to any other."

Resolved, That all laws which prevent woman from occupying such a station in society as her conscience shall dictate, or which place her in a position inferior to that of man, are contrary to the great precept of nature, and therefore of no force or authority.

Resolved, That woman is man's equal – was intended to be so by the Creator, and the highest good of the race demands that she should be recognized as such.

Resolved, That the women of this country ought to be enlightened in regard to the laws under which they live, that they may no longer publish their degradation by declaring themselves satisfied with their present position, nor their ignorance, by asserting that they have all the rights they want.

Resolved, That inasmuch as man, while claiming for himself intellectual superiority, does accord to woman moral superiority, it is pre-eminently his duty to encourage her to speak and teach, as she has an opportunity, in all religious assemblies.

Resolved, That the same amount of virtue, delicacy, and refinement of behavior that is required of woman in the social state, should also be required of man, and the same transgressions should be visited with equal severity on both man and woman.

Resolved, That the objection of indelicacy and impropriety, which is so often brought against woman when she addresses a public audience, comes with a very ill-grace from those who encourage, by their attendance, her appearance on the stage, in the concert, or in feats of the circus.

Resolved, That woman has too long rested satisfied in the circumscribed limits which corrupt customs and a perverted application of the Scriptures have marked out for her, and that it is time she should move in the enlarged sphere which her great Creator has assigned her.

Resolved, That it is the duty of the women of this country to secure to themselves their sacred right to the elective franchise.

Resolved, That the equality of human rights results necessarily from the fact of the identity of the race in capabilities and responsibilities.

Resolved, therefore, That, being invested by the Creator with the same capabilities, and the same consciousness of responsibility for their exercise, it is demonstrably the right and duty of woman, equally with man, to promote every righteous cause by every righteous means; and especially in regard to the great subjects of morals and religion, it is self-evidently her right to participate with her brother in teaching them, both in private and in public, by writing and by speaking, by any instrumentalities proper to be used, and in any assemblies proper to be held; and this being a self-evident truth growing out of the divinely implanted principles of human nature, any custom or authority adverse to it, whether modern or wearing the hoary sanction of antiquity, is to be regarded as a self-evident falsehood, and at war with mankind.

Resolved, That the speedy success of our cause depends upon the zealous and untiring efforts of both men and women, for the overthrow of the monopoly of the pulpit, and for the securing to woman an equal participation with men in the various trades, professions, and commerce.

Elizabeth Cady Stanton

Letter to Mary Ann White Johnson and the Ohio Women's Convention (April 7, 1850)[24]

DEAR MARY ANNE:——

How rejoiced I am to hear that the women of Ohio have called a Convention preparatory to the remodeling of their State Constitution. The remodeling of a Constitution, in the nineteenth century, speaks of progress, of greater freedom, and of more enlarged views of human rights and duties. It is fitting that, at such a time, woman, who has so long been the victim of ignorance and injustice, should at length throw off the trammels of a false education, stand upright, and with dignity and earnestness manifest a deep and serious interest in the laws which are to govern her and her country. It needs no argument to teach woman that she is interested in the laws which govern her. Suffering has taught her this already. It is important, now that a change is proposed, that she speak, and loudly too. Having decided to petition for a redress of grievances, the question is for what shall you first petition? For the exercise of your right to the elective franchise – nothing short of this. The grant to you of this right will secure all others, and the granting of every other right, whilst this is denied, is a mockery. For instance: – What is the right to property, without the right to protect it? The enjoyment of that right to-day is no security that it will be continued to-morrow, so long as it is granted to us as a favor, and not claimed by us as a right. Woman must exercise her right to the elective franchise, and have her own representatives in our national councils, for two good reasons:

1st. Men cannot represent us. They are so thoroughly educated into the belief that woman's nature is altogether different from their own, that they have no idea that she can be governed by the same laws of mind as themselves. So far from viewing us like themselves, they seem, from their legislation, to consider us their moral and intellectual antipodes; for whatever law they find good for themselves, they forthwith pass its opposite for us, and express the most profound astonishment if we manifest the least dissatisfaction. For example: our forefathers, full of righteous indignation, pitched King George, his authority and his tea chests, all into the sea, and because forsooth, they were forced to pay taxes without being represented in the British government. "Taxation without representation," was the text for many a hot debate in the forests of the new world, and for many an eloquent oration in the parliament of the old. Yet, in forming our new government, they have taken from us the very rights which they fought, and bled, and died, to secure to themselves. They have not only taxed us, but in many cases they strip us of all we inherit, the wages we earn, the children of our love; and for such grievances we have no redress in any court of justice this side of Heaven. They tax our property to build Colleges, then pass a special law prohibiting any woman to enter there. A married woman has no legal existence; she has no more absolute rights than a slave on a Southern plantation. She

[24] From *Proceedings of the Ohio Women's Convention, Held at Salem, April 19th and 20th, 1850; with an Address by J. Elizabeth Jones* (Cleveland: Smead and Cowles, 1850), pp.15–19.

takes the name of her master, holds nothing, owns nothing, can bring no action in her own name; and the principle on which she and the slave is educated is the same. The slave is taught what is considered best for him to know – which is nothing; the woman is taught what is best for her to know – which is little more than nothing; man being the umpire in both cases. A woman cannot follow out the impulses of her own immortal mind in her sphere, any further than the slave can in his sphere. Civilly, socially, and religiously, she is what man chooses her to be – nothing more or less – and such is the slave. It is impossible for us to convince man that we think and feel exactly as he does, that we have the same sense of right and justice, the same love of freedom and independence. Some men regard us as devils, and some as angels; hence, one class would shut us up in a certain sphere for fear of the evil WE might do, and the other for fear of the evil that might be done to us; thus, except for the sentiment of the thing, for all the good it does us, we might as well be thought the one as the other. But we ourselves have to do with what we are and what we shall be.

2nd.   Man cannot legislate for us. Our statute books and all past experience teach us this fact. His laws, where we are concerned, have been, without one exception, unjust, cruel, and aggressive. Having denied our identity with himself, he has no data to go upon in judging of our wants and interests. If we are alike in our mental structure, then there is no reason why we should not have a voice in making the laws which govern us; but if we are not alike, most certainly we must make laws for ourselves; for who else can understand what we need and desire? If it be admitted in this government that all men and women are free and equal, then must we claim a place in our Senate Chambers and Houses of Representatives. But if after all, it be found that even here we have classes, and caste – not "Lords and commons," but Lords and women – then must we claim a lower House, where our Representatives can watch the passage of all bills affecting our own welfare, or the good of our country. – Had the women of this country had a voice in the Government, think you our national escutcheon would have been stained with the guilt of aggressive warfare upon such weak defenceless nations as the Seminoles and Mexicans? Think you we should cherish and defend, in the heart of our nation, such a wholesale system of piracy, cruelty, licentiousness and ignorance, as is our slavery? Think you that relic of barbarism, the gallows, by which the wretched murderer is sent with blood upon his soul, uncalled for, into the presence of his God, would be sustained by law? Verily, no, or I mistake woman's heart, her instinctive love of justice and mercy, and truth.

Who questions woman's right to vote? We can show our credentials to the right of self-government; we get ours just where man got his; they are all Heaven-descended, God-given. It is our duty to assert and re-assert this right, to agitate, discuss and petition, until our political equality be fully recognized. Depend upon it, this is the point to attack, the stronghold of the fortress – the one woman will find most difficult to take. the one man will most reluctlantly [*sic*] give up; therefore let us encamp right under its shadow – there spend all our time, strength and moral ammunition, year after year, with perseverance, courage and decision. Let no sallies of wit or ridicule at our expense, no soft nonsense of woman's beauty, delicacy and refinement, no promise of gold and silver, bank stock, road stock, or landed estate, seduce us from our position, until that one stronghold totters to the ground. This done, the rest will they surrender at discretion. Then comes equality in Church and State, in the family circle, and in all our social relations.

The cause of woman is onward. For our encouragement, let us take a review of what has occurred during the last few years. Not two years since, the women of New York held several Conventions. Their meetings were well attended by both men and women; and the question of woman's true position was fully and freely discussed. The proceedings of those meetings and their Declaration of Sentiments were all published and scattered far and near. Before that time, the newspapers said but little on that subject. Immediately after, there was scarcely a newspaper in the Union that did not notice these Conventions, and generally in a tone of ridicule. Now, you seldom take up a paper that has not something about woman; but the tone is changing – ridicule is giving way to reason. Our papers begin to see that this is no subject for mirth, but one for serious consideration. Our literature also is assuming a different tone. The heroine of our fashionable novel is now a being of spirit, of energy, of will, with a conscience, with high moral principle, great decision and self-reliance.

[. . .] Woman seems to be preparing herself for a higher and holier destiny. That same love of liberty which burned in the hearts of our sires, is now being kindled anew in the daughters of this proud Republic. From the present state of public sentiment, we have every reason to look hopefully into the future. I see a brighter, happier day yet to come; but Woman must say how soon the dawn shall be, and whether the light shall first shine in the East or the West. By her own efforts the change must come. She must carve out her future destiny with her own right hand. If she have not the energy to secure for herself her due position, neither would she have the force or stability to maintain it, if placed there by another.

Farewell! yours, sincerely,

E. C. STANTON.

Article in The Revolution (January 14, 1869)[25]

[In the article, Stanton is replying to Gerrit Smith's refusal to sign a petition from the State of New York to Congress, requesting that "in any change of amendment of the Constitution you may propose to extend or regulate suffrage, there shall be no distinctions made between men and women."]

[. . .] He [Gerrit Smith] does not clearly read the signs of the times, or he would see that there is to be no reconstruction of this nation, except on the basis of universal suffrage, as the natural, inalienable right of every citizen. The uprising of the women on both continents, in France, England, Russia, Switzerland, and the United States, all show that advancing civilization demands a new element in the government of nations. As the aristocracy in this country is the "male sex," and as Mr. Smith belongs

[25] From " Chapter XXI: Reconstruction" in E. Cady Stanton, S. B. Anthony, and M. Joslyn Gage (eds.), *History of Woman Suffrage*, Vol. II: *1861–1876* (Rochester, NY: Privately published, 1882), pp. 317–19.

to the privileged order, he naturally considers it important for the best interests of the nation, that every type and shade of degraded, ignorant manhood should be enfranchised, before even the higher classes of womanhood should be admitted to the polls. This does not surprise us. Men always judge more wisely of objective wrongs and oppressions, than of those in which they are themselves involved. Tyranny on a Southern plantation is far more easily seen by white men at the North than the wrongs of the women of their own households.

[...] While philosophy and science alike point to woman as the new power destined to redeem the world, how can Mr. Smith fail to see that it is just this we need to restore honor and virtue in the Government? There is sex in the spiritual as well as the physical, and what we need to-day in government, in the world of morals and thought, is the recognition of the feminine element, as it is this alone that can hold the masculine in check.

Again; Mr. Smith refuses to sign the petition because he thinks to press the broader question of "universal suffrage" would defeat the partial one of "manhood suffrage"; in other words, to demand protection for woman against her oppressors, would jeopardize the black man's chance of securing protection against his oppressors. If it is a question of precedence merely, on what principle of justice or courtesy should woman yield her right of enfranchisement to the negro? If men can not be trusted to legislate for their own sex, how can they legislate for the opposite sex, of whose wants and needs they know nothing? It has always been considered good philosophy in pressing any measure to claim the uttermost in order to get something. [...] But their intense interest in the negro blinded our former champions so that they forsook principle for policy, and in giving woman the cold shoulder raised a more deadly opposition to the negro than any we had yet encountered, creating an antagonism between him and the very element most needed to be propitiated in his behalf. It was this feeling that defeated "negro suffrage" in Kansas.

But Mr. Smith abandons the principle clearly involved, and intrenches himself on policy. He would undoubtedly plead the necessity of the ballot for the negro at the south for his protection, and point us to innumerable acts of cruelty he suffers to-day. But all these things fall as heavily on the women of the black race, yea far more so, for no man can ever know the deep, the damning degradation to which woman is subject in her youth, in helplessness and poverty. The enfranchisement of the men of her race, Mr. Smith would say, is her protection. Our Saxon men have held the ballot in this country for a century, and what honest man can claim that it has been used for woman's protection? Alas! we have given the very hey day of our life to undoing the cruel and unjust laws that the men of New York had made for their own mothers, wives, and daughters.

As to the "rights of races," on which so much stress is laid just now, we have listened to debates in anti-slavery conventions, for twenty years or more, and we never heard Gerrit Smith plead the negro cause on any lower ground than his manhood; his individual, inalienable right to freedom and equality and thus, we conjure every thoughtful man to plead woman's cause to-day. Politicians will find, when they come to test this question of "negro supremacy" in the several States, that there is a far stronger feeling among the women of the nation than they supposed. We doubt whether a constitutional amendment securing "manhood suffrage" alone could be fairly passed in a single State in this Union. Women everywhere are waking up to their own God-given rights, to their true dignity as citizens of a republic, as mothers of the race.

Although those who demand "woman's suffrage" on principle are few, those who would oppose "negro suffrage" from prejudice are many, hence the only way to secure the latter, is to end all this talk of class legislation, bury the negro in the citizen, and claim the suffrage for all men and women, as a natural, inalienable right. [...]

Frederick Douglass *Speech at the American Equal Rights Association Convention* (May 12, 1869)[26]

I came here more as a listener than to speak, and I have listened with a great deal of pleasure to the eloquent address of the Rev. Mr. Frothingham and the splendid address of the President [Stanton]. There is no name greater than that of Elizabeth Cady Stanton in the matter of woman's rights, but my sentiments are tinged a little against *The Revolution*. There was in the address to which I allude the employment of certain names, such as "Sambo," and the gardener, and the bootblack, and the daughters of Jefferson and Washington., and all the rest that I can not [*sic*] coincide with. I have asked what difference there is between the daughters of Jefferson and Washington and other daughters. (Laughter.) I must say that I do no not see how anyone can pretend that there is the same urgency in giving the ballot to woman as to the negro. With us, the matter is a question of life and death, at least, in fifteen States of the Union. When women, because they are women, are hunted down through the cities of New York and New Orleans; when they are dragged from their houses and hung upon lamp-posts; when their children are torn from their arms, and their brains dashed out upon the pavement; when they are objects of insult and outrage at every turn; when they are in danger of having their homes burnt down over their heads; when their children are not allowed to enter schools; then they will have an urgency to obtain the ballot equal to our own. (Great applause.)

[AN AUDIENCE MEMBER INTERRUPTED: Is that not true about black women?]

Yes, yes, yes; it is true of the black woman, but not because she is a woman, but because she is black.

Suggested Readings

Ralph Waldo Emerson, "Man the Reformer" [1841] in K. Sacks (ed.), *Political Writings* (Cambridge: Cambridge University Press, 2008), pp.101–14.

Henry David Thoreau, *Walden, or Life in the Woods* (Boston: Ticknor and Fields, 1854).

---

[26] From "Chapter XXII: National Conventions – 1869" in Cady Stanton, Anthony, and Joslyn Gage (eds.), *History of Woman Suffrage*, Vol. II, pp. 382–3.

Walt Whitman, *Leaves of Grass* (Brooklyn, 1855).

Bob Blaisdell (ed.), *Great Speeches of Native Americans* (Mineola: Dover, 2000).

Judith Sargent Murray, "On the Equality of Sexes" [1770], *Massachusetts Magazine*, 2:2–3 (1790), pp. 132–5, 223–6.

Elizabeth Cady Stanton, Susan B. Anthony, and Matilda Joslyn Gage, *History of Woman's Suffrage*, Vol. I: *1848–1861*, and Vol. II: *1861–1876* (Rochester, 1881/1882).

Ann. D. Gordon (ed.), *The Selected Papers of Elizabeth Cady Stanton and Susan B. Anthony*, Vol. I: *In the School of Anti-Slavery, 1840–1866* (New Brunswick, NJ: Rutgers University Press, 1997).

10 The United States "Is"

We have seen how, throughout the entire founding era, various attempts were made to protect, on the one hand, the <u>common good</u> of the people and, on the other hand, <u>individual interests and rights</u>. In order to balance the <u>majority principle</u> with <u>minority rights</u> and <u>collective identities</u> with <u>particular ones</u>, appeals were made, depending on the circumstances, to the people's two bodies and to both republican and liberal *Weltanschauungen*. More often than not, the best solution proved to be some form of compromise between opposite poles. Yet the series of political compromises in the nineteenth century also made the tragic survival of slavery possible, well into the second half of the century.

Embarrassing as it is, one must acknowledge that, in the early 1800s, the issue of slavery was far from the forefront of political debates. Most people treated it more as a *political* rather than a *moral* problem. Even when it did become a central issue of division, the emphasis remained on the future of the Union rather than the institution of slavery itself. As late as August 1862, **Abraham Lincoln** displayed this kind of <u>political pragmatism</u> when claiming in a famous letter to Horace Greely, the editor of the influential *New York Tribune*:

> My paramount object in this struggle is to save the Union, and is not either to save or to destroy slavery. If I could save the Union without freeing any slave I would do it, and if I could save it by freeing all the slaves I would do it; and if I could save it by freeing some and leaving others alone I would also do that. What I do about slavery, and the colored race, I do because I believe it helps to save the Union; and what I forbear, I forbear because I do not believe it would help to save the Union.[1]

But if slavery was not the cornerstone of American politics during the first part of the nineteenth century, what was? Since by then the idea of the <u>people's sovereignty</u> had become a widely accepted doctrine, the answer is rather straightforward – the proper definition of "the people." The groundwork for the **Gettysburg Address** was laid decades earlier when, in 1830, **Daniel Webster** (Chapter 8) told **Robert Hayne**:[2] "It is, Sir, the people's Constitution, the people's government, made for the people,

---

[1] R. P. Basler et al. (eds.), *The Collected Works of Abraham Lincoln*, Vol. V (New Brunswick, NJ: Rutgers University Press, 1953), p. 389.

[2] Robert Young Hayne (1791–1839), US Senator, Governor of South Carolina, mayor of Charleston, was a fervent supporter of states' rights.

made by the people, and answerable to the people."[3] Twenty years later, furious at Webster's position during the **Compromise of 1850**, **Theodor Parker** accused Webster himself of betraying "a government of all the people, by all the people, for all the people."[4] In Lincoln's own words, even the war was nothing other than "essentially a people's contest." But, once again, which people? In the end, "We the people of the Confederate States," as the first words of the Constitution of the Confederate States read, clashed on the battlefield with "We the people of these United States" in the name of the same revolutionary principle of popular sovereignty that had earlier been employed by the Patriots.

A crisis long in the making, it began before the end of the eighteenth century, when Thomas Jefferson and James Madison penned the **Virginia and Kentucky Resolutions** (1798/1799), both of which alluded to the right of a state to <u>nullify</u> a federal law if found unconstitutional by its own state constitution. This appeal cracked open the door for the possibility of secession. And even though both Jefferson and Madison toned down their positions after becoming presidents, the **Nullification Crisis** exploded in 1832–1833, when South Carolina threatened to secede over tariffs designed to protect Northern manufactories. Eventually the crisis was resolved by a compromise (the **Tariff of 1833**) proposed by **John C. Calhoun** and **Henry Clay**. It wasn't the first major compromise that Clay – who would come to be known as the Great Compromiser – managed to orchestrate in order to avoid a secession crisis, and it wouldn't be the last. The first one was the (second) **Missouri Compromise** of 1821, upon which Maine was admitted into the Union as a free state while Missouri was admitted as a slave state in order to maintain the balance of power between free states (North) and slave states (South) in the US Senate.

While both Calhoun and Clay professed their dedication to the Union and embraced compromise as the founding principle of the United States, they ended up on opposite sides of history. **John C. Calhoun** (1782–1850) started his career as a supporter of a strong central government and of modernization, yet by the end of the 1820s he believed that the Southern states had been treated unfairly by the Northerners. He subsequently changed his position and became a strong supporter of state rights. That he understood "we, the people" to mean the people of each state in their corporate capacity is obvious in his *Exposition*, which he penned in opposition to what he called "the **Tariff of Abomination**," while serving as the seventh Vice President of the United States under John Quincy Adams.[5]

Calhoun's main argument centered on the "striking distinction between Government and Sovereignty." The separate governments of the several States have the executive, the legislative, and the judiciary *powers*, but "the *sovereignty* resides in the *people* of the States respectively." The same applies to the federal government, in which case "*the sovereignty resides in the people of the several States*

---

[3] *The Writings and Speeches of Daniel Webster*, 18 vols., Vol. VI (Boston: Little, Brown, 1906), p. 54, quoted in D. T. Rodgers, *Contested Truths: Keywords in American Politics since Independence* (Cambridge, MA: Harvard University Press, 1987), p. 91.

[4] T. Parker, *The Slave Power* (New York: Arno, 1969 [1916]), p. 250. Theodor Parker (1810–1860) was a Unitarian minister, a transcendentalist, and a moral abolitionist.

[5] For obvious reasons, the text was circulated anonymously, even though the author was an "open secret."

who created it." The right to judge whether the powers of state governments had been infringed upon was, for Calhoun, "an essential attribute of sovereignty, of which the States cannot be divested without losing their sovereignty itself." He developed his political theory further in his ***Disquisition of Government***, during another crisis that threatened the Union and ended with the **Compromise of 1850**.

Calhoun built his theory from the ground up, starting with <u>human nature</u>. In accordance with the **republican** *Weltanschauung*, he claimed that "man is so constituted as to be a social being." Yet, as classic **liberalism** had it, he conceded that "each [. . .] has a greater regard for his own safety or happiness, than for the safety or happiness of others; and, where these come in opposition, is ready to sacrifice the interests of others to his own." <u>Government</u>, therefore, is the result of "this twofold constitution of his nature." But individual abuses aside, abuses of government must also be prevented. How? By a <u>constitution</u> that "stands to *government*, as *government* stands to *society*."

Like Madison (Chapter 7), Calhoun argued that, since men are far from perfect, "power can only be resisted by power – and tendency by tendency." The <u>right of suffrage</u> is a *necessary* condition for preventing abuses, but not a *sufficient* one; something more is needed. The distinction Calhoun drew between **numerical (absolute) majorities** and **concurrent (constitutional) majorities** is in essence the distinction between the people understood as a collection of individuals (Chapter 3), and the people understood as a whole (Chapter 2). While not rejecting the majority's right to make decisions that will affect all people, he claimed that the minority should have the constitutional right to <u>veto</u> the decisions of the majority, thus compelling the majority to find workable <u>compromises</u> and serving as an alternative to the use of <u>force</u>.

Like Calhoun, **Henry Clay** (1777–1852) fervently supported "that great principle of compromise and concession which lies at the bottom of our institutions, which gave birth to the constitution itself." Yet by "the people" he did not understand "the people of several states," but the people of the United States. Like Calhoun, he acknowledged that it would be too much to ask from human nature to even "forget for a moment [. . .] party feeling and party causes," yet he believed that no "man who is entitled to deserve the character of an *American* statesman, would [. . .] disturb this treaty of peace and amity." In the end, he noticed, "nullification has been put down, and put down in a manner more effectually than by a thousand wars or a thousand armies – by the irresistible force, by the mighty influence of *public opinion*." While the compromise of 1833 temporarily abated the danger of secession and increased the popularity of the Whig Party (Chapter 8), it did not help Clay win the presidency of the United States. However, this failure did not affect his unshakeable belief in the principle of compromise. The last settlement he helped to orchestrate, together with the Democrat Stephen Douglas, was the **Compromise of 1850**: a series of five bills meant to solve the question of slavery in the new territories acquired after the **Mexican–American War** (1846–1848).

Daniel Webster, Clay's fellow Whig, adopted the same approach intended to preserve the Union in a controversial speech known as ***The Constitution and the Union***. Webster attacked all of Calhoun's arguments and enthusiastically supported Clay's compromise. His position was made clear from the opening remarks: "I wish to speak today, not as a Massachusetts man, nor as a northern man, but as an *American*." Without mincing his words, he acknowledged "the question which has so long harassed the country [. . .] – the question of slavery." According to Webster, it was not, as many Southerners claimed, a matter of honor and justice, or of state rights; "[i]t was the cotton interest that gave a new desire to promote slavery, to spread it and to use its labor." And yet, to the dismay of many, he agreed with the Fugitive Slave Act (1850), making it easier for Southerners to recover fugitive slaves from the Northern states. No matter what one's judgment about slavery was, Webster argued, it was a constitutional obligation to uphold the law. For the hardcore abolitionists, his endorsement of the amendment to the Act was anathema. A *Liberator* headline read, "*On the Late Satanic Speech of Daniel Webster*," and Ralph Waldo Emerson (Chapter 9) proclaimed that it put Webster on "the side of abuse and oppression and chaos" rather that the "side of humanity and justice."[6]

These were the **moral abolitionists**, like **William Lloyd Garrison**, who refused to treat slavery as a *political* problem, and insisted on its intrinsic evilness.[7] They did not agree with the step-by-step approach, embraced by the **pragmatic abolitionists**, claiming that freedom and slavery cannot be "espoused." Using the very words of the Declaration of Independence, "the corner-stone upon which [was] founded the Temple of Freedom," **The Declaration of Sentiments of the American Anti-Slavery Society** (1833) insisted that "the slaves ought instantly to be set free." For Garrison, all compromises involving slavery were off the table. "How has the slave system grown to its present enormous dimensions? Through compromise. How is it to be exterminated? Only by an uncompromising spirit."

For a long time, Southerners were convinced that they occupied the higher ground politically speaking, since the institution of slavery was acknowledged by the Constitution. After all, three clauses mention it specifically: Art. I, § 2, cl. 3, also known as the Three-Fifths Compromise; Art. I, § 9, cl. 1, on the slave trade; and Art. V, § 2, cl. 3, requiring the return of persons "held to service of labor" escaping into other states. The only concern of the pro-slavery camp were the "political speculatists, who deriving their ideas of government from abstract theorems, and estimating man more by what he ought to be, than what he is, [wish] to erect an Utopian Constitution on a sandy basis."[8] According to the pro-slavery camp, these were the **philosophical abolitionists** who, like the French revolutionaries, were foolishly trying to impose some abstract ideals on an existing reality for which they did not feel responsible.

Hence, moral battles were followed by theoretical ones and the idea of natural, inalienable rights was the first target. "The Declaration of Independence is to be taken with a great qualification. It declares men have an inalienable right to life; yet we hang criminals – to liberty, yet we imprison – to the pursuit of happiness, yet we must not infringe upon the rights of others. If the Declaration of Independence is

---

[6] S. M. Reznick, "On Liberty and Union: Moral Imagination and Its Limits in Daniel Webster's Seventh of March Speech," *American Political Thought: A Journal of Ideas, Institutions, and Culture*, 6 (2017), p. 372.

[7] William Lloyd Garrison (1805–1872) was the founder of the abolitionist paper *The Liberator*, and of the New England Anti-Slavery Society. After the Civil War, but before the freed slaves were granted the right to vote, he considered the objective of his fight fulfilled.

[8] William Smith in an Independence Day oration at Charleston in 1796, quoted in W. Sumner Jenkins, *Pro-Slavery Thought in the Old South* (Chapel Hill: University of North Carolina Press, 1935), p. 61.

taken in its fullest extent, it will warrant robbery."[9] Two of the most influential pro-slavery arguments claimed to be based on "sociology." **George Fitzhugh**'s *Sociology for the South* was the first book published in the English language to use the word "sociology" in its title, and **James H. Hammond**'s "mudsill theory," according to which every society must have a lower class on which civilization can be raised, was presented as a "sociological theory."

George Fitzhugh (1806–1881) vituperated against the "unobservant, abstract thinkers and closet scholars, who deal with little of the world and see less of it." According to him, the idea that men were free and equal was part of the laissez-faire philosophy (market economy), meant to promote the interests of the strong at the expense of the weakest, including women, the poor, and the ignorant. "In free society none but selfish virtues are in repute. [...] In such society virtue loses all her loveliness, because of her selfish aims. Good men and bad men have the same end in view: self-promotion, self-elevation." Shocking phrases such as "liberty is an evil which government is intended to correct," or "some were born with saddles on their backs, and others booted and spurred to ride them" abound in his writings. But when he proposed to extend slavery to white men, in order to protect them, his fellow Southerners began to dissociate themselves from what they judged the words of a crackpot.

In the end, the most powerful enemy of the slaveholders proved to be not, as they had thought for decades, the "abstract thinkers and closet scholars," and not even the seasoned politicians. Their main enemy was a new public opinion roused mainly by **Harriet Beecher Stowe**'s *Uncle Tom's Cabin*, which sold 310,000 copies in 1852 alone. Under popular pressure, the second party system crumbled; the Whig Party disintegrated and the Know Nothing Party, nativist and resentful, enjoyed only an ephemeral success (Chapter 8). Disregarding the change in public mood, an over-confident **Stephen Douglas** (1813–1861) pushed the **Kansas–Nebraska Bill**, which effectively repealed the Missouri Compromise. In addition to the new Fugitive Slave Act, which nationalized slavery, it proved to be the straw that broke the back of the Democratic Party, preparing the ground for the rise of the **new Republican Party**.

During the famous **Lincoln–Douglas debates**, Douglas found himself caught between the two definitions of "the people." He made appeal to the sovereignty of the people at state (and territory) level in deciding whether to accept slavery or not, and to the people at a national level when supporting the Fugitive Slave Act. This apparent contradiction did not go unnoticed, and on a banner during the Galesburg, Illinois, debate he was depicted trying unsuccessfully to ride two donkeys at the same time. Henry Clay's professed disciple, Abraham Lincoln, observed during his first debate with Douglas that "Public sentiment is everything. With it, nothing can fail; against it, nothing can succeed." He was proven right.

In 1852, the **Free Soil Party**'s presidential candidate, **John P. Hale** (1806–1873), gathered less than 5 percent of the popular vote. Yet two years later the new Republican Party was born, and by 1856 its national platform advocated "the

---

[9] J. Clay, *Annals of the Congress of the United States* (9th Congress, 2nd Session, December 29, 1806), p. 227.

maintenance of the principles promulgated in the Declaration of Independence" while inviting "the affiliation and cooperation of the men of all parties, however differing from us in other respects, in support of the principles herein declared."[10] The remnants of the nativist Know Nothings and of the Free Soil Party answered the invitation, including Hale. The promise to restore the principles of the Declaration appealed simultaneously to the supporters of state rights and to the "philosophical abolitionists." Shuffling the cards of "the people" allowed the new Republicans to claim to be the true Democrats.

In the end, the **moralist abolitionists** and their all-or-nothing approach helped mold public opinion, but the **political abolitionists** and their step-by-step approach delivered the practical results. A case in point: **Frederick Douglass** (1817–1895). After escaping from slavery, he acquired a great reputation as an orator and writer, advocating for the equal treatment not just of African Americans but also women, Native Americans, and Chinese immigrants (Chapter 9). Douglass started his career as a moral abolitionist, supporting Garrison and the Anti-Slavery Society. Yet he came to realize that "its doctrine, of 'no union with slaveholders,' carried out, dissolves the Union, [. . .]. It ends by leaving the slave to free himself." Initially, he refused to support the new Republican Party, considering that its position was too compromising when it came to abolition, and directed his followers to support the **Liberty Party** instead. However, just four months later, after realizing that only the Republicans had a real shot at an electoral victory against the pro-slavery Democrats, he changed his mind, arguing that some progress is better than none.

Abraham Lincoln (1809–1865) remains the most famous example of political abolitionism. Lincoln's desperate attempts to find a compromise between radical abolitionists and radical supporters of states' rights were not enough to prevent secession. His conciliatory **First Inaugural Address** fell on deaf ears. Southerners were too obsessed with what they perceived to be a direct threat to their particular identities to be willing to compromise, and the Civil War commenced soon after. The days of compromise were, indeed, gone. In a **Special Session Message**, Lincoln told Congress: "No compromise by public servants could in this case be a cure; not that compromises are not often proper, but that no *popular* government can long survive a marked precedent that those who carry an election can only save the government from immediate destruction by giving up the main point upon which the *people* gave the election." What was at stake for him was more than the issue of slavery; it was the definition of "the people."

As Lincoln put it in his **Gettysburg Address**, it was a war to guarantee that "government of the people, by the people, for the people, shall not perish from the earth." More than 600,000 deaths later, the institution of slavery was formally eradicated and a new era had begun: The United States *are* became the United States *is*. As a *Washington Post* article from April 24, 1887, read, "There was a time a few years ago when the United States was spoken of in the plural number. Men said 'the United States are.' [. . .] But the war changed all that. [. . .] The

---

[10] Quoted in Brown, *Moderates*, p. 106.

surrender of Mr. Davis and Gen. Lee meant a transition from the plural to the singular."

This change from "are" to "is" put the question of whether there is an American people to rest forever; although not whether this *one* people has but one or two bodies. Yet if there is only one single lesson to be learned from the foundations of American political thought, it might be simply this: favoring *theoretically* one of the people's two bodies at the expense of the other comes with dangerous *practical* consequences. There will always remain a gap between ideals and reality, or between theory and practice. Yet whenever the two divorce, one thing is for sure: the first to suffer is reality. Ideals can survive even the most atrocious facts.

COMPROMISES: STATES V. UNION

John C. Calhoun *South Carolina Exposition and Protest* (1828)[11]

[...] In drawing the line between the powers of the two – the General and State Governments – the great difficulty consisted in determining correctly to which of the two the various political powers ought to belong. This difficult task was, however, performed with so much success that, to this day, there is an almost entire acquiescence in the correctness with which the line was drawn. It would be extraordinary if a system, thus resting with such profound wisdom on the diversity of geographical interests among the States, should make no provision against the dangers to which its very basis might be exposed. The framers of our Constitution have not exposed themselves to the imputation of such weakness. When their work is fairly examined, it will be found that they have provided, with admirable skill, the most effective remedy; and that, if it has not prevented the danger with which the system is now threatened, the fault is not theirs, but ours, in neglecting to make its proper application. In the primary division of the sovereign powers, and in their exact and just classification, as stated, are to be found the first provisions or checks against the abuse of authority on the part of the absolute majority. The powers of the General Government are particularly enumerated and specifically delegated; and all powers not expressly delegated, or which are not necessary and proper to carry into effect those that are so granted, are reserved expressly to the States or the people. The Government is thus positively restricted to the exercise of those general powers that were supposed to act uniformly on all the parts – leaving the residue to the people of the States, by whom alone, from the very nature of these powers, they can be justly and fairly exercised, as has been stated. [...]

In order to have a full and clear conception of our institutions, it will be proper to remark that there is, in our system, a striking distinction between Government and Sovereignty. The separate governments of the several States are vested in their Legislative, Executive, and Judicial Departments; while the sovereignty resides in the people of the States respectively. The powers of the General Government are also vested in its Legislative, Executive, and Judicial Departments, while the sovereignty resides in the people of the several States who created it. [...]

If it be conceded, as it must be by every one who is the least conversant with our institutions, that the sovereign powers delegated are divided between the General and State Governments, and that the latter hold their portion by the same tenure as the former, it would seem impossible to deny to the States the right of deciding on the infractions of their powers, and the proper remedy to be applied for their correction. The right of judging, in such cases, is an essential attribute of sovereignty, of which the States cannot be divested without losing their sovereignty itself, and being reduced to a subordinate corporate condition. In fact, to divide power, and to give to one of the parties the exclusive right of judging of the portion allotted to each, is, in reality, not to

---

[11] From R. M. Lence (ed.), *Union and Liberty: The Political Philosophy of John C. Calhoun* (Indianapolis: Liberty Fund, 1992), pp. 311–66.

divide it at all; and to reserve such exclusive right to the General Government (it matters not by what department) to be exercised, is to convert it, in fact, into a great consolidated government, with unlimited powers, and to divest the States, in reality, of all their rights. [. . .] But the existence of the right of judging of their powers, so clearly established from the sovereignty of States, as clearly implies a veto or control, within its limits, on the action of the General Government, on contested points of authority; and this very control is the remedy which the Constitution has provided to prevent the encroachments of the General Government on the reserved rights of the States; and by which the distribution of power, between the General and State Governments, may be preserved for ever inviolable, on the basis established by the Constitution. It is thus effectual protection is afforded to the minority, against the oppression of the majority. [. . .]

Have the States, as members of the Union, distinct political interests in reference to their magnitude? Their relative weight is carefully settled, and each has its appropriate agent, with a veto on each other, to protect its political consequence. May there be a conflict between the Constitution and the laws, whereby the rights of citizens may be affected? A remedy may be found in the power of the courts to declare the law unconstitutional in such cases as may be brought before them. Are there, among the several States, separate and peculiar geographical interests? To meet this, a particular organization is provided in the division of the sovereign powers between the State and General Governments. Is there danger, growing out of this division, that the State Legislatures may encroach on the powers of the General Government? The authority of the Supreme Court is adequate to check such encroachments. May the General Government, on the other hand, encroach on the rights reserved to the States respectively? To the States respectively each in its sovereign capacity is reserved the power, by its veto, or right of interposition, to arrest the encroachment. [. . .]

Henry Clay *On Introducing the Compromise Tariff Bill* (February 12, 1833)[12]

[. . .] When I survey, sir, the whole face of our country, I behold all around me evidences of the most gratifying prosperity, a prospect which would seem to be without a cloud upon it, were it not that through all parts of the country there exist great dissensions and unhappy distinctions, which, if they can possibly be relieved and reconciled by any broad scheme of legislation adapted to all interests, and regarding the feelings of all sections, ought to be quieted; and leading to which object any measure ought to be well received.

In presenting the modification of the tariff laws, which I am now about to submit, I have two great objects in view. My first object looks to the tariff. [. . .]

On one side we are urged to repeal a system which is fraught with ruin; on the other side, the check now imposed on enterprise, and the state of alarm in which the public mind has been thrown, renders all prudent men desirous, looking ahead a little

---

12 From D. Mallory (ed.), *The Life and Speeches of the Hon. Henry Clay, in Two Volumes*, Vol. II (New York: Van Amringe and Bixby, 1844), pp.106–21.

way, to adopt a state of things, on the stability of which they may have reason to count. Such is the state of feeling on the one side and on the other. I am anxious to find out some principle of mutual accommodation, to satisfy, as far as practicable, both parties – to increase the stability of our legislation; and at some distant day – but not too distant, when we take into view the magnitude of the interests which are involved – to bring down the rate of duties to that revenue standard, for which our opponents have so long contended. The basis on which I wish to found this modification, is one of time; and the several parts of the bill to which I am about to call the attention of the senate, are founded on this basis. I propose to give protection to our manufactured articles, adequate protection for a length of time, which, compared with the length of human life, is very long, but which is short, in proportion to the legitimate discretion of every wise and parental system of government; securing the stability of legislation, and allowing time for a gradual reduction, on one side; and, on the other, proposing to reduce the duties to that revenue standard, for which the opponents of the system have so long contended. [...]

I want harmony. I wish to see the restoration of those ties which have carried us triumphantly through two wars. I delight not in this perpetual turmoil. Let us have peace, and become once more united as a band of brothers. [...]

The security against any chance of the system proposed by the bill, is in the character of the bill, as a compromise between two conflicting parties. [...] Sir, if you carry your measure of repeal without the consent, at least, of a portion of those who are interested in the preservation of manufactures, you have no security, no guarantee, no certainty, that any protection will be continued. But if the measure should be carried by the common consent of both parties, we shall have all security; history will faithfully record the transaction; narrate under what circumstances the bill was passed; that it was a pacifying measure; that it was as oil poured from the vessel of the union to restore peace and harmony to the country. When all this was known, what congress, what legislature, would mar the guarantee? What man who is entitled to deserve the character of an American statesman, would stand up in his place in either house of congress, and disturb this treaty of peace and amity? [...]

I will admit that my friends do not get all they could wish for; and the gentlemen on the other side do not obtain all they might desire; but both will gain all that in my humble opinion is proper to be given in the present condition of this country. It may be true that there will be loss and gain in this measure. But how is this loss and gain distributed? Among our countrymen. What we lose, no foreign land gains; and what we gain, will be no loss to any foreign power. It is among ourselves the distribution takes place. The distribution is founded on that great principle of compromise and concession which lies at the bottom of our institutions, which gave birth to the constitution itself, and which has continued to regulate us in our onward march, and conducted the nation to glory and renown.

It remains for me now to touch another topic. [...] When I came to take my seat on this floor, I had supposed that a member of this union had taken an attitude of defiance and hostility against the authority of the general government. I had imagined that she had arrogantly required that we should abandon at once a system which had long been the settled policy of this country. [...] But since my arrival here, I find that South Carolina does not contemplate force, for it is denied and denounced by that state. She disclaims it; and asserts that she is merely making an experiment. That experiment is this: by a course of state legislation, and by a change in her fundamental laws, she is endeavoring by her civil tribunals to prevent the general government from carrying the laws of the United States into operation within her limits. That she has professed to be her object. Her appeal is not to arms, but to another power; not to the sword, but to the law. [...] She thinks she can oust the United States from her limits; and unquestionably she has taken good care to prepare her judges beforehand by swearing them to decide in her favor. [...] She disclaims any intention of resorting to force unless we should find it indispensable to execute the laws of the union by applying force to her. [...] I think that she has been rash, intemperate, and greatly in error; and, to use the language of one of her own writers, made up an issue unworthy of her. From one end to the other of this continent, by acclamation, as it were, nullification has been put down, and put down in a manner more effectually than by a thousand wars or a thousand armies – by the irresistible force, by the mighty influence of public opinion. Not a voice beyond the single state of South Carolina has been heard in favor of the principle of nullification, which she has asserted by her own ordinance; and I will say, that she must fail in her lawsuit. [...]

A state might take it upon herself to throw obstructions in the way of the execution of the laws of the federal government; but federal legislation can follow at her heel quickly, and successfully counteract the course of state legislation. The framers of the constitution foresaw this, and the constitution has guarded against it. What has it said? It is declared, in the clause enumerating the powers of this government, that congress shall have all power to carry into effect all the powers granted by the constitution, in any branch of the government under the sweeping clause; for they have not specified contingencies, because they could not see what was to happen; but whatever powers were necessary, all, all are given to this government by the fundamental law, necessary to carry into effect those powers which are vested by that constitution in the federal government. [...]

If we can forget for a moment – but that would be asking too much of human nature – if we could suffer, for one moment, party feelings and party causes – and, as I stand here before my God, I declare I have looked beyond those considerations, and regarded only the vast interests of this united people – I should hope, that under such feelings, and with such dispositions, we may advantageously proceed to the consideration of this bill, and heal, before they are yet bleeding, the wounds of our distracted country.

John C. Calhoun *A Disquisition of Government* (1849; published 1851)[13]

[...] What is that constitution or law of our nature, without which government would not exist, and with which its existence is necessary?

---

[13] From Lence (ed.), *Union and Liberty*, pp. 3–78.

In considering this, I assume, as an incontestable fact, that man is so constituted as to be a social being. His inclinations and wants, physical and moral, irresistibly impel him to associate with his kind; and he has, accordingly, never been found, in any age or country, in any state other than the social. In no other, indeed, could he exist; and in no other – were it possible for him to exist – could he attain to a full development of his moral and intellectual faculties, or raise himself, in the scale of being, much above the level of the brute creation.

[. . .] [W]hile man is created for the social state, and is accordingly so formed as to feel what affects others, as well as what affects himself, he is, at the same time, so constituted as to feel more intensely what affects him directly, than what affects him indirectly though others; or, to express it differently, he is so constituted, that his direct or individual affections are stronger than his sympathetic or social feelings. I intentionally avoid the expression, selfish feelings, as applicable to the former; because, as commonly used, it implies an unusual excess of the individual over the social feelings, in the person to whom it is applied; and, consequently, something depraved and vicious. [. . .]

But that constitution of our nature which makes us feel more intensely what affects us directly than what affects us indirectly through others, necessarily leads to conflict between individuals. Each, in consequence, has a greater regard for his own safety or happiness, than for the safety or happiness of others; and, where these come in opposition, is ready to sacrifice the interests of others to his own. And hence, the tendency to a universal state of conflict, between individual and individual; accompanied by the connected passions of suspicion, jealousy, anger and revenge – followed by insolence, fraud and cruelty – and, if not prevented by some controlling power, ending in a state of universal discord and confusion, destructive of the social state and the ends for which it is ordained. This controlling power, wherever vested, or by whomsoever exercised, is GOVERNMENT.

It follows, then, that man is so constituted, that government is necessary to the existence of society, and society to his existence, and the perfection of his faculties. It follows, also, that government has its origin in this twofold constitution of his nature; the sympathetic or social feelings constituting the remote – and the individual or direct, the proximate cause. [. . .]

But government, although intended to protect and preserve society, has itself a strong tendency to disorder and abuse of its powers, as all experience and almost every page of history testify. The cause is to be found in the same constitution of our nature which makes government indispensable. The powers which it is necessary for government to possess, in order to repress violence and preserve order, cannot execute themselves. They must be administered by men in whom, like others, the individual are stronger than the social feelings. And hence, the powers vested in them to prevent injustice and oppression on the part of others, will, if left unguarded, be by them converted into instruments to oppress the rest of the community. That, by which this is prevented, by whatever name called, is what is meant by CONSTITUTION, in its most comprehensive sense, when applied to GOVERNMENT.

Having its origin in the same principle of our nature, *constitution* stands to *government*, as *government* stands to *society*; and, as the end for which society is ordained, would be defeated without government, so that for which government is ordained would, in a great measure, be defeated without constitution. But they differ in this striking particular. There is no difficulty in forming government. It is not even a matter of choice, whether there shall be one or not. Like breathing, it is not permitted to depend on our volition. Necessity will force it on all communities in some one form or another. Very different is the case as to constitution. Instead of a matter of necessity, it is one of the most difficult tasks imposed on man to form a constitution worthy of the name; while, to form a perfect one – one that would completely counteract the tendency of government to oppression and abuse, and hold it strictly to the great ends for which it is ordained – has thus far exceeded human wisdom, and possibly ever will. From this, another striking difference results. Constitution is the contrivance of man, while government is of Divine ordination. Man is left to perfect what the wisdom of the Infinite ordained, as necessary to preserve the race.

With these remarks, I proceed to the consideration of the important and difficult question: How is this tendency of government to be counteracted? Or, to express it more fully – How can those who are invested with the powers of government be prevented from employing them, as the means of aggrandizing themselves, instead of using them to protect and preserve society? It cannot be done by instituting a higher power to control the government, and those who administer it. This would be but to change the seat of authority, and to make this bigger power, in reality, the government; with the same tendency, on the part of those who might control its powers, to pervert them into instruments of aggrandizement. Nor can it be done by limiting the powers of government, so as to make it too feeble to be made an instrument of abuse; for, passing by the difficulty of so limiting its powers, without creating a power higher than the government itself to enforce the observance of the limitations, it is a sufficient objection that it would, if practicable, defeat the end for which government is ordained, by making it too feeble to protect and preserve society. [...]

What I propose is [...] to explain on what principles government must be formed, in order to resist, by its own interior structure – or, to use a single term, organism – the tendency to abuse of power. This structure, or organism, is what is meant by constitution, in its strict and more usual sense; and it is this which distinguishes, what are called, constitutional governments from absolute. It is in this strict and more usual sense that I propose to use the term hereafter.

How government, then, must be constructed, in order to counteract, through its organism, this tendency on the part of those who make and execute the laws to oppress those subject to their operation, is the next question which claims attention.

There is but one way in which this can possibly be done; and that is, by such an organism as will furnish the ruled with the means of resisting successfully this tendency on the part of the rulers to oppression and abuse. Power can only be resisted by power – and tendency by tendency. Those who exercise power and those subject to its exercise – the rulers and the ruled – stand in antagonistic relations to each other. The same constitution of our nature which leads rulers to oppress the ruled – regardless of the object for which government is ordained – will, with equal strength, lead the ruled to resist, when possessed of the means of making peaceable and effective resistance. Such an organism, then, as will furnish the means by which resistance may be systematically and peaceably made on the part of the ruled, to oppression and abuse of power on the part of the rulers, is the first and indispensable step towards forming a constitutional government. And as this can only be effected by or through the right of suffrage – (the right on the part of the ruled to choose their rulers at proper intervals, and to hold them thereby responsible for their conduct) – the responsibility of the rulers to the ruled, through the right of suffrage, is the indispensable and primary principle in the foundation of a constitutional government. When this right is properly guarded, and the people sufficiently enlightened to understand their own rights and the interests of the community, and duly to appreciate the motives and conduct of those appointed to make and execute the laws, it is all-sufficient to give to those who elect, effective control over those they have elected.

I call the right of suffrage the indispensable and primary principle; for it would be a great and dangerous mistake to suppose, as many do, that it is, of itself, sufficient to form constitutional governments. [. . .] If the whole community had the same interests, so that the interests of each and every portion would be so affected by the action of the government, that the laws which oppressed or impoverished one portion, would necessarily oppress and impoverish all others – or the reverse – then the right of suffrage, of itself, would be all-sufficient to counteract the tendency of the government to oppression and abuse of its powers; and, of course, would form, of itself, a perfect constitutional government. The interest of all being the same, by supposition, as far as the action of the government was concerned, all would have like interests as to what laws should be made, and how they should be executed. All strife and struggle would cease as to who should be elected to make and execute them. The only question would be, who was most fit; who the wisest and most capable of understanding the common interest of the whole. This decided, the election would pass off quietly, and without party discord; as no one portion could advance its own peculiar interest without regard to the rest, by electing a favorite candidate.

But such is not the case. On the contrary, nothing is more difficult than to equalize the action of the government, in reference to the various and diversified interests of the community; and nothing more easy than to pervert its powers into instruments to aggrandize and enrich one or more interests by oppressing and impoverishing the others; and this too, under the operation of laws, couched in general terms – and which, on their face, appear fair and equal. Nor is this the case in some particular communities only. It is so in all; [. . .] the more extensive and populous the country, the more diversified the condition and pursuits of its population, and the richer, more luxurious, and dissimilar the people, the more difficult is it to equalize the action of the government – and the more easy for one portion of the community to pervert its powers to oppress, and plunder the other.

Such being the case, it necessarily results, that the right of suffrage, by placing the control of the government in the community must, from the same constitution of our nature which makes government necessary to preserve society, lead to conflict among its different interests – each striving to obtain possession of its powers, as the means of protecting itself against the others – or of advancing its respective interests, regardless of the interests of others. For this purpose, a struggle will take place between the various interests to obtain a majority, in order to control the government. If no one interest be strong enough, of itself, to obtain it, a combination will be formed between those whose interests are most alike – each conceding something to the others, until a sufficient number is obtained to make a majority. The process may be slow, and much time may be required before a compact, organized majority can be thus formed; but formed it will be in time, even without preconcert or design, by the sure workings of that principle or constitution of our nature in which government itself originates. When once formed, the community will be divided into two great parties – a major and minor – between which there will be incessant struggles on the one side to retain, and on the other to obtain the majority – and, thereby, the control of the government and the advantages it confers. [. . .]

As, then, the right of suffrage, without some other provision, cannot counteract this tendency of government, the next question for consideration is – What is that other provision? [. . .] There is but one certain mode in which this result can be secured; and that is, by the adoption of some restriction or limitation, which shall so effectually prevent any one interest, or combination of interests, from obtaining the exclusive control of the government, as to render hopeless all attempts directed to that end. There is, again, but one mode in which this can be effected; and that is, by taking the sense of each interest or portion of the community, which may be unequally and injuriously affected by the action of the government, separately, through its own majority, or in some other way by which its voice may be fairly expressed; and to require the consent of each interest, either to put or to keep the government in action. This, too, can be accomplished only in one way – and that is, by such an organism of the government – and, if necessary for the purpose, of the community also – as will, by dividing and distributing the powers of government, give to each division or interest, through its appropriate organ, either a concurrent voice in making and executing the laws, or a veto on their execution. [. . .]

It results, from what has been said, that there are two different modes in which the sense of the community may be taken; one, simply by the right of suffrage, unaided; the other, by the right through a proper organism. Each collects the sense of the majority. But one regards numbers only, and considers the whole community as a unit, having but one common interest throughout; and collects the sense of the greater number of the whole, as that of the community. The other, on the contrary, regards interests as well as numbers – considering the community as made up of different and conflicting interests, as far as the action of the government is concerned; and takes the sense of each, through its majority or appropriate organ, and the united sense of all, as the sense of the entire community. The former of these I shall call the numerical, or absolute majority; and the latter, the concurrent, or constitutional majority. I call it the constitutional majority, because it is an essential element in every constitutional government – be its form what it may. So great is the difference, politically speaking, between the two majorities, that they cannot be confounded, without leading to great and fatal errors; and yet the distinction between them has been so entirely overlooked, that when the term majority is used in political discussions, it is applied exclusively to designate the numerical – as if there were no other. [. . .]

If the numerical majority were really the people; and if, to take its sense truly, were to take the sense of the people truly, a government so constituted would be a true and perfect model of a popular constitutional government; and every departure from it would detract from its excellence. But, as such is not the case – as the numerical majority, instead of being the people, is only a portion of them – such a government, instead of being a true and perfect model of the people's government, that is, a people self-governed, is but the government of a part, over a part – the major over the minor portion. [. . .]

It is this negative power – the power of preventing or arresting the action of the government – be it called by what term it may – veto, interposition, nullification, check, or balance of power – which, in fact, forms the constitution. They are all but different names for the negative power. In all its forms, and under all its names, it results from the concurrent majority. Without this there can be no negative; and, without a negative, no constitution. The assertion is true in reference to all constitutional governments, be their forms what they may. It is, indeed, the negative power which makes the constitution – and the positive which makes the government. The one is the power of acting – and the other the power of preventing or arresting action. The two, combined, make constitutional governments.

But, as there can be no constitution without the negative power, and no negative power without the concurrent majority – it follows, necessarily, that where the numerical majority has the sole control of the government, there can be no constitution; as constitution implies limitation or restriction – and, of course, is inconsistent with the idea of sole or exclusive power. And hence, the numerical, unmixed with the concurrent majority, necessarily forms, in all cases, absolute government. [. . .]

From this there results another distinction, which, although secondary in its character, very strongly marks the difference between these forms of government. I refer to their respective conservative principle – that is, the principle by which they are upheld and preserved. This principle, in constitutional governments, is compromise – and in absolute governments, is force – as will be next explained.

It has been already shown, that the same constitution of man which leads those who govern to oppress the governed – if not prevented – will, with equal force and certainty, lead the latter to resist oppression, when possessed of the means of doing so peaceably and successfully. But absolute governments, of all forms, exclude all other means of resistance to their authority, than that of force; and, of course, leave no other alternative to the governed, but to acquiesce in oppression, however great it may be, or to resort to force to put down the government. But the dread of such a resort must necessarily lead the government to prepare to meet force in order to protect itself; and hence, of necessity, force becomes the conservative principle of all such governments.

On the contrary, the government of the concurrent majority, where the organism is perfect, excludes the possibility of oppression, by giving to each interest, or portion, or order – where there are established classes – the means of protecting itself, by its negative, against all measures calculated to advance the peculiar interests of others at its expense. Its effect, then, is, to cause the different interests, portions, or orders – as the case may be – to desist from attempting to adopt any measure calculated to promote the prosperity of one, or more, by sacrificing that of others; and thus to force them to unite in such measures only as would promote the prosperity of all, as the only means to prevent the suspension of the action of the government – and, thereby, to avoid anarchy, the greatest of all evils. It is by means of such authorized and effectual resistance, that oppression is prevented, and the necessity of resorting to force superseded, in governments of the concurrent majority – and, hence, compromise, instead of force, becomes their conservative principle. [...]

To perfect society, it is necessary to develop the faculties, intellectual and moral, with which man is endowed. But the main spring to their development, and, through this, to progress, improvement and civilization, with all their blessings, is the desire of individuals to better their condition. For this purpose, liberty and security are indispensable. Liberty leaves each free to pursue the course he may deem best to promote his interest and happiness, as far as it may be compatible with the primary end for which government is ordained – while security gives assurance to each, that he shall not be deprived of the fruits of his exertions to better his condition. These combined, give to this desire the strongest impulse of which it is susceptible. For, to extend liberty beyond the limits assigned, would be to weaken the government and to render it incompetent to fulfil its primary end – the protection of society against dangers, internal and external. The effect of this would be, insecurity; and, of insecurity – to weaken the impulse of individuals to better their condition, and thereby retard progress and improvement. On the other hand, to extend the powers of the government, so as to contract the sphere assigned to liberty, would have the same effect, by disabling individuals in their efforts to better their condition.

[...] Liberty, then, when forced on a people unfit for it, would, instead of a blessing, be a curse; as it would, in its reaction, lead directly to anarchy – the greatest of all curses. No people, indeed, can long enjoy more liberty than that to which their situation and advanced intelligence and morals fairly entitle them. If more than this be allowed, they must soon fall into confusion and disorder – to be followed, if not by anarchy and despotism, by a change to a form of government more simple and absolute; and, therefore, better suited to their condition. [...]

It follows, from what has been stated, that it is a great and dangerous error to suppose that all people are equally entitled to liberty. It is a reward to be earned, not a blessing to be gratuitously lavished on all alike – a reward reserved for the intelligent, the patriotic, the virtuous and deserving – and not a boon to be bestowed on a people too ignorant, degraded and vicious, to be capable either of appreciating or of enjoying it. Nor is it any disparagement to liberty, that such is, and ought to be the case. On the contrary, its greatest praise – its proudest distinction is, that an all-wise Providence has reserved it, as the noblest and highest reward for the development of our faculties, moral and intellectual. [...]

There is another error, not less great and dangerous, usually associated with the one which has just been considered. I refer to the opinion, that liberty and equality are so intimately united, that liberty cannot be perfect without perfect equality. [...] These great and dangerous errors have their origin in the prevalent opinion that all men are born free and equal – than which nothing can be more unfounded and false. It rests upon the assumption of a fact, which is contrary to universal observation, in whatever light it may be regarded. It is, indeed, difficult to explain how an opinion so destitute of all sound reason, ever could have been so extensively entertained, unless we regard it as being confounded with another, which has some semblance of truth – but which, when properly understood, is not less false and dangerous. I refer to the assertion, that all men are equal in the state of nature; meaning, by a state of nature, a state of individuality, supposed to have existed prior to the social and political state; and in which men lived apart and independent of each other. [...] But such a state is purely hypothetical. It never did, nor can exist; as it is inconsistent with the preservation and perpetuation of the race. [...] As, then, there never was such a state as the, so called, state of nature, and never can be, it follows, that men, instead of being born in it, are born in the social and political state; and of course, instead of being born free and equal, are born subject, not only to parental authority, but to the laws and institutions of the country where born, and under whose protection they draw their first breath. [...]

Daniel Webster *The Constitution and the Union* (Senate Speech, March 7, 1850)[14]

Mr. President, I wish to speak today, not as a Massachusetts man, nor as a northern man, but as an American, and a member of the Senate of the United States. [...] I speak today for the preservation of the Union. "Hear me for my cause." I speak today, out of a solicitous and anxious heart, for the restoration to the country of that quiet and that harmony which make the blessings of this Union so rich and so dear to us all. [...]

[I]t is obvious that the question which has so long harassed the country, and at times very seriously alarmed the minds of wise and good men, has come upon us for a fresh discussion – the question of slavery in these United States. [...] Now, sir, upon the general nature, and character, and influence of slavery there exists a wide difference between the northern portion of this country and the southern. It is said, on the one side, that if not the subject of any injunction or direct prohibition in the New Testament, slavery is a wrong; that it is founded merely in the right of the strongest; and that it is an oppression, like unjust wars – like all those conflicts by which a mighty nation subjects a weaker nation to their will; and that slavery, in its nature, whatever may be said of it in the modifications which have taken place, is not in fact according to the meek spirit of the Gospel. [...] The South, upon the other side, having been accustomed to this relation between the two races all their lives, from their birth; having been taught, in general, to treat the subjects of this bondage with care and kindness – and I believe, in general, feeling for them great care and

---

[14] From the *Congressional Globe*, 31st Cong., 1st sess., Appendix, pp. 269–76.

kindness – have yet not taken this view of the subject which I have mentioned. There are thousands of religious men, with consciences as tender as any of their brethren at the North, who do not see the unlawfulness of slavery; and there are more thousands, perhaps, that, whatsoever they may think of it in its origin, and as a matter depending upon natural right, yet take things as they are, and, finding slavery to be an established relation of the society in which they live, can see no way in which – let their opinions on the abstract question be what they may – it is in the power of the present generation to relieve themselves from this relation. And, in this respect, candor obliges me to say, that I believe they are just as conscientious, many of them – and of the religious people, all of them – as they are in the North, in holding different opinions. [...]

What, then, have been the causes which have created so new a feeling in favor of slavery in the South – which have changed the whole nomenclature of the South on the subject – and from being thought of and described in the terms I have mentioned, but will not repeat, it has now become an "institution," a "cherished institution," in that quarter; no evil, no scourge, but a great religious, social, and moral blessing, as I think I have heard it lately described. I suppose this, sir, is owing to the sudden uprising and rapid growth of the cotton plantations of the South. So far as any motive of honor, justice, and general judgment could act, it was the cotton interest that gave a new desire to promote slavery, to spread it and to use its labor. [...]

Well, sir, we know what followed. The age of cotton became a golden age for our southern brethren. It gratified their desire for improvement and accumulation, at the same time that it excited it. The desire grew by what it fed upon, and there soon came to be an eagerness for other territory – a new area or new areas for the cultivation of the cotton crop; and measures leading to this result, were brought about somewhat rapidly, one after another, under the lead of southern men at the head of the government, they having a majority in both branches, to accomplish their ends. The honorable member from Carolina [Calhoun] observed, that there has been a majority all along in favor of the North. If that be true, sir, the North has acted either very liberally and kindly, or very weakly; for they never exercised that majority five times in the history of the government. Never. Whether they were out-generalled, or whether it was owing to other causes, I shall not stop to consider, but no man acquainted with the history of the country can deny, that the general lead in the politics of the country, for three-fourths of the period that has elapsed since the adoption of the Constitution, has been a southern lead. [...]

And lastly, sir, to complete those acts of men, which have contributed so much to enlarge the area and the sphere of the institution of slavery, Texas – great, and vast, and illimitable Texas – was added to the Union, as a slave state, in 1845; and that, sir, pretty much closed the whole chapter and settled the whole account. That closed the whole chapter – that settled the whole account – because the annexation of Texas, upon the conditions and under the guaranties upon which she was admitted, did not leave an acre of land, capable of being cultivated by slave labor, between this Capitol and the Rio Grande, or the Nueces, or whatever is the proper boundary of Texas – not an acre, not one. From that moment, the whole country from this place to the western boundary of Texas, was fixed, pledged, fastened, decided, to be slave territory forever, by the solemn guaranties of law. And I now say, sir, as the proposition upon which I stand this day, and upon the truth and firmness of which I intend to act until it is overthrown, that there is not, at this moment, within the United States, or any territory of the United States, a single foot of land, the character of which, in regard to its being free-soil territory or slave territory, is not fixed by some law, and some irrepealable law, beyond the power of the action of this government. [...]

On other occasions, in debates here, I have expressed my determination to vote for no acquisition, or cession, or annexation, north or south, east or west. My opinion has been, that we have territory enough, and that we should follow the Spartan maxim, "Improve, adorn what you have, seek no farther." [...] But now that, under certain conditions, Texas is in, with all her territories, as a slave state, with a solemn pledge that if she is divided into many states, those states may come in as slave states south of 36°30', how are we to deal with this subject? [...]

I may not then be here – I may have no vote to give on the occasion; but I wish it to be distinctly understood, today, that according to my view of the matter, this government is solemnly pledged, by law and contract, to create new states out of Texas, with her consent, when her population shall justify such a proceeding, and so far as such states are formed out of Texan territory lying south of 36°30', to let them come in as slave states. The time of admission, and requisite population, must depend, of course, on the discretion of Congress. But when new states shall be formed out of Texas, they have a fixed right to come into the Union as slave states. That is the meaning of the resolution which our friends, the northern Democracy, have left us to fulfill; and I, for one, mean to fulfill it, because I will not violate the faith of the government. [...]

Sir, wherever there is a particular good to be done, wherever there is a foot of land to be staid back from becoming slave territory – I am ready to assert the principle of the exclusion of slavery. I am pledged to it from the year 1837; I have been pledged to it again and again; and I will perform those pledges; but I will not do a thing unnecessary, that wounds the feelings of others, or that does disgrace to my own understanding. [...]

Mr. President, in the excited times in which we live, there is found to exist a state of crimination and recrimination between the North and the South. There are lists of grievances produced by each; and those grievances, real or supposed, alienate the minds of one portion of the country from the other, exasperate the feelings, subdue the sense of fraternal connection, and patriotic love, and mutual regard. [...] I will state these complaints, especially one complaint of the South, which has in my opinion just foundation; and that is, that there has been found at the North, among individuals and among the legislatures of the North, a disinclination to perform, fully, their constitutional duties, in regard to the return of persons bound to service, who have escaped into the free states. In that respect, it is my judgment that the South is right, and the North is wrong. Every member of every northern legislature is bound, by oath, like every other officer in the country, to support the Constitution of the United States; and the article of the Constitution, which says to these states, they shall deliver up fugitives from service, is as binding in honor and conscience as any other article. No man fulfills his duty in any legislature who sets himself to find excuses, evasions, escapes from this constitutional obligation. [...] And I desire to call the attention of all sober-minded men, of all conscientious men in the North, of all men who are not carried away by any fanatical idea, or by any false idea whatever, to their constitutional obligations. I put it to all the sober and sound minds at the North, as a question of morals and a question of conscience, what right have they, in their legislative capacity, or any other, to endeavor to get round this Constitution, to embarrass the free exercise of the rights secured by the Constitution, to the persons whose slaves escape from them? None at all – none at all. Neither in the forum of conscience, nor before the face of the Constitution, are they justified, in my opinion. Of course, it is a matter for their consideration. They probably, in the turmoil of the times, have not stopped to consider of this; they have followed what seemed to be the current of thought and of motives as the occasion arose, and neglected to investigate fully the real question, and to consider their constitutional obligations, as I am sure, if they did consider, they would fulfill them with alacrity. [...]

Mr. President, I should much prefer to have heard, from every member on this floor, declaration, of opinion that this Union could never be dissolved, than the declaration of opinion that in any case, under the pressure of any circumstances, such a dissolution was possible. I hear with pain and anguish, and distress the word secession, especially when it falls from the lips of those who are eminently patriotic, and known to the country, and known all over the world, for their political services. Secession! Peaceable secession! Sir, your eyes and mine are never destined to see that miracle. The dismemberment of this vast country without convulsion! The breaking up of the fountains of the great deep without ruffling the surface! Who is so foolish – I beg everybody's pardon – as to expect to see any such thing? Sir, he who sees these states, now revolving in harmony around a common centre, and expects to see them quit their places and fly off without convulsion, may look the next hour to see the heavenly bodies rush from their spheres, and jostle against each other in the realms of space, without producing the crush of the universe. [...] Is the great Constitution under which we live here – covering this whole country – is it to be thawed and melted away by secession, as the snows on the mountain melt under the influence of a vernal sun – disappear almost unobserved, and die off? No, sir! no, sir! I will not state what might produce the disruption of the states; but, sir, I see as plainly as I see the sun in heaven – I see that disruption must produce such a war as I will not describe, in its twofold character.

Peaceable secession! peaceable secession! The concurrent agreement of all the members of this great republic to separate! A voluntary separation, with alimony on one side and on the other. Why, what would be the result? Where is the line to be drawn? What states are to secede? What is to remain American? What am I to be – an American no longer? Where is the flag of the Republic to remain? Where is the eagle still to tower? or is he to cower, and shrink, and fall to the ground? [...] I know, although the idea has not been stated distinctly, there is to be, a southern confederacy. I do not mean, when I allude to this statement, that anyone seriously contemplates such a state of things. I do not mean to say that it is true, but I have heard it suggested elsewhere, that that idea has originated in a design to separate. I am sorry, sir, that it has ever been thought of, talked of, or dreamed of, in the wildest flights of human imagination. But the idea must be of a separation, including the slave states upon one side, and the free states on the other. Sir, there is not – I may express myself too strongly, perhaps – but some things, some moral things are almost as impossible as other natural or physical things; and I hold the idea of a separation of these states – those that are free to form one government, and those that are slaveholding to form another – as a moral impossibility. We could not separate the states by any such line, if we were to draw it. We could not sit down here today, and draw a line of separation, that would satisfy any five men in the country. There are natural causes that would keep and tie us together, and there are social and domestic relations which we could not break, if we would, and which we should not, if we could. [...]

THE ABOLITIONISTS

The Declaration of Sentiments of the American Anti-Slavery Society (1833)[15]

The Convention assembled in the city of Philadelphia, to organize a National Anti-Slavery Society, promptly seize the opportunity to promulgate the following Declaration of Sentiments, as cherished by them in relation to the enslavement of one-sixth portion of the American people.

More than fifty-seven years have elapsed, since a band of patriots convened in this place, to devise measures for the deliverance of this country from a foreign yoke. The corner-stone upon which they founded the TEMPLE OF FREEDOM was broadly this – "that all men are created equal; that they are endowed by their Creator with certain inalienable rights; that among these are life, LIBERTY, and the pursuit of happiness." At the sound of their trumpet-call, three millions of people rose up as from the sleep of death, and rushed to the strife of blood; deeming it more glorious to die instantly as freemen, than desirable to live one hour as slaves. They were few in number – poor in resources; but the honest conviction that TRUTH, JUSTICE and RIGHT were on their side, made them invincible.

We have met together for the achievement of an enterprise, without which that of our fathers is incomplete; and which, for its magnitude, solemnity, and probable results upon the destiny of the world, as far transcends theirs as moral truth does physical force. [...]

[T]hose, for whose emancipation we are striving [...] are recognized by law, and treated by their fellow-beings, as marketable commodities, as goods and chattels, as brute beasts; are plundered daily of the fruits of their toil without redress; really enjoy no constitutional nor legal protection from licentious and murderous outrages upon their persons; and are ruthlessly torn asunder – the tender babe from the arms of its frantic mother – the heart-broken wife from her weeping husband – at the caprice or

---

[15] *Declaration of Sentiments of the American Anti-Slavery Society. Adopted at the Formation of Said Society, in Philadelphia, on the 4th Day of December 1833* (New York: American Anti-Slavery Society, 1833) via the Library of Congress digital archive, www.loc.gov/collections/.

pleasure of irresponsible tyrants. For the crime of having a dark complexion, they suffer the pangs of hunger, the infliction of stripes, the ignominy of brutal servitude. They are kept in heathenish darkness by laws expressly enacted to make their instruction a criminal offence. [...]

Hence we maintain – [...] that no man has a right to enslave or imbrute his brother – to hold or acknowledge him, for one moment, as a piece of merchandise – to keep back his hire by fraud – or to brutalize his mind, by denying him the means of intellectual, social and moral improvement.

The right to enjoy liberty is inalienable. To invade it is to usurp the prerogative of Jehovah. Every man has a right to his own body – to the products of his own labor – to the protection of law – and to the common advantages of society. It is piracy to buy or steal a native African, and subject him to servitude. Surely, the sin is as great to enslave an AMERICAN as an AFRICAN.

Therefore we believe and affirm – that there is no difference, *in principle*, between the African slave trade and American slavery:

That every American citizen, who detains a human being in involuntary bondage as his property, is, according to Scripture, (Ex. xxi. 16,) A MAN-STEALER:

That the slaves ought instantly to be set free, and brought under the protection of law:

That if they had lived from the time of Pharaoh down to the present period, and had been entailed through successive generations, their right to be free could never have been alienated, but their claims would have constantly risen in solemnity.

That all those laws which are now in force, admitting the right of slavery, are therefore, before God, utterly null and void; being an audacious usurpation of the Divine prerogative, a daring infringement on the law of nature, a base over-throw of the very foundations of the social compact, a complete extinction of all the relations, endearments and obligations of mankind, and a presumptuous transgression of all the holy commandments; and that therefore they ought instantly to be abrogated.

We further believe and affirm – that all persons of color, who possess the qualifications which are demanded of others, ought to be admitted forthwith to the enjoyment of the same privileges, and the exercise of the same prerogatives, as others; and that the paths of preferment, of wealth, and of intelligence, should be opened as widely to them as to persons of a white complexion.

We maintain that no compensation should be given to the planters emancipating their slaves;

Because it would be a surrender of the great fundamental principle, that man cannot hold property in man:

Because slavery is a crime, and therefore is not an article to be sold:

Because the holders of slaves are not the just proprietors of what they claim; freeing the slave is not depriving them of property, but restoring it to its rightful owner; it is not wronging the master, but righting the slave – restoring him to himself:

Because immediate and general emancipation would only destroy nominal, not real property; it would not amputate a limb or break a bone of the slaves, but by infusing motives into their breasts, would make them doubly valuable to the masters as free laborers; and

Because, if compensation is to be given at all, it should be given to the outraged and guiltless slaves, and not to those who have plundered and abused them.

We regard as delusive, cruel and dangerous, any scheme of expatriation which pretends to aid, either directly or indirectly, in the emancipation of the slaves, or to be a substitute for the immediate and total abolition of slavery.

We fully and unanimously recognise the sovereignty of each State, to legislate exclusively on the subject of the slavery which is tolerated within its limits; we concede that Congress, *under the present national compact*, has no right to interfere with any of the slave States, in relation to this momentous subject:

But we maintain that Congress has a right, and is solemnly bound, to suppress the domestic slave trade between the several States, and to abolish slavery in those portions of our territory which the Constitution has placed under its exclusive jurisdiction.

We also maintain that there are, at the present time, the highest obligations resting upon the people of the free States to remove slavery by moral and political action, as prescribed in the Constitution of the United States. They are now living under a pledge of their tremendous physical force, to fasten the galling fetters of tyranny upon the limbs of millions in the Southern States; they are liable to be called at any moment to suppress a general insurrection of the slaves; they authorize the slave owner to vote for three-fifths of his slaves as property, and thus enable him to perpetuate his oppression; they support a standing army at the South for its protection and they seize the slave, who has escaped into their territories, and send him back to be tortured by an enraged master or a brutal driver. This relation to slavery is criminal, and full of danger: IT MUST BE BROKEN UP. [. . .]

William Lloyd Garrison *No Compromise with the Evil of Slavery* (1854)[16]

[. . .] Let me define my positions, and at the same time challenge any one to show wherein they are untenable.

I   I am a believer in that portion of the Declaration of American Independence in which it is set forth, as among self-evident truths, "that all men are created equal; that they are endowed by their Creator with certain inalienable rights; that among these are life, liberty, and the pursuit of happiness." Hence, I am an Abolitionist. Hence, I cannot but regard oppression in every form – and most of all, that which turns a man into a thing – with indignation and abhorrence. Not to cherish these feelings would be recreancy to principle. They who desire me to be dumb on the subject of Slavery, unless I will open my mouth in its defence, ask me to give the lie to my professions, to degrade my manhood, and to stain my soul. I will not be a liar, a poltroon, or

---

[16] W. L. Garrison, *No Compromise with Slavery: An Address Delivered in the Broadway Tabernacle, New York* (New York: American Anti-Slavery Association, 1854).

a hypocrite, to accommodate any party, to gratify any sect, to escape any odium or peril, to save any interest, to preserve any institution, or to promote any object. Convince me that one man may rightfully make another man his slave, and I will no longer subscribe to the Declaration of Independence. Convince me that liberty is not the inalienable birthright of every human being, of whatever complexion or clime, and I will give that instrument to the consuming fire. I do not know how to espouse freedom and slavery together. [...]

Notwithstanding the lessons taught us by Pilgrim Fathers and Revolutionary Sires, at Plymouth Rock, on Bunker Hill, at Lexington, Concord and Yorktown; notwithstanding our Fourth of July celebrations, and ostentatious displays of patriotism; in what European nation is personal liberty held in such contempt as in our own? Where are there such unbelievers in the natural equality and freedom of mankind? Our slaves outnumber the entire population of the country at the time of our revolutionary struggle. In vain do they clank their chains, and fill the air with their shrieks, and make their supplications for mercy. In vain are their sufferings portrayed, their wrongs rehearsed, their rights defended. As Nero fiddled while Rome was burning, so the slaveholding spirit of this nation rejoices, as one barrier of liberty after another is destroyed, and fresh victims are multiplied for the cotton-field and the auction-block. For one impeachment of the slave system, a thousand defences are made. [...] Everywhere to do homage to it, to avoid collision with it, to propitiate its favour, is deemed essential – nay, *is* essential to political preferment and ecclesiastical advancement. Nothing is so unpopular as impartial liberty. The two great parties which absorb nearly the whole voting strength of the Republic are pledged to be deaf, dumb and blind to whatever outrages the Slave Power may attempt to perpetrate. Cotton is in their ears – blinds are over their eyes – padlocks are upon their lips. [...]

The reasons adduced among us in justification of slaveholding, and therefore against personal liberty, are multitudinous. I will enumerate only a dozen of these: 1. "The victims are black." 2. "The slaves belong to an inferior race." 3. "Many of them have been fairly purchased." 4. "Others have been honestly inherited." 5. "Their emancipation would impoverish their owners." 6. "They are better off as slaves than they would be as freemen." 7. "They could not take care of themselves if set free." 8. "Their simultaneous liberation would be attended with great danger." 9. "Any interference in their behalf will excite the ill-will of the South, and thus seriously affect Northern trade and commerce." 10. "The Union can be preserved only by letting Slavery alone, and that is of paramount importance." 11. "Slavery is a lawful and constitutional system, and therefore not a crime." 12. "Slavery is sanctioned by the Bible; the Bible is the word of God; therefore God sanctions Slavery, and the Abolitionists are wise above what is written."

Here, then, are twelve reasons which are popularly urged in all parts of the country, as conclusive against the right of a man to himself. If they are valid, in any instance, what becomes of the Declaration of Independence? On what ground can the revolutionary war, can any struggle for liberty, be justified? Nay, cannot all the despotisms of the earth take shelter under them? [...] But they are not valid. They are the logic of Bedlam, the morality of the pirate ship, the diabolism of the pit. They insult the common sense and shock the moral nature of mankind. [...]

III   The Abolitionism which I advocate is as absolute as the law of God, and as unyielding as His throne. It admits of no compromise. Every slave is a stolen man; every slaveholder is a man-stealer. By no precedent, no example, no law, no compact, no purchase, no bequest, no inheritance, no combination of circumstances, is slave-holding right or justifiable. While a slave remains in his fetters, the land must have no rest. Whatever sanctions his doom must be pronounced accursed. The law that makes him a chattel is to be trampled under foot; the compact that is formed at his expense, and cemented with his blood, is null and void; the church that consents to his enslavement is horribly atheistical; the religion that receives to its communion the enslaver is the embodiment of all criminality. [...]

No man is to be injured in his person, mind, or estate. He cannot be, with benefit to any other man, or to any state of society. Whoever would sacrifice him for any purpose is both morally and politically insane. Every man is equivalent to every other man. Destroy the equivalent, and what is left? "So God created man in his own image – male and female created he them." This is a death-blow to all claims of superiority, to all charges of inferiority, to all usurpation, to all oppressive dominion. [...]

How has the slave system grown to its present enormous dimensions? Through compromise. How is it to be exterminated? Only by an uncompromising spirit. This is to be carried out in all the relations of life – social, political, religious. Put not on the list of your friends, nor allow admission to your domestic circle, the man who on principle defends Slavery, but treat him as a moral leper. [...]

Some men are still talking of preventing the spread of the cancer, but leaving it just where it is. They admit that, constitutionally, it has now a right to ravage two-thirds of the body politic – but they protest against its extension. This is moral quackery. Even some, whose zeal in the Anti-Slavery cause is fervent, are so infatuated as to propose no other remedy for Slavery but its non-extension. Give it no more room, they say, and it may be safely left to its fate. Yes, but who shall "bell the cat?" Besides, with fifteen Slave States, and more than three millions of Slaves, how can we make any moral issue with the Slave Power against its further extension? Why should there not be twenty, thirty, fifty Slave States, as well as fifteen? Why should not the star-spangled banner wave over ten, as well as over three millions of Slaves? Why should not Nebraska be cultivated by Slave labour, as well as Florida or Texas? If men, under the American Constitution, may hold slaves at discretion and without dishonour in one-half of the country, why not in the whole of it? If it would be a damning sin for us to admit another Slave State into the Union, why is it not a damning sin to permit a Slave State to remain in the Union? [...] The South may well laugh to scorn the affected moral sensibility of the North against the extension of her slave system. It is nothing, in the present relations of the States, but sentimental hypocrisy. It has no stamina – no back-bone. The argument for non-extension is an argument for the dissolution of the Union. [...] Not a solitary slaveholder will I allow to enjoy repose on any other condition than instantly ceasing to be one. Not a single slave will I leave in his chains, on any conditions, or under any circumstances. I will not try to make as good a bargain for the Lord as the Devil will let me, and plead the necessity of a compromise, and regret that I cannot do any better, and be thankful that I can do so much. [...] My motto is, "No union with slaveholders, religiously or politically." [...]

I would to God that we might be, what we have never been – a united people; but God renders this possible only by "proclaiming liberty throughout all the land, unto all the inhabitants thereof." By what miracle can Freedom and Slavery be made amicably to strike hands? How can they administer the same Government, or legislate for the same interests? [...] The present American Union, therefore, is only one in form, not in reality. [...]

These are solemn times. It is not a struggle for national salvation; for the nation, as such, seems doomed beyond recovery. The reason why the South rules, and North falls prostrate in servile terror, is simply this: With the South, the preservation of Slavery is paramount to all other considerations – above party success, denominational unity, pecuniary interest, legal integrity, and constitutional obligation. With the North, the preservation of the Union is placed above all other things – above honour, justice, freedom, integrity of soul, the Decalogue and the Golden Rule – the Infinite God himself. All these she is ready to discard for the Union. Her devotion to it is the latest and the most terrible form of idolatry. She has given to the Slave Power a *carte blanche*, to be filled as it may dictate – and if, at any time, she grows restive under the yoke, and shrinks back aghast at the new atrocity contemplated, it is only necessary for that Power to crack the whip of Disunion over her head, as it has done again and again, and she will cower and obey like a plantation slave – for has she not sworn that she will sacrifice everything in heaven and on earth, rather than the Union?

What then is to be done? Friends of the slave, the question is not whether by our efforts we can abolish Slavery, speedily or remotely – for duty is ours, the result is with God; but whether we will go with the multitude to do evil, sell our birthright for a mess of pottage, cease to cry aloud and spare not, and remain in Babylon when the command of God is, "Come out of her, my people, that ye be not partakers of her sins, and that ye receive not of her plagues." [...] Living or dying, defeated or victorious, be it ours to exclaim, "No compromise with Slavery! Liberty for each, for all, forever! Man above all institutions! The supremacy of God over the whole earth!"

Frederick Douglass *The Anti-Slavery Movement* (1855)[17]

[In his address to the Rochester Ladies' Anti-Slavery Society, Douglass critiques the four branches of the anti-slavery movement: the Garrisonian Anti-Slavery Society; the American and Foreign Anti-Slavery Society; the Free Soil Party, or Political Abolitionists; and the Liberty Party.]

[...] I shall consider, first, the Garrisonian Anti-Slavery Society. [...] Its peculiar and distinctive feature is, its doctrine of *"no union with slaveholders."* This doctrine has, of late, become its bond of union, and the condition of good fellowship among

[17] F. Douglass, *The Anti-Slavery Movement: A Lecture by Frederick Douglass, before the Rochester Ladies' Anti-Slavery Society* (Rochester: Lee, Mann & Co., Daily American Office, 1855), pp. 28–35.

its members. Of this Society, I have to say, its logical result is but negatively, anti-slavery. Its doctrine, of "no union with slaveholders," carried out, dissolves the Union, and leaves the slaves and their masters to fight their own battles, in their own way. This I hold to be an abandonment of the great idea with which that Society started. It started to free the slave. It ends by leaving the slave to free himself. It started with the purpose to imbue the heart of the nation with sentiments favorable to the abolition of slavery, and ends by seeking to free the North from all responsibility for slavery [. . .]. It has given up the faith, that the slave can be freed short of the overthrow of the Government. [. . .]

I dissent entirely from this reasoning. It assumes to be true what is plainly absurd, and that is, that a population of slaves, without arms, without means of concert, and without leisure, is more than a match for double its number, educated, accustomed to rule, and in every way prepared for warfare, offensive or defensive. This Society, therefore, consents to leave the slave's freedom to a most uncertain and improbable, if not an impossible, contingency.

But, "*no union with slaveholders.*"

As a mere expression of abhorrence of slavery, the sentiment is a good one; but it expresses no intelligible principle of action, and throws no light on the pathway of duty. [. . .]

But this is not the worst fault of this Society. Its chief energies are expended in confirming the opinion, that the United States Constitution is, and was, intended to be a slave-holding instrument – thus piling up, between the slave and his freedom, the huge work of the abolition of the Government, as an indispensable condition to emancipation. My point here is, first, the Constitution is, according to its reading, an anti-slavery document; and, secondly, to dissolve the Union, as a means to abolish slavery, is about as wise as it would be to burn up this city, in order to get the thieves out of it. [. . .]

The fourth division of the anti-slavery movement is, the "*Liberty Party*" – a small body of citizens, chiefly in the State of New York, but having sympathizers all over the North. It is the radical, and to my thinking, the only abolition organization in the country, except a few local associations. It makes a clean sweep of slavery every-where. It denies that slavery is, or can be legalized. It denies that the Constitution of the United States is a pro-slavery instrument, and asserts the power and duty of the Federal Government to abolish slavery in every State of the Union. Strictly speaking, I say this is the only party in the country which is an abolition party. The mission of the Garrisonians ends with the dissolution of the Union – that of the Free Soil party ends with the relief of the Federal Government from all responsibility for slavery; but the Liberty Party, by its position and doctrines, and by its antecedents, is pledged to continue the struggle while a bondman in his chains remains to weep. [. . .] The slave as a man and a brother, must be the vital and animating thought and impulse of any movement, which is to effect the abolition of slavery in this country. Our anti-slavery organizations must be brought back to this doctrine, or they will be scattered and left to wander, and to die in the wilderness, like God's ancient people, till another generation shall come up, more worthy to go up and possess the land. [. . .]

SOUTHERN REACTIONARY ENLIGHTENMENT

George Fitzhugh *Sociology for the South, or The Failure of Free Society* (1854)[18]

Chapter I Free Trade

Political economy is the science of free society. Its theory and its history alike establish this position. [...] Political economy is quite as objectionable, viewed as a rule of morals, as when viewed as a system of economy. Its authors never seem to be aware that they are writing an ethical as well as an economic code; yet it is probable that no writings, since the promulgation of the Christian dispensation, have exercised so controlling an influence on human conduct as the writings of these authors. The morality which they teach is one of simple and unadulterated selfishness. The public good, the welfare of society, the prosperity of one's neighbors, is, according to them, best promoted by each man's looking solely to the advancement of his own pecuniary interests. They maintain that national wealth, happiness and prosperity being but the aggregate of individual wealth, happiness and prosperity, if each man pursues exclusively his own selfish good, he is doing the most he can to promote the general good. They seem to forget that men eager in the pursuit of wealth are never satisfied with the fair earnings of their own bodily labor, but find their wits and cunning employed in overreaching others much more profitable than their hands. *Laissez-faire*, free competition begets a war of the wits, which these economists encourage, quite as destructive to the weak, simple and guileless, as the war of the sword. [...]

It arrays capital against labor. Every man is taught by political economy that it is meritorious to make the best bargains one can. In all old countries, labor is superabundant, employers less numerous than laborers; yet all the laborers must live by the wages they receive from the capitalists. The capitalist cheapens their wages; they compete with and underbid each other, for employed they must be on any terms. This war of the rich with the poor and the poor with one another, is the morality which political economy inculcates. [...] A beautiful system of ethics this [is], that places all mankind in antagonistic positions, and puts all society at war. What can such a war result in but the oppression and ultimate extermination of the weak? In such society the astute capitalist, who is very skilful and cunning, gets the advantage of every one with whom he competes or deals; the sensible man with moderate means gets the advantage of most with whom he has business, but the mass of the simple and poor are outwitted and cheated by everybody.

Woman fares worst when thrown into this warfare of competition. The delicacy of her sex and her nature prevents her exercising those coarse arts which men do in the vulgar and promiscuous jostle of life, and she is reduced to the necessity of getting less than half price for her work. To the eternal disgrace of human nature, the men

---

[18] G. Fitzhugh, *Sociology for the South, or The Failure of Free Society* (Richmond: A. Morris, 1854), pp. 7, 20–5, 34–7, 45–8, 82–4, 177–80.

who employ her value themselves on the Adam Smith principle for their virtuous and sensible conduct. "Labor is worth what it will bring; they have given the poor woman more than any one else would, or she would not have taken the work." Yet she and her children are starving, and the employer is growing rich by giving her half what her work is worth. Thus does free competition, the creature of free society, throw the whole burden of the social fabric on the poor, the weak and ignorant. They produce every thing and enjoy nothing. They are "the muzzled ox that treadeth out the straw."

In free society none but the selfish virtues are in repute, because none other help a man in the race of competition. In such society virtue loses all her loveliness, because of her selfish aims. Good men and bad men have the same end in view: self-promotion, self-elevation. The good man is prudent, cautious, and cunning of fence; he knows well, the arts (the virtues, if you please) which enable him to advance his fortunes at the expense of those with whom he deals; he does not "cut too deep"; he does not cheat and swindle, he only makes good bargains and excellent profits. He gets more subjects by this course; everybody comes to him to be bled. He bides his time; takes advantage of the follies, the improvidence and vices of others, and makes his fortune out of the follies and weaknesses of his fellow-men. The bad man is rash, hasty, unskilful and impolitic. He is equally selfish, but not half so prudent and cunning. Selfishness is almost the only motive of human conduct in free society, where every man is taught that it is his first duty to change and better his pecuniary situation. [...]

Chapter II Failure of Free Society and Rise of Socialism

[...] The advocates of universal liberty concede that the laboring class enjoy more material comfort, are better fed, clothed and housed, as slaves, than as freemen. The statistics of crime demonstrate that the moral superiority of the slave over the free laborer is still greater than his superiority in animal well-being. There never can be among slaves a class so degraded as is found about the wharves and suburbs of cities. The master requires and enforces ordinary morality and industry. We very much fear, if it were possible to indite a faithful comparison of the conduct and comfort of our free negroes with that of the runaway Anglo-Saxon serfs, that it would be found that the negroes have fared better and committed much less crime than the whites. [...] Their numbers have multiplied a hundred-fold, but their poverty has increased faster than their numbers. Instead of stealing and begging, and living idly in the open air, they work fourteen hours a day, cooped up in close rooms, with foul air, foul water, and insufficient and filthy food, and often sleep at night crowded in cellars or in garrets, without regard to sex. [...]

How slavery could degrade men lower than universal liberty has done, it is hard to conceive; how it did and would again preserve them from such degradation, is well explained by those who are loudest in its abuse. A consciousness of security, a full comprehension of his position, and a confidence in that position, and the absence of all corroding cares and anxieties, makes the slave easy and self-assured in his address, cheerful, happy and contented, free from jealousy, malignity, and envy, and at peace with all around him. His attachment to his master begets the sentiment of loyalty, than which none more purifies and elevates human nature. [...]

Socialism and every other heresy that can be invoked to make war on existing institutions, prevail to an alarming extent. [...] But it is probable [that] the constant arrival of emigrants makes the situation of the laborer at the North as precarious as in Europe, and produces a desire for some change that shall secure him employment and support at all times. Slavery alone can effect that change; and towards slavery the North and all Western Europe are unconsciously marching. The master evil they all complain of is free competition – which is another name for liberty. Let them remove that evil, and they will find themselves slaves, with all the advantages and disadvantages of slavery. They will have attained association of labor, for slavery produces association of labor, and is one of the ends all Communists and Socialists desire. A well-conducted farm in the South is a model of associated labor that Fourier might envy.[19] One old woman nurses all the children whilst the mothers are at work; another waits on the sick, in a house set aside for them. Another washes and cooks, and a fourth makes and mends the clothing. It is a great economy of labor, and is a good idea of the Socialists. Slavery protects the infants, the aged and the sick; nay, takes far better care of them than of the healthy, the middle-aged and the strong. They are part of the family, and self-interest and domestic affection combine to shelter, shield and foster them. A man loves not only his horses and his cattle, which are useful to him, but he loves his dog, which is of no use. He loves them because they are his. What a wise and beneficent provision of Heaven, that makes the selfishness of man's nature a protecting aegis to shield and defend wife and children, slaves and even dumb animals. The Socialists propose to reach this result too, but they never can if they refuse to march in the only road Providence has pointed out. Who will check, govern and control their superintending authority? Who prevent his abuse of power? Who can make him kind, tender and affectionate, to the poor, aged, helpless, sick and unfortunate? *Qui custodiat custodes?* [...] None but lawyers and historians are aware how much of truth, justice and good sense, there is in the notions of the Communists, as to the community of property. [...] But it is domestic slavery alone that can establish a safe, efficient and humane community of property. It did so in ancient times, it did so in feudal times, and does so now, in Eastern Europe, Asia and America. Slaves never die of hunger; seldom suffer want. [...] A Southern farm is a sort of joint stock concern, or social phalastery [*sic*], in which the master furnishes the capital and skill, and the slaves the labor, and divide the profits, not according to each one's in-put, but according to each one's wants and necessities.

Socialism proposes to do away with free competition; to afford protection and support at all times to the laboring class; to bring about, at least, a qualified community of property, and to associate labor. All these purposes, slavery fully and perfectly attains. [...]

Chapter V Negro Slavery

We have already stated that we should not attempt to introduce any new theories of government and of society, but merely try to justify old ones, so far as we could

---

[19] Charles Fourier (1772–1837) was a French philosopher and influential early socialist thinker.

deduce such theories from ancient and almost universal practices. Now it has been the practice in all countries and in all ages, in some degree, to accommodate the amount and character of government control to the wants, intelligence, and moral capacities of the nations or individuals to be governed. A highly moral and intellectual people, like the free citizens of ancient Athens, are best governed by a democracy. For a less moral and intellectual one, a limited and constitutional monarchy will answer. For a people either very ignorant or very wicked, nothing short of military despotism will suffice. So among individuals, the most moral and well-informed members of society require no other government than law. They are capable of reading and understanding the law, and have sufficient self-control and virtuous disposition to obey it. Children cannot be governed by mere law; first, because they do not understand it, and secondly, because they are so much under the influence of impulse, passion and appetite, that they want sufficient self-control to be deterred or governed by the distant and doubtful penalties of the law. They must be constantly controlled by parents or guardians, whose will and orders shall stand in the place of law for them. Very wicked men must be put into penitentiaries; lunatics into asylums, and the most wild of them into straight jackets, just as the most wicked of the sane are manacled with irons; and idiots must have committees to govern and take care of them. Now, it is clear the Athenian democracy would not suit a negro nation, nor will the government of mere law suffice for the individual negro. He is but a grown up child, and must be governed as a child, not as a lunatic or criminal. The master occupies towards him the place of parent or guardian. We shall not dwell on this view, for no one will differ with us who thinks as we do of the negro's capacity, and we might argue till dooms-day, in vain, with those who have a high opinion of the negro's moral and intellectual capacity.

Secondly. The negro is improvident; will not lay up in summer for the wants of winter; will not accumulate in youth for the exigencies of age. He would become an insufferable burden to society. Society has the right to prevent this, and can only do so by subjecting him to domestic slavery.

In the last place, the negro race is inferior to the white race, and living in their midst, they would be far outstripped or outwitted in the chase of free competition. Gradual but certain extermination would be their fate. We presume the maddest abolitionist does not think the negro's providence of habits and money-making capacity at all to compare to those of the whites. This defect of character would alone justify enslaving him, if he is to remain here. In Africa or the West Indies, he would become idolatrous, savage and cannibal, or be devoured by savages and cannibals. At the North he would freeze or starve. [...]

Chapter XIX Declaration of Independence and Virginia Bill of Rights

[...] It is, we believe, conceded on all hands, that men are not born physically, morally or intellectually equal, – some are males, some females, some from birth, large, strong and healthy, others weak, small and sickly – some are naturally amiable, others prone to all kinds of wickednesses – some brave, others timid. Their natural inequalities beget inequalities of rights. The weak in mind or body require guidance, support and protection; they must obey and work for those who protect and guide them – they have a natural right to guardians, committees, teachers or masters. Nature has made them slaves; all that law and government can do, is to regulate, modify and mitigate their slavery. In the absence of legally instituted slavery, their condition would be worse under that natural slavery of the weak to the strong, the foolish to the wise and cunning. The wise and virtuous, the brave, the strong in mind and body, are by nature born to command and protect, and law but follows nature in making them rulers, legislators, judges, captains, husbands, guardians, committees and masters. [...]

Men are not "born entitled to equal rights!" It would be far nearer the truth to say, "that some were born with saddles on their backs, and others booted and spurred to ride them," – and the riding does them good. They need the reins, the bit and the spur. No two men by nature are exactly equal or exactly alike. No institutions can prevent the few from acquiring rule and ascendency over the many. Liberty and free competition invite and encourage the attempt of the strong to master the weak; and insure [*sic*] their success.

"Life and liberty" are not "inalienable"; they have been sold in all countries, and in all ages, and must be sold so long as human nature lasts. It is an inexpedient and unwise, and often unmerciful restraint, on a man's liberty of action, to deny him the right to sell himself when starving, and again to buy himself when fortune smiles. Most countries of antiquity, and some, like China at the present day, allowed such sale and purchase. The great object of government is to restrict, control and punish man "in the pursuit of happiness." All crimes are committed in its pursuit. Under the free or competitive system, most men's happiness consists in destroying the happiness of other people. This, then, is no inalienable right. [...]

James Henry Hammond *Speech to the US Senate* (March 4, 1858)[20]

[Hammond gave this speech during Senate's consideration of the bill for admission of Kansas into the Union. He originally addresses the legitimacy of the Lecompton Constitution, one of the constitutions proposed for the new state of Kansas, and then turns to the economic power of the South and the issue of slavery.]

[...] In all social systems there must be a class to do the menial duties, to perform the drudgery of life. That is, a class requiring but a low order of intellect and but little skill. Its requisites are vigor, docility, fidelity. Such a class you must have, or you would not have that other class which leads progress, civilization, and refinement. It constitutes the very mud-sill of society and of political government; and you might as well attempt to build a house in the air, as to build either the one or the other, except on this mud-sill. Fortunately for the South, she found a race adapted to that purpose to her hand. A race inferior to her own, but eminently qualified in temper, in vigor, in docility, in capacity to stand the climate, to answer all her purposes. We use them for

---

[20] J. H. Hammond, *Speech of Hon. James H. Hammond on the Admission of Kansas under the Lecompton Constitution* (Washington, DC: Printed by Lemuel Towers, 1858), pp. 13–15.

our purpose, and call them slaves. We found them slaves by the common "consent of mankind," which, according to Cicero, "*lex naturae est.*" The highest proof of what is Nature's law. We are old-fashioned at the South yet; slave is a word discarded now by "ears polite"; I will not characterize that class at the North by that term; but you have it; it is there; it is everywhere; it is eternal.

The Senator from New York [William H. Seward] said yesterday that the whole world had abolished slavery. Aye, the *name*, but not the *thing*; all the powers of the earth cannot abolish that. God only can do it when he repeals the *fiat*, "the poor ye always have with you"; for the man who lives by daily labor, and scarcely lives at that, and who has to put out his labor in the market, and take the best he can get for it; in short, your whole hireling class of manual laborers and "operatives," as you call them, are essentially slaves. The difference between us is, that our slaves are hired for life and well compensated; there is no starvation, no begging, no want of employment among our people, and not too much employment either. Yours are hired by the day, not cared for, and scantily compensated, which may be proved in the most painful manner, at any hour in any street in any of your large towns. Why, you meet more beggars in one day, in any single street of the city of New York, than you would meet in a lifetime in the whole South. We do not think that whites should be slaves either by law or necessity. Our slaves are black, of another and inferior race. The *status* in which we have placed them is an elevation. They are elevated from the condition in which God first created them, by being made our slaves. None of that race on the whole face of the globe can be compared with the slaves of the South. They are happy, content, unaspiring, and utterly incapable, from intellectual weakness, ever to give us any trouble by their aspirations. Yours are white, of your own race; you are brothers of one blood. They are your equals in natural endowment of intellect, and they feel galled by their degradation. Our slaves do not vote. We give them no political power. Yours do vote, and, being the majority, they are the depositories of all your political power. If they knew the tremendous secret, that the ballot-box is stronger than "an army with banners," and could combine, where would you be? Your society would be reconstructed, your government overthrown, your property divided, not as they have mistakenly attempted to initiate such proceedings by meeting in parks, with arms in their hands, but by the quiet process of the ballot-box. You have been making war upon us to our very hearthstones. How would you like for us to send lecturers and agitators North, to teach these people this, to aid in combining, and to lead them?

LINCOLN'S SPEECHES

Lincoln–Douglas *Debate at Freeport, Illinois* (August 27, 1858)[21]

Abraham Lincoln [. . .] [I]n regard to the Fugitive Slave Law. I have never hesitated to say, and I do not now hesitate to say, that I think, under the Constitution of the

---

[21] From R. O. Davis and D. L. Wilson (eds.), *The Lincoln–Douglas Debates* (Urbana and Chicago: The Knox College Lincoln Studies Center and the University of Illinois Press, 2008), pp. 48, 58–9.

United States, the people of the Southern States are entitled to a congressional fugitive slave law. Having said that, I have had nothing to say in regard to the existing Fugitive Slave Law, further than that I think it should have been framed so as to be free from some of the objections that pertain to it, without lessening its efficiency. And inasmuch as we are not now in an agitation in regard to an alteration or modification of that law, I would not be the man to introduce it as a new subject of agitation upon the general question of slavery. [...]

Stephen Douglas [...] The next question propounded to me by Mr. Lincoln is, "Can the people of a territory, in any lawful way, against the wishes of any citizen of the United States, exclude slavery from their limits prior to the formation of a state constitution?" I answer emphatically, as Mr. Lincoln has heard me answer a hundred times from every stump in Illinois, that in my opinion the people of a territory can, by lawful means, exclude slavery from their limits prior to the formation of a state constitution. Mr. Lincoln knew that I had answered that question over and over again. He heard me argue the Nebraska bill on that principle all over the state in 1854, in 1855, and in 1856, and he has no excuse for pretending to be in doubt as to my position on that question.

It matters not what way the Supreme Court may hereafter decide as to the abstract question whether slavery may or may not go into a territory under the Constitution. The people have the lawful means to introduce it or exclude it as they please, for the reason that slavery cannot exist a day or an hour anywhere, unless it is supported by local police regulations, furnishing remedies and means of enforcing the right to hold slaves. Those police regulations can only be established by the local legislature, and if the people are opposed to slavery, they will elect representatives to that body who will, by unfriendly legislation, effectually prevent the introduction of it in their midst. If, on the contrary, they are for it, their legislation will favor its extension. Hence, no matter what the decision of the Supreme Court may be on that abstract question, still the right of the people to make a slave territory or a free territory is perfect and complete under the Nebraska bill. I hope Mr. Lincoln deems my answer satisfactory on that point. [...]

I want Lincoln's answer. He says he was not pledged to repeal the Fugitive Slave Law, that he does not quite like to do it. He will not introduce a law to repeal it, but thinks there ought to be some law. [...] Upon the whole, he is altogether undecided, and don't know what to think or to do. That is the substance of his answer upon the repeal of the Fugitive Slave Law. I put that question to him distinctly, whether he endorsed that part of the Black Republican platform which calls for the entire abrogation and repeal of the Fugitive Slave Law. [...] Why cannot he speak out and say what he is for and what he will do?

First Inaugural Address (March 4, 1861)

Fellow-Citizens of the United States:

In compliance with a custom as old as the Government itself, I appear before you to address you briefly and to take in your presence the oath prescribed by the Constitution of the United States to be taken by the President before he enters on the execution of this office.

I do not consider it necessary at present for me to discuss those matters of administration about which there is no special anxiety or excitement.

Apprehension seems to exist among the people of the Southern States that by the accession of a Republican Administration their property and their peace and personal security are to be endangered. There has never been any reasonable cause for such apprehension. Indeed, the most ample evidence to the contrary has all the while existed and been open to their inspection. It is found in nearly all the published speeches of him who now addresses you. I do but quote from one of those speeches when I declare that –

I have no purpose, directly or indirectly, to interfere with the institution of slavery in the States where it exists. I believe I have no lawful right to do so, and I have no inclination to do so.

Those who nominated and elected me did so with full knowledge that I had made this and many similar declarations and had never recanted them; and more than this, they placed in the platform for my acceptance, and as a law to themselves and to me, the clear and emphatic resolution which I now read:

Resolved, That the maintenance inviolate of the rights of the States, and especially the right of each State to order and control its own domestic institutions according to its own judgment exclusively, is essential to that balance of power on which the perfection and endurance of our political fabric depend; and we denounce the lawless invasion by armed force of the soil of any State or Territory, no matter what pretext, as among the gravest of crimes.

I now reiterate these sentiments, and in doing so I only press upon the public attention the most conclusive evidence of which the case is susceptible that the property, peace, and security of no section are to be in any wise endangered by the now incoming Administration. I add, too, that all the protection which, consistently with the Constitution and the laws, can be given will be cheerfully given to all the States when lawfully demanded, for whatever cause – as cheerfully to one section as to another. [. . .]

I hold that in contemplation of universal law and of the Constitution the Union of these States is perpetual. Perpetuity is implied, if not expressed, in the fundamental law of all national governments. It is safe to assert that no government proper ever had a provision in its organic law for its own termination. Continue to execute all the express provisions of our National Constitution, and the Union will endure forever, it being impossible to destroy it except by some action not provided for in the instrument itself.

Again: If the United States be not a government proper, but an association of States in the nature of contract merely, can it, as a contract, be peaceably unmade by less than all the parties who made it? One party to a contract may violate it – break it, so to speak – but does it not require all to lawfully rescind it?

Descending from these general principles, we find the proposition that in legal contemplation the Union is perpetual confirmed by the history of the Union itself. The Union is much older than the Constitution. It was formed, in fact, by the Articles of Association in 1774. It was matured and continued by the Declaration of Independence in 1776. It was further matured, and the faith of all the then thirteen States expressly plighted and engaged that it should be perpetual, by the Articles of

Confederation in 1778. And finally, in 1787, one of the declared objects for ordaining and establishing the Constitution was "to form a more perfect Union."

But if destruction of the Union by one or by a part only of the States be lawfully possible, the Union is less perfect than before the Constitution, having lost the vital element of perpetuity.

It follows from these views that no State upon its own mere motion can lawfully get out of the Union; that resolves and ordinances to that effect are legally void, and that acts of violence within any State or States against the authority of the United States are insurrectionary or revolutionary, according to circumstances.

I therefore consider that in view of the Constitution and the laws the Union is unbroken, and to the extent of my ability, I shall take care, as the Constitution itself expressly enjoins upon me, that the laws of the Union be faithfully executed in all the States. Doing this I deem to be only a simple duty on my part, and I shall perform it so far as practicable unless my rightful masters, the American people, shall withhold the requisite means or in some authoritative manner direct the contrary. I trust this will not be regarded as a menace, but only as the declared purpose of the Union that it will constitutionally defend and maintain itself.

In doing this there needs to be no bloodshed or violence, and there shall be none unless it be forced upon the national authority. The power confided to me will be used to hold, occupy, and possess the property and places belonging to the Government and to collect the duties and imposts; but beyond what may be necessary for these objects, there will be no invasion, no using of force against or among the people anywhere. Where hostility to the United States in any interior locality shall be so great and universal as to prevent competent resident citizens from holding the Federal offices, there will be no attempt to force obnoxious strangers among the people for that object. While the strict legal right may exist in the Government to enforce the exercise of these offices, the attempt to do so would be so irritating and so nearly impracticable withal that I deem it better to forego for the time the uses of such offices.

The mails, unless repelled, will continue to be furnished in all parts of the Union. So far as possible the people everywhere shall have that sense of perfect security which is most favorable to calm thought and reflection. The course here indicated will be followed unless current events and experience shall show a modification or change to be proper, and in every case and exigency my best discretion will be exercised, according to circumstances actually existing and with a view and a hope of a peaceful solution of the national troubles and the restoration of fraternal sympathies and affections. [. . .]

All profess to be content in the Union if all constitutional rights can be maintained. Is it true, then, that any right plainly written in the Constitution has been denied? I think not. Happily, the human mind is so constituted that no party can reach to the audacity of doing this. Think, if you can, of a single instance in which a plainly written provision of the Constitution has ever been denied. If by the mere force of numbers a majority should deprive a minority of any clearly written constitutional right, it might in a moral point of view justify revolution; certainly would if such right were a vital one. But such is not our case. All the vital rights of minorities and of individuals are so plainly assured to them by affirmations and negations, guaranties and prohibitions, in the Constitution that controversies never arise concerning them.

But no organic law can ever be framed with a provision specifically applicable to every question which may occur in practical administration. No foresight can anticipate nor any document of reasonable length contain express provisions for all possible questions. Shall fugitives from labor be surrendered by national or by State authority? The Constitution does not expressly say. May Congress prohibit slavery in the Territories? The Constitution does not expressly say. Must Congress protect slavery in the Territories? The Constitution does not expressly say.

From questions of this class spring all our constitutional controversies, and we divide upon them into majorities and minorities. If the minority will not acquiesce, the majority must, or the Government must cease. There is no other alternative, for continuing the Government is acquiescence on one side or the other. If a minority in such case will secede rather than acquiesce, they make a precedent which in turn will divide and ruin them, for a minority of their own will secede from them whenever a majority refuses to be controlled by such minority. For instance, why may not any portion of a new confederacy a year or two hence arbitrarily secede again, precisely as portions of the present Union now claim to secede from it? All who cherish disunion sentiments are now being educated to the exact temper of doing this.

Is there such perfect identity of interests among the States to compose a new union as to produce harmony only and prevent renewed secession?

Plainly the central idea of secession is the essence of anarchy. A majority held in restraint by constitutional checks and limitations, and always changing easily with deliberate changes of popular opinions and sentiments, is the only true sovereign of a free people. Whoever rejects it does of necessity fly to anarchy or to despotism. Unanimity is impossible. The rule of a minority, as a permanent arrangement, is wholly inadmissible; so that, rejecting the majority principle, anarchy or despotism in some form is all that is left. [. . .]

In your hands, my dissatisfied fellow-countrymen, and not in mine, is the momentous issue of civil war. The Government will not assail you. You can have no conflict without being yourselves the aggressors. You have no oath registered in heaven to destroy the Government, while I shall have the most solemn one to "preserve, protect, and defend it."

I am loath to close. We are not enemies, but friends. We must not be enemies. Though passion may have strained it must not break our bonds of affection. The mystic chords of memory, stretching from every battlefield and patriot grave to every living heart and hearthstone all over this broad land, will yet swell the chorus of the Union, when again touched, as surely they will be, by the better angels of our nature.

Special Session Message (July 4, 1861)

Fellow-Citizens of the Senate and House of Representatives:

Having been convened on an extraordinary occasion, as authorized by the Constitution, your attention is not called to any ordinary subject of legislation.

At the beginning of the present Presidential term, four months ago, [. . .] the purpose to sever the Federal Union was openly avowed. In accordance with this purpose, an ordinance had been adopted in each of these States declaring the States respectively to be separated from the National Union. A formula for instituting a combined government of these States had been promulgated, and this illegal organization, in the character of Confederate States, was already invoking recognition, aid, and intervention from foreign powers. [...]

By the affair at Fort Sumter [...] the assailants of the Government began the conflict of arms, without a gun in sight or in expectancy to return their fire [...]. In this act, discarding all else, they have forced upon the country the distinct issue, "Immediate dissolution or blood."

And this issue embraces more than the fate of these United States. It presents to the whole family of man the question whether a constitutional republic, or democracy – a government of the people by the same people – can or can not maintain its territorial integrity against its own domestic foes. It presents the question whether discontented individuals, too few in numbers to control administration according to organic law in any case, can always, upon the pretenses made in this case, or on any other pretenses, or arbitrarily without any pretense, break up their government, and thus practically put an end to free government upon the earth. It forces us to ask, Is there in all republics this inherent and fatal weakness? Must a government of necessity be too strong for the liberties of its own people, or too weak to maintain its own existence?

So viewing the issue, no choice was left but to call out the war power of the Government and so to resist force employed for its destruction by force for its preservation. [...]

It might seem at first thought to be of little difference whether the present movement at the South be called "secession" or "rebellion." The movers, however, well understand the difference. At the beginning they knew they could never raise their treason to any respectable magnitude by any name which implies violation of law. They knew their people possessed as much of moral sense, as much of devotion to law and order, and as much pride in and reverence for the history and Government of their common country as any other civilized and patriotic people. They knew they could make no advancement directly in the teeth of these strong and noble sentiments. Accordingly, they commenced by an insidious debauching of the public mind. They invented an ingenious sophism, which, if conceded, was followed by perfectly logical steps through all the incidents to the complete destruction of the Union. The sophism itself is that any State of the Union may consistently with the National Constitution, and therefore lawfully and peacefully withdraw from the Union without the consent of the Union or of any other State. The little disguise that the supposed right is to be exercised only for just cause, themselves to be the sole judge of its justice, is too thin to merit any notice.

With rebellion thus sugar coated they have been drugging the public mind of their section for more than thirty years, and until at length they have brought many good men to a willingness to take up arms against the Government [...].

This sophism derives much, perhaps the whole, of its currency from the assumption that there is some omnipotent and sacred supremacy pertaining to a State – to each State of our Federal Union. Our States have neither more nor less power than that reserved to them in the Union by the Constitution, no one of them ever having been a State out of the Union. The original ones passed into the Union even before they cast off their British colonial dependence, and the new ones each came into the Union directly from a condition of dependence, excepting Texas; and even Texas, in its temporary independence [1836–1845], was never designated a State. The new ones only took the designation of States on coming into the Union, while that name was first adopted for the old ones in and by the Declaration of Independence. Therein the "United Colonies" were declared to be "free and independent States." [...] Having never been States, either in substance or in name, outside of the Union, whence this magical omnipotence of "State rights," asserting a claim of power to lawfully destroy the Union itself? Much is said about the "sovereignty" of the States, but the word even is not in the National Constitution, nor, as is believed, in any of the State constitutions. What is a "sovereignty" in the political sense of the term? Would it be far wrong to define it "a political community without a political superior"? Tested by this, no one of our States, except Texas, ever was a sovereignty; and even Texas gave up the character on coming into the Union, by which act she acknowledged the Constitution of the United States and the laws and treaties of the United States made in pursuance of the Constitution to be for her the supreme law of the land. The States have their status in the Union, and they have no other legal status. If they break from this, they can only do so against law and by revolution. The Union, and not themselves separately, procured their independence and their liberty. By conquest or purchase the Union gave each of them whatever of independence and liberty it has. The Union is older than any of the States, and, in fact, it created them as States. Originally some dependent colonies made the Union, and in turn the Union threw off their old dependence for them and made them States, such as they are. Not one of them ever had a State constitution independent of the Union. Of course it is not forgotten that all the new States framed their constitutions before they entered the Union, nevertheless dependent upon and preparatory to coming into the Union. [...]

What is now combated is the position that secession is consistent with the Constitution – is *lawful* and *peaceful*. It is not contended that there is any express law for it, and nothing should ever be implied as law which leads to unjust or absurd consequences. The nation purchased with money the countries out of which several of these States were formed. Is it just that they shall go off without leave and without refunding? [...] The nation is now in debt for money applied to the benefit of these so-called seceding States in common with the rest. Is it just either that creditors shall go unpaid or the remaining States pay the whole? A part of the present national debt was contracted to pay the old debts of Texas. Is it just that she shall leave and pay no part of this herself? Again: If one State may secede, so may another; and when all shall have seceded none is left to pay the debts. Is this quite just to creditors? [...]

Our adversaries have adopted some declarations of independence in which, unlike the good old one penned by Jefferson, they omit the words "all men are created equal." Why? They have adopted a temporary national constitution, in the preamble of which, unlike our good old one signed by Washington, they omit "We, the people," and substitute "We, the deputies of the sovereign and independent States." Why? Why this deliberate pressing out of view the rights of men and the authority of the people?

This is essentially a people's contest. On the side of the Union it is a struggle for maintaining in the world that form and substance of government whose leading object is to elevate the condition of men; to lift artificial weights from all shoulders; to clear the paths of laudable pursuit for all; to afford all an unfettered start and a fair chance in the race of life. Yielding to partial and temporary departures, from necessity, this is the leading object of the Government for whose existence we contend. [...]

Our popular Government has often been called an experiment. Two points in it our people have already settled – the successful *establishing* and the successful *administering* of it. One still remains – its successful *maintenance* against a formidable internal attempt to overthrow it. It is now for them to demonstrate to the world that those who can fairly carry an election can also suppress a rebellion; that ballots are the rightful and peaceful successors of bullets, and that when ballots have fairly and constitutionally decided there can be no successful appeal back to bullets; that there can be no successful appeal except to ballots themselves at succeeding elections. Such will be a great lesson of peace, teaching men that what they can not take by an election neither can they take it by a war; teaching all the folly of being the beginners of a war. [...]

Gettysburg Address (November 19, 1863)

Fourscore and seven years ago our fathers brought forth, on this continent, a new nation, conceived in liberty, and dedicated to the proposition that all men are created equal.

Now we are engaged in a great civil war, testing whether that nation, or any nation so conceived, and so dedicated, can long endure. We are met on a great battle-field of that war. We have come to dedicate a portion of that field, as a final resting-place for those who here gave their lives, that that nation might live. It is altogether fitting and proper that we should do this. But, in a larger sense, we cannot dedicate, we cannot consecrate – we cannot hallow – this ground. The brave men, living and dead, who struggled here, have consecrated it far above our poor power to add or detract. The world will little note, nor long remember what we say here, but it can never forget what they did here. It is for us the living, rather, to be dedicated here to the unfinished work which they who fought here have thus far so nobly advanced. It is rather for us to be here dedicated to the great task remaining before us – that from these honored dead we take increased devotion to that cause for which they here gave the last full measure of devotion – that we here highly resolve that these dead shall not have died in vain – that this nation, under God, shall have a new birth of freedom, and that government of the people, by the people, for the people, shall not perish from the earth.

Second Inaugural Address (March 4, 1865)

Fellow-Countrymen:

[...] On the occasion corresponding to this four years ago all thoughts were anxiously directed to an impending civil war. All dreaded it, all sought to avert it. [...] Both parties deprecated war, but one of them would make war rather than let the nation survive, and the other would accept war rather than let it perish, and the war came.

One-eighth of the whole population were colored slaves, not distributed generally over the Union, but localized in the southern part of it. These slaves constituted a peculiar and powerful interest. All knew that this interest was somehow the cause of the war. To strengthen, perpetuate, and extend this interest was the object for which the insurgents would rend the Union even by war, while the Government claimed no right to do more than to restrict the territorial enlargement of it. Neither party expected for the war the magnitude or the duration which it has already attained. Neither anticipated that the cause of the conflict might cease with or even before the conflict itself should cease. Each looked for an easier triumph, and a result less fundamental and astounding. Both read the same Bible and pray to the same God, and each invokes His aid against the other. It may seem strange that any men should dare to ask a just God's assistance in wringing their bread from the sweat of other men's faces, but let us judge not, that we be not judged. The prayers of both could not be answered. That of neither has been answered fully. The Almighty has His own purposes. "Woe unto the world because of offenses; for it must needs be that offenses come, but woe to that man by whom the offense cometh." If we shall suppose that American slavery is one of those offenses which, in the providence of God, must needs come, but which, having continued through His appointed time, He now wills to remove, and that He gives to both North and South this terrible war as the woe due to those by whom the offense came, shall we discern therein any departure from those divine attributes which the believers in a living God always ascribe to Him? Fondly do we hope, fervently do we pray, that this mighty scourge of war may speedily pass away. Yet, if God wills that it continue until all the wealth piled by the bondsman's two hundred and fifty years of unrequited toil shall be sunk, and until every drop of blood drawn with the lash shall be paid by another drawn with the sword, as was said three thousand years ago, so still it must be said "the judgments of the Lord are true and righteous altogether."

With malice toward none, with charity for all, with firmness in the right as God gives us to see the right, let us strive on to finish the work we are in, to bind up the nation's wounds, to care for him who shall have borne the battle and for his widow and his orphan, to do all which may achieve and cherish a just and lasting peace among ourselves and with all nations.

Suggested Readings

John Taylor, *Arator* 13, "Slavery," and 14, "Slavery, Continued" [1813] in *Arator, Being a Series of Agricultural Essays, Practical and Political: In Sixty-One Numbers* (Georgetown: J. M. Carter, 1814).

John C. Calhoun, Fort Hill Address, July 26, 1831 (Richmond: Virginia Commission on Constitutional Government, 1967).

John C. Calhoun, *A Discourse on the Constitution and Government of the United States* (Columbia: Johnston, 1851).

David Walker, *An Appeal, In Four Articles; to the Coloured Citizens of the World*, 3rd ed. (Boston: David Walker, 1830).

William Leggett, "The Question of Slavery Narrowed to a Point" (newspaper editorial, April 15, 1837), in L. H. White (ed.), *Democratick Editorials: Essays in Jacksonian Political Economy by William Leggett* (Indianapolis: Liberty Fund, 1984), pp. 224–8.

Harriet Beecher Stowe, "What Is Slavery?" and "Slavery Is Despotism" in *A Key to Uncle Tom's Cabin: Presenting the Original Facts and Documents upon Which the Story is Founded* (Boston: John P. Jewett & Co., 1853).

Frederick Douglass, "What to the Slave Is the Fourth of July?" (speech before the Rochester Ladies' Anti-Slavery Society, July 5, 1852), in *My Bondage and My Freedom* (New York and Auburn: Miller, Orton, & Mulligan, 1855), pp. 441–5.

Frederick Douglass, "What Is My Duty as an Anti-Slavery Voter?" (essay published in *Frederick Douglass' Paper*, April 25, 1856).

Roger B. Taney, *Dred Scott v. Sanford* (60 U.S. 393; 1857).

Edmund Ruffin, *The Political Economy of Slavery, or, The Institution Considered in Regard to Its Influence on Public Wealth and the General Wealth* (Washington, DC: L. Towers, 1857).

George S. Sawyer, "The Relative Position and Treatment of the Negroes" [1858] in B. Frohnen (ed.), *The American Republic: Primary Sources* (Indianapolis: Liberty Fund, 2002), pp. 665–80.

J. D. B. De Bow, *The Interest in Slavery of the Southern Non-Slave-Holder: The Right of Peaceful Secession. Slavery in the Bible* (Charleston: Evans & Cogswell, 1860).

Index

9 781108 733557